A DICTIONARY
OF
CATCH PHRASES

Other Works by Eric Partridge

Routledge & Kegan Paul:

ORIGINS: AN ETYMOLOGICAL DICTIONARY OF MODERN ENGLISH; 4th edn (US: Macmillan).
A DICTIONARY OF THE UNDERWORLD; 3rd edn (US: Macmillan).
A DICTIONARY OF SLANG AND UNCONVENTIONAL ENGLISH: vol. 1, 5th edn; vol. 2, 7th edn (US: Macmillan).
A DICTIONARY OF HISTORICAL SLANG – that is, up to 1914, ed. Jacqueline Simpson (US: Macmillan).
A SMALLER SLANG DICTIONARY; 2nd edn (US: Philosophical Library). Also in British paperback.
SLANG TODAY AND YESTERDAY; 4th edn.
SHAKESPEARE'S BAWDY: AN ESSAY AND A GLOSSARY; 3rd edn (US: Dutton). Also in a British, and
 an American, paperback.
A DICTIONARY OF CLICHÉS; numerous printings (US: a Dutton paperback).
COMIC ALPHABETS: A LIGHT-HEARTED HISTORY (now available only in US: Hobbs, Dorman).

André Deutsch:

SWIFT'S 'POLITE CONVERSATION': A COMMENTARY EDITION (US: Westview Press).
CHAMBER OF HORRORS: OFFICIALESE, BRITISH AND AMERICAN (US: Westview Press).

Hamish Hamilton:

USAGE AND ABUSAGE: A GUIDE TO GOOD ENGLISH; numerous edns. (Also in a Penguin paperback,
 both British and American.)
NAME THIS CHILD: A DICTIONARY OF CHRISTIAN OR GIVEN NAMES; many printings. (Also an Evans
 Brothers paperback: *Name Your Child.*)

Books for Libraries, Inc. (Plainview: New York State):

Many republications of books out of print in Britain, including: Francis Grose's A CLASSICAL
DICTIONARY OF THE VULGAR TONGUE, a commentary edn; NAME INTO WORD, a dictionary of proper
names become common property; ENGLISH: A COURSE FOR HUMAN BEINGS; (with John Brophy)
THE LONG TRAIL, being songs and slang of the British soldier in WW1, and (with Wilfred
Granville and Frank Roberts) A DICTIONARY OF FORCES' SLANG, of all three services in WW2; A
NEW TESTAMENT WORD-BOOK; LEXICOGRAPHY: A PERSONAL MEMOIR; and seven volumes of essays
on language (general) and words (particular). Also some books literary rather than linguistic, e.g.:
GLIMPSES (short stories); JOURNEY TO THE EDGE OF MORNING (autobiographical essays); THE FRENCH
ROMANTICS' KNOWLEDGE OF ENGLISH LITERATURE; EIGHTEENTH-CENTURY ENGLISH ROMANTIC POETRY.

A DICTIONARY OF CATCH PHRASES

British and American,
from the Sixteenth Century
to the Present Day

ERIC PARTRIDGE

Routledge & Kegan Paul
London and Henley

First published in 1977
by Routledge & Kegan Paul Ltd
39 Store Street,
London WC1E 7DD and
Broadway House,
Newtown Road,
Henley-on-Thames,
Oxon RG9 1EN
Set in 8/9 Monophoto Times
and printed in Great Britain by
Butler & Tanner Ltd, Frome and London
© Eric Partridge 1977

British Library Cataloguing in Publication Data

Partridge, Eric

A dictionary of catch phrases.
1. English language – Terms and phrases
I. Title
423'.1   PE1689

ISBN 0 7100 8537 0

For Norman Franklin
worthy son of a worthy father
and, in his own right,
a brilliant and generous publisher

PREFACE

After a longish period of *ad hoc* reading and note-making (with, since, a continual 'spare-time' reading) I began to write, not merely compile, this dictionary in September 1973 and completed the writing almost exactly two years later.

I have been deeply interested in catch phrases ever since during the First World War when, a private in the Australian infantry, I heard so many; in both *Slang Today and Yesterday* and, 1937 onwards, *A Dictionary of Slang and Unconventional English*, I have paid them considerable – and increasing – attention. Moreover, as I have always read rather widely in American fiction and humour, I did not start from scratch in that vast field.

But I could not have adequately treated either the catch phrases of the United States or those of the British Commonwealth of Nations without the constant, faithful, extraordinarily generous assistance of friends and acquaintances and pen-friends. In the list of acknowledgments, I have named all the more copious and helpful – at least, I like to think that I've done so. Probably there are a few unforgivable omissions; I can but ask forgiveness.

There are, however, three acknowledgments, in a different order of things, to be made right here. I have to thank *Newsweek* for permission to quote a long passage from an article by the late John – son of Ring – Lardner; and Mr Edward Albee for his unqualified permission to quote freely from his perturbing and remarkable plays, so sensitive to the nuances of colloquial usage. In yet another order, I owe a very special debt to Mr Norman Franklin, who has, a score of times, saved me from making an ass of myself and, several score of times, supplied much-needed information.

The Introduction is intentionally very brief: I don't pretend to an ability to define the indefinable: I have merely attempted to indicate what a catch phrase is, there being many varieties of this elusive phenomenon; a phenomenon at once linguistic and literary – one that furnishes numerous *marginalia* to social history and to the thought-patterns of civilization.

Finally, a caution. I have, although very seldom, written an entry in such a way as to allow the reader to see just how it grew from a vague idea into a certainty or, at least, a virtual certainty.

Late 1976   EP

ACKNOWLEDGMENTS

I have not counted the number of entries; it can hardly be less than 3,000 – a figure that will, I hope, be increased both by my own further research and by further contributions from my loyal helpers, as well as from all those reviewers and general readers who will have noticed omissions and defects.

To generous friends and acquaintances and pen-friends I owe much: and of these, perhaps the most helpful have been the following (an asterisk* indicates a very considerable indebtedness):

*Mr Laurie Atkinson, who has contributed so much to the later editions of *DSUE* – and so much to this book.

The late Mr Sidney J. Baker, author of *The Australian Language.*

*Mr Paul Beale of Loughborough.

British Library, the: the staff for courteous assistance.

Rear-Admiral P. W. Brock, CB, DSO.

*Mr W. J. Burke, for many years the head of *Look*'s research department.

*Professor Emeritus John W. Clark, University of Minnesota, invaluably and from the beginning.

The late Mr Norris M. Davidson of Gwynedd, Pennsylvania.

Professor Ralph W. V. Elliott of University House, Canberra.

Professor John T. Fain, University of Florida.

*Mr Norman Franklin, the Chairman of Messrs Routledge & Kegan Paul. As if he hadn't already more than enough 'on his plate'!

*The late Julian Franklyn, heraldist and an authority on Cockney custom and speech.

Mr Christopher Fry, welcomely 'out of the blue' on several occasions.

*The late Wilfred Granville – like Mr Franklyn, an indefatigable helper – who died on 23 March 1974.

Mr Ben Grauer, the well known interviewer (etc.) on American radio and TV – like most extremely busy men, this dynamo has always been courteous, patient, helpful.

Mr Arthur Gray of Auckland, New Zealand.

Dr Edward Hodnett, American scholar.

*Dr Douglas Leechman, an authority on Canadiana.

Mr Y. Mindel of Kfar Tabor, Lower Galilee.

*Colonel Albert Moe, United States Marine Corps, ret.; over a long period.

Professor Emeritus S. H. Monk of the University of Minnesota.

Mrs Patricia Newnham of Hampstead.

*Mr (formerly Squadron Leader) Vernon Noble, journalist, author, BBC man (ret.).

Mr John O'Riordan, Librarian of Southgate Library, North London, for keeping me supplied with contemporary fiction.

Professor Emeritus Ashley Cooper Partridge, University of the Witwatersrand.

Mr Fernley O. Pascoe of Camborne, Cornwall.

Mrs Shirley M. Pearce of West Wickham, Kent.

Mr Ronald Pearsall, authority on Victorian and Edwardian themes.

*Mr Albert B. Petch of Bournemouth, Hampshire; a good and fruitful friend for many, many years.

*Mr Barry Prentice of Sydney, Australia; copiously and perspicaciously.

Professor Emeritus F. E. L. Priestley, University of Toronto.

Mrs Camilla Raab of Routledge & Kegan Paul.

*Mr Peter Sanders of Godalming, Surrey.

Professor Harold Shapiro, University of North Carolina.

*The late Frank Shaw, authority on 'Scouse' – the speech of the Merseyside. (See the note at *do the other* in the dictionary.)

*Dr Joseph T. Shipley of New York; patiently and most helpfully.

Miss Patricia Sigl, an American resident in London; authority on the eighteenth-century theatre.

Mr Lawrence Smith of Totley, Sheffield.

*Mr Ramsey Spencer (bless him too) of Camberley, Surrey.

Mr Oliver Stonor of Morebath, Devonshire; several valuable reminders.

Mrs Margaret Thomson of Bray-on-Thames.

Mr Cyril Whelan of St Brelade, Jersey, CI; contributions of much distinction.

The late Colonel Archie White, VC, author of *The Story of Army Education*.

Miss Eileen Wood of Routledge & Kegan Paul.

Mr and Mrs Arthur Wrigglesworth, the friends with whom I lived surrounded by comfort and considerateness: he for unwittingly supplying me with indirect evidence; she for her exceptional knowledge of music, whether classical or popular (not 'pop'), including songs.

INTRODUCTION

Man is a creature who lives not by bread alone, but principally by catchwords.
R. L. Stevenson, *Virginibus Puerisque* (Part II), 1881

Friends – and others – have often asked me, 'What the devil *is* a catch phrase?' I don't know. But I do know that my sympathy lies with the lexicographers.

Consult the standard dictionaries, the best and the greatest: you will notice that they tacitly admit the impossibility of precise definition. Perhaps cravenly, I hope that the following brief 'wafflings' will be reinforced by the willingness of readers to allow that 'example is better than precept' and thus enable me to 'get away with it'. A pen-friend, who has, for thirty years or more, copiously contributed both slang terms, on the one hand, and catch phrases (not, of course, necessarily slangy) on the other, tells me that the best definition he has seen is this: 'A catch phrase is a phrase that has caught on, and pleases the populace.' I'll go along with that, provided these substitutions be accepted: 'saying' for 'phrase'; and 'public' for the tendentious 'populace'.

Frequently, catch phrases are not, in the grammarians' sense, phrases at all, but sentences. Catch phrases, like the closely linked proverbial sayings, are self-contained, as, obviously, clichés are too. Catch phrases are usually more pointed and 'human' than clichés, although the former sometimes arise from, and often they generate, the latter. Occasionally, catch phrases stem from *too* famous quotations. Catch phrases often supply – indeed they are – conversational gambits; often, too, they add a pithy, perhaps earthy, comment. Apart from the unavoidable 'he-she' and 'we-you-they' conveniences, they are immutable. You will have perceived that the categories Catch Phrase, Proverbial Saying, Famous Quotation, Cliché, may co-exist: they are not snobbishly exclusive, any one of any other. All depends on the context, the nuance, the tone.

Precepts mystify: examples clarify. Here, in roughly chronological order, are a few catch phrases.

The proverbial *no one can say black is my eye* developed, probably late in the sixteenth century, into the catch phrase, *black* is – later, *black's* – *your eye*, you're at fault, you're guilty, whence *black's the white of my eye*, a nautical protestation of innocence. Nor is this catch phrase entirely extinct.

I'll have your guts for garters, a threat originally serious, but in late nineteenth to twentieth century usually humorous, has likewise had an astonishingly long history. In Robert Greene's *James the Fourth*, 1598, we find, 'I'll make garters of thy guts, thou villain'; and in an early seventeenth-century parish register, my formidably erudite friend, Dr Jack Lindsay, discovered the prototype: *I'll have your guts for garter points*. In the twentieth century, the modern form has been mostly a Cockney, and often a racecourse, semi-humorous threat.

Another catch phrase with an historical background is *hay is for horses*, which duly acquired the variant *'ay is for 'orses*. In Swift's *Polite Conversation* (the most fertile and valuable single literary source of them all), 1738, we read:

NEVEROUT: Hay, Madam, did you call me?
MISS: Hay! Why; hay is for horses.

Nowadays, the catch phrase is usually addressed to someone who has used either *hey* (as in 'Hey there, you!') or *eh?* for 'I beg your pardon.' This refreshing domesticity – compare, for instance, *'she' is a cat's mother* – became, inevitably in its colloquial form, *'ay is for 'orses*, incorporated in the Comic Phonetic Alphabet. You know the sort of thing: '*B* is for honey' – '*C* is for fish' – and the rest of it. Perhaps, however, I should add that, in Swift, *hay* is a mere phonetic variant of the exclamatory *hey* and is therefore associated with *eh*, whence the entirely natural *'ay is....*

A characteristically nineteenth-century catch phrase is *Lushington is his master*, he's a drunkard, which has derived from the synonymous eighteenth to nineteenth-century *Alderman Lushington is concerned*. Clearly there is both a pun on *lush*, an old low-slang term for strong liquor, and on that convivial society or club known as *the City of Lushington* (recorded by the indispensable *Oxford English Dictionary*).

Originating early in the present century, *hullo, baby! – how's nurse?* was an urban and civilian jocularity before the licentious soldiery blithely adopted and popularized it during those extraordinarily formative years, 1914–18. It was spoken to any girl pushing a perambulator. So far as I'm aware, it had, in the army and the air force at least, fallen into disuse by the time the Second World War arrived; it does, however, exemplify the wit and the humour that mark so many catch phrases.

A WW2 phrase that has impressed me with its wit (and its realism) is the mock-Latin *illegitimis non carborundum*, which, after the war, spread to civilians throughout the British Commonwealth, even to those who had no Latin. Meaning 'Don't let the bastards grind' – idiomatically 'wear' and colloquially 'get' – 'you down', it is generally supposed to have been coined by Military Intelligence. *To coin a phrase – that figures.* (Two other post-WW2 catch phrases.)

But *illegitimis non carborundum* does not stand alone in its gravity. I'll cite only two other, at first intensely serious, catch phrases: the First World War's *hanging on the old barbed wire*; and the socially and sociologically, racially and historically, far-reaching and important creation of the (probably early) 1930s, a catch phrase remaining predominantly grave – to wit, *some of my best friends are Jews*, to which I shall attempt to do justice.

Watch how you go!

ABBREVIATIONS

Adams	Franklin P. Adams (1881–1960), *Baseball's Sad Lexicon*, 1936(?)
Am	John Russell Bartlett, *Americanisms*, 1848; 2nd edn, 1859; 4th edn, 1877
anon.	anonymous
Apperson	G. L. Apperson, *English Proverbs and Proverbial Phrases*, 1929
AS	Sidney J. Baker, *Australia Speaks*, 1953
Baker	Sidney J. Baker, *Australian Slang*, 1942; 3rd edn, 1943; revised edn, 1959
Bartlett	John Russell Bartlett, *Bartlett's Familiar Quotations*, 14th edn, 1968
Baumann	Heinrich Baumann, *Londinismen*, 1887
BE	B.E., Gent, *Dictionary of the Canting Crew*, 1698–9
Benham	Gurney Benham, *Dictionary of Quotations*, 1907, revised edn, 1948
Berrey	Lester V. Berrey and Melvin Van Dan Bark, *The American Thesaurus of Slang*, 1942
B & L	A. Barrère and C. G. Leland, *Dictionary*, 2 vols, 1889–90
Bowen	F. Bowen, *Sea Slang*, 1929
B & P	John Brophy and Eric Partridge, *Songs and Slang of the British Soldier: 1914–1918*, 1930; 3rd edn, 1931; republished as *The Long Trail*, 1965
BQ	Burton Stevenson, *Book of Quotations*, 5th edn, 1946
Brewer	E. C. Brewer, *Dictionary of Phrase and Fable*, revised and enlarged edn, 1952
Brophy	John Brophy, *English Prose*, 1932
C	century
c.	*circa* (about the year — —)
cf	compare
Clarke	John Clarke, *Paroemiologia*, 1639. Sometimes noted as *P*
CM	Clarence Major, *Black Slang: A Dictionary of Afro-American Talk*, 1970 in US, 1971 in Britain
Cobb	Irvin S. Cobb, *Eating in Two or Three Languages*, 1919
Cohen	J. M. and M. J. Cohen, *Penguin Dictionary of Quotations*, 1960
Collinson	W. E. Collinson, *Contemporary English: A Personal Speech Record*, 1927
c.p.	catchphrase; pl., c.pp.
DAE	W. L. Craigie and R. J. Hulbert, *A Dictionary of American English*, 1938–44
D. Am.	M. M. Mathews, *A Dictionary of Americanisms*, 1950
DCCU	Helen Dahlskog, *A Dictionary of Contemporary and Colloquial Usage*, 1971
DD	Oliver Herford, *The Deb's Dictionary*, 1931
DNWP	Anne Baker, *A Dictionary of Northamptonshire Words and Phrases*, 1854
DSUE	Eric Partridge, *A Dictionary of Slang*, 1937; edn quoted is 7th edn, 1970, unless otherwise stated
ed	edited
EDD	Joseph Wright, ed., *The English Dialect Dictionary*, 1896–1905
edn	edition

e.g.	for example
Egan	edition of Grose (q.v.), 1823
EJ	Edward B. Jenkinson, *People, Words and Dictionaries*, 1972
EP	Eric Partridge
esp.	especial; especially
Farb	Peter Farb, *Word Play*, 1973 in US, 1974 in Britain
Farmer	John S. Farmer, *Americanisms – Old and New*, 1889
F & G	E. Fraser and J. Gibbons, *Soldier and Sailor Words and Phrases*, 1925
F & H	John S. Farmer and W. E. Henley, *Slang and Its Analogues*, 1890–1904
Folb	Edith A. Folb, *A Comparative Study of Urban Black Argot*, 1972
Foster	Brian Foster, *The Changing English Language*, 1968
Fr.	French
Fuller	Thomas ('Proverbs') Fuller, *Proverbs*, 1732
G	Thomas Fuller, *Gnomologia: Adagies and Proverbs*, 1732
Ger.	German
Gr.	Greek
Granville	Wilfred Granville, *Dictionary of Theatrical Terms*, 1952
Greig	J. Y. T. Greig, *Breaking Priscian's Head; or English as She Will be Wrote and Spoke*, 1928
Grose	Francis Grose, *A Classical Dictionary of the Vulgar Tongue*, 1785; 2nd edn, 1788; 3rd edn, 1796; Pierce Egan edn, 1823
Heywood	John Heywood, *Proverbs*, 1546
HLM	H. L. Mencken, *The American Language*, 1921; 2nd edn, 1922; 4th edn, 1936; Supp. 1 = Supplement One, 1945; Supp. 2 = Supplement Two, 1948
Holt	Alfred A. Holt, *Phrase Origins*, 1936
H & P	J. L. Hunt and A. G. Pringle, *Service Slang*, 1943
Hotten	John Camden Hotten, *The Slang Dictionary*, 1859; 2nd edn, 1860; 3rd edn, 1864; 4th edn, 1870; 5th edn, 1874
Howell	James Howell, *Proverbs*, 1659
ibid.	*ibidem*, in the same authority or book
Irwin	Godfrey Irwin, *American Tramp and Underworld Songs and Slang*, 1931
It.	Italian
Jamieson	John Jamieson, *An Etymological Dictionary of the Scottish Language*, 1808
JB	'Jon Bee', *Dictionary*, 1823
Kelly	James Kelly, *Collection of Scottish Proverbs*, 1721
L.	Latin
LB	*The Lexicon Balatronicum*, 1811
l.c.	in or at the passage or book cited
Lyell	T. Lyell, *Slang, Phrase and Idiom in Colloquial English*, 1931
M	James Maitland, *The American Slang Dictionary*, 1891
Mackay	Charles Mackay's essay 'Popular Follies of Great Cities', in *Memoirs of Extraordinary Popular Delusions*, 1841. Available in reprint
McKnight	G. H. McKnight, *English Words and Their Background*, 1923
Manchon	J. Manchon, *Le Slang*, 1923

Matsell	George Matsell, *Vocabulum*, 1859
Moncrieff	W. T. Moncrieff, *Tom and Jerry, or Life in London* (a comedy), 1821
NZS	Sidney J. Baker, *New Zealand Slang*, 1941
ODEP	*The Oxford Dictionary of English Proverbs*, 3rd edn, 1970
ODQ	*The Oxford Dictionary of Quotations*
OED	*The Oxford English Dictionary: OED* Supp.: Supplement, 1933
P	See Clarke
PG	Francis Grose, *A Proverbial Glossary*, 1787
PGR	E. Partridge, W. Granville and F. Roberts, *A Dictionary of Forces' Slang: 1939–1945*, 1948
pl.	plural
RAF	Royal Air Force
Ray	John ('Proverbial') Ray, *English Proverbs*, 1670; 2nd edn, 1678; enlarged edn, 1813
RS	Edwin Radford and Alan Smith, *To Coin a Phrase*, 1973
S	Jonathan Swift, *Polite Conversation*, 1738, in EP's edn, 1963
Safire	William Safire, *The New Language of Politics*, 1968
Sailors' Slang	Wilfred Granville, *A Dictionary of Sailors' Slang*, 1962
sc.	L: scilicet, namely
SE	Standard English
SS	Wilfred Granville, *Sea Slang of the Twentieth Century*, 1949
Stevenson	Burton Stevenson, *Dictionary of Quotations*, 5th edn, 1946
STY	Eric Partridge, *Slang Today and Yesterday*, 1933
Thornton	R. H. Thornton, *American Glossary*, 1912
U	Eric Partridge, *A Dictionary of the Underworld*, 2nd edn, 1961; *U3*=3rd edn supplement, 1968
US	United States of America; also as adjective, American
V	Schele de Vere, *Americanisms*, 1871; 2nd edn, 1872
Vaux	John Hardy Vaux, 'Glossary of Cant', in *Memoirs*, written *c.* 1812, published 1818
Ware	J. Redding Ware, *Passing English*, 1909
Webster	Noah Webster (1758–1843). *The Living Webster Encyclopedia of the English Language*; *American Dictionary of the English Language*, 1828; *Webster's New International Dictionary*, 1909, 2nd edn, 1934; *Webster's Third New International Dictionary*, 3rd edn
Weekley	Ernest Weekley, *An Etymological Dictionary of Modern English*, 1921
W & F	H. Wentworth and S. B. Flexner, *A Dictionary of American Slang*, 1960
W-J	C. H. Ward-Jackson, *It's a Piece of Cake, or RAF Slang Made Easy*, 1943
WW1	First World War (1914–18)
WW2	Second World War (1939–45)
YB	Henry Yule and A. C. Burnell, *Hobson-Jobson*, 1886: edn by W. Crooke, 1903
[.....]	signifies that the entry so enclosed, although doubtfully eligible, is yet worthy of comment

à d'autres! Tell that to the Marines! It occurs in Shadwell, *The Sullen Lovers*, 1668, Act IV: '*Ninny.* Pshaw, pshaw, ad'autre, ad'autre, I can't abide you should put your tricks upon me' – glossed thus by George Saintsbury in his edn of four Shadwell plays: 'I.e. "à d'autres" ("tell someone else that"). It was a specially fashionable French catchword among English coxcombs and coquettes of the time. See Dryden's *Marriage à la Mode*', 1673. In short, fashionable in the fashionable London of *c.* 1660–80.

about as high as three penn'orth (or **pennyworth**) **of coppers** is a C20 c.p. applied to very short persons, but seldom heard after *c.* 1950.

[**Abyssinia!** belongs to ONE-WORD CATCH PHRASES. It means 'I'll be seein(g) you' and dates from the Abyssinian War, 1935–6.]

accidentally on purpose. Only apparently accidental, but really – and often maliciously – on purpose: since *c.* 1880 in Britain and since *c.* 1885 in US, according to W & F, who add that, in the latter, it was 'in popular student use *c.* 1940'.

according to plan was, in WW1 *communiqués*, a distressingly frequent excuse for failure, e.g. an enforced retreat; it soon became used ironically for anything, however trivial, that did *not* go according to plan. 'Oh, nonsense, old man! All according to plan, don't you know.?' (The Germans, in their *communiqués*, used an equivalent: *planmässig*.) In WW2, there was the similar phrase, *withdrawing to a prepared position*.

act your age! Act naturally – not as if you were much younger than, in fact, you are: adopted, *c.* 1920, from US, where it had an alternative – **be your age!**, likewise adopted. (*DSUE*; Berrey.)

[**apa changhol dua malam.** 'An example of "mangled Malay" from the 1950s. Literally the whole was meant to translate "What-ho to-night?" Intelligence Corps people during the Malayan Emergency (late 1940s–early 1950s).' Thus Paul Beale, on 6 November 1975.]

after his end, usually preceded by *he's*. This is a C20 workmen's c.p., applied to a man 'chasing' a woman, *end* connoting 'tail', as the variant **after his hole** makes clear.

after the Lord Mayor's show; or, in full, **after the Lord Mayor's show comes the shit-cart**. Originally (late C19) a Cockney c.p. applied to the cleaning-up (especially of horse-dung) necessary after the Lord Mayor of London's annual procession and soon extended to any comparable situation; hence in WW1 it was, mostly on the Western Front, addressed to a man returning from leave, esp. if he were just in time for a 'show' – as 'the troops', with a rueful jocularity, described an attack. Among civilians, it is extant, although not in cultured or highly educated circles.

after you, Claude – no, after you, Cecil! Characterizing an old-world, old-time, courtesy, this exchange of civilities occurred in an 'ITMA' show, produced by the BBC in (I seem to remember) 1940. Although it was already, in 1946, slightly obsolescent, yet it is still, in the latish 1970s, far from being obsolete. The Canadian version, as Dr Douglas Leechman informed me in 1959, is **after you, my dear Alphonse – no, after you, Gaston**, with variant **after you, Alphonse** (Leechman, January 1969. 'In derision of French bowing and scraping') – and was, by 1960, slightly obsolescent, and by 1970, very; current also in US, where, however, it often took the form, **you first, my dear Alphonse** (or **Alfonso**). Note that all of them were spoken in an ingratiating manner. Cf:

after you I come first is an American variant of **after you, Claude ....** (Berrey.) Cf:

after you is manners implies the speaker's consciousness, usually jocular and ironic, of inferiority: since late C17; by 1900, obsolescent – and by 1940, virtually obsolete. As so often happens, the earliest printed record occurs in S, 1738 (Dialogue II): 'Oh! madam: after you is good manners.' Elliptical for: 'For me to come after you – to make way for you – is only right.'

after you, miss, with the two two's and the two b's. See **two white ....**

after you, my dear Alphonse (or **Alfonso**). See **after you, Claude.**

after you with the po, Jane! A jocular domestic c.p. of – very approximately – *c.* 1840–90. The reference is obviously to a *pot* (*de chambre*) or *vase de nuit*, the *milieu* non-aristocratic, the form an elaboration of **after you with** this or that. (Laurie Atkinson, 25 December 1974.)

after you with the push! A street – esp. London – c.p. addressed no less politely than ironically to one who has rudely pushed his way past the speaker: *c.* 1900–14. (Ware.)

after you with the trough! Addressed to someone who has belched and implying not only that he has eaten too fast but also that he has the manners, or the lack of manners, expectable of a pig: originating, *c.* 1930 or a little earlier, in the North Country and still, in 1970 anyway, used mostly there.

age before beauty is mostly a girl's mock courtesy addressed to an old – or, at best, an elderly – man: late C19–20, but rarely heard after (say) 1960.

On entering a room, two people would joke:
'Age before beauty!'
'No, dust before the broom.'
(With thanks to Mrs Shirley M. Pearce, 12 January 1975.)

age of miracles is past – the, was contentiously used by free-thinkers during C18, challengingly by agnostics during C19 and by all cynics and most sceptics in C20. By (say) 1918, it had become a cliché; by 1945 or 1946, it was so often employed, both derisively and in such varied applications, that since then it has been also a c.p. A manifest miracle, yet I've never seen it posed, is recorded in the penultimate paragraph of **some of my best friends are Jews.**

agents. See **I have my agents**.

ah! que je can be bête! What a fool – or, how stupid – I am! This c.p. of c. 1899–1912 is, by Redding Ware, classified as 'half-society', by which he presumably means 'the fashionable section of the *demi-monde*'. Macaronic: Fr. *que*, how, and *je*, I, and *bête*, stupid.

ah there! 'What can be more revolting than phrases like *Whoa, Emma*; *Ah there!*; *Get there, Eli*; *Go it, Susan, I'll hold your bonnet*; *Everybody's doing it*; *Good night, Irene*; *O you kid!* in vogue' – that is, in the US – 'not long ago.' Thus McKnight. Cf:

ah there, my size – I'll steal you. In a footnote on p. 566 of the 4th edn, 1936, HLM includes this phrase among half a dozen of which he says that when the 'logical content' of the phrase is sheer silliness the populace quickly tires of it: 'Thus "Ah there, my size, I'll steal you", "Where did you get that hat?" ... and their congeners were all short-lived.' Obviously it's US, but, so far, I've been unable to determine, even approximately, how long it did last – or precisely when.

aid of? – what's this in. See **what's this in aid of?**

ain't ain't grammar is a humorous phrase, elicited by someone using *ain't*, as, e.g., in 'That ain't funny': since c. 1920.

ain't coming!, indicating a firm refusal, was current among US negroes during the 1940s, as CM tells us.

ain't it a fact? and **ain't it the truth?** are US phrases dating from c. 1910 – or earlier – and recorded in Berrey; the latter is also recorded by McKnight. Both are exclamatory rather than interrogative.

ain't it grand to be blooming well dead! – current in the 1930s, but naturally WW2 killed it – comes from a Leslie Sarony song of the period. (Vernon Noble, 10 May 1976.) Clearly a pun on 'Ain't it grand (just) to be alive!'

ain't love grand! expresses pleasure, originally at being in love, derivatively in other situations; and often either ironically or derisively. US at first (and still so), it became, c. 1930, also British; I heard it, 1919 or 1920, in Australia. Cf:

ain't Nature grand (? or !) is a 'c.p. apposite to anything from illegitimate offspring to tripping over a muddy path' (Laurie Atkinson, late 1974): late C19–20.

ain't that a laugh? Well, that's really a joke: US: C20. (Colonel Albert Moe, 15 June 1975). Cf the next two:

ain't that nothin'! implies a usually irritated displeasure, is characteristically US, dates from c. 1920, and derives from – and forms – the opposite of:

ain't that something – or, in rural dialect, **somepin'!** Indicative of considerable pleasure, this pleasantly terse US c.p. dates from c. 1918. Like the preceding, it is recorded in Berrey.

ain't that the limit? Can you beat that?: US: C20. (Colonel Moe, 15 June 1975.)

ain't that the truth? An emphatic, c.p. form of 'Well, that really is the truth, isn't it?': US: C20. (Colonel Moe, 15 June 1975.)

ain't we got fun (? or !) This late C19–20 US c.p. roughly answers to the British **we don't get much money – but we do see life!** (Colonel Moe, 15 June 1975.)

ain't you right! This US c.p. was 'circulating in the year 1920'

(McKnight) – esp. among students; it seems to have become obsolete by 1930.

ain't you (or yer) wild you (or ye') can't get at it? was, c. 1910–30, loudly and jeeringly intoned, at young girls passing, by Cockney adolescent youths, as Julian Franklyn told me in 1968. From the louts, who usually added *yer muvver's sewn yer draws up*, it ascended, c. 1920, to Cockney children as a 'taunting call, especially by children able to keep some desired object to themselves' (Laurie Atkinson, also in 1968).

Alamo. See **remember the Alamo!**

alas, my poor brother! A generalization of a famous Bovril advertisement of the 1920s. It showed a fine-looking bull mourning the brother quintessenced in a tin of Bovril. (Recorded in 1927 by the late Professor W. E. Collinson in his valuable book; I remember seeing it in the *Strand Magazine*, where so many famous advertisements appeared – and not a few c.pp. originated.)

Alderman Lushington is concerned and **Lushington is his master**, respectively 'Well, he *drinks*, you know' and 'He's a hopeless drunkard' – indeed *Lushington* (or *lushington*) soon came to mean 'drunkard'. The former belongs to c. 1780–1900, the latter to c. 1825–90. Perhaps a pun on the low-slang *lush*, strong liquor, and *Lushington*, the brewer; with influence from *the City of Lushington*, a convivial society that, flourishing c. 1750–1895, is recorded by *OED*. This use of *concerned* occurs in several C18–19 c.pp.

'alf a mo, Kaiser! belongs to the years 1915–18: it was, in fact, a 1915–16 recruiting poster thus captioned, the picture showing 'a "Tommy" lighting a cigarette prior to unslinging his rifle and going into action. The catch phrase was widely adopted in England' (F & G). Cf **Kitchener wants you**. The phrase survived, in civilian use, until the late 1930s, and not only in Britain.

alive and well and living in –. See **God is alive and well ...**.

all alive and kissing. See **still alive and kissing**.

all ashore as is going ashore! 'Used, outside of the original context, by, e.g., the driver of a car hastening his passengers – or rather the passengers' friends – taking over long to say good-bye' (Professor John W. Clark, in a letter dated 5 December 1968). US: apparently since the middle 1950s. Also, I surmise, a Cockneyism.

all behind – like a fat woman (or – **like Barney's bull**), often shortened to **like Barney's bull**. A low c.p. applied, late C19–20 and esp. in Australia, to one who is extremely late, or much delayed, in arriving, also to one who is physically exhausted or otherwise distressed. To the *bull* version (the commoner), either *hitched, buggered and bewildered* or (*well*) *fucked and far from home*, is added; both, however, often stand by themselves. The *fat woman* version is often used literally, 'having a very large bottom', and is then often shortened to **all behind** – cf **all bum**; in Western Australia, there exists the variation, **all behind in Melbourne** – a sly 'dig', not notably true. With the connotation of lateness or delay, the Australian version is ... **like Barney's bull**. A later variant is **all behind – like a cow's tail**, which a friend assures me was used in a BBC TV play on 3 December 1970.

all betty! (or **it's all betty!**) It's all up – the 'caper' is over, the game lost – we've completely failed: an underworld c.p. of c.

1870–1920; the opposite of **it's all bob** or **Bob's your uncle**. this sort of pun (*Bob – Betty*) being not rare in cant; but also deriving from **all my eye and Betty Martin**. (Recorded by B & L.)

all bum! was, *c*. 1860–1900, a street – esp. a London street – cry directed at a woman wearing a bustle; therefore cf **all behind – like a fat woman**.

all chiefs and no Indians, sometimes elaborated, esp. in Sydney, by the addition of **like the University Regiment**. This Australian c.p. arose *c*. 1940 and, whereas the longer form became obsolete very soon after the end of WW2, the shorter is still active; no longer restricted to Australia, it has also. since *c*. 1950, been much more widely applied: from 'all Officers and no Other Ranks' (in John Braine's *The Pious Agent*, 1975, ' "Well, we're a merchant bank, after all. More officers than privates, so to speak." '), it means 'all bosses and no workers' – 'all presidents (or chairmen) and no, or too few, executives' – and similar nuances.

all contributions gratefully received, with **however small** originally and still often added. Used literally, it does not, of course, qualify; used allusively or in very different circumstances, it has, since *c*. 1925, been a c.p., as in ' "Dying for a smoke! Anyone give me a cigarette?" A long silence. Then "All I have left is half a cigarette – the one behind my ear. Welcome to that, if you want it." No silence. "All contributions gratefully received. Ta." ' (From a novel published in 1969, Catherine Aird's *The Complete Steel*.)

all coppers are is a 'truncated version of the c.p. "All coppers are bastards", current since, at latest, 1945. This itself is only the last line of the chanted jingle, "I'll sing you a song, it's not very long: all coppers ..., etc." Obviously one would choose one's company with care before letting this dangerously abusive statement loose, even in jest' (Paul Beale, 18 July 1974). I heard it first in the late 1920s, and I suspect that it has existed throughout C20 and, among professional criminals and crooks, for at least a generation longer. It is a slanderous misstatement at the expense of an, in the majority, fine body of men, grossly underpaid ever since it was founded. Cf, semantically, 'once a policeman, always a policeman', which is not a c.p., for it follows the pattern of 'once a schoolteacher, always a schoolteacher', a much-exaggerated piece of dogma. Every profession, trade, occupation, has its black sheep.

all day! is a children's and young people's rejoinder to the query 'What's the date – is it the *X*th?' If the question is simply 'What's the date?' the answer is 'The *X*th – *all day*.' Arising *c*. 1890 – if not a decade or two earlier – it was, by 1960, very slightly obsolescent, yet it doesn't, even now, look at all moribund.

all done by kindness! This ironic late C19–20 phrase occurs in that unjustly forgotten novel, W. L. George's *The Making of an Englishman*, 1914. It is often used in jocularly explanatory response to, e.g., 'How on earth did you manage to do *that*?'; also as in 'Not at all! All done by kindness, I assure you' – 'a nonchalant c.p. of dismissal of thanks for an action that is done to someone else's advantage' (Wilfred Granville, in a letter dated 14 January 1969). It seems, as Professor T. B. W. Reid has (6 December 1974) reminded me, to have originated with performing animals and the assurances of their trainers. Cf and contrast:

all done with (occasionally **by**) **mirrors**, often preceded by **it's**. A phrase uttered when something very clever or extremely ingenious has been done: since *c*. 1920, at latest. It probably originated either among or, at the least, in relation to stage conjurors. In Noël Coward's *Private Lives*, performed and published in 1933, occurs (Act II) this illuminating example:

> AMANDA [*wistfully clutching his hand*]: That's serious enough, isn't it?
> ELYOT: No, no, it isn't. Death's very laughable, such a cunning little mystery. All done with mirrors.

Occasional variant: *all done with pieces of string*, probably in reference to Heath Robinson's contraptions.

all dressed up and no place (US) (or **nowhere**) **to go** originated, *c*. 1915, in 'a song by Raymond Hitchcock, an American comedian' (Collinson); by 1937 it was obsolescent – as it still is, yet, like **all day!** above, very far from obsolete.

all dressed up like Astor's horse. US: since '*c*. 1930 (? obs.). Perhaps largely Broadway lingo; possibly invented by Damon Runyon. Intended to suggest that someone was overdressed' (Edward Hodnett, 18 August 1975).

all fine ladies are witches: C18. In S, Dialogue II, we find:

> LADY SM.: You have hit it; I believe you are a Witch.
> MISS: O, Madam, the Gentlemen say, all fine Ladies are Witches; but I pretend to no such Thing.

An allusion to women's intuition?

all gas and gaiters is the shortened – the c.p. – form of 'All is gas and gaiters' in Dickens's *Nicholas Nickleby*, 1838–9. In civilian life, the c.p. is often applied to bishops and archbishops: a reference to the gaiters they wear and to the facile eloquence beloved by so many of them: indeed *gas and gaiters* has come to mean 'mere verbiage'. But the c.p. has not been much used after *c*. 1950. See also **attitude is the art of gunnery ....**

all honey or all turd with them, usually preceded by **it is**. They are either close friends or bitter enemies – they fly from one extreme to the other: mid C18–mid C19. (Grose, 3rd edn, 1796.)

all I know is what I read in the papers, which we owe to Will Rogers, the so-called 'cowboy philosopher', is the c.p. form of the words beginning his 'letter' of 21 May 1926: 'Dear Mr Coolidge: Well all I know is just what I read in the papers' (Will Rogers, *The Letters of a Self-Made Diplomat to His President*, 1927): by which he meant that all he knew of events in the US was what he could glean from the English newspapers. A particular and topical reference became, as is the way in the genesis of c.pp., general and enduring: and this one has 'worn very well', esp. in US, where, very properly, it has always been far more popular than in Britain, not that it's in the least rare even in Britain. Mr W. J. Burke has, on 9 March 1975, told me that, in the US, it continues to be very widely used.

The interpretation made above is very British, however natural it may sound. An old friend, Dr Joseph T. Shipley, wrote thus to me on 3 December 1974:

> I showed [your 'item'] to ... a publisher. He said: 'This misses the point. Wherever Will Rogers was, the expression means: "*I'm just an ordinary citizen. I don't read the highbrow journals, the magazines that tell you the news isn't so; I'm not a professor; I don't go to listen to men that call themselves experts: all I know is what I read in*

the papers – and that makes me as good a citizen as the next man."

'The sentence also implies: "I don't trust them pernickety persuaders always telling you they know what isn't so. I get my facts from the papers, and that's good enough for me." '

Then, on his own account, Dr Shipley adds:

(Note the naïve implication: 'All I *know* ...'. If it's in the papers, it's true. A man may try to lie to me; print doesn't lie!) The catch phrase 'All I know is what I read in the papers' is an implied assertion that all *you* (i.e., anyone) can know is what you read in the papers; and my opinion is therefore as good as the next man's, and that's the way it is and should be in this democracy. That's what Will Rogers felt, and that's the spirit underlying his humor and a main source of his popularity.

A long discussion for a short sentence! But it does mean more than it says. And I think the final implication above (that the simple man is as qualified a citizen as the self-styled expert) deserves mention.

Yes, indeed!

all in the seven. See **it's all in the seven.**

all in the twelve. See **it's all in the twelve.**

all is bob. See **Bob's your uncle.**

all is rug. See **all's rug.**

all jam and Jerusalem is a slightly derogatory c.p. directed at Women's Institutes since *c.* 1925. Whereas *jam* arises from the jam-making contents, *Jerusalem* refers to Blake's 'Jerusalem' being sung at every meeting – less in piety than as a signature. A very English phrase concerning a very English institution.

all Lombard Street to a Brummagem sixpence is a c.p. – a jocular variation of **all Lombard Street to a china orange.** Meaning 'heavy odds', the original and originating **all Lombard Street to a china orange** (a piece of chinaware) has the further variants **... to ninepence** and **... to an egg-shell;** all three variants arose in C19 – and all, as c.pp., are obsolete. The reference is to the wealth of this famous London street.

all my eye (and Betty Martin), often preceded by **that's.** 'That is utter nonsense.' The shorter form seems to have been the earlier, Goldsmith using it in 1768; yet Francis Grose, in his dictionary, shows the variant *that's my eye, Betty Martin* to have been already familiar in 1785. Grose's form became obsolete before 1900, as did such variants as *all my eye, Betty* (Thomas Moore, 1819) and *all my eye and Tommy* (John Poole's *Hamlet Travestied,* 1811), this mysterious *Tommy* recurring, as Ernest Weekley long ago pointed out, in the phrases *like Hell and Tommy* and the earlier *play Hell and Tommy.* The predominant short form is (*that's*) *all my eye,* which recurs in, e.g., R. S. Surtees, *Hillingdon Hall; or, The Cockney Squire,* 1845; there, in chapter XVI, we read, ' "The land's worked out!" says another, slopin' off in the night without payin' his rent. "That's all my eye!" exclaimed Mr Jorrocks.' Surtees uses it again in *Hawbuck Grange,* 1847.

I think that the original form was *all my eye!,* which later acquired the variant *my eye!:* perhaps cf the slangy and synonymous Fr. *mon oeil!,* which could, indeed, have generated *all my eye,* if, in fact, the Fr. phrase preceded the English, although probably each arose independently of the

other and was created by that 'spontaneous combustion' which would account for so much that is otherwise unaccountable in English. The full *all my eye and Betty Martin* is less used in the 1970s than it was in the 1870s, but 'there's life in the old girl yet'.

Inevitably the *and Betty Martin* part of the complete phrase has caused much trouble and even more hot air: who *was* she? I suspect that she was a 'character' of the lusty London of the 1770s and that no record of her exists other than in this c.p. In *The Disagreeable Surprise: A Musical Farce,* ?1828, George Daniel makes Billy Bombast say, 'My first literary attempt was a flaming advertisement ... My next was a Satirical Poem ... I then composed the whole art and mystery of Blacking or Every Man his own Polisher; which turned out all Betty Martin ...' and thus offers us yet another variant: and in the Earl of Glengall's *The Irish Tutor; or, New Lights: A Comic Piece,* performed in 1823 and published *c.* 1830, the spurious Dr O'Toole says to his tutor, 'Hark ye, sirrah, hem – [*Aside to him*] It's all Betty Martin. I have demaned myself by brushing your coat, to *tache* you modesty.' 'Jon Bee' in his dictionary, 1823, propounded a theory silently adopted a generation later by William Camden Hutton, that *Betty Martin* derives from, and corrupts the L. *o(h), mihi, beate Martine* (St Martin of Tours), which, they said, occurs in a prayer that apparently doesn't exist. Slightly more probable is the theory advanced by Dr L. A. Waddell in his highly speculative book, *The Phoenician Origin of Britons, Scots, and Anglo-Saxons,* 1914; to the effect that *all my eye and Betty Martin* derives, entire, from L. *O mihi, Britomartis,* 'Oh, (bring help) to me, Britomartis', who, we are told, was the tutelary goddess of Crete and whose cult was either identical or, at the least, associated with the sun-cult of the Phoenicians – who traded with Britons for Cornish tin. Such etymologies lose sight of a basic problem: how did – how *could* – the Cockneys, among whom the phrase originated, ever come to even encounter either of these two religious and erudite L. phrases? The relationship appears wildly improbable.

Such energetic ingenuity is supererogatory, these erudite imaginings being inherently much less convincing than the theory of simple English origin. To me, anyway, *all my eye and Betty Martin!* no more than elaborates *all my eye!;* and as for Betty Martin, well! the English language, in its less formal aspects, affords many examples of mysterious characters appearing in a phrase and recorded nowhere else. In this instance, however, there was, in the (?) latter part of C18, 'an abandoned woman' named Grace, an actress, who induced a Mr Martin to marry her. She became notorious as Betty Martin: and favourite expressions of hers were *my eye!* and *all my eye,* as Charles Lee Lewis tells us in his *Memoirs,* 1805. Even that immensely erudite poet, Southey, remarked, in *The Doctor,* 1834–7, that he was 'puzzled by this expression'. (And Mr Ronald Pearsall, of Landscove, Devon, imparts *his* erudition to me on 12 January 1975.)

In South Africa, *Betsy.* (Professor A. C. Partridge.)

all my eye and my elbow! and **all my eye and my grandmother!** are London variants of **all my eye and Betty Martin:** strictly, the *grandmother* version stems from the *elbow* version. The latter is recorded by Ware for 1882, and seems to have fallen into disuse by 1920; the former is recorded in Baumann, 1887, and was obsolescent by 1937 and obsolete by 1970. Note also *so's your grandfather!*, which, expressing incredulity, has been current since late C19, is still very much alive, although, by 1970, mildly obsolescent, and has been general throughout England.

all my eye and Peggy Martin, often preceded by **that's**. A C20 (and earlier?) North Country variant of **all my eye and Betty Martin**. Vernon Noble, on 9 December 1974, glosses it: 'Romantic nonsense, not to be believed. Long common in the north of England. There probably was a romancer named Peggy Martin.'

all my (or **me**) **own work** is a c.p. only when used figuratively – chiefly when the tone is either jocular or ironic, esp. if ironically self-deprecatory. Dating from *c.* 1920, it originated, I believe, in the drawings and paintings displayed by pavement artists. Cf **alone I did it**, which is not, of course, synonymous.

all on top. That's untrue!: a c.p. of the British underworld; dating from *c.* 1920. The evidence is all – but *only* – on top; in short, superficial.

all over – bar (occasionally **but**) **the shouting**, often preceded by **it's**. Originally – the earliest record apparently occurs in C. J. Apperley's *The Life of a Sportsman*, 1842 – both the British and the US form was (*it's*) *all over but the shouting*, but in late C19–20 it has predominantly been ... *bar the shouting*. As c.pp. they developed, late in C19, from the proverbial or semi-proverbial *all is over but shouting* (Apperley's version); the *bar* form occurs in Adam Lindsay Gordon's poem, *How We Beat the Favourite*, 1869, as 'The race is all over, bar shouting'. In Henry Arthur Jones, *The Manoeuvres of Jane*, 1898, near end of Act IV, there is a rare variant:
STEPHEN: Well, George, how goes it?
SIR G: All over, I think, except the shouting.
This is a particularly interesting example, for it is sometimes a genuine proverbial saying and sometimes a genuine c.p.; in C20, almost entirely a c.p.

all over the place like a mad woman's shit. Used in Australia to describe a state of complete untidiness or confusion. (Camilla Raab.)

all part of the service – it's. See **just part of ....**

all parts bearing an equal strain. All is well – 'no complaints': Naval: since *c.* 1930. Derivatively, since *c.* 1945, it is also applied to oneself, or to another, lying down comfortably.

all pissed-up and nothing to show (sc. *for it*) is a working-class phrase addressed – or used in reference – to one who has spent all his wages or all his winnings on drink; since *c.* 1920. On the analogy – indeed, moulded to the shape – of **all dressed up and nowhere to go**.

all present and correct! All correct; all in order, as in Ronald Knox, *Still Dead*, 1934, ' "Is that all present and correct?" "Couldn't be better." ' It comes from the sergeant-major's phrase, used in reporting on a parade to the officer in charge.

all profit! is a C20 barbers' c.p., spoken usually to the customer himself, when no 'dressing' is required on the hair.

all quiet on the Potomac; **all quiet in the Shipka Pass** and **all quiet on the Western Front**. The first is the earliest, although decidedly not the model for the other two. It is, obviously, US: and it naturally arose during the Civil War (1861–5) from its frequent application – either by Secretary of War Cameron or by General McClellan or, as is probable, by

both – to a comparatively quiet period in 1861–2 on that sector. It enraged a public that wanted action and soon caught on, esp. in jocular and often somewhat derisive irony; it remained a very general c.p. for the whole of a generation and even for some forty years; Berrey adjudges it to have become obsolete by 1910. (For fuller information, see notably *D. Am.*)

In the US, *all's quiet* – but usually *all quiet – on the Western Front* derives 'from the standard official phrase as issued daily by the War Department during relatively calm ... periods during ... WW1' (Berrey), but as a c.p. it was, of course, applied to periods or situations devoid of fighting or quarrelling or mere bickering, precisely as in Britain 'at home and abroad'; indeed, the US official phrase was adopted from the War Office's *communiqués*, which, even during the latter half of that war, roused the derision and ribaldry of the men fighting it instead of writing about it – it was *they* who originated the c.p., which persisted right up to WW2 and is still used. Erich Maria Remarque's *Im Westen Nichts Neues* (Berlin, 1929), admirably translated by A. H. Wheen as *All Quiet on the Western Front* and published by Putnam in 1929, reinforced the popularity and still further widened the use of the phrase. On 3 January 1969, Professor John W. Clark wrote to tell me that it was 'a real c.p., at least in this country [US], in that it is indiscriminately used, without reference to WW1'.

The c.p. *all quiet on the Western Front* owes nothing to the US *all quiet on the Potomac*: it was suggested by *all quiet in the Shipka Pass*, which, current in 1915–16, refers to – or, rather, was prompted by – Vasily Vereshchagin's bitter cartoons of a Russian soldier being gradually, ineluctably, buried in falling snow during the Russo-Turkish War of 1877–8; this is a pass through the Balkan Mountains and was the scene of exceptionally bloody fighting; and Vereshchagin's paintings acquired a just fame far beyond Russia. That fame led to a revival of interest in Vereshchagin's war paintings and cartoons, an interest culminating in the journalistic, hence also a brief military, c.p., *all quiet in the Shipka Pass*. (I myself never heard it during WW1, either on Gallipoli or in Egypt or on the Western Front.)

all right, all right, as in Dorothy L. Sayers, *Murder Must Advertise*, 1933, ' "She's a smart jane, all right, all right" '. intensifies a simple *all right*. It goes back to early C20, perhaps to late C19.

all right – don't pipe it! Belonging to the Royal Navy's lower-deck, it is 'addressed to a man who speaks too loud, in the manner of a Tannoy, for all to hear when *not* all should hear' (Wilfred Granville, in letter of 7 August 1970): since *c.* 1930.

all right for *some*! 'Some people have all the luck. A c.p. of disgruntlement by one of the luckless' (Wilfred Granville, 13 January 1969): C20. Cf:

all right for you is ironically addressed to those who are worse off than oneself: the fighting Services': since *c.* 1940.

all right on the night (that is, on the first night – the opening night), an actors' c.p., applied to a bad – esp. a very bad – dress rehearsal, dates from *c.* 1890. (Granville.) It has, since *c.* 1920, gained a wider acceptance – an application, in the larger world, to small things going wrong, but optimistically hoped to go right – to judge by its extension and allusiveness in Nichol Fleming's *Hush*, 1971, 'I've always found the soft sell

almost irresistible.... "It'll be all right on the night," I said.'
This, perhaps the most famous of all theatrical c.pp., shortens
it will all come right on the night, which has a variant: *it will
be all right on the night*.

all right up to now. All is well – so far: 1878–*c.* 1915: originally,
and always, mostly feminine. 'Used by Herbert Campbell ...
in Covent Garden Theatre Pantomime, 1878', as Ware, himself a writer of light comedies, tells us; he adds that it derives
from '*enceinte* women making this remark as to their condition'; the phrase became used also in other circumstances.

all right – you did hear a seal bark indicates a resigned, long-
suffering, vocal agreement (and mental disagreement) with
someone who insists that something odd is indeed happening: US: since *c.* 1950. It was occasioned by James Thurber's
famous caption and sketch (of a seal leaning over the head-
board of a bed and barking as it looks down at a married
couple, the woman insistent and the man sceptical), appearing originally in the *New Yorker* and reprinted in one of his
inimitable collections of sketches.

all round my hat! was a derisive, originally and always predominantly Cockney, retort, connoting 'What nonsense you're
talking': approximately *c.* 1834–90. Perhaps from the broadside ballad, 'All Round my Hat I Wears a Green Willow'.
A derivative sense appears in *spicy as all round my hat*, a
slangy expression meaning 'sensational' and occurring in
Punch, 1882.

That comic song, written by John Hansett, with music by
John Valentine, was – according to the British Museum
Library's *Modern Music Catalogue* – first sung in 1834; it was
included in *The Franklin Square Song Collection*, 8 parts,
1881–91, published in New York.

Mackay noted the c.p. in his long essay. The phrase and
the song became so popular that George Dibdin Pitt's
'domestic drama', *Susan Hopley; or, The Vicissitudes of a
Servant Girl*, 1841, Act III, Scene ii, ends with the stage directions: '*Music ... Dicky sings "All Round My Hat" and leads
the Donkey off*.' And in R. S. Surtees, *Handley Cross*, 1854,
vol. II, the chapter titled 'The Stud Sale', we find:

'Well done!' exclaimed Mr Jorrocks, patting the orator's
back.
'Keep the tambourine a rowlin'!' growled Pigg, turning
his quid, and patting the horse's head.
'All round my 'at!' squeaked Benjamin in the crowd.

all round St Paul's – not forgetting the trunkmaker's daughter
was a book-world c.p. used in late C18–early 19 and applied
to unsalable books. The *OED* quoted *The Globe* of 1 July
1890: 'By the trunkmaker was understood ... the depository
for unsalable books.' At that period – and, indeed, until 'the
London blitz' of 1940–1 – the district around St Paul's was
famous for its bookshops and its book-publishers.

all serene!, short for *it's all serene* (quiet, safe, favourable),
is enshrined in Dickens's comment, 1853: 'An audience will
sit in a theatre and listen to a string of brilliant witticisms,
with perfect immobility; but let some fellow ... roar out "It's
all serene", or "Catch 'em alive, oh!" (this last is sure to take),
pit, boxes, and gallery roar with laughter.' M. has the entry:
'**Serene** (Eng.). "all serene", all right; a phrase taken from a
comic song and used, when first introduced, on all occasions.
Now it is seldom heard.' That sharp observer of current
speech, R. S. Surtees, in *Plain or Ringlets*, 1860, chapter LV,

writes, 'On this auspicious day, however, it was "all serene",
as old Saddlebags said.' It was, in England, still being used
right up to WW2.

[all Sir Garnet! and **all Sirgarneo!** All right!: since *c.* 1885,
the former; since *c.* 1895, the latter, on the analogy of such
locutions as *all aliveo*; both slightly obsolescent by 1915, very
much so by 1935, and obsolete by 1940. From *c.* 1890 there
existed the Cockney variant, *all Sir Garny*, as in Edwin Pugh,
Harry the Cockney, 1912. From the military fame of Sir Garnet (later Viscount) Wolseley (1833–1923) – almost as famous
in his day as Lord Roberts ('Bobs') was in his – who served
both actively and brilliantly from 1852–85. He did much to
improve the lot of the Other Ranks, who often debased *Sir
Garnet* to *Sirgarneo*, whence *Sigarneo*, whence *Sigarno*. In the
debased forms it was quite common among Common-
wealth troops. (B & P) But I'd say that none of them is a true
c.p.]

all smoke, gammon and spinach (occasionally **pickles**). All
nonsense: *c.* 1870–1900. An elaboration of the slangy *gammon
and spinach* (used by, e.g., Dickens in 1849), nonsense, hum-
bug, itself an elaboration of *gammon*, nonsense.

all systems go, 'literally the statement of readiness for launch-
ing manned and unmanned rocket systems for space exploration from Cape Canaveral, esp. for the moon landings in the
late 1960s and early 1970s was popularized through world-
wide television coverage. The words were taken up in Britain
[*c.* 1970] and America [*c.* 1969] as a c.p. for preparedness
for any endeavour, often used humorously' (Vernon Noble,
26 February 1974). *DCCU*, independently in 1971 after
appearing, 1970, in some editions of Webster, with this
example, 'It's *all systems go* here, so let's take off'.

[all talk and no cider. That's 'a great deal of talk and no
results' (Berrey, 1942): US: C20; by 1970, obsolescent – and
by 1975, as Colonel Albert Moe tells me on 14 July, obsolete.

And then, on 31 July 1975, Colonel Moe, after remarking
that the phrase is 'of long standing, but still heard occasionally', quotes from *Salmagundi*, I, 7 (4 April 1807) – where
Washington Irving, in 'Letter from Mustapha Rub-a-dub
Keli Khan', has this passage:

Now after all it is an even chance that the subject of this
prodigious arguing, quarrelling and talking is an affair of
no importance and ends entirely in smoke. May it not then
be said, the whole nation have been talking to no purpose?
The people, in fact, seem to be somewhat conscious of this
propensity to talk, by which they are characterized, and
have a favourite proverb on the subject, viz. 'all talk and
no cider'.

In short, all talk and no cider should perhaps be classified,
not as a c.p. but as a proverbial saying, apparently from late,
maybe mid, C18. To me it sounds like a mislaid aphorism
coined by that master of aphorism, Benjamin Franklin
(1706–90) – as in his *Poor Richard's Almanack*, 1732–57.
Clearly reminiscent is Artemus Ward's 'What we want is
more cider and less talk'. Nevertheless, I have included the
phrase in deference to several US friends whose opinion is
never to be ignored.]

all that the name implies is 'a c.p., which originated in a
chance expression used during the *cause célèbre* of the Rev.
Henry Ward Beecher' (Farmer): US: *c.* 1875–90. The trial
took place in 1875; Beecher died in 1889.

all the better for seeing you! is the cheerfully courteous answer to 'How *are* you?': late C19–20. Contrast *none the better for your asking!*, q.v. at **better for your asking**.

all the same in a hundred years. See **it'll all be the same ....**

all the traffic will bear, often preceded by *that's*. Literally, it relates to fares and freights; only figuratively it is a c.p., meaning that the situation, whether financial or other, precludes anything more. Originally – ? *c.* 1945 – US, it was adopted *c.* 1948 in Canada and *c.* 1955 in Britain. It is – Dr Douglas Leechman tells me – said to derive from a US magnate's cynicism.

all there and a ha'p'orth over was, *c.* 1870–1914, the superlative of *all there* used as a term of approval. (M.)

all there but the most of you! was a low, raffish c.p. applied (as if you hadn't guessed!) to copulation: mid C19–20 – but by *c.* 1950, extinct.

all things – occasionally **everything** – **to all men** – **and nothing to one man** is aimed at prostitutes or at 'enthusiastic amateurs' or at promiscuous girls or women in general. I first heard it in 1940 – and rather think it didn't much precede that date.

all tits and teeth. (Of a woman) having protrusive breasts and large teeth: a low c.p. of C20. Hence, a still low but predominantly Cockney c.p., dating from *c.* 1910 and applied to a woman wearing an insincere smile and exhibiting a notable skill in displaying the amplitude of her bosom (*il y a du monde au balcon*). An alert and erudite friend, writing to me in March 1967, recalled that he had sometimes heard this phrase elaborated to ' "... like a third-row chorus girl", i.e. one who can neither sing nor dance, and depends upon the display of her exceptional physique to keep her on the stage'.

all together like Brown's (or **Browne's**) **cows**, often preceded by *we're*. We're alone: an Anglo-Irish c.p. of late C19–20. This fellow Brown – a creature merely of anecdotal tradition, not a character in history – possessed only one cow. Clearly of rural, probably of rustic, origin. (Owed to the late Frank Shaw, the authority on Scouse.)

all very large and fine! indicates either ironic approval or incredulity or even derision: 1886, from 'the refrain of a song sung by Mr Herbert Campbell' (Ware) and much in vogue for a couple of years; by 1935, slightly obsolescent, and by 1950, obsolete, its place having, *c.* 1920 if not earlier, been taken by *all very fine and large*, usually preceded by *it's* or *that's*.

all white and spiteful. See **white and spiteful.**

all wind and piss like a barber's cat is contemptuous of a man given to much talk, esp. to much boasting, and little, if any, performance: probably since *c.* 1800, for it clearly derives from the semi-proverbial C18–19 *like the barber's cat, all wind and piss*. Cf also the C20 slang phrase, *pissing like the barber's cat*, applied to prolific output – which I owe (17 January 1975) to Mr C. A. Worth.

all's rug (or **all rug** or **it's all rug**). '*It's all Rug*, *c.* [i.e., cant]. The Game is secured' (B.E., Gent, 1698) – all is safe: late C17–mid 19. Cf both the proverbial *snug as a bug in a rug* and:

all's snug! All is safe: an underworld c.p. of C18–mid 19. A variant of *all rug* or *all's rug* or *it's all rug*, qq.v. in entry preceding this. See *U* for a more detailed treatment.

alone I did it is both British and US. My only early record of this latish C19–20 c.p. occurs in Act I of Alfred Sutro's *The Fascinating Mr Vanderbildt*, performed and published in 1906:

> VANDERBILDT: Your doing, of course?
> CLARICE: Alone I did it.

By 1940, obsolescent; by 1970, almost obsolete – but not yet entirely so. Cf the rather different **all my own work**.

⎡**although** (or **though**) **I say it who** – occasionally **that – shouldn't**, with originally illiterate, but soon deliberately jocular, variant **(al)though I says it as shouldn't**. A borderline case, which, after much thought, I adjudge to be not a c.p. but a hackneyed quotation, going at least as far back as *though I say it that should not say it* (often, in C19–20, ... *that shouldn't*) in Beaumont and Fletcher's *Wit at Several Weapons*, Act II, Scene ii.⎤

always be nice to people on your way up – you may meet them (again) on your way down; but perhaps more often without *always*. I did not become conscious of this as a c.p. – for several years I had regarded it as merely a cynical epigram – until mid-1975: and then, within a month, I read John Braine's exemplarily intelligent, witty, genuinely exciting novel of espionage, *The Pious Agent*, 1975. There, a senior official of the KGB said to an up-and-coming young agent, 'And, as the saying goes, always be nice to people on your way up. You may meet them again on your way down.' Cf this from 'Number Ten' in John Osborne's *The Entertainer* (produced and published in 1957), where Billy, the old-timer, says: 'Well, Eddie's still up there all right. He's still up there. (To Jean.) I always used to say to him, we all used to say: "Eddie, always be good" ', etc. Occasionally either *good* or *kind* has been substituted for *nice*.

It seems, however, that it was originally US: Bartlett attributes it (with a cautionary 'also attributed to Jimmy Durante', who was born in 1893) to Wilson Mizner, in the form *be nice to people on your way up because you'll meet 'em on your way down*.

always in trouble like a Drury Lane whore is a late C19–20 phrase reprehending one who wallows in self-pity, also one who deplores a series of personal misfortunes. Prostitutes frequenting this area have always tended to dramatize their troubles – or so the legend goes.

am I burned up! Am I angry! – or irritated! – or resentful! A US c.p. dating since *c.* 1920. (Berrey.) Cf:

am I insulated! and **am I irrigated!** Am I insulted – am I irritated! Both of these US c.pp., recorded by Berrey, were short-lived: say 1930–45. Clearly intentional puns, not malapropisms.

am I is or am I ain't?, am I or am I not?; **are we is or are we ain't?**, are we or aren't we? The former is a derivative of **is you *is* or is you *ain't*?**, q.v.

AMERICAN HISTORICAL BORDERLINERS
Of the various candidates, three stand out from the rest:
1 **damn the torpedoes – full steam ahead!**;
2 **don't fire till you see the whites of their eyes**;
3 **you may fire when you are ready, Gridley**.

The first is listed in, e.g., Burton Stevenson's *Book of Quotations* as **damn the torpedoes!** and attributed to David Glasgow Farragut, at the Battle of Mobile Bay on 5 August 1864. As a c.p., from *c.* 1880, it = damn it all, we'll take the risk!

The second was the command issued by the US commander at the Battle of Bunker Hill on 17 June 1775. Being the only one of the three to have attained British currency, this has been accorded an individual entry.

The third is, in *BQ*, attributed to Admiral George Dewey as having been said to the Captain of his flagship at the Battle of Manila on 1 May 1898. (It occurs in Dewey's *Autobiography* at p. 214.)

Of the trio, Professor John W. Clark, in a letter dated 25 September 1968, says that he thinks they qualify as c.pp. 'When they are used, they are almost always used *without* reference to the original situation. But I will agree that, if there is a clear and valuable distinction between famous quotation, cliché, and catch phrase, they may be the first or the second rather than the third.' I'd say that *damn the torpedoes* and *you may fire when you are ready, Gridley* are both famous quotation *and* cliché and that *don't fire till you see the whites of their eyes* is both quotation and c.p., but in C20 predominantly the latter.

AMERICAN POLITICAL SLOGANS JUST FAILING TO MAKE THE GRADE

Dr Joseph T. Shipley, in a letter dated 1 April 1974, writes thus pertinently and convincingly:

> **remember the Alamo**: after the garrison was wiped out, became the battle cry of General Houston in Mexico, 1836, when Texas was annexed to the US.
> **remember the *Maine***: after the battleship was attacked in Havana Harbor in 1896, the battle cry for the war against Spain.
> **remember Pearl Harbor**: after the airplane strike of 6 December 1941, the battle-cry rallying our country against Japan.
> All of these seem to me to be propaganda slogans, rather than catch phrases.

I agree, but include them, none the less.

amuse yourself – don't mind me! Meaning 'Have your fun!', it was originally US, mostly teenagers' and students' of the early 1920s, as recorded by McKnight; adopted in Britain *c.* 1924, but by 1960 virtually obsolete.

an hour past hanging time, a C18 rejoinder to 'What's the time?', appears in S. Cf **kissing time**.

and all that (i.e., and all such things) was Standard English until 1929, when Robert Graves changed all that in his very distinguished war book, *Goodbye to All That*.

and all that jazz. And all that sort of thing; 'and all the rest concerning the subject under discussion, as in "sex and all that jazz". 1960 plus' (Wilfred Granville, in letter dated 23 January 1969). Adopted in Britain from the US, perhaps via Canada; by W & F recorded in a quotation from a newspaper article of 16 February 1958, but already current a year or two earlier. In US, it bore – as indeed it came, in Britain, to bear – the further sense 'and all that nonsense'.

and Bob's your uncle! And all will be well; all will be perfect: since *c.* 1890. 'You go and ask for the job – and he remembers your name – and Bob's your uncle.' Australian as well as British, a fairly late example occurring in Michael Gilbert's 'Modus Operandi', a story in the collection entitled *Stay of Execution*, 1971, and an earlier in John Arden's *When Is a Door Not a Door?*, produced in 1958, published 1967. The origin remains a mystery; just possibly it was prompted by the cant (then low-slang) phrase, *all is bob*, 'all is safe'. Folk-etymologically, the origin is said to lie in the open and unashamed nepotism practised by some British premier or other famous politician, as the late Frank Shaw reminded me late in 1968.

and call it 'it'. Let's say the job is done, as in 'I'll just take the duster round the room and call it done' (Wilfred Granville, 11 February 1969): mostly domestic: since *c.* 1950.

and did he marry poor blind Nell? An Australian c.p. dating from *c.* 1910 or perhaps a little earlier. I cannot – nor should I try to – do better than to quote my pen-friend Barry Prentice:

> A rhetorical question asked about anything improbable. Also as a euphemism for *like fucking hell*. Ex the saga of *Poor Blind Nell*. (Cf *Ballocky Bill the Sailor*, *The Bastard from the Bush*, etc.) As in 'and did he marry ...?' – 'He did! – (*softly*) Like fuckin(g) hell!' *Poor Blind Nell* itself is used to describe any simple girl who is over-trusting where men are concerned.

and don't you forget it! – *and* being often omitted. A c.p. originally (–1888) US; adopted *c.* 1890. After being admonitory, it became an almost pointless intensive. The expression so infuriated John Farmer that, in 1889, he inveighed thus: 'One of the popular catch-phrases which every now and then seize hold of the popular taste (or want of taste) and run their course like wildfire through all the large centres of population. They convey no special idea, rational or irrational, and can only be described as utterly senseless and vulgar.' Vulgar they often are; only rarely are they senseless, for although the meaning is often imprecise, the general purport is usually very clear indeed. Berrey, 1942, classifies it as a c.p. of affirmation.

and he didn't! is a tailors' c.p., referring to – or implying – a discreditable action: *c.* 1870–1920.

and his name is mud! An exclamatory c.p., commenting on a foolish speech in the House of Commons or on one who has been heavily defeated or disgraced: since *c.* 1815. In C20 the meaning is weaker: merely 'he has been discredited; he is out of favour with, e.g., a woman'.

and how! indicates intensive emphasis of what one has just said or intensive agreement with what someone else has just said: originally US (Berrey), dating from *c.* 1925 and probably translating the *e come!* of the very large Italian population; adopted in Britain by 1935 at latest: Frank Shaw, in a letter dated 1 September 1969, says that it came from early US 'talkies' and had 'v. much 30's vogue U.K.' – i.e., very much of a vogue in the United Kingdom during the 1930s, the vogue, by the way, lasting until at least 1945 and the usage still (1975) fairly active; it was, moreover, recorded by EP in *A Dictionary of Clichés*, 1940. In Gelett Burgess, *Two O'Clock Courage*, 1934: 'I said: "But I'm afraid you're ill!" – "*And* how!" she said dreamily. "Ain't I got a right to be if I want to, mister?" Her eyes didn't even open.'

> Clarence B. Kelland, *Speak Easily*, *c.* 1935:
> 'Is a drinking-song essential?' I asked.
> 'And how!' said Mr Greb.

The phrase recurs in Kelland's *Dreamland*, 1938. An early English example occurs in Maurice Lincoln's witty novel, *Oh! Definitely*, 1933; and in Alec Waugh's *Wheels within Wheels*, 1933. A young American exclaims: 'Oh boy, if you could see the look in my mother's face at times! She thinks she's living in a fairy tale. And as for that girl, oh boy and how! You should just see her!' Cf:

and I don't mean maybe! (or occasionally ... **perhaps!**) – with *and* often omitted. Berrey, 1942, records both as Americanisms: and Americanisms they remained. They seem to have arisen *c.* 1920. An early example is afforded by Clarence B. Kelland's *Dance Magic*, 1927, ' "Leach is a bearcat and I don't mean maybe." '

and it takes a small mind to notice it! See **and only** ....

and like it! 'A naval expression anticipating a grouse and added to any instruction for an awkward and unwanted job' (H & P); it probably arose during WW1.

and no error! See **and no mistake!**

and no flies. And no doubt about it at all: a c.p. tag of the lower and lower-middle classes of *c.* 1835–70. Mayhew, 1851. No flies are allowed to settle on it and thus obscure the patent truth.

and no kidding! I mean it. An extension of **no kidding!**, q.v. (Berrey.)

and no mistake, dating from *c.* 1810 (*OED* records it for 1818) and meaning 'undoubtedly', has generated the much later, rather less used, *and no error* (recorded by Baumann): very general until *c.* 1920, but not yet (1976) obsolete. Both of these phrases were adopted in the US: M records them in 1891 and illuminatingly adds, ' "Don't you make no error" is the ungrammatical method of asserting that what has been said is a fact.' Berrey notes *and no mistake* as an 'expression of affirmation'.

and no mogue? A tailors' c.p., implying slight incredulity, 'That's true?': since *c.* 1880. Something of a mystery, *mogue* perhaps derives from Fr. *moquerie* but more probably derives from gypsies' and Ger. underworld *mogeln*, to mock, reaching into England by way of Yiddish.

and no whistle is another tailors' c.p., implying that the speaker is, in the fact, although not in appearance, referring to himself: *c.* 1860–1900.

and not a bone in the truck imputes time-wasting during hours of work, as in 'Ten o'clock – and not a bone in the truck' (loading hasn't even been started): mostly in factories and mostly Australian: C20.

and one for the road, the *and* being often omitted, is a C20 – originally commercial travellers' – c.p., either applied to the last of several drinks or proposing a final drink to keep one warm on the journey.

and only small minds would notice (i.e., observe and remark upon) **it!** Variant: **and it takes a small mind to notice it.** These variants belong to late C19–20.

[**and so he died** and **and then she died** are Restoration-drama tags verging on c.pp.; but only verging. See Dryden's plays in Montague Summers's edn at p. 419.]

and so she prayed me to tell ye (with slight variations) is an almost meaningless c.p. originating in Restoration comedy – for instance, in Duffet's burlesque, *The Mock Tempest*, 1675.

and so to bed! is both a famous quotation from Pepys's *Diary* (1659 onwards) and a c.p. since 1926, when James Bernard Fagan (1873–1933) had his very successful comedy, *And So*

to Bed, played on the London stage; when published in 1927, it bore the sub-title 'An Adventure with Pepys'.

But, as Vernon Noble has kindly reminded me, in a letter dated 9 December 1974, it had been becoming a c.p. for perhaps seventy years before the play established it as one: '*The Diary of Samuel Pepys* became familiar to the public with Lord Braybrooke's text, especially his fourth edition of 1854. Revisions in the latter part of the century extended the Diary's popularity.'

and so what? A variant of **so what?**

and that ain't hay! is recorded by W & F as occurring always after the mention of a specific sum and as meaning 'that's a lot of money', e.g. in 'He makes $30,000 a year, and that ain't hay'. They neither assign nor hazard a date. The late John Lardner, brilliant son of famous father, Ring Lardner, writes in the 'Minstrel Memories' article forming part of *Strong Cigars and Lovely Women*, a selection, published in 1951, of pieces appearing in *Newsweek*, 1949–51:

> If Louie Ambers
> Should come our way,
> He brings the title,
> And that ain't hay.

an extension showing how very familiar the phrase must have been by (say) 1950.

and that goes. That's final – there's no more to be said. US: since *c.* 1925, perhaps much earlier, but I lack a record earlier than Berrey. Cf:

and that goes double! The same to you!: US: since *c.* 1930. (Berrey.)

and that is that. See **and that's that!**

and that's flat! – *and* occasionally omitted. Of *that's flat*, Berrey, 1942, says that it is 'used to emphasize or conclude a preceding remark'. I'd guess that it has been in US use since late C19. In British use it has been so long established – it occurs as early as Shakespeare – that it cannot be rated as a c.p. at all.

and that's no lie, a c.p. of emphasis, implies that the speaker isn't too sure that he'll be believed: since *c.* 1920.

and that's that! – *and* occasionally omitted; emphatic variant, **and that is that**; also **well, that's that!** The first is both British and US, Berrey explaining it as 'that is the end of the matter, so much for that'; so too the second; the third, connoting a rueful resignation, occurs in Terence Rattigan's *While the Sun Shines*, performed on Christmas Eve, 1943, at the Globe Theatre, London, and published in 1944;

> MABEL: ... When I read you were getting married I thought, well, that's that. He'll just fade quietly away and I won't ever see him again.

I cannot remember having heard the phrase before I came to England in 1921; certainly not during WW1, although I strongly suspect that the phrase (*and*) *that's that!* arose precisely then.

The apparently formal, but really the emphatic, *and that is that* occurs in Edward Albee, *Who's Afraid of Virginia Woolf?*, produced and published in 1962:

> GEORGE TO WIFE MARTHA: I'll hold your hand when it's dark and you're afraid of the bogey man ... but I will not light your cigarette. And that, as they say, is that.

and that's your lot! That's all you're going to receive, so don't expect any more: since *c*. 1920. Often used by wives to their husbands, or by women to their lovers.

and the best of British (luck). See **best of British luck to you – the.**

and the rest! has, since *c*. 1860, sarcastically and trenchantly implied that something important or, at the least, essential has been omitted – or that reticence has been carried too far.

and then some! This Americanism goes back to *c*. 1910 and – on the evidence of *OED* – was anglicized in or *c*. 1913. The thoroughness of its adoption by Britain is proved in an odd way: Professor J. W. Mackail in his *Aeneid*, 1930, finds a parallel in Book VIII, line 487, *tormenti genus*.

The US phrase seems to have arisen as a mere elaboration of the Scots *and some* ('and much more so'), as in Ross's pastoral poem *Helemore*, 1768, and, perhaps more significantly, in lexicographer Jamieson's exemplification, 'She's as bonny as you, and some'; and again in *EDD*.

and then the band played; variant **and the band played on**. See **then the band began to play.**

and to prove it, I'm here was a frequent tag of comedians playing the halls; it added a finishing touch to the preceding 'spiel'. Naturally it became an almost meaningless c.p. of late C19-mid 20; not much used after 1940. (Cyril Whelan, 14 January 1975.)

and very nice too! Indicative of warm approval, e.g. of feminine charms: late C19-20.

and what's the matter with Hannah? is 'a slangy c.p., generally tailed on to a statement or remark without the slightest sense of congruity' (Farmer): US: ? *c*. 1875-1900.

and when she bumps she bounces. See **when she bumps ....**

and whose little girl are you? And who may *you* be?: a male c.p., dating from *c*. 1905. Perhaps it originated in the film world, where, at parties, the stars sometimes took their children. On the cover of the *Sunday Times* Magazine of 11 June 1972 appeared the face of a lovely girl and her famous and lovely film actress mother, the caption being 'And whose little girl are you?' – with the explanatory sub-title, 'The stars and their daughters'.

and you too!, occasionally shortened to **and you!** A C20 c.p. addressed to someone suspect of unexpressed insult or recrimination. In the Armed Forces, it has, since 1914 or 1915, presupposed an unvoiced *fuck you!*, as, e.g., from a soldier awarded detention, with the officer saying or, more usually thinking, *and you (too)!*.

Angus or Agnes. See **I don't know whether ....**

Annie's room. See **up in Annie's room.**

[**anniversary of the siege of Gibraltar, the.** 'Since the great siege lasted from 1779 to 1883, this could be unofficially celebrated whenever desired' (Rear-Admiral P. W. Brock, 1 January 1969): naval toast: late (? middle) C19-20.]

another clean shirt oughta (ought to) see ya (or you) out. You look as if you might die at any moment; New Zealanders': since *c*. 1930 or a little earlier. It occurs in, e.g., Gordon Slatter, *A Gun in My Hand*, 1959. Clumsily humorous rather than callously hard-boiled.

another county heard from! 'A c.p. used when one of a company breaks wind or interjects something' (Douglas Leech-

man): Canadian: since *c*. 1935. From 'the receiving of election results from various counties'.

another day, another dollar. 'Said thankfully at the end of a hardworking day. I have often used this myself and have heard many others use it' (Mrs Shirley M. Pearce, 23 January 1975). Since the late 1940s and presumably adopted from the US, where it has been current since *c*. 1910: 'We meet someone and inquire: "How goes it?" or "How's tricks?" or "How you doing?" and more often than not our friend answers, "Another day, another dollar", meaning he is "keeping his head above water", holding on, not getting rich, but still working.... I have heard the expression most of my adult life' (W. J. Burke, 13 May 1975). In his *The Kidnap Kid*, 1975, Tony Kendrick employs it allusively.

another fellow's is applied to something new – not by its possessor but by some wag: *c*. 1880-1910. (B & L.)

another good man gone! A men's ruefully regretful remark passed on a man either engaged to be married or, esp., very recently married: late C19-20.

another little drink won't do us any harm: since *c*. 1920. From the refrain of a very popular song.

another nail in my coffin. On 7 May 1974, Vernon Noble sent me this note: 'Long before medical science officially condemned cigarettes as a hazard to health there was a catch phrase "Another nail in my coffin" as a person lighted a cigarette. This was an ironical answer to those who rebuked a cigarette-smoker who coughed: usually to an anxious wife. I have known this phrase in the North of England for something like 50 years': and I have known it used by Australians since *c*. 1910 and in the South of England since 1921.

another one for the van! Someone else has had to be taken to the lunatic asylum: Cockneys': since *c*. 1920.

another push and you'd have been a Chink (or **a nigger**). A brutal c.p. employed by workmen in a slanging match, or by youths bullying boys in a factory: C20, but, for *nigger*, esp. since *c*. 1950. This insult imputes a colour-no-objection promiscuity in the addressee's mother.

answer is a lemon – the; also **the answer's a lemon**. A derisive reply to a query – or a request – needing a 'yes' or a 'no' but hoping for 'yes'; a 'sarcastic remark – acidic in its conclusion', as Vernon Noble aptly calls it: originally (*c*. 1910) US – cf the US slang *lemon*, used since *c*. 1900, for 'a sharp verbal thrust, criticism, or retort' (W & F); adopted in England *c*. 1919. Its origin lies either in a lemon's sourness or, according to legend, in an improper, indeed an exceedingly smutty, story circulating during the 1920s. In Maurice Lincoln's novel, *Oh! Definitely*, 1933, occurs this illuminating dialogue:

'Written by some fellow with long hair who lives in Bloomsbury, I expect,' said Horace.

'Why?' said Peter.

'Why what?'

'Well, why would he have long hair like that and live where you said?'

'The answer's a lemon,' said Horace.

In the US, the thought is expressed a little differently. On 14 December 1974, my loyal old friend W. J. Burke wrote to me thus:

In the US we have a phrase *I drew a lemon* or *It turned*

out to be a lemon, etc. If we buy a new car which has 'bugs' in it, isn't working properly, we say, *It's a lemon*.

For years we have had slot machines in gambling joints. You put in a coin, pull a lever, and a row of the conventional objects appear on the face of the machine, bells, plums, etc. If you get a whole row of the same objects, all balls, say, you win, and out drops a handful of coins. If you hit the 'jackpot', as they say, you win big. You probably know all about this. But the point I want to make is that you may draw a whole row of yellow *lemons*, and *you get nothing*. Lemons mean a bust, a disappointment. Hence, when someone says *I drew a lemon*, the slot machine connotation is well understood.

answer's in the infirmary – my (or **the**). See **infirmary** ....

any B.F. (or **b.f.** or **bloody fool**) **can be uncomfortable**. 'Alleged to be a Guards' maxim. It certainly expressed the attitude of the Guards Armoured Division when I had dealings with them in Schleswig-Holstein in 1946. Wonderful chaps!' (Rear-Admiral P. W. Brock, CB, DSO, 1 January 1969): whether maxim or not, certainly a c.p. and, later, enjoying a much wider currency.

any day you 'ave the money, I 'ave the time. A prostitutes' or, derivatively, an enthusiastic amateurs' or near-amateurs' c.p., dating since *c.* 1910 and used mostly by Londoners. See Charles Drummond, *Death at the Furlong Post*, 1967, where the c.p. is employed allusively: The Inspector ... laid down seven pound notes. 'Fair and square?' – 'Yes, love, any day you 'ave the money, I 'ave the time.' Ag. laughed.

any joy? Any luck?: US: since *c.* 1930.

any more for any more? Does anyone want a second helping?: military mess-orderlies' c.p. of WW1 – and, figuratively, later; by 1939, slightly obsolescent – yet still far from obsolete. In WW1, 'also used by the man running a Crown and Anchor board or a House outfit, asking others to join in before the game commenced' (B & P).

any more for the Skylark? A jocular c.p. of C20. The invitation of seaside pleasure-boat owners, so many of these boats so named, became a generalized invitation.

any of these men here? Dating from *c.* 1910, this is a military Other Ranks' c.p. A wag, imitating a sergeant-major at a kit inspection, would ask, 'Knife, fork, spoon' and sometimes a reply would come, 'Yes, *he* is'; either the wag or a third party would obligingly ask, '*Who* is?' and would receive the obliging reply, 'Arseholes'.

anyone for tennis? See **tennis, anyone?**

anyone here seen Kelly? – with K-E-double L-Y often added and with variant **anyone here seen Kelly, Kelly from the Isle of Man?** – which, indeed, forms the original and comes straight from a popular song. Recorded, as *anyone here seen Kelly?*, by Collinson. C20; by 1937, slightly obsolescent and, by 1970, virtually obsolete.

anything for a quiet wife is a c.p. variant – less vaguely, 'a jocular perversion' (Petch) – of *anything for a quiet life*. itself a proverbial saying; the former dates from *c.* 1968; the latter probably from late C17 (see *ODEP*). Cf **deft and dumb**.

anything goes! Anything is permissible; 'do exactly as you please': since *c.* 1960. Adopted *c.* 1966 from US, where

current since the mid 1930s. (Mr A. B. Petch records its use in Bournemouth's *Evening Echo* of 26 January 1967.)

anything! so help me! God help me!: originally euphemistic and almost proletarian: since *c.* 1918; by 1940, obsolete. (Manchon.)

anything that can go wrong will go wrong, with *can* and *will* emphasized. 'This c.p. is known as Murphy's law. Why?' asks Barry Prentice on (?) 1 May 1975. I don't know why, but I believe the expression *Murphy's law* is also US. The c.p., as BP words it, is Australian and it dates, I think, from the middle or late 1940s.

anyway, it's winning the war. See **it's winning** ....

anywhere down there! A c.p. uttered by tailors when something is dropped on the floor: *c.* 1860–1910.

Appleby? – who has any lands in. See **how lies the land?**

apples a pound pears derides barrow boys, who often use strange or even nonsensical cries, deemed by some customers to be misleading: since *c.* 1925.

apples swim! – how we. See **how we apples swim!**

appray (or **appree**) **la guerre**, often written *gare*; **après la guerre**. 'Sometime – or perhaps never'; or, simply, 'never'; a British army, esp. a Tommy, c.p. of 1915–18. Often *appray la gare finee*, being the Fr. *après la guerre finie*, after the end of the war. 'A hopeless soldier would often be heard to say, for instance: "When shall I see my happy home again?" or "When shall I get my back pay? Appree la Gare" – i.e., Never' (F & G). '*Après la guerre* carried two connotations for the soldier: It was used jokingly for the indefinite and remote future, e.g. "When will you marry me? – Oh, après la guerre".... And, secondly, the phrase was a depository of secret sentiment. The two usages are clearly seen in the ribald ditty composed by some unknown warrior – "Après la guerre finie" [sung to the tune of 'Sous les ponts de Paris']' (B & P, who failed to note the third connotation: 'Never').

[**Arbroath!** belongs to ONE-WORD CATCH PHRASES.]

Archer up! He – or it – is certain to win: a London c.p. of 1881–6. From the very famous, very great, jockey, Fred Archer, who, having achieved fame in 1881, died in 1886. He is, I think, the only jockey to have occasioned a c.p.

Archibald, certainly not! A c.p. satirizing a prim and prudish feminine refusal of sexual intimacy: *c.* 1911–20 for its heyday; by 1940, virtually obsolete. From the title and refrain of a music-hall song written by John L. St John – a well-known song-writer usually known as Lee St John; the song owed most of its popularity to George Robey. The c.p. was noted by Collinson.

are there any more at home like you? A C20 c.p. addressed to a (very) pretty girl; by 1940, obsolescent; by 1970, obsolete – except among those with long memories. From the very popular musical comedy *Floradora*, which, performed first in 1900, contained the song, 'Tell me, pretty maiden, are there any more at home like you?'

are we downhearted? Political in origin (*c.* 1906) it did not achieve the status of a true c.p. until WW1 and was not, I believe, at all – if at all – general before late 1915. In B & P, John Brophy, at p. 194, wrote:

The original –
Are we downhearted? No!

soon became the vehement –
　　Are we downhearted? – Yes!
But this was intended as humorous comment. Sometimes
it would be expanded, and declaimed by alternate voices,
thus:
　　Are we downhearted?
　　No!
　　Then you damn (or bloody) soon will be!

are we is or are we ain't? See **is you** *is* **or is you** *ain't*?

are yew werkin'? is a Liverpool c.p. of 'the hungry Twenties'
and in frequent use until *c.* 1940 – and in occasional use for
some ten years longer. (Frank Shaw, communication made
in November 1968.)

are you a man or a mouse? Originally and predominantly
US, Berrey glossing it thus: 'disparagingly of a timorous person'. Adopted in England *c.* 1945 and there used jocularly,
esp. by female to male.

are you anywhere? Do you possess – or have on you – any
drugs? A US negroes' c.p., since *c.* 1950. (CM.)

[**are you for real?**, like **it's for real**: not catch, but ordinary
colloquial, phrases.]

are you getting too proud to speak to anyone now? – with *are*
often omitted – is addressed to one who has failed to notice
the speaker when passing: C20.

are you going to walk about – or pay for a room? is 'an impatient whore's question after a client has dithered too long'
(a correspondent, in 1969): C20.

are you happy in the Service? and **are you happy in your work?**
Ironic queries addressed to someone engaged in dirty or
dangerous work: the Services; the latter mostly RAF at first
(1939 or 1940), the former originally (since *c.* 1935) naval.
Whereas the former had become obsolescent by 1946, the latter is still with us, and, ever since 1945, very common among
civilians. In his novel, *Virgin Luck*, 1963, Laurence Meynell
wrote, ' "You like it here? Are you, as they facetiously say,
happy in your work?" '

are you in my way? is 'a c.p. reminder of egotistical oblivious-
ness' (Laurie Atkinson, in a letter): since *c.* 1925. Also US;
Berrey solemnly explains it as 'am I in your way?' Paul Beale
glosses it somewhat differently: 'Jocular phrase used as
"Excuse me" or to forestall another's having to ask one to
make room.'

are you is or are you ain't? A variant of **is you** *is* **or is you**
ain't?

are you keeping it for the worms? A Canadian c.p., dating
from *c.* 1940, and addressed to a female rejecting sexual advances. (Here, 'it' is the hymen.) Accidentally reminiscent of
Shakespeare's famous attack on the value of virginity as such.

are you kidding? Are you joking? But also an ironically derisive exclamation = Surely you're not serious? Dating since
c. 1945, it was probably suggested by the US c.p., *no kidding?*,
and in its turn, it probably occasioned the British *you must
be joking!*
　　In Act I, Scene i, of Terence Rattigan's *Variation on a
Theme*, both performed and published in 1958:
　　RON: You'll get a good settlement, I hope. [On remarry-
ing.]
　　ROSE: Are you kidding? I'm settling for half the Ruhr.

are you pulling the right string? Are you going the right way
about it? or, occasionally, are you correct? A cabinet-
makers' c.p., dating from 1863, says Ware; apparently obsolete by 1940. From small measurements being often made
with string.

are you there with your bears? There you are again! – esp. with
a connotation of 'so soon': *c.* 1570–1840. It occurs in Lyly,
1592 – James Howell, 1642 – Richardson (the novelist), 1740 –
Scott, 1820. (Apperson.) From the itinerant bear-leaders'
regular visits to certain districts.

are you winning? 'A rhetorical greeting: since *c.* 1960' (Paul
Beale, 30 September 1975).

are your boots laced? Do you understand what I'm saying
or what I'm talking about?: US negroes': since *c.* 1965. (CM.)

aren't we all? – often preceded by *but*. But surely we're all
alike in *that*? Since *c.* 1918 or perhaps ten or even twenty
years earlier. In Frederick Lonsdale's comedy, *Aren't We All*,
1924, occurs this passage:
　　VICAR: Grenham, you called me a bloody old fool.
　　LORD GRENHAM: But aren't we all, old friend?
Berrey, in 1942, records it as US – which it had become by
adoption.

aren't you the one! expresses admiration whether complete
or quizzical or rueful: US: since *c.* 1942; not much used since
c. 1972. (Mr Ben Grauer, in conversation, on 24 August 1973.)
It is a counterpart of the British **you are a one!**

'ark at 'er! See **hark at her!**

army, left! and **army, right!** is an army drill instructors' c.p.
addressed to a recruit turning, or wheeling, in the wrong
direction and dating, I think, since WW1. (PGR.)

arse, so is my (early **mine**) and **kiss my arse!** Coarse exclamatory phrase, indicative of contempt or incredulity – or both:
the former, C17–20, and occurring in, e.g., Ben Jonson; the
latter, C18–20, and occurring in, e.g., Swift. Cf **ask my arse!**
and see also **kiss my arse!**

arse and shite through his ribs – he would lend his. A c.p.
applied to 'anyone who lends his money inconsiderately'
(Grose, 2nd edn, 1788): *c.* 1770–1860. Here, inconsiderately
= unthinkingly.

arse from a hole in the ground – (he) doesn't know his. See **he
doesn't know his arse ....**

arse if it was loose – he would lose his refers to a careless, esp.
very forgetful, person: *c.* 1770–1860. (Grose, 2nd edn, 1788.) Cf:

arsehole is bored or punched (now mostly ... **punched or bored**)
– (he) doesn't know if his. He's a complete fool: since *c.* 1910.
Probably it originated in engineering workshops. The
earliest form seems to have been '... *bored, punched or coun-
tersunk*', which, indeed, is extant. Among Canadian Army
officers, during WW2, the c.p. ran *that guy don't know if his
ass-hole was drilled, dug, seamed, bored or naturally evagi-
nated.* Cf **you don't know whether you want ....**

arsehole of the world. See **you know the old saying....**

art thou there (? or !). Oh! so the penny has dropped – you
understand at last – you've tumbled to it: *c.* 1660–1730.
Thomas Shadwell, *The Scowrers*, Act III, opening scene:
　　CLAR[A]: Oh, Sister, the Sight of this Man has ruin'd me:
　　I never shall recover it.

EUG⌈ENIA⌉: Ah! Art thou there, 'faith, recover it! Why, who would put a Stop to Love? Give Reins to it, and let it run away with thee.

Arthur or Martha. See **I don't know whether** ... .

as common as shit and twice as nasty. See **as soft as shit** ....

as easy as shaking the drops off your John, often preceded by *it's*. It's dead easy: essentially masculine: since *c.* 1945 – if not ten, twenty, thirty years earlier. (*John = John Thomas*, now a rather outmoded euphemism.)

[**as ever is** is not a c.p., but a cliché tag connoting emphasis, as in 'this next winter as ever is' (Edward Lear, *c.* 1873).]

as good a scholar as my horse Ball. No scholar at all – indeed, these words may have formed the second half of the saying. Used by John Clarke in 1639, it seems to have been current *c.* 1620–70.

as hasty as a sheep – as soon as the tail is up, the turd is out. A low, mostly rural c.p. dating since *c.* 1850; by 1950, obsolescent.

as I am a gentleman and a soldier belongs apparently to the approximate period 1570–1640, is an asseveration or occasionally a remonstration, and for its meaning should be compared with the C19–20 stock phrase, yet hardly a c.p., *an officer and a gentleman*. Ben Jonson, in his *Every Man in His Humour*, staged in 1598 and published in 1601, has Cob the water-bearer say of Captain Bobadil: 'O, I have a guest ⌈a lodger⌉ – he teaches me – he swears the legiblest of any man christened: "By St George! – the foot of Pharaoh! – the body of me! – as I am a gentleman and a soldier!" – such dainty oaths' (Act I, Scene iii). At Act I, Scene iv, Bobadil himself says, 'I protest to you, as I am a gentleman and a soldier, I ne'er changed words with his like.'

The shortened form, *as I am a gentleman*, occurs frequently in the comedies of *c.* 1580–1640, e.g. John Fletcher's *The Pilgrim*. Act IV, Scene ii, where Pedro exclaims:

Murdering a man, ye Rascals?
Ye inhumane slaves, off, off, and leave this cruelty,
Or as I am a Gentleman: do ye brave me?

Beaumont and Fletcher, *Love's Cure*, written not later than 1616, in Act III, Scene ii, has:

BOB: You'll come, Sir?
PIO: As I am a Gentleman.
BOB: A man o' the Sword should never break his word.

as I am a person. This c.p. of emphasis, apparently current *c.* 1660–1750, comes, for instance, in Congreve's *The Way of the World*, staged and published in 1700, at Act IV, Scene ii, where Lady Wishfort says: 'Well, Sir Rowland, you have the way – you are no novice in the labyrinth of love – you have the clue. But, as I am a person, Sir Rowland, you must not attribute my yielding to any sinister appetite, or indigestion of widowhood ...' Later (Act V, Scene ii) she declares, 'As I am a person 'tis true; – she was never suffered to play with a male child, though but in coats; nay, her very babies [i.e. dolls] were of the feminine gender.' Cf **as I live**.

as I am honest (i.e. honourable) and **truly as I live** are c.pp. of asseveration, reassurance, or mere emphasis: late C16–17. In Beaumont and Fletcher's *The Chances* (probably by Fletcher alone), written not later than 1625 and published in 1639, at Act II, Scene ii, John, a lusty young Spanish gentle-man designing to pay ardent court to a lovely woman, saying woefully:

Now may I hang myself; this commendation
Has broke the neck of all my hopes: for now
Must I cry, no forsooth, and I ⌈i.e. ay⌉ forsooth, and surely,
And truly as I live, and as I am honest. He
Has done these things for 'nonce too; for he knows
Like a most envious Rascal as he is,
I am not honest, nor desire to be,
Especially this way.

The latter phrase elaborates *truly*, honestly, certainly, and connotes 'as certain as the fact that I am alive'. Cf **as I am a gentleman** above.

as I have breath and **as I have life**. The former, a variant of **as I live and breathe**, is more often **as I've breath**; it occurs in Mark Lemon's *Hearts Are Trumps*, performed and published in 1849, thus at Act I, Scene ii:

GOAD: One morning a silver spoon was missing, and the next day you were ditto.
JOE: But I didn't steal it! As I've breath, I didn't, master!

The latter, also a variant of **as I live**, occurs in R. B. Sheridan's *The Duenna*, staged and published in 1775:

ISAAC: Good lack, with what eyes a father sees! As I have life, she is the very reverse of all this.

And again in Sheridan's *The School for Scandal*, performed in 1777 and published in 1779, at Act V, Scene iii.

as I hope to be saved is a c.p. of (originally, solemn) asseveration: *c.* 1650–1850; and then it gradually lost currency until, by 1920 at latest, it had entirely disappeared. In *The Sullen Lovers*, staged and published in 1668, Thomas Shadwell writes in Act II, Scene iii:

NINNY: But I'll tell you; there are not above ten or twelve thousand lines in all the poems; and, as I hope to be saved, I asked him but twelve pence a line, one line with another.

Sly, in Act IV, of Colley Cibber's *Love's Last Shift* (or, as a Frenchman gleefully translated it, *La Dernière chemise de l'amour*), performed in 1694 and published the next year, says: 'Bless me! O Lord! Dear Madam, I beg your pardon: as I hope to be sav'd, Madam, 'tis a mistake: I took him for Mr –.'

In 1720, Charles Shadwell (son of Thomas) uses it in *The Plotting Lovers; or The Dismal Squire*: Samuel Foote's, *The Minor*, 1760, in Act I, in the scene between Sir William Wealthy and Samuel Shift, the latter says:

Would you believe it, as I hope to be saved, we dined, supped, and wetted five-and-thirty guineas ... in order to settle the terms; and, after all, the scoundrel would not lend us a stiver.

It can also be found in Foote's *The Maid of Bath*, 1778, and Thomas Shadwell uses it again in *The Woman Captain*, 1680.

In 1816, in Samuel James Arnold's *Free and Easy. A Musical Farce*, Act I, Scene ii, Mr and Mrs Courtly discuss an unexpected and cavalier guest:

COU: Did you ever see such an original?
MRS C: Very amusing, indeed!
COU: Vastly pleasant!
MRS C: Familiar – free and easy.
COU: And d-d disagreeable, as I hope to be saved.

There are variants, dating from Chaucer and even earlier; but this particular form is the only one to have become a c.p. – and it probably arose among pious Nonconformists.

as I hope to live likewise asseverates, during the very approximate period 1650–1820. Thomas Shadwell, *The Sullen Lovers*, 1668, at Act III, Scene i, has: 'Not I, sir, as I hope to live.'

In 1784, in Hannah Cowley's *A Bold Stroke for a Husband*, at Act II, Scene ii, Don Caesar exclaims: 'Beginning! as I hope to live; aye, I see 'tis in vain.'

In George Colman the Younger's *Ways and Means; or a Trip to Dover*, 1788, the whimsical Sir David Dunder, apropos of a man cramped into the corner of a coach, exclaims: 'Took him for dead, as I hope to live.'

as I live and breathe – rarely *if* – often shortened to **as I live**, which, however, sometimes appears to be the more emphatic form. Indicating confidence or assurance, it arose, very approximately, *c*. 1645. Of the numerous examples, these will perhaps serve:

Thomas Killigrew, *The Parson's Wedding*, 1664, Act II, Scene i at end, Lady Love-all, 'an old Stallion Hunting Widow', being ardently pressed by the lively Mr Jolly, exclaims: 'Hang me, I'll call aloud; why, *Nan!* you may force me; But, as I live, I'll do nothing' – yet does.

In Thomas Shadwell's *Epsom Wells*, performed in December 1672 and published in 1673, at Act IV, Scene i (lines 210–12 of D. M. Walmsley's edn), Mrs Jilt soliloquizes thus: 'Miserable Woman, how unlucky am I? but I am resolv'd never to *give* over 'till I get a Husband, if I live and breath [*sic*].' Cf also Act IV, Scene i (lines 651–62), Fribble speaking: 'Oh monstrous impudence! the Woman's possess'd, as I hope to breathe.'

John Crowne, in Act II of *The Country Wit*, performed in 1675 (published 1693), makes Ramble exclaim: 'Oh dull rogue that I am! I have staid till she's gone: gone as I live!'

In Colley Cibber's *Woman's Wit; or, The Lady in Fashion*, 1697, in the first scene of Act V, Leonora exclaims: 'Ha! muffled in a cloak! O! for a glimpse of him! – My Lord *Livermore*, as I live!'

In William Burnaby's *Love Betray'd* (an adaptation of Shakespeare's *Twelfth Night*), performed and published in 1703, Act I, Scene i (p. 354, lines 6–7 of F. E. Budd's edn of Burnaby's plays), Emilia exclaims to Villaretta: 'Cousin *Frances* drunk, as I live!'

Arthur Murphy, *The Apprentice*, 1756, at Act II, Scene i; Charlotte speaks: 'Dear Heart, don't let us stand fooling here; as I live and breathe, we shall both be taken, for heaven's sake, let us make our escape.'

Samuel Foote, *The Author*, 1757, Act I, Sprightly to Cape: 'Cape, to your post; here they are, i' faith, a coachful! Mr and Mrs Cadwallader, and your flame, the sister, as I live!'

In George Colman's *The Deuce Is in Him*, 1763, in Act II, Scene i, Tamper exclaims: 'Belford's Belleisle lady, as I live!' where *as I live* = well, I'm damned!

George Colman and David Garrick, *The Clandestine Marriage*, 1766, Act III, Scene i ('Scene Changes to another Apartment'); Miss Sterling remarks: 'As I live, Madam, yonder comes Sir John.' Garrick employs it twice in another play of the same year, *Neck or Nothing*. George Colman uses *as I live* again in *The English Merchant*, 1767, Act V.

In 1784, John O'Keeffe, *The Young Master*, employs it very effectually in Act IV, Scene i.

In 1787, Elizabeth Inchbald, *The Midnight Hour* (a translation from the Fr.), has the shorter form.

In 1792, Thomas Holcroft, *The Road to Ruin*, at Act III, Scene i, also has the shorter form.

Arthur Murphy, *The Way to Keep Him*, 1794, Act III, Scene i:

MRS BELL [MOUR]: I really think you would make an admirable Vauxhall poet.

LOVE [MORE]: Nay, now you flatter me.

MRS BELL.: No, as I live, it is very pretty.

Frederick Reynolds, an extremely popular light dramatist, in *The Delinquent; or, Seeing Company*, 1805, has Old Doric soliloquize thus: 'I'm safe at home at last – [*Looking round*] and, as I live – our villa is a pretty partnership concern – so snug – so tasty!'

In J. V. Millingen's *The Bee-Hive: A Musical Farce*, 1811, at Act I, Scene ii, Cicely exclaims: 'As I live, the very uniform!'

W. C. Oulton, *The Sleep-Walker; or, Which Is the Lady? A Farce*, 1812, in Act I, Scene i, causes Squire Rattlepate to burble, 'As I live, here is Mr Jorum, the landlord of the George.'

In 1820, Theodore Hook, in his very popular comedy, *Exchange No Robbery*, employs the shorter form, which had, by 1790 at latest, become the predominant form.

In 1829, George Colman the Younger uses it in *X.Y.Z.: A Farce*, at Act II, Scene i; in 1830, both J. B. Buckstone, *Snakes in the Grass*, another farce, at Act I, Scene i, and Caroline Boaden, *The First of April; A Farce*, at Act I, Scene iii, also use it; all three, in the short form.

In 1845, to go to a novelist for a change, R. S. Surtees, *Hillingdon Hall; or The Cockney Squire*, beginning chapter III with the heading:

'Ecce iterum Crispinus,'

Here's old Jorrocks again, as we live! – *Free Translation*.

A late example occurs in Thomas Morton the Elder, *'Methinks I See My Father!' or, 'Who's My Father?'*, ?1850, Act I, Scene i, 'Why, as I live, here he comes.' The phrase had always occurred frequently·in connection with someone's arrival on the scene.

The phrase, even in its shorter form, began to become slightly obsolescent *c*. 1900; yet it is extant; it appears as late as in Terence Rattigan's comedy, *French without Tears*, performed on 6 November 1936 and published in 1937. In Act I:

(*Enter Marianne, the maid, with a plate of scrambled eggs and bacon, placing them in front of Brian.*)

BRIAN: Ah, mes œufs, as I live.

I find it again, this time in Anglo-Irish, in Peter Driscoll, *In Connection with Kilshaw*, 1974: ' "Kilshaw's handwriting? Are you sure?" – "As I live, Harry." '

And the full phrase appears in May Mackintosh, *The Double Dealers*, 1975, ' "You're in love with him!" he said accusingly. "As I live and breathe, love at first sight, no less." '

Moreover, *as I live and breathe* had US currency from I don't know when until at least 1942, when it was recorded by Berrey.

as I live by bread exemplifies how very easy it is to 'slip up' with c.pp.: I had some record of it and then mislaid it! But, if I remember correctly, it belongs to mid C17–mid 18. It may have been prompted by the long-obsolete oath, *God's bread*, literally the sacramental bread.

as I used to was is a jocular variant of 'as I used to be': C20; by 1950, obsolescent, and by 1970, obsolete. Somerset Maugham, *Cakes and Ale*, 1930, ' "I'm not so young as I used to was." '

as if I'm ever likely to forget the bloody place! – the place being Belgium. *Remember Belgium!*, originally a recruiting slogan-become-c.p., 'was heard with ironic and bitter intonations in the muddy wastes of the Salient. And some literal-minded, painstaking individual, anxious that the point be rubbed well in, would be sure to add: "As if I'm ever likely to forget the bloody place!" ' (John Brophy at p. 194 of the first edn [1930] of B & P, reprinted, after a generation, as *The Long Trail*).

as large as life and twice as natural, it may astonish and even surprise many Britons to learn, was originally US: T. C. Haliburton in *The Clockmaker*, 1837 (Series I, pp. 159–60), has his central character, Sam Slick of Slicksville, say, 'He marched up and down afore the street door like a peacock, as large as life and twice as natural'. The expression caught the public fancy and became a c.p., adopted by Britain well before the end of C19. It survives; indeed, it has – and enjoys – good health. Such is its vitality that it has fathered the frequent variation (which I owe to Cyril Whelan): *as large as life and twice as ugly*, which is British and hardly earlier than *c.* 1910.

as long as I can buy milk I shall not keep a cow. Why go to the expense of a wife so long as I can visit a whore? – or, since *c.* 1950 – while there are so many willing girls available? Current throughout C17–20, although slightly obsolescent since *c.* 1940.

as many faces as a churchyard clock, usually preceded by **he has.** He's thoroughly unreliable: C19–early C20. 'Old navy' (F & G).

as Moss caught his mare napping: *c.* 1500–1870; in mid C18–early 19, often *Morse*; in C19, mainly dialectal. Refers to catching someone asleep, hence by surprise. 'The allusions to this saying and song in C16–17 are very numerous,' says G. L. Apperson in his pioneering and excellent book. Moss – ? a mythical farmer – appears to have caught his elusive mare by feeding her through a hurdle, as in a cited quotation dated 1597.

as much chance as a fart in a windstorm. No chance whatsoever: Canadian: C20. But **like a fart in a windstorm** is British for 'puny' – hence 'incommensurate' or 'ineffectual': low: C20.

as much chance as a snowball in hell. None at all: late C19–20: US, hence Canadian, hence British (in narrower sense – usually as **snowflake**), hence Australian and New Zealand. Probably the prompter of the preceding entry.

as much use as a (sick) headache. See **headache** ....

as much use as my arse, often preceded by **you're**, is a low and very abusive c.p. of late C19–20.

as much wit as three folks – two fools and a madman – he has. He's a fool; but also, he's rather cunning: C17–19: said to be mostly a Cheshire phrase; bordering on the proverbial. (Notably in Apperson.)

as old as my tongue .... See **old as** ....

as soft as a whore-lady's heart. Not soft at all; hard-hearted: C19–20. Contradictory to the legend that prostitutes have hearts of gold.

as soft as shit and twice as nasty is a rural c.p., belonging to S-E England and applied by rustics to those pasty-faced and loose-living urban owners of weekend 'cottages' in the country: late C19–20. (First heard by me in Kent, during the summer of 1932.) Contrast the workman's *soft as shit*, which they apply to a man habitually speaking without filth and occasionally thinking of something other than booze and soccer and 'birds'; but cf the Cockney's probably derivative C20 **as common as shit and twice as nasty**, applied either to a social inferior or, less frequently, to a very inferior article.

as straight as my leg – and that's crooked at knee. In S, published 1738 but concerned mainly with the language of Queen Anne's reign (1702–14), we find in the first conversation this exchange:

> LADY ANSW[ERALL]: But, Mr *Neverout*, I wonder why such a handsome strait [*sic*] young Gentleman as you, does not get some rich Widow.
>
> LORD SP[ARKISH]: Strait! ay, strait as my Leg, and that's crooked at Knee.
>
> NEV[EROUT]: Faith, Madam, if it rain'd rich Widows, none of them would fall upon me ...

The phrase was probably current throughout C18.

as the actress said to the bishop – and vice versa. An innuendo scabrously added to an entirely innocent remark, as in 'It's too stiff for me to manage it – as the actress said to the bishop' or, conversely, 'I can't see what I'm doing – as the bishop said to the actress'. Certainly in RAF use *c.* 1944–7, but probably going back to Edwardian days; only very slightly obsolescent by 1975, it is likely to outlive most of us.

A good example occurs in John Osborne's *A Sense of Detachment*, produced on 3 December 1972 and published 1973, in Act I:

> INTERRUPTER: You're trying to have it all ways, aren't you?
>
> GIRL: As the actress said to the bishop.

Another excellent example occurs in Len Deighton's remarkable WW2 novel *Bomber*, 1970:

> 'He worked out the position of the short circuit on paper, but it was enough to make a strong man weep, watching him trying to fix it: gentleman's fingers.'
>
> 'As the actress said to the bishop,' said Digby.

Another in Martin Russell's novel, *Double Hit*, 1973:

> Alongside a turntable in an alcove stood an open record-case ... The player was a stereo job in moulded mahogany ...
>
> 'Admiring my equipment?' Adrian re-emerged with a sandwich on a plate. 'As the actress said to the bishop. You get a terrific tone ... at least, so the man assured me as he installed it all: I've never yet managed to do exactly what he did, as the bishop said to the actress.'

'As the bishop said to the actress = *Not having jokes of its own, spoken English turns ordinary statements into jokes by adding this phrase afterwards*' (Punch, 10 October 1973). (Cf **bit of how's-your-father.**)

Either form tends to attract the other to cap it. Cf the next.

as the girl said to the sailor (less often **the soldier**) – and vice versa. An end-c.p., to soften a double, esp. if sexual, meaning: like the preceding phrase, it seems to have arisen in Edwardian times. Based – or so I've been told – upon a prototype about someone coming into money. Cf the C20 *as the monkey said*, a tag to a smoking-room story. Example: ' "We didn't come here just to look at the scenery," as the soldier said to the girl in the park.'

as the Governor of North Carolina said to the Governor of South Carolina: it's a long time between drinks; either part is often used separately, the former allusively and with a significant pause, the latter either literally or figuratively: a famous quotation that, *c.* 1880, became a c.p., almost entirely US, although known to – and used by – Americanophiles since *c.* 1920 – witness, e.g., Alec Waugh, *So Lovers Dream*, 1931:

> 'I suppose we've all got a barmaid side to us,' said Gordon [an Englishman].
> 'I know I've got a barman side to me,' said Gregory [an American].
> 'As the Governor of North Carolina said to the Governor of South Carolina,' said Francis [another American].

In the inestimable, rather than merely estimable, Bartlett, the *quotation* is given as 'Do you know what the Governor of South Carolina said to the Governor of North Carolina? It's a long time between drinks, observed that powerful thinker.' In *BQ* (5th edn, 1946), the formidable editor states that *it's a long time between drinks* 'is undoubtedly an invention' and adds that 'the expression antedates the Civil War'. See also **it's a long time between drinks**.

as the man in the play says occurs frequently in the comedies and farces of *c.* 1780–1840; it lends humorous authority to a perhaps frivolous statement. A felicitous example comes in Andrew Cherry's extremely popular and enviably durable comedy, *The Soldier's Daughter*, 1804, Act IV, Scene i, where the drily humorous Timothy, to Frank Heartall's 'Tim! Timothy! – Where are you hurrying, my old boy?' replies:

> Hey sir! Did you speak to me? Lord, I ask pardon, sir! – As the man in the play says, 'My grief was blind, and did not see you.' Heigho!

as the man said was, *c.* 1969, imported from US ('heard in the last year or two' A. B. Petch, 4 January 1974): in the fact, a little earlier), where current since *c.* 1950. It lends authority – occasionally a humorous warning – to what *has* been said.

as the monkey said. 'In English vulgar speech the monkey is often made to figure as a witty, pragmatically wise, ribald simulacrum of unrestrained mankind. Of the numerous instances, "You must draw the line somewhere, as the monkey said when peeing across the carpet" is typical. The phrase "... as the monkey said" is invariable in this context' (Laurie Atkinson, 1969): since *c.* 1870. Cf the four entries preceding this – esp. **as the girl said to the sailor**.

as we say in France, apparently current *c.* 1820–1900, was mainly a Londoners' c.p. It occurs in, e.g., R. S. Surtees, *Handley Cross*, 1854, vol. II, in the chapter entitled 'The Cut-'Em-Down Quads':

> 'I vish we may!' exclaimed Mr Jorrocks, brightening up; 'Somehow the day feels softer; but the hair [i.e. air] generally is after a fall. Howsomever, *nous verrons*, as we say in France: it'll be a long time before we can 'unt, though – 'edges will be full o' snow.'

as wears a head is a tag c.p., current *c.* 1660–1730 and meaning 'as a human being can be'. In Thomas Shadwell's *The Scowrers: A Comedy*, 1691, at Act III, Scene i, we read:

BLUST[ER]: I am glad to hear you say so: Your Worship's as wise a Man——

WHACK[UM]: As wears a Head in the City.

DING[BOY]: As wears a Pair of Horns there. [*Aside.*]

The phrase occurs often in Shadwell and other – and later – writers of comedies.

as you are stout, be merciful! A middle- and upper-class c.p. of C18. S (Dialogue I), 1738:

COL[ONEL]: Have you spoke with all your Friends?

NEV[EROUT]: Colonel, as you are stout, be merciful.

LORD SP[ARKISH]: Come, agree, agree, the Law's costly.

It had been recorded in 1721 by Kelly.

Here, *stout* does not mean 'obese, corpulent' but 'strong' or 'brave', as a gallant soldier is brave and fearless – and needs to be strong.

In C19 *stout* gave way to *strong* (*ODEP*, 3rd edn, 1970). But this proverb-c.p. did not, I think, long survive WW1.

as you were! 'Used ... to one who is going too fast in his assertions' (Hotten, 1864): mid C19–early C20. But since *c.* 1915, it has signified 'Sorry! *My* mistake'. The origin of the latter sense (and, of course, of the former) is made clear by F & G: 'The ordinary military word of command, used colloquially by way of acknowledging a mistake in anything said, e.g. "I saw Smith – as you were – I mean Brown." ' Much used in WW2: 'The [military] phrase spread to ordinary conversation. "See you at Groppi's [in Cairo] at 9.30 – as you were, 10 o'clock" ' (PGR).

ask a silly question and you'll get a silly answer: also **ask silly questions and you'll get silly answers**; the latter, often shortened to **ask silly questions**, the former rarely to **ask a silly question**. This is, in late (?mid) C19–20, the c.p. evolved from an old proverb, *ask no questions and you'll be told no lies*.

ask another!; also **ask me another!** Don't be silly!: mostly Cockneys': late C19–20, originally addressed to someone asking a stale riddle. Ware records *ask another!* for 1896. In 1942 Berrey records *ask me another!*, which, originally English, probably goes back to the 1890s. In Allan Monkhouse's play, *The Rag*, 1928, in Act I, occurs this dialogue:

WALLINGFORD: Certain houses?

WELBY: Bawdy houses.

WALLINGFORD: What?

ANTHONY: How did I know?

WELBY: Ask me another.

ask cheeks near Cunnyborough! A low London – female only – c.p. of mid C18–mid C19. Literally, 'Ask my arse!' (Grose, 1785.) *Cunnyborough* = the borough, hence area, of *cunny* = *cunt*. Cf the male **ask mine**, or **my, arse!**

ask me! was common among US students at the beginning of the 1920s. Recorded by McKnight.

ask me another! See **ask another!**

ask mine (later **my**) **arse!** Originally nautical, always low, c.p. of evasive reply to a question: mid C18–20. (Grose, 1788.) Cf **ask cheeks near Cunnyborough** and also **so is mine** – later **my – arse**.

[**ask no questions and you'll hear** (or **be told**) **no lies** is not a c.p. but a proverb.]

ask silly questions and you'll get silly answers! See **ask a silly question** ....

ask yourself! Be reasonable – be sensible: Australian: since *c*. 1925. (Sidney J. Baker, *Australian Slang*, 1942.) Probably elliptical for *Well, just ask yourself!*

asking – not by your. See **not by your asking**.

asking – that's. See **that's asking!**

astonish me! An educated, cultured, intelligent c.p., dating from early 1960s. In Derek Robinson, *Rotten with Honour*, 1973:

    '... There is still a good chance.'
    Hale waited. 'Go on,' he muttered. 'Astonish me.'
    'I think I might.'

at a church with a chimney in it. S. 1738, Dialogue I (p. 103, my edn):

    LADY ANSW[ERALL]: Why, Colonel; I was at Church.
    COL[ONEL]: Nay, then I will be hang'd, and my Horse too.
    NEV[EROUT]: I believe her Ladyship was at a Church, with a Chimney in it [i.e. at a private house; but also applicable to an inn].

This c.p. has been current throughout C18–20, although little since *c*. 1920 and, by *c*. 1970, virtually obsolete.

at least she won't die wondering. See **she will die wondering**.

at this moment in time was being used to a nauseating extent in 1974 – as, indeed, it is still – and Vernon Noble, writing on 11 September 1974, remarks:

    As you know, it's become a cliché. But I now find that its use is considered so ridiculous by the more sensitive kind of people that it is coming into their conversation sarcastically as a catch phrase. It is one of those American importations that had at first a use for emphasis but has outstayed its welcome.

John W. Clark has noted that the cliché *at that point in time* was very frequently used during the Watergate hearings.

atta boy! is how Edward Albee writes the next, in Act III of *Who's Afraid of Virginia Woolf?*, 1962.

attaboy! is only apparently a 'one-word c.p.', for, via *'at's the boy!*, it stands for *that's the boy!*, an expression of warm approval, either for something exceptionally well done or for especially good behaviour; exclamatory approbation: since *c*. 1910 in US (W & F); adopted in Britain in the last year (1918) of WW1 – recorded by F & G, 1925, and see, e.g., Dorothy L. Sayers, *Murder Must Advertise*, 1933, ' "Picture of nice girl bending down to put the cushion in the corner of the [railway] carriage. And the headline [of the advertisement]? *Don't let them pinch your seat.*' " "Attaboy!" said Mr Bredon [Lord Peter Wimsey].'

    Much less common were *attababy!* (Berrey) and *attagirl!* (W & F, 1960 – although in use long before that date). See also **thatta boy**.

attention must be paid. 'Last week, on a theater program, I saw a few reminiscences. Among them was the remark: "Arthur Miller's *Death of a Salesman*" – it opened in New York, 10 February 1949 – "gave us a catch phrase, Mildred Dunnock's line: 'Attention must be paid'." The sentence has had some general use, but was, I think, rather a vogue expression than one making any lasting stay in the language' (Joseph T. Shipley, 14 February 1975).

attitude is the art of gunnery and whiskers make the man. This c.p. has – by the rest of the Royal Navy – been applied to gun-

nery officers, who were also said to be 'all gas and gaiters': 'the gas being their exaggerated emphasis on the word of command, and the gaiters being worn by officers and men at gun drill and on the parade ground' (Rear-Admiral P. W. Brock, CB, DSO, on 1 January 1969): since *c*. 1885. Naval gunnery became much more important when John Arbuthnot Fisher (1841–1920) was appointed the captain in charge of the gunnery school in the late 1880s; he and his disciples vastly improved both the standard of gunnery and the status of gunnery officers and men.

    The lower-deck version is *h'attitude is the h'art of gunnery and whiskers make the man*, recorded by Granville.

au reservoir! '*Au revoir!*' According to Frank Shaw – I'm not doubting his word – this c.p. valediction was occasioned by *Punch* when, in 1899, 'two engineering experts went to Egypt to survey the Nile water resources': the phrase apparently caught on almost immediately; by 1940, obsolescent, and by 1950, obsolete. The slangy truncation, *au rev!*, however, did not rise to the pinnacle or status of c.p.

aw, forget it! A US c.p. current at least as early as 1911. ('The Function and Use of Slang' in *The Pedagogical Seminary*, March 1912.) It became **forget it**, q.v.

'aw, shit, lootenant!' – an' the lootenant shat. 'Borrowed from the US army; a scornful c.p. used by the other ranks to describe ineffective and easily browbeaten subalterns. Often, to utter the first half of the phrase is enough' (Paul Beale, 6 September 1974): US, since *c*. 1942; also British by the latish 1950s.

aw shucks! 'The conventional US and Canadian expression of yokel embarrassment. "Aw shucks! I couldn't say that to a lady!" ' (Dr Douglas Leechman): since *c*. 1910 and, as used by others than yokels, often jocular and always a c.p. It occurs, with a reference to Huckleberry Finn, in John D. MacDonald's *The Girl, the Gold Watch and Everything*, 1962.

aw, your fadder's (occasionally **father's**) **mustache!** An elaboration of **your fadder's mustache!**, q.v.

away with the mixer! Either 'Let's go ahead!' or derivatively 'Now we're going ahead': since *c*. 1946. A concrete-mixer or a cocktail-mixer?

'ay is for 'orses. See **hay is for horses**.

ay thang yew! I thank you! Since the mid-1930s, when comedian Arthur Askey constantly used it on radio – notably in 'Band Wagon' – and elsewhere, but, from *c*. 1955, less and less general. That great comedian reputedly 'borrowed it from the London bus conductors' (*Radio Times*, 28 June–4 July 1975).

aye, aye, that's yer lot. And that's all – that's the end of the music-hall number. A comedian's tag, converted by the public into a c.p. with a much wider application: post-WW2 (Cyril Whelan, 14 January 1975). A few weeks later, Mr Whelan had narrowed it down to either 'Arthur English, the archetypal "spiv" comedian of the [late 1940s and] early 1950s ... or the somewhat older Jimmy Wheeler who had a longer and broader experience in Variety'. And then, on 7 March 1975, Mr Paul Beale wrote: 'Jimmy Wheeler, music-hall and radio comedian, who worked to mid-1950s at least, said it as he finished his little fiddle piece at the end of his act.' And Jimmy Wheeler it was!

B.E.F. will all go home – in one boat – the. 'In 1917 old expressions such as "a bon time" and "trays beans" were not much heard; another had arisen, "The B.E.F. will all go home – in one boat" ' (Edmund Blunden, *Undertones of War*, 1928). More officers' than men's: 1917–18 only. The BEF was, of course, the British Expeditionary Force.

B.F.N. See **good-bye for now!**

baby wants a pair of shoes; also, in Australia, **... a new pair** .... A dicing gamblers' c.p. of C20: originally underworld, esp. in prisons; by 1940, also fairly general.

back in your kennel! See **get back into your box!**

back o' me hand to ye! – the. An Anglo-Irish retort: late C19–20. Probably literally 'a slap', but perhaps euphemistic.

back pedal! Steady – that can hardly be true; in short, tell that to the marines: c. 1910–35. From cycling. (Collinson.)

back teeth are afloat (occasionally **floating**) – **my**, implies a need – a strong desire – to urinate: C20; by 1960, slightly obsolescent:

back to square one, often shortened to **square one!**; in full, **let's go back to square one**. Let's start again – by going back to the point of starting: since the late 1930s. Via the BBC's football commentaries of the period, the reference being to the listeners' 'maps'; but the commentators themselves took it from such games as Snakes and Ladders, where an unlucky fall of the dice took one from the top to the bottom line. In *The Deadly Joker*, 1963, 'Nicholas Blake' (Cecil Day Lewis) uses it in this short form. But it has also been suggested that the phrase derives from the game of hopscotch. 'The grid from which football commentators worked did indeed resemble a hopscotch pitch' (Ramsey Spencer, 17 July 1974). On 4 January 1974, Mr A. B. Petch notifies me that 'the latest form used' is *back to square one – and the one before that –* with the variant *back to square nought* ('a square worse than when it started': Richard Miers, *Shoot to Kill*, 1959), as Paul Beale tells me.

back to the cactus! An Australian navy's c.p., dating from the 1930s and meaning 'back to duty – after leave'. The reference is to the prickly pear that forms a feature of the Australian rural scene, esp. in the outback. Dal Stivens, for instance, uses it in a story written in 1944 and published, 1946, in *The Courtship of Uncle Henry*. Cf **back to the war!**

back to the drawing-board! is 'used when one has to make an agonizing reappraisal' (Barry Prentice). Concerning his 'Oscar', David Niven has, in *The Moon's a Balloon*, 1971, remarked, 'King for a day?... Certainly! After that, it's back to the old drawing-board.' Common to the US (Edward Hodnett, 18 August 1975) and to Britain; I'd hate to have to decide the national primacy in this grave matter. But it soon became well known also in Canada, Australia, New Zealand. In the US there exists, as in the David Niven quotation, the slight variant, *back to the old drawing-board* (con-

firmed by Colonel Albert Moe, 15 June 1975). It probably arose, during WW2, among aircraft designers. Probably, also, it stems from **oh, well! back to the grindstone!**

Note that in Anthony Tucker's article ('Magnetic Field') in the *Guardian*, 15 September 1975, there occurs this illuminating example: 'The monopole would certainly "rule out the existence of free quarks or other fractionally charged particles," say the Houston team. Curiouser and curiouser, said Alice. Back to the drawing board.'

back to the jute mill! is a solely US variant of the next but one: 'I first heard it ... in 1938 by military personnel serving in the Far East' (Colonel Moe, 11 July 1975).

back to the kennel! is a US c.p. of contemptuous disparagement: c. 1925–50. (Berrey.) Speaking to a person as if to a dog. Cf **get back into your box!**

back to the salt mines! – *salt* being often omitted and *well* often preceding. I first heard it early in the 1950s, but its British use probably goes back to c. 1945. It was imported from the US and, there, may have originated late in C19. Colonel Albert Moe thinks *back to the mines!* is the earliest form and attributes it to a play of the 1890s, *Siberia*, with its dramatic poster of a party of Russians proceeding to Siberia 'under the lashes of the Cossacks'. He cites Henry Collins Brown, *In the Golden Nineties*, 1928, chapter III, 'The Theatre. (Old Time Posters)'. In Irving S. Cobb, *Murder Day by Day*, 1933: ' "That would be Terence," he said. "Well, Gilly, it's back to the mines for me, and this day I'll need to have my brain grinding in two–three different places at once." '

From the Western idea – not so far wrong at that! – that, in both imperial and in communist Russia, political prisoners were sent to do hard labour in the salt mines of Siberia. Berrey records the addition of *ye slaves*.

There are two variants quite well known in the US but unknown in Britain: **back to the jute mill!** and *back to the chain gang*, the former noted by Colonel Moe (1975) and the latter by Berrey (1942).

back to the war! This WW1 c.p. was used by Tommies returning to the Line after a leave or, esp., after a tour of duty in back areas.

back up! A US c.p., dating c. 1919–40. George Ade, in Act I of *The College Widow* ('A Pictorial Comedy in Four Acts'), 1924: 'She wanted me to come back and board with her mother this year. (One of the [college] boys says, "Back up?" Another chuckles – another whistles....)' Here, *back up* probably = 'to corroborate, to prove', rather than 'to explain in detail'.

backwards – the way Mollie went to church, or with *backwards* omitted. She *didn't* go; hence, 'reverse what has just been said!': Anglo-Irish wit: C20.

bad luck to him! See **luck to him....**

bad manners to speak when your arse is full. See **it's bad manners to speak when....**

[**bad show!** See **good *on* you!**]

bail him out! See LIVERPOOL CATCH PHRASES.

balderdash, poppycock and piffle! That's nonsense: Australian educated and cultured, or merely cultured, c.p., dating from the early 1960s. A euphemism for the low slang *balls!*

But apparently the Australian phrase adapts the English *balderdash, piffle and poppycock*, used by Harcourt Williams on the West End stage as early as 1946, as Mr Norman Franklin tells me (late 1974).

Ballocky Bill the Sailor (originally **BB the S**) **just returned from the sea**; less correctly but very frequently spelt *bollicky*. This mythical character has been commemorated in a low ballad of late C19–20 and he becomes the subject of a c.p. when either the short or the long version was, by way of evasion, used by British soldiers in WW1. Ballocky Bill was – and is – reputed to have been most generously genital'd: cf the vulgar *ballocks*, testicles; but at least partly operative is the dialectal *ballocky*, left-handed, hence clumsy.

[**balloon?** All right?: an underworld one-word c.p., current in the 1930s. James Curtis, *You're in the Racket Too*, 1937.]

balloon go up?, when does the. See **when does the balloon go up?**

balls, bees and buggery!; also **balls, picnics and parties!** The former, a c.p. of late C19–20, seems to have occasioned the latter, a c.p. dating from *c.* 1925. They are punning and stylized amplifications and elaborations of the exclamatory *balls!*, nonsense.

[**'balls!' cried the King – the Queen laughed because she wanted to** and **'balls!' cried the Queen – the King laughed because he wanted to (two).** Separately or together. Professor John W. Clark roundly declares that this US pair of phrases 'not only never were, but could not have become, catch phrases, because they don't and can't apply to a situation' (10 July 1975). Colonel Albert Moe, on the other hand, thinks (11 July 1975) that they have two applications: (1) 'referring to nonsense or foolishness: "It's ridiculous" – "That's a laugh" – "Don't be an Airedale" ...'; and (2) 'expletive of profanity, cursing, or oath: "Go to hell!" – etc.'. Both of these gentlemen place it as far back as the 1930s (JWC) or the 1920s (AM), and one adjudges it to have been, originally, current among students; both, moreover, say that it is extant.]

balls on him like a scoutmaster, usually preceded by **he has.** A low New Zealand and Canadian c.p. dating from *c.* 1925 and based upon the scurrilous idea, formerly – and still? – current among the ignorant, that many scoutmasters are active homosexuals.

balls to that lark! There's nothing doing *or* I don't think much of that idea: New Zealand (and elsewhere): since *c.* 1910. A c.p. extension of *balls to that*, common in Britain late C19–20.

balls to you, love! is a C20 variant – an elaboration – of the rather older *balls to you* itself, of course, also a c.p., low and masculine. It reflects both the workman's contempt for the white-collar worker and his own ignorance of lawn tennis, the precise reference being to the game of mixed doubles at the suburban lawn tennis club level.

Banagher. See **bangs Banagher.**

bang, bang, you're dead! – often written **bang! bang! you're dead.** In Britain, it is mostly a children's c.p., dating from *c.* 1960 and resulting from an excessive televiewing of 'Westerns'. Originally it was US: indeed, in US slang, a *bang-bang* is a 'Western' (a cowboy movie) – 'from the high incidence of gunshots in such films' (W & F); as a US c.p., *bang-bang!* = *drop dead!*, q.v., and antedates 1960. It is perhaps worth recalling that, in 1929, the brilliant, witty, entertaining George Ade published a collection of narratives first appearing in the late 1890s and called them *Bang! Bang!*

In Jack D. Hunter's 'thriller', *Spies Inc.*, 1969, occurs this significant use of the c.p.: 'I could not visualize Carl strolling into the motel office and saying, Hey, pal.... I could, though, visualize Carl strolling into the motel office and saying, Bang, bang – you're dead.'

In 1973, June Drummond, an English novelist, named one of her books *Bang! Bang! You're Dead!*

The variant *boom! boom! you're dead!*, based on US soldiers WW2 *boom-boom*, a small calibre rifle or a pistol, is used by Donald MacKenzie (Canadian-born) in his novel, *The Kyle Contract*, 1970.

bang goes sixpence! This originally Scottish c.p., current since the 1870s and re-popularized by Sir Harry Lauder, after having been originated by Charles Keene in *Punch*, on 5 December 1868, in the form *bang went sixpence*, is jocularly applied to any small expense incurred, esp. for entertainment and with a light heart, although it has also, in C20, been increasingly addressed to someone exceedingly careful about small expenses. Weekley shrewdly suggested that *bang* suggests abruptness.

bang on! was a bomber crews' c.p. of WW2 and it meant that everything was all right; in the nuances 'dead accurate' and 'strikingly apposite', it was adopted by civilians in 1945, a notable early example occurring in Nicholas Blake's *Head of a Traveller*, 1948.

bang to rights! 'A fair cop' – a justifiable arrest for an obvious crime: underworld, since before 1930. Hence, a police and London's East End c.p. by 1935 at latest, and a fairly general slangy c.p. since *c.* 1950. Note Frank Norman's engaging criminal reminiscences, *Bang to Rights*, 1958. For the *bang* part of the phrase, cf **bang on!**; *to rights* = rightfully.

bangs Banagher and Banagher bangs the world – that or **this.** The mainly Anglo-Irish *bang*, to defeat, to surpass, supplies the key, as also does the variant, *that* (or *this*) *beats Banagher and Banagher beats the world*. The original and predominant Anglo-Irish proverbial saying is *this bangs ...*; it dates from not later than 1850, and it seems to have become a c.p. within a decade. It occurs in, e.g., Rolf Boldrewood, *My Run Home*, 1897, in a passage concerning a period *c.* 1860. See P. W. Joyce, *English as We Speak It in Ireland*, 1910, and note that *Banagher*, a village in King's County, Ireland (now Co. Offaly), as Weekley, neatly aligning [to] *beat creation*, once noted, was perhaps chosen because of its echoic similarity to *bang*.

In 1891, M records the composite variant, *that bangs Banagher, and Banagher beats the devil*, and adds, 'An Irish expression [equivalent] to "that beats the Dutch"' – by which, clearly, it has been influenced: cf, therefore, **that beats the Dutch.** Subsidiarily cf **that beats the band.**

barber. See *that's the barber*.

Barkis is willin' indicates to a girl that a man is willing and ready to marry her: a famous quotation become, *c.* 1870, a c.p. Later (C20) extended loosely to indicate willingness to do anything short of risking life or limb, money or position. In Dickens, *David Copperfield* (chapter V), 1849, Barkis sends this message to Peggotty.

Barney's bull. See *all behind, like Barney's bull*.

bash it up to you! Run away and stop bothering me: Australian: esp. in WW2, among Servicemen, but apparently surviving until *c.* 1960. (*AS.*)

basinful of that. See *I'll have a basinful ....*

[**baw-haw, quoth Bagshaw.** You're a liar!: half a proverbial saying, half a c.p.: *c.* 1550–1700. F & H cite Levins and Nashe. It seems that *baw-haw* may be a variant of *baw-baw*, an echoic term of derision or contempt, and that the surname *Bagshaw* was chosen solely because it rhymed.]

be a devil! or, in full, **oh, come on – be a devil** (or even **a real devil**) is an ironically merry invitation to someone to be, for once, generous or audacious, as in 'Oh, come on, Billy, be a devil and buy yourself a beer' or in 'Be a real devil, Joe, and buy her a whisky': since *c.* 1945. This c.p. belongs to the thought-pattern connoted by Lilian Jackson Braun, when, in *The Cat Who Could Read Backwards*, 1966, she wrote: ' "Come on, have another tomato juice," Ron invited. "Live it up." '

be a good girl and have a good time! A predominantly Canadian c.p., addressed to someone – not necessarily female – setting off for a party or a dance: since *c.* 1930. Inevitably it invited the comment, 'Well, make up your mind!' – which itself, *c.* 1935, became a c.p.

be good! is a c.p. substitute, both American and British, for *au revoir!* It dates from 1907, when, in the USA, lyricist Harrington and composer Tate produced the song, *Be Good! If You Can't Be Good, Be Careful!* – introduced by actress Alice Lloyd, as Edward B. Marks, who sometimes omitted first names, tells us in *They All Sang*, 1934. (By courtesy of Mr W. J. Burke.) It somewhat facetiously exhorts the departer to behave well. In B & P, 1930, John Brophy noted that, during WW1, it was used mostly by officers, sometimes extended to *be good – and if you can't be good, be careful* – perhaps adopted from the pre-1914 musical, *The Girl in a Taxi*, as Mr Ronald Pearsall suggests. But, on 12 January 1975, a correspondent (Mr G. Maytum of Strood, Kent) tells me: 'I have a humorous postcard dated 16 September 1908 and depicting a couple on a couch; the caption reads "Be good, and if you can't be good, be careful, and if you can't be careful, get married." ' Colonel Moe, 15 June 1975, notes a US variation for ... *get married* – and that is *be sanitary*. It had, originally, a sexual meaning that soon disappeared in the simple form. An excellent example occurs in Terence Rattigan's *Who Is Sylvia?* (played in 1950 and published in 1951), where Williams the manservant, going off for the evening, says to the two mannequins visiting his lordship: 'Well, goodnight, ladies. Be good!' (he knowing that that's the last thing they're expected to be, or intend to be). Since the middle 1930s, the longer form has often become still longer by the addition of *and if you can't be careful, buy a pram*, which, among Americans, becomes ... *name it after me*. Its US use is recorded by Berrey, 1942, and occurs in, e.g., E. V. Cunningham, *Phyllis*, 1962, 'He was proud of his Americanisms, that man Gorschov. "Be good," he said to me.' Certainly it caught on in US. Mr Derrick Kay records, as current in 1934: 'Be good! If you can't be good, be careful. If you can't be careful, name the first child after me.' Alan Brien, in the *Sunday Times* of 12 January 1975, recalls that during his schooldays in the 1930s, the c.p. ran: 'Be good! And if you can't be good, be careful! And if you can't be careful, remember the dates.'

On 19 January 1975, Mr F. G. Cowley of Swansea, gleefully writing to the *Sunday Times*, pointed out that 'Salimbere, the Franciscan chronicler writing in the thirteenth century, reports that the phrase (*sinon caste, tamen caute*) was frequently used by Italian priests and attributed by them to St Paul.... I have failed to trace the catch phrase in the Epistles of St Paul.' The L. may be rendered, 'If not chastely, yet cautiously' (or prudently), and it affords an excellent example of the medieval monastic fondness for alliteration. But surely Mr Cowley doesn't believe that a thoroughly English c.p., as *if you can't be good, be careful* certainly is, could have been originated by anything so remote as the L. Here is a neat example of the inevitable recurrence of a thought-pattern, such as we find also in **does your mother know you're out?**, q.v.

be like dad – keep mum!, a punning WW2 slogan, became, for a short period ending *c.* 1955, something of a c.p., esp. among Service and ex-Service men and women. Neat; for the slogan means, be like father – keep mum, i.e. maintain mother, but also keep quiet, refrain from loose talk. In Catherine Aird, *A Late Phoenix*, 1970:

'Walls have ears,' murmured Dr Dabbe, getting into his surgical gown.

'Be like Dad, keep Mum.' Sloan was surprised to hear himself responding.

be like that – see if I care! Addressed to someone disagreeing or refusing, esp. in a matter of personal importance: originally – *c.* 1971 – at Oxford, then more generally.

be lucky! is, originally, an underworld, esp. ex-convicts', c.p., synonymous with *au revoir!* or *cheerio!*: since *c.* 1930; by *c.* 1950, general Cockney. P. B. Yuill, *Hazell Plays Solomon*, 1974, two Cockneys parting:

'I'll let you know, Tel.'

'Be lucky.'

Lucky, in one's criminal activities.

be my Georgie Best! is an Association Football world variation – in Britain – of the next: since 1970. From Georgie Best, the wayward 'soccer' star; always far commoner among spectators and other 'fans' than among players and managements. The fact that this variation is rhyming slang serves to heighten the importance of **be my guest** by showing how firmly it was embedded in colloquial usage at all levels: otherwise the meaning wouldn't have been obvious.

be my guest! is said to someone wishing to borrow something not valuable, nor otherwise important, enough to be worth returning, or wishing to do something trivial; often equivalent to 'You're welcome!'; since *c.* 1950. It was current in Australia before 1967, the date of Frank Hardy's *Billy Borker Yarns Again*. A pleasant English example occurs in Dick Francis's novel, *Forfeit*, 1968, where wife and husband, after making love, say:

'Goodnight, Ty.'
'Goodnight, honey.'
'Thanks for everything.'
'Be my guest.'

The c.p. is also US (the earliest example I've noticed being in Ellery Queen, *Death Spins the Platter*, 1962, at the end of chapter XIV) – as in Hugh Pentecost's novel, *The Gilded Nightmare*, 1968:

'I am now ... in search of a surface fact.'
'Be my guest.'
'Do you know what time the Countess Zetterstrom is supposed to arrive today?'

There are many examples of this phrase in British and US fiction, as well as two in John Mortimer's witty play, *Collaborators*, produced in 1970 and published in 1971: e.g. in Hillary Waugh, *Finish Me Off*, 1970: Ellery Queen, *A Fine and Private Place*, 1971; Frederic Mullally, *The Malta Conspiracy*, 1972 ('"Be my guest, as they say."'); Mickey Spillane, *The Erection Set*, 1972, but already in 1966 (*The By-Pass Control*). By 1972, indeed, the phrase had become so much a part of everyday speech that several big horse-races 'over the sticks' were won by a horse named Be My Guest. That so agreeable a c.p. should so thoroughly have established itself is a fact worth recording.

be nice to people on your way up .... See **always be nice** ....

be seeing you! – in US, often **be seein' yuh!** – is short for *I'll be seeing you* and is itself often shortened to *seeing you!* or *see you!*: a very common non-final valediction since the middle 1940s, 'especially among the young and the vulgar' (John W. Clark, 17 February 1975), it has even been punningly modified as *Abyssinia* (q.v.). Terence Rattigan, *Who Is Sylvia?*, played in 1950 and published in 1951, causes a 'gentleman's gentleman' to end a telephone conversation with: 'O.K. Be seeing you.'

be thankful for small murphies! See **little fish are sweet.**

be your age! Stop being childish! Act like a grown-up and use your intelligence! Adopted, c. 1934, from the US. Gelett Burgess, US wit, provides an early example in *Two O'Clock Courage*, 1934, thus:

'I don't know,' I said. 'I don't believe I did.'
'You don't know? How come? See here, be your age. You can tell me, you know.' Then she sat back in her chair silently studying me.

An early English example occurs in Denis Mackail, *Back Again*, 1936, ' "And now go to bed, will you, and be your age." ' In 1942, Berrey glosses it as = don't be ridiculous!; he adduces the synonym, *act your age!*, q.v.

Since the middle 1940s, current in Australia – witness, e.g., the story 'The Unluckiest Man in the World' in *Billy Borker Yarns Again*, 1967.

Cf **get wise to yourself!**: **grow up!**: **hurry up and get born!**: **why don't you get wise to yourself?**

be yourself! Pull yourself together! – i.e., be your *better* self! Adopted c. 1934 – cf the preceding entry – from US. (It was, as a British phrase, recorded in the Supplement of the 3rd edn of *The Concise Oxford Dictionary*.) Berrey glosses it as = don't be ridiculous!

bear, it would bite you, – if it were a: also **if it had been a bear, it would have bitten you**. See **if it were a bear.** ...

beat it while the going is good! was originally a US young students' c.p. from before 1912; it had become general US by 1915 at latest and adopted in Britain by c. 1919.

beats the band – it (or **that**). That beats everything; that's excessive or remarkable; since c. 1880 in Britain and soon going to the Commonwealth and to the USA, where usually *don't that beat the band*, often preceded by *now*, and, as in Britain, rare after c. 1940.

beats the Dutch. ... See **that beats the Dutch.**

beautiful but dumb, originally (? late 1920s) US, became Canadian in late 1930s; foisted on far too many 'dizzy blondes' less stupid than they seemed to be. In WW2 a Services' slogan-poster was captioned 'She's not so dumb; careless talk costs lives.'

becalmed, the sail sticks to the mast. See **I am becalmed, the sail.** ...

because I cannot be had is a ? C16 also an early C17 rhyming reply to the question, *why are ye so sad?*, as in Nicholas Udall's comedy, *Ralph Roister Doister*, 1544, Act III, Scene iii (lines 11–13 in F. S. Boas's edn, *Five Pre-Shakespearean Comedies*):

MERRYGREEK: ... But why speak ye so faintly? or why are ye so sad?
ROISTER DOISTER: Thou knowest the proverb – because I cannot be had.

Such a question with such an answer can hardly form a proverb: and the lack of sense in itself indicates that the status is: c.p.

because it's there, originally the mountain-climber's reason for the literal climbing, or attempted climbing, of literal mountains, became a c.p. when it was humorously or wryly advanced as 'a foolish reason for a foolish act', mostly among those who were conscious of the origin. I don't know who first said it literally; but I'd, not in the least dogmatically, guess that it commenced its new, its c.p., career during the middle or late 1950s, both in Britain (hence in the Dominions) and in the US. (John W. Clark in two letters – early and mid March 1975.)

because the higher the fewer is a mainly Cockney c.p. answer to the mainly Cockney c.p. question *what does a mouse do when it spins?* or, perhaps more often, to *why is a mouse when it spins?* Hardly before 1900. (With thanks, both to the late Julian Franklyn and to Mr Ramsey Spencer.) For other examples of the same kind of deliberate *non sequitur*, cf **do they have ponies down a pit?** – **what was the name of the engine-driver?** – **which would you rather, or go fishing?**

been a long day – hasn't it? 'Almost meaningless – fills a conversational pause' (Frank Shaw, 1 September 1969): since c. 1950.

been and gone (or **gorn**) **and done it**, preceded by **I've** or **you've** or **he's** or **she's**, etc. A jocular, occasionally rueful, emphatic form of *been and done it*, itself tautologically emphatic for *done it*, as in 'Well, I've been and gone and done it' = I've got married: late C19–20. An early example comes in one of P. G. Wodehouse's school stories, his earliest form of humour: *Tales of St Austin's*, 1903, 'Captain Kettle had, in the expressive language of the man in the street, been and gone and done it.'

been robbing a bank? is addressed to someone who, clearly in funds, is rather throwing his money about: C20.

been to see Captain Bates? is a greeting to one recently released from prison: late C19–early 20. 'Captain Bates was a well-known prison-governor' (Ware).

beer, bum and bacca (tobacco). The reputed, almost legendary, pleasures of a sailor's life; since *c.* 1870. Since *c.* 1910, there has existed the variant *rum, bum and bacca*.

beer is best, a brewers' slogan, became, *c.* 1930, a c.p. – and by 1970, slightly obsolescent. John G. Brandon, *The Pawn Shop Murder*, 1936, 'Sterling blokes these, all of whom agreed ... with Mr Pennington that, in moments of relaxation, Beer is Best.'

beer today, gone tomorrow is a c.p. punning parody of *here today (and) gone tomorrow*, connoting brevity: *c.* 1941–60.

[**bee's knees – that's the** suggests the very peak of perfection or the ultimate in beauty, attractiveness, desirability: *c.* 1930–40, in Britain. In 1936 I overheard a girl described as 'a screamer, a smasher, a – oh! the bee's knees'. Originally (*c.* 1925) US – as was *the cat's meow*, which, arising in 1926 (W & F), hardly survived the great economic depression and did not, so far as I know, reach Britain. Neither of these is strictly a c.p. at all.]

before you bought your shovel – which should be compared with the next – is a tailors' c.p., implying that something has been either done or thought of before, and it hardly antedates the C20: before you were even old enough to use a toy shovel.

before you came (or, illiterately yet generally, **come**) **up**, either 'before you came up to the front line' or 'before you joined up' (esp. to a bumptious young soldier), suggests to the man addressed a vast ignorance and inexperience of warfare; army Other Ranks': WW1, but obviously not before late 1915. Variants were *'fore you 'listed*; *before you had a regimental number* or the much commoner *before your number was dry* (on your kit bag) or *up* or *your number's still wet*, never very general – and current only in 1917–18 – or *before you knew what a button-stick was* (a button-stick being a gadget that protected one's uniform from polish overflowing from buttons being polished); *before you was breeched* (wore trousers) or *before you nipped* (went to school); *before your ballocks dropped* or *before you lost the cradle-marks off your arse*; *when your mother was (still) cutting bread on you*; *while you were clapping your hands at Charlie* (Chaplin, of course); *when you were off to school* (with several tags); *I was cutting barbed wire while you was* – or *were – cutting your milk teeth*. (All these were recorded by B & P.)

The prototype was the proverbial saying, *your mamma's milk is scarce out of your nose yet*, recorded by 'proverbial' Fuller in 1732. There exists, moreover, a Shakespearean adumbration; occurring in *Troilus and Cressida*: 'Whose wit was mouldy ere your grandsires had nails on their toes.'

By far the most used form was *before you come* (or *came*) *up*: 'the classic crushing retort of the private soldier. The unanswerable argument from experience and seniority' (John Brophy in B & P). It survived into WW2, when 'the reply of one who was asked to believe something that did not seem credible was: "Do you think I came up yesterday?" ' (PGR).

being fatted for the slaughter. See **fatted ....**

believe it or not! Miss Monica Baldwin, who was a nun from 1914 until 1941, found herself puzzled and often bewildered by all the new words and phrases, as by all the new features of life, when she emerged to a new Britain. She was 'equally bewildered when friends said, "It's your funeral" or "Believe it or not" ' (Foster) – as she attested in her autobiographical *I Leap over the Wall*, 1949.

believe me! seems to have, as a c.p., originated among young US students *c.* 1910 or 1911: A. H. Melville, 'An Investigation of the Function and Use of Slang' – in *The Pedagogical Seminary*, March 1912. Also in Berrey, 1942.

believe me, baby! is a US c.p., 'circulating in the year 1920', esp. among students, as McKnight remarks; obsolete by 1930, at latest.

believe you me! A vaguely emphatic, somewhat conventional c.p. of C20. In PGR, Wilfred Granville notes that 'this is the [naval] Gunnery Instructor's emphasis to any statement. "Believe you me, that is the only way to do the job." ' A more recent example occurs in Lynton Lamb's urbane 'thriller', *Return Frame*, 1972: ' "Well, mister, we was soon out to Renters Hard. Lot going on, believe you me." ' Also in Berrey. Cf **believe me!** and **you'd better believe it!**

belly and wipe my eyes with it – I could take up the slack of my. I'm damned hungry! A nautical c.p., common on ships inadequately rationed: late C19–20.

belly up! belly up to the bar, boys! Drinks on the house, boys!: Canadian: C20. Cf the US underworld, mostly pickpockets', c.p., *belly up?*, Have a drink! – *c.* 1930–50. Prompted by the English-speaking world's toast, *bottoms up!*

Benjamin Brown. See **my name is Benjamin Brown.**

Berlin by Christmas! and **Berlin or bust!** The former is British, referring to Christmas 1914; the latter is US, partially adopted by British soldiers; and both are blush-making. For both, see B & P; for the latter, note esp. Ring W. Lardner, *Treat 'Em Rough* (Letters from Jack the Kaiser Killer), 1918. Of this 1917–18 c.p., used by the US army even before the users reached Europe, Lardner says little in Jack's first letter (23 September); but of the attitude, he implies much – by noting the patriotic hyperboles affected by the vain, gabby, boastful ex-'busher' named Jack Keefe, and apparently that attitude offended him as much as it did John Brophy.

best by (taste) test was a US c.p. of *c.* 1945–7. It arose as Royal Crown Cola's slogan for a soft-drink: *best by (taste) test*. W & F remark that it became 'generalized in meaning to have some ... fad use' – the sense being 'I like it' and the application being to almost anything likable.

best of British luck to you! – the. A c.p., dating since *c.* 1943 or 1944, and meaning exactly the opposite, the intonation being ironic – or even sardonic. Originally an army phrase: in 1942–early 1944, things weren't going any too well for the British, and the phrase was characteristically British in its ironic implications; by 1950, fairly – and by 1955, quite – general. It perhaps owes something to **over the top and the best of luck!**, q.v., and it was, by the late Frank Shaw (of Scouse fame), described as that 'amazing modern phrase in mock-hearty tone'; he also remarked that it is used 'in false "old boy" tone. "You'll lose – but – good luck, friend" – sardonic. Emphatic "British" mocking of such phrases in old patriotic plays.'

Sometimes preceded by **and** and, since *c.* 1960, often shortened to (and) the best of British (as Albert Petch tells me, 31 October 1974).

[**bet you a million to a bit of dirt! – bet your boots! – bet your bottom dollar! – bet your life!** These 'bets' are asseverative exclamations at the colloquial level. They are not true c.pp.]

better for your asking – never (or **no** or **none**) **the.** An abrupt rejection of conventional solicitude: the first, late C17–early 18, and occurring in e.g. S, early in Dialogue I; the second, late C18–20; the third, late C18–20, but slightly obsolescent by c. 1970. Cf **not you by your asking.**

better fuckers (or, euphemistically, **pickers**) **than fighters,** often preceded by **they're.** Applied to those soldiers in WW1 who frequented Fr. or Belgian brothels whenever they had the money: WW1.

better in health than good condition, usually preceded by **he's** or **she's:** C18. S (1738), first dialogue:

LADY SM[ART]: How has your Lordship done this long Time?

COL[ONEL]: Faith, Madam, he's better in Health than good Condition.

Better, that is, than he looks – perhaps a shade too fat, but healthy.

better Red than dead. 'It is better to live under communist rule than to die. This c.p. is probably not of folk origin' (Barry Prentice, 9 June 1975): in Australia, and elsewhere: probably since the late 1940s; and probably literary – suggested, I suspect, by Hilaire Belloc's epigram,

When I am dead, I hope it may be said:
'His sins were scarlet, but his books were read.'

better since you licked them. See **how's your poor feet?**

better than a dig in the eye with a blunt stick or, more generally, ... **than a poke in the eye with a sharp stick;** ... **than a kick in the pants** or **up the arse,** the Canadian version being ... **than a kick in the ass with a frozen boot;** ... **than a slap in the belly with a wet fish;** ... **than sleeping with a dead policeman.** Better than nothing or, since c. 1920, very much better than nothing. They all seem to have originated late in C19. Contrast:

better than a drowned policeman. Of a person: attractive; very pleasant; expert: c. 1900–15. In e.g., J. B. Priestley, *Faraway,* 1932. Contrast the preceding entry.

Betty-all. See **all betty.**

Betty Martin. See **all my eye and Betty Martin.**

beware of your latter end. See **remember you, next astern.**

Big Brother is watching you! This jocularly, often emphasized finger-waggingly, monitory, indeed minatory, c.p., became one within a few weeks after George Orwell's prophetic novel, *Nineteen Eighty-Four,* salutarily shocked the British public in 1949; at first, only in literary and cultured circles, then very soon, among the educated, and by c. 1955, among the remainder of the at least moderately intelligent, esp. those who take some interest in political and sociological history; then it gradually spread by sheer force of hearsay until, by c. 1960, it had gained fairly wide currency, those users who had never read Orwell tending to burlesque the somewhat sinister undertone into a painfully obvious overtone.

The reference occurs in Book 1, chapter I. 'Before that, "Big Brother" was used in the sense of someone being protective –

as in a family. But Orwell changed all that, with his tale of a TV set in every home and officialdom watching', as Vernon Noble remarked in a letter dated 28 July 1975; he appended a quotation from his *Nicknames Past and Present,* 1976: 'Big Brother: watchful officialdom, dictatorial in its powers, from the sinister omnipotent leader of a subservient country in George Orwell's [book].'

Of its US usage, Colonel Albert Moe remarked (31 July 1975): 'It has appeared here in cartoons criticizing governmental surveillance and supervision over private affairs with a lessening of personal freedom. It had frequent usage when the Internal Revenue Service began using computers to check the personal income tax returns.... It has been applied to any sort of "thought control".' And on 1 August, John Clark wrote: 'It has been widely current – increasingly so, since Watergate and especially the current scandal about the CIA and more recently about the FBI – ever since the book was published. It may not be common among the uneducated, but it certainly is among the educated, or at least the "socially aware" educated.'

I also have to thank Colonel Moe for this revealing reference in *Washington Star* of 16 August 1975, in a letter to the editor:

FBI Director Clarence Kelley's appearance before the American Bar Association in Montreal is another reason why Congress should drastically overhaul and reorganize the FBI so that it cannot further infringe upon the civil liberties and democratic freedoms of the American people. Kelley's Big-Brother-is-watching-you philosophy, in the name of 'national security', smacks of police-state dictatorship rationale. Shades of Beria!

big conk – big cock; complementarily, **big conk – big cunt.** This earthy c.p. implies that a big nose implies a large penis or a large vulva: late C19–20, perhaps since c. 1800. Cf **big man ....**

big deal! has, say W & F, 1960, been very widely used by US students and that its employment as a c.p., deflating the addressee's pretensions or enthusiasm or eagerness of attitude or of proposal or proposition, is (in, of course, 1960) 'fast supplanting the earlier uses' (*non*-c.pp.); they add that it was 'popularized by comedian Arnold Stang ... c. 1946, and [again, on a different radio programme] c. 1950'. The c.p. rapidly 'caught on' in both Canada, c. 1947, and Australia, c. 1950, perhaps a few years earlier than in Britain, where, Frank Shaw opined on 1 September 1969, it appeared in the early 1950s.

big man, big prick – small man, all prick. Literally, this vulgar yet vigorous expression extols virility; but figuratively – and only thus does it become a c.p. – it is satirical, 'apostrophizing dolts, dupes, or dunderheads', as one of my wittiest correspondents puts it: C20. Cf **big conk...** above.

big mouth. See **large mouth.**

big shot? – big shit! A c.p. derisive of someone who has just been called 'a big shot'; often shortened to *big shit.* Since c. 1910, but less and less used since c. 1950.

bigger the balls, the better the man – the. An army instructors' c.p. of 1948 – witness Edmund Ions. *A Call to Arms,* 1972 – and probably for some years earlier. Another of those myths which are so common among men addicted to preferring quantity to quality. (With thanks to Paul Beale, 6 September 1974.)

bigger the fire, the bigger the fool – the. An Australian, originally (late 1890s) – and with deadly literalness – bushwhackers' c.p. that had, by *c.* 1900, been generalized to mean 'the more noise a man makes, the less sense he speaks' – esp. applicable to politicians.

bigger they are, the harder they fall – the; occasionally, **the taller they are the further (or farther) they fall**. This indicates a fearless defiance of one's superiors: late C19–20; used also in US; very common in the army of WW1. Probably it originated in the boxing-booths; its popularity has been attributed to Bob Fitzsimmons on the eve of his match with James J. Jeffries, a much bigger man.

bip bam, thank you, ma'am! (I'd have expected *bim bam ...*) and **wham, bam, thank you** (or ye), **ma'am!** The former is a negro c.p. – a 'descriptive phrase expressing gratitude to a woman after love-making, from a popular song' (CM) – which adapted it from the latter phrase, which, literally, has, since *c.* 1895, afforded an either cynical or jocularly brutal comment on sexual intercourse. The *wham bam* part of the phrase is, as you might expect, the slangy US adjective and adverb, *wham-bam*, 'rapid(ly) and roughly' – hence 'displaying more energy and enthusiasm than finesse' (W & F), hence, in love-making, without tenderness or considerateness.

bird is flown – the, is an underworld c.p. of *c.* 1810–60; it signifies that a prisoner has escaped from jail or that a criminal has left his hiding-place. (JB.) It is just possible that here is a reference to 'Charles I in pursuit of Pym, Hampden & Co.', as Mr Norman Franklin has proposed.

bishop! (rarely) is short for **oh, bishop!** and it greets, derisively, the announcement of (very) stale news: on the *Conway* training ship during the 1890s. Attested by John Masefield, the English poet and laureate, who served on her.

bishop hath blessed it – the, was a C16 c.p., applied 'when a thing speedeth not well' (Tyndale, 1528).

bishop's sister's son – he is the, is another C16 c.p., this time ecclesiastical, yet again authorized by Tyndale in 1528; it implies that 'he' has influence in high places – nepotism, in fact.

bit of all right – a. See **this is a bit of all right**.

[**bit of how's-your-father – a**, and **a bit of the other**. 'A bit of the other, something on the side, a bit of how's-your-father, slap and tickle, etc. = "An expression of tenderness for a member of the other sex." (Spoken English is very rich in these poetic romantic phrases)': *Punch*, 10 October 1973, 'Complete Vocabulary of Spoken English', anonymously but wittily, satirically, ironically written by Miles Kington, the literary editor: since *c.* 1950. Strictly, these two phrases are sited on the no-man's-land that lies between cliché and c.p.]

bit of string with a hole in it – I've (or **I've got**) **a** ... See **I've got a....**

[**bit of the other – a**. See **bit of how's-your-father – a**.]

bit tight under the arms – a. A C20 jocularity, for it refers to a pair of trousers much too large for the wearer.

bit you? – what's. See **what's bit you?**

bite in the collar or the cod-piece? – usually preceded by **do they**: a piscatorial c.p. of *c.* 1750–1830. Captain Francis

Grose, who was himself something of a wag, and a wit, described this as 'water wit to anglers'.

biting you? – what's. See **what's biting you?**

black cat and a tin of Vaseline – a. 'Proverbially the last resort in cases of sexual frustration' (a correspondent, 24 September 1973): fairly common in the Fighting Services during WW2; also civilian, both before and after that war.

black friars! or **Blackfriars!** Beware! Look out!: underworld: *c.* 1830–1914. Perhaps *black* because it's an ominous colour and *friars* used in a hostile way; or *Blackfriars* because it was once a very shady district indeed.

black is beautiful has, since *c.* 1950, been a slogan of US negroes, and as such it is clearly ineligible, but when it is jocularly misused by 'Whitey' it *is* a c.p. – white men's only, of course – dating from *c.* 1960.

black is – later, often **black's – your eye!** These are the c.p. forms of the proverbial *no one* – occasionally *you* or *he*, etc. – *can say black is* – or *black's – my eye*, no one can justly accuse me of wrongdoing, no one can justifiably find fault with me; the c.p., therefore, means 'you are at fault' or 'you are guilty'. The proverbial forms date C15–19 and C17–20; *black's your eye*, although increasingly obsolescent since *c.* 1910, is not yet entirely obsolete; the c.p. forms, probably from C16 and C18. Formal documentation is given by the admirable 3rd edn (ed. by F. P. Wilson and, later, his wife) of the *ODEP*. Less formal evidences are these:

The comparable and apparently derivative *black's the white of my eye* is 'an old-time sea protestation of innocence' (Bowen); Beaumont and Fletcher, *Love's Cure*, or *The Martial Maid*, written not later than 1616, Act III, Scene i, in which Alguazier, a corrupt constable, says to a whore:

Go to, I know you, and I have contrived;
Y'are a delinquent....

....

I can say, black's your eye, though it be grey.

In James Shirley's, *The Bird in a Cage*, performed in 1632 and published a year later, Act II, Scene i (p. 397 of the Dyce edn), Bonamico says, 'If you have a mind to rail at them, or kick some of their loose flesh out, they shall not say *black's your eye*, nor with all their lynxes' eyes discover you' – where 'them' = the importunate or the troublesome or the hostile; and in Thomas Shadwell, *The Amorous Bigot: With the Second Part of Tegue O Diodly. A Comedy*, 1690, at Act II, Scene i:

TEG[UE]: Out and avoyd my Presence; I will lose my Reputation, if I will be after speaking vid dee in de Street indeed.
GRE[MIA]: I defy any one to say Black's my Eye; I beseech your Reverence, come into my House.

bless your little belly! This lower-middle class c.p. was certainly current *c.* 1910 and probably goes back to *c.* 1890; by 1940, archaic. Addressed to a child zestfully eating a lot of food (Laurie Atkinson, late 1974). Cf:

bless your little cotton socks! Thank you!: a middle-class c.p., dating from *c.* 1905 and becoming, by 1960, archaic. The elaboration, *bless your little heart and cotton socks!*, arose *c.* 1910 and disappeared *c.* 1918. Although the two phrases are always benevolent, they never exceed affection.

Blighty.... See **roll on, Blighty!**

blimey, Charley (or **Charlie**)! A New Zealand and Australian c.p. used as a safety-valve for pent-up emotions: C20. Australia offers a synonym: *blimey, Teddy*. But why *Charley* or, for that matter, *Teddy*, I don't know, yet have the temerity to suggest that they are friendly and companionable diminutives.

blind Freddie would see it or, even more emphatically, **even blind Freddie wouldn't miss it**: an Australian witticism, imputing the obvious: since *c.* 1930. (*AS*.)

blinded with science is an Australian and New Zealand c.p., celebrating the victory of intelligence over mere physical strength: late C19–20. From boxing: 'it arose when the scientific boxer began, *c.* 1880, to defeat the old bruisers' (Julian Franklyn), perhaps with Jim Corbett's defeat of John L. Sullivan. Cf the WW2's clearly derivative army *blind with science*, to explain away – e.g., to a commanding officer – an offence, esp. by talking busily and technically.

block goes on – the. An underworld c.p., dating from *c.* 1920 and meaning 'an illegal practice has been forestalled or circumvented by Law' or that 'something desirable comes to an end' (Frank Norman's immensely readable *Bang to Rights*, 1958).

blood for breakfast, usually preceded by **there's**. A naval c.p. indicating (late C19–20) that the admiral's or the captain's temper is very bad this morning. In WW2, it had spread to the other two fighting Services, but predominantly as *there'll be blood for breakfast, let alone tea* (last three words often omitted) and notably as a warning from NCOs, either to other NCOs or to privates or their equivalents; moreover, by *c.* 1943, it had spread to civilians.

The navy has, throughout C20, had its own variant, strictly an intensive: *there'll be blood and fur for breakfast*, a hint – from e.g. the Commander's messenger – that 'a Hate is brewing' (John Laffin, *Jack Tar*, 1969).

blood's worth bottling. See **yer blood's . . . .**

blow, Gabriel, blow! is a US negro c.p., imputing credulity and simplemindedness in 'Whitey': (?) since *c.* 1920. CM explains it as springing from a US folk-tale. Among US musicians, *Gabriel* is a (usually professional) trumpet player.

blow in the bell – a. See **there's a blow in the bell**.

blow the bloody ballet! is a philistines' c.p., addressed – since the early 1950s – to lovers of ballet as shown on TV.

blown in! – look (or **see**) **what the wind has**. See **look what the wind . . . .**

blue shirt at the masthead – a, usually preceded by ·**there's**. There is a call for assistance in an emergency: nautical: late C19–20. From the blue flag shown on the occasion.

blurt, master constable! In his edn of *The Works of Thomas Middleton* (3 vols, 1885–6) A. H. Bullen says of the title of Middleton's earliest extant play, *Blurt, Master Constable*, published in 1602: ' "Blurt" was a contemptuous interjection; and "Blurt! Master Constable!" appears to have been a proverbial expression'; but 'catch phrase' would be an apter description and classification. Howell says, 'Blurt, Mr Constable, spoken in derision'. The phrase is recorded by Apperson but excluded by *ODEP*. Cf the early sense of *blurt*, 'to puff scornfully', but also note that, in C19–20, *blurt* has been euphemistic for 'to fart'; cf, further, the theatrical and music-hall 'raspberry'. Apparently *blurt, master con-*

stable was current *c.* 1570–1700. Middleton's titular use indicates that the general intent of this lively play should be apprehended before the play even begins; in other words, the phrase indicates the widespread and well-established character of the saying.

Cf Thomas Dekker, *The Honest Whore*, Part One (1604), Act I, Scene v:

FLUELLO: Will you not pledge me then?
CANDIDO: Yes, but not in that: Great love is shown in little.
FLUELLO: Blurt on your sentences! [Wise sayings.]
Dyce's comment on *blurt* is, 'An exclamation of contempt, equivalent to "a fig for".'

boat sails on Tuesday – the. A 'stock remark by London managers when an American act fails upon its first performance' (Berrey): theatrical and music-hall: since *c.* 1920, but little used since *c.* 1950. Contrast:

boat's left – the. This naval c.p., dating since *c.* 1910, means 'you're too late' – 'you've "had it" '. The boat referred to is that which takes men ashore on short leave.

bob down – you're spotted! Your argument – reason – excuse – etc. – is so feeble that you needn't continue: since *c.* 1920.

Bob's your uncle! See **and Bob's your uncle**.

boil your head! See **go and boil your head!**

boloney. See **it's boloney**.

boo hoo! Cry on – *I'm* not at all sorry for you!: US: since *c.* 1930. A mocking, taunting c.p., based on *boo hoo!* as a conventionally indicative imitation of young children's crying. (W & F.)

'book!' (or **'book! book!'**) **he says – and can't (even) read a paper yet**. This c.p., dating *c.* 1890–1914, is addressed to one who has broken wind 'on a short note' not merely emphatically but explosively. Dr Douglas Leechman (4 March 1976) further states that it is of East Anglian origin. But why *book*? My guess is that whereas a book is long, an item in a newspaper is comparatively short although rarely so short as a single-note fart.

boom! boom! you're dead! See **bang! bang! you're dead!**

[**boomps-a-daisy** is hardly a c.p. – but rather a nursery and general domestic formula of comfort addressed to a child that has knocked its head or, more commonly, fallen down: late (?mid) C19–20. Clearly modelled on *ups-a-daisy!* – which nobody, I hope, would classify as a c.p.]

boots – it didn't go into his. See **it didn't go . . . .**

boots – not in these. See **not in these boots**.

born a gentleman – died an actor is a theatrical c.p. of late C19–20; by 1960, slowly dying – yet by 1973, far from dead. Apparently recorded first in Granville, 1952.

born in a barn? See **were you born in a barn?**

born with a pack of cards in one hand, a bottle of booze in the other, and a fag in his (or **her**) **mouth** refers to one who is born to the raffish manner: since *c.* 1950.

born with the horn. A coarse c.p., applied to a womanizer: late C19–20. This is the slang *horn*, an erection.

bots biting? – how are the. See **how are the bots biting?**

[**bottoms up!**, like **no heeltaps!**, could, I suppose, be called a drinking c.p.; but then drinking phrases, unless they are otherwise used, are excluded as ordinary slang.]

bow-wow! See **wow-wow (-wow)!**

box open – box shut! was a soldiers' c.p. of WW1. It implied that the donor, although glad to be generous, had, in company, to curb his generosity: he possessed only a few cigarettes. (B & P.) Cf **canteen open ....**

boy! is the shortened form, as **boy! oh boy** is the elaboration, of **oh boy!**

boys call 'meal' after her. 'You could eat her!': c. 1950–75: perhaps mostly Liverpudlian. (Frank Shaw, 11 September 1969.)

boys scout: girls guide, a pun on 'Boy Scouts and Girl Guides'; meaning *boys scout* on the look-out for girls, and *girls guide* the boys to the desired spot; current among the older members of the complementary movements: certainly during the 1920s and 1930s and perhaps both before and since.

bra is a girl's best friend – a – occasionally preceded by **square shape** or **pear shape** – is an Australian feminine c.p., dating from c. 1950. Because it helps her to keep in good shape.

brace up! warns the person addressed that what is to follow, whether in speech or in writing, will probably come as a shock; for instance, in telling the recipient that he has been rebuffed or snubbed: since c. 1940. (Royston Lambert, *The Hothouse Society*, 1968.) The c.p. shape of the colloquial *brace yourself!*

brains he was (or, as a c.p., **you were) born with – he hasn't** (as c.p., **you haven't) the.** See **you haven't the brains you were born with.**

Bramah knows – I don't is a euphemism (c. 1880–1910) for 'God knows – I don't!' Better spelt *Brahma.*

brandy is Latin for (a) goose – and tace is Latin for a candle (or, much later, **fish**); also in shorter form, **brandy is Latin for goose** (or **fish**), the former dating from late C16, the latter from c. 1850. Brewer has neatly posed the pun: '*What is the Latin for goose? (Answer) Brandy.* The pun is on the word *answer. Anser* is Latin for goose, which brandy follows as surely and quickly as an answer follows a question.' Then why *fish?* Mayhew tells us that the richer kinds of fish produce queasiness, the stomach's stability being restored best by a drink of good brandy.

And what of the appendage, 'and *tace* is Latin for a candle'? It occurs as early as 1676, and also in S, 1738; *tace* = Latin *tace!* (be, or keep, silent) and therefore the appendage forms a warning against indiscreet speech. The precise connection with a candle remains disputable – indeed, mysterious.

Both parts of the whole, whether in combination or separately, are, among the classically educated, extant (although only just). L. used to be the requisite, and the badge of a gentleman: since WW2, it seems to be unrequired of even a scholar.

brandy is Latin for pig and goose is, according to Halliwell, 1847, 'an apology for drinking a dram after either': a perhaps mainly rural variant of the first part of the preceding c.p.: C19–early C20.

brass monkey. See **it's so cold ....**

brayvo, Hicks! and **brayvo, Rouse!** The former covers the approximate period 1850–1910; the latter, probably prompted by the former, c. 1900–14; mean 'splendid!' or 'well done!'; the former belongs to music-halls and theatres, the latter to East London in general; the former was, late C19–early 20, used esp. in South London. Of the former, J. Redding Ware, who was always very good in the entire field of entertainment, writes, 'In approbation of muscular demonstration.... From Hicks, a celebrated ... actor ... more esp. "upon the Surrey side ...", e.g. "Brayvo Hicks – into 'er again".' Of the latter phrase, Ware remarks that it derives from 'the name of an enterprising proprietor of "The Eagle" ...; a theatre ... in the City Road' A very successful, though unauthorized, presenter of French light opera, notably 'all the best of Auber's work'.

Brazen Nose College. See **you were bred in ....**

bread. See **as I live by bread.**

break a leg! A US actors' c.p., meaning 'Good luck!' and anecdotally dated since mid-April 1865. It has been said (by whom originally, I don't profess to know) to have originated in that incident in which John Wilkes Booth, little-known but fanatical actor, who, on 14 April 1865, assassinated Abraham Lincoln at Ford's Theatre, Washington, D.C., and broke his leg when, immediately after, he jumped on to the stage. I owe this anecdotal origin to Edward C. Lawless, MD, of San Francisco; he added: 'The phrase was more popular in the 30's and 40's [than it is now: 1 August 1975]. It was used among actors just before one of them [was due to go] before an audience for the first time.'

But the consensus of opinion among scholars and theatrical people dismisses that origin, mainly because the phrase does not appear to have arisen before C20.

Colonel Albert Moe (31 July 1975) cites Sherman Louis Sergel, editor of *The Language of Show Biz.* Chicago, 1973. Mr Sergel, after quoting the phrase as *break a leg* or *go break a leg,* writes:

> What you are supposed to tell someone just before he goes onstage on opening night. Also used, though more rarely, for any performance. It is a way of wishing him well without breaking the superstitious injunction against saying the words, 'good luck'. This is to avoid tempting the gods. It seems to be a widespread custom in the theater. In Germany you are invited to suffer a *Hals und heinbruch,* or neck and bonebreak. Sometimes this is accompanied by the application of the well-wisher's knee in the rump, just to get things started.... (Note: no one seems to know the [place of] origin or the history of the phrase, though a number of our editors suspect it to be English in origin.)

Colonel Moe adds: 'An offshoot of the theater usage seems to be to a person about to embark on a voyage – in the nature of "Bon Voyage" or "Have a nice trip".'

To take a risk ('Partridge is always game', my best friend, who died in action in the autumn of 1918, mendaciously punned in the summer of 1916 on the Somme): I gravely doubt the currency of the phrase before WW1; like Colonel Moe, I propose its origin in 'a variant translation from the German'.

Mr Ramsey Spencer, a fine German scholar, compares the perhaps WW1 and certainly the WW2 (and probably since 1936 when the Luftwaffe was reconstituted) *Hals- und Beinbruch,* 'Break your neck and leg!' = 'Happy landings!' He thinks that the aviation c.p. *may* have existed since the earliest days of flying. In short, the Ger. pilots' phrase could well have been adopted by the Ger. theatre, whence, in translation, it passed – just possibly via the British theatre – to the US as early as the 1920s.

In the US theatre, as Professor John W. Clark wrote to me on 1 August 1975, 'the c.p. may also be spoken by a director or a producer or a stage manager or a property man or a dresser or a costumes mistress or a stage hand'; he noted that 'any or all of these deplore and despise its use by a "layman"'.

Concerning its Canadian currency, Dr Douglas Leechman, on 11 August 1975, sent me this comment: 'Theatre, radio, etc. Do your best! Go in and win! A facetious cry of encouragement, heard on radio, 29 December 1974. The speaker implied that it was frequently used.'

Cf **fall through the trap door!**

But there is a second US usage, probably quite independent: 'a sarcastic refusal to comply with a request', recorded in *American Speech*, April 1947, by Jane W. Arnold, 'The Language of Delinquent Boys'. (Owed to Colonel Moe.)

break it down! Stop talking like that! Also, change the subject!: Australian: since *c.* 1920. It occurs in, e.g., Lawson Glassop's fine war novel, *We Were the Rats* [the 'Desert Rats'], 1944. Contrast:

break it up! Disperse! Hence, get moving and keep moving! A Canadian official c.p., adopted, *c.* 1930, from US; adopted by Britain *c.* 1935. Hence, a couple embracing may be exhorted, 'Break it up!': since the late 1930s, and as much British as Canadian or US.

bridges, bridges!, a printers' c.p. of *c.* 1890–1930, is 'a cry to arrest a long-winded story', says Ware, who, perhaps correctly, proposes as origin the Fr. *abrégeons*, let us shorten it!

bright-eyed (or **bright eyes) and bushy tailed**, meaning 'alertly active – and ready for anything', may have been US – Colonel Albert Moe vouches for its use in 1933 – before it became Canadian. Dr Douglas Leechman remembers hearing it in 1956 and in 1959 tells me that it was 'incorporated in a current popular song'. From the usual aspect of squirrels and other such quadrupeds.

brinded pig will make a good brawn to breed upon – a. This c.p. of *c.* 1670–1760 is recorded in Ray's *Proverbs* with the comment, 'A red-headed man will make a good stallion.'

bring anything with you? – the laconic abridgement of **did you bring anything with you?** – is a Canadian drug addicts' c.p. of *c.* 1950–60 – and means 'have you any narcotics on you?'

bring on the body! A US film-industry c.p.: since *c.* 1930. Berrey clarifies, thus: 'request that actor come into camera range'.

bring on the dancing girls! Let's watch – or do – something more entertaining or exciting, for *this* is a crashing bore: since *c.* 1930. From the pleasant practice of Oriental potentates: when bored with their guests, they order the dancers to appear.

[**bring us back a parrot?** Addressed, in late C19–20, but obsolescent by 1940, to someone leaving for a hot country, this is a 'borderliner': c.p. or cliché? The latter, I think.]

Britons never shall be slaves (or **wage slaves**) – **not willingly**. These c.p. adaptations of 'Britons never, never shall be slaves' date from the early 1920s.

broom up at the masthead. See **she carries the broom....**

[**brother, can you spare a dime?** dates, as a candidate, since the song so titled – the lyricist being Harburg, the composer Gorney – became popular in 1932, at the height of the Depression. It failed to gain election.]

brutal and licentious soldiery. Dating from 1891, when Kipling used it in *Life's Handicap*, where Private Mulvaney ironically satirizes a Victorian civilian attitude to the Regular Army, an attitude not yet extinct; common among army officers, wryly jocular. Kipling's phrase seems to have been an unconscious merging of two late C18 phrases: *a rapacious and licentious soldiery*, occurring in Burke's *Speech on Fox's East India Bill*, 1783; and *the uncontrolled licentiousness of a brutal and insolent soldiery*, in Thomas, Baron Erskine's *Defence of William Stone*, 1796; both of these two phrases are cited in *ODQ*.

Buckley. See **who struck Buckley?**

[**buddy, can you spare a dime**. 'Not a catch phrase – title of post-Depression popular song *c.* 1932, sung by Harry Richman ... recounting tear-jerk saga of a rich man reduced to street begging'. Ben Grauer on Christmas Day 1975.]

built like a brick shit-house, mostly preceded by **he's**. A low Canadian phrase, meaning 'he's a very well-made fellow': C20.

bullet with my name on it – there's a, refers to a fear, a belief, that one will be killed – or, at the least, severely wounded – in action: WW1, certainly, but I suspect that it may have arisen twenty to twenty-five years earlier. A. W. Bacon, *Adventures in Kitchener's Army* has, '... and every soldier believed that unless the bullet with your name on came your way, no other one would hit you' (a quotation I owe to Colonel Archie White, VC). Cf **when your name's on it ....**

bullshit baffles brains is an army officers' c.p. of WW2. The bullshit comes from others, the brains from the speaker. Cf **excrementum vincit cerebellum.**

bully for you! Capital! Splendid! Fine! Well done! In 1864–1866, it had a tremendous vogue in the US and lingered on well into C20; it reached England *c.* 1870 and lasted until *c.* 1920. Then, among the middle-class young, it has had a vogue, but only as used mockingly during the early 1970s.

bumps! – now she and **what ho! she bumps!** Well, that's splendid or excellent!: esp., *c.* 1895–1910 and since *c.* 1899 'about the time of the South African War' (Collinson): at first, Londoners' and then, by *c.* 1914, general; the latter is satirically applied to 'any display of vigour – especially feminine' (Ware).

Bush Week. See **what do you think this is – Bush Week?**

business as usual (with 'despite difficulty and danger' understood) was a c.p. of WW1; during the 1930s, it was used, in the main, ironically; during WW2 – if used at all – (mostly) literally; since then, it has been derisively condemnatory of a blind complacency. Its post-WW2 history is lucidly and wittily treated in Safire.

but that's a mere detail. See **detail....**

but yes indeed! was, in 1923, recorded by McKnight as being regarded by youthful US students as 'old fogeys' ': late (?mid) C19–20. Cf the homely US *yes indeed!*, which is, in part, dialectal.

butcher's horse.... See **that must have been a butcher's horse ....**

butts on you, ducks! was, in the 1940s, a US army request for a partially smoked cigarette. (Berrey.) Apparently *ducks* is used merely because it approximates to a rhyme.

buy a bewk (i.e., book)! See LIVERPOOL CATCH PHRASES.

buy a prop! Buy some stock!: stockbrokers': c. 1885–1940. The market needs to be supported.

buy me one of those, daddy. See **oh, mummy ....**

by Christchurch, houya? A New Zealand juvenile c.p. of C20. A euphemistic and 'Maorified' shape of *by crikey, who are you?*

by Jove, I needed that! (A drink understood.) A 'gag' popularized by Ken Dodd, who presumably 'thought it up'; he used it as an 'opener', after playing 'a quick burst on me banjo'. It also occurs as a 'line' in the Goon Show. (Paul Beale, 7 May 1975.)

by the grace of God and a few Marines 'has been used to indicate the accomplishment of some difficult task even though only one Marine may have been involved.... It received extensive coverage and publicity in WW2 when General MacArthur waded ashore on his "return" to the Philippines. The Marines that preceded him and were already there erected a sign on the beach to greet him with "By the grace of God and a few Marines, MacArthur returned to the Philippines"': which shows that the implication is that God needed a little help from the Marine Corps' (Colonel Albert Moe, 15 June 1975). Its use preceded WW2, perhaps by a generation, and clearly it is a Marine Corps c.p.

And then, on 28 June, Colonel Moe notes that an occasional variant:

appears as WW1 book title by a USMC general, Albertus Wright Catlin, *With the Help of God and a Few Marines* (1919). Walter A. Dyer in the Introduction, p. xvi, [writes]: 'With the help of God and a few Marines is a phrase that has been attributed to nearly every naval hero from John Paul Jones to Admiral Dewey, and it fits. It ... somehow expresses the very spirit of the Corps'. ... I am inclined to doubt ... that the phrase was used by either John Paul Jones or Admiral Dewey.

by the great god Bingo. A c.p. of asseveration – and of satire on the popularity of – indeed, the craze for – that game: since c. 1962.

'bye for now! See **good-bye for now.**

C.O.D. 'A blessing on an outgoing, a comment on an incoming, shell' (B & P): British Other Ranks': WW1. Literally 'cash on delivery'.

cabbage-looking .... See **not so green** ....

cable home about – nothing to. See **nothing to** ....

cackle .... See **cut the cackle and** ....

cake .... See both **it's a piece of cake** and **that takes the cake**.

cake is getting thin – the. One's money is running short: Cockneys': C20. In Cockney slang of C20 (obsolescent by 1950), *a cake* is a pile of currency or bank notes.

calf .... See **you are a calf**.

California, here I come! I'm on my way to success: US: C20. Originally in reference to the film industry, as Professor John W. Clark tells me in a letter of 11 September 1968. In Jean Pott's novel, *The Little Lie*, of that same year, a man says, 'Nineteen years since I took off in that good old jalopy. California, here I come. Only I never made it': yet he had indeed intended to go to California and he *was* using the c.p. deliberately and allusively. I seem to have a vague memory – *can* one be vaguer than that? – of Al Jolson singing a very popular song either thus or similarly titled; also an equally vague impression that it was this song which 'sparked off' the c.p. itself. Well, for once, an impression was – in the main – correct. In 1923, Al Jolson interpolated this song, the words by himself and Buddy de Sylva and the music by Joseph Meyer, into a musical comedy, *Bombo*, first mounted in 1921. But I was lucky, for three friends at the Savile Club, Dallas Bower and the late Luthar Mendes and John Foster White, whose aggregate knowledge of the film industry's history is encyclopedic, came to my aid in December 1973 and thus spared me the blushes proper to ignorance exposed.

The phrase has exercised at least some small influence in Britain: a clear allusion occurs in Robert Crawford's 'thriller', *Kiss the Boss Goodbye*, 1970:

'We can't afford to wait,' he said ...

'Thrumbleton,' I said, 'here I come.'

And the *New Yorker*, on 6 August 1973, heads a review of books about the state thus: 'California, Here I Come'.

call it eight bells! This nautical, mostly naval, c.p. dates, so far as I've been able to ascertain, from *c.* 1890: and it serves as a convenient and most acceptable excuse for drinking before noon, before which time it has long been held unseemly to take strong liquor. (Ware, 1909. See also *Sailors' Slang*.)

call me (or **you can call me**) **anything** (or **what**) **you like, so** (or **as**) **long as you don't call me late for breakfast.** This mostly Australian c.p., belonging to late C19–20, is used by one who has been addressed by the wrong name – or by a hesitant or embarrassed no-naming.

call me cut. In Act IV, Scene ii, of Nathaniel Field's *A Woman Is a Weathercock*, performed and published in 1612:

PENDANT: ... For profit, this marriage (God speed it!) marries you to it; and for pleasure, if I help you not to that as cheap as any man in England, call me cut.

In the Mermaid Series, A. Wilson Verity's footnote runs thus: 'A proverbial phrase and a term of reproach, "cut" being commonly used to designate a horse with a cut tail'; rather, I'd say, an asseveration – 'call me a liar!' – than a reproach, and a c.p. rather than a proverbial phrase, apparently of the very approximate period, 1570–1650.

calves' heads are best hot is jeeringly spoken by a third party in apology for someone so ill-mannered as to sit down to eat with his hat on: C19–20, but obsolescent by 1940. (I've lost the authorizing reference: in *DSUE*, 1937, it appears without one.)

came over with the onion boat! is a C20 c.p. – rare before 1920 – spoken with the well-known British insularity and contempt for foreigners; originally it referred to the Breton onion-vendors, who still (late 1975) contribute to the saving of the London scene from drabness. Sometimes it occurs in the form, 'You don't think that I came over in the onion boat, do you?' Occasionally 'cattle boat' is used, at first in reference to cargo boats from Ger. ports; or of Italians it is often said, 'Came over with an icecream barrow'. Two rarer phrases – both used jocularly – are 'came over with the Mormons' or 'came over with the morons', the latter not before 1930. (The last two are owed to an old contributor, Mr Albert B. Petch, in a letter dated 5 September 1946.)

came up with the rations; in full, **it** – or **they** – **came up** .... A soldiers' c.p. of both WW1 and WW2, when it was either derisively or bitterly applied to medals easily won or haphazardly apportioned because a (say) brigade was due for at least some sort of metallic recognition. (PGR.) This is not to say that the recipients had not deserved *some*thing: merely that a 'mentioned in despatches' would normally have sufficed. The most trenchant of all adverse criticisms of a certain type – or, rather, types – of medal-acquirers occurs in a brilliant story by C. E. Montague. I once remarked to my friend the late Colonel Archie White, VC, that nobody could say anything nasty about *his* award; he replied, 'All the *truly* brave men were dead before WW1 ended.'

camp as a row of tents, usually preceded by **as**. Spectacularly histrionic and affected in gesture and speech, as also in manner and movement; literally, of an extremely homosexual male – or, in the sophisticated slang of the 1960s and 1970s, 'a roaring queer'. The pun, manifestly, is on the noun *camp* (or encampment) and the slang adjective *camp*, literally 'homosexual' or 'Lesbian', hence 'excessively affected or theatrical in speech or manner'. I didn't see this c.p. in print until I read John Gardner's amusing essay on that recognized sport which was formerly known as *épater les bourgeois*.

can do? and **can do!** 'Can you do it?' and 'Yes, I can do it':

originally and still pidgin (mid C19–20); hence in naval, hence also in army, use for 'All right?' and 'Yes, all right!' Used literally, it occurs, 1914, in 'Bartimeus', *Naval Occasions*, where it is put into the mouth of a Chinese messman employed on one of HM ships 'on the China Station'; as Colonel A. White, VC, has remarked, in a letter dated 22 October 1968, 'The Chinese store-keeper's OK in any part of Asia. "Have you got Navy Cut medium?" – "Can do!" ' The negative reply is *no can do!* – so general that, in the navy, it is often 'abridged' to *NCD* (PGR and *Sailors' Slang*.)

can I do you now, sir? In his book *Itma, 1939–1948*, published in December 1948, Frank Worsley, the producer of the show and, along with Ted Kavanagh, the brilliant script-writer, and Tommy Handley, who presented and, indeed, 'made' Mr 'ITMA' himself, having written about the period September 1939 – July 1940, comes to the renewal of the radio programme 'ITMA' with these words:

It will be noticed that up to now there has been no mention of one of our most popular characters, the beloved Cockney Charlady, *Mrs Mopp* (played by Dorothy Summers). This famous personage did not make her first appearance through the equally famous ITMA door until 10th October 1940, when, with a clatter of bucket and brush, she burst into the Mayor's Parlour and that delightful hoarse voice was heard to ask – CAN I DO FOR YOU NOW, SIR?

Surely there is something wrong with this picture? There is indeed. 'Can I do *for* you now, sir?' – one word too many for the nation-wide slogan [*sic*] that swept the whole country, indeed the entire English-speaking globe, in a few months. Yet those were her very first words. Later – by a sheer accident – they became 'Can I *do* you *now*, sir?' and that's how they remained.

The immortal words were spoken by Mrs Mopp to Tommy Handley. And, inevitably Ted Kavanagh also, in his rushed, yet very readable, biography of Tommy Handley – it appeared in 1949, within a few months of Handley's death – refers to the phrase. For an account of the phrases themselves, Frank Worsley's is by far the better book.

Note, however, that this justly famous c.p. had what seems to have been its forerunner, certainly its adumbration: Frank Worsley had, earlier in his book, recorded that within six weeks of 13 September 1939, when the show began, at least three phrases had become established as c.pp.: *Funf speaking* – *I always do my best for all my gentlemen* – and *I wish I had as many shillings*. (Cf the separate entries for the first and third.) Worsley had remarked that among the early characters playing in 'ITMA' was '*Mrs Tickle*, the office charlady (played in the pantomime tradition by a man – Maurice Denham). Lola Tickle, it may be remembered, kept asserting that she "always did her best for all her gentlemen", particularly her favourite, MR ITMA.' Yet it is doubtful whether this admirable sentiment prevailed for even a week after *can I do you now, sir?* hit Britain like a tornado.

'The extraordinary thing is that such phrases [as Mrs Mopp's 'Can I do you now, sir?' – 'I go, I come back' – etc., from 'ITMA'] are still used by people who were not born when Tommy Handley flourished' (Vernon Noble, for many years associated with the BBC in Manchester, in a letter dated 4 December 1973).

can I help you with that? I'd like to have some of that: c. 1895–

1940. Ware remarks, 'When said to the fairer sex the import is different': in Shakespearean phrase, ' "Let us exchange flesh." '

can the comedy! Cut out the funny stuff!: US, mostly students': 1920s. (McKnight; Berrey.)

can you beat it? (or, more specifically, *that?*) This colloquial c.p. is both British, recorded in e.g. *DSUE*, 1937, and US, recorded in e.g. Berrey, 1942; the preponderance of evidence suggests that the phrase was adopted by Britain from US. The general sense is 'Can you better that – for impudence or excellence or unexpectedness?' and it seems to have been current throughout the C20. A fairly recent example occurs in Noël Coward's *Nude with Violin*, produced and published in 1956:

CLINTON: Why did she never divorce him?
SEBASTIEN: She is a woman of the highest principles, and a Catholic.
CLINTON: Can you beat that?

Clinton, it should be added, is a US journalist. Cf the following from his *Pretty Polly Barlow* (Section 3), in *Pretty Polly Barlow and other stories*, 1964:

'She died about half an hour ago in the hospital.'
'Can you beat that?' Lorelei's fluent English had recently been idiomatically enriched by the visit to Singapore of an American aircraft carrier.

can you 'ear (or **hear**) **me, Mother?** Of the *hear* form, Mr Laurie Atkinson, in a letter written in December 1968, says that it is employed to 'prompt [a] reluctant or [a] hesitating reply, originating from popularity of its repetition by Sandy Powell, comedian, from line in radio script, Blackpool, 1928, used and repeated *ad lib*. while picking up and rearranging script that fell to floor'. Mr Vernon Noble, in a letter written on 4 December 1973, quotes the phrase as *can you 'ear me, mother?* and likewise attributes it to Sandy Powell. And Sandy Powell it was! In the *Guardian* of 12 March 1975, Stephen Dixon, in a nostalgic, witty article, 'Haul of Fame', a set of memories of music-hall and radio comedians, writes:

'Can you hear me, mother?' Another great music hall comedian ripe for revival is Sandy Powell, now 75.... His fraudulent, harassed ventriloquist and inept conjurer acts.... [In these] Powell's routines have been polished to perfection ... the routines are a master humorist's brilliant evocation of all that was seedy and third-rate in variety. Moreover, Harry Stanley's appreciation, *Can You Hear Me, Mother?* – subtitled *Sandy Powell's Lifetime in Music*, appeared later in 1975.

Can you 'ear me, Mother? is most appositely and delightfully burlesqued in Act I, Scene i, of John Osborne's *Look Back in Anger* (produced in 1956 and published in 1957), where Jimmy, well launched in a rousingly eloquent tirade against his upper-class mother-in-law, says: 'She's as rough as a night in a Bombay brothel, and as tough as a matelot's arm. She's probably in that bloody cistern, taking down every word we say. (*Kicks cistern*.) Can you 'ear me, mother?'

can you feature that? Literally, 'Can you understand that?' but, in slangy usage, it indicates astonishment: US students': in 1920 and for a few more years. (McKnight; Berrey.)

can you hear me, Mother? See **can you 'ear me, Mother?**

can you say uncle to that? is a dustmen's c.p. of c. 1900–14. Clearly, *say uncle* means 'reply'. Ware notes that the c.p.

answer to the question is *Yes – I can*; the emphasis on *can* in both the question and the answer rather suggests that there is a pun on dust*bins*.

can you see him coming, Sister Anne? A 'woman's mock-stagy whisper to any other female on look-out for caller or visitor' (Laurie Atkinson, late 1974): late C19–20; obsolescent by 1970. An allusion to the Bluebeard fairy-tale.

· **can you tell which is the white goose, or the grey goose the gander?** occurs in S (Second Conversation), 1739, where young Neverout asks Miss Notable this 'trick' question – the sort that admits of no answer, like *which would you rather, or go fishing?* Miss neatly replies, 'They say, a Fool will ask more Questions, than twenty wise men can answer.' I doubt whether this 'trick' long outlived its century.

can you tie that? is a US c.p., expressive of amazement or profound admiration – or both; recorded by Berrey in 1942, but existing from much earlier.

cant a slug into your bread room! was a nautical c.p. of mid C18–early C19; it meant 'Drink a dram' and was recorded by Grose, 1788.

can't be bad! is a 'cliché response, which I heard in the latter half of 1973, as a term of approbation or congratulation, e.g. "Hey! I've just got an Income Tax rebate of ninety quid." – "Can't be bad!" Fairly loosely used in army circles' (Paul Beale, 11 December 1974). Cf semantically **is that good?**

And then, on 1 May 1975, he adds: 'From a Beatles' song, at the height of their fame, "... she loves you, yeah, yeah, and you know it can't be bad ...".'

can't be did! (or, in full, **it can't be did!**) This jocularity, arising *c.* 1890, was by 1937 (*DSUE*) 'very ob.' and by 1970 fatally moribund; yet even in late 1973 I heard it – from, odd though this may seem, a teenager. These deliberate mispronunciations were tiresomely common during the approximate period, 1890–1914; one of the few salutary effects of WW1 was to kill off most of 'em.

can't claim a halfpenny (or **ha'penny**) indicates that one has 'a complete alibi which is carefully concocted when one is about to face a charge' (H & P). It dated from *c.* 1930, was mostly army, and, by *c.* 1970, virtually obsolete. Understand: 'They cannot claim even a ha'penny from me, chum!'

can't complain! and **no complaints!** I have nothing to *really* complain about: British (perhaps rather the former) and US (perhaps rather the latter): C19–20, for the former, since *c.* 1920 the latter. A US example occurs in, e.g., Jean Potts, *An Affair of the Heart*, 1970, 'Hilda had sounded exactly the same way she always did.... Had said the things she always said: "How's tricks?" and "Can't complain" and "Bye now".' A much earlier English example occurs in R. S. Surtees, *Hawbuck Grange; or, The Sporting Adventures of Thomas Scott, Esq.*, 1847, in Chapter I:

'It was the fifteenth season of my hunting the country, and now I'm in my thirty-eighth – *time flies*.'

'It passes lightly over you, Sir, though,' observed Tom.

'Middling,' replied he, cheerfully. 'Middling – can't complain ...'

In C20, a frequent variant is *can't grumble*, as in *Punch*, 1 October 1973, 'Complete Vocabulary of Spoken English': 'Can't grumble = *"I am about to give you a long list of my complaints."*'

can't have my telly! and **the old man must be working overtime** are references, the former by the victim and the latter by others, to a woman with many (young) children; the former since *c.* 1950, the latter of late C19–20. (Supplied by Mr Frederick Leech on 15 May 1972.)

can't help it – he (or **she**), is used jocularly when someone is seen acting, or heard talking, eccentrically or oddly: C20. (Mr Albert Petch.)

can't see it is a lower-middle-class and lower-class c.p. of *c.* 1890–1914 and it means 'I don't see why I should – *esp.*, do it' (Ware).

can't you feel the shrimps? was a Cockney c.p. of *c.* 1870–1914 and it meant 'Don't you smell the sea?' (Ware.)

canteen open – mind your fingers! – canteen closed. A naval lowerdeck c.p., dating from *c.* 1920 and spoken by a seaman offering, rather summarily, a packet of cigarettes to a group of messmates. (*Sailors' Slang.*) Cf **box open ....**

Captain Bates. See **been to see ....**

captain is at home (or **is come) – the.** She is having her period: mid C18–19. A pun on *catamenia*, menstruation. (Grose, 1796.) Cf **(the) Cardinal is come** below.

captured a sugar-boat, usually preceded by **they** – occasionally, **we – must have.** A New Zealand c.p., current during WW1 and serving to explain the issue of an unusually liberal ration of sugar.

card. See **that's a sure card.**

Cardinal is come – the. She is having her period: mid C18–mid C19. (Grose, 1796.) By a pun on *red*, the colour held to characterize a Cardinal of the Catholic Church. Cf **captain is at home** above.

care if I do – I don't. See **I don't care if I do.**

Carl the caretaker's in charge. The front line – on the Western Front only – is quiet: a soldiers' c.p. of WW1, esp. during 1917–18 and, in the latter year, among US as well as British troops. Quite a saga arose about this quiet, methodical, mythical old man

whom the Kaiser left in charge while the troops were elsewhere ... sometimes he was credited with a family, a 'Missus' and 'three little nippers'. Sometimes he was 'Hans the Grenadier', owing to an occasional fancy for a night bombing party. Sometimes he was called 'Minnie's husband' [a Minnie being the Ger. *Minenwerfer* or trench mortar] (F & G, who were so very good at this sort of thing).

carrot. See **take a carrot.**

carry me out and bury me decent! (or **decently!**) indicated the speaker's incredulity – occasionally his displeasure – at something he has just seen or just heard: *c.* 1770–1930; during the period *c.* 1870–1930, usually shortened to **carry me out!** Post-1850 variants included *carry me out and leave me in the gutter – carry me upstairs – carry me home* – and *whoa, carry me out*. (Ware.) Cf **good night!** and **let me die!** A US equivalent was, *c.* 1870–1910, *you can have my hat*, as M remarked in 1891.

carry on, London! This public-spirited c.p. was frequently heard during the period from mid-June to early September 1944, when London suffered from the Ger. V1 (flying bomb) blitz, and then from early September of that year until March 1945, when it suffered from the V2 (rocket) blitz. It derived from the 'sign-off' of a BBC radio weekly magazine programme 'In Town Tonight', which ran for many years. The c.p. lasted beyond March 1945, but in a more jocular spirit and in even the most trivial circumstances.

carry on, Sergeant-Major! 'Go ahead! – oh, yes, do that! – I've finished, so *you* do as you like': military (mostly Other Ranks'): ever since early 1915. It originated in the company commander's order to his SM, but was also used by any officer inspecting a parade; in the latter instance, it signified that the officer had completed his inspection of the parade and that the paraded troops were now the SM's responsibility; now and then, it was spoken by a lazy or an incompetent officer 'passing the buck'.

carrying all before her is a raffishly jocular or facetious c.p., dating from *c.* 1920 and indicating that the woman or girl to whom it is applied either has a liberally developed bust or is rather prominently pregnant.

cartload of monkeys and the wheel won't turn – a. A children's c.p., 'shouted after a crowd of people cycling, or riding, slowly past, or sitting in a bus, or a coach, awaiting departure' (Peter Ibbotson, in a letter of 9 February 1963): since *c.* 1890; by 1960, slightly obsolescent, but not yet obsolete.

cat? – who shot the. See **who shot the cat?**

cat got your tongue? See **has the cat got your tongue?**

cat in hell.... See **no more chance than a cat in hell.**

cat laugh – enough to (or **it would**) **make a.** (It is) very funny or ludicrous: since *c.* 1820. Apperson cites Planché, 1851, and Stanley Weyman, 1898.

catch 'em all alive-o! Originally – *c.* 1850 – a fishermen's c.p., it had, by 1853 or a year or two earlier, gained a tremendous general vogue; yet by 1880, or very soon after, it fell into disuse.

catch 'em young, treat 'em rough, tell 'em nothing – with the second and third injunctions sometimes reversed – has, since *c.* 1920, been popular as a male jocularity, occasionally more serious than jocular; not much heard since *c.* 1960 – which is perhaps just as well, such a masculine attitude offending more sensitive minds.

catch me at it! – often, and in C20 always, shortened to **catch me!**, with a complementary **catch you (at it)!** It dates from *c.* 1770. The former occurs in, e.g., Mrs Hannah Cowley (1743–1809), dramatist, and in Scottish novelist, John Galt (1779–1839); the latter in Dickens, in an allusive form: ' "Catch you at forgetting anything!" exclaimed Carker.'

cats have nine lives – and (or **but**) **women ten cats' lives** is obviously an elaboration of the proverb, *cats have nine lives*, in reference to their exceptional and, indeed, notable powers of survival; the c.p. belongs to the very approximate period, 1750–1850 and it appears in Grose.

cat's meow – the. See **bee's knees – that's the.**

cats of nine tails of all prices – he has is a low and callous c.p. of *c.* 1770–1840: it is applied to the public hangman. (Grose, 1796, at **cart.**)

caught cold by lying in bed barefoot – he (or **she**). Grose, 2nd edn, 1788, records this mid C18–mid C19 c.p. and explains that it was applied both to outright valetudinarians and to persons merely fussy, not neurotic, about their health.

cavalry are coming (or **are here**) – **the.** Help is coming or has arrived: late C19–20, but after *c.* 1940 always ironic. From the literal military sense. Cf the US **the marines have landed.**

c'est la guerre! is a military c.p., offered as an apology or excuse for – or as an explanation of – any shortage or shortcoming. Cf Anon., *C'est la Guerre: Fragments from a War Diary*, 1930. From the continual, the constant, Fr. apology for any deficiency or failure whatsoever, adopted in 1915 by the British soldier and in late 1917 by the US. In Clarence B. Kelland's war novel, *The Little Moment of Happiness*, 1919, occurs this passage:

> She shrugged her shoulders and said, with that calm resignation which is so much to be met with, '*C'est la guerre....* It is the war.' That is a phrase which explains everything, excuses everything in France today [1918]. '*C'est la guerre.*' One offers it to explain the lateness of trains, the price of cheese, poverty. The lack of sugar, morale, everything great or small. '*C'est la guerre*' is the countersign of the epoch. It embraces everything.

chain? – who pulled your. See **who pulled....**

chalk it up! Just look at that!: *c.* 1920–40. Recorded in Manchon: *regarde-moi ça!* Worthy of at least ephemeral admiration or astonishment. Contrast:

challik it oop! Esp. in a tavern, 'Put it to my credit!': a theatrical c.p., presumably introduced by some comedian, not necessarily a professional 'funny man', who deliberately perverted *chalk*; phonetically, *challik* is a vocalization of the S-E word. Recorded in 1909 by Ware, it seems to have arisen in the 1890s; by 1930, obsolescent. Dialectal *challik* is, of course, *chalk*: notations of credit were – although less after *c.* 1960 – chalked up on a board at the back of the bar.

chance as a fart in a windstorm, as much. See **as much chance....**

[**chance is** (or, less commonly, **would be**) **a fine thing**, where *chance* is misused for *opportunity* and where, in the *would be* form, *opportunity* sometimes displaces *chance*, was originally and still predominantly a c.p., but it has, I should have thought, become a proverb; yet it figures neither in the dictionaries of proverbs nor in (at least most of) those of quotations. Its general sense is either 'I only wish I had the opportunity!' or, more often, 'You don't know what you'd do if you got the chance or had the opportunity'; it is said esp. to a girl or, come to that, a woman, with an implication of sexual opportunity – and then 'madam' is usually appended as in ' "I wouldn't have anything to do with him, no matter how much I wanted a man." – "Chance is a fine thing, madam." ' It is also a stock reply by a married woman to a spinster declaring that she doesn't want to marry. It must go back a long way, perhaps as far as Restoration times; I have to admit that the earliest example I've found in literature occurs in William Stanley Houghton's rightly famous play, *Hindle Wakes*, 1912. The sexual sense appears to have been the original sense, for clearly the c.p. owes much to the C16–17 proverb, *opportunity is whoredom's bawd* (see notably *ODEP*).]

chance your arm! is the c.p. shape of *chance it!*, in the nuances 'have a go, anyway' – 'give it a try, you never know your luck': since *c.* 1870. It originated among tailors, but before the turn of the century it had become, and it remained, predominantly a soldiers' saying, as it was a soldiers', esp. Other Ranks', attitude: 'Take a risk in the hope of achieving your purpose, esp. as it's a worthwhile purpose, even though you may lose your stripes.' Yet 'arm' suggests an origin, not in tailoring but in boxing. The variant *chance your mitt* belongs to C20; in comparison, however, it is so little used – at least as a c.p. – that it hardly ranks as a c.p.

change the record! See **put another record on!**

Charley's dead is current among schoolgirls 'to indicate that one's slip or petticoat is showing below the hem of her skirt; cf "it's snowing" or a reference to "next week's washing" ' (Paul Beale, 18 July 1974): since *c.* 1945.

chase me, Charley (or **Charlie**) is recorded by Brophy, who says, 'We should not' – we Britons – 'pharisaically (stifling all memories of our sinful past, such as "Chase me, Charlie!" and "Keep your hair on!") talk and think as if American slang consisted only of "Says you!" and "Oh, yeah!" and "big boy" '; belongs esp. to the years *c.* 1890–1914, and probably, as Vernon Noble tells me, either springs from, or owes much to, a music-hall song. It clearly survived until after WW2, to judge by the fact that the Royal Navy, in 1940–5, applied *chase-me-Charley* to a radio-controlled glider bomb used by the Germans; and may well owe something to:

chase me, girls!, an Edwardian c.p., going back to *c.* 1895 and forward to 3 August 1914, indicates high male spirits and a gloriously assured optimism. Contrast:

chase yourself! Oh, run away – or, at the least, *go away*!: Australian: *c.* 1910–20. In, e.g., C. J. Dennis's 'classic' of Australian, mostly Sydneysiders', sentiment and slang, *The Songs of a Sentimental Bloke*, 1915.

cheap and nasty – like Short's in the Strand was recorded in the *Athenaeum* of 29 October 1864, in reference to the ordinary phrase *cheap and nasty*, 'or, in a local form, "cheap and nasty, like Short's in the Strand", a proverb' – not, of course, a proverb at all – 'applied to the founder of cheap dinners', a gibe applicable certainly no later than WW1: Londoners': *c.* 1860–1940.

cheap at half the price, often preceded by **it's** or **it would be**. That's a very reasonable price: a c.p. applied when one is well satisfied with a price either asked or charged, and dating from at least as early as 1920 – I suspect as far back as *c.* 1890. The implication is: 'At half the price you're asking, it would be cheap; yet the article is so good that one can hardly object to the charge' – sometimes with the nuance 'It's cheap – since you're asking only half the price that is being asked in some shops.' This is one of those intensely idiomatic phrases which, in their general ostensible meaning, are taken for granted, yet which, on examination, prove to be hard to explain.

cheaper to grow skin than to buy it, often preceded by **it's**, is a western US phrase 'said by one who does not wear gloves' (Berrey): C20.

cheated the starter, usually preceded by **they**, is applied to a married couple whose first child arrives before it is conventionally expectable: C20.

[**cheats never prosper**. 'This', writes Barry Prentice early in 1975, 'may be a proverb, but it is not in *ODEP*.' I myself have never heard it in Britain; I did hear it, more than once, in Australia, 1908–early 1915 and 1919–21. Yet, as I am told (December 1975) it has been used by English children since *c.* 1955 at latest. Probably it *is* to be classified as a proverb. Semantically cf the parallel *crime doesn't pay*, which, clearly, is a cliché.]

cheeky monkey! A gag of Al Read's, since the late 1950s.

cheer up – the first seven years are the worst. See **first seven years....** Cf:

cheer up – the worst is yet to come is a US c.p. of ironic encouragement: since (?)*c.* 1918. (Berrey.)

cheer up (or **cheer up, cully**) **you'll soon be dead!** is a C20 British c.p., occurring in, e.g., W. L. George's fine novel, *The Making of an Englishman*, 1914, and either deriving from or, at the least, occurring in, an early C20 music-hall song, 'I've got a motter, "Always be merry and bright" ' – rendered, as Julian Franklyn informed me in 1968 – 'in a painfully miserable tone'. In H. V. Esmond's *The Law Divine*, first performed on 29 August 1918 although not published until 1922, there comes in Act III, referring to a Ger. air raid of 1918, this piece of dialogue:

> JACK: ... Where's cook?
> NELLIE: She's sitting on the stairs, sir, for the moment.
> BILL: Let's have her in.
> TED (*calls*): Cheer up, cooky – you'll soon be dead.

cheers are running up my legs – the. 'Used to deflate (especially senior to junior) importance of local "buzz" [rumour; commendatory report in newspaper; 'and all that']. Sarcasm cannot come more scathing than this' (Laurie Atkinson, 18 July 1975): since *c.* 1950. The reverberations of the cheering are so loud that they set up vibrations affecting one's legs.

cheers for now! 'Goodbye and good luck!' By itself hardly a c.p., but in conjunction with the dovetail reply, (*and*) *screams for later*, it is one: since *c.* 1950. (Cyril Whelan, 14 January 1975.)

cheese won't choke her! is partly a proverbial saying and partly – predominantly, I'd say – a c.p. It occurs in, e.g., S in the First Conversation, where the company is discussing a rakish toast of the town and Lady Answerall says, 'She looks as if Butter would not melt in her Mouth; but I warrant Cheese won't choak her' – where the latter statement implies that she is physically intimate with men. *Cheese*, as used here, is familiar English for what is physiologically and medically known as smegma.

chicken – that's your. See **that's your chicken.**

chicken got the axe – where the. See **where the chicken....**

child – not for this. See **not for this child.**

China – not for all the tea in. See **not for all....**

Chinaman – I must have killed a. See **I must have....**

chips are down – the. This is final – the situation is both grave and urgent; this could mean 'the end', be disastrous; anything you now do could be irrevocable. The English-Language Institute of America's *DCCU* 1971 (earlier – 1970 – in some editions of Webster), glosses it as 'The time has come when we can no longer avoid making a fateful decision'. Of this US c.p., the earliest quotation in W & F is of 1949, 'When the chips are down, a man shows what he really is'; but the c.p. goes back, I believe, to well before WW1. The 'chips' concerned are the counters used in poker and other games of chance.

chocks away! 'Get on with the job!': RAF: since *c.* 1920. In their timely little Fighting Services' glossary, H & P explain that the literal meaning is 'Remove the wooden chocks and let the 'planes get off the ground'; *chocks away!*, therefore, is short for *pull the chocks away!* Hence applied to '*any* first run of anything mechanical' (Lawrence Smith, 15 January 1975).

choice. See **you pays your money and you takes your choice.**

choke away – the churchyard's near! A callously jocular admonition to anyone coughing badly: mid C17–early C19. It is recorded by, e.g., Ray in 1678 and Grose in 1796. Cf the slang *churchyard cough*, a severe one. Cf:

choke, chicken: more are hatching is a synonymous c.p.: C18–early C19, then mostly dialectal. It occurs in S and also Grose, 1796.

choke you? – didn't that and **it's a wonder that didn't choke you!** C19–20 comments, mostly good-natured, on a thundering great, or a truly notable, lie. Probably prompted by the C17–18 semi-proverbial 'If a lie could have choked him, that would have done it' (Ray, 1678).

[**choose, proud fool – I did but ask you** comes towards the end of the First Conversation in S, and looks rather like a c.p., but I can't feel sure about it:

    MISS: Every fool can do as they're bid ... do it yourself.
    NEV[EROUT]: Chuse, proud Fool; I did but ask you.]

Christian born, donkey-rigged – and throws a tread like a cabby's whip has, esp. in the Bethnal Green area of London, been, throughout C20 and probably also in latish C19, applied to a 'stout fellow', generously-genital'd, and strong. (Mr C. A. Worth, who in letter dated 14 January 1975, says he first heard it, as a young man, in 1938.) Cf the low-slang *chuck a tread* (of the male), to coit.

'Christmas comes but once a year' – thank God! is a c.p. dating from *c.* 1945 and is spoken by those who hate to see what the profiteers have made of Christmas. The quotation part of the c.p. is a cliché, uttered by those who feel that the celebration of Christmas justifies any expense or excess.

church – I'll see you in; or ... **in jail**. See **I'll see you ....**

church with a chimney in it – at a. See **at a church ....**

cinch – it's a. It's a certainty; hence, that's dead easy: since *c.* 1890: US, originally south-western but by 1900 at the latest, general throughout the US. In his celebrated essay 'The Function of Slang' (*Harper's Magazine*, July 1893), the even more celebrated Brander Matthews, university professor and dean, wrote thus: 'From the Southwest came "cinch" [a certainty], from the tightening of the girths of the pack-mules, and so by extension indicating a grasp of anything so firm that it cannot get away'; W & F add, 'From the cinch of a saddle, which secures it' – but it has to be a *strong* girth.

city morgue: duty corpse speaking is a telephone c.p.: army, mostly in the orderly rooms and among other headquarters personnel: late 1960s and early 1970s. 'American influence obvious here' (Paul Beale, 12 March 1974).

clank! clank! A derisive cry, used against Australians: C20. A friend of mine writes: 'I learned this from an Aussie!' He also writes: 'From the sound of convicts' chains' – an allusion to the days when Australia was utilized as a dumping-ground for Britain's criminals. Contrast:

clank, clank, I'm a tank. 'A taunt directed at any member of RAC or RTR whose mental ability is not up to the speaker's; usually delivered in a stupid, ponderous voice' (Paul Beale, 12 June 1974): since *c.* 1950.

clap your hands! is a 'silly witticism [addressed] to person carrying something like large tray (in bar); and, if he drops it or anything breakable, *don't bother to pick it up!*' (Frank Shaw in letter dated 25 February 1969): since *c.* 1940.

class will tell. Quality or, esp., ability is what counts the most; for instance, the best man – or the best horse – usually wins: C20. In 1968, in my original entry for this c.p., I wrote, 'This c.p. may easily become a proverb of the more colloquial kind': it hasn't yet (1976) done so, but it's still a possibility.

clean! – keep it. See **keep it clean!**

clean and polish – we're winning the war! This military c.p. of 1915–18 was scathingly applied by the Other Ranks, notably in or near the front line, to the 'spit and polish' attitude adopted by a number of antediluvian officers. Note that, for *clean, spit* was often substituted and that, if additional irony were felt to be desirable, *no wonder* was inserted before 'we're winning ...'.

'If one wished to pretend a justification of someone else's routine order, especially of an exasperating triviality, one exclaimed: "Well, I suppose it's winning" – or "helping to win" – "the war" ' (B & P). Cf:

clean, bright and slightly oiled. This WW1 advice to the infantryman on the condition in which his rifle should be kept was already, by 1917, an officers' jocular c.p., with a pun on the slang *oiled*, tipsy, and it is extant, although, by *c.* 1960, slightly obsolescent. A post-WW2 example: 'We find the guns.... Everything is clean, bright and, where necessary, slightly oiled' (Jack Ripley, *Davis Doesn't Live Here Any More*, 1971): clearly reminiscent of and allusive to the old army phrase and probably of Gerald Kersh's volume of short stories, *Clean, Bright and Slightly Oiled* (1946) – its own title richly allusive.

clear as mud (or **as clear as mud**) is a jocular or, rather, a jocularly ironic c.p., mud being anything but clear: as clear as muddy water: obscure: since *c.* 1820 or perhaps a generation earlier. It occurs in, e.g., Barham's *Ingoldsby Legends*, 1842, 'That's clear as mud' (*OED*). Contrast the late C19–early C20 school slang *as sure as mud*, utterly sure.

Normally such similes do not rank as c.pp., but because of its ironic character, as in the exchange 'Is that quite clear to you now?' – 'Yes, as clear as mud!', this one, I think, does.

clever chaps (often **devils**) **these Chinese!**; also occasionally **damned clever** (or **dead clever**) **chaps these Chinese!** This Royal Navy c.p., which came to be heard in the other two Services and became, in the later 1940s, fairly general among ('U' rather than 'non-U') civilians, did not, so far as I've been able to discover, antedate the C20, is used as a quizzical, or an ironical, comment upon an explanation of some device or process, esp. if it hasn't been fully understood. It's a somewhat back-handed compliment to Chinese inventiveness and ingenuity. There must be much earlier examples in print, but I'm ashamed to admit that the earliest I have noted occurs at p. 154 of John Winton's *We Saw the Sun*, 1960. Since *c.* 1945, *Chinese* has been now and then displaced by *Japs*.

The phrase seems to have some currency in the US, to judge by this quotation from Patrick Buchanan, *A Requiem of Sharks*, 1973:

'May you live in interesting times,' she said.
'What's that?'
'An ancient Chinese curse.'
'Very clever, those Chinese,' I said.

climbing trees to get away from it. See **getting any?**

close as God's curse to a whore's arse, or **close as shirt and shitten arse**, both often preceded by **as**, stands in the No-Man's-Land between c.p. and proverbial saying and is characteristic of its earthy, outspoken, too often brutal, period, mid C18–early 19. (Grose, 1785.)

close hangar (or **the hangar**) **doors!**; variant, **hangar doors closed!** An RAF c.p., signifying 'Stop talking shop!' and dating from *c.* 1935. (Recorded H & P: *close hangar doors!* And by C. H. Ward-Jackson, *It's a Piece of Cake*, same year: *close the hangar doors*. And EP, *A Dictionary of RAF Slang*, 1945: *hangar doors closed*.) Wilfred Granville, in a letter dated 1 January 1969, has glossed *close the hangar doors* thus, 'Catch phrase addressed to anyone in the RAF or ex-RAF who is fond of indulging in reminiscences or shop when in mixed or civilian company.' By 1974, slightly obsolescent even among the most conservative ex-RAF 'types'.

close your eyes and guess what God has sent – sometimes **brought** – **you!** is a playful, or even a jocular, c.p. of C20 and often accompanies the gesture of a girl placing her hands over your (masculine) eyes.

close your eyes and think of England! is a late C19–20 c.p., employed by Britons living in distant countries (and esp. if in difficult conditions) when life has become particularly hard or distressing. Barry Prentice, in a letter dated 13 June 1975, says:

If it is not used in Australia [that is, by Australians] I have heard it on British television programs. In her *Journal* of 1912, Lady Hillingdon wrote, 'I am happy now that Charles calls on my bedchamber less frequently than of old. As it is, I endure but two calls a week and when I hear his steps outside my door I lie down on my bed, close my eyes, open my legs and think of England.' I do not know whether the *Journal* was published in full, but this passage is frequently quoted.

Used as title of an article in the *Economist*, 12 April 1975. Cf **think of England!**

cloth-ears – **he has** (or **has got** or **he's got**) is a Cockney c.p. of C20 and is applied to one who, not wishing to hear, pretends that he doesn't. From caps with heavy ear-flaps.

clothes sit on her .... See **her clothes** ....

clumsy as a cub bear handling his prick, often preceded by *as*. A low Canadian c.p. applied to an extremely clumsy person: C20.

coaches won't run over him – **the**. A c.p. of, I'd guess, mid C18–mid 19, for it first appears, 1813, in an enlarged edn of Ray. It means 'He's in gaol'. Semantically, it is comparable with **where the flies won't get it**.

cock won't fight – **that**. See **that cock** ....

coconut. See **that accounts for the milk in the coconut**.

coffee, 5 cents; coffee (aber coffee), 10 cents. 'It originated among (esp. New York) Jews, in self-mockery. The "aber" is specifically Yiddish rather than generally Ger. [literally "but"]. A paraphrase would be something like this: "The price of 'coffee' in this lunch room is five cents; oh, of course, if you want *real* coffee, it's ten cents" ' (John W. Clark, 18 March 1975): since (very approximately) *c.* 1955.

cold enough to freeze the balls off a brass monkey, exceedingly cold: very common in both Australia and Canada; in the latter, *ears* is, in polite company, substituted for *balls*. But it's almost equally common in New Zealand and in Great Britain and Ireland; indeed, in any country where English is 'the first language'. Euphemisms are expectably common; for instance, the TV comedy 'The Two Ronnies' (very late 1973 or very early 1974) offered *cold enough to freeze the brass buttons off a flunkey*, but it didn't, so far as I know, 'catch on'; then there was the euphemism once printed in 'a Manchester University *Rag-Bag*: "The cold in Moscow was so intense that the brass monkeys on top of the Kremlin were heard to utter a high falsetto shriek" ' – which also, more subtly, alludes to that other testicular c.p., **too late! too late!**

The army, *c.* 1900–40, had the variant *cold enough to make a Jew drop his bundle*.

Colney Hatch for you! You're crazy! This topographical imputation belongs to *c.* 1890–1914 and might be compared to the WW1 army's *stone Win(n)ick*, insane; Colney Hatch belongs to London, Winnick to Lancashire.

come again (**!** or, more often, **?**). Repeat that, please! or Please explain! As a question, *come again?*, What do you mean? Current in the British Empire, later Commonwealth of Nations, since *c.* 1919; Noël Coward uses it in *Relative Values*, 1951 (at Act II, Scene ii) and Terence Rattigan a little earlier in *While the Sun Shines*, 1943 (Act II); although by *c.* 1960 less used than before, it is still far from being even obsolescent, probably because it is at once terse and picturesque; I read it as recently as 1972 in Philip Cleife's speech-alert and speech-sensitive novel, *The Slick and the Dead*, and in John Godey's *The Three Worlds of Johnny Handsome* (US), the latter offering

'I'm interested in locating a man named Jappy Schroeder.'
'Come again?'

And also in Michael Gilbert's 'thriller', *The Ninety-Second Tiger*, 1973. W & F, oddly enough, cite no US example earlier than 1952, although it must, I think, have been current there since *c.* 1910; and CM notes it as having been popular among US negroes of the 1940s.

come aloft! is a c.p. of *c.* 1670–1700 or probably for much longer. Meaning – approximately – 'Let's enjoy ourselves', perhaps with reference to, or an undertone of, 'high with wine', it was probably, at first, naval. It occurs in Thomas Shadwell, *The Virtuoso*, performed and published in 1676, at Act I, Scene i, where Sir Samuel Hearty ('one that, by the Help of humourous, nonsensical By-words, takes himself to be a great Wit') speaks: 'We were on the high Ropes, i' faith. Hey poop – troll – come aloft, Boys, ha, ha. Ah Rogues, that you had been with us, i' faith. Ha, ha, ha.'

And very early in Act II, the same foolish coxcomb exclaims, '... if any man manages an Intrigue better than I,

I will never hope for a Masquerade more, or expect to Dance my self again into any Lady's Affection, and about that Business [i.e., and set about the business of making love]. Come aloft, Sir *Samuel*, I say –.'

come along, Bob! See **go along, Bob!**

come and get it! Come and eat! Dinner *or* lunch *or* tea *or* supper is ready: originally, in the army, the cooks' or the orderlies' cry, deriving from the British army's bugle-call, 'Come to the cookhouse door, boys, come to the cookhouse door'; from the British army it passed to the US and to the Dominions armies: latish C19–20. Adopted in camps of all sorts everywhere; Berrey, for instance, noting it as a dinner call in the US West. It was naturally taken up by cowboys, drovers, sheepshearers, lumbermen, labour – esp. construction – camps. Then finally – say about 1950 – it became also a sort of c.p.: 'Mother facetiously calls to meals, from cowboy films' (Frank Shaw, letter of November 1968). In James Hadley Chases's US novel, *You're Dead without Money*, 1972, occurs this passage, which shows it very clearly indeed as a c.p.:

> He turned off the T.V. as Judy came out of the bathroom. He got to his feet and stared at her.
> 'Come and get it,' she said and going to the bed, she lay down, swung up her longs legs and beckoned to him.

'Universal and frequent. A real c.p., I think': thus John W. Clark, 17 February 1975, of its US usage.

come and have a pickle was, in 1878–*c.* 1914, English Society, 'an invitation to a quick unceremonious meal' that rapidly became a c.p. Cf:

come and have one – come and see your pa – come and wash your neck: invitations to come and have a drink: respectively general, dating from *c.* 1880; general, of *c.* 1870–1910; nautical, of *c.* 1860–1914. Ware records the first and the third.

come ashore, Jack!, as a c.p. addressed by civilians to sailors, antedates WW2 and perhaps WW1. It is a 'warning to a sailor who is fond of telling salty stories [*sea* stories, not ribald or obscene stories as such] or indulging too freely in NAVALESE' (*Sailors' Slang*).

come back – with or without **Fred – all is forgiven**. A 'humorously despairing c.p., sometimes used of someone who has left a certain post or organization on posting, transfer, demob, etc., in which his know-how would now be helpful' (Paul Beale, 12 June 1974): army: since *c.* 1950.

Come back, all is forgiven is itself a c.p., of much wider application and clearly the source of the army's specialized c.p.: dating from, I think, the 1920s, but perhaps from as far back as the late C19. From 'the agony column' of *The Times*. For that source, cf **have gun – will travel**. Cf **come home – all is forgiven**.

come down from the flies! A C20 theatrical c.p.: 'Corresponds to "come off it" and is addressed to an actor or actress with a tendency to self-inflation over a minor success' (Granville).

come from Wigan. See **comes from Wigan.**

come home – all is forgiven is a late C20 c.p., deriving from a frequent pre-1914 advertisement in 'the agony column' of *The Times*. I've even, on a 1973 in-lieu-of-a-Christmas-card 'spoof' map, enlivened with comic directions, seen it burlesqued as 'Go back – all is forgiven.'

A rather pleasant example occurs in Ted Allbeury's novel,

A Choice of Enemies, 1973: ' "... They've got a message for you from Joe Steiner." Bill grinned. "Joe said 'Come home all is forgiven'." And oddly enough that rather weak joke made me feel I was back in the club again.'

come home with your knickers torn and say you found the money!, preceded by an understood *you* (or *you have*). Do you expect me to believe *that?*: C20. Based upon a perhaps true story of an irate, probably lower-middle-class, mother addressing her errant, usually teenage, daughter. It is, indeed, indicative (as a friend of mine has remarked) of 'extreme scepticism'. Cf **you'll be telling me ....**

come hup, I say, you hugly beast! See **come up, I say ....**

come in and see how the poor live! As a c.p., a jocular 'Come in!' – 'but often to deprecate relatively straitened circumstances. (Early 1900s [; but still] used by surviving Victorians [and Edwardians])': Laurie Atkinson, 18 June 1975.

come in – don't knock! is addressed ironically to someone entering a room, an office, without permission and without even knocking: C20. Occasionally it is both ironic and ungracious.

come in if you be fat appears in S, 1738: to someone knocking at the door, Lady Smart calls, 'Who's there? You're on the wrong Side of the Door; come in if you be fat'; current throughout most of C18–19, except that in C19 the form is usually ... *if you're fat*. Either because fat people are commonly supposed to be jolly and therefore good company, or because thin ones may be more expensive to entertain. Ramsay Spencer (7 January 1971) has pertinently asked, 'May not Swift have had in mind Shakespeare's *Julius Caesar*, "Let me have men about me that are fat;/Sleek-headed men and such as sleep o'nights;/Yond Cassius hath a lean and hungry look;/He thinks too much; such men are dangerous"?'

come into my parlo(u)r, said the spider to the fly is a British c.p., dating from the 1880s. Probably a slight adaptation of the song, *Will You Walk into My Parlor, Said the Spider to the Fly*, published at that time and sung by Kate Castleton. (W. J. Burke.)

come off! Elliptical for the next, it arose, *c.* 1910, in US and was adopted in Britain *c.* 1919 and fell into disuse *c.* 1935. It occurs, *c.* 1917, in S. R. Strait's 'Straight Talk' in the *Boston Globe*.

come off it! See:

come off the grass! Originally US, it was, *c.* 1890, adopted in Britain, where, since *c.* 1910, it has predominated in its shortened form, *come off it* which, since *c.* 1918, is also US [W & F]. Its senses waver between 'don't show off!' and 'don't exaggerate, don't tell lies!' From the signboard in parks and gardens, 'Keep off the grass!'

come off the roof! Don't be so superior! Don't be so high and mighty: lower-middle and lower class c.p.: *c.* 1880–1940, but obsolescent by 1930. It occurs in, e.g., W. Pett Ridge, *Minor Dialogues*, 1895. Cf:

come off your perch (or **horse**). Don't act so superior! Come down to earth! Don't be so high-falutin'! US, esp. students' in the early 1920s (McKnight), but also general US (witness, e.g., Berrey, 1942, and W & F, 1960); note, however, that *come off your horse!* derives from 'to *come off one's high horse*', which clearly is not a c.p.

come on in out of the war! is a WW2 c.p., used by civilians during bombing raids and clearly meaning 'Take shelter!' and no less clearly burlesquing 'Come on in out of the rain!'

[**come on in – the water's fine** (or **really warm**), a seaside cliché, has long been knocking at the c.p. door, but has never, I think, quite gained an entry. (Cyril Whelan, 14 January 1975.)]

come on – let's be having you! Let go of yer (or **your**) **cocks and put on yer** (or **your**) **socks!** A reveille call, or rather the lower-deck c.p. version of it: Royal Navy: late C19–20. Cf **let's have you!**

come on, my lucky lads; also **come on – you don't want to live for ever!**; sometimes the latter was added to the former. During WW1 these two c.pp. were addressed by company, or by regimental, sergeant-majors to their men in the moment before the jump-off (mostly it was a scrambling from the trenches) for an attack; occasionally a rallying-cry; and in neither moment possessing always the inspiriting quality they were, by these heroic fellows, deemed to possess. For a notable example, see Hugh Kimber's arresting and remarkable novel, *Prelude to Calvary*, 1933. Perhaps the injunction had been used ever since early in the Napoleonic Wars. The US version (*come on, you sons of bitches, do you want to live for ever?*) was immortalized by Carl Sandburg in his poem, 'Losers'. Of the US form, Colonel Albert Moe writes on 15 June 1975: 'It finds usage to encourage someone to "get on with it" and not to slacken or stop in an effort.... It may be classed as of "limited usage". I have never heard it used in the singular, ... even though a single individual may be the target of the phrase.'

come on, Steve! Get a move on! Hurry up!: mostly Cockney: *c.* 1923–40. From the fame of Steve Donohue, the jockey.

come on tally plonk (or, carrying the process of 'Hobson-Jobson' a stage further) **come on taller** [tallow] **candle!** How are you?: British army on the Western Front during WW1. A masterly attempt by the Tommy to adapt the Fr. *comment allez-vous?* to his own need and measure.

come out and fight dacent! is an Anglo-Irish c.p. of late C19–20; it is also the older version of the literal – and figurative – C20 *come outside and say that!*, which, when figurative, almost qualifies as a c.p.

come out of it! Cheer up!: US: since *c.* 1930 (Berrey). Literally, 'Come out of your fit of despondency!'

come out of that hat – I can't see your feet! is a (mostly boys') street cry to a man wearing a 'topper' or top hat: *c.* 1875–1900. Cf **crawl out of that hat!**

come to cues! This theatrical c.p. is 'directed at anyone fond of long-winded narrative, or garrulously explanatory. "Come to cues, old boy, I'm busy"' (Granville): 'Come to the point!' – 'Cut it short!' – 'Get on with the story!' It arose, *c.* 1880 or earlier, from 'rehearsal practice of giving a hesitant actor the cue line only' (WG, letter dated 12 April 1948).

come to Hecuba! See **cut to Hecuba!**

come to papa! A US dicing gamblers' exclamation as they throw dice – 'an entreaty for a winning throw' (Berrey): C20. Of domestic origin: a father's blandishment addressed to his (very) young daughter.

come up 'n' see me some time! Originally (1934) US – a 'gag' of the famous Mae West – it probably became a widely used US c.p.: in 1942, Berrey, in a synonymy for a 'flirtatious glance', includes the 'come-up-and-see-me-some-time look'. Moreover, this humorously euphemistic sexual invitation very soon crossed the Atlantic; in Dodie Smith's comedy, *Call It a Day*, performed in 1935 and published in 1936, occurs, at Act II, Scene iii, this passage:

BEATRICE: Why not bring all the papers up to my flat this evening?

ROGER: Am I being invited to come up and see you some time?

BEATRICE (*a moment's pause and then she looks straight at him*): Yes.

In a letter dated 10 January 1969, Professor Samuel H. Monk tells me that this was Miss West's famous line in the play *Diamond Lil*, first performed on 9 April 1928 and having a long run (it didn't reach London until early in 1948); her own adaptation, *Come On Up – Ring Twice*, appeared in 1952; but it was probably the film version, *She Done Him Wrong*, he says, which, first shown in 1933, brought a worldwide currency to an invitation already well known: 'her rendering of the invitation with postures became immediately famous. I've even seen a young child in the '30s perform the act. I feel confident that it moved from the streets as a sentence, to art via Miss West, to American students and the world at large'. For the male counterpart, see:

come up and see my etchings was, perhaps, originally a US students' c.p. that rapidly gained a much wider currency: throughout the US, thence in Canada and Britain and, probably indicative of US influence in 1943–5, Australia. Formerly I suspected that it was prompted by **come up and see me some time!**; yet it could well have been the other way about. In his letter dated 10 January 1969, Professor S. H. Monk writes:

I am certain that I knew this sentence by the midtwenties. Actually I knew no one who had a collection of etchings or who was suave enough to seduce a young thing in this manner. But the phrase certainly floated in and out of cartoons and jokes. To me, it has an 1890-ish or Edwardian tone, and I suspect that it existed in 'sophisticated' urban society before it ever reached me. I think that this can still sometimes be heard, but it is definitely 'corny'.

Perhaps confirmatory of Professor Monk's shrewd remarks is the fact that in Susannah Centlivre's comedy, *The Man's Bewitched* (1710), Act III, where Belinda, Maria, Constant and Lovely are in the study, and Lovely exclaims, 'Interrogating! Nay, then 'tis proper to be alone; there is a very pretty Collection of Prints in the next Room, Madam, will you give me leave to explain them to you?' Maria answers, 'Any Thing that may divert your Love – Subject.'

It should, however, be noted that this c.p. perhaps derives from Surreyside melodrama – the villain enticing the innocent maiden.

come up for air! Rest a while!: Australian: since late 1940s. Perhaps from pearl-diving, but prompted by 'End the kissing for a while, I need air': Canadian: since *c.* 1930.

come up (but correctly **hup**). **I say, you hugly beast!** *Handley Cross* was not a success when it was first published. It was only later in the [19th] century that Jorrocks and his *bons mots* ("Come hup, I say, you hugly beast") became household words' (J. F. C. Harrison, *The Early Victorians* (1832–51), published in 1971). Except among hunting people, this c.p. has been little heard since *c.* 1940.

come with me to the Casbah! 'Always said with a suggestive leer, or a snigger' (Paul Beale, who, on 7 May 1975, adds: 'I believe it came originally in a Hollywood film' and that it 'is sufficiently well known and misapplied to be a c.p.'). The Casbah was originally the citadel and palace of an Arab state, hence the surrounding native quarter of any North African city, e.g. Algiers or Cairo, and supposed to be a scene of romance, but usually disappointing and dangerous.

comes and goes. See **he comes and goes.**

comes from Wigan, with or without *he* (rarely *she*) preceding, means that he's thoroughly or hopelessly provincial, a real 'hayseed': as a c.p., it dates from *c.* 1920; but derogatory references to Wigan – in the fact, a rather attractive Lancashire town – go back to *c.* 1890; cf its use in George Orwell's *Wigan Pier,* 1937.

coming? Ay, so is Christmas! is a C18–20 c.p. addressed to one who, saying 'Coming!' (in a minute), takes an inordinately long time to arrive. S, 1738 (First Conversation) has:

LADY SM[ART]: Did you call *Betty?*

FOOTMAN: She's coming, Madam.

LADY SM: Coming? Ay so is *Christmas.*

By *c.* 1850, the *ay* was often omitted; but in R. S. Surtees, *Plain or Ringlets,* 1860, chapter LXVIII, we still find:

'His Grace *is* coming, and the Earl too,' replied Mr Haggish ...

'Coming! aye, so is Christmas,' sneered Mr Ellenger.

coming, Mother! has been described by W & F in 1960 as a 'synthetic fad expression' – i.e., a c.p. that achieved a vogue. W & F attribute it to some popular comedian as both coiner and popularizer. I have no other record of the phrase, which I take to derive ironically from an obsequious youth's or young man's answer to a peremptory mother's summons and to have arisen *c.* 1945 and to have become obsolescent by *c.* 1960. (In the hundreds of post-1960 US novels I've read, I've never seen the expression.)

coming up on a lorry, often preceded by *it's,* is a jocular c.p., dating from *c.* 1910 and referring to something small – a letter, a packet – that has failed to arrive when it was expected.

common as cat-shit and twice as nasty!, often preceded by **as.** This Cockney c.p. dates from *c.* 1920 – if not from twenty years earlier – and it is applied either to a person one regards as beneath oneself or, less often, to an inferior article. (Communicated by Julian Franklyn on 3 January 1968.) More frequent is *common as dirt* ..., probably going back to mid C19. The North Country form is *...mucky...* which itself possesses a variant, dating from 1973: *common as muck! – no! commoner,* used by, e.g., Frankie Howerd in 'Up Pompeii', a TV comedy series. Cf **soft as shit and twice as nasty.**

confess and be hanged! is a late C16–18 semi-proverbial c.p.: 'You lie!' Literally, be shriven and be hanged! (Apperson.) Cf the proverbial 'Tell the truth and shame the Devil!'

Confucius he say. This is an introductory gag to words of homely wisdom – homespun philosophy that is often cynical in an engagingly ingenuous way; it is couched in a supposedly Chinese grammar and style. Although heard earlier, it did not, I think, achieve full status until *c.* 1920; certainly it had, by 1960, become slightly obsolescent. In Colin Dexter's *Last Bus to Woodstock,* 1975:

Tomsett drained his glass. '... I've always been a bit dubious about this rape business.'

'Confucius, he say girl with skirt up, she run faster than man with trousers down, eh?'

The two older [dons] smiled politely at the tired old joke, but Melhuish wished he hadn't repeated it; off-key, over-familiar.

It may also be applied by auditor to a speaker's sage generalization. A tribute to the fame of the ancient Chinese moralist and philosopher.

[**consult your friendly neighbourhood** – or **local** – whoever's in your mind as the expert in the trade, profession, sport, or what not. This isn't a c.p., for the operative final word is variable. It is a cliché pattern; cf the syntactical pattern of, e.g., *came the dawn,* hence the show-down, the crunch, or whatever.]

cool it! Simmer down! Calm down! Relax!: US: since *c.* 1955 (W & F); it became, by the late 1960s, common also in Britain – and in the rest of the Commonwealth. A natural development from SE *cool,* unafraid, unflustered. In the US, mostly a teenagers', and negroes', phrase; in a Philadelphia newspaper of late May or early June 1970, Sidney J. Harris, in a witty poem entitled 'This Cat Doesn't Dig All that Groovy Talk', declares:

If I were king, I'd promptly rule it

Out of bonds [sic] to murmur, 'cool it'.

An elaboration, first mostly negro and beatnik and hippie and jazz, arose almost immediately: *cool it, man!*

cop that lot! This Australian c.p., dating since *c.* 1930 and alluded to by Nino Culotta in his book, *Cop This Lot,* 1960, means 'Just look at those people or that incident or scene or display!' and implies either astonishment or admiration – or, on the other hand, derision or contempt.

cop this, young Harry! Another Australian c.p., dating since *c.* 1950 and used during horse-play, e.g. throwing things about. (One of many Australianisms I owe to Mr Barry Prentice of Sydney.) Cf the US **sock it to me.**

cor! chase me Aunt Fanny round the clock tower and **cor! chase me, winger, round the wash-house!** Both of these c.pp. are used by naval ratings to express either astonishment or incredulity: but whereas the former belongs to Chatham, where the clock tower forms a very prominent feature of the landscape, and has been current for most, if not all, of C20, the latter was a fairly general c.p. of the approximate period 1947–57. A *winger* is naval for a chum, a pal.

corvette would roll on wet grass – a. A Royal Navy's and very soon also the other English-speaking navies' c.p. of WW2. In the *Sunday Times* Weekly Review of 9 August 1970, Nicholas Montsarrat records it and glosses it thus: 'Corvettes were abominable ships to live in, in any kind of weather; ... they pitched and rolled and swung with a brutal persistence as long as any breeze blew.'

cost yer!, literally 'You may have it – providing you're prepared to pay for it' and used thus in prisons since the 1920s, has come, among friends there, hence among ex-convicts, hence also among their relatives and among their friends and acquaintances, to be used jokingly, e.g. in affectionate irony.

cotton socks. See **bless your little ....**

could eat the hind leg off a donkey; often preceded by *I*, occasionally by *he*; the Canadian shape (*teste* Dr Douglas Leechman) being **could eat a horse, if you took his shoes off.** I'm (etc.) extremely hungry: late C19–20.

could I have that in writing? – to which *please* is courteously but not very often added. Addressed to one who has spoken very flatteringly or, at the least, complimentarily of the speaker's abilities or character: since *c.* 1945. Cf **thank you for those few kind words** – of which it forms, in essence, a synonym or, at worst, an approximate equivalent.

couldn't agree more. See **I couldn't agree more.**

couldn't care fewer, often preceded by *I*, is a jocular – occasional – short-lived (*c.* 1959–64) – variant of the next.

couldn't care less, usually preceded by *I*, occasionally by *he* or *she*, I'm entirely indifferent. Dating from *c.* 1940, it was originally upper-middle class, but by 1945 fairly general; moreover, since *c.* 1948, it has been rampant, although since 1969 or 1970 it has, I've noticed, seemed to have become a shade less ubiquitous. It had been prompted by **I couldn't agree** (with you) **more**, which, flourishing *c.* 1937–49 and still heard occasionally, arose in society and was, by 1940, common among officers in all three Services, although it never spread so widely as the 'care less' plague. In his *God Help America!*, 1952, Sydney Moseley writes, 'Ordinary citizens "couldn't have cared less" – to use a cant post-war phrase current in England.' In the US, by the way, the phrase was, well before 1970, so thoroughly naturalized that it could be employed allusively, as in Stanley Ellin, *The Man from Nowhere*, 1970.

'How did she react.... Did it seem to hit a nerve?'
Elene shook her head. 'She couldn't have cared less.'
Cf also:

couldn't care less if the cow calves or breaks its leg! – usually preceded by *I* – is a New Zealand extension – or, if you prefer that angle – elaboration of the preceding.

couldn't do it in the time. See **you couldn't do it ....**

couldn't hit the inside of a barn (polite) or **a bull in the arse with a scoop-shovel**; either version is, naturally, often preceded by *you*. A C20 Canadian c.p. addressed to a very poor marksman.

couldn't knock the skin off a rice pudding. See **he couldn't knock ....**

couldn't organize a fuck in a brothel; or **piss-up** – i.e., a drinking bout – **in a brewery**; or **sell ice-water in hell** (elliptical for *he* or *you* ...). The first two belong to the Other Ranks (or the ratings) in the British fighting Services, hence also among civilians, date from ?1920s or 1930s, are as low as they're picturesque, and are derisively directed at grossly inefficient superiors. The third is US, dates probably from the early 1920s (? during the torrid days of Prohibition), and is 'said of an incompetent salesman' (Berrey).

couldn't punch his way out of a paper bag. See **he couldn't knock the skin off a rice pudding.**

couldn't speak a threepenny bit, or, in full, with *I* preceding. I just couldn't speak at all: London streets': *c.* 1890–1914. (Ware.)

cow climbed up a hill. See **there was a cow climbed up a hill.**

'cracked in the right place' – as the girl said, often preceded by *yes! but*, is the low c.p. reply to an insinuation or an imputation or an allegation of insanity or extreme eccentricity or foolhardy rashness. 'You really must be *cracked!*' I first heard it in 1922, but it's a good deal older than that: it rather sounds as if it originated among raffish Edwardians. (Cf **you must have been sleeping near a crack.**)

crackling is not what it was. This sadly wistful, or a wryly nostalgic, male c.p. voices the feeling, states the conviction, of one's later years that, 'whatever the crackling, the savour of the bite is not as it was in one's former years' (Laurie Atkinson, late 1974); since *c.* 1920 or perhaps a decade earlier. Here, *crackling* = girls regarded as sexual pleasure; *crackling* is bar-room slang for the female pudenda.

crawl out of that hat! is a US c.p. – see the quotation at **pull down your vest!** – of *c.* 1870–80.

crazy mixed-up kid – a (or **just a**) was originally and still is a US c.p.; in the late 1940s, it was adopted in Britain. It applies to a youth confusingly troubled with psychological problems (aren't most of us?), esp. if he is, or if he pretends to be, unable to distinguish between the good and the bad, an inability that tends to disappear when the failure operates to his disadvantage as opposed to his advantage.

cricket, it's (or **that's**) **not.** See **it's not cricket.**

cripples. See **go it, you cripples!**

cross, I win – pile, you lose, synonymous with **heads, I win – tails, you lose**, was current, so far as I've been able to determine, in C17–18. It occurs in Butler's *Hudibras*, 1678, thus:

That you as sure, may Pick and Choose,
As Cross I win, and Pile you lose. (Apperson.)

The *cross* is the 'face', the *pile* the reverse, of a coin.

cross my heart! is a c.p. of declaration that one is telling the truth: mid C19–20. Originally, a solemn religious guarantee. It is short for (*I*) *cross my heart and may I die*, itself probably elliptical for *cross my heart and may I die, if I so much as tell a lie*. 'Schoolgirls' c.p. protestation of honesty. "Is this true, Janet?" – "Cross my heart!"' (Wilfred Granville, late December 1968).

Since *c.* 1920, perhaps more usually *cross my heart and hope to die!*

crutches are cheap is a jocularly ironic comment upon very strenuous, esp. if violent, physical effort, notably in athletics: mid C19–20; by 1935, slightly obsolescent, but still far from obsolete. It has the variant *wooden legs are cheap*.

crutches for meddlers and legs for lame ducks seems to be a variant of **lareovers for meddlers.** (Brought to my notice, on 14 January 1975, by Mr B. Bass of Marshfield, Avon.) 'Sticking my neck out' I hazard the guess that it arose *c.* 1870.

cry all the way to the bank, either as *I'll cry ...* or as *He cried....* A US c.p. dating from *c.* 1950 and adopted in Britain in the late 1950s, is ironically used by someone, or of someone, whose work is adversely criticized on literary or artistic or musical grounds – that is, by such criteria – but who has had the temerity to make a fortune by it.

cry mapsticks! I cry you mercy: lower-class c.p. of late C17– mid C18. It occurs in Swift (*OED*) and appears to be a perversion, jocular not illiterate, of SE *cry mercy* and *mopsticks*.

curdles one's milk, usually introduced by *it*, is directed at – not necessarily addressed to – one whose behaviour sours 'the milk of human kindness': since *c*. 1925. (One of the many c.pp. I owe to the alertness and kindness of Mr Laurie Atkinson.)

curse is upon me – the. A female's notification, humorously formal and deliberately archaic, that she is having her period: a domestic c.p.: probably ?mid C19–20; certainly throughout C20. Often laconically shortened to *the curse*; *the curse* is itself elliptical for *the curse of Eve*.

curse of the drinking classes – the, often preceded by *it's*, means 'work', by a pun on the cliché (untrue since WW2 and grossly exaggerated since WW1), *drink is the curse of the working classes*: since the late or, at earliest, the middle 1940s.

curtains for you! is explained by Berrey in 1942 as 'the end for you, enough from you' – that's enough argument or talk from you; but originally this US c.p. implied 'the end of life', whether literally by death or figuratively by imprisonment or a totally disabling accident or disease: since *c*. 1920. In *c*. 1944, it was adopted in Britain from US Servicemen on leave (or, indeed, duty). Originally from the curtain that is dropped upon – and therefore conceals – the stage upon which a play has just ended. Often shortened to *curtains!*

custom – it's an old Southern. This line from a popular song became a c.p. in 1935 and by the end of the year (in fact by October) other words began to be substituted for *Southern*, but no variant has ever achieved c.p. status. In the *Evening News* of 4 January 1936, I read an account of a man who, on being upbraided for kissing a girl in a square in London W2, explained that 'It's an old Bayswater custom.' The explanation, one regrets to say, was not accepted.

[**customer is always right – the**, teeters on the tightrope with c.p. at one end and cliché at the other. Commercial: C20.]

cut off my legs and call me Shorty! A US c.p., dating from before 1945 and bearing no very precise meaning. (Peter Sanders, 28 April 1975.) But Harold Shapiro, on 13 May 1975, writes:

> A jocular exclamation of surprise, verging on wonderment if not disbelief.... It's the sort of exclamation ordinarily introduced by 'Well'.... There is also a conflation of this c.p. with another exclamation of surprise, *Well, shut my mouth*, producing *Well, shut my mouth and call me Shorty*. This last was popularized, I think, if not invented by Phil Harris in the early 1940s. Harris was a radio personality, bandleader and comedian, who presented himself as a mock whiskey-guzzling Southerner.

cut the cackle and come to the 'orses! Let's get down to business! late C19–20. It occurs in, e.g., Dorothy Sayers, *Unnatural Death*, 1927. Either from horse-dealing or from horse-racing. Oddly enough, this c.p. apparently does not figure in the dictionaries of either quotations or proverbs (and proverbial sayings). Occasionally *'osses*.

cut to Hecuba (or **come to Hecuba**) is a 'relic from Shakespeare and was an artifice employed by many old producers to shorten matinées by cutting out long speeches' (Michael Warwick, 'Theatrical Jargon of the Old Days' in *Stage*, 3 October 1968): theatrical: *c*. 1880–1940. The reference is to

> What's Hecuba to him or he to Hecuba
> That he should weep for her?

in Act II, Scene ii, of *Hamlet*.

cut your kiddin'! was a US students' and teenagers' c.p. of the early 1920s. (McKnight, a scholarly, very readable, attractive book.)

cut yourself a piece of cake! is recorded, as an English c.p., in Supplement 2 (p. 645, fn. 1), 1948, of HLM, along with *how's your poor feet?*, *does your mother know you're out?*, *keep your hair on!*. I myself have never heard it; I hazard the guess that it belonged to the extremely approximate period *c*. 1890–1914.

cuts no ice. See **that cuts no ice**.

D

'dab!' quoth Dawkins when he hit his wife on the arse with a pound of butter was applied, mid C18–mid 19, to any noisy impact; it appears in Grose, 1785; to *dab* is 'to pat, to give with a pat' – and it was presumably a witticism prompted by a *dab*, or pat, of butter. Cf:

dab, says Daniel was a nautical c.p. of *c.* 1790–1860: applied to 'lying bread and butter fashion' in bed or bunk. It occurs in 'A Real Paddy', *Real Life in Ireland*, 1822.

daddy, buy me one of those. See **oh, mummy!**...

daddy wouldn't buy me a bow-wow is mostly 'used in a seemingly petulant manner as a complaint that the speaker's request for something (probably trivial ...) has been denied. As you suspected, it was the title of a song and appeared in the refrain. TABRAR, Joseph, "Daddy Wouldn't Buy Me a Bow-Wow" (1892). It has been referred to as "delightful bit of nonsense, whose comedy lay in the infallible trick of having a grown person talk like a child". The "comic success" was one of the major hits of the decade' (Colonel Albert Moe, 11 July 1975). Sung by Vesta Victoria, it is memorialized in Edward B. Marks, *They All Sang*, 1934, as William J. Burke tells me.

dam of that was a whisker – the. This was a colloquial and dialectal c.p. of *c.* 1660–1810 and was applied to a great lie. (Ray, 1678 – cited by Apperson.) Could *whisker* have been a pun on whisper? That it wasn't a misprint is virtually proved by the existence of the almost synonymous **the mother of that was a whisker.**

damn a horse if I do! A strong – almost a violent – refusal or rejection: *c.* 1810–60. 'Jon Bee', in his dictionary of slang and cant, 1823, shrewdly postulates an origin in *damn me for a horse if I do* (any such thing).

damn the torpedoes – full steam ahead! See AMERICAN HISTORICAL BORDERLINERS – and cf the Irvin S. Cobb quotation at **where do we go from here?.**

damned clever these Chinese! See **clever chaps these Chinese!** and cf **darn' clever these Armenians!**

dance at your funeral – I'll (but occasionally **he'll** or **she'll**). 'An old slanging-match catch phrase' (Albert B. Petch, who has helped me for well over thirty years): since *c.* 1880 – pure guesswork, this; almost certainly current at least as early as 1900. In essence, this is a taunt and, by the speaker, regarded as a 'finalizer'.

darn' clever these Armenians! (or **Chinese!**) is the US version of **damned clever these Chinese**, q.v. at **clever chaps these Chinese!** Berrey, 1942, has it – and notes what was presumably the earlier form, **darn' clever these Chinese!**

date – you. See **you date!**

David (or Davy) send it down. See **send it down, David!**

Davy putting on the coppers for the parson (or **parsons**) is a nautical c.p. comment on an approaching storm at sea: since *c.* 1830; by 1945, virtually extinct. The sailors' belief that there is an arch-devil of the sea is clearly implied.

day the omelette hit the fan – the. 'The day when everything went wrong', is a not very common variant of **when shit hits the fan** and was adopted, *c.* 1966, from the US.

days to do're getting fewer is a jingle (*do're – fewer*) c.p. 'I was in Cyprus at the end of the 1950s and of national servicemen – who were, naturally, greatly preoccupied with questions of time: done and time to do. Catch phrases like "Days to do're getting fewer" and question and answer rituals like "Days to do?" "Very few" were common' (Paul Beale, 10 February 1974).

dead! and she never called me 'mother', with *she* often omitted; also with the fairly frequent variant, **dead, dead, and she....** This c.p., dating from the 1880s to 1890s, is used satirically of melodrama, esp. of the Surreyside, or 'Transpontine', Drama, which flourished at that period, although it survived, heartily enough, until WW1, and from which, of course, it came; thence it was transferred to similar or reminiscent situations. It occurs in, e.g., Christopher Bush, *The Case of the April Fool*, 1933.

The wording is based upon – for the words of the c.p. do not occur in – T. A. Palmer's dramatized version, 1874, of Mrs Henry Wood's *East Lynne*. (See *ODQ*; and cf the entry in Granville.)

I heard it often, as a soldiers' derisive chant, during WW1; much less often during WW2.

My good friend, Mr Albert B. Petch, writing on 18 November 1974, recalls 'an old morality picture that my mother had in her parlour: it showed a poor ragged woman peering through the window of a mansion at a little coffin, and the caption read, "Dead – and never called me Mother!"'

dead but he won't lie down (usually preceded by **he's**), current since *c.* 1910, does not, as one might suppose, imply great courage; what it implies is great stupidity – a complete lack of common sense. It was, on ITV, used in a series called 'Sam', showing mining life in Yorkshire about WW1 period (as Mr Albert B. Petch informed me on 16 September 1974).

dead clever these Chinese! See **clever chaps these Chinese!**

deal of glass about – a, often preceded by **there's.** Mostly it was applied to a flashy person or a showy thing, but it did almost mean 'first-class' or 'the thing', the ticket': *c.* 1880–1940, for the secondary meaning; the first is extant, although slightly obsolescent. Probably from large show-windows or show-cases. In form, cf:

deal of weather about – a, mostly prefaced by **there's.** There's a storm approaching – we're in for bad weather: nautical: mid C19–20. (Ware.)

dear Mother, I am sending you ten shillings – but not this week is a lower- and lower-middle-class – hence a WW1 army

(Other Ranks')–c.p. of C20; less common among soldiers in WW2 than it had been in 1914–18, when it served as a kind of self-mockingly humorous, jocularly cynical, chant. (B & P.) Cf:

dear Mother, it's a bastard, with the 'dovetail'–**dear Son, so are you**–is later than, and was perhaps generated by, the next. Not, I think, before *c.* 1920. (Paul Beale, 17 February 1975.)

dear Mother, it's a bugger–**sell the pig and buy me out**. This is another army (Other Ranks') c.p., dating since *c.* 1910 and expressing disgust with Service life and at the loss of home comforts.

dear Mother, respectful–or **dear Mum**, affectionate,
Please send me one pound and 'The Christian Herald'.
P.S. Don't bother with 'The Christian Herald'.
Your loving son, ——
This c.p. belongs to WW2 and was common among Servicemen–other ranks, naturally; not among officers.

dear Mother, sell the pig and buy me out! Cf **dear Mother, it's a bugger** ... and **sell the pig** ....

dear old pals! 'A derisive chanted cat-call or song when boxers funk action or are in a clinch' (Albert B. Petch): boxing spectators': C20. It no less neatly than humorously derives from the song 'Dear Old Pals, Jolly Old Pals'–very popular on festive occasions.

death-warrant is out–**his** (or, occasionally, **my** or **your**). This police c.p. dates from late C19. In his *London Side-Lights*, 1908, Clarence Rook informs us that 'when a constable is transferred against his will from one division to another, the process is alluded to in the phrase, "His death-warrant is out". For this is a form of punishment for offences which do not demand dismissal.'

deft and dumb is a c.p. that, obviously parodying *deaf and dumb*, arose *c.* 1940; it indicates the speaker's idea of an ideal wife or mistress. Cf **anything for a quiet wife**.

deliver de letter–**de sooner de better** is an Australian 'message to the postman that is put on the back of envelopes, in the same way as SWALK [sealed with a loving kiss], etc.' (Barry Prentice, 1 May 1975): since *c.* 1950, if not a little earlier. But whereas SWALK and its variants are non-cultured conventionalisms, *deliver de letter* ... is a deliberate travesty or 'guying' or 'send-up' of 'New Australians'' illiteracies.

demure as a whore–notably **an old whore**–**at a christening**, often preceded by *as*, is picturesquely and earthily synonymous with 'extremely demure': C18–20. Grose records it in 1788, but it appears, in the shorter form, in Captain Alexander Smith's *The Life of Jonathan Wild*, 1726; and I've seen it in one or two C18 comedies.

depending on what school you went to. 'A c.p. used by cowards who give two pronunciations of a rare, or a foreign, word' (Barry Prentice): Australian: since *c.* 1950. Not unheard–although not yet, I believe, a c.p.–elsewhere; I've encountered it in England–in the grammatical variant, *depending on which school you went to*.

depends on what you mean. See **it all depends** ....

desist! curb your hilarity! 'And there were the George Robey quips which became, for a period, catch phrases–"Desist! Curb your hilarity" was one, I think: there were several, all

ephemeral, but common talk in their time' (Vernon Noble, 11 December 1973). Cf:

desist, refrain, and cease–cf the preceding–was a Robey 'gag' that, current in June 1911–14 and then heard decreasingly, did not die until *c.* 1960; and even then it lingered in the memory of many. The Coronation (of George V) number of *Punch*, 7 June 1911, 'paraded caricatures of eminent men named George. These included George Robey, with the couplet
    To all who would invade your Royal peace
    Three words have I–"Desist", "Refrain", and "Cease".'
(Thus Vernon Noble, on 19 February 1975.)

detail!–**but that's a mere**; *but* is occasionally omitted, and the shortened form, *a mere detail!*, has always, in C20, been fairly frequent. It dates from the 1890s, when the complete phrase was used humorously to make light of something either very difficult or rather important–in short, a meiosis entirely characteristic of British, perhaps most notably of English, *mores*.
    It need not, I hope, be added that, used literally, the phrase does not qualify as a c.p.; for some, unfortunately, it does so need.

devil a bit, says Punch–**the**. This jocular yet decidedly firm negative belongs to the very approximate period 1850–1910. It elaborates a merely colloquial, general, non-c.p., *the devil a bit*, current since *c.* 1700–if not a decade or so earlier.

[**Devil is alive and well and living at** –– (locality variable)–**the**. Probably the original of **God is alive and well** ..., q.v.]

Devil's in Ireland–**as sure as the**. See **sure as the Devil's** ....

devil's own luck and my own (too)–**the**, provides a c.p. variation of *the devil's own luck*, very bad luck: late C19–20.

dice are cold–**the**, and **the dice are hot**. Few gamblers are winning–or, many are winning: dicing gamblers': C20.

did it drop (occasionally *fall*) **off a lorry?** In the shady fringes of crime–e.g., in shady public-houses–and esp. among transport men, this is a graceful, delicate way of asking 'Was it stolen?' or even 'And you stole it, I suppose': since *c.* 1950 (Albert B. Petch, 16 January 1974). Used as a synonym of the very much more general euphemism, 'found before it was lost'.

did it hurt? This jocular C20 c.p. 'is heard in jocular use in several ways, as "Did it hurt?" when a chap has said that he had been thinking' (Albert Petch, May 1966). Ironic? Often. Unkindly? Rarely.

did she fall or was she pushed? was originally–that is, in the raffish 1890s–as still, applied to a girl deprived of her virginity; then to a person stumbling; in C20, occasionally shouted (not, of course in the most respectable theatres) at an old style actress. In 1936 appeared (in Britain) the much-lamented witty and wildly humorous Thorne Smith's novel of the punning title, *Did She Fall?*, which reinforced the phrase's applicability to murder cases. But the phrase is of English origin, perhaps as early as 1908, in a (true) murder case–that of Violet Charlesworth, found dead at the foot of a cliff near Beachy Head.

did you bring anything with you? See **bring anything** ....

did you enjoy your trip, often shortened to **enjoy your trip?** 'I'll tell you a catch-phrase which used to delight me when

I was very small. It used to be said by my grandmother's maid when I was playing about in the kitchen. If I got too obstreperous and shuffled up one of the mats on the floor, she always said "Mind my Brussels!" [i.e., Brussels carpet]. I found it marvellously witty at the time. A later version, often heard in the 1930s, was "Did you enjoy your trip?" or simply "Enjoy your trip?" when anyone caught a toe on anything' (Christopher Fry, 11 December 1974).

I don't think *mind my Brussels!* did truly become a c.p. The other certainly did and has, I believe, been current from *c.* 1920; also it contained a neat pun on *trip*, a short voyage or journey, and *trip*, a near-fall.

And then, on 18 December 1974, CF wrote to inform me that Mrs Robert Gittings (the biographer Jo Manton) had, a day or so before, heard one workman say to another on a scaffolding, apropos a luckily non-fatal stumble, 'Enjoy your trip?' So the phrase has lingered on: and it deserves its longevity.

did you ever?, indicating surprise or astonishment or admiration, is elliptical for 'Did you ever see or hear (or hear of) the like?'; arose *c.* 1875 and was originally US. In *Doc Horne*, 1899, George Ade wrote:

'I could see the train coming along through the woods, and I made a final spurt.'

'Did you ever!' observed Mrs Milbury, with an upward roll of the eyes.

By 1900 at latest, it was also British.

did you ever see a dream walking? 'In a Kipling story you may read that "the houses" – the audiences of the music-halls – "used to coo" over Nellie Farren. Only for Vesta Tilley have I heard houses coo. A later [than 1900] song asked, "Did you ever see a dream walking?" I saw Vesta Tilley walk' (Harold Brighouse in *What I Have Had: Chapters in Autobiography*, 1953).

One still (in 1975) occasionally hears the same question asked as a c.p.

did you get the rent? Did you find a customer? This – or had you guessed? – is a prostitutes' c.p., dating, apparently, from late C19. (*U.*)

did you hear anything knock? See **do you hear...?**

did you now! and **do you now!** Of the former, Wilfred Granville said that it is a 'sarcastic c.p. addressed to one who boasts of bringing off a coup or achieving something of which he was not thought capable'; of the latter, 'Much the same as [did you now!]; 1960's; via TV' (letter of 7 January 1969). The former is the commoner and the earlier – it goes back at least as far as 1930 and has (I think) been used throughout the century; nor would it surprise me if I were to discover it in a publication issued in the 1890s or even the 1880s.

did you say something? and **did you speak?** are addressed to someone who has just broken wind: late C19–20. They belong to the raffishly polite conversation of the public bar.

didn't have a pot to pee (or **piss**) **in.** See **pot to pee....**

didn't he do well! See **didn't we do well!**

didn't that choke you? See **choke you....**

didn't they do well! 'During 1973 Bruce Forsyth in "The Generation Game" on BBC1 on Saturday evenings had the catch phrase "Didn't they do well!" after competitive games

in the studio for which prizes were given. You now hear it in pub conversation, with attempts to imitate his chuckling voice' (Vernon Noble, letter dated 18 January 1974). Cf:

didn't we do well! comes from the world of BBC entertainment; it soon acquired a rival: *didn't he do well!*: (?late 1960s) 1970s. In the *Evening News* of 24 January 1975 a full-page advertisement issued by Messrs Tate and Lyle was headed 'Didn't he do well!'; the 'he' refers to their advertisement 'little man', Mr Cube. And in March 1975 I noticed that the London Co-operative Society's milk bottles bore, printed on them, 'Didn't we do well!' – where 'we' referred to careful housewives.

didn't win any (illiterately *no*) **medals**, mostly thus tersely; sometimes preceded by *he*, rarely by *she* or *you*. He made no profit or gained no advantage: a Cockney c.p., dating from late 1918.

didn't you sink the *Emden*? – expressing a profound contempt either of arrogance or of a colossal conceit induced by an excessively laudatory 'Press' – was frequently heard in the Australian army, 1915–18. The Australian cruiser *Sydney* had, at the Cocos Islands in 1914, destroyed the roving Ger. cruiser *Emden*. (Recorded both by F & G and by B & P.)

died of wounds, likewise recorded by F & G and by B & P as current in the army throughout WW1, is synonymous with other such expressions as *hanging on the* (*old*) *barbed wire* and *up in Annie's room*; they were the standardized replies to queries about an absent man's whereabouts.

Dieu et mon droit (pronounced *dright*) – **fuck you, Jack, I'm all right** was, notably in 1914–15, a variant of **fuck you, Jack, I'm all right**, the Fr. phrase being dragged in to form a jingle but itself acquiring independent status and surviving until 1970 at least, although not much heard after *c.* 1960. (Julian Franklyn.)

different ships – different long-splices (or **cap tallies**). Different countries, different customs: nautical: the former, C19–20, is recorded by Bowen; the latter, naval only, belongs to C20 only. A cap tally, by the way, is a cap ribbon bearing the name of a man's ship.

dig in and fill your boots; often *and* is omitted. Eat hearty!: fill not only your belly but, if you wish, your boots as well: naval: C20. (PGR, 1948.)

dig you later! was a negro 'expression of farewell' current during the 1930s and decreasingly so in the 1940s.

digging a grave (or **digging for worms**) (in full, **he is** or **they are ...**) is a C20 cricketers' c.p. applied to a batsman, or batsmen, doing a bit of 'gardening', i.e. patting the pitch and picking up loose pieces of turf, often a deliberate ploy in the art of gamesmanship.

dimple in chin, devil within was partly a potential proverb, but predominantly a c.p., 'jingle used as a challenge to a girl, in the hope of learning more of the devil within: ?C19–1930, at least' (Laurie Atkinson, late 1930). It's one of those sayings that, like **I'll have your guts for garters**, turn out to be a century or two earlier than even a wild surmise.

dipped into my pockets – it (or **that**) **has.** That has occasioned me a great deal of expense: *c.* 1875–1914. Recorded in that rare book, Baumann.

dirt – the. See **what's the dirt?**

dirt before the broom. See **age before beauty.**

dirty face. See **who are you calling dirty face?**

dirty work at the crossroads! Sexual intercourse, but also minor amorous intimacies; in jocular innuendo: C20. Hence, also applied to anything 'fishy'. From the literal sense, 'foul play', which so often takes – or used to take – place at cross-roads.

A reference to, a comment upon, a love affair or a piece of love-making occurs in the play, *The Law Divine*, performed on 29 August 1918, published in 1922, and written by H. V. Esmond: TED (*slowly*): I believe Pop's a bit of knut.' Then, a few lines later, 'Hot work at the cross-roads – eh, my lad?'

Throughout WW1, the phrase was continually being used as a jocularity, rendered the more trenchant because cross-roads were invariably a target for the Ger. guns.

ditto here was a US c.p. – attested by Berrey – of *c.* 1925–50. General meaning is 'The same goes for me' – 'I think so too' – 'So do I.' Cf **that makes two of us.**

do as Garrick did. The reference being to the famous David Garrick (1717–79), greatest English actor of C18, the c.p. is naturally theatrical – current among actors (and actresses) – and this, Granville tells us, is 'the advice given to a disgruntled star who is upset by an adverse press notice. The great David Garrick is said' – erroneously – 'to have written his own notices'.

do as I do was, *c.* 1860–1914, a c.p. used – not only in public-houses – as an invitation to someone to have a drink; current on both sides of the Atlantic. (Farmer.)

do as my shirt does! is, so far as the nature of the invitation allows, a polite variation of **'Kiss my arse!'**: C18–20, but, except among the literary, obsolete by 1940. Whether Tom Durfey (1653–1723), using it towards the end of his life, coined it or was, as I suspect, popularizing it, I don't know.

do I ducks! is a Cockney c.p. of C20 and less a euphemism than a humorously polite variation (an exercise of wit) of the somewhat abrupt 'I do not!' Perhaps via 'Do I hell!' – itself standing for the robust, vigorous, earthy 'Do I *fuck!*' The *s* of *ducks* is a 'confuser' of *duck*, itself a rhyme.

do I not! is a c.p. asseverative of 'I certainly do': 'Heard on and off' (Albert B. Petch, 4 January 1974), it has, I'd say, existed throughout C20.

do I owe you anything? or **what do I owe you?** is, late C19–20, an indirect, yet remarkably effectual, remark addressed to someone who has been staring either persistently or without reason at oneself.

do it! was a US negro c.p. of the 1920s and 1930s. In effect, it unnecessarily encouraged 'one who was already demonstrating any sort of cultural refinement or artistic skill' (CM).

do it again, Ikey – I saw diamonds! Please say it again, because it sounds a bit too good to be true: a proletarian c.p. of *c.* 1890–1914. It occurs in W. L. George's novel, *The Making of an Englishman*, which, historically, is all the more important because of its year of publication: 1914.

do it now! originated as a business slogan, but clearly, by lending itself to jocular, even to semi-irrelevant, misuse, it became a c.p., at first in the world of business, yet very soon also socially: it preceded 1910 but, as a c.p., it fell, in Britain, into disuse slightly before, rather than because of, WW2; but

in Australia was still common in 1965 – and presumably later. (Recorded in 1927 in the late Professor W. E. Collinson's invaluable book; at a time, that is, before the study of spoken or other familiar English became almost *de rigueur*.)

do it – or else! If you don't do it, you can expect trouble: a reasonably polite and almost reasonable threat: US: since *c.* 1925. (Berrey.)

do it the hard way! is a Canadian c.p., dating from *c.* 1910, and often preceded by *that's right!* and often either elaborated or rounded off with *standing up in a hammock* (copulation insinuated): derisively shouted at a (very) awkward workman struggling, somewhat unsuccessfully, to do his job. (Douglas Leechman.)

do me a favour! (Illiterate, or mock-illiterate, **do us a favour.**) See **look! do me a favour.** Arnold Wesker employs this form several times in *Chicken Soup with Barley*, produced in 1958 and published in 1959, the first being:

MONTY: Ten thousand bloody sightseers! Do me a favour, it wasn't a bank holiday [but a 'demo' and a clash with the police].

do one for me! is a predominantly male jocularity addressed to someone going into a public convenience, esp. in bitterly cold weather: C20. (Wilfred Granville, letter dated 11 January 1969.) Cf **have one for me.**

do others before they do you! is a post-1918 c.p., a jocularly cynical adaptation of *do unto others as you would be done by*. Often it implies 'Get them before they get *you!*'

do tell! You don't say so! Used literally, it obviously isn't a c.p.; used either ironically or sarcastically or with a deceptive incredulity, it *is* one. As a Canadian c.p., it dates from *c.* 1945. But the Canadian c.p. is simply an adoption of the US, mostly New England. M recorded it in 1891; and in 1889 Farmer called it:

a senseless catch-phrase, lugged in everywhere, in season and out of season.... It forms a very useful non-committal interjection for listeners who feel that some remark is expected of them; it is thus equivalent to the 'really?' 'indeed?' of English people. A similar phrase in the South is ... 'You don't say so?' which a Yankee will vary by 'I want to know!' 'Do tell' is also used as a decoy.

V confirmed it as having originated among, and been confined to, New Englanders.

But the phrase long antedates 1889. In 1848 *D.Am.* described it as 'a vulgar exclamation common in New England, and synonymous with really! indeed! is it possible!'

A year later, the famous British geologist Sir Charles Lyell, in *A Second Visit to the United States in the Years 1845–6*, 2 vols, revealingly says:

Among the most common singularities of expression are the following: 'I should admire to see him' for 'I should like to see him', 'I want to know' and 'Do tell', both exclamations of surprise, answering to our 'Dear me'. These last, however, are rarely heard in society above the middling class [vol. I, p. 163, October 1845].

To date it as at least as early as 1820 seems reasonable, for it occurs in John Neal's *The Down-Easters*, 2 vols, 1833, at chapter I, p. 61, thus:

Why that are [= that there] chap you was with below, said the Down Easter.

George Middleton, hey? – do tell! – is that his name?

And it was still common at least as late as 1920, when Clarence Budington Kelland, in his novel, *Catty Atkins*, writes:

'It would be runnin' away. We've been runnin' away right along.'
'Do tell,' says I. 'From what?'

Oddly enough, Kelland had already in 1919 written this passage:

'I'm no Sunday-school boy –' said Dick O'Meara.
'Do tell,' gibed Eldredge.

And in 1838, T. C. Haliburton in *The Clockmaker; or, The Sayings and Doings of Samuel Slick, of Slicksville*, 2nd Series (p. 118), has Sam Slick of Connecticut saying, 'Why, he'll only larf at it [a painting] – he larfs at everything that ain't Yankee. Larf! said I, now do tell: I guess I'd be very sorry to do such an ungenteel thing to any one – much less, miss, to a young lady like you.'

Probably some US scholar has written an article on *do tell!* If not, the oversight should promptly be remedied, for this is one of the most persistent, perhaps the *most* persistent, of all US c.pp.: and – intentionally, of course – I've merely scratched a square foot of the surface.

do the other! is a c.p. retort to 'I don't like it'; has the variant, *well, lump it*; and belongs to C20. (One of the many sent to me – this, on 1 April 1969 – by the late Frank Shaw, the authority on Scouse, the dialect of the Merseyside. He had long been an Excise Officer before he became a writer and a radio man. His knowledge of popular speech, of general colloquialism, of the language of music-hall and theatre was immense: and he was immensely generous with that knowledge.)

do they have ponies down a pit? is one of the better-known Cockney c.pp. used derisively and by way of provocative interrogation; two others are *what was the name of the engine driver?* and *why is a mouse when it spins?* These C20 phrases either express the deepest boredom or are designed to start a violent argument or even a quarrel.

do what comes naturally dates from *c.* 1920 and is a c.p. of advice to a young man doubtful how he should treat a girl he's fond of, yet perhaps excessively respects; a generalization – not a euphemism for – the less polite (and less brutal than it sounds) frequently proffered 'I should screw the girl if I were you'. Common among lusty young males and also among maturer, would-be helpful males.

do you feel like that? was, *c.* 1880–1940, a satirical c.p. addressed to workmen, and by others of the working class, either to anyone engaged in unusual work or to a lazy person doing any work at all. (Ware.)

do (or did) you hear anything knock? was a cant c.p. of *c.* 1810–70 and it meant either 'Do – or Did – you understand this?' or 'Do – or Did – you take the hint?' (See *U*, at *hear anything knocking*.)

do you hear the news? A nautical c.p., almost a formula, 'used in turning out the relief watch' (Bowen): mid C19–20.

[**do you know?** may have been a c.p. in 1883–*c.* 1890, after its adoption in 1884 by Beerbohm Tree in *The Private Secretary*, as Ware tells us; but it is one of those almost meaningless tags which should, I think, be classified as clichés rather than as c.pp.]

do you know any other funny stories? dates from *c.* 1935 and

either signifies 'Do you think I'm green *or* a fool?' or implies 'You're a great leg-puller *or* kidder!' or even, very discreetly, 'You're a liar!' The sting resides in 'other'.

do you know something? is partly a tag, introducing gently what might otherwise come abruptly or unkindly, and partly a c.p., 'heard on and off' (Albert B. Petch, 4 January 1974), of quietly humorous intent, as when a fellow says to a girl, 'Do you know something? I rather *like* you.' Cf:

do you know what? is a mainly US variation of *you know what?*, q.v. It occurs in e.g. Damon Runyon's 'Brooklyn Is All Right', the second story in his *My Wife Ethel*, 1939:

Dear Sir the other night my wife Ethel was reading the paper and she says Joe do you know what? I ses here Ethel why do you always start to say something by asking me a question? ... Ethel ses why Joe that is not a question at all. That is just to get you to notice me so I can tell you something.

Who could have put it more neatly than that?

do you know where I'm coming from? Do you understand what I'm saying?: a US c.p., dating from *c.* 1969 (Norris M. Davidson, in letter dated 19 July 1971).

do you mind (? or ! – or both). 'Very common a few years ago, now dying but not fast enough' (Peter Sanders, 27 November 1968), and still not obsolescent, let alone obsolete: dating since the early 1950s. On 2 January 1969, Wilfred Granville glossed the expression thus: 'Addressed to an intruder into conversation or into any circle where the addressee is not wanted or is otherwise unwelcome'; on 10 May 1969, Ramsey Spencer mentioned that it is 'spoken emphatically and on a descending scale; a sarcastic and barely courteous form of "Mind your own business"'; and on 1 July 1975, Paul Beale described it as 'a very common [expression] of reproach or expostulation, perhaps used more by girls and women than by men. Usually uttered in a rather whining tone.' Cf. Laurie Atkinson, late 1974: 'A woman's facetiously affected indignation at imputation of unladylike behaviour'. A good example is '"You wouldn't much like it if *you* went mad." – "*Do* you mind?"' In the *New Yorker* of 26 May 1973, there is a drawing of a 'snooty' couple examining the pieces in an *avant-garde* exhibition, and the woman says to her husband, 'Do you mind? I'm forming an opinion.' The phrase seems to have reached the US *c.* 1970.

An equally, though differently, effective example comes in John Mortimer's percipient comedy, *Collect Your Hand Luggage*, produced in 1961:

OFFICIAL: Have you checked your luggage, sir?
CRISPIN (*embracing both girls*): This is all the luggage I possess.
SUSAN (*wriggling away from him*): Do you mind?

Cf this slightly earlier example, occurring in John Osborne's *Look Back in Anger*, produced at the Royal Court Theatre, London, on 8 May 1956, and published in 1957 – in Act I, concerning cigarettes and music:

ALISON: ... Do you want one, Jimmy?
JIMMY: No thank you. I'm trying to listen. Do you mind?
CLIFF: Sorry, your lordship.

Note that in the collection of stories, *Pretty Polly Barlow*, 1964, in the one titled 'Me and the Girls', Noël Coward makes one of his characters say, 'She's got this "thing" about me not really being queer but only having caught it like a bad habit. Would you mind!' In itself a never very general c.p. of the 1950s–60s, *would you mind?* is important only because it so obviously varies *do you mind?* An illuminating example of the parent c.p. occurs in Martin Russell's novel, *Deadline*, 1971:

> 'Does that mean [that] at present you're bogged down [in your investigations]?'
>
> 'Do you mind?' The superintendent raised a pained hand.
>
> 'Police are actively pursuing a number of theories ... that'll do till we hit on something promising.'

Like **do yourself a favour**, q.v., this c.p. reminds me of a line in some melodramatic novel of the Edwardian period: 'Under the innocent exterior there lurks a veiled menace' (where a self-respecting writer would have preferred 'innocuous' to 'innocent'). Clearly it possesses a trenchant terseness that has attracted the susceptible minds of its multitudinous users.

do you need a knife and fork? See **sort 'em out!**

do you now? See **did you now?**

do you see any green in my eye? You must take me for a fool! *or* What do you take me for – an inexperienced idiot?: since c. 1840. Noted both by Benham and by Collinson. Cf the Fr. *je la connais* (understood: *cette histoire-là*). In late C19–20, although very rarely since c. 1940, *do you see any green stuff in my eye?* – cf **not so green as I'm cabbage-looking**; *green* has for centuries implied either inexperience or credulity – or both.

do you see what I see? A c.p. serving 'to express astonishment at unexpected "vision" of former fellow members of army or RAF unit turning up again *en route* to another posting, or home to Blighty; hence in similar general use. 1942–6 [in the Armed Forces]. I still use it' (Laurie Atkinson, 18 July 1975).

do you spit much with that cough? was, c. 1910–30, a Canadian c.p. addressed to one who has just broken wind.

do you take? – short for *do you take my meaning?* – was an English c.p. of c. 1780–1930. George Colman the Younger, in his comedy, *The Poor Gentleman*, published in 1802, has in Act I, Scene ii:

> OLL[APOD].... He he! – Do you take, good sir? do you take?
>
> SIR C[HARLES]: Take! – Oh, nobody can miss.

Then in Act II, Scene i, we find this:

> OLL: Right – the name's nothing; merit's all. Rhubarb's rhubarb, call it what you will. Do you take, corporal, do you take?
>
> FOSS: I never took any in all my life an' please your honour.
>
> OLL: That's very well – very well indeed! Thank you, corporal; I own you one. [Cf **I owe you one.**]

Foss, a corporal, newly returned from long years of campaigning abroad, would not know the civilian c.pp. of the day.

do you think I came up yesterday? See **before you came up**, final paragraph.

do you think (or, if addressed to a third person, **does he think**) **I can shit miracles!** This mainly Londoners' c.p. dates from c. 1920, for certain; but probably from a decade or two earlier.

do you think I'm made of money? See **you must think I'm made of money**.

do you think I've just been dug up? is often shortened to *think I've just been dug up?* Do you think I'm a fool? Dating since c. 1915, it is to be related to **do you see any green in my eye?**, the implication being that a plant 'just dug up' is – naturally – green.

do you think you'll know me again? (or **you'll know me again, won't you?**) is addressed to someone staring at the speaker, esp. if the addressee does not, in soberest fact, know him: C20. The former is polite; the latter aggressive and pointed.

do you want a knife and fork? See **sort 'em out!**

do you want to bet on it? See **want to bet on it?**

do you want to borrow something? is a late C19–20 c.p. addressed to a flatterer.

do you want to buy a battleship? (or, abruptly, **want to buy a battleship?**) often slovened to *wanna buy* ... This RAF c.p., dating from 1940, means 'Do you want to make water?' and is addressed to a fellow Serviceman whom one has, with exquisite humour, awakened with the express purpose of asking him this infuriating question. An elaboration of 'to pump ship', to urinate, and a (somewhat veiled) ironic allusion to flag days.

do your own thing!, a US hippies' c.p., dating from the late 1950s, is ambiguous, for it can mean either 'Do your own (esp., dirty) work!' or 'Mind your own business!' or, as usually, 'Follow your own bent!'

do your own time! Work out your sentence quietly and uncomplainingly – don't foist your woes upon others!: US underworld, since c. 1919. Occurring in Lewis E. Lawes's, *20,000 Years in Sing-Sing*, 1932, thus, 'You mustn't let anyone else do your bit. Do your own time. Be careful of the wolves in the institution.' It forms the title of Don Castle's *Do Your Own Time*, 1938.

do yourself a favour!, dating from c. 1945, introduces a warning, as in 'Do yourself a favour! Watch out for that fellow – he's an informer'. The meaning current in 1976 is, rather, 'go away!'; 'Buzz off!'; 'Scram!' (Norman Franklin).

doan't tha thee-tha me! Thee-tha thasen an' see 'ow tha likes it! A 'jocular assumption of dignity from one Yorkshireman to another; protesting need of the dignified distance and respect of "you"' (Laurie Atkinson, late 1974): mostly Yorkshire since the 1920s.

Doctor Livingstone, I presume is both a famous quotation and a remarkably persistent c.p.; the words were spoken in 1871 by H.M., later Sir Henry, Stanley (1841–1904), when he, a journalist, at last came up with David Livingstone (1813–73) in central Africa. Livingstone, physician, missionary, explorer, was thought to be lost; the well-known proprietor of the *New York Herald*, James Gordon Bennett, financed a search party; Stanley, as hard-working as he was alert to the main chance, 'cashed in' by publishing, the very next year, *How I Discovered Livingstone* – and later became even more famous with *In Darkest Africa*.

As a c.p., it arose, c. 1885, as a skit upon Englishmen's traditional punctiliousness in no matter what circumstances, even to dressing for dinner at night, but it was almost immediately extended to almost any fortuitous, or any unexpected, meeting, whether between strangers or even between friends. In Anthony Hope's *Father Stafford*, 1891, occurs this passage:

> As they went in, they met Eugene, hands in pockets and pipe in mouth, looking immensely bored. 'Dr Livingstone, I presume?' said he. 'Excuse the mode of address, but I've not seen a soul all the morning and thought I must have dropped down somewhere in Africa.'

The quotation – or perhaps rather the c.p. – has become so embedded in the structure of English that it can be alluded to in a US 'thriller', Thomas Patrick McMahon's *The Issue of the Bishop's Blood*, 1972, in this way:

> His tailoring had changed. Either he had bought a boat, or he was made up for a party. He was wearing a blue brass-buttoned yachting jacket, improbably white pants and spotless, white, rubber-soled shoes.
>
> 'Sir Thomas Lipton, I presume,' I said sourly.
>
> He raised his bushy eyebrows. 'Still the same nasty bastard, aren't you? Sit down, long time no see.'

For those unfamiliar with yachting history, Sir Thomas Lipton (1850–1931) was equally famous for the brands of tea he sold and for his five gallant attempts ('the world's best loser'), from 1899 to 1930, to win the America's Cup with his various yachts, all named *Shamrock*.

A strange and pleasant footnote to the history of the phrase is the apparent foreshadowing that occurs early in Act V, Scene i, of Sheridan's celebrated comedy *The School for Scandal*, performed in 1777 (but unpublished until 1799); Joseph Surface, having just entered, says: 'Sir, I beg you ten thousand pardons for keeping you a moment waiting – Mr Stanley, I presume.'

Rather odd, isn't it? Now, if it could be proved that H. M. Stanley had seen a performance of the play, or merely read it, not long before he set out for Africa ...

does he think I can shit miracles? A variant of **do you think I can ...?**

does it? A sarcastic retort: c. 1870–1940.

does it hurt? See **did it hurt?**

does your bunny like carrots? '[Heard in] 1915–16 and no doubt existing earlier. Street boys to girls, jocular familiarity, with sexual symbolism' (Laurie Atkinson, November 1969): mostly London: probably late C19–20. With *bunny*, cf. the slang *pussy*, female pudend.

does your mother know you're out? This c.p., sometimes jocular, sometimes sarcastic, but esp. addressed derisively to someone displaying either an exceptional simplicity or a youthful conceit or presumption, is, all in all, perhaps the most remarkable – certainly one of the three or four most remarkable – of all British c.pp. It dates, according to the admirably dependable Benham, from 1838; it recurs in *Punch*, 1841; and heaven knows how often since! The *OED* pinpoints the 1838 reference by quoting *Bentley's Miscellany*: '"How's your mother? Does she know that you are out?"' Baumann cites the variants *what will your mother say?* and *did you tell your mother?*, neither of which I have ever heard: they presumably flourished only briefly. There has, however, been, since c. 1900, a c.p. reply, used mainly by Cockneys and virtually obsolete by 1950: *yes, she gave me a farthing to buy a monkey with – are you for sale?*, recorded in Manchon's valuable little dictionary. Frank Shaw, early in November 1968, noted that this national c.p. was 'addressed

to jolly girls', but that, in Liverpool, from c. 1920 onward, it was 'very sarcastic, like *we had* [one or other expletive] *dozens of these*'.

A very early critical commentary on this remarkably and continuously popular phrase occurs in Mackay:

> The next phrase [after *flare up!*] that enjoyed the favour of the million was less concise and seems to have been originally aimed against precocious youths who gave themselves the airs of manhood before their time. '*Does your mother know you're out?*' was the provoking query addressed to young men of more than reasonable swagger, who smoked cigars in the streets, and wore false whiskers to look irresistible. We have seen many a conceited fellow who could not suffer a woman to pass him without staring her out of countenance, reduced at once into his natural insignificance by the mere utterance of this phrase.... What rendered it so provoking was the doubt it implied as to the capability of self-guidance possessed by the person to whom it was addressed. '*Does your mother know you're out?*' was a query of mock concern and solicitude, implying regret and concern that one so young and inexperienced in the ways of a great city should be allowed to wander about without the guidance of a parent.

This agrees entirely with the impression created by the earliest US reference I've found.

Twice in vol. I of the Robert Surtees novel *Handley Cross; or Mr Jorrocks's Hunt*, 1854, the phrase occurs; in the chapter 'Another Sporting Lector' it is mentioned as 'a familiar inquiry that may safely be hazarded to a bumptious boy in a jacket'; and in an early chapter ('Belinda's Beau') it figures more topically in a scene where a couple of 'real swells' (Mr Jorrocks and a handsome young fellow), visiting a bulldog fight, are greeted with ribald cries:

> 'Make way for the real swells wot pay!' roared a stentorian voice from the rafters.
>
> 'Crikey, it's the Lord Mayor!' responded a shrill one from below.
>
> 'Does your mother know you're out?' inquired a squeaking voice just behind.
>
> 'There's a brace of plummy ones!' exclaimed another, as Bowker and Jorrocks stood up together.

It had also occurred notably in R. H. Barham's *The Ingoldsby Legends*, 2nd Series, 1842, concerning a 'poor old Buffer' victimized by a clever swindler ('Misadventures at Margate'):

> I went and told the Constable my property to track;
> He asked if 'I did not wish that I might get it back?'
> I answered, 'To be sure I do! – It's what I've come about.'
> He smiled and said, 'Sir, does your mother know that you are out?'

Note that this c.p. was also US, 'very popular c. 1900, but long obsolete' (W. J. Burke, in letter of December 1968); and popular long before 1900, witness T. C. Haliburton, *The Clockmaker*, 3rd Series, 1840; a dancing girl, backstage at a New York theatre, and a country lad, having been taken there, proceed thus: 'Comin' up and tappin' me on the shoulder with her fan, to wake me up like, said she, Pray, my good feller "Does your mother know you're out?" – The whole room burst out a-larfin' at me.'

In *The Life of the Party*, 1919, Irvin S. Cobb – that genuinely US humorist – describes how a group of young people 'rag' a fancy-clothes-party reveller thus: '"Algernon, does your mother know you're out?" "Three cheers for Algy, the walkin' comic valentine." "Algy, Algy – oh, you cutey Algy!" These jolly Greenwich Villagers were going to make a song of his name.'

In 1942, Berrey merely lists the phrase as US.

But there is yet another noteworthy aspect of this phrase; has it ancient prototypes? On 31 December 1971, my old and dauntingly learned friend Jack Lindsay, after 'doing a Macaulay' ('As every schoolboy knows') on me, tells me that 'this question occurs in the Memnonia. (Ancient Thebes, Egypt, Valley of the Kings – J. Baillet, *Descriptions grecques et latines des tombeaux des rois ou syringes*, 1926, Nos 1922 and 1926. See my *Gods on the Roman Nile*, p. 338.) The fact that it occurs twice shows that it was not a chance invention but a Gr. slang phrase.'

Independently, Dr Brian Cook, of New York, had, on 10 March 1969, written to me about these two examples, the Gr. words being ἡ ποῦ σε μήτηρ 'εκτὸς 'όντ' 'επίσταται, first published, with appropriate comment, by M. N. Tod in *Journal of Egyptian Archaeology*, XI, 1925, p. 256; where it is also related that a famous Classical scholar, John Conington, was, while a schoolboy at Rugby (1838–43), challenged by a friend,

'You're a swell at Greek verses, Conington: turn this into an iambic – "Does your mother know you're out?"''

Promptly came the reply, 'Μῶν οἱ μήτηρ, τεκνον, ὡς θυραῖος εἶ?'

This prototype does not, of course, justify a justification for deriving the English c.p. from an ancient *graffito*: such coincidences arise from the fact that, throughout the ages and in all countries, certain *thought-patterns* are discernible: and in the sphere of informal and unconventional speech, they almost inevitably occur. Cf **be good – and if you can't be good, be careful** and **Kilroy was here**.

does your mother like a monkey? is a C20 school taunt c.p., from one boy to another. (Wilfred Granville, late December 1968.)

does your mother take in washing? belongs to a *c.* 1900–30, although it continued to be heard, now and then, for a decade or more after that. A vague phrase, with (I think) no specific insult implied but with a mild imputation of poverty. It occurs in Howard Spring's novel, *My Son, My Son*, 1918.

does your mother want a rabbit? is a c.p. of *c.* 1890–1914. It derives from the stock question (addressed to a child) of the itinerant rabbit-vendors and is therefore not scabrous in origin – whatever may have happened to it in its c.p. stage. (B & P.)

does your nose swell (or **itch**)? – often completed, as logic would demand, by **at this** or **at that**. Are you angry (usually ... **swell**) or annoyed (usually ... **itch**)?: C20.

doesn't buy groceries, often preceded by **it**. A US c.p., implying that such or such an act or activity brings in no money: since *c.* 1920 (Berrey). Cf the British **this won't buy Baby a frock**.

doesn't care what he (or **she**) **spends when he** (or **she**) **has no money**, often preceded by **he** or **she**. This c.p. hits very effectively at one who, penniless, talks as if 'rolling in the stuff': since *c.* 1925. I've heard it very seldom since *c.* 1950.

doesn't have a pot to piss (later, also **pee**) **in**. See **pot to pee in**.

doesn't it make you want to spit?! That is, in disgust: since the late 1930s. An Arthur Askey 'gag' in 'Band Wagon', 1st Series (?late) 1937, 2nd Series 1938, 3rd Series soon after WW2 started. (*Radio Times*, 28 June–4 July 1975, in notice of AA's autobiography.)

doesn't know enough to pee down wind is 'a c.p. directed against a very stupid fellow': mostly Canadian: since *c.* 1920. (Douglas Leechman.)

doesn't know his ass (or **ear**) **from a hole in the ground** (or **a hot rock**), preceded by **he**. He's completely ignorant or a complete simpleton: US: C20. (Colonel Albert Moe, 15 June 1975.)

doesn't know if (or **whether**) **he wants a shit or a haircut**, with or without **he** preceding. To describe someone rather distrait: mainly nautical: C20. (On 16 January 1975, I received this from a helpful contributor who stated neither his address nor even his name. Anyway, I'm grateful for it.)

doesn't know which way he's (occasionally **she's**) playing – **he** (or **she**). This is said of 'one who sets about a job or embroils himself in argument without knowledge or understanding or with wrong-headed idea' (Laurie Atkinson, late 1974): since *c.* 1920.

dogs are barking it in the street – **the**. This Australian c.p., dating since *c.* 1920, is applied to something that, supposed to be a secret, is in fact very widely known – in short, an open secret.

dogs are pissing on your bluey (swag) – **the**. As exhortation, 'Wake up!' More generally, 'something unpleasant is happening to your little world': in the glossary to Alexander Buzo's *Three Plays*, 1973. The former sense recurs in his *The Roy Murphy Show*, performed in 1971. Australian.

dogs have not dined – **the**. Recorded by Grose in 1785, this mid C18–early C19 c.p. is addressed to one whose shirt is hanging out at the back and therefore inviting the attention of any playful dog.

donkey! – **a penny** (or **twopence** or **threepence**) **more and up goes the!** This lower-class London c.p. expresses derision, arose a few years before 1841, and fell into disuse either during or just before WW2. From an itinerant, esp. a street, acrobat's stock finish to a turn.

donkey? – **who stole the**. See **who stole the donkey?**

don't act so daft or I'll buy you a coalyard is a jocular c.p., dating since *c.* 1956 (Julian Franklyn). Why a coalyard? 'Your guess is as good as mine'; even so, I'll hazard the conjecture that then the addressee could blacken his face as much and as often as he liked, and act like a 'black and white' comedian.

don't all speak at once! is used by someone who, having made an offer or a suggestion, is greeted with a conspicuous lack of enthusiasm: since *c.* 1880, if not considerably earlier; both British and US. Walter Woods, US playwright, in *Billy the Kid*, produced in 1907, has this passage in Act II:

MOLLY: [*Enters from dance hall.*] Who wants to dance? Well – don't all speak at once.

don't answer that! There's no need to make any comment, much less to answer the question! *or* Well, no – perhaps you'd better *not* answer that!: as a genuine c.p., only since *c.* 1960. (Literally, it goes – expectably – back as far as modern

English does.) A good example occurs in David Craig's novel, *Contact Lost*, 1970: '"Why am I doing all the talking? Don't answer that!"'

don't be an Airedale! Don't be such a bitch!: US: early 1920s. (Colonel Albert Moe, 15 June 1975; and W & F.) Unfair to this breed of dog.

don't be filthy! Don't be foul-mouthed *or* bawdy *or* suggestive!: since the late 1930s; not much heard since *c.* 1960. A 'gag' by Arthur Askey in 'Band Wagon', *c.* 1937–40. (*Radio Times*, 28 June–4 July 1975; AA's autobiography *Before Your Very Eyes*.)

don't be funny! Don't be ridiculous – I'd never dream of doing such a thing: Canadian: since *c.* 1930, perhaps five or ten years earlier. (Leechman.)

don't be like that! and **don't be that way!** These US c.pp. date from the late 1920s; Berrey records the former; in *DSUE* I've noted its adoption, *c.* 1948, into Britain. The general sense is 'Don't behave in that objectionable – or in that unreasonable and ludicrous – way.'

don't bother me now – my hands are wet. This British soldiers' c.p. of 1914–18 – it seems to have disappeared before WW2 – arises from 'the weary impatience of harassed mothers' repelling the attention-claiming of young children. (B & P.)

don't bother to pick it up! See **clap your hands!**

don't bully the troops! is another WW1 soldiers' c.p., this one being addressed to a noisy or aggressive or excessive talker. (B & P.)

don't call us – we'll call you. Thank you for coming to be interviewed – we'll let you know *or* We have your letter – esp. letter of application for a job or an interview – and we'll let you know our decision: either a businessman's polite brush-off or a gentle intimation of probable rejection or a selection board's (or committee's) final remark to a candidate whose interview has, in effect, ended: since *c.* 1945; originally US, arising either in the film or in the theatrical world, with the one reinforcing the other, and the c.p. becoming general in the early 1950s and then very soon becoming British as well. (Mr W. J. Burke, former head of *Look*'s research department, in a letter of December 1968.)

In Bill Turner's novel, *Circle of Squares*, 1969, a man, having been shadowed by detectives instead of by crooks (as he had suspected them of being), goes into a police station to complain and finds himself being greeted by one of his shadowers, 'Don't call us, we'll call you.'

Then in Peter Townsend's novel *Out of Focus*, 1971, occurs this passage:

'Be in the bar of the Reina Cristina in Algeciras at nine o'clock to-morrow evening.'
Konrad laughed. 'Don't call us, we'll call you.'

In the same year, a well-known novelist described the slight variant *don't call me – I'll call you* as 'a threadbare joke' – and indeed the joke had begun to lose its pristine charm.

'It is generally understood that this is mere prevarication, and the result will turn out unfavourable. "How d'you get on?" – "Oh, you know; Don't call us, *etcetera*"' (Paul Beale, 17 February 1975).

The pertinence and popularity of the phrase had rendered it virtually inevitable that the predominant form should generate a variant or two. It did, by late 1970: *don't ring us – we'll ring you*. Moreover, on 12 October 1970, the *Guardian* could head an article 'Don't Tell Us – We'll Tell You' in the justifiable expectation of being not merely understood but even appreciated.

don't chant the poker! and **don't sing it!** Don't exaggerate!: a proletarian c.p. of *c.* 1870–1914 (B & L, vol. I, 1889). Here, *chant* is 'to advertise, as with a street cry'; but as for *poker* – well, I don't know precisely why, but clearly *chant the poker* was at the barrow-boy, or the Petticoat Lane, level.

don't clap so hard – you'll bring the house down (– **it's a very old house**)! An ironic call to the audience by a comedian greeted with resounding silence at one of his best jokes: music-hall: since the 1870s or 1880s; by 1960, obsolescent; now (1975) a nostalgic survival. John Osborne uses it two or three times in *The Entertainer*, 1957; I had heard it, 1925 or 1926, at either the Victoria Palace or the old Holborn Empire.

don't come it – you never used to! is a 'protest at putting on "side" or pretence. (The rider seems to me to be a music-hall elaboration, or embellishment, and undercurrent)' (Laurie Atkinson, in letter written in December 1968). Since *c.* 1910; by 1970, slightly obsolescent.

don't come (or **give me**) **the old abdabs!** Don't tell me the tale – don't try to fool me or throw dust in my eyes: C20, but esp. in 1939–45. By itself, *abdabs* was, during WW2, occasionally used for 'afters' (a second course of a meal): so perhaps the phrase basically means 'Don't elaborate!' It may have been influenced by 'the screaming abdabs', an attack of *delirium tremens*.

don't crow so loud, rooster – you might lay an egg! Oh! Do stop boasting or bragging: a US c.p., dating from *c.* 1920; recorded by Berrey in 1942; slightly out of date by 1950, but still used by – or, at the least, familiar to – old-timers as late as 1970; and never adopted in Britain, despite its homely picturesqueness.

don't do anything I wouldn't do! is an English – and an Australian and, by adoption, US – c.p., dating from *c.* 1910 or from a lustrum or even a decade earlier, and intended as merely jocular advice. (Cf **be good – and if you can't be good, be careful!**) During 1939–45, in the Services, it served as a 'c.p. addressed to anyone going on leave, especially if suspected of going on a "dirty week-end"' (Wilfred Granville, 7 January 1969).

Examples later than WW2 abound, as, for instance, in Anne Morice, *Death in the Grand Manor*, 1970:

''Bye, 'bye,' Mary called after us. 'And don't do anything I wouldn't do.'

'I wonder what there is that Mary wouldn't do?' I said. Although less frequent than before WW2, this c.p. is still very far from being obsolete.

Usually there is a sexual connotation as in Owen Sela, *The Kiriov Tapes*, 1973, 'Paul . . . threw open the door with a flourish. "There, lovelies," he cried, "it's all yours. And don't do anything I wouldn't do."'

'I have an idea,' writes Mr Peter Sanders on 27 November 1968, 'this comes from *Punch*. The counter is "That gives me plenty of scope".'

Since *c.* 1918, also US. In Ring W. Lardner ('The Facts' – in *How to Write Short Stories*, 1926): 'I will let you know how I come out that is if you answer this letter. In the mean wile girlie au reservoir and don't do nothing I would not do.' Berrey records it.

don't do anything you couldn't eat! is an Australian c.p., dating from c. 1930 and meaning 'Don't take on anything you can't do' – 'Don't start something you can't finish.' (Baker.) By 1960, rather old-fashioned.

It was prompted by *to bite off more than one can chew*; and perhaps it forms a deliberate elaboration of that phrase.

don't dynamite! Don't be angry!: 1883–c. 1900: a non-cultured, non-aristocratic phrase, 'result of the Irish pranks in Great Britain with this explosive' (Ware). Cf:

don't excite! Keep cool! Elliptical for 'Don't excite yourself!': c. 1895–1939. Recorded by *The Concise Oxford Dictionary*, in the Supplement of 1934, it occurs as early as in E. H. Hornung's once extremely popular *Raffles*, 1899: ' "All right, guv'nor," drawled Raffles: "don't excite. It's a fair cop." '

don't fear! See **don't you fear!**

don't fire until (or, loosely, **till**) **you see the whites of their eyes.** At the Battle of Bunker Hill, 1775, the US General Israel Pitman or, according to other authorities, General Joseph Warren or Colonel William Drescott – such being the stuff of which history is made and such the evidence from which so much of it has been written – issued this order to his troops: 'Men, you are all marksmen – don't one of you fire until you see the whites of their eyes.'

This famous US quotation became, at some point early in C20, also a c.p.: a c.p. when used, as since c. 1940 it has been used, without reference to the original situation; in this respect it should be aligned with the two other US historical c.pp. noted at AMERICAN HISTORICAL BORDERLINERS. John W. Clark has, 17 February 1975, pointed out that, as a c.p., it is used 'always with reference to a comparable situation (metaphorically comparable, never literally; never, that is, of an armed conflict, but only of a debate or dispute or the like)'.

By 1945 at latest, *don't fire*. . . . was also a British c.p. and, as such, it has often been employed allusively, as in this passage in John Welcome's *Hard to Handle*, 1964, where the second speaker is a girl:

'I won't be more than a few minutes. If you see anyone taking an undue interest in the car . . . watch him until I come back.'

'I won't shoot until I see the whites of his eyes.'
Here, *shoot* represents an occasional variant, *but* only in Britain.

don't forget the diver! During the short run of six 'ITMA' broadcasts, in the summer of 1940, while the relevant departments of the BBC were at Bangor,

the Diver [played by Horace Percival] made the first of his lugubrious entrances and his even more doleful exits [with the words] 'Don't forget the Diver!'. . . . His few words very soon became part of the country's vocabulary . . . and it was not long before 'Don't forget the Diver' was heard on all sides, in bars, in buses, on stations, even from disembodied voices in the blackout, and practically no lift descended without someone saying, in those weak tones, 'I'm going down now, sir!'
So tells us the producer himself, Frank Worsley, in his *Itma*, (December) 1948. Referring to latish 1948, Worsley says 'Even now I sometimes hear someone mutter "Don't forget the Diver!" ' He might have added that 'going down now, sir' was, as a c.p., often the preferred form.

The late Stephen Potter, in *The Sense of Humour*, 1954, wrote concerning the landlord of a certain public house:

Every now and then he utters some of the accepted comic phrases of our age, quite isolated, quite without reference, 'Mind my bike' he will say. Then a little later: 'Time I gave it the old one-two'. Gave what he does not say . . . Then 'Don't forget the diver' is perhaps the next phrase which happens to come to the surface.

don't fret! See **don't you fret!**

don't get smart! Don't try to be clever or smart or 'Smart Alec'!: US: since c. 1925. (Berrey.)

don't get your arse (occasionally **balls** or **bowels**) **in an uproar** and **don't get your shit hot** and **don't get your knickers in a twist** (or **twisted**). Don't get so excited or, esp., angrily excited: all are low; none, I think, precedes C20; the second is Canadian: but whereas the first and second are addressed by men to men, the third (i.e., the last) is addressed, by either sex, to male or female – or, as Laurie Atkinson puts it, 'a reproof to (over-)indignant man by treating him as a flustered woman'. The US version is *don't get your bowels in an uproar*, which carries no social taboo.

don't get your back up! 'There is, of course, little that is distinctively American in the idea of putting one's back up when inclined to be angry; but as a street catch phrase, one time very popular, it claims a place' (Farmer): c. 1880–90.

don't get your knickers in a twist! See **don't get your arse in an uproar!**

don't give me that! Tell that to the Marines!: since c. 1920. The implication is, 'Don't take me for a fool when you talk like that!' In Terence Rattigan's *Love in Idleness*, first performed on 20 December 1944 and published in 1945, in the opening speech, Olivia Brown on the telephone says:

'Treasury? Hullo, Dicky? Olivia. Is there a chance of a word with the Chancellor? . . . . Don't give me that. If I know him he's in the middle of a nice game of battleships with you at this moment.'

It became also Canadian and US, Berrey recording it in 1942 in the forms *don't give me* – or *us* – *that!* and, less commonly, *don't give me* – or *us* – *one of those!* A US elaboration is *don't give me that jive*, noted by HLM in Supp. 2 and by W & F, 1960; it was adopted in Britain, esp. among jazz addicts, as early as 1950. Contrast:

don't give me that toffee! Don't give me that wrapped-up, glib explanation!: this c.p. is exceptional in having a very limited currency – among RAF airmen in Malta since c. 1950; by 1970, slightly old-fashioned; but worthy of inclusion for its value in comparison with the preceding c.p. and **don't give me the old abdabs**, q.v. at **don't come** . . . . (Laurie Atkinson, in letter of 11 September 1967.)

don't give up the ship!, noted by Berrey as a c.p., is one of those which began their chequered careers as famous quotations. The full words, spoken, as his final order, by Captain James Lawrence, commanding the US frigate *Chesapeake* on 1 June 1813, as he was carried below fatally wounded, before the capture of his ship by the British frigate *Shannon*, were: 'Tell the men to fire faster and not to give up the ship; fight her till she sinks', which, strictly, form the famous quotation, whereas *don't give up the ship!* forms the c.p. (with thanks to Bartlett) – a conflated abridgement of a kind familiar to all historians.

Don't give up the ship! has, since *c.* 1870, if not far earlier, been a US c.p. of encouragement; nor has it, in C20, been entirely unknown in Britain and the Commonwealth.

In Bert Leston Taylor and W. C. Gibson's *Extra Dry*, 1906, 'Hennessy Martel's farewell words, as he breathed his last sober breath in Gottlieb Kirschenwasser's arms, were: "Don't give up the ship!"' is a mock-heroic allusion. Contrast, at **where do we go from here, boys?**, Irvin S. Cobb's mention in his patriotic *The Glory of the Coming*, 1919.

don't go down the mine, daddy! comes from a famous old tear-jerking song that, in WW1, formed a soldiers' chant and very soon after it – say in 1920 – became a c.p.; not much heard since WW2 and very little heard since 1970.

don't hold your breath! is elliptical for 'Don't hold your breath in expectation or excitement' and has the special sense 'Don't count on it': originally – ?during WW2 – and predominantly US, as in Anne Blaisdell, *Practice to Deceive*, 1971:

> 'That air conditioning! You suppose they'll ever get around to us?'
> 'Don't hold your breath,' said Rodriguez.

The implication is that, even if it did happen, they would have to wait some considerable time.

An English example occurs in Donald MacKenzie's novel of suspense, *The Spreewald Collection*, 1975:

> 'Up yours,' grunted the warder. 'I know your kind. You'll be back for a certainty!'
> Hamilton closed his right eye. 'Don't hold your breath. And take good care of those ulcers!'

don't hurry, Hopkins! was, *c.* 1865–1900, a US c.p., addressed to (very) slow persons; Farmer remarks that it is 'used ironically in the West in speaking to persons who are very slow in their work, or tardy in meeting an obligation'. It derived from the C17–18 English proverbial or semi-proverbial *as well come* – or *as hasty – as Hopkins, that came to jail overnight and was hanged the next morning*, which clearly implied 'Don't be too hasty!'

don't I know it!, expressing, somewhat ruefully, 'How well I know it!' – is both US (recorded by, e.g., Berrey) and British – and arose *c.* 1880, if not considerably earlier.

don't it beat the band! Current in US in C20; recorded in, e.g., the *Boston Globe* of *c.* 1970. A variant of **that beats the band.**

don't just stand there – do something! originated, very naturally, as a literal exhortation. But it has been so frequently employed that, *c.* 1940, it became a c.p., both British and US, with a connotation either humorous or allusive or, indeed, both, as in the title of the US Charles Williams's exciting and delightful novel, *Don't Just Stand There*, 1966. It was, I suppose, inevitable that some wit should reverse it to *don't do anything – just stand there!*

don't keep a good woman waiting! 'Advice in a social context, with sexual innuendo' (Laurie Atkinson, November 1969): humorous rather than euphemistic: late C19–20.

don't knock the rock! was originally (1956) the title of the main song in the Columbia film so titled and featuring Bill Haley and the Comets. A year earlier, Bill Haley and his

Comets had appeared in *Rock Around the Clock*, which contained a valedictory c.p. that became famous: *see you later, alligator*. (Ronald Pearsall, 7 February 1975.) It promptly migrated to Britain, where it tended to be used to express resentment at criticism of Rock-and-Roll. An illuminating commentary has, on 17 February 1975, been sent to me by Mr Cyril Whelan:

> [It] can be placed more or less precisely at 1957 [that is, as a c.p.]. Small-town America, pre-Vietnam ... fresh-faced youth worries only about acne, high-school grades, Peggy-Sue next door, and the new Rock 'n' Roll developing from jazz and black rhythm and blues into a white mainstream of music exclusively for the newly *post-pubescent....* *The Rock* was Rock 'n' Roll. Hence *don't knock the rock* = Mummy and Daddy, don't chastise the new music, it symbolizes once and for all [the belief] that Generation is private property (the myth of every generation?). The phrase was extremely powerful until the late 1950s, when 'the Rock' became increasingly *passé* – until it was embarrassingly outmoded by the new popular music developments.

But Mr Ben Grauer has, on Christmas Day, 1975, assured me that it lives again, and means 'Don't ignore the strength and reliability of *X*' – person, institution, custom – with ultimate reference to the Rock of Gibraltar.

don't know which side his arse hangs, often preceded by **he**. This low C20 c.p. implies that the poor fellow is either hopelessly bewildered or in a state of complete indecision. Other forms occur; esp. *I don't know which side my arse hangs*, but the third person predominates and is the only one to have attained to the status of c.p. Contrast:

don't know who's which from when's what, usually preceded by **I**. I know nothing whatever about it: lower classes' c.p., according to Ware: 1897–*c.* 1905.

don't laugh, lady – your daughter may be inside! was, during the Australian 1950s, painted on old cars driven by young people, but was also used by young people in general in reference to such cars. 'Young people rarely own old cars in this more affluent era' (Barry Prentice, 1 May 1975).

don't let anyone sell you a wooden nutmeg! This prototype of **don't take any wooden nickels** 'stems from Colonial days when sharpers or itinerant peddlers in Connecticut sold imitation nutmegs carved out of wood [and] was a common admonition to the unwary' (W. J. Burke, 13 May 1975; he adds that 'Connecticut is sometimes called "The Nutmeg State"'). These wooden nutmegs are mentioned by Timothy Flint in his *Recollections*, 1886. The saying, therefore, seems to belong to *c.* 1850–1900.

don't let me catch you bending! was, *c.* 1890–1960, a jocular c.p., implying 'Don't let me catch you at a disadvantage.' (P. G. Wodehouse, *Psmith in the City*, 1910; Lyell.) A person bending invites a kick.

don't let your braces dangle in the shit! is a workmen's, by adoption a Servicemen's, c.p. of late C19–20, but I never heard it in the WW2 army or RAF. In the army of 1914–18 it was sometimes chanted.

don't let your mouth overload your ass – less commonly, **don't let your mouth buy what your ass can't pay for** – least commonly, **don't let your mouth write a check your ass can't cash**

all mean 'Don't talk too much' and esp. 'Don't boast': 'argot elicited from Black male youths living in the South central Los Angeles ghetto' (Folb): since *c.* 1960, at a guess. Extremely localized, but because of its pungent earthiness and vividness, worth recording. (In localization, cf **don't give me that toffee!**)

don't let's be beastly to the poor Germans was current from the middle 1920s to the very early 1930s, and then rapidly less up to WW2, and was very popular among those inhabitants of Great Britain, particularly the 'intellectuals', who hadn't suffered much during WW1; especially perhaps among the women writers and artists and musicians.

Then, in WW2, a shortened form – *don't let's be beastly to the Germans*, arose: Noël Coward dignified the original by that omission of *poor*, to retain which would have been farcical. The long lyric was sung by Coward in his inimitably conversational 'throw-away' manner, so much more effectual than an emphatically jingoistic treatment could ever have been. He both created and, in a sense, revived this c.p.

don't let's play games! is 'used when a person tries to evade the issue by quibbling or prevaricating' (A. B. Petch, 9 January 1974), the sense being 'Don't waste time by fooling about'. I first heard it *c.* 1960, but I think it arose very soon after the end (1945) of WW2.

don't look down – you'd soon find the hole if there was hair round it! is an army drill-sergeant's admonition to recruits as they fumble to fix bayonets – when practised, they don't need to look: late C19–20. Ribald and pertinent. (B & P.)

don't look now, but I think we're being followed (or **but I think someone's following us**) became, *c.* 1933, a c.p., jocularly allusive to timorous women's mostly imaginary fear; by 1960, obsolete, the fear remaining, but mostly of *not* being followed.

don't make a Federal case out of it! Don't exaggerate the importance of something! Don't exaggerate the seriousness of my action – e.g., of a mistake in judgment – US: since *c.* 1950. (W & F.) Cf **it's not a hanging matter**.

don't make a Judy (Fitzsimmons) of yourself! Don't make a fool of yourself *or* Don't be a fool: Anglo-Irish: C20, but perhaps not until *c.* 1920. To *make a judy of oneself* is 'to play the fool' and, originally US, became anglicized *c.* 1850; the full form, therefore, is an elaboration, prompted by a real Judy Fitzsimmons, whoever *she* may have been. Note that John Brougham, in the final scene of *Po-Ca-Hon-Tas, or The Gentle Savage* (a play full of puns, mostly outrageous), performed in 1855, allows himself this absurdity:

SMITH: *Judas!* You haven't yet sub*dued* John Smith!
KING: Don't make a *Judy* of yourself!

don't make a production of it! – often preceded by **all right!** – dates from the late 1930s and is addressed to one who makes a simple matter seem difficult and very important; very common among Servicemen during WW2; obsolescent by 1970, but still far from obsolete. It derives from film (moving picture)-makers' productions; cf Royal Navy's slang phrase, *make an evolution*, to do something with maximum fuss.

don't make I laugh, it makes I pee I's drawers! '(Mock-yokel, mock-feminine, used by boys and men). Indicates "protest" at being overcome by fooling and jocularity, and thus keeps jollity going' (Laurie Atkinson, late 1974). An elaboration of the next.

don't make me laugh – I've got a split lip! (or **I've cut my lip!**) This C20 c.p., moribund by 1940, yet not, in its shorter form, dead by 1976, occurs in, e.g., Leonard Merrick's *Peggy Harper*, 1911, in the form ... *I've got a split lip* and in Collinson, as ... *I've cut my lip*; since *c.* 1920, mostly shortened to *don't make me laugh*, whence, since *c.* 1925, *don't make me smile*, which has, since *c.* 1930, had a humorous variant, *don't make I smile* (mercifully a short-lived variant). An excellent example of the shortened form comes in John Mortimer's *Gloucester Road*, one of the four short plays comprising John Mortimer's *Come As You Are*, all produced at the New Theatre, London, on 27 January 1970 and published in 1971:

BUNNY: [*To Mike, her husband.*] You're jealous!
MIKE: Jealous! Of that (*Lost for words*) ... four letter man. That wet handshake with his co-respondent's shoes and a bit of Brillo pad stuck under his nose.... Jealous ... of Toby Delgado! Don't make me laugh!

Don't make me laugh! was adopted by the US, apparently *c.* 1918 or 1919, Berrey recording also the predominantly US variant, *don't make me laugh – I've got a cracked lip*. The earliest printed record of the US use of *don't make me laugh* I happen to have noted occurs in Leonard Hastings Nason, *A Corporal Once*, 1930; and I owe that to Colonel Albert Moe.

don't mensh! was a lower-middle-class c.p. of *c.* 1900–39, WW2 apparently and creditably killing it off. Obviously it derives from the polite formula, *don't mention it!*, itself probably elliptical for ... (*for*) *it's a trifle*. Cf:

don't mention that! was current only *c.* 1882–4; arising topically from a notorious libel case, as Ware tells us, it naturally disappeared soon after the case lost its attraction for the public. In form, it deliberately varies the *don't mention it* of the preceding entry.

don't mind me! Go ahead – don't mind me!: usually ironic: late C19–20. Cf **are you in my way?**

don't pick me up before I fall, applied to a premature correction or criticism, probably goes back to late C18: cf Bill Truck, 'The Man-of-War's Man' in *Blackwood's Edinburgh Magazine*, January 1822, 'O ho! my smart fellows, don't you be after picking me up before I fall.'

don't push the panic button! Don't panic!; esp., Whatever you do, don't panic unnecessarily: 'nuclear age' (as John T. Fain describes it) – but, as a c.p., only since *c.* 1950. The reference is to a button that, once pressed, will cause a nuclear warhead to be released.

don't ring us – we'll ring you, an occasional variant of **don't call us ...**, q.v., occurs in, e.g., John Mortimer, *Collaborators*, 1973 – in Act II, allusively.

don't rock the boat! Don't disturb the *status quo!* Everything's going nicely – don't start spoiling things: since *c.* 1950, at least as an established c.p., as in Philip Purser, *The Holy Father's Navy*, 1971:

'Maybe we don't want to rock the boat.'
'Don't rock the boat! – It could be the BBC call-sign these days.'

See also **sit down – you're rocking the boat!** Note also the 'usage in politics and the City to prevent a maverick from going his own way'. (Norman Franklin, March 1976.)

don't say I told you! is an Anglo-Irish c.p. of late C19–20.

It forms the title of a book by Honor Tracy. A more truly Irish form is **mind you, I've said nothing**. (Frank Shaw, 25 February 1969.)

don't say No until (usually **till**) **you are** (usually **you're**) **asked!** Addressed to one who has declined an offer or an invitation before it has been made: C18–20. Originally, *don't you say no.....* as in Dialogue I of S. In C19–20 *before* is occasionally substituted for *until*, and *invited* for *asked*. Also, mid C19–20: *it's manners to wait until you are* – or *till you're – asked*.

don't see it! See **I don't see it!**

don't sell me a dog! Don't deceive, don't cheat, me!: society: *c.* 1860–80. (Ware.) Cf the slangy *to sell someone a pup*, to swindle him.

don't shit the troops! See **you wouldn't shit the troops**.

don't shoot the pianist! (or, as originally, **don't ...**) – **he's doing his best** was adopted, *c.* 1918, from the US, where current, at first as a saloon notice in the Wild West, since *c.* 1860. A US variant was *don't shoot the piano-player: he's doing the best he can*. According to Stevenson, the correct form was *please do not shoot the pianist – he is doing his best*, and Stevenson's gloss is: 'Oscar Wilde, telling of a notice seen by him in a Western bar-room during his American tour, in a lecture delivered in 1883.'

don't shoot until you see the whites of their eyes. See **don't fire ....**

don't sing it! See **don't chant the poker!**

don't some mothers 'ave (occasionally **have**) **'em!** You do meet funny [i.e., odd or peculiar] people, don't you? (itself almost a c.p.): North Country; popularized on radio by the Jimmy Clitheroe Show of the 1930s, but dating from at least as early as 1920. (The late Frank Shaw, November 1968 and January 1969; he used to take endless trouble to help his friends.)

don't spare the horses. See the third paragraph of **home, James....**

don't spend it all at once! See **here's a ha'penny ...!**

don't spit – remember the Johnstown Flood originated in – and probably began to be used very soon after – the great flood on 31 May 1889 and was 'killed' either by the disaster of Pearl Harbor on 10 December 1941, as I used to think, or by Prohibition, as Dr Joseph T. Shipley expounded the matter in a letter written to me on 1 April 1974:

In the saloons* that abounded before Prohibition [1919–33] some had sawdust strewn on the floor (even in the big cities like New York) for readier absorption of spilled beer and expectorations, for easier sweeping. And of course they all had NO SPITTING signs. I remember signs with comic turns – used in the saloons, but also on sale in the stores that specialize in party novelties, signs, and practical jokes: NO SPITTING ALOUD: DON'T SPIT: REMEMBER THE JOHNSTOWN FLOOD.

During Prohibition, the speakeasies had a different make-up, with emphasis on quiet drinking, mainly of hard liquors. And after repeal, in 1933, the law required every place that sold liquor also to sell food – hence a different structure, with a front bar where usually both men and women congregated, and no longer any promiscuous spitting – no spittoon.

In 1912 – I remember the date because it was my Senior year at college – I saw a burlesque act. Two bums see a pretty girl, sitting on a park bench. They plot to 'make' her. The dominant one tells the other to go by and insult her; then he will come along, chase him away, comfort the girl – and win her. They start; when the second drives the first away, and she turns to her rescuer, she cries on his shoulder – and he says: DON'T CRY: REMEMBER THE JOHNSTOWN FLOOD. The audience howled at the turn of the known expression.

In *The American Language*, HLM wrote thus (on p. 424 of the 2nd edn, 1921): 'It would be difficult to match, in any other folk-literature, such examples [of extravagant and pungent humour] as "I'd rather have them say 'There he goes', than 'Here he lies' " or "Don't spit: remember the Johnstown flood".'

don't strain yourself! 'C.p. sarcasm at slow, as if indifferent, co-operation' (Laurie Atkinson, late 1974): C20, perhaps earlier. I first heard it, *c.* 1913, in Australia.

don't sweat it! 'Take it easy – above all, don't worry!': American: since *c.* 1960. Recorded by *DCCU*.

don't take any wooden nickels! is described by W & F as 'a *c.* 1920 fad phrase' and glossed as 'Take care of yourself; protect yourself' (a wooden nickel having, of course, no legal value): but this US c.p. lasted right up to WW2 and dates, I suspect, since *c.* 1900. It was adopted by Canadians; Douglas Leechman, in May 1959, remarking in a letter to me, 'A c.p. of the last fifty years, and still heard occasionally'. And note that in Ring W. Lardner's *The Real Dope*, 1919, it occurs in Jack Keefe's letter of 16 May 1918, thus: 'In the mean wile' – until we meet again – 'don't take no wood nickles and don't get impatient and be a good girlie and save up your loving for me.' Cf **don't let anyone sell you a wooden nutmeg!**

don't take it out, Chiefie – I'll walk off. This Royal Navy c.p., dating since *c.* 1930 (? a decade earlier), is a seaman's conciliatory joke to the Chief Petty Officer after a reprimand.

don't take me up until I fall, an Anglo-Irish c.p. of late C19–20, is used 'when a person attempts to correct you when you are not in error' (P. W. Joyce, *English in Ireland*, 1910).

don't tear it, lady! was a C20 c.p. of *c.* 1910–40; originating, I suspect, among London stall-holders (e.g., Petticoat Lane and the Caledonian Market) and barrow boys and remaining a street witticism of rather vague meaning. Frank Shaw, in a letter dated 14 February 1969, sent me a bare notification of the phrase itself: and before I got round to asking him or, failing him, Julian Franklyn, also tremendously knowledgeable about such c.pp., both of them had died.

don't tell me! and **never tell me!** Don't tell me that – it's too silly (or too preposterous or too incredible) to believe: respectively mid C18–20 and, by 1935, slightly obsolescent; and C17–20 and, by 1935, extremely obsolescent and, by 1970, obsolete. The *OED* quotes Shakespeare in *Othello* and Foote (*don't ...* ').

don't tell *me* – I'll tell *you*! is either repressive or merely anticipatory – of someone clearly about to impart a piece of news or scandal already known to the speaker: since the latter half of WW2. (Frank Shaw, November 1968.) It soon came (*c.*

* His footnote: 'Saloons were open to men only. Spittoons everywhere!'

1950) to acquire the nuance 'I already know the answer, perhaps better than you do'. On 1 January 1969, a well-known diagnostician told me about one of his clients, a man self-confident and something of a know-all, who visits him several times a year and always initiates the encounter by saying 'Don't tell me – I'll tell you'. Contrast:

don't tell me – let me guess! This humorous anticipatory c.p. dates from c. 1940 and, in its early period, was often preceded by **no!** and occasionally by **now.** Also in the early days, the predominant form was ... *I'll guess.*

don't tell more than six. A jocularly roundabout way of saying 'Don't tell anyone!': Londoners': June 1937–August 1939. (I can no longer remember why, in the Supplement to *DSUE*, I could be so precise; there once existed an excellent reason.)

don't throw the baby out with the bath water is a c.p. often – since c. 1946 – addressed, in gentle warning, to theorists, esp. the theorists in politics and sociology, but also to those who carry some commercial practice beyond the bounds of good, or even of merely common, sense, and it springs immediately from the colloquialism *to throw the baby out with the bath water*, to go too far in reform-making. My loyal and learned correspondent (better, contributor) Ramsey Spencer compares the Ger. proverbial *Das Kind mit dem Bad ausgiessen,* which, he rightly hints, forms the origin of *to throw....*

don't turn that side to London. This commercial c.p., condemning either goods or persons, implies that in London only the best is wanted. Ware records it in 1909 and I'd guess that its approximate life began c. 1890 and ended in 1914.

don't wake him up! is enshrined in HLM, 1921. 'Poor fellow! He lives in the past – or in a pleasant day dream – or in a state of euphoria; and it'd be a pity to wake him.' Contrast:

don't wake it up! Don't talk about it – it's better to drop and forget the subject. In short, Let sleeping dogs lie! Australian, it dates from c. 1920 and was, by 1970, in an advanced state of decomposition.

don't want to know! In British jails of C20 this is a prisoners' plea of ignorance. It amounts to 'I don't know and I don't want to know – safer *not* to'.

don't wear it – eat it!, a US c.p. of very approximately 1930–45, was addressed to 'a sloppy eater' (Berrey).

don't worry – it may never happen is intended as salutary advice to the worried-looking or, still more jocularly, to the merely thoughtful-looking: since c. 1916. Current during WW1, but chiefly among civilians, was an elongated version, 'thought up' by one of the intellectuals of the day. Cf **don't worry your fat!**

don't worry – use Sunlight! was current during the first thirty years of C20 and was adopted from a famous advertisement for Sunlight Soap. (Collinson.) The late Alexander McQueen, that very erudite Englishman who migrated to the US, vouched, in a letter written in 1953, for its use by, or slightly before, 1905.

don't worry your fat! is crudely addressed to someone who is patently worrying: c. 1910–40. 'Don't lose weight by worrying!' Cf **don't worry – it may never happen!**

don't you fear! (or **don't fear!**) has two nuances: 'Take my word for it!' and 'Certainly not!': since c. 1870; by 1940, rather old-fashioned; by 1970, virtually obsolete. Cf **never fear!**

don't you forget it! See **and don't you forget it!**

don't you fret! (or **don't fret!**) You have no cause to worry – addressed sarcastically to someone worrying needlessly: late C19–20; by 1950, the former was decidedly old-fashioned, and by 1970, the latter was falling into disuse. Cf **I should worry.**

don't you know there's a war on? See **remember there's a war on!**

don't you wish you knew! Wouldn't you like to know? *or* I won't tell you: US: since c. 1920; by 1970, slightly obsolescent. (Berrey.)

don't you wish you may get it! was a c.p. of c. 1830–60; it means 'I don't think much of your chance of getting it' and therefore 'I'll bet you don't get it!' It occurs in R. H. Barham, *The Ingoldsby Legends*, Second Series, 1842 (see the quotation at **does your mother know you're out?**), and in a couple of the very early issues of *Punch*, i.e. in the early 1840s.

[**doubled over like a dog fucking a football** was, in WW2, a Canadian soldiers' c.p. variant, still literal, of *doubled right over* and therefore may, perhaps, be more sensibly regarded as a slangily earthy, ostensibly humorous, variant of the originating phrase.]

down in the forest something stirred; burlesqued as **down in the forest something's turd.** This domestic c.p., referring sometimes to incipient sexual desire in either partner or esp. in both, and sometimes to a consummated coition, dates from 1915, when Sir Landon Ronald's very popular song was published. A few years later (1920 at latest) the irrepressible Cockney parodied that c.p. by applying it to a bird's, mostly a pigeon's, droppings landed on someone, the remark being uttered by onlooker or, wryly, by victim.

down on his knees and at it! A male 'facetious exclamation at [the sight of] a man kneeling down to do a job of work' (Laurie Atkinson, late 1974); hence, a jocular reference to a man performing a marital duty: since the 1920s.

[**down the hatch!** is a drinking toast, or admonition, not truly a c.p. This remark applies to all such toasts. Cf **here's mud in your eye!**]

down went McGinty was an American c.p. of 1889–c. 1914. This was a song, words by Joe Flynn, who sang it with Sheridan in 1899 and thus fathered the c.p. (W. J. Burke.) Cf **up goes McGinty's goat.**

drag! – it's a and **what a drag!** It's a bore, a tremendous nuisance. What a bore *or* nuisance!: since the early 1950s, when it came to England from the US.

dressed up. See **all dressed up ....**

drop dead! and its variant, **why don't you drop dead!**, are likewise US in origin and, in US, date from the late 1930s (F & W's earliest recording is for 1951, but the longer phrase appears in Berrey, 1942). Only the terse, more telling, form migrated to England c. 1949, to become almost a status symbol of teenagers, probably via Canada, where well-established by c. 1946. It is only fair to the US and Canada to add that there, too, it was used mainly by teenagers; although, in all three countries rather old-fashioned by 1965, it was still being employed by British teenagers as late as 1974; not unnaturally, this particular callousness, being so vigorous and effective, was fostered by the film companies.

An illuminating late British example occurs in Paul Geddes's novel. *A November Wind*, 1970:

'I don't have to worry.' said Wetherton. 'You do.'

The man smiled briefly. 'Do you mind if I ask you a favour? Drop dead.' It wasn't mint fresh, but he said it well, even with panache.

Cf also this example from John Osborne's *Look Back in Anger* (produced 1956 and published in 1957), Act III, Scene i:

JIMMY: ... Let's have that paper, stupid!

CLIFF: Why don't you drop dead!

drop dead twice! intensifies the c.p. preceding this one: American: since early 1960s. Recorded by *DCCU*. Often 'initialled' *D.D.T.*

drop your traces and rest awhile, addressed to a coach- or a buggy-driver; **fall off and cool your saddle**, variants **get off and rest your hat** and **light and rest your saddle**, addressed to a horse-rider: Western US c.pp. of late C19–20, but rare even in the wildest and woolliest West, by 1945. (Berrey.)

dropped right in it, with preceding I stated or, at least, understood. I really fell in the shit!; occasionally 'I really did put my foot in it' – but mostly, 'I truly got into serious, or very awkward, trouble': since *c.* 1910; 'still heard on and off' (A. B. Petch, 4 January 1974).

dry up and blow away! Go away – don't bother me!: teenagers', esp. the coffee-bar set: *c.* 1957–9. A blend, probably inconscient, of the slang *dry up!* ('Stop talking!') and *blow!* ('Go away! Depart!'). Inherently artificial, this witticism soon perished. Recorded by Michael Gilderdale in his article, 'A Glossary of Our Times' in the *News Chronicle*, 22 May 1958.

Duchess! – ring up the, and, with the same meaning but from a different angle, **I must ring up the Duchess**. Applicable to the resolution of a doubt or to the solution of a problem.

this c.p. arose in January 1935 from the play *Young England*; originally and predominantly a society c.p., it had a very lively, yet very brief currency, for it was, by the end of 1936, already obsolescent and, by the outbreak of WW2, already obsolete.

duchess of deathless memory – the. See **hell! said the Duchess**.

dun is (but usually **dun's**) **the mouse** is both a c.p. and a quibble, made when someone says 'done'; when spoken urgently, it implies 'Keep still and quiet!' It was current *c.* 1580–1640. A mouse is dun-coloured and therefore, if still, hard to see. A later form (C17) is *dun as a mouse*, which seems to have arisen from a confusion of *dun's*: 'dun is', and *duns*: 'dun as'. (Apperson.)

[**Dutch have taken Holland – the**, is a mid C17–early C18 prototype of the proverbial *Queen Anne's dead* and is therefore not strictly a c.p.]

Dutchman if I do! – I'm a. See **I'm a Dutchman...!**

d'you know something? was adopted, *c.* 1945, from the US, where it had existed since *c.* 1930. It could, originally, have been prompted by the Ger. *Weisst du 'was* (short for *etwas*), 'Do you know what?' – and have come into US speech via the Ger. immigrants, as Foster suggests.

d'you mind? is the more colloquial form of **do you mind?**

d'you need (or **want**) **a knife and fork?** See **sort 'em out!**

d'you (occasionally **d'ye**) **want jam on both sides?** is a British Army c.p., essentially of WW1, although it lingered on, among the older men, into WW2; it was addressed to someone making an unreasonable request. (B & P.)

But the more usual – and general – form was *d'you want jam on it?*. Haven't you had enough? Aren't you satisfied? This seems to have been the earlier, perhaps an elaboration of *jam on it*, a most agreeable surplus – and common to all three Services – and lasting rather longer.

'e don't know where 'e lives. See **he doesn't know where he lives.**

'e dunno where 'e are! was a c.p., predominantly Cockney, of the 1890s; it was applied to a half-wit or, at best, a moron or, rather, to someone acting in such a way; and esp. to one who has lost his sense of reality. Julian Franklyn, who knew so much of and about the music-halls, once told me that this c.p. arose in a music-hall song: 'Since Jack Jones come into a 'arf a'nounce o' snuff, 'e dunno where 'e are. 'E's got the cheek and impudence to call 'ee's muvver Ma.' Frank Shaw (1 September 1969) adduces a variant – *she dunno where she are* – and thinks that this was a joke from *Punch*.

ears (put) back – get your. See **get your ears back!**

earwig! earwig! – often shortened to **earwig!** – 'Be quiet – there's someone listening': British underworld: c. 1830–1914 and perhaps later. It occurs in the invaluable *Sessions Papers* (which, incidentally, I was the first scholar to examine linguistically and systematically), 10 April 1849, thus, 'He said "earwig, earwig" ... they were then silent.' A pun both on the literal sense of *earwig* and on ear – cf the US underworld pun in (*Lake*) *Erie*, 'eary'.

easy as you know how or, in full, **it's as easy ....** It is simplicity itself – if you know how; in the RAF slang of WW2, 'It's a piece of cake'. It originated either in 1940 or, at the latest, in early 1941; by 1950, slightly obsolescent, and by 1970, virtually obsolete. (Wilfred Granville, near the end of 1968.)

easy does it! Take it easy – take your time!: since c. 1840; by 1940, obsolescent. Cf **softly, softly, catchee monkey.**

easy over the pimples! (or the **stones!**) Go more slowly! Be a bit more careful!: since c. 1870; by 1940, obsolescent; by 1970, obsolete. The former derives from a nervous youth's plea to a barber, the latter from a cry to a coachman driving fast on a bad road.

eat more fruit! was a c.p. of c. 1926–34. (Collinson.) From the famous trade slogan.

eat up – you're at your auntie's is a Scottish c.p. invitation to 'eat hearty': late C19–20. (Mrs M. C. Thomson of Bray-on-Thames, 15 January 1975.) Aunts being notably generous to their nephews and nieces.

education has been sadly neglected, mostly – and, as c.p., always – introduced by *your*. This is usually jocular but occasionally said in friendly seriousness, dating from c. 1905; and applied mostly to matters of quite unremarkable unimportance.

ee, it was agony, Ivy! 'A popular c.p. from the radio show, "Ray's a Laugh", late 1940s. It was uttered falsetto by a character addressed by "Ivy" as "Mrs 'Oskins"' (Paul Beale, 1 May 1975). Vernon Noble, on the other hand, remembers it as having never really 'caught on'. (21 April 1976.)

ee, what a do! – by 1965, seldom heard and, by 1976, dead –

enjoyed a brief popularity; it had originated in a gag of Rob Wilton's. (Vernon Noble, 21 April 1976.)

effort, St Swithin's! 'An urging, rallying cry, used by, I think, Joyce Grenfell in one of her games-mistress roles. It achieved a certain popularity at the time, late 1940s' (Paul Beale, 25 May 1975). *St Swithin's*, as used here, particularizes 'English girls' Public Schools'. Cf **jolly hockey sticks.**

eggs are cooked – the. That's done it! or 'His number is up': New Zealand: since c. 1910.

Egyptian medal. See **you're showing an ....**

eh? to me! – strictly **'eh?' to me** – **(why,) you'll be saying 'arse-holes' to the C.O. next!** 'A c.p. of jocularly dignified reproof' (Laurie Atkinson): RAF: since c. 1930.

eight eyes. See **I will knock out ....**

either piss (or shit) or get off the pot! See **shit – or get off the pot!**

elbow in the hawser – an, with introductory **there's** either stated or understood: a nautical c.p., applied to a ship that, with two anchors down, swings twice the wrong way, causing the cables to take half a turn round one another. (Bowen.) Since c. 1810 or perhaps 1800. It occurs in W. N. Glascock, *Sketch-Book I*, 1825.

elementary, my dear Watson! – occasionally distorted as **obvious, my dear Watson** – is an educated c.p. current throughout C20. 'I notice that the revival of interest in Sherlock Holmes – a play, books and a TV programme – has reintroduced "Elementary, my dear Watson". This must be one of the most persistent of literary catch phrases since Conan Doyle coined it' (Vernon Noble, 18 January 1974). It is not a literal quotation, for it rationalizes Arthur Conan Doyle's, '"Excellent!" I [Dr Watson] cried. "Elementary," said he [Sherlock Holmes]' in *The Memoirs of Sherlock Holmes*, 1893, in the story titled 'The Crooked Man', where also occurs 'You know my methods, Watson'. These two quotations and the resultant two c.pp. have generated the further c.p., **Sherlock Holmes!**, q.v.

A good supporting quotation is this, from Harold Brighouse's *What's Bred in the Bone*, performed in 1927 and published in 1928:

> JOAN: ... I knew from the moment we came in to-night that you couldn't intend to go on living here.
> ETHEL: Tell me, Sherlock. My name is Watson.
> JOAN: Your dress, my child. Your dress and this room. They don't match.

eleven o'clock and no poes emptied. 'Factory wit of mock dismay at being behind with work' (Laurie Atkinson, November 1969): late C19–20. But, in the form *no poes emptied, no babies scraped*, it is a man's jibe at woman's dismay at delay in her work, no beds made, no potatoes peeled.

Eliza smiles is a British, esp. an English, underworld c.p., dating from c. 1870–1910 and applied to a planned robbery that looks like being very successful. Eliza probably represents the generic servant girl – a class eminently serviceable to fore-sighted burglars. (*U.*)

Emden – the. See **didn't you sink the *Emden*?**

end is (or **end's**) **a-wagging – the.** The end of the job is in sight: naval: mid C19–20. According to the late Wilfred Granville, 'From sailing days when, after much "pulley-hauley", the end of a rope was in sight.'

end of the bobbin. See **that's the end of the bobbin!**

English as she is spoke. The broken English spoken by many foreigners; hence, as a c.p., the English spoken by the illiterate, the semi-literate – and the abominably careless: C20. With a pun on *broke* for *broken*, as we see from the short-lived variant (never a c.p.), *English as she is broke.*

enjoy your trip? See **did you enjoy your trip?**

enjoy yourself and have a go! Drive, so as to scatter the head (presumably the cluster of bowls or 'woods' at the Jack end): South African c.p. employed by players in the game of bowls: C20. (Professor Ashley Cooper Partridge in a letter dated 18 November 1968.) Cf **it's in your eye!** and **you're not here!**

enough said! is a c.p. of hearty agreement, both British (late C19–20) and derivatively US (C20), recorded by Berrey. Cf **nuff said!**

enough to give you a fit on the mat. Very amusing or laugh-able: non-cultured, non-aristocratic, non-upper-middle class: *c.* 1890–1920, then rapidly fading to complete obsoleteness by 1930. (W. L. George's novel *The Making of an Englishman*, 1914.) Cf the next, which is, in fact, its probable prompter.

enough to (or **it would**) **make a cat laugh.** It is extremely funny, very droll, ludicrous: C19–20. The US form – *teste* Berrey – tends to be *that's enough....* Recorded by Apperson, it verges on the proverbial.

enough to make my gran turn in her urn is applied to acts and attitudes that would have shocked grandma: since *c.* 1960 ('heard on and off, these permissive days': A. B. Petch in a communication dated 16 January 1974); notably lower- and lower-middle-class in origin and predominantly so in practice.

'ere! what's all this? Sometimes **'ere! 'ere! what's all this?** See **you can't do that there 'ere!**

Eric or Little by Little (or **little by little**) is a c.p. addressed to, or directed at, very shy, esp. sexually slow, youths; since *c.* 1860; by 1950, obsolescent, and by 1970, obsolete. It derives from the phenomenal popularity of Dean F. W. Farrar's novel of Public School life, *Eric; or Little by Little*, 1858, the antithesis of the sunny *St Winifred's; or The World of School*, 1862: *Eric* tells the story of a boy going slowly to the bad and ending tragically.

'e's lovely, Mrs Hoskins – 'e's lovely! 'From Ted Ray and Kitty Bluett in radio comedy series "Ray's a Laugh" late 1940s and 1950s' (Vernon Noble, 8 February 1975).

even blind Freddie wouldn't miss it. See **blind Freddie ....**

even the Admiralty can't boil you in the coppers or put you in the family way. Well, things might be worse *or* When things go badly, always remember this: naval: C20. (Rear-Admiral

P. W. Brock, in letter of late 1968.) An apt comparison is afforded by **they can make you do anything....**

even you had a mother once. See **you once had a mother.**

ever since Adam was an oakum boy. 'A colloquial Navy phrase to indicate that something goes back to ancient history' (F & G): mid C19–20; by 1950, obsolescent.

every barber knows that. That's common gossip: US: C20. (Berrey.) Implying that barbers are commonly the repository of gossip and rumour, whether at the strictly local or, preferably, at the national – or even international – level.

[**every bullet has its billet.** ' "Every bullet has its billet" ... may be true, but fortunately it is usually in or on the ground. But if you met "A bullet (*or* a shell) with your name on it", then you were a dead man' (B & P, 1931). The quotations in the *OED* and esp. in Apperson show that this is a proverb, not a c.p.]

every day and in every way, to which, in the original form, is added **I am getting better and better.** This, the slogan enunciated by Dr Coué, almost immediately became a fashionable c.p. of 1923–6; the c.p. accompanied the fad's meteoric decline, which began very soon indeed after his death in 1926.

Emile Coué, born in 1857, was, in brief, the Fr. originator of a psychotherapeutic system of autosuggestion called, for short, Couéism. In 1910 he established, at Nancy, a clinic where his system might be practised; his patients were in-structed to repeat as frequently as possible his formula, which his enemies slightly misrepresented as a slogan, 'Day by day, in every way, I am getting better and better.' He lectured in both England and the US. His teachings are summarized in the book translated as *Self-Mastery through Conscious Auto-suggestion,* published on both sides of the Atlantic in 1922. In its wake came such expositions and popularizations as Frank Bennett's *M. Coué and His Gospel of Health* and Cyrus Brooks's *The Practice of Autosuggestion by the Method of Emile Coué,* with a foreword by Coué himself, both published in 1922; and during the next three or four years several other writers 'jumped on the band wagon'. While I attended the University of Oxford in 1921–3, a vast battery of wit and witticism was, in 1922 onwards, turned on the numerous dis-ciples: and the formula-become-c.p. had what it would be cowardly to describe as other than a furore, for it amounted to far more than a mere vogue.

'Up like a rocket and down like a stick': Coué's claims were falsified by sadly inadequate results in physical betterment.

every hair a rope yarn; every finger a marline-spike; every drop of blood, Stockholm tar is 'an old nautical phrase [or, rather, a trio of linked phrases] descriptive of the real dyed-in-the-wool sailor of the windjammer era' (*Sailors' Slang*): only very approximately *c.* 1850–1910.

every home should have one, originally an advertising slogan, has, both in Britain and in the US, been applied – since, I think, the 1920s – to all sorts of things, ranging from common objects to babies to non-material things, as in Ivor Drum-mond, *The Power of the Bug*, 1974:

'With a new car we are clean. We go a little further away, get a new car, and make a plan.'

'Yeah, we want one of those,' said Colly. 'Every home should have one.'

every little helps – as the old woman said when she pissed in the sea is a c.p. uttered when one urinates into sea or stream, hence to any tiny contribution to a cause, esp. a subscription or a street, or other, collection of funds: mid C19–20.

every night about this time is an Australian c.p., dating from c. 1955 and originating in radio announcements and referring to habitual sexual intercourse.

every one a coconut! derives from a fairground barker's cry, uttered to induce the crowd to join in the coconut shy, where the prize awarded for success was a coconut. In the late C19 and right through (although decreasingly) to this day, the 'event' or competition has existed: and very soon, it became a c.p., by being applied in other ways and acquiring the general sense of 'You've gained a success every time you try', as, for instance, a famous novelist with successive novels; I heard it, as a c.p., used by an educated and highly reputed professional man, as late as September 1974.

every picture tells a story. This, the exact wording that accompanied 'the distressing pictures of human suffering amenable to treatment by Doane's Backache Kidney Pills, supplies us with the useful Every picture tells a story – often used derisively of anecdotal paintings' (Collinson) and of anyone clutching his lumbago-afflicted back: C20; obsolescent by 1935 and, excepting among those of fifty or over, obsolete by 1960. These advertisements appeared regularly in such magazines as *The Strand*, above all, and *The Windsor*. The picture showed a person bent over with pain. The c.p. had an occasional variant, **oh, my aching back!** – which was resuscitated, with a new bearing, during the latter half of WW2 (so see **oh, my achin' back!**).

every time he opens his mouth he puts his foot in it. Both British and US (Berrey), this c.p. dates from c. 1920 (I first heard it in the early 1920s) or perhaps a decade earlier. By a pun on *put one's foot in it*, to make a social mistake.

everybody works but father, originally an English song, published in the 1890s, was, in US, revived by Jean Hayes and sung by Lew Dockstader. Edward B. Marks, *They All Sang*, 1934. (Thanks to W. J. Burke.)

everybody's doing it, doing it, doing it characterizes the years 1912–14 at least, up to 4 August; it comes from a wildly popular song, the reference being to the ragtime dance known as the Turkey trot, 'the rage' in 1912–13 – and is recorded in, e.g., Robert Keable's wildly popular novel, *Simon Called Peter*, 1921. Ragtime, precursor of jazz, arrived c. 1910: and this particular dance was extremely popular during the war years 1914–18, esp. among naval and army officers.

The words come from Irving Berlin's song, *Everybody's Doing It Now*, copyrighted in New York in 1912. The chorus runs: 'Everybody's doin' it, doin' it, everybody's doin' it now'; and the song ends: 'Everybody's doin' it now'.

everything in the garden's lovely! All goes well: C20; slightly obsolescent by 1935, yet, among people aged (say) fifty or more, still far from obsolete in 1974; for instance I heard a 'real Cockney' cleaner on the British Museum staff use it, in the portico, on 28 February 1974. It was prompted by **everything is nice in *your* garden**, q.v. below, and a fairly early Commonwealth example occurs in G. B. Lancaster's *Jim of the Ranges*, 1910 (at p. 110). Cf **everything is lovely and the goose hangs high.**

everything in the garden's lovely – except the gardener 'refers to Dad, who often looks like a scarecrow when he is gardening' (A. B. Petch, 16 September 1974): suburban witticism, at almost any social level below that of the upper-middle class, and manifesting an affectionate malice: since c. 1945. Obviously an elaboration of the preceding entry.

everything in the shop window – nothing in the shop. All shadow and no substance – all promise and no (or very poor) performance: since c. 1920. It is applied to, e.g., those girls who do their damnedest to catch a man, get him, but lack the qualities to keep him, for, having displayed all their wares, they have exhausted their repertoire and lack the permanent, retentive graces.

everything is George. All goes well, esp. for me: a beatnik c.p. of c. 1959–70. Why George and not Tom or Bill or John, I don't know. An origin as topical and fortuitous as this one is usually impossible to ascertain – unless one's exceptionally lucky.

everything is lovely and the goose hangs high. All goes well: US rural: since c. 1860; obsolescent by 1940, but not yet obsolete in 1976. Farmer glosses it, '…all is going swimmingly; all is serene'; *D.Am.* cites the shortened phrase, *the goose hangs high*, as meaning 'prospects are bright; things look encouraging' – and adds that no satisfactory origin has been found. The reference seems to be to a plucked goose hanging high and well out of a fox's reach.

everything is marvellous for you. See **you have it made.**

everything is nice in *your* garden, originating in society and passing well beyond it, was, in 1896–c. 1910, 'a gentle protest against self-laudation', as Ware, who supplies an anecdotal origin, put it in 1909; he also developed the link with **everything in the garden's lovely.** Note that whereas *everything is nice. …* is always used ironically, the later c.p. is rarely so used.

everything is (or **everything's**) **under control**; also **everything under control.** A Services' c.p., dating from c. 1930 and applicable to any situation where things are 'ticking over nicely'. (Recorded by H & P.) Noël Coward, in *Peace in Our Time*, performed and published in 1947, has, in Act I, Scene iv, this piece of dialogue:

FRED (*brokenly*): Stevie … How did you get here? It's all too much to believe – all in a minute.…
STEVIE: It's all right, Dad – everything's under control.

everything on top and nothing handy. See **just like a midshipman's chest ….**

excrementum bellum vincit is a humorously erudite WW2 army officers' 'translation' into L. of **bullshit baffles brains.** Cf **illegitimis non carborundum.**

excuse me! I beg to differ: South African: since c. 1930. (Ashley Cooper Partridge, 13 August 1974.)

excuse me reaching! A lower-middle-class c.p. that has, in C20, been uttered when one reaches for something at the mealtime table; by 1935, slightly obsolescent – and by 1950 obsolete. With a pun on *retching*.

excuse my abbrev (pronounced *abbreve*) – **it's a hab.** A c.p. either addressed to or, at mildest, directed at someone addicted to trivial and constant abridgement; literally, 'Excuse my *habit* of *abbreviating*.' It belongs to a very brief period indeed: *c.* 1910–12. Such abbreviations were much commoner *c.* 1890–1912 than before – or since.

excuse my dust! Excuse me, please; I'm sorry: US, originally Western: C20. From the inconvenience caused by a vehicle to the occupants of the one immediately following it along a dusty road. My friend Professor John W. Clark's comment, made on 5 December 1968, is: ' "I'm 'way ahead of you, and you're not very bright". Possibly antedates the automobile, but I doubt it. At any rate, common for at least 50 years, [that is, since *c.* 1920] and even now, when few roads are dusty.'

excuse my (or **the**) **French!** See **pardon my French!**

excuse my pig – he's a friend! 'A c.p. used when a companion disgraces one by, e.g., breaking wind while drinking at the bar' (Paul Beale, 1 October 1974): since *c.* 1950. By jocular inversion of *friend* and *pig*. Cf **is he with you?** and **you can't take him anywhere**.

extra two inches you're supposed to get after you're forty – the. This Armed Forces' c.p. of 1939–45 referred to an entirely imaginary phallic compensation for the years that have gone before and perhaps been wasted or, at the least, misused. One of the numerous myths that sex, whether male or female, has evoked.

eye! eye! In his popular and very readable *The Underworld*, 1953, Jim Phelan, who knew what he was talking about, writes, 'Every time Alf said "Eye-eye", it was a call for vigilance'. Dating since *c.* 1920, this British underworld c.p. derives from – in the sense that it stands for – 'Keep your *eye*, yes your *eye*, on' somebody or something.

eye it – try it – buy it! is a US trade slogan (for Chevrolet automobiles, to be precise) that, W & F tell us in 1960, 'finds some generalized use [for] looking at, trying, or sampling anything': since the early 1950s, but by 1970 obsolescent.

eyes and ears of the world – the. An Australian c.p. dating since *c.* 1950 and ironically addressed to – or aimed at – someone who speaks as if he has all the latest information. It comes from the motto of Gaumont British News. (Barry Prentice.)

eyes in the boat! Keep your eyes on the job: nautical: late C19–20. Watch your oars – not that pretty girl over there.

eyesight. See **it will do ....** and **there's eyesight in it**.

f.h.o. See **family – hands off!**

face would stop a clock. See **her face would ....**

fair cop! See **it's a fair cop.**

fair do's, mostly written **fair doo's.** At first, it was written *fair dues*, as in C. T. Clarkson and J. Hall Richardson, *Police*, 1889, 'Now then, fair dues; let everybody be searched. I have no money about me' – so it must have gone back to 1880 or earlier. After *c.* 1930, the original two-worder became a four-worder: *fair doo's all round.*

fair enough! is elliptical for 'Well, *that*'s fair enough' – 'that sounds plausible', *or* 'I'll accept that statement or offer', but also used as a question (common among instructors), 'Satisfied?' *or* 'Convinced?' *or* 'Is that agreeable to you?' It dates from the 1920s, and until *c.* 1946 it remained a predominantly Services', esp. RAF, c.p., which, *c.* 1940, spread to Australia and New Zealand.

fair, fat and forty goes back much earlier than I should have thought: recorded in anon., *The New Swell's Night Guide*, 1846, it may safely be originated in the raffish 1820s (Egan, Moncrieff, *et al.*). A vulgar parody, current – although not very widely so – during the 1940s but mercifully killed by WW2, was *fair, fat and farty*, which, perhaps earthily true, fell rather short of being *très galant*.

fair to middling is a mainly Australian jocular reply to 'How are you?'. It dates from *c.* 1945; the jocularity takes the form of a pun, 'fair' and 'middling' being synonymous.

fall into a cart and **fall into the shit.** See **he could fall....**

fall off and cool your saddle. See **drop your traces....**

fall out and dust your medals! 'A derisive dismissive sometimes used to end an argument among Army contemporaries, who may not in fact have any medals to dust' (Paul Beale, 23 June 1974): post WW2.

fall through the trap door! is an occasional variant, likewise US and dating not earlier than 1904, not later than 1916, of **break a leg!** 'I have heard [it]. Sothern once tried for the first 15 minutes of a play to whisper to Julia Marlowe that the trap on that stage was faulty; she thought he was trying to "upstage" her and kept shying away' (Joseph T. Shipley, 16 August 1975). Edward Hugh Sothern (1859–1936), born in New Orleans, the son of English actor Edward Sothern (1826–81), 'led', in Shakespearean drama, with Julia Marlowe (retired 1924) at the Lyceum Theater in New York during the periods 1904–7 and 1909–16. Cf **break a leg!**

fallen away from a horse-load to a cart-load dates *c.* 1650–1850, is recorded by Grose (1796) and earlier by S, and by Ray, and somewhat ironically means 'grown suddenly fatter – and very fat'.

family, hands off! *or* **family, hold off**, but – for obvious reasons – customarily abbreviated to *f.h.o.*, is a domestic c.p. employed by the middle class as a warning that a certain dish is not to be eaten by members of the family when guests are present, there being insufficient for all: mid C19–20. The variant *family, hold back*, abbreviated to *f.h.b.*, was very usual before WW2. The corollary was *m.i.k.* (more in kitchen).

famous last words! 'A catch-phrase rejoinder to such fatuous statements as "Flak's not really dangerous"' (PGR): RAF, thence to the other two Services: since 1939 and, 1945 onwards, among civilians. A jocular, when not a jeering, reference to the 'famous last words' of History, e.g. 'It can't – or it could never – happen here' or, notably, 'in this country', whichever country the speaker or writer belongs to; see the separate entry at **it can't happen here.**

Famous last words originated as 'a satirical comment on the kind of feature once popular in such magazines as *Great Thoughts* and *Titbits* and was directed especially at such daring statements as could easily be refuted with proof often tragic' (Frank Shaw, in letter dated 1969).

A neat example occurs in Terence Rattigan's comedy, *Variation on a Theme*, 1958, Act I, Scene ii:

ROSE: No, it's red, impair and my age tonight. At chemmy it's bancos. The banks won't run.

MONA: Famous last words.

The phrase was adopted by the US, as in Hartley Howard, *Million Dollar Snapshot*, 1971:

'If you had any sense you'd ask me to stick around until you whistled up some reinforcements.'

'No need for that. Sergeant Goslin will be back soon.'

'Famous Last Words,' I said.

This c.p. has become so embedded in colloquial English that the words can be employed allusively, as in Karen Campbell's *Suddenly in the Air*, 1969: 'I smiled. "We're doing remarkably well." These were famous last words.'

In short, one of the most memorable and trenchant of all c.pp.

far better off in a home, mostly introduced by **you'd be**, is a rather vague c.p., dating from *c.* 1920 and presumably aimed at an institutional home, esp. a State-provided home for old people. There was a popular song with that refrain.

farewell and a thousand, with a comma or a dash after *farewell*. A thousand times farewell! *or* Farewell – and a thousand thanks! *or* Farewell – and the best of luck! Belonging, so far as I've been able to discover, to the very approximate period *c.* 1550–1640. It occurs in, e.g., George Peele's play, *The Old Wives' Tale*, 1595 (lines 248–9 in A. H. Bullen's edn):

ERESTUS: ... Neighbour, farewell.

LAMPRISCUS: Farewell, and a thousand.

Alexander Dyce compares Thomas Middleton's 'Let me hug thee: farewell, and a thousand' in *A Trick to Catch an Old One*, 1608. Semantically, cf the slangy C20 *thanks a million!* (times, not dollars).

fart's the cry of an imprisoned turd – a. Dating from *c.* 1930 (or a little earlier), this c.p., as essentially poetical as it is superficially coarse, either satirizes – pungently yet benevolently – the condition of one who, having just broken wind, might properly go to the water-closet or unrepentingly apologizes for having broken it. Clearly an allusion to the cry of a bird imprisoned in a cage.

fate worse than death – a, the rape of a female, or even a genteel seduction (probably since mid C18), became, in the raffish period, 1880–1910, a callously jocular, then, 1910 onwards, a merely humorous, often derisive, c.p. applied to girls willing enough, and finally, c. 1915, applied by girls themselves – or, come to that, women – to intercourse between the unmarried or between a married and an unmarried person.

When used literally, it is a cliché.

father keeps on doing it! comes from a popular song, dates from c. 1920, refers to a man with a repetitiously large family.

father's backbone. See **I was doing it when . . . .**

fattened for the slaughter, usually preceded by **being**, refers to a 'rest' period, i.e. one – a week, ten days, a fortnight – spent out of the line; esp. for the very lucky, at a rest camp: jocular among infantrymen, mostly on the Western Front in 1917–18.

favour. See **look! do me a favour, will you?**

fear God and tip the crusher! is a naval lower-deck motto of C20. A *crusher* is slang for a Regulating Petty Officer, a Warrant Officer in the naval police. (PGR.)

fed at both ends, as they say – in full, **she should get a bit fatter, fed . . .** – is a low c.p., applied to a slim bride and dating from before 1958, when I first heard it. Contrast:

feed the brute!, introduced by one or other of these: 'Always remember' or 'All you have to do is . . .', or 'The secret is . . .' or 'The great, or main thing, is to . . .', none of which, obviously, can be part of the c.p. itself, far the commonest form being simply *feed the brute!* This feminine c.p. is used either by mothers to daughters about to marry or by wives, esp. if young. Often there's the overt meaning 'That'll keep him amiable, content, happy – and you too'. The covert implication is that a well-fed man is the more readily amorous and the more capable of attending to his wife vigorously and frequently. This, one of the best-known and widest-spread of all c.pp., arose in *Punch*, 1886 (vol. LXXXIX, p. 206), where, to a young wife complaining of her husband's absences from home and of his neglect of her, a widow speaks these fateful words. But it is no longer apprehended as a famous quotation.

Felix keeps on walking. In Collinson we read of 'the popular phrase "Felix keeps on walking" from Felix's loping walk in the picture-house' – the reference being, of course, to Felix the Cat. This c.p. belongs to the 1920s and has a variant: *Felix kept on walking*, which Benham gives as originating in 1923.

Ferguson. See **you can't lodge here . . . .**

fetch your bed and we'll keep you! is a C20 c.p. addressed either to an over-frequent visitor or 'sometimes among workingmen to one who is always hungry and who can eat up any spare bait that is going around' (Albert B. Petch, September 1946).

fie upon pride when geese go bare-legged! A proverbial c.p.

retort made to a lowly person showing undue pride: late C17–18. (BE.)

figures can't lie – but liars can figure is an Australian c.p. rejoinder to the cliché, *figures can't* (or *don't*) *lie*: since c. 1960. (Barry Prentice, 1 May 1975.)

find, feel, fuck – and forget is the navy's mainly lower-deck sexual motto, dating from c. 1890 and often, in C20, alluded to as *the four F method.*

fine and large. See **all very fine and large.**

fine day for the (young) ducks – a, and **fine weather for ducks** and **great weather for ducks.** A jocular way of referring to an extremely wet day: respectively mid C19–20, but obsolete by 1920 – late C19–20 – and since c. 1820. The second is the commonest; Dickens used the third in 1840. (Apperson.)

fine fellow. See **he's a fine fellow.**

fine morning to catch herrings on Newmarket Heath – a, is the mid C17–mid C18 equivalent of **fine weather for ducks** above. (Apperson.)

fine night to run away with another man's wife – a. An elaborate way of saying 'It's a fine night': late C16–early 19. Apperson cites Florio, Rowley, S (in the variant *a delicate night . . . .*).

fine weather for ducks. See **fine day . . . .** above.

finger of suspicion points at you! – the. This cliché of the old-style (say c. 1870–1940) crime story has, since c. 1925, become a humorous c.p., often employed in the most trivial circumstances. (With thanks to Paul Beale for the reminder: 23 March 1975.)

fings ain't wot they used ter (or **t'**) **be.** Things aren't what they used to be (as if they ever had been!): this Cockney form of a very general impression and conviction going back perhaps centuries became a c.p. only in 1960 when Frank Norman's play, *Fings Ain't Wot They Used t' Be*, with lyrics by Lionel Bart, achieved a considerable success.

To quote only one novel, Karen Campbell's *Suddenly in the Air*, 1969, offers this:

'Then I've a few dollars I managed to hang on to. But even they aren't worth what they used to be.' I hummed 'Fings ain't what they used to be' under my breath.

fireman – save my child! 'I've often heard this derisive cry but am not sure whether in England or in Canada' (Douglas Leechman, December 1968); both, I suspect: C20. Probably from the Surreyside melodramas of late C19–20. I've not heard it since the 1920s, but think that it was probably current up to WW2.

fire's gone out – the, literally 'An engine has stopped', was a Fleet Air Arm saying that, in that Arm, became a c.p.; the phrase probably arose during the 1930s, but it didn't rank as a c.p. until during WW2 and didn't last for many years after it. An example of characteristically British *sang-froid* and manly meiosis. (PGR.)

first catch your hare is the c.p. counterpart of that sage and salutary proverb which runs *don't count your chickens before they are hatched,* which Barry Prentice, in reference (1 May 1975) to Australian usage, interprets as 'Make sure that you have the raw materials before starting' an enterprise. As a c.p., it goes back to well before 1900 and is the very usual misquotation of a piece of culinary advice given to house-wives by 'A Lady' (Mrs Hannah Glasse) in her book, *The Art of Cookery*, 1747: 'Take your hare when it is cased' or skinned; but who was the first person effectually to misquote, we do not know.

first hundred years are the hardest – (US) (or **worst**) (British) – **the**, belongs to the C20. Berrey glosses it thus: 'the first difficulties are the greatest'; perhaps rather 'the earliest-encountered difficulties seem to be the worst'; cf this predominantly civilian c.p. with the next entry and also with **the first seven years are the worst** and **they say the first hundred years ....**

first million is the hardest – **the**. The first million dollars are the hardest to make or, as Berrey puts it, 'the first earnings are the most difficult': since *c.* 1920.

first on the top-sail and last on the beef-skid was, in the Royal Navy of *c.* 1860–1920, applied to an able-bodied seaman; it meant that he was first-class, 'first on the job and last at the mess table'. (Ware.)

first seven years are the worst – **the** – often introduced by **cheer up!** – was a British Army c.p. of late 1915–18. Glossed thus by John Brophy in B & P: 'Ironic with a jocular despair. ... Usually either Job's comfort to a grouser or a whimsical encouragement to oneself; it was rarely heard before that 1916–17 winter which drove the iron fairly into men's hearts and souls.'

Paul Beale (17 February 1975) says: 'A rueful c.p. concerning, for example, the 2-year National Service [in Britain for some years, after WW2]; "Oh, well, never mind, they say the first two years are the worst". The time-measure is, of course, variable.'

For a much less bitter, much more generalized, reaction to one aspect of *la condition humaine*, see **first hundred years ...** above.

first term too early, second term too cold, third term too late is an Australian, esp. a Sydney, undergraduates' c.p., dating from *c.* 1925. Supplied by Mr Barry Prentice, who has also supplied the comparable *freshers work first term, nobody works second term, everybody works third term*, which originated at about the same time. (I never heard either when, 1914 and 1919–21, I was a Queensland undergraduate.)

first turn of the screw cancels all debts – **the**. A 'catch phrase used when someone is worried about his dues ashore. A cheer-up from a messmate' (Wilfred Granville, in letter dated 22 November 1962): naval: since the late 1940s. The screw mentioned is, naturally, the ship's: and the sentiment is so optimistic as to verge upon the mythical.

first up, best dressed is an Australian domestic c.p.: C20. Employed 'where members of a family use each other's [or one another's] clothes' (Barry Prentice, *c.* 6 March 1975).

firty-free fevvers on a frush's froat, sometimes preceded by **free fahsend free 'undred and**, dates apparently from the 1920s and is, in Mr Laurie Atkinson's compact language, 'the two-way dialect speech class chaffing formula of and by Cockneys'. An analysis of this c.p., both semantically and phonetically, would either cause any self-respecting phonetician *un véritable frisson d'horreur* or afford him a saturnalia of sensual recognition.

fish and find out! is an evasive reply to a question one doesn't

wish to answer: since *c.* 1890; by 1940, becoming obsolescent, yet, by 1975, not quite obsolete. At once pert and pointed.

fish – or cut bait! Please finish what you're trying to do, or else stop, so that someone else can try or get the chance to do it: US: 'since *c.* 1876; archaic and dial[ectal]' (W & F, who, 1960, compare **shit or get off the pot**).

fishing. See **what shall we do....**

fit where they touch; fits where it touches. See **it fits....**

five eggs, and four of them rotten. See **putting your two pen-n'orth in.**

flag of defiance is out – **the**; also **the bloody flag is out**. He has a red face caused by drink; also, he is drunk: nautical: late C17–early C19. (BE; Grose.)

flare up! This c.p. of *c.* 1832–45, and then, for perhaps twenty years probably a nostalgic survival, was a cry of joy or triumph or jubilation or, indeed, of joyous defiance to the world in general or to a particular situation: 'Let 'em all come!' Mackay says, 'It took its rise in the time of the Reform riots, when Bristol was nearly half burned by the infuriated populace. The flames were said to have *flared up* in the devoted city.' (Mackay's long passage on the phrase is well worth reading.) In the c.p., the sense is sometimes that of the verb *flare up* and sometimes that of the noun *flare-up*.

flattery will get you nowhere. Don't go to the trouble of trying to persuade me by flattering me: esp. from women to men, and perhaps commoner in US than in Britain and the Commonwealth ('This is a very common c.p.': Barry Prentice); 'unheard by me before 1950, but probably going back to *c.* 1945' (John W. Clark, 22 October 1968). In Ellery Queen's *A Fine and Private Place*, 1971, I note:

'You're a clever adversary indeed. One of the cleverest in my experience.'

'Flattery will get you nowhere, Queen,' the murderer said. 'Gallop along on your fairy tale.'

The phrase has become so much a part of the British colloquial composite that it occurs thus in a sports page title of an article – 'Flattery Will Get You Nowhere' – in the *Evening Standard* of 29 March 1974. There is even a humorous variation, *flattery will get you everywhere* – not very common.

Fleet's lit up – **the**. 'Not used now, but never forgotten,' writes Frank Shaw, November 1968. 'BBC announcer, ex-R.N. officer, hiccuped this and nothing else in Spithead BBC broadcast from battleship, King George V Jubilee, 1935. Sensation.' Another correspondent, however, attributes it to John Snagge in 1937. Often until WW2 heard in hilarious reminiscence and reference.

follow the man from Cook's! 'Come along, follow me; etc. All my life!' says Douglas Leechman, in early 1969, thus placing it as British, C20, and Canadian, since *c.* 1908. The reference is, obviously, to Cook's celebrated tours.

follow your nose! – often supplemented with **and you can't go wrong** or **you are sure to go straight** – is a non-cultured c.p. addressed to someone asking the way: since before 1854. Other forms, e.g. *... and you will be there directly* (C17) are earlier; moreover, the phrase was clearly adumbrated in C14. (Apperson.) BE glosses *follow your nose!* thus: 'Said in a jeer to those that know not the way, and are bid to smell it out.' Contrast:

follow your own way – you'll live the longer occurs in S, Dialogue I, and seems to be a c.p. of *c.* 1700–60.

Foo was here was, in 1941–5, the Australian equivalent of **Kilroy was here**. In the Royal Australian Air Force, Foo was a favourite gremlin whose name may have come from a very popular US cartoon strip, 'Smokey Storer', where the titular character used *foo* as a stop-gap name for anything of which he couldn't be bothered to remember the correct name.

fool at one end and a maggot at the other – a; and **a fool at the end of a stick** are mid C18–early C20 'gibes on an angler' (Grose, 1788).

fools seldom differ. See **great minds think alike**.

for half a farthing I'd do it, I'd need very little encouragement to be persuaded to do it: *c.* 1860–1914. (Baumann.)

for kicks. See **I only do it for kicks**.

for king and cunt is a Services' reply to the question, 'What are *you* fighting for?': earlier half of C20. With an obvious pun on 'for king and country'.

for my next trick, followed by a significant pause. Uttered by someone, whether the culprit or one of his 'audience', who has just made a mess of things: since the early 1930s, for certain, but probably since *c.* 1900. 'From the patter of stage magicians, who traditionally and blasphemously attribute the *gaffe* to Jesus Christ' (Frank Shaw, November 1968). As Mr Shaw phrased it some six months later (1 April 1969): 'Comic apology after a minor mishap. From music-hall acrobat or juggler or magician. World of entertainment. Hence in more general use for *any* minor mishap.'

for show and not for blow. This Australian c.p., meaning 'for display rather than for use', was originally applied to a neatly folded handkerchief in the breast pocket and, when used literally, was not, of course, a c.p. at all; only when, *c.* 1950 onwards, it was applied to comparable things, did it achieve the dignified status of a genuine c.p.

for the birds. See **that's for the birds**.

for the hell of it and its elaborations, **just for the hell of it** (US, hence also British) and **for the sheer hell of it** (British only). Simply – or merely – or just – for the pleasure of doing it, experiencing it, seeing it, etc.; to express a reckless independence: originally – ?c. 1910 – US, hence also – ?early 1940s – British; of the elaborations, the former since *c.* 1930 in the US and since *c.* 1945 in Britain, and the latter (...*sheer*...) since *c.* 1950. (Based, for US usage, on a letter, dated 5 June 1975, from Harold Shapiro.)

The best British example I happen to have encountered of *just for the hell of it* occurs in Norman F. Simpson's *The Hole*, performed in 1958. Early in this diabolically clever surrealist play Lorna remarks, referring to boxer Spider, 'I know people who claim to have seen him hold his opponent off with the ace of diamonds just long enough to reload his dice, and then perhaps he'd huff him two or three times just for the hell of it, and then you'd see it! Then you'd see the real *coup de grâce* ...'

for the widows and orphans – it's; or, in full, **all the money I take goes to the widows and orphans**. A cheapjacks' and market grafters' cynical c.p., dating from late C19 or very early C20; by 1960, slightly outmoded and by 1970, virtually obsolete. (A. B. Petch, April 1966.)

for this relief – much thanks! is the c.p. form, applied in late C19–20 to a much-needed urination, of the quotation from Shakespeare's *Hamlet*, Act I, Scene i, lines 8–9:
For this relief much thanks; 'tis bitter cold,
And I am sick at heart
The relief of a military guard.

for those few kind words – many (occasionally **my best**) **thanks**. (Only the *many* form is strictly a c.p.) A jocular, often 'hammed up' but, no less often, ironic, exclamation of gratitude, esp. from one who is or has very recently been, suffering much misfortune. Cf:

for what we are about to receive. Of this mid C18–20 Royal Navy c.p., C. S. Forester, in *The Happy Return*, 1937, has written, '"For what we are about to receive—," said Bush, repeating the hackneyed blasphemy quoted in every ship awaiting a broadside.'

From the Grace said before meals, 'For what we are about to receive, the Lord make us truly thankful'.

for you the war is over was, 1940–5, a c.p. used by British prisoners of war in Italy, where they were thus addressed, on their arrival, by the It. authorities. It was used jocularly.

for your information is a sarcastic reply to an impertinent question asked by a nosy busybody: since *c.* 1955. (Albert B. Petch, 10 January 1974.) With ironic allusion to the legitimate queries of commerce – and bureaucracy.

fore you listed. Before you enlisted: a variant of **before you came** – or **come-up**.

forget it! – a variant of **and don't you forget it!** – occurs in S. R. Strait's 'Straight Talk' in the *Boston Globe* in *c.* 1917. But it also, since the 1930s in the US (Berrey, 1942) and derivatively since *c.* 1950 in Britain and the Commonwealth, has a different sense, 'It's not worth worrying, or even thinking, about'. Among US negroes, it 'implies that the listener has not properly understood what is in question or being explained; *example*, "if you think this dictionary was easy to put together, *forget it!*"' (CM).

forgive me for swearing! See S, Dialogue I: 'MISS: [*stooping for a Pin.*] I have heard 'em say, a Pin a-Day, is a Groat a Year. Well, as I hope to be married (forgive me for Swearing) I vow it is a Needle.' This C18 c.p. means no more than 'if I may mention it'. Contrast rather than cf **pardon my French!**

fork in the beam! is a late C19–20 naval c.p. – and a firm order from the sub-lieutenant for all junior midshipmen to retire from the gunroom, which they thereupon did, to remain outside until recalled. '*Fork in the beam* was merely an intimation that there was too much noise being made, and the banishment a hint for them to keep quiet in the future' (*Sailors' Slang*). Granville explains that there was an old gunroom – i.e., midshipmen's mess – 'custom of placing a fork in a deck beam above the sub-lieutenant's head, which was a sign that he wanted privacy'.

formerly I could eat all – but now I leave nothing. S, Dialogue II, has:
LADY ANSW[ERALL]: God bless you, Colonel, you have a good Stroak with you. [That is, you're a notable trencherman.]
COL: O Madam, formerly I could eat all, but now I leave nothing; I eat but one Meal a-Day.

MISS: What? I suppose, Colonel, that's from Morning till Night.

The precise meaning: 'My appetite remains excellent.' Tone: waggish. Date: C18–19.

forty-acre field. See **wouldn't be seen crossing a....**

forty-foot pole – wouldn't touch it with a. See **wouldn't touch it ....**

forty pounds of steam behind him; occasionally preceded by **with**. This Royal Navy c.p., dating from *c.* 1900, is applied to someone receiving an order to go immediately on draft, and derives from the fact that, at one time in the Navy's history, safety valves 'went off' at a pressure of forty pounds. (*Sailors' Slang.*)

four exits from jail is a US convicts' c.p. of C20. 'Spindrift' – an English ex-member of a gang – has, in *Yankee Slang*, 1932, explained it as 'Pay out, run out, work out (serve the term), and die out – meaning to die in [jail]'.

fourteen hundred (new fives). There's a stranger in the Exchange: a Stock Exchange warning cry, dating from *c.* 1870. For a very long time, the Stock Exchange had only 1,399 members; by 1930, the cry was obsolescent. Why 'fives'? Perhaps because one of its slang senses was 'a hand' (four fingers plus thumb).

foxes always smell their own hole first. A c.p., dating *c.* 1890–1914 and uttered by the culprit trying to shift the blame of a wind-breaking on to the first person complaining.

free, gracious and for nothing is a c.p. variant, would-be witty, of the colloquial *free, gratis and for nothing*, and lasting only *c.* 1885–1900.

free trade or protection? A raffish c.p., applied since *c.* 1905 to women's knickers or panties loose and open or tight-fitting and closed. By the early 1970s, obsolescent.

French! – excuse (or **pardon**) **the** or **my.** See **pardon....**

fresh hand at the bellows – a; often **there's a ....** A sailing-ship c.p. of mid C19–early C20; said when, esp. after a lull, the wind freshened.

fresh kiss, fresh courage. In *Yours Unfaithfully*, written by Miles Malleson and published in 1933, a writer speaks thus in Act III:

STEPHEN ... Damn it! No, Alan! I'm not going to have 'special treatment' as a writer! Temperament, and all that. There's a proverb [*it isn't one*] among 'business' men in the 'city' – have you ever heard it? – 'Fresh Kiss, Fresh Courage'. Business men! They aren't supposed to deal in temperaments. 'Fresh Kiss, Fresh Courage.'

Apparently *c.* 1925–39.

freshers work first term. See **first term ....**

fret! – don't (you). See **don't you fret!**

friend has come – my (little) and **I have friends to stay** are female euphemistic c.pp., announcing that the menstrual period has begun: C19–20; by 1935, obsolescent, and by 1950 obsolete. A variant, dating since *c.* 1830 and obsolete by 1950, was *I have my auntie* – or *grandmother* – *to stay*. Cf **(the) captain is at home.**

[**from Alice Springs to breakfast time**, 'from one end of the country to the other, everywhere' (from Alice Springs, 'the isolated chief town of Central Australia'): Australian, the quotation coming from the glossary to Alexander Buzo's *Three Plays*, 1973; it occurs in *Norm and Ahmed*, performed in 1968. Half-way between a c.p. and an ordinary slang phrase.]

from marbles to manslaughter. A raffish London c.p. of *c.* 1830–70. In *An Autobiography*, 1860, Renton Nicholson wrote: 'About the year 1831 or 1832, play [i.e., gambling] first became common. Harding Ackland ... an inveterate and spirited player at anything, "from marbles to manslaughter", as the saying is, opened the first shilling hell in the metropolis.'

from the sublime to the gorblimey. 'General, as an occasional [c.p.] variant of [the cliché] *from the sublime to the ridiculous*' (Paul Beale, 15 April 1975). Since *c.* 1950 – if not a decade or two earlier. (Thanks to Oliver Stonor.)

from Tinker to Evers to Chance – but usually **from** is omitted – was a US baseball c.p. referring to a clever 'play' concerted by three players, the names deriving from the trio that had devised and perfected it. For a while, it became so widespread that the following allusion in 'The Score in the Stand', part of Robert Benchley's *Love Conquers All*, 1923, must have been clear to many readers:

SEVENTH INNING: Libby called 'Everybody up!' as if he had just originated the idea, and seemed proudly pleased when every one stood up. Taussig threw money to the boy for a bag of peanuts who tossed the bag to Levy who kept it. Taussig to boy to Levy.

Apparently it has been current since *c.* 1920; and on 9 November 1968, John W. Clark comments thus, 'Certainly is used generally of any triumph achieved by adroit and quick-witted co-ordination of two or more persons. ... Everybody understands its origin in baseball.'

In Franklin P. Adams occur the touching lines:
These are the saddest of possible words:
'Tinker to Evers to Chance'
....
....
Words that are heavy with nothing but trouble:
'Tinker to Evers to Chance'.

He adds a gloss:

Joe Tinker, Johnny Evers and Frank Chance were members of the Chicago Cubs, the first at shortstop, the second at second base, and the third at first base. With a runner at first base, Tinker would stop a ground hit, toss the ball to Evers, and Evers would whip the ball to first before the man who hit the ball could get there, making a double play which was frequently repeated. [Cited in *BQ*.]

fry your face! See **go and fry your face!**

fuck a day keeps the doctor away – a. See **shit a day ....**

fuck anything – he'd. See **he'd ....**

fuck 'em all! expresses a (usually cheerful) defiance to the world in general or to this or that circumstance or situation in particular: since *c.* 1919. In the famous old army song *Bless 'Em All*, the original words were *fuck 'em all*. Cf:

fuck 'em all – bar six; and they can be the pall-bearers. 'I first heard this expansive expletive or c.p. in 1960,' writes Paul Beale on 22 August 1974. It arose *c.* 1944 and was adopted from the US Army. Mr Beale tells me that James Crumley's novel about the US Army, *One to Count Cadence* (1969), 'carried as a prologue what the author labelled an "old Army prayer"':

Fuck 'em all bar nine –
Six for pall-bearers,
Two for road-guards,
And one to count cadence.

fuck 'em and leave 'em is 'proverbially the correct way to treat women. Very commonly used' (a correspondent, 24 September 1973): late (?mid) C19–20.

'fuck me!' said the Duchess – more in hope than in anger, current since *c.* 1910, is a variant of the much more frequent **'hell!' said the Duchess.**

fuck that for a comic song! (or a **top hat!**) I emphatically disagree; I strongly disapprove: sporting world and raffish world: C20. (Frank Shaw, 1 April 1969.)

Literally, *that's* no comic song or *that's* not a real top hat.

fuck that (or **this**) **for a lark!** 'Expression of dissatisfaction and disgust at some uncongenial task or situation' (Paul Beale, 1 October 1974): C20. 'There is also a military variant: *fuck this* [or *that*] *for a game of soldiers!*' (ibid.): since the late 1940s.

fuck you, buddy, I'm shipping out is an American version of the next. Recorded by *DCCU*, 1971.

fuck you, Jack, I'm all right.

> Among inverted sayings ... one was general and typified concisely the implied and the often explicit arrogance of' many senior officers towards the ranks. This was (the first word is a polite synonym for the one actually used) [in those days, *fuck* could not be printed] –
> Curse you, Jack, I'm all right!

Thus John Brophy in Appendix A, Chants and Sayings, of B & P, published in 1930 – and over thirty years later, 'consolidated' and revised as *The Long Trail*. In the 2nd edn, Brophy adds: 'The original form, i.e. in 1914, was:

> Dieu et mon droit,
> F— you, Jack, I'm all right.

pronounced with a strong Cockney accent, *droit* rhyming with *right*. By 1916, the original saying had been almost completely forgotten.' But this longer form was, I'm pretty sure, an elaboration of the at first nautical *fuck you, Jack, I'm all right*, which seems to have arisen *c.* 1880.

The spread of that phrase to the army caused the unbeatable and ever-ingenious Royal Navy to coin a new c.p. of its own: *fuck you, Jack, I'm inboard* or, 'in other words, "Pull the ladder up, Jack, I'm all right"' (PGR).

Not to be outdone, the RAF, having adopted *fuck you, Jack, I'm all right*, decided to invent its own c.p. This they did – *fuck you, Jack, I'm fire-proof*, i.e. invulnerable; an officers' pun on this: *per ardua asbestos*.

The original phrase has, since WW2, experienced many euphemisms, allusions, translations, absorptions, mostly as the result of its own virility and trenchancy, but, in part, also as a result of the tremendous success of the film, *I'm All Right, Jack*, starring Peter Sellars and Ian Carmichael, 1960. A good example of euphemism appears in Terence Rattigan, *Variation on a Theme*, 1958, near the end of Act I, where Ron says, 'But that's how I was told when I was a kid – in this world, Ron boy, they said, you've got to work it so it's "F.U., Jack, I'm all right", or you go under.'

An illuminating allusion-*cum*-absorption occurs in Laurence Meynell's excitingly entertaining novel, *Virgin Luck*, 1963: 'I could afford to have no ill feelings. I had made the bus; she hadn't. She was Jack; I was all right.'

fucked and far from home, feeling utterly miserable, mentally and physically: an army c.p. of WW1, but believed to have had a civilian existence since *c.* 1905 or a little earlier: originally, it was supposed to represent the despair of a girl seduced and abandoned – and stranded. The earliest form of the phrase, recorded in 1899, seems to have been *fucked-up and far from home*.

full march by the [e.g.] **Crown Office – the Scotch Greys are in!** The lice are crawling down his, e.g., head: a low c.p. of *c.* 1800–30. This particular regiment was chosen for no better reason than that body lice are predominantly *grey* in colour. (Recorded *LB*, which, published in 1811, would have more fittingly been called Grose's *Vulgar Tongue*, 4th ed.)

full of fuck and half-starved, often preceded – but occasionally followed – by **like a straw-yard bull**, was, *c.* 1870–1940, a low but friendly reply to 'How goes it?'

full of larceny, often ushered-in by **it's**, is a US theatrical c.p., 'said of an act which has stolen its "gags"' (Berrey, 1942): apparently dating from the 1920s.

Funf speaking! or, originally and better, **this is Funf speaking!** At the second programme – 26 September 1939 – of 'It's That Man Again', later to be known as 'ITMA', 'the supreme telephone character of them all – the notorious FUNF ... the embodiment of all the nation's spy-neuroses, a product of the times ... an ineffective, comic spy' arrived, to become immediately famous. 'Those blood-curdling tones, so soon to be heard being reproduced all over the country, were actually obtained by Jack Train speaking into a tumbler.' The name *Funf*, pronounced *foonf*, derives from the Ger. for 'five': the producer, Francis Worsley, had overheard his small son counting in Ger. and decided that this was precisely what he needed.

In his book, *Itma*, published in 1948, Frank Worsley continues:

> Although his first series was a comparatively short one, finishing in February, 1940, it was really the FUNF SERIES, for very soon after his introduction he became a nation-wide craze. Children everywhere began playing Funf, just as they do now with Dick Barton, and no person with a family reputation for wit would dream of prefacing a telephone conversation with any other words than 'This is FUNF SPEAKING!' ... Everywhere one went, Funf kept cropping up. In the black-out two people would collide. 'Sorry. Who's that?' one would say, and like a flash would come the answer 'Funf!' Perhaps a workman would accidentally drop a brick down near a mate below. ''Ere, who threw that?' and from somewhere up in the scaffolding a raucous voice would bellow 'Funf!'

The heyday of this c.p. was brief: late 1939–all 1940. But throughout the rest of the war, it continued to be one; and it would occasionally be heard at least as late as 1950.

funny peculiar or funny ha-ha? is the c.p. comment upon the frequent statement that 'Something funny happened today': since *c.* 1924. One of the earliest dependable examples of the c.p. occurs in Act III of Ian Hay Beith's *Housemaster*, 1938. An Australian example occurs in Alexander Buzo's *Rooted*, at Act I, Scene iii. Prompted by the dual-sense *funny* – causing amusement, and the derivative *funny* – odd, strange, peculiar, puzzling, with the '*funny* bone' probably intervening. Cf **ha! ha! ha!**

It is inevitable that there should be variations, as in Nichol Fleming, *Czech Point*, 1970:

> She planted a kiss on my cheek. The car almost ran off the road.
> 'You are a funny creature.'
> 'Funny ha-ha or funny peculiar?' I asked.
> 'A bit of both.' We both laughed.

funny thing happened on my way (mostly **to** a named locality) – **a**; or, rather, the c.p. – as opposed to the 'free' localization – is **a funny thing happened on my way to the Forum**; dating since 1966 and deriving immediately from these words used as the title of the film first shown in 1966 but ultimately from such statements as 'A funny thing happened while, *or* when, I was doing or being something', as in '... while I was having my bath'. A very early printed use of the 'free' composition occurs in that exceptionally alert novelist John D. Mac-Donald's *One Fearful Yellow Eye*, 1966: 'A funny thing happened to me on my way to the hotel room.'

Cf the preceding entry.

fusilier. See **you're a Fusilier!**

future. See **no future ....**

gall not yet broken or, in full, **his gall is not yet broken.** A British underworld c.p. that, used in mid C18–mid C19, was applied ironically to a clearly dispirited, even despairing, prisoner, either by the warders or by his fellow-prisoners. (Recorded by Grose, 1785.) A pun on the long-obsolete *gall,* or *galls,* courage.

galley down your back. See **put a galley** ....

gamble on that!; originally, **you can** – or **may** – **gamble on that.** A c.p. synonym of 'assuredly!' or 'certainly!': adopted *c.* 1870 from the US, where used since before 1866, when humorist Artemus Ward used it; in Britain, obsolete by 1960 and obsolescent by 1940, and in US apparently obsolete by 1940, obsolescent by 1920.

game and the name – **the.** See **if I have the name** ....

Gamp is my name and Gamp my natur' is, literally, a familiar quotation from Dickens, but if another surname is substituted, the quotation, no longer such, becomes a c.p., educated and, indeed, cultured, of late C19–20 (cited by Collinson) but rather less used after, than before, 1940.

gangway for a naval officer!; or **gangway! make way for** .... The latter is the English, the former the Australian and New Zealand, WW1 c.p. F & G give the longer form only and gloss it thus: 'An expression, heard sometimes among New Zealand Army men, anywhere and on any occasion, meaning "Get out of the way", "Stand back", "Clear a passage" ' – but chiefly the third. ' "Gangway!" is ordinarily a common warning call on board ship' for bystanders to make way for someone, or a party, engaged on the ship's business. In B & P, John Brophy writes, 'GANGWAY FOR A NAVAL OFFICER! – A facetious method of asking for a passage through a group of soldiers, or of announcing *sotto voce* the approach of some self-important officer or NCO.'

garbage in – **garbage out.** 'The computermen's c.p. *par excellence.* Now so well known as to have the recognized abbreviation GIGO (pronounced with a long *i*). It means simply that if one feeds into the machines, for processing, material that is rubbish, then rubbish will be churned out in return. From US and current since the widespread use of data-processing machines' (Paul Beale, 25 May 1975).

gassed at Mons (and **on the wire at Mons**). See **hanging on the wire** and **Mons** ....

gate's shut, short for **my gate's shut,** means 'I'll say no more'; 'I have no more to say': Australian: since *c.* 1920. See D'Arcy Niland, *Call Me When the Cross Turns Over,* 1958:
'No,' she insisted. 'I want to know.'
'No good prodding me. My gate's shut.'
Of rural origin.

Gaw, or **Gawd, cast me** – **don't ask me!** A horse-racing c.p., dating from the late 1940s. In the *Sunday Telegraph,* 7 May 1967, in an anonymous article its author says, 'An expression by a racing chap, such as "Gaw-cast-me-don't-ask-me"

means blood-pressure soaring. It usually denotes that a fancied horse has fell over or something – says Danny' (who, on the inside, is telling the reporter, who, relatively, is on the outside). A sort of rhyming slang: indeed *cast* probably rhymes on the illiterate *ast,* ask.

Gawd forgive him the prayers he said! He did curse and swear! This, according to Ware in 1909, is an evasive Cockney comment: *c.* 1880–1930.

gee, lookit! This Canadian children's c.p. of astonishment, or of excited interest, was adopted, *c.* 1950, from the US, where current since the middle 1940s. Dr Douglas Leechman, writing in May 1959, adds, 'I recently read the next step: "Oh, lookit at that!" ' By itself, *lookit,* means 'look here' and presumably slovens *look at it.*

gentlemen present, ladies, usually preceded by **there are** or **there're,** is a jocular, yet also satirical and slightly censorious, variation – dating from 1945 – of the like (*there are*) *ladies present, gentlemen,* so please mind your language.

gently Bentley! – Take it easy! *or* Gently does it – was current *c.* 1945–50 and was taken from a radio show of the middle 1940s. (Wilfred Granville, late December 1968.) Paul Beale tells me that **gently Bentley** comes from 'Take it from here' (BBC radio), with Joy Nichols, Jimmy Edwards and Dick Bentley; J.E. used to growl it at D.B. whenever the latter became excited.

George! – **let's join,** and **where's George?** were a pair of linked c.pp. that originated, in 1935, in advertisements set forth by Messrs Joseph Lyons, who, in elucidating the mystery, state that George is *at Lyonch* and that George has *gone to Lyonch* or lunch at a 'Joe Lyons's'. This *George* may be regarded as typical of any middle- (though not upper-middle) class householder, esp. if he is married; it had earlier been, as it still is, a conventionalized, rather plebeian, English form of address to a stranger: cf the US *Mac.*

Both of these phrases lasted only for the years 1935–6; and *where's George?* – consecrated in Benham – almost immediately came to be applied to any male person noticed as being unexpectedly absent. Messrs Lyons's advertisement-pictures showed a pathetically vacant stool or chair.

get a bag! is a cricket spectators' cry to a fielder missing an easy catch, mostly in Australia and New Zealand, late C19–20. The implication is twofold: that he should be the team's twelfth man, who carries the bag, but also and predominantly that, if he were to hold out an open and empty bag instead of his bare hands, he'd stand a much better chance of making the catch.

get a horse! According to Mr Norris M. Davidson, a retired radio commentator on music, including opera, and very widely read, who was born *c.* 1908, this
was a common American phrase in my childhood, when the motor car or automobile, as we called it, was a novelty.

The roads not being paved were full of mud holes; tires were apt to burst, engines conked out and publications like *Life*, *Puck* and *Judge* were filled with illustrations about stranded motorists. Many showed the car being towed ignominiously by a horse. Urchins would shout 'Get a horse!' at every daring motorist. *Punch* used to be filled with similar illustrations, but I'm not sure whether the English lads used this phrase. One would think they would have. 'Get a horse!' is sometimes heard even to-day. [Letter dated 3 November 1968.]

The c.p. has a fairly common variant, *hire a horse!* In December 1968, Mr W. J. Burke wrote: 'Obsolete. Phrase used in disparagement of early automobiles.'

get a load of that! (or ... **of this!**) Just look at that!; Just listen to this!: both were originally US, dating from the 1930s, and both phrases bore both senses: adopted in Britain *c.* 1943.

get a number! See **get some service in!**

get along with you! and **go along with you!** Be quiet and stop talking nonsense! Stop flattering me – stop fooling me!: used playfully and jocularly or, at the very least, good humouredly. The former, used by Dickens in 1837 (*OED*), arose *c.* 1830; the latter, *c.* 1850.

get away closer! is, as Ware coyly puts it, an 'invitation to yet more pronounced devotion': late C19–20; obsolescent by 1935 and virtually obsolete by 1945. At first a costers', it very soon became a general Cockneys', c.p.

get back into your box! We've heard enough from you, be quiet: originally (1880s) US, it was anglicized by *c.* 1900. Apparently it comes from the stables.

get back to your kennel! See **back to the kennel**.

get fell in! fall in!: among NCOs, it amounted to a c.p. – grammatically interesting, because, from being a mere illiteracy, it became consecrated; originally and always army, it spread to the other Services. (PGR.)

get in, knob, you're posted! An RAF c.p., uttered when one has heard of an imminent posting to another camp or district and is gaily determined to have a last fling, usually sexual: 1939–45. Then mostly historical (*knob* being slang for the *glans penis*). Cf the low c.p., **get in, knob, it's your birthday!**, in joyous exclamation at the sight of intimate female flesh: army: C20. Also cf **you wouldn't knob it!**

get in there! was, *c.* 1930–50, a US Negro c.p. – a 'command to become active toward a positive end' (CM). It derives from:

get in there and pitch! 'Instead of dreaming and endlessly talking, take an active physical part in the effort, the attempt, the struggle' – or, more generally, 'Stop talking and work or act!' A US c.p. of C20, from the game of baseball.

get in there, Murdoch! 'was a catch phrase in my younger days; and I believe it had something to do with a popular footballer' (Vernon Noble, 12 February 1974): *c.* 1920–35.

get inside and pull the blinds down! Get out of the public view and hide in shame!: a Cockney c.p. that, *c.* 1860–1940, was addressed to a poor horseman. (Recorded both by Ware and in Benham.)

get it! is 'a cry of encouragement to one engaged in doing something positive and exciting' (CM): US negroes': 1920s–

50s. Make sure you get what you want *or* Do what you intend.

get lost! Oh run away and stop bothering me! Adopted from the US, *c.* 1944 in Australia, from US Servicemen, and *c.* 1949 in Britain. For an English example see Dominic Devine, *Dead Trouble*, 1971:

> Sarah kept pace with her. 'I need your help, Betty,' she said.
> 'Get lost.'

Also Canadian, with variant *go and get lost*: 'of long standing' (Douglas Leechman, January 1969).

get Maggie's drawers! See **give him Maggie's drawers!**

get me, Steve? See **got me, Steve?**

get off and milk it! 'Shouted by schoolboys at passing cycling-club riders. (1950s),' says Mrs Shirley M. Pearce (23 January 1975), who continues:

> *up, up, up!* was a similar cry, but was also uttered by groups of sports cyclists when passing members of the more sedate CTC (Cyclists' Touring Club). 1950s.
> *King of the Road!* was an advertising slogan of, I believe, Lucas cycle lamps and dynamos. This would be shouted at lone racing or sports cyclists or at the leader of a bunch of touring cyclists. The same slogan [the first of the three] was used to embarrass large-breasted lady cyclists, as the connection between the shape of the Lucas dynamo lamp and the breasts of the lady in question was supposed to be obvious. 1950s.

get off me barrer! is purely Cockney; a comic ending 'to fit any number of music-hall songs. ... On chromatic scale, very roughly goes CBCED. I'd date its origin with *good evening, friends* at 1880s; and its currency stretches to the present. Both are a pleasant self-parody of fairly simplistic group melody-making' (Cyril Whelan, 17 February 1975). But it more probably dates from late 1940s or early 1950s, when used by a radio comedian – ?Arthur English.

get off my back! and **get off my neck!** The former means 'Stop being a nuisance! Leave me alone!'; the latter, 'Stop trying to bluff *or* fool me!' The former, Australian, dates from *c.* 1940, and is recorded in the entertaining *AS*; the latter, mostly English military, dates from *c.* 1915 and derives from the synonymous *oh, Gertie, get off my neck!* – a predominantly Cockney c.p. of *c.* 1905–15.

get off your knees! is a Services', but esp. RAF, c.p., which, when directed by a NCO to an airman, signifies that the latter's job seems too much for him or that he is just plain lazy, but which, when spoken by a friend, was an encouraging 'shout to a comrade coming in tired from a march, or showing similar signs of distress' (PGR): since *c.* 1920. Behind the impatience lies the encouragement of 'You're *not* beaten to your knees'. The RAF occasionally employed the variant: **get off your chin-strap!**

get out! Stop flattering me! Tell that to the Marines: the former sense, used predominantly by females, the latter by males: since *c.* 1830. Dickens was one of the earliest to honour it in print.

get out and get under! was 'heard by my father in the Sheffield Empire *c.* 1895–1900, when the motor car began to appear' (Lawrence Smith, 26 March 1976). Apparently it survived up to WW1 and after; for Smith, on 12 March 1976, recounts that he heard it, during the late 1940s, in Australia, where. after being literally applied to the need to get under a car or a truck and see, then if necessary repair what was wrong, it 'caught on' as a c.p. and, perhaps independently, also in Yorkshire at least. But it wasn't only a Yorkshire and Australian c.p., as Ramsey Spencer makes clear in this excerpt from some notes dated 22 March 1976: 'An elaboration of *get out!* especially in the Cockney form, *git out an' git under!* From a briefly popular song, *Get Out and Get Under the Moon, c.* 1910.' Vernon Noble, 30 March 1976, writes, 'The date I have for the song is 1913. ... The song tells of a man taking his girl for a ride, and the car breaking down....

"He'd have to get under, get out and get under" [it]. It was a very popular music-hall song, and **get out and get under** was a catch phrase right into the First World War.' The date 1913 is supported by James Laver's *Edwardian Promenade*, 1958. It looks, therefore, as if the two songs reinforced each other, as frequently happens.

get out and push! is derisively addressed to a motorist whose car keeps on stalling: since *c.* 1920; little heard since *c.* 1960.

get some dirt on your tapes! Get some experience as an NCO – esp., before you start throwing your weight about: Services': since *c.* 1920. Cf:

get some service in! and **get some time in!**, often shortened to **get some in!**; and **get a number!**, the last being the most insulting: Services' c.pp., dating from *c.* 1920 – although the last may date from *c.* 1917.

get stuck in! 'A form of exhortation used by New Zealand Rugby supporters in addressing the players, means "Play much harder". Used also in other games, and in general contexts, e.g., when a job is being done. The idea seems to be that adhesiveness connotes vigour and enthusiasm. In common use since about 1920' (Arthur Gray, in a list of New Zealand c.pp. he sent me in late March 1969). Still current in Australia, this c.p. has migrated to Britain.

get (often **git**) **the ambulance!** An urban c.p. addressed to a drunk person: 1897–*c.* 1940. (Ware.)

get the cat to lick it off! and **try a piece of sandpaper!** Unkind advice to youths with down on their cheeks or their upper lip: C20; but little heard since WW2.

get the drift? Do you understand what I'm saying?: US: since the late 1920s. (W & F.) From 'the (general) *drift* of the conversation'. Cf **got me, Steve?**

get the lead out of your pants! is the US 'pop' musicians', but also a general US, slangy c.p., synonymous with **get stuck in!**: since *c.* 1930. (Berrey.)

The phrase soon became reduced to *get the lead out*, of which, on 17 February 1975, John W. Clark writes: 'Universal; though always humorous; recognized as vulgar, but used by educated people – to each other only, however – as a kind of *healthy* vulgarism.' On 20 May 1975, he added the 'definition', 'Get up and get busy', and the gloss, 'It originated (I *think*) in the language of sergeants (perhaps especially drill sergeants) in Hitler's war.'

get the shilling ready! Prepare to subscribe!: 1897–8, esp. with reference to the *Daily Telegraph's* shilling fund for the London hospitals, one of the charities characterizing the sixtieth year of Queen Victoria's reign. (Ware.)

get up, Joe! is the c.p. involved in 'asking a fellow "viper"

to accept a marijuana cigarette' (the US Senate Hearings, *Illicit Drug Traffic*, 1955). For how long the phrase was current, I lack any evidence.

get up them stairs! A Services', perhaps esp. RAF, c.p. addressed by his comrades to a man (mostly if married) about to go on leave: since *c.* 1940. Before the phrase achieved widespread use and radio renown, i.e. in 1942, **Blossom** – generic for a woman – either preceded or followed the rest.

A valuable sidelight on the vitality of this c.p. occurs in Margaret Powell, *The Treasure Upstairs*, 1970: 'So I told her a thing or two I'd seen going on on the backstairs between the men of the house and the housemaids and parlour-maids. It wasn't romantic love I told her about, it was plain, straightforward "Get up them stairs!"' And Paul Beale, writing on 11 December 1974, remarks that it 'has lasted well'.

get wise to yourself! Don't be ridiculous – grow up! This US c.p. goes back to *c.* 1910, if not earlier. (Berrey.) Cf **why don't you get wise ....**

get with it! Be alert to – or conversant with – or understanding of and sympathetic to – the current state of affairs or condition or information: US: since *c.* 1950; adopted by Britain, as well as the Commonwealth, *c.* 1960. To *get with it* is to make oneself, to be, familiar with life as it is lived right now.

get you! (emphasis on *you*) and **he's got ten bob each way on himself** are female teenagers' 'deflaters' addressed to conceited young men: *c.* 1957–9.

get (or **go and get**) **your brains examined!** is either derisive or disparaging, or both, and dates from *c.* 1920, the former, and from *c.* 1925, the latter.

get your ears dropped! A facetious Canadian c.p., dating since *c.* 1955 and addressed to one whose hair is so long that it hides the ears. (Douglas Leechman.)

get your ears put back! Get your hair cut! – or, rather, keep your hair closely trimmed: the army in WW1. Cf **get your hair cut!**

get your eye in a sling! – a proletarian c.p. of *c.* 1890–1930 – was, in effect, 'a warning that you may receive a sudden and early black eye, calling for a bandage – the sling in question' (Ware).

get your feet wet! was 'originally said to a timid bather. Universally understood and used, as a c.p., and as an imperative, usually addressed to someone faced with a task he is fearful of' (John W. Clark, 28 October 1968): US: C20.

get your finger out! is a variant of **take ....**

get your hair cut! was a 'non-U' c.p. of *c.* 1882–1912; Dr Douglas Leechman judges its heyday to have been *c.* 1900. (B & P; Benham.) It has the variant *go and get your hair cut*, as in Collinson, who adds, 'From a song, I think'; Benham prefers an origin in the London streets; it could be both. My friend Jerry Burke (W. J. Burke) directs me to two passages in A. A. Milne's *Autobiography*, where, at pp. 27 and 85 of the US edn, 1939, the author, referring to the period 1882–93, has some interesting things to say about this c.p.; including a suggestion that he himself and his middle-class exact contemporaries may have inspired the music-hall song. Vernon Noble tells me that it comes from a song with that title sung by George Beauchamp, a famous comedian of the late Victorian music-hall.

get your knees brown! 'Men with Overseas Service to their credit tell Home Service chaps to do this' (H & P): since *c.* 1925.

get your knickers untwisted! – often preceded by **you want** (i.e., need) **to** – is a male c.p., dating from *c.* 1950, and it means, in general, 'You should clarify your ideas', and, in particular, to do this in order to extricate yourself from a troublesome impasse.

get your steel helmets! (or **tin hats!**) is the army's counterpart (1940–5) to the RAF's *line!*, 'That's a piece of line-shooting'; 'often accompanied,' as John Bebbington, librarian, tells me, 'by the gesture of handle-turning, like that of a street organist, to the tune of da-di-di-da'.

getting a big boy now, i.e. of age, is 'applied satirically to strong lusty young fellows' since the 1880s, Ware tells us, and that it comes from the 'leading phrase of the refrain of a song made popular by Herbert Campbell'. But it is also used defensively by a man made to feel that he is being excessively mothered and patronized.

getting a big girl now. See **you're getting…**.

getting any (or **any lately**) or **enough?** is an Australian male c.p., dating from *c.* 1930 and used mostly by manual workers, esp. on one meeting another; it implies, 'Have you "made" any girls lately?' Sidney J. Baker, 1959, lists these 'formulas of reply': *climbing trees to get away from it* – *got to swim under water to dodge it* – and *so busy I've had to put a man on* (*to help me*): all of which sound like 'line-shoots' to end all 'line-shoots'.

ghost walks on Friday – the; the ghost does not walk; when will the ghost walk?; has the ghost walked yet? There is – or is not – any money for salaries and wages; when will there be – has there been – such money? These are theatrical c.pp., dating from the 1840s; the first printed recording was in *Household Words*, 1853. The origin: Shakespeare's *Hamlet*, Act I, Scene i.

Friday is the traditional pay-day in the theatre. The related **what time's Treasury?** is clearly derivative; it dates from *c.* 1870.

gi' us a kiss and call me Charlie! is applied to 'one who sets about a job or embroils himself in argument without knowledge or understanding or with wrong-headed ideas' (Laurie Atkinson, late 1974): since *c.* 1920.

gi' us y' hand! Among men, a jocular reply to solicitous 'How do you feel (, Jock)?': imitation Scottish: 1941–5, mostly in the Armed Forces. (Laurie Atkinson, late 1974.)

giddy little kipper (or **whelk**) is a Cockney c.p., dating from the 1880s and addressed to another or to oneself in approbation of the clothes one is wearing, esp. on a festive occasion; it became obsolete by 1940 at latest.

gift of the grab – (he) has the. He is successfully 'on the make'; he is making easy money: since the late 1940s. An easy pun on *the gift of the gab*. (A. B. Petch, 16 September 1974.)

giggles nest? – have you found a. See **have you found…**.

gimme! gimme! gimme! Literally 'Give me – give me – give me', it characterizes the attitude of the taker, not the giver: since *c.* 1960. Originally US, it was duly adopted in Britain, where the attitude is equally common. (Mrs M. C. Thomson of Bray-on-Thames, 15 January 1975.)

Ginger, you're barmy! is a good-humoured streets' and, in general, non-aristocratic c.p. of C20's first decade; Vernon Noble (30 March 1976) thinks that it originated in a music-hall song *Barmy* = mentally deficient, crazy. A 1940s–50s schoolchildren's cry addressed to any red-headed male was … – *you ought to join the army*.

'gip' – quoth Gilbert when his mare farted was a C17–18 c.p. addressed to one who is 'pertish and forward'. It occurs in Howell's collection of proverbs, 1659, and it had the variant noted by Ray in 1678: '*gib with an ill rubbing' – quoth Badger when his mare kicked*. (Apperson.)

girdle? … See **ne'er an M by your girdle?**

girls are hauling on the tow-rope – the, is 'an old navy expression applied to a ship coming home to pay off' (F & G): *c.* 1870–1914.

git the ambulance! See **get the ambulance!**

give her twopence! was an Australian c.p. of late 1945–7 (the cost then rose) – 'used on sighting a beautiful female child, i.e. Give her twopence to ring you when she is sixteen' (the age of consent). (Barry Prentice.)

give him a card! Just hark at him boasting!: naval: since *c.* 1940. Legend has it that, in eastern Mediterranean waters, early in WW2, it was customary to pass to anyone boasting of his exploits a card bearing the comforting words, 'Carry on! I'm a bit of a bull-shitter myself.' By 1970, obsolescent.

give him a rolling for his all-over! A Cockney c.p., punning on and synonymous with 'Give him a *Roland* for his *Oliver*', i.e. tit for tat: *c.* 1890–1914. (Ware.)

give him Maggie's drawers! Perhaps more frequently **get Maggie's drawers!** A US army (and then also Marine Corps) c.p.: C20.

Originally it referred to the use of a red flag which was waved in front of the target to indicate a miss. At one time, it had a limited usage away from the rifle range to convey the idea that the teller of a tale had failed to make a point and was hooted down in derision; [or] that the listener to a tale had failed to understand or get the point being made; that someone had made a mistake, or that someone had failed to achieve his objective. [Colonel Albert Moe, 15 June 1975.]

give him the money, Barney. In a letter dated 18 January 1974, Vernon Noble writes:

This was for a long time after the war [WW2] a phrase introduced by Wilfred Pickles in the very long-running 'Have a Go' radio broadcasts and repeated by millions of people. The 'Barney' referred to was Barney Colehan, producer of the show in BBC North Region, where it originated, and the man who handed out the money prizes to contestants in the simple general knowledge contests.

give it a drink! 'A cat-call of disapproval directed at a bad singer or actor' by the audience: C20. (Granville.)

give it a name! See **name yours!**

give it a rest! For heaven's sake, stop talking – or, indeed, making a noise of any kind!: C20. From **give us a rest** below. Cf:

give it air! Stop talking nonsense! A US c.p., mostly in student use, of the early 1920s. (McKnight.)

give it to the Belgians! was, among New Zealand soldiers serving in WW1 – more precisely in the latter half of that war, the humorous advice offered to a comrade either complaining about the food or his clothes or enquiring what the hell he was expected to do with some unwanted equipment.

give me some skin! Shake hands – esp. with one person's flat palm brushing the other's flat palm: US jive c.p. of *c.* 1935; it caught on and acquired a rhyme: *give me some skin, Flynn!* Cf *slip me five!*, which, current since WW1, prompted the *skin* phrase. (W & F.) CM regards it as a distinctly Negro c.p.

give me strength (short for the literal *God give me strength* to bear it) is, as Barry Prentice (1 May 1975) neatly puts it, 'a secular prayer. Used when one hears of some new misfortune or of an example of imbecility.' Originally Australian: since *c.* 1920. But also current in Britain.

The literal *God give me strength* was probably the earlier as a c.p., the shortened being a weakened form; and, based on a ribald myth, it expresses exasperation at the folly or stupidity or clumsiness of others, or at interruptions by others. Since *c.* 1950, it has gradually become, not obsolescent, but less and less used, as Laurie Atkinson reminded me in late 1974.

give my regards to Broadway! is an American c.p. of *c.* 1904–50, initiated by George M. Cohan's song, so titled, in *Little Johnny Jones.* (W. J. Burke.)

give the gentleman a coconut! Addressed to anyone making a successful effort, as in 'Right first time – give the gentleman a coconut!': C20. Originally a fair-ground stall-holder's congratulation to a successful competitor at a coconut-shy booth: with a ball he has knocked a coconut off its perch. (Wilfred Granville, 6 December 1968.)

give us a little of the old McGoo! is, Berrey tells us in 1942, a US film director's 'way of asking a star to display some sex appeal, as with exposed limbs'; obsolete by 1945, W & F in 1960 curtly dismissing it as 'Sex appeal. *Some c. 1930 use. Obs[olete].*' Who McGoo was, I don't know; there seems to be some reference to the US slang, *goo,* a sticky mess, itself perhaps from *glue.*

give us a rest!, writes James Maitland in 1891, was 'a slang phrase of recent introduction used when a tedious story is being told. Equivalent to *you make me tired*': US: *c.* 1885–1910.

give your arse a chance!, often preceded by **shut up** (or **stop talking) and**, is a low C20 c.p. It was particularly common in the Australian Forces, 1914–18. The politer *give your ears a chance!* arose *c.* 1920; 'sometimes said to one who never stops talking' (A. B. Petch, 4 January 1974).

give your face a joy-ride! is a cheery admonition, addressed to someone looking mournful: since *c.* 1930, but heard decreasingly little after *c.* 1950, and by 1970, obsolete.

give your head a bump! 'Pull yourself together. Wake up. Bestir yourself' (F & G): army: *c.* 1900–20, esp, during WW1. As a means of sharp arousing; perhaps also an allusion to phrenological bumps.

give yourself a bit of an overhauling! Go and have a wash and a general clean-up!: *c.* 1912–40. Probably from cleaning a motor car.

given away with a pound of tea is 'a Cockney c.p. of jocular disparagement, as in "Mum's new hat looks as if it was given away with a pound o' tea" and "Jack says his new bike was *not* given away with a pound o' tea" ' (Julian Franklyn): since *c.* 1880, but much less general since *c.* 1914 than before that date; and by 1940 obsolescent, by 1960 obsolete. From the pre-WW1 grocers' practice of making a free gift with every pound of tea or with any fair-sized order.

In F. Anstey's *Mr Punch's Model Music-Hall Songs and Dramas,* 1892, No. 3, 'A Democratic Ditty' entitled 'Given Away with a Pound of Tea' begins thus:

Some Grocers have taken to keeping a stock
Of ornaments – such as a vase, or a clock –
With a ticket on each where the words you may see:
'To be given away – with a Pound of Tea!'

In a later 'Vice-Versa' Anstey book, *Salted Almonds,* 1906, the story 'At a Moment's Notice' contains the passage: 'I had heard Monty discuss the Reggie Ballimore that was [the narrator] and give him away with a pound of tea, so to speak – and I hadn't turned a hair.'

But much the earliest record appears to occur towards the end of Act I of Arthur Wing Pinero's comedy, *The Rocket,* performed in 1883 (although not published until 1905):

WALK[INSHAW]: ... Go, sir, fetch my child.
JOSLYN: Do I understand then, Sir, that you consent?
WALK: The daughter of the Chevalier Walkinshaw and the son of a tea dealer. The arms of the Walkinshaws crossed with a pair of scales and a pig-tailed Chinaman. Motto, 'Given away with a pound of tea.' Go, sir, fetch my child, my heart is broken.

(The old hypocrite!)

glazier? – is (occasionally **was**) **your father a.** Addressed to one who blocks the light, originally that from a window, but soon also that from a lamp, a candle, a fire: C18–20, but little used since *c.* 1950. In S (Dialogue I), occur the words, 'I believe your father was no glazier'; and in Grose, 1788, we find the gloss: 'If it is answered in the negative, the rejoinder is – I wish he was, that he might make a window through your body to enable us to see the fire or light.' In late C19–20 Australia, ... *glassmaker?* (BP.) Cf **were you born in a barn?**

glimpses of the obvious dates either from the very late C19 or from the very early C20; heyday, *c.* 1920–40; partially eclipsed during the next fifteen years or so; partially revived since the middle 1950s. It can, obviously, be employed as a headline, but its more important usage is that of a usually smiling interposition into, or comment upon, a truism or a cliché.

glue did not hold – the. You were baulked: you missed your aim. (Ray, enlarged edn, 1813.) *c.* 1780–1860. Perhaps originally a proverbial saying, but probably always a true c.p.

glue-pot has come unstuck – the. His body emits the odour of a genital sweat or, strictly, of a seminal emission: a low c.p., dating from *c.* 1880 but obsolete – or, at the least, obsolescent – by 1940. I first heard it used by a rather coarse lower-middle-class woman in 1913.

go along, Bob! and **come along, Bob!**, current *c.* 1800–30 and recorded by JB, are obscure in meaning and, apparently, dubious in taste.

go along with you! See **get along with you!**

go and bag your head! Oh, shut up and run away!: an Australian c.p., dating from *c.* 1920. Cf **go and chase yourself!**

go and boil your head! Oh! don't be silly: a proletarian injunction: C20; little used since *c.* 1945. It occurs in, e.g., Compton Mackenzie, *Water on the Brain*, 1933. Of the Cockney variant, *garn, boil yer 'ead!* Douglas Leechman has remarked, 'Heard in England before 1904.' Cf the preceding and the next two.

go and chase yourself! 'Oh, run away and stop bothering me!' American; arising *c.* 1910 or even a decade earlier, it was recorded by S. R. Strait in the *Boston Globe* of *c.* 1917. (W. J. Burke.) But more often as **go chase yourself!** – the form cited by Strait.

go and eat coke! This c.p. of the London slums indicates a lively and impatient contempt: *c.* 1870–1940. It is used rather often in the school novels and short stories by 'Frank Richards' (i.e. Charles Hamilton). F & H cite the coarse variant *go and shit cinders!* – not a schoolboy phrase.

go and fetch the crooked straight-edge! (or **rubber hammer** or **wall-stretcher!**) is an 'April Fool catch': mid C19–20; one or other of them may go back considerably earlier. To discriminate: carpenters tend to prefer the first; engineers' shops, the second; and warehousemen, the third. There exists the occasional variant with *left-handed screwdriver.*

go and find another man to bring the money home! is addressed by husband to nagging wife: C20. It is reputed to be a certain stopper of a domestic difference or even a quarrel. A certain dry humour makes it memorable.

go and fry your face! – belonging to the approximate period, 1870–1905 – is hardly an educated c.p. It expresses either incredulity or derision or contempt; cf the obsolete Suffolk *fry your feet!*, don't talk nonsense (*EDD*).

go and get lost! See **get lost!**

go and get your brains examined! See **get your brains examined!**

go and get your mother to take your nappies off! (or **go and get your nappies changed!**) is a working-class girls' retort to callow youths' **does your mother know you're out?** (q.v.): C20. (Julian Franklyn.)

go and have a ride! – the first two words being sometimes omitted. Run away and stop bothering me! *or* Go to hell!: since *c.* 1920; obsolescent by 1970. Like *go and take a running jump* (*at yourself*) it is occasionally a euphemism for *fuck off!* – with allusions to the slangy *jump* and *ride*, (of the male) to copulate with.

go and play in the traffic! is a Canadian variant ('very recent', says Douglas Leechman, January 1969) of **get lost!** He simultaneously notes the further Canadian variant, *take a running fuck at the moon!* – '30 or 40 years ago'.

go and play trains! See **run away and play trains!**

go and see a taxidermist! was, in 1943–5, an RAF variation on the theme of 'Go and get *stuffed!*'

go and shit cinders! See **go and eat coke!**

go away, boy, you're bothering me, a US c.p., dates from early in C20; not much used since WW2. See the entry **it's an old army game**. I'd say that it had been prompted by **shoo, fly, don't bother me**.

go back and cross the T's! This naval c.p. has, since *c.* 1920, been ironically directed at any helmsman, but usually a learner coxswain, who has 'written his name' in the ship's wake by steering an erratic course. (*Sailors' Slang*, 1962; recorded earlier in PGR, 1948.)

go break a leg! See **break a leg!**

go chase yourself! See **go and chase yourself!**

[**go easy, Mabel!** 'Take it easy! Don't get excited! Cool it! Let up on me!' Based on a popular song 1909, it may have achieved a brief period of c.p. success; Mr W. J. Burke, however, in letter dated 8 March 1976, doubts its eligibility.]

go 'er on! An exclamatory c.p. made when a broker or a jobber wishes to continue buying or selling the same shares: Stock Exchange: C20, but less used since WW2. A sort of financial *attaboy!*

go have your hair bobbed, occasionally preceded by **aw**. Shut up!: US: 1920s. Robert Benchley uses it in *Love Conquers All*, 1923 – see the quotation at **oh, is that so?**

go it, Ned! is a naval c.p. of encouragement: *c.* 1810–50. It occurs in W. N. Glascock's lively *Sailors and Saints*. 1829.

go it, Susan, I'll hold your bonnet. 'What can be more revolting than phrases like *Whoa, Emma; Ah, there!; Get there, Eli; Go it, Susan, I'll hold your bonnet; Everybody's doing it; Good night, Irene; Oh you kid!* in vogue not long ago' (McKnight): *c.* 1919–29.

go it, you cripples! (occasionally **cripple!**) An ironic, often senseless, adjuration, originally to the crippled or disabled, but soon to anyone, esp. in sports and games, to move sharply, to 'get a move on': C19–20; by 1940, slightly obsolescent. Often added: **wooden legs are cheap**, seldom heard after WW1. It occurs in Thackeray, 1840. Its senseless usage or aspect is very clearly seen in Robert Surtees, *Mr Sponge's Sporting Tour*, 1853 (in vol. II, chapter L, 'Farmer Peastraw's Dîné-Matinée'):

> '... Who the Dickens are you?'
> 'Who the Dickens are you?' replied I.
> 'Bravo!' shouted Sir Harry.
> 'Capital!' exclaimed Seedybuck.
> 'Go it, you cripples! Newgate's on fire!' shouted Captain Quod.

Surtees uses it again in *Mr Pacey Romford's Hounds*, 1865 (he had died in 1862): or rather, he uses *go it, you cripples! Newgate's on fire!* – which leads one to suspect that the double adjuration was the original form: it at least makes sense.

Mr Lance Tonkin of Dunedin, New Zealand, has, on 15 December 1974, sent me two useful pieces of information: a newspaper published, 1845, in Hobart, Van Diemen's Land (later, Tasmania), reported that a group of women, presumably convicts, fighting in the streets, used this c.p.; and that, in his New Zealand schooldays, *c.* 1908, he and his companions 'used this ... as an encouraging phrase'. I suspect that it didn't, in Britain, Australia, New Zealand (and perhaps elsewhere) fall into disuse until between WW1 and WW2.

go, man, go! is an extension of the slang *go!*, an 'exhortation to dig, get with it, swing' (the *Daily Colonist* – Victoria, British Columbia – 16 April 1959). This US jazz c.p., dating from *c.* 1946, rapidly became also Canadian and, in or *c.* 1948, English. (The *locus classicus* is Norman D. Hinton's article in the American Dialect Society's periodical, November 1958.) A Negro jazz-players' coinage.

go on back to the kennels! A pejorative, (mildly) insulting, derisive US c.p. that arose *c.* 1950. (Professor John T. Fain, in letter dated 25 April 1969.) Also occasionally **get back to your kennel!**

go see the chaplain! – with **go** often omitted. 'The meaning = shut up, quit bitching, stop complaining, e.g. "Stop telling me your troubles and woes – I'm not interested – but go tell them to the chaplain and he will issue you a crying towel." WW2 [US] armed forces usage.' (Colonel Albert Moe, 11 July 1975.) And Professor John W. Clark writes: 'Certainly very common, and as a c.p., in the US Army 30 years ago. Now seldom heard (at least among civilians) except among ex-Servicemen'; he adds, 'often with the subaudition, "Your complaint is trivial, or commonplace, or both".'

go shoe the goose! A derisive – or an utterly incredulous – retort: late C16–18. (Recorded by, e.g., BE) Cf **go to hell and pump thunder!** for sense; of rural origin.

go sit on a tack! is a slangy US c.p. meaning 'Run away and don't bother me!' (cf **shoo, fly**) and dating from *c.* 1930. (W. J. Burke, in a letter of December 1968.)

go to father! Go to hell!: late C19–20; obsolete by 1940. Taken from a music-hall song; 'father' being dead. Probably suggested by *ask father* and *go farther*.

go to grass! is, said Hotten in 1859, 'a common answer to a troublesome or inquisitive person': obsolescent by 1880 and obsolete by 1900. Said to have been originally US. Perhaps from putting an old horse out to grass.

go to hell and pump thunder! indicates either derision or unmitigated incredulity: late C19. Cf the much earlier **go shoe the goose!**

go to Hell or Connaught! In 1909, Ware, having said 'historical', wrote thus: 'Be off. From the time of Cromwell, but still heard, especially in Protestant Ireland. Means utter repudiation of the person addressed. The Parliament (1653–54) passed a law, driving away all the people of Ireland who owned any land, out of Ulster, Munster, and Leinster.' More precisely, the meaning is, 'Go where you like but don't bother me with where you're going'; and Connaught was one of the ancient kingdoms – later, provinces – of Ireland.

go to the back of the class! See **join the back of the class!**

go to the pub, Dad! 'This expression I have overhead (in my occupation as a photographer) from teenagers ... mostly Maori; used in the situation where a poor type has said or suggested a course of action that is "square" or out of type for the spokesman or -woman' (Colin Keith, letter of 10 August 1974): New Zealand: since *c.* 1970.

go to the top of the class! is a remark one makes to somebody who has answered quickly and accurately: since *c.* 1948. Cf:

go up one! Excellent! Good for you!: late C19–20. From a schoolteacher's promotion of a bright and successful pupil. Cf the preceding entry – and contrast:

go 'way back and sit down! A US students' c.p. of the 1920s (McKnight); it survived, in general usage, until WW2 at least.

go West, young man, go West is a mainly British elaboration of *go West, young man*, often credited to Horace Greeley

(1811–72), who indeed popularized it; but the man originating it was John Barsone Lane Soule (1815–91), who, in 1851, used it in an article published in the *Express* at Terre Haute, Indiana, as Bartlett informs us. 'At first meaning exactly what it says, the expression at length became a mere catch-phrase, and was used in season and out of season' (Farmer) – a most revealing early comment upon its transition from famous quotation to equally famous c.p., with an astonishingly long life. No less significant is the fact that, in George Ade, *The Slim Princess*, 1908, we find this allusion:

'Strange,' she murmured. 'You are the second person I have met to-day who advises me to go away to the west.'

'That's the tip!' he exclaimed with fervor. 'Go west and when you start, keep on going.'

The two characters being an Oriental princess and a rich young American. It had, slightly modified, appeared in James J. McClosky's *Across the Continent; Or, Scenes from New York Life and the Pacific Railroad*, performed in 1870, although 'the version here reproduced is largely the work of ... Oliver Doud Bryson'; not published until 1940. In Act II:

JOE: [Interrupts.] I trust that our paths may lie in different directions, but if in our walk through life we should ever meet, fear will never cause me to turn aside from avenging a wrong.

AND[ERLY]: Nor me from avenging an insult.

JOHN: Oh, go West, young fellow, and shoot snipe.

But when *go West, young man* was adopted in Britain, it is difficult to say: my own impression is that it did so *c.* 1950 and that the Laurel and Hardy film had something to do with its British popularization.

God bless the Duke of Argyll! is, according to Hotten, a Scottish c.p., addressed to one who shrugs his shoulders or scratches himself as if he were troubled with lice: C19–20. An allusion to certain posts erected in Glasgow by his Grace's authority – or so Southern report has it! Mr Andrew Haggard, in a letter dated 28 January 1947, tells me these posts were erected

on certain large tracts of land belonging to [his Grace] where there were no trees or boulders and where sheep, in consequence of having nothing to rub against, were always getting 'cast'. The shepherds, who were not uncommonly verminous, used these posts to scratch their backs against and, when doing so, blessed the Duke.

Contrast:

God bless you! Addressed to one who sneezes: C18–20. Fuller (1732) says, 'He's a friend at a sneeze: the most you can get out of him is a *God bless you*.'

God bless you both! is 'the ironic aside (*sotto voce*) when a "thin" laugh greets a comedian's best gag' (Wilfred Granville): theatrical and music-hall: C20. Cf **it must be the landlady**.

God give me strength! See **give me strength!**

God have mercy – but usually **Godamercy – horse!** 'An almost meaningless proverbial exclamation' (Apperson) that was, *c.* 1530–1730, also a c.p. In Tarlton's *Jests*, 1611, it is mentioned as 'a by word thorow London'.

**[God is alive and well and living in —— (locality variable) has, by Mr D. R. Bartlett, MA, FLA, to whom I owe it, been glossed as a 'parody of a religious slogan of some kind, popularized recently on lavatory walls' (mid March 1975). I had never heard it or, come to that, seen it. The slogan was itself, I suspect, drawn from the frequent reply in any such dialogue as this:

'I haven't seen X for ages. Is he dead, d'you know?'

'Oh, no! He's alive and well and living in Manchester' [or any other place or area].

Moreover, I think that *God* is a deliberate variation of the ecclesiastical c.p., *the Devil is alive and well and living at—*, which may go back to early in C20, although I must admit that I had never heard of it until 4 April 1975 (from Paul Beale). Frankly, I doubt whether either saying is a true c.p.

These alternatives have set going a sentence-pattern, a syntactical pattern, if you prefer that description. As Mr Beale has pointed out, the following passage from a review (*The Times Literary Supplement*, 4 April 1975) of Constantine Fitzgibbon's *The Golden Age* exemplifies the fact: 'Orpheus then makes a pact with Mephistopheles and thereby recovers his memory in full. The Monster is alive and well, and living in the New Bodleian in the guise of a gently retiring Byzantine emperor.' This kind of thing had begun to happen at least as early as the 1920s, as we see in the progeny – e.g., 'came the crunch' – engendered by the films' *came the dawn*.]

God (or **God only) knows – I don't** and **God knows – and He won't split!** The former c.p. of emphatic reply to a question belongs to C19–20; it is the modern shape of the mid C16–18 *God himself tell you, I cannot*, recorded in Florio's dictionary, 1598. The irreverent *He won't split!* variation belongs to C20; I first heard it in 1912 in Australia, but it isn't either specifically or predominantly Australian. Douglas Leechman recalls that, during WW1, it was, in the form GOK, a 'cryptic medical annotation for any undiagnosed complaint'.

God pays and the synonymous **if I don't pay you, God Almighty will.** The former, current in late C16–18, appears thus in Ben Jonson's *Epigrams*, 1612:

To every cause he meets, this voice he brays,
His only answer is to all, God pays.

The latter belongs to C19–20. Used esp. by discharged naval seamen and by soldiers, who assumed a right to public charity.

Godamercy, horse! See **God have mercy, horse!** above.

goes for my money – usually **he** but occasionally **she**. He's the man (or woman) for me – the person I favour: c. 1540–1660. (See esp. the *OED*.) Cf the Standard English *he's the man for my money*, which isn't a c.p., because the form can be varied according to persons and the saying can be applied also to quadrupeds or even to inanimate objects.

goffer .... See **I'll draw you off a goffer.**

going down now, sir. See **don't forget the diver**, at end of the opening paragraph.

going home to eat cucumber sandwiches on the lawn? is one of those envious c.pp. still applied by a non-existent lower class to a non-existent upper class; more specifically by one who has a regional accent to one who speaks Standard English with a pure accent. As if the eating, by a 'gracious liver', of cucumber sandwiches on the lawn were somehow offensive to one who eats whelks in a kitchen 'fug'.

going through 'L' is applied to 'learner drivers, who have to stand a lot from instructors and the police' (A. B. Petch): since c. 1950; but little used since 1970. Obviously a pun on *going through hell*, having a thoroughly bad time, and on the '*L* for learner' sign hung on the back of cars.

going to buy anything? was, in 1896–c. 1930, an urban c.p.: an 'evasive request for a drink' (Ware, who elaborates).

going – until c. 1940, often **going out – to see a man about a dog.** See **see a man about a dog ....**

golden eagle shits on Friday – the; also **the eagle shits on pay-day**; and **the golden eagle lays its eggs.** The first is the British army and the RAF version, dating since 1941, of the second, which is the US army's c.p., dating since before WW2 and meaning 'Pay-day is on Friday'; the third is British and it means 'It's pay-day'. In the Services, the normal weekly pay-day is a Friday; the eagle concerned is that which figures on the US dollar.

Gomorrah to you! Good morning to you: a raffish c.p. of c. 1900–14. (Ware.) Punning on *good morrow!*, archaic for 'good morning!', and on '*sod* you!' – *Sodom and Gomorrah*.

gone for a Burton and **gone for a shit with a rug round him**. usually preceded by **he's.** He's 'had it' – 'bought it' – 'been killed', e.g. in an air raid over Germany: RAF: since 1939 – or at least I've found no earlier record. Hence, 1941 and onwards, loosely 'He's absent' or 'He's not to be found' – 'He's missing'. It remains an open question whether the phrase refers to a glass of Burton ale or, as I think, a suit made by Messrs Montague Burton, as the longer phrase seems to indicate, esp. as it too seems to have arisen in 1939. This longer phrase refers to a general practice in Service hospitals and, as a c.p., predominantly means 'He's been a long time absent'. Often **blanket** for **rug.**

There is another explanation of *he's gone for a Burton*, but I think it so much less probable than either of the other two that I refrain from noting it.

gone north about. See **he's gone north about.**

gone to lift his lying (or **lying-on**) **time** is an Anglo-Irish c.p. of C20. It occurs in, e.g., Patrick MacGill and is applied to a labourer recently dead.

gone to lyonch, 'gone to lunch' or, come to that, anywhere else: c. 1930–9. Recorded by James Street in *Carbon Monoxide*, 1937. From a famous advertisement issued by Messrs Joseph Lyons, the London multiple caterers.

good a scholar as my horse Ball – as. See **as good a scholar ....**

good blood .... See **you come of good blood ....**

good business! That's good! or I'm glad to hear *that!*: since c. 1880. Arthur Wing Pinero, in the opening scene of *Playgoers*, 1913, has:

THE MISTRESS   ... Darling, I am convinced that at last our miseries are ended and that we are in for a run of luck.

THE MASTER: (*lighting a cigarette*) Good business, if that's the case!

Earlier, Pinero's great rival, Henry Arthur Jones, in *The Lackey's Carnival*, 1900, writes in Act IV:

SIR G: And, Bertie, you might bring your men round from the Compasses.

BERTIE: What? Good business!

good-bye – and bolt the door, bugger you!, with the last two words omitted when the c.p. is uttered in polite company: 'a parting without a blessing' is how Frank Shaw described it (25 February 1969): lower and lower-middle class: C20.

good-bye-ee! This was, *c.* 1915–20, the c.p. form of *good-bye!* (Collinson.) It occurred in several popular songs of the period.

good-bye for now! has been very frequent, esp. over the telephone, since *c.* 1960, and it should be compared with **ta-ta for now**, q.v. at TOMMY HANDLEY CATCH PHRASES. It was soon used also in the shorter form *'bye for now*, itself further shortened to *BFN*.

good-bye to all that! is a regretful, often nostalgic, c.p., dating from 1929, when Robert Graves's autobiographical *Good-bye to All That* appeared, to invest an old cliché with a much wider currency and a much wider application, as, e.g., in James Leasor's *Passport to Peril*, 1966.

good evening, friends! is, like **get off me barrer**, a comic ending 'to fit any number of music-hall songs. ... On the chromatic scale goes (e.g.) ABAC, played very slowly ... originated as a convenient end sequence for part-singing like Barber's-shop quartets. Cf **get off me barrer**.' (Cyril Whelan, 17 February 1975.) But Ramsey Spencer thinks it may be a radio-programme opening of the middle 1950s.

good evening, Mrs Wood, is fourpence any good? lasted from *c.* 1910 to *c.* 1950; that it lasted so long was due to its rhyme – and its implication.

good field, no hit (literally, a good fielder, but a poor hitter, i.e. batter). W. J. Burke writes on 9 April 1975:

A baseball catch phrase which caught on and is still current is 'Good field, no hit'. ... In the spring of 1924 the Brooklyn 'Dodgers' were training at Clearwater, Florida. One of the 'Dodger' players was Moe Berg, who later became America's No. 1 atomic spy. Miguel Gonzales, a coach for the St Louis 'Cardinals', was also in Clearwater at that time. Mike Kelley of Minneapolis wanted to buy Berg for his team and wired Gonzales for his opinion of Berg's potentialities. Gonzales wired back the four-word message 'Good field, no hit'. The expression ... has been used ever since as a description of anyone good in one field and inept in another. My authority is ... *Moe Berg Athlete, Scholar, Spy*, by Louis Kaufman, Barbara Fitzgerald and Tom Sewell, 1974, pp. 137–8. The authors wrote: 'It is ironic that the suave and polished Berg should have been the subject of baseball's most illiterate message.' Berg wrote and spoke several languages, including Japanese and Chinese. It was touch and go whether German scientists in WWII would produce an atomic bomb before the U.S. did. With such a weapon the Germans could have won the war. Berg was sent to Switzerland to spy on visiting German scientists known to be working on the bomb. Berg spied on Professor Werner Heisenberg, the leading scientist working for the Germans.

good goods! is 'addressed to one who has donned a new suit; said with Jewish intonation and an industrious feeling of the quality of the cloth' (Douglas Leechman): Canadian: since *c.* 1950.

good (or **sweet**) **herbs!** (or **'erbs!**) Excellent or excellently: a mostly postmen's c.p. of *c.* 1910–30. (Manchon.) From a street vendors' cry.

good hunting! This, at first a sportsmen's c.p., dates from the 1890s – and means, without elaboration or deviousness, 'Good luck!' The phrase was popularized, perhaps even started on its career as a c.p., by Kipling's *The Jungle Book*, 1894, 2nd edn in 1895. In his *Shadow Play*, published in 1936, Noël Coward uses it thus:

YOUNG MAN: Will you excuse me – I have to dance with Lady Dukes.
VICKY: Certainly.
YOUNG MAN: Good hunting.

And in the final scene of *Blithe Spirit*, both played and published in 1941, he has Madame Arcati, who is addicted to the fashionable slang of the 1920s, saying, 'Don't trouble – I can find my way. Cheerio once more and good hunting!'

good idea (pause) – **son** (emphatic)! This was a Max Bygraves 'gag' of (?) the late 1950s–early 1960s. 'I think that he eventually made it the chorus punch line of a song (Paul Beale, 8 December 1975).

good in parts – like the curate's egg. It was Professor W. E. Collinson who, in 1927, noticed it as a c.p. – and so it has remained ever since. During WW1 and for a few years afterwards, it justified H. W. Fowler's condemnation, 'a battered ornament'; during the first decade, it was, rather, a cultured allusion.

From an illustrated joke in *Punch*, 1895 (vol. CIX, p. 222). A curate is taking breakfast in his Bishop's home:

'I'm afraid you've got a bad egg, Mr Jones.'
'Oh no, my Lord, I assure you! Parts of it are excellent.'

The same sort of 'rationalization' – or, if you prefer that angle, of conflation – occurs in **elementary, my dear Watson!**

[**good lawyer must be a good liar – a**, is, I'd say, a proverb, not a c.p.; G. L. Apperson the dependable classifies it as proverb.]

good look round – have a. See **have a good look round** ....

good luck to him! See **luck to him** ....

good men are scarce – not many of us left. 'With the cliché-maker, this follows **look after yourself!** (Frank Shaw) as a pendant: since at least as early as 1920. By itself, *good men – occasionally folk(s) – are scarce* is a cliché: the c.p. elaborates it.

good morning! have you used Pear's soap? was originally an advertising slogan issued by a famous old soap firm in the late 1880s; it almost immediately became a c.p., by 1930 moribund and by 1950 extinct. The slogan had been devised by Thomas W. Barratt, a well-known advertising man, who later became the chairman of the company. Cf **since when I have used no other.**

good morning, sir! Was there something? was Sam Costa's weekly entry line in the BBC's 'Much Binding in the Marsh' (?1944–5 and after), as Paul Beale reminds me (21 April 1975). The 'gag' caught on. The second member of the line is, of course, elliptical for 'Was there something you needed?'

good night! This c.p. retort vigorously expresses the height of incredulity or the depth of comic despair or undiluted delight; it arose *c.* 1880; by 1935 it was obsolescent, by 1976 – virtually obsolete, yet still heard occasionally – and not only among the old.

In the late C19 it acquired the nuance 'That's *done* it' – cf **that's torn it**: since *c.* 1920, indeed, the predominant sense of *good night!* has been 'That's finished it' – 'That's the end'.

A notable adumbration occurs in Shakespeare's I *Henry IV*, Act I, Scene iii, lines 191 ff.:

WORCESTER: As full of peril and adventurous spirit
As to o'er-walk a current roaring loud
On the unsteadfast footing of a spear.
HOTSPUR: If he fall in, good night!

Inevitably, the phrase was, apparently *c*. 1910, adopted in the US: and in 1960, W & F remarked that it expressed 'surprise, disgust or anger' and that it served also as a euphemism for *good God!* Unfortunately they supply no date, no other information, no comment. It is therefore worth recording that, in the essay titled 'Lesson Number One' in *Of All Things*, 1922, Robert Benchley wrote: 'As he cranked it again, George said ... that he could take a joke as well as the next man, but that, good night! what was the use of being an ass?' At about the same time, H. L. Mencken noted the phrase in *The American Language*: and what finer consecration could a phrase receive than this dual mention? An earlier example occurs in S. R. Strait's 'Straight Talk' in the *Boston Globe* of *c*. 1917. (W. J. Burke.)

Cf the next three entries.

good night, Irene! 'Common in my Alabama world *c*. 1910–14 to express surprise or even mild dismay. It had its currency about then, and I am sure that I used it. It *may* be a phrase from the title of, or the principal song, in a musical comedy' (Professor S. H. Monk, 9 November 1968). It was also current among US students of the second decade, as McKnight declares. Cf **good night, nurse!**

good night, McGuinness! A New Zealand version of the next: *c*. 1910–35. I've no idea who this briefly famous McGuinness may have been.

good night, nurse!, although it probably dates from *c*. 1910, became popular during – and largely because of – WW1, with particular reference to the naval and military hospitals for Other Ranks. It is synonymous with and clearly prompted by the simple, the basic, **good night!** Cf **good night, Irene!** and such other phrases as **carry me out!** – **let me die!** – **that's torn it!**

good night, Vienna comes from the title of a romantic operetta, 1932, book and lyrics by Eric Laschwitz, music by George Posford, the whole serving as a vehicle for Richard Tauber. 'Its main song was "Good night, Vienna" (you city of a million melodies)' (Ronald Pearsall, 7 February 1975). As a c.p. it has been described by Cyril Whelan on 17 February 1975, as 'a pen-knife phrase, in that it can be put to a variety of different uses – often apparently contradictory. "If the officer catches us up to this, it's Good Night, Vienna, for the lot of us." – "So I met the girl. We had a few drinks. Back to her place, and Good Night, Vienna".' Its appeal and currency are due only to the fact that it's mildly pleasing to the tongue in a racy sort of way and bounces quite happily on the ear of the listener.

good old England! and **good old terra firma!** are railwaymen's ironic c.pp., applied since *c*. 1920, to 'off the railroad, at trap points'.

[**good on you!** Good for *you*! Excellent! Well done! Splendid news!: Australian: C20. This is not strictly a c.p.; rather, a colloquial cliché. The same remark applies to **good show!** – therefore also to **bad show!**]

good question. Michael Innes, in the *The Mysterious Commission*, 1974, has:

'Do particular gangs going after this sort of thing have their regular and identifiable techniques?'

'Good question.' It was to be presumed that Detective Superintendent Keybird was in the habit of conducting seminars at police colleges.

See also **that's a good question** and **very good question**.

good shit would do you more good – a. This is a low c.p. addressed to one who says 'I could do with a woman': late C19–20, but by 1970 slightly obsolescent.

good soldier never looks behind him – a, is an originally – ?1914 or 1915 – military c.p., become by 1918 common enough among civilians, but I've not heard it for many years. Meaning 'You have no right to criticize the heels of my boots or shoes', it is an ingenuously ironic misapplication of an old army adage.

good thinking!, often introduced by **that's**. That's a sound – an excellent – idea; What a wonderful suggestion!: heard from *c*. 1960 onwards, but not a genuine British c.p. until *c*. 1969. Originally a serious comment; but as c.p., jocular. In the *Daily Telegraph* colour supplement, 27 October 1972, I noticed this advertisement:

'I've brought you a glass of BLUE NUN, sir ...'

'Good thinking, Cranston – just hold it there while I land this killer pike.'

And on the evening before, a Congregational minister had used it to an intelligent member of the congregation at a church meeting.

In 1974, Marshall Pugh, in *A Dream of Treason*, uses it thus:

'Arab terrorists,' Max said. 'How would you set about it?'

'Well, I'd keep a sharp eye out for sandals,' Middlemass said. ...

'Good thinking,' Max said.

The phrase came from the US, where it had arisen, *c*. 1950, among the advertising and publicity agencies of New York's Madison Avenue and had, by the middle or late 1950s, become a US c.p. – not unassisted by the 'Good thinking, Batman' of the Batman 'comic' strips.

good time was had by all – a. In 1937, the late Miss Stevie Smith's book of verse, *A Good Time Was Had by All* appeared: and within five years in Britain and by 1950 at latest in the US, the words of the title had become a c.p. – so thoroughly that it is employed allusively in Clarence Budington Kelland's *Counterfeit Gentleman*, 1956: '"One night at dinner we had a justice of the Supreme Court, the president of a university, a truck driver who did card tricks and an Aleutian Islander with a trained seal. A good time was had by all."'

It had not, by 1974, attained a general currency: it has remained a predominantly literary and cultured phrase. But it has become so integrated in the speech of cultured Britons and Americans that it can occur with devastating naturalness, as in Amanda Cross's US novel, *Poetic Justice*, 1970, thus: 'How they got through the subsequent two hours ... Kate never properly knew. But such a good time was had by all that they quite happily voted Mr Cornford a distinction.' And in May Mackintosh's British novel,

Appointment in Andalusia, 1972: 'Once the Spanish police start getting suspicious they are liable to clap you in gaol and then start thinking the matter over. It's their policy not to rush their thinking, so I assure you a good time is not had by all.'

Perhaps six months before Stevie Smith's death, I wrote to her and asked whether she had coined the phrase or adopted and popularized it. Her explanation was startlingly simple: she took it from parish magazines, where a church picnic or outing or social evening or other sociable occasion, almost inevitably generated the comment, 'A good time was had by all.'

She herself asked, 'Are you the Eric Partridge of the Slang dictionary. But no! he must by now be dead.' I assured her that I, at any rate, suffered from the delusion – and lived within the illusion – that I was still alive and busy and *compos*. Then she died rather unexpectedly: but then, don't we all live under the dispensation of a *D.V.*?

good to the last drop. 'Maxwell House's coffee slogan – "good to the last drop" – has seen some generalized use – "thoroughly or completely good or enjoyable" ' (W & F, p. 604). Berrey, 2nd edn, 1952, had included it in the synonymy for 'excellent'.

In a letter dated 5 December 1968, John W. Clark writes: 'Disused (I think) by then, because people were always saying, "What's wrong with the last drop?" But still a c.p., used of other things than beverages – speeches, e.g.'

This US c.p. was, *c.* 1960, adopted in Britain.

good trumpeter. See **he would make a . . . .**

good tune . . . . See **there's many a good tune . . . .**

good voice to beg bacon – a, was, *c.* 1680–1770, a c.p. derisive of a poor, or even a thoroughly bad, voice. (BE.)

[**good work!** Well done! Not a true c.p. – cf **good show!** at **good *on* you!**]

good young man – a, was, 1910–*c.* 1914, a trenchant proletarian c.p. applied to a hypocrite. Originated, Ware tells us, by Arthur Roberts in a song.

good yunting! 'Employed jocularly by costermongers as a means of wishing the next-stall neighbour (and some regular, understanding customers) a Merry Christmas, a Happy New Year, a pleasant Easter, and so on' (Julian Franklyn, 3 January 1968): since *c.* 1918. Influenced by **good hunting!** in sense and by Yiddish pronunciation.

goodness me, it's number 3 is of the consecrated c.pp. in the game of bingo; brevity and a rhyme being the prime essentials: since the early 1950s.

goose hangs high – the. See **everything is lovely and the goose hangs high.**

got a clock – or, in full, **he's got a clock.** He's carrying a bag with a time-bomb in it: a Londoners' c.p. of 1883, in reference to the activities of the dynamitards. *Plus ça change . . .*

got a feather in your trousers? is addressed to a boy giggling suddenly and, it seems, inexplicably, as in 'What's the matter, son? Got . . .?' C20.

got a snake in your pocket? See **snake in . . .?**

got any hard? This was, *c.* 1920–40, a c.p. addressed, in Southampton (England) bars to a stranger and implying that he may have been to sea and therefore may, just possibly, have some hard tobacco, i.e. tobacco in blocks, to spare. It was more of a joke than a serious question.

got it off or **got it all off** – or **got it all off pat,** preceded by **I** or **you** or **he** (or **she**), means that the lesson has been thoroughly learnt: schoolchildren's: since *c.* 1920.

got (or **get**) **me, Steve?** Do you understand? This US c.p., dating from very early in C20, was anglicized by 1910. As *got me, Steve?*, it was recorded as early as 1914 by W. L. George in his striking novel, *The Making of an Englishman*, and, as *got me? or got me, Steve?*, it was, in 1925, glossed thus by F & G: '. . . A phrase current in the War from an American film drama in which the "hero" kept producing a revolver to stress his points.' Agatha Christie in *Why Didn't They Ask Evans?*, 1934: ' "I get you, Steve" . . . and . . . the queer phrase represented sympathy and understanding.' The positive form is either *I get you, Steve* or *I've got you, Steve.*

The simple *got me?* was noted by A. H. Melville in 'An Investigation of the Function and Use of Slang', a long article published in *The Pedagogical Seminary* of March 1912 and based on a school test made in 1911. *I get you, Steve* is the form in which it was recorded by Berrey in 1942.

got to swim under water to dodge it! See **getting any?**

got your eyeful? Have you had a good look?: raffish: since *c.* 1910 or a little earlier. Cf **take an eyeful,** to look long or carefully, slang current in late C19–early 20.

grandmother and mine had four elbows – her (or **his**). In S, Dialogue I, we read:

> LORD SP: Pray, my Lady *Smart*, what kin are you to Lord *Pozz*?
>
> LADY SM: Why, his Grandmother and mine had four Elbows.

We are both human beings – there's no closer relationship than that.

Apparently a c.p. of late C17–mid 18.

grandmother is with me. See **friend has come.**

granted as soon as asked is a lower-middle-class c.p. of C20. In Noël Coward's sketch, 'Cat's Cradle' (written in 1928), we come upon this:

> MISS M: False modesty's one thing, Miss Tassel, and loose thinking's another.
>
> MISS T: I beg your pardon.
>
> MISS M: Granted as soon as asked.

Cf the next.

granted, I'm sure. A lower-middle-class genteel reply to an apology: C20. Cf the preceding entry.

grateful and comforting – like Epps's cocoa, often with the last three words omitted, as in Collinson. It was taken from a famous advertisement issued by Epps's Cocoa. The c.p. arose in the very late C19 and was, apparently, still flourishing during the 1920s.

In Act I, Scene ii, of Noël Coward's perturbing play, *Peace in Our Time*, performed and published in 1947, George Bourne remarks that 'One quick brandy, like Epps's cocoa, would be both grateful and comforting' and when Ger. Albrecht asks 'Who is Epps?' George replies, 'Epps's Cocoa – it's an advertisement that I remember when I was a little boy – "Epps's Cocoa – Both grateful and comforting".'

[**great American dream – the**; and **the great American novel**, tempting although it be to treat them as c.pp., originally and predominantly US, are fundamentally clichés, employed mostly by journalists, publicists, satirists.]

great life if you don't weaken – a – often preceded by **it's**. Arising among British soldiers very early in WW1, it survived into civilian life; it occurred in, e.g., George Ade's excellent and shrewdly prophetic essay 'Golf', in *Single Blessedness and Other Observations*, 1922: 'A great life, my friends, if you don't weaken, and you can't weaken where the match is all square and a small bet riding' – which tends to show that it was familiar also to Americans, probably via the US soldiers on the Western Front in 1918; in G. D. H. and M. Cole's novel, *Burglars in Bucks* (Buckinghamshire), 1930; and it is still heard quite often. It has always been jocular – sometimes ruefully so.

great minds think alike does not appear in the dictionaries of quotations, nor in those of proverbs. It seems to have arisen *c.* 1890, perhaps a decade earlier, as a c.p., and a c.p. it has remained: any remark, esp. about a trivial matter, that could be answered by 'I happen to think the same' or by 'We agree entirely on that point' can be capped by *great minds think alike*, a phrase that has become so embedded in ordinary, everyday English that, on 7 October 1973, one of London's 'nationals' had an article headed 'Great Minds Think Unalike'.

A stock – indeed, a c.p. – reply is, *fools –* or *small minds – seldom differ* (C20).

great weather for ducks. See **fine day** ....

greedy, but he (or **she**) **likes a lot – not** – usually preceded by **he's** or **she's** – is a late C19–20 c.p., sarcastically implying greediness.

[**Greeks had a word for it – the**. Occurs in Zoë Akins's play, *The Greeks Had a Word for It*, 1929; and in a letter to Burton Stevenson, the author of two famous dictionaries of quotations, she explains that, in Stevenson's words, 'the phrase is original and grew out of the dialogue'. It 'caught on' with a notable celerity: by 1930, it was common both in the US and, by virtually instantaneous adoption, in Britain (whence, by 1931, in the Commonwealth). Had Zoë Akins's words appeared in the text – they had done so, originally, but were cut out – this would indisputably have ranked as a famous quotation; as they did not, but were preserved only in the title, I'm tempted to classify it as a c.p.]

green as I'm cabbage-looking – I'm not so. See **not so green** ....

green bag .... See **what's in the green bag?**

green in my eye .... See **do you see any green in my eye?**

green lime, please! is a C20 theatrical c.p., 'sometimes murmured today when a line savours of melodrama', as Granville told us. He explained its origin thus: 'A melodrama villain indicated his diabolical intentions in the light of a green lime. At rehearsals when mouthing his lines he used to remind the stage manager that he would require the green limelight in that speech, "on the night".'

gremlins have got into it – the. See the Vernon Noble quotation at **press on, regardless**.

grow on trees – it doesn't or, of currency and bank-notes, **they don't** ....; and **you seem to think money grows on trees**. These are c.pp. addressed to – or directed at – those who think that money just happens to be always and immediately available or is, at worst, very easily obtained; an exasperated reply to an unanswerable request for money: late C19–20. 'The mass of men lead lives of quiet desperation' (Thoreau).

grow up! and **why don't you grow up?** are synonymous with **be your age!**: since the late 1930s in Britain. Perhaps originally US: Berrey records it. The general sense is 'Don't be ridiculous!'.

growl you may – but go you must! A nautical c.p. uttered 'when the watch below have to turn out of their bunks to shorten sail in bad weather' (Bowen): *c.* 1870–1910.

guess who's back! is an Australian c.p. 'uttered with one hand on hearer's back' (Barry Prentice): since *c.* 1950. A pun on *whose back.*

[**guess who's here!** 'You'll (*or* You'd) never guess who has arrived *or* is here!' It lies in the no-man's land between c.p. and cliché: C20.]

Guinness is good for you, as a c.p. deriving from a famous advertisement for Guinness stout, dates from the late 1920s. It occurs in fiction at least as early as 1930, the year when Dorothy L. Sayers's 'deteccer', *Strong Poison*, appeared.

In Act I of H. M. Harwood's *The Man in Possession*, published in the same year, Raymond asks his draper father, 'Why shouldn't you advertise, too? Think of it! Worthington's Beer woven into one leg and Eno's Fruit Salt into the other. "Guinness is good for you", on the back of every tie. You couldn't miss it – you'd see it every day.'

I recorded it in the first edn, 1933, of *STY*.

[**guns before butter** is Dr Josef Goebbels's famous pronouncement, made in 1942. Almost a c.p., when used facetiously.]

guns, gas and gaiters. This C20 c.p. of the Royal Navy was 'applied to the gunnery officers, who were the first to introduce the polished gaiters for work in the mud at Whale Island' (Bowen, 1929). Since *c.* 1940, also ecclesiastical. Cf both **all gas and gaiters** and **attitude is the art of gunnery** ....

guts for garters .... See **I'll have your guts for garters**.

guy could get hurt that way – a was in WW2, and before and after it, applied by Americans ('stunt men' – Servicemen – and others) to any particularly hazardous enterprise. (Arthur Wrigglesworth, 13 April 1975.)

ha, ha, bloody ha! is 'a sarcastic c.p. that greets any stupid question' (Wilfred Granville, 19 February 1969); or 'Exposing feebleness of a sarcastic or apt rejoinder' (Laurie Atkinson, November 1969); since *c.* 1950. Cf **that's a good question** and contrast:

ha! ha! ha! 'This mocking pretence to be amused, [with] last *ha* emphasized, I believe to come from [Frank] Richards [proper name, Charles Hamilton]. But it was often in the old "comics". Still used' (Frank Shaw, November 1968); and still occasionally in 1974. Cf both the preceding and **funny peculiar or funny ha-ha?**

[**had it – I've** (or **you've** or **he's** or **she's**). Not a true c.p. See esp. **have had it** and **had it in a big way**, both in the *DSUE* post-War Supplements and in *PGR* at *had it*.]

had one but (occasionally **and**) **the wheel came off**, mostly preceded by *we*. A lower- and lower-middle-class, hence also a military (Other Ranks') c.p. directed at an unintelligible speaker or speech, often a *gamin* comment on words, or even a single word, not understood; but also expressive of a feigned helpfulness, or a droll regret, or a *gamin* comment: since *c.* 1890; a little less frequent since WW2. Perhaps slightly commoner in Liverpool than elsewhere in England; but very widely used – in, e.g. Australia.

had your penn'orth or do you want a ha'penny change? is, notably among Londoners, addressed to someone staring at the speaker: since *c.* 1920. (Laurie Atkinson, 11 September 1967.) A good example of Cockney sarcasm at its humorously trenchant best.

had your time. See **you've had your time.**

haha! heehee! 'Briefly *c.* 1920 ... was used as a greeting – without any counter' (Ramsey Spencer, 15 August 1975): *c.* 1921–4. Cf **pip-pip!** and **tootle-oo!**

hail, hail, the gang's all here! was originated and popularized by a 1917 song so titled, words by Estrom, music by Morse, sung by Sullivan, as one learns from Edward B. Marks, *They All Sang*, 1934, and as I learned from my friend, Mr W. J. Burke. Ed McBain uses it as a c.p. title for one of his detective novels.

Haines. See **my name is Haines!**

hair. See **there's hair!** as well as **his hair grows through his hood.**

half an hour is soon lost at dinner. In S, Dialogue II, Lord Smart says, 'Pray edge a little to make more room for Sir *John*. Sir *John*, fall to, you know half an Hour is soon lost at Dinner', which is the only record I have of this c.p., jocularly ironic and reminiscent of very long sessions: probably *c.* 1690–1760.

half an hour past hanging time, mostly preceded by *it's*. Also in S is this c.p. reply to 'What's the time?':

NEV[EROUT]: [to Lady Answerall] Pray, Madam, do you tell me, for I let my Watch run down.
LADY ANSW: Why, 'tis half an Hour past Hanging Time.
Common in C18–19, but now rare; displaced by:

half past kissing time and time to kiss again. This c.p. belonged mostly to London and flourished *c.* 1880–1930, although it has lingered on. The phrase is recorded by B & L in 1889. It comes from a popular song by one G. Anthony:

It's half-past kissing-time, and time to kiss again,
For time is always on the move, and ne'er will still remain;
No matter what the hour is, you may rely on this:
It's always half-past kissing-time, and always time to kiss.

half your luck! I wish I had even a half of your good luck: Australian: since *c.* 1915. (Baker, 1942) Spoken with a semi-humorous ruefulness.

hallo, baby – how's nurse? was a civilian c.p., dating from early in C20, before it was adopted by the licentious soldiery for use in WW1; obsolete (so far as I know) by the time WW2 began. It was 'addressed to any girl pushing a perambulator' (B & P, 1931).

hallo, playmates! see **hello, playmates!**

[**halt the –, steady the –, and let the – go by**, where 'the first two dashes represent the speaker's unit, the third the squad or battalion encountered', exemplified the fact that in WW1, 'on the line of march, greetings were usually exchanged by meeting regiments' or battalions or other units (B & P, 1931). But this was a chant rather than a c.p. The same remark applies to *Gorblimey! here comes* – or *come – the* – and to **here they come – mooching along, all of a bloody heap.** Cf **steady, the Buffs!**]

Hamlet, I am thy father's gimlet is a punning theatrical c.p., based on the ghost of Hamlet's father: very approximately *c.* 1880–1925. (Frank Shaw, 30 October 1968.)

Hamlet in its eternity. 'An actors' jocular phrase descriptive of a performance of Shakespeare's *Hamlet* in its *entirety*. It goes on for ever' (Granville): C20. As *Macbeth* is the shortest of the tragedies, so is *Hamlet* the longest of all Shakespeare's plays.

hands off your cocks and pull up your socks! A British Army, esp. an orderly corporals', reveille call to men in barracks: C20 and perhaps going back a further twenty-or-so years. A late example occurs as the opening speech of Act II of Arnold Wesker's *Chips with Everything*, published in 1962.

hands up! Oh, for heaven's sake, stop talking!: originally a lower-class c.p.: *c.* 1885–1914. From the police command to surrender. (Recorded in a history of the police published in 1888.) Semantically cf:

hang crape on your nose – your brains are dead! Stop talking nonsense!: a US students' c.p. of the early 1920s. (Recorded by McKnight.)

hang in there, baby! – with **baby** soon discarded and with **in** emphasized: US: 'It means "Stick with it" and is addressed to someone doing a good job in difficult circumstances; it's a word of encouragement' and has been current 'for possibly as long as five years' (Paul Beale – with fair US assistance – 10 February 1975).

On 25 March 1975, W. J. Burke described it as:

a common expression, an everyday one. It is simply an admonition to keep fighting when the odds are against you, probably an expression around the prize ring to begin with, then applied to other sports. [It] is addressed pleadingly or encouragingly both to individual participant and to the team as a whole, and is often heard at football games, baseball games, etc. Its application to non-athletic endeavours, such as telling your friend to 'buck up' when he is 'down' or 'blue' or 'licked' was an easy transition from your *playing fields of Eton* to the common situations of downheartedness. 'Hang in there' goes back a long ways, predating our 'Hippie' era.

The Hippies, however, adopted it early in the 1960s; 'lately taken up by sports and politics, to advocate fortitude' (Ben Grauer, 25 December 1975).

In the *New York Post*, 20 February 1976, Max Lerner noted the 'bid' being made by the phrase and added, 'But will it hang in there?'

hang saving! In S, Dialogue II, see:

COL[ONEL]: Faith, my Lord ... I wish we had a Bit of your Lordship's *Oxfordshire* Cheese.

LORD SM[ART]: Come, hang saving, bring us a halfporth of Cheese.

This is a jocular c.p. rather than a proverb and has been used over a very long period: C17–20, although little before 1650 and very little since c. 1940. Phonetically, *halfporth* is a clumsy contraction of *halfpennyworth*: ha'p'orth is both scripturally and phonetically perfect. It has been displaced by *hang the expense!*: mid C19–20.

hang the Kaiser!, often oh, hang...., was a humorous c.p. current among soldiers during the latter half of WW1, when the men had become unutterably bored by the newspaper talk about him. It was not, in the c.p., meant literally, although, inevitably, the phrase implied a reference, still humorous and tolerant, to that possibility.

hang your number out to dry! A post-1918 variant of **before you came up**: Services'. (H & P.)

hangar doors closed! See **close hangar doors!**

hanging on the (usually **the old**) **barbed wire**, with the topical variant **hanging on the barbed wire at**, e.g. Loos, both versions being often shortened to **on the barbed wire**, was an army (mostly among the Other Ranks) reply to the query 'Where is So-and-So?': late 1915–18. The reference is to men left dead on the enemy wire entanglements after an attack.

The gloss in B & P (3rd edn) is worth quoting: 'These [other replies] referred only to a person whose whereabouts was unknown– or not to be disclosed:

Died of wounds. –
Hanging on the (barbed) wire. –
On the wire at Mons. –
Gassed at Mons.

There was, of course, no wire at the Retreat from Mons and gas was unknown at that time.' This retreat began on 24 August 1914 and was halted at Le Cateau, where the Anglo-French forces repulsed the enemy; and the Battle of Loos took place thirteen months later.

Hannah – that's the man as married; occasionally **that's what's the matter with the man as married Hannah**. A proletarian c.p. of c. 1850–1905. (Hotten.) Originally denoting a good, or a happy, beginning, it soon came to mean 'Good for you!' or 'Excellent!'; hence, simply a hearty agreement. Hotten implies that this c.p. migrated from Shropshire to, esp., London.

Just who Hannah was, history is apparently silent; probably some forgotten song or ballad affords a clue.

Hans the Grenadier is in charge. See **Carl the caretaker's in charge**.

happy days are here again was originally an American song, words by Agar and music by Yellen; sung and published in 1929. 'Incidentally, this song became Franklin D. Roosevelt's political theme song' (W. J. Burke, 23 September 1975). It also became an American c.p. and, at the end of WW2 in Europe, an immensely popular British sentimental song.

happy in the Service? or, in full, **are you happy ... ?** is the Royal Navy's, hence also the RAF's, version of the army's **are you happy in your work?**: phrases that, arising in 1940 or perhaps in late 1939, are addressed to someone who is engaged in work either dirty or difficult or downright dangerous. PGR's comment is, 'Cheery greeting to someone who obviously isn't'; irony in moments of harassment'.

hard in a clinch – and no knife to cut the seizing is a nautical c.p. of c. 1860–1910, refers to cordage, and means 'in an extremely difficult situation, with apparently no way out'.

hard on the setting sun was, c. 1895–1914, a journalistic c.p., expressive of contempt for the Red Indian: the *People*, on 13 June 1897, referred to it as 'a characteristic by-word'. (Ware, 1909.)

hard titty! See **tough titty!**

harder than pulling a soldier off your sister, preceded mostly by **it's** but sometimes by **that's**. This low, mostly naval, c.p. dates from c. 1939 and applies to circumstances in which compliance would be disagreeable or repugnant.

hark (but usually 'ark) at her, more often **'er**. A derisive C20 c.p., directed at a woman, 'uttering supposedly well-meaning or high-sounding sentiments' (Laurie Atkinson). Evocative of back-street disputes in which one woman derides another.

harpers. See **have among you, blind harpers**.

Harwell. See **no return ticket**.

Harwich. See **they're all up at Harwich**.

has anybody here seen Kelly? was originally, 1909, an English song, words by Murphy and music by Letters, and the c.p. followed immediately; now (1976) seldom heard. In US, Nora Bayes popularized the song, in McKenna's American version as it appeared in *Jolly Bachelors*. (W. J. Burke.)

has his ballocks in the right place, often preceded by **he**, expresses warm approval of a man well set-up and levelheaded: C20.

has more money than I (or **you**) **could poke a stick at**, with **has** often omitted; often, too, preceded by **he** or **she**. He's (she's) very rich: Australian: since c. 1920. See, in Frank

Hardy, *Billy Booker Yarns Again*, 1967, 'The Parrot ... tells Hot Horse: "Your tips have cost me more money than I could poke a stick at."' Perhaps it would be more precise to say that the c.p. is *more money*....

has Mr Sharp come in yet? is a monitory c.p. addressed by one shopkeeper or other trader to another 'to signify that a customer of suspected honesty is about' (Hotten, 1864): *c.* 1850–1940. Cf **two upon ten**.

has the cat got your tongue? – often, as at Act I, Scene 5, of John Mortimer's *The Judge*, produced and published in 1967, shortened to **cat got your tongue?** A mid C19–20 c.p., British and US, meaning 'Have you lost your tongue? Can't you speak?' It forms one of the small group of domestic phrases; often used in speaking to a child that, after some mischief, refuses to speak or to answer questions. A late example occurs in Janet Green's novel, *My Turn Now*, 1971: 'Taken totally by surprise, I couldn't speak. I just stood there ... literally gaping. He laughed. "What's the matter? Cat got your tongue?"'

A still later example occurs in E. V. Cunningham, *Millie*, 1973 (British edn, 1974):

'Peace,' I replied, and ... sat and stared at Millie.
'Cat got your tongue?'

has the ghost walked yet? See **ghost walks on Friday – the**.

has your mother sold her mangle? An urban, chiefly Londoners', c.p. of no precise application: rather low: since the 1830s. There is apparently some reference to a woman taking in washing – or no longer doing so.

Mackay, immediately after having dealt with **there he goes with his eye out!**, writes:

Another very odd phrase came into repute in a brief space afterwards, in the form of the impertinent and not universally apposite query, '*Has your mother sold her mangle?*' But its popularity was not of that boisterous and cordial kind which ensures a long continuance of favour. What tended to impede its progress was, that it could not well be applied to the older portions of society [because it hadn't long been invented?]. It consequently ran but a brief career, and then it sank into oblivion.

hasn't got a Chinaman's chance, often preceded by **he**. He has no chance at all: US: since 1849 or 1850. It originated, W & F tell us, in the California Gold Rush, when Chinese, in the hope – it could hardly have been expectation – of finding gold, worked streams and old claims abandoned by white prospectors; an origin to which was added the contributory factor of 'the hard life and times' of Chinese immigrants living in a virtual enclave of society.

The phrase was taken to Australia by those optimists who had joined, somewhat late, in the Rush of 1849 onwards. When, many years later, I first (in 1908) heard the phrase, it was always in the form *he hasn't* – or *hasn't got – a Chinaman's chance in hell*.

The form commonest in Britain is ... *a snowflake's chance* ... C20.

Cf **as much chance as a snowball** ... and **no more chance** ....

hasn't had it so long. See **she hasn't had it so long**.

hasn't sucked that out of his fingers. See **he hasn't sucked** ....

hasty as a sheep. See **as hasty** ....

hat – all round my. See **all round my hat**.

hat – I'll have your, and **shoot that hat.** See **shoot that hat!**

hat – what a shocking bad. See **what a shocking** ....

hat? – where did you get that. See **where did you** ....

hatter? – who's your. See **who's your hatter?**

h'attitude is the h'art of gunnery is the lower-deck version of **attitude is the art of gunnery**, q.v.

have? – is that a catch or a. See **is that a** ....

have a banana! was, *c.* 1900–39, a low – or, rather, a lower-class – c.p. expression of contempt; by association with the popular music-hall song, 'I had a banana/With Lady Diana', a sexual implication accrued. Not unknown in the British Army during WW1. Cf **yes, we have no bananas today**.

have a feel till Friday. 'Until pay-day, enjoy what is offered. A feel instead of a fuck, and pay on Friday. Cockney girls' (a correspondent, writing on 6 February 1969): C20.

have a go! See **enjoy yourself!**

have a go, Joe, your mother will (or **mother'll**) **never know**, often shortened to **have a go, Joe!** A c.p. of encouragement addressed to a very shy, or a reluctant, man: Cockneys' and Armed Forces': since *c.* 1935.

[**have a good day**, 'often heard after saying "Goodbye!"' (Douglas Leechman): Canadian: since *c.* 1970. Then, in 1975, it became a vogue in the US: witness especially Max Lerner's 'Have a Good Phrase' in the *New York Post* of 20 February 1976. It lies somewhere between a mere conventionalism and a remotely potential c.p. and it could go either way. My own opinion is that, wherever used, it is no more a c.p. than, say, 'have a good time'.]

have a good look round – or, in full, **have a good look round – for you won't see anything but the ceiling for a day or two.** This military c.p. of WW1 – and, although perhaps less generally, WW2 – was applied to the ardour of soldiers on leave towards their wives (whether fully legal or common-law). Cf the slangy *lie feet uppermost*, of women receiving a man sexually.

have a gorilla? (sometimes preceded by **here –**) was Neddy Seagoon's (Harry Secombe's) offer of a cigarette in the BBC 'Goon Show' of the 1950s. The standard reply was 'No thanks, I only smoke baboons'; later, the invitation was declined in the undying words, **I'm trying to give them up**.

have a heart! Don't be so hard-hearted! Steady! Go easy! Current since *c.* 1880, it has been a little less common after *c.* 1940 than before. Common also in US: H. L. Mencken recorded it in *The American Language* in a list of c.pp once very popular, but soon become threadbare and void of either piquancy or any precise meaning; and Berrey in 1942. Its American heyday was *c.* 1910–18; cited as *now* ... by S. R. Strait in the *Boston Globe* in *c.* 1917 (W. J. Burke.)

have a nice trip? is an Australian variant of **did you enjoy your trip?** (Barry Prentice, 9 June 1975.)

have a scratch! has two meanings, both of which I owe to friends as loyal and helpful as they are – or were – intelligent and well-informed. Apparently the slightly earlier is a 'c.p. of satirical encouragement to someone at a loss for answer or information' (Laurie Atkinson): C20. From advice given to someone fidgeting as if at the bite of a flea.

The second, originally and predominantly Cockney, dating from *c.* 1910, is a c.p. of contemptuous dismissal, as in 'Oi, go orn! 'Op it! Go and 'ave a scratch!' (the late Julian Franklyn).

And a third friend, Douglas Leechman, remarks of sense 1, 'Is this not a suggestion that the puzzled one should scratch his head in bewilderment?' He is, clearly, right.

have a snort! See **oh, bloody good ....**

have among (or **at**) ye (later **you**), **my blind harpers!** – with **my** very frequently omitted. Look out for your heads! Look out for yourselves!: this c.p. was, C16–early C19, 'used in throwing or shooting at random among a crowd' (Grose). It lay on the borderline between c.p. and proverbial saying; as early as 1546, Heywood adjudged it to be the latter; but by (say) 1660, at latest, it had, I believe, become the former. Perhaps from coppers thrown to several blind beggars.

This is so notable and expressive a phrase that it merits exemplification. In John Day's comedy, *Humour out of Breath*, both performed and published in 1609, we read, in Act IV, Scene iii:

PAGE: Lord, what scambling [i.e. scrambling] shift has he made for a kiss, and cannot get it neither; a little higher, so so; are you blind, my lord?

HORTENSIO: As a parblind poet: have amongst you, blind harpers.

John Dryden, *The Wild Gallant*, 1662, at Act IV, Scene i, has:

[*They Dance a round Dance, and Sing the Tune.*]
Enter Isabella *and* Constance.
ISA: Are you at that Sport, i' faith? Have among you, blind Harpers.
[*She falls into the Dance.*]

There the sense has become, 'Here goes!'

In *The London Cuckolds*, performed in 1681 and published in 1682, Edward Ravenscroft, at Act III, Scene ii, has Drodle firing a musket into a cellar where he thinks some thieves to be and he announces the action with the words *have amongst you, blind harpers*.

George Farquhar in *The Constant Couple*, performed 1699 and published in 1700, at Act V, Scene i, employs an occasional variant:

FOOTMAN: Sir, we must do as our young mistress commands us.
SIR HARRY: Nay, then have among ye, dogs. [*Throws money among them; they scramble, and take it up.*]

In *The Relapse; or, Virtue in Danger*, 1696, Sir John Vanbrugh uses a common derivative variant at Act IV, Scene v:

SIR TUN: [*Within*] Fire [the blunderbuss], porter.
PORTER: [*Fires.*] Have among ye, my masters.

Much later, David Garrick, in his comedy, *The Male Coquette*, 1757, in Act II, 'Scene, the Club-Room', uses a very frequent C18 form, thus:

DAF[FODIL]: There, then, have among you. [*Throws the letter upon the table.*]

That is to quote a very few from among very many examples occurring in C17–18 literature, principally in comedies.

have among ye (or **you**), **my masters.** See preceding – the quotation from Vanbrugh.

have at the plum-tree! is a late C17–19 c.p., either semi-pro-

verbial or, more likely, in allusion to some popular bawdy song, for there is clearly a reference to *plum-tree*, the female pudenda. It occurs several times in the plays of Thomas Middleton, e.g. *The Widow*, performed *c.* 1614.

have at thee (or **ye** or **you**). 'Take this!' – whatever 'this' may be – uttered in defiance or offer or challenge; sometimes, Look out for yourself! *or* yourselves! *also*, Here's good luck or good health to you!: frequently in the literature, mostly the comedies, of *c.* 1540–1750 and even later. Among playwrights using it are John Fletcher, Beaumont and Fletcher, Thomas Shadwell, Colley Cibber, John Till Allingham, George Macfarren.

Clearly owing much to **have among ye, blind harpers**, this ubiquitous c.p. may be amusingly exemplified by Shadwell's *The Amorous Bigot*, 1690; in Act I, Scene i, Elvira, having made up her face, exclaims, 'Ha, my dear unknown Love, have at thee!' (Look out for yourself!) – and by Allingham's *Mrs Wiggins: A Comic Piece*, 1803, at Act I, Scene ii ('A Tavern'), where Old Wiggins, a mighty trencherman, exclaims over 'a Basin of Turtle': 'Ah! The smell is delicious – (*Tucks the napkin under his chin*) – the taste must be exquisite – come, have at you!'

In its C18–early C19 period very often, and occasionally earlier, the phrase was used playfully or jocularly, with a light ironic touch.

have gun – will travel is taken from the personal advertisement column ('the agony column') of *The Times*, where, of course, it was entirely serious; something comic about it ensured its promotion to the status of a c.p., dating, I suspect, since *c.* 1900, certainly from as early as *c.* 1920, although I have to admit that I didn't often hear it before WW2. Perhaps it also owed something to 'the thick-ear' novel of the Bulldog Drummond type, for, as a c.p., it bears an undertone of 'I'm ready, or game, for anything'. Something of a vogue phrase, it generated such frivolities as *have pen – will write*. The phrase became so engrained in the language that in the *Daily Mail* of 21 October 1969, in the 'Showpiece' section, Harold Wale titles his notice of the film *Hard Contract*, 'Have bed, will travel'.

have one for me. Have a drink for me, as I've no time to go into the pub, or remain in the club, for one: C20. (Wilfred Granville, 11 January 1969.) Cf **do one for me**.

have you a licence? was a mid C18–early C19 c.p., addressed to someone clearing his throat noisily. Grose, 1785, refers to the Act against hawkers and pedlars – and there's an obvious pun on the double sense of *hawking*.

have you any kind thoughts in your mind? introduces a request for a loan, a kindly intervention, any other favour: C20.

have you any more funny stories? and **now tell me the one about the three bears.** Tell me another! These are c.pp. of polite scepticism, or of polite boredom: mostly in Britain and Australia: since the late 1920s or the early 1930s.

have you ever been tickled, lady? See Vernon Noble's comment at **can you 'ear me, Mother?** In a letter dated 11 December 1973, Vernon Noble mentions that this 'Ken Dodd phrase usually begins as an "intro" to his act. "I was tickled to death. Have *you* ever been tickled, lady?"'

have you found a giggles nest? is a lower-class C19 c.p. addressed to someone giggling or tittering or to someone laughing senselessly or excessively. By a pun on an imaginary *giggle's nest* and on '(a fit of the) giggles'. If there's a *laughing* jackass (the kookaburra), why not a *giggle* bird?

have you got the weight? Have you 'caught on'? – do you understand? Naval: since *c.* 1930. Semantically cf 'the *onus* of the proof'.

have you heard any good stories lately? exemplifies the use of c.pp. as social gambits and dates from (if I remember rightly) *c.* 1930. Noël Coward's *Relative Values*, performed in 1951 and published in 1952. Act II, Scene i, ends with precisely this gambit.

In the 1920s, another such gambit used to be. 'Have you been to – *or* seen – any good plays lately?': but it didn't so take the public fancy as to have 'made the grade'.

have you heard the latest? – to which the reply, with or without a pause to enable one's interlocutor or audience the opportunity to say, 'No! Tell me' – is *It's not out yet*. A jocular c.p., employed predominantly, in fact almost exclusively, among men: C20. (Mr A. B. Petch, 16 September 1974, reminds me of this one; I first heard it, *c.* 1920, in Australia.)

have you heard the news? The squire (or **the squire's daughter**) **has been foully** (or **most foully**) **murdered**. This c.p., very common *c.* 1905–30, satirizes the late Victorian and early Edwardian melodrama. It was much used by the British soldier in WW1, as B & P testify. It occurs in Philip MacDonald's 'thriller', *Rope to Spare*, 1932; and in a letter dated 5 September 1946, Mr A. B. Petch remarks, 'Jokers still come on with it.'

have you heard this one? – often shortened to **heard this one?** A c.p. that inexorably introduces a (usually so-called) funny story: C20.

have you pigs in your belly? See **what? have you pigs … ?**

have you *quite* **finished?** – for instance, talking in general or complaining or adversely criticizing or merely rambling pointlessly on and on: 'since the 1920's (? earlier). Very genteelly "sarky"' (Frank Shaw).

have you read any good books lately? is a conversational gambit originating – if I remember correctly – in the middle 1940s. The smart literary-world rejoinder is, 'No, but I've written one', which arose *c.* 1955.

have you seen a dream walking? is a variant of **did you ever see a dream walking?**, q.v.

have you seen the Shah? This late C19 c.p., current mostly among Londoners but derivatively heard often enough among provincials, arose from a visit of the Shah of Persia to Queen Victoria. (The late Frank Shaw, in a letter dated 28 October 1968, suggested *Punch* as the originator.)

have you shit the bed? A low late C19–20 c.p., addressed to one who has got out of bed rather earlier than usual. As pointed as it is earthy.

have you shook? was a late C18–mid C19 underworld c.p., explained thus by J. H. Vaux in the glossary written in 1812 and included in his *Memoirs*, published in 1818: 'Have you *shook*? … did you succeed in getting any thing? When two persons rob in company, it is generally the province, or part, of one to *shake* (that is, obtain the *swagg*), and the other to carry, that is, bear it to a place of safety.'

haven't his best friends told him? is a jocular c.p., arising in the middle or late 1950s, and based upon the advertisements of a well-known deodorant. Not necessarily applied to body odour.

having a good arm? A C20, esp. a WW1, military c.p. applied to a soldier wearing numerous badges on his sleeve – e.g., 'farrier' or 'Lewis gunner' or 'marksman'. Perhaps influenced by *having a good war*, a successful or very lucky war.

[**having a wonderful time – wish you were here**, a favourite cliché, usually scrawled on a postcard from a friend on holiday, and probably dating from the 1870s or 1880s, has, by its exacerbating frequency, naturally been good-humouredly derided – and therefore become almost a c.p. It was not unknown among soldiers serving in the grim, wet, bitterly cold trenches on the Western Front, 1914–18.]

having fun? is an ironical c.p., dating since *c.* 1950 and addressed to someone obviously having difficulties or in trouble. Cf **are you happy in the Service** or **in your work?**

hay is for horses or, in the Comic Phonetic Alphabet and as a c.p. reminiscent of the CPA, **'ay is for 'orses**, the latter perhaps prompted by the conversion of the exclamatory *hey* to *eh*. This is a c.p. addressed to someone who says *hey!* or *eh?* for 'I beg your pardon': C18–20. It is one of the longest-lived of all c.pp. (**black is your eye!** having flourished notably longer), and was recorded in S, towards the end of Dialogue I:

NEV[EROUT]: Hay, Madam, did you call me?
MISS: Hay! Why; Hay is for Horses.

For a fuller treatment of this refreshing domestic c.p., see my *Comic Alphabets*, 1961, and cf my commentary edn (1963) of S's witty book.

hay (or **hey**), **lass, let's be hammered for life on Sunday!** A lower classes', perhaps originally a metal-workers', c.p. of late C19–early C20. Ware, however, plausibly advances the theory that the phrase came from 'the work of the blacksmith at Gretna Green. It was said of him jocularly that he hammered couples together rather than married them': an attractive guess, and probably accurate.

he beats Akeybo – and Akeybo beats the devil arose before 1874 and fell into disuse during the late 1930s. (Hotten, 5th edn.) *Akeybo* remains, I believe, a mystery; there is, just possibly, a link with Welsh Gypsy *ake tu!*, a toast, literally 'Here thou art!' – cf **here's to you!**

he broke his pick is, in the US, said of a man discharged from a job: *c.* 1920–60. (Berrey.) Without a pick, a certain type of manual labourer is obviously useless.

he can make it sit up and beg indicates that a man has become exceptionally skilful in working some material, esp. a metal: originally among metalworkers; since *c.* 1930 or maybe a decade earlier. Perhaps it derives from the late C19–20 low c.p., *it sits up and begs* or *it is sitting up and begging*, where *it* is clearly the male organ and the allusion is to making a dog sit up and beg for, e.g., a piece of meat.

he can pick the bones out of that! See **pick the bones!**

he can put his shoes under my bed any time he likes. He's sexually acceptable to *me*: feminine, mostly in Australia: since *c.* 1920 (Barry Prentice, 15 December 1974.)

he comes and goes is 'an occasional usage' – *not* a very frequent c.p. – 'for a man of the *Love 'em and leave 'em* type, with emphasis on the *come*' (A. B. Petch, 30 March 1976): not only public-house humour: since *c.* 1950, or perhaps a decade or two earlier.

he could eat me without salt. See **I could eat that** ....

he could fall into shit (or **the shit** or, Canadian, **into the shit-cart**) **and come up smelling of violets**; Cockney variant, **he could fall into a cart** (or **dump** or **heap** or **load** or **pile**) **of shit and come out with a gold watch** (or **with a new suit on**). This late C19–20 c.p. is applied either to an exceptionally, or an habitually lucky person or to someone extraordinarily lucky upon a specific occasion.

he couldn't hit the side of a barn! US: dating since *c.* 1920. 'Origin obscure, but rural. Main lease of life in baseball: the opposing pitcher is so wild *he couldn't etc.* (and so can't get the ball over the plate)' (Edward Hodnett, 18 August 1975).

he couldn't knock the skin off a rice pudding expresses extreme contempt of a weakling or a coward: C20, but particularly common in army or navy during WW1. A US – and British – variant is *he couldn't punch his way out of a paper bag*: since *c.* 1910. (Colonel Albert Moe, 15 June 1975.) Cf **now then, shoot** ....

he couldn't see a joke except by appointment – and he'd probably be late for that has, since *c.* 1955, been applied to a very, very 'dim' or slow-witted fellow. (Wilfred Granville, in a letter written in late December 1968.)

he cut me some slack. He did me a favour: US teenagers': a vogue for a brief period, *c.* 1968–72. (Norris M. Davidson, in letter dated 15 June 1971.)

he doesn't know his arse from his elbow, late C19–20; Canadian variant, C20, **... from a hole in the ground.** He's extremely or hopelessly ignorant. Cf the next two.

he doesn't know if his arsehole is bored or punched. See **arsehole** ....

he doesn't know the difference between shitting and tearing his arse. He ignores – or is ignorant of – the golden mean: low Canadian: since the 1920s.

he doesn't know where he lives or, originally an illiteracy, but soon an intentional jocularity, **'e don't know where 'e lives.** A contemptuous c.p., applied to a person painfully futile; dating from *c.* 1920. The latter and slightly later form owes something, I suspect, to some radio comedian.

he doesn't know whether it's Pancake Tuesday or half-past breakfast time. He doesn't know what's what; he's bewildered: since *c.* 1965 (? much earlier). Mr A. B. Petch records that he heard it, 16 June 1968, on television.

he doesn't miss a beat. He's very alert and well-informed: since *c.* 1950. From music. (Wilfred Granville, 11 February 1969.)

he fought the battle of Paris is a US witticism of the 1920s and 1930s; 'said of one who was stationed in Paris during the First World War' (Berrey).

he goes around with thumb in bum and mind in neutral. See **with thumb in bum** ....

he goes for my money. See **goes for my money.**

he hangs up his fiddle when he comes home. See **he leaves his fiddle behind the door.**

he has a pain in the little finger. See **pain** ....

he has a rag on every bush. See **rag on every bush.**

he has as much wit as three folks, explained by the c.p. it curtails: **he has as much wit as three folks, two fools and a madman.** It belonged to the approximate period mid C18–mid C19. (Grose, 1796.)

he has cloth ears. See **cloth-ears** ....

he has gone to visit his uncle was a mid C18–19 c.p., applied to 'one who leaves his wife soon after marriage' (Grose, 1785).

he has swallowed a stake and cannot stop. See **swallowed a stake.**

he hasn't sixpence to scratch his arse with. See **scratch his arse with** ....

he hasn't sucked that out of his fingers. That's not *his* idea *or* He hasn't thought of *that* all by himself; in a rather different nuance, He has mysterious – *or* closely-guarded – authentic information: mostly Londoners' and esp. Cockneys': late C19–20. I haven't heard it since *c.* 1950, but that's not to say that it doesn't linger on.

he hath been at shrift! This C16 ecclesiastical c.p. was applied to a man betrayed he knows not how. (Tyndale, *The Obedience of a Christian Man*, 1528.) The implication is that, contrary to almost inviolable practice, he has been betrayed by the priest to whom he confessed.

he hath eaten the rump is partly a proverbial saying and partly a c.p. of *c.* 1660–1800; said of one who is constantly talking. Perhaps cf, semantically, **give your arse a chance!**

he is digging a grave or **...digging for worms.** See **digging** ....

he is in his skin. See **in his skin** ....

he is like a rope-dancer's pole – (with) lead at both ends was, *c.* 1770–1830, applied to a dull, sluggish fellow. (Grose, 1788.)

he is like a winter's day – short and dirty. This probably, at first, rural mid C18–mid C19 c.p. is recorded in Grose, 1788. Cf the dialectal *winter Friday*, a cold and wretched-looking person.

he is none of John Whoball's children. He's not easy to fool: late C16–17. Cf **whoa-ball**, a milkmaid, itself probably a compound of *whoa!* and *Ball*, a common name for a cow.

he is (or **he's**) **not greedy but he likes a lot.** See **greedy** ....

he is only fit for Ruffians (or **Ruffins**) **Hall** is a mid C17–early C19 Londoners' c.p., applied to an overdressed apprentice. Ruffians Hall was that part of Smithfield 'where Trials of Skill were played by ordinary Ruffianly people with Sword and Buckler' (Blount's dictionary, 1674). The c.p. was recorded in C17 and again in *PG*.

he is so mean that he wouldn't give you his cold. Very late C19–20. (Wilfred Granville, in letter of 6 December 1968.)

he leaves his fiddle behind the door (or **he hangs up his fiddle**) **when he comes home.** He is great fun, and very witty, when he's out of the house but not when he's in it: *c.* 1800–1940. It probably derives from the synonymous C18–20 Derbicism, *to hang the fiddle at the door.*

he looks as if he could eat me without salt is the feminine complement and counterpart of the masculine **she looks** ....

he looks as if he had pissed on a nettle is 'a c.p. evoked on seeing a doleful countenance' (Douglas Leechman): late C19–20. From the colloquial – later, dialectal – mid C16–20 expression, *to have pissed on a nettle*, to be ill-tempered, or very uneasy.

he looks as if he has lost a pound and found sixpence or **a sixpence**; occasionally ...**lost a shilling and found a ha'penny**, obsolete by *c.* 1940. He looks either ruefully pleased or, more frequently, very miserable: C19–20.

he may be trusted alone. He is very experienced and shrewd: *c.* 1800–50. Recorded in Pierce Egan's enlargement, 1823 – one cannot call it an improvement – of Grose. It sarcastically suggests that he can safely go anywhere alone.

he never does anything wrong! ironically or satirically implies that he never does anything right; arising on 'the halls' in 1883 (Ware), it soon became general – and by 1920 obsolete. Another source, however, puts the origin in a Gaiety Theatre play that enshrines the song containing the optimistic words, 'In me you see the Rajah of Bong/Who never, no never, did anything wrong.'

he never had no mother – he (or **he just) hatched out when his dad pissed against a wall one hot day** is a low military c.p. of C20. (I regret to admit that never did I hear it in either WW1 or WW2: and I spent most of my time in the ranks. I suspect that by 1945 it had become obsolete.)

he numbers the waves. See **numbers**....

he pisses more than he drinks was a semi-proverbial c.p., preceded by **vainglorious man** and directed at a braggart: late C17–early C19. (BE; Grose.)

he plays as fair as if he had (or **he'd) picked your pocket** was, in C19, applied to a dishonest gambler.

he plays at hide and seek was *c.* 1750–1880, 'a saying of one who is in fear of being arrested ... and therefore does not choose to appear in public' (Grose, 1785.)

he rides like a sack of flour is applied to a poor horseman: Canadian: since (?) *c.* 1950 (Douglas Leechman, December 1968.)

he should be pissed on from a great height. He's beneath contempt: Australian naval: WW2 and after. I cannot prove it, but I'd say that this c.p. was prompted by the RAF's *to shoot* (someone) *down from a great height*, to defeat him in argument or on a matter of procedure or protocol.

he that is at a low ebb at Newgate may soon be afloat at Tyburn was *c.* 1660–1810, a c.p. implying that he who was condemned at Newgate might end by being hanged – his heels afloat, i.e. dangling in the air – at Tyburn. ('Proverbs' Fuller, *PG*.)

he thinks he holds it. He's conceited and vain: *c.* 1870–1930: originally a sporting, it soon became a general, c.p. (Ware.) By *it* is meant either a championship or a prize.

he thinks it's just to pee through is applied to an unsophisticated youth: C20.

he was little – but oh my! See **little – but oh my!**

he was on the wrong side of the hedge when the brains were given away. He is brainless or stupid or, at the very least, extremely dull: *c.* 1810–80. In late C19–20, the form has been *he was on the wrong side of the door when the brains were handed out.*

he was wrapped in the tail of his mother's smock. See **wrapt up**....

he washes clean and dries dirty. 'The classic excuse for a slovenly rating who disgraced his Division on an important occasion by appearing unshaven and unwashed: now a part of naval folklore, and applied to any "scruffy" rating' (*Sailors' Slang*); so far as I know, first recorded in *SS* in 1949, but going back, I think, to *c.* 1920.

he will be pleased! – emphasis on *will*. This ironic c.p. dates from *c.* 1910.

he will never louse a grey head of his own. He will never live to be old: C18–early C19. (Grose.)

he will never shit a seaman's turd. He'll never be a good seaman: naval: late C19–20 (*DSUE*, 1937).

he will piss when he can't whistle. He will be hanged: perhaps originally an underworld c.p.: mid C18–19. (Grose.) A reference to the *post-mortem* release of waste.

he worships his creator was a society c.p. of *c.* 1900–40; applied to a *self-made* man holding an excessively high opinion of himself. Punning on *the Creator*, God. (Ware.)

he would make a good trumpeter – for he smells strong, with the second part omitted increasingly often: mid C18–mid C19. In Grose, 1788, the latter part of the c.p. is **for he has a strong breath**. It means 'He has fetid breath'; and it plays on *strong breath*, bad breath, but good lungs.

he would (or **he'd) tap the Admiral.** He'd do anything for a drink of strong liquor: Naval: midC19–early C20. According to Bowen, 'From the old naval myth that when Lord Nelson's body was being brought home, seamen contrived to get at the rum in which it was preserved.'

he wouldn't say 'shit' even if he had his mouth full – or **a mouthful** – of it. This low Canadian c.p. satirizes a man excessively mealy-mouthed: since *c.* 1930 or perhaps a little earlier.

he wouldn't work in an iron lung. 'He is so lazy that he would not work if his breathing were done for him' (Barry Prentice, *c.* 6 March 1975): Australian: since *c.* 1950.

headache – as much use as a; no more use than a headache. Useless: C20. The former occurs in, e.g., Dorothy L. Sayers, *Unnatural Death*, 1927.

heads I win – tails you lose. This is a mock wager; 'I cannot fail!': since *c.* 1830. It was anticipated by Thomas Shadwell, *Epsom Wells*, 1672, thus: 'Worse than *Cross I win*, *Pile you lose*'. (Apperson.)

It became also US before – probably well before – the end of C19. John W. Clark says (24 July 1975), 'Certainly common here'.

heads on 'em like boils is an Australian two-up players' c.p., referring to coins that have yielded a long run of heads: since *c.* 1910. For a wonderful account of a two-up game, Lawson Glassop's gambling story, *Lucky Palmer*, 1948, could hardly be bettered. Cf Australian card-players' c.p., **heads on 'em like mice**, indicating a very strong hand.

hear anything knock? See **did you hear...?**

hear my tale or kiss my tail! – originally and often preceded by **either**. At line 120 of George Peele's *The Old Wives' Tale*, 1595, in A. H. Bullen's edn of Greene's and Peele's plays and poems, Madge, the blacksmith's wife, telling an old wives' tale, is interrupted by Frolic; she promptly exclaims 'Nay, either hear my tale or kiss my tail', i.e. Don't interrupt my story. In 1595. *tail* meant either 'posterior' or 'penis' or, as perhaps here, the female pudend; in general, *kiss my tail* was an early equivalent of *kiss my arse*. There is, I think, little doubt that (*either*) *hear my tale or kiss my tail* is a homely c.p. of Elizabethan and Jacobean and probably Caroline and perhaps even Restoration times.

heard the news? See **have you heard the news?**

heard this one? See **have you heard this one?**

heart. See **have a heart!**

heavy-heavy hangs over your head was, very approximately *c*. 1910–50, a warning 'to duck something overhead' (Berrey); not, one would have thought, an urgent warning – it's far too wordy.

he'd drink the stuff if he had to strain it through a shitty cloth! A low Canadian c.p. that, dating from *c*. 1920, means that he's a hopeless drunkard.

he'd fuck (or **shag**) **anything on two legs** (or **anything with a hole in it**) is an admiring, mostly Services c.p. that pays tribute to a reputedly spectacular sexual urge and potency, but not necessarily implying satyriasis. A late C19–20 general synonym, applying to an inveterate womanizer, is **he will** (or **he'll**) **shag anything from seventeen to seventy.**

he'd skin a turd. He's parsimonious: low Canadian: late C19–20.

he'll clog ag, again. C20: Vernon Noble, 11 September 1974, says:

> He'll live long enough to wear out another clog sole. Still current in the West Riding, although far fewer clogs are worn to need repairing. (Similarly: 'He'll mucky another clean collar.') The West Riding [of Yorkshire] is rich in 'sayings', some, like this one, becoming catch-phrases with wider connotations than the original meaning.

he'll leap over your head was a hunting c.p. of *c*. 1830–1900. In R. S. Surtees, *Handley Cross*, 1854, vol. I, in the chapter headed 'Another Sporting Lector' (lecture by Mr Jorrocks), occurs this passage. 'If a chap axes if your neg will jump timber, say, "He'll leap over your 'ead".'

he'll make nineteen bits (or **bites**) **of a bilberry** is a pejorative c.p. of *c*. 1640–1700. He'll make a meal of what's only a mouthful. (Ray.)

he'll shag anything from seventeen to seventy. See **he'd fuck anything on two legs.**

he'll spit brown and call the cat a ring-tailed bustard. An 'ironic c.p. directed against a young naval rating who is seen to be acting "stroppy"' – i.e., bloody-minded – 'after a short time in the Service. A potential "skate" or Queen's hard bargain' (Wilfred Granville, late December 1968): since the late 1940s.

he'll take off any minute now. He's in a 'flap' – exceedingly excited; also, He's very angry indeed – likely to 'hit the ceiling': RAF: since 1938. From aeroplanes taking off in departure.

hell hath (or **holds**) **no fury like a woman's corns.** This jocular punning c.p., apparently not antedating the C20, obviously burlesques the famous quotation from William Congreve's *The Mourning Bride*, 1697:

> Heaven has no rage like love to hatred turn'd,
> Nor hell a fury like a woman scorn'd.

hell! said the Duchess when she caught her teats in the mangle, often shortened, allusively, to the opening four words. Dating from *c*. 1895, it was frequently used in WW1, although seldom in the ranks; after WW1, the shorter form has predominated, often with no reference whatsoever to the original: cf Michael Arlen's novel, *Hell! Said the Duchess*, 1934. So well established by that time was the phrase that, on 11 January 1936, *The Times Literary Supplement* could wittily caption a review of Daniel George's *A Peck of Troubles*, with the words, 'Said the Duchess'. On 20 March 1937, in the same newspaper supplement, the reviewer of *DSUE* remarked that 'The saga of the Duchess, "who had taken no part in the conversation", was on men's lips at least forty years ago'.

A C20 variant is *hell! said the Duke, pulling the Duchess on like a jack-boot*; another C20 variant, but Canadian, is *hell! cried the Duchess and flung down her cigar*.

hello, hello, hello! See **hullo, hullo, hullo!**

hello, playmates! is 'Arthur Askey's cheerful greeting introduced (and long used) in his record-running pre-Second World War radio entertainment "Band Waggon", described by Gale Pedrick in BBC Year Book 1948 as "grandfather of all BBC series", continued through the war and after' (Vernon Noble, 8 February 1975). It would be safe to say that it had become a very widely used general c.p. by 1945 at the latest.

[**hello, sucker!** is a sort of c.p. greeting by a night-club proprietor or manager to a prospective customer: US: *c*. 1930–50. (Berrey.)]

hell's a-poppin', occasionally with **loose** added. 'Said of one on a spree' (Berrey), but also = Things are really swinging: US: *c*. 1930–60. A crazy, zany US film, bore a similar title.

help! sharks! see **too late! too late!**

help yourself! Please *do!* – Please yourself! – Just as you please!: since *c*. 1917. It occurs in, e.g., Richard Blaker, *Enter, a Messenger*, 1926. 'Often said in reply to "Can – or may – I use your 'phone?"' (A. B. Petch, March 1967).

It passed to the US *c*. 1918. Irvin S. Cobb, *Murder Day by Day*, 1933, writes,

> He asked ... if he might be permitted to take a last look at the deceased.
> 'Help yourself.' said the widow. 'He's laid out upstairs in the front room. Just you walk up, Mr McKenna.'

Other enlightening examples are these:
June Drummond, *The Saboteurs*, 1967:

> 'I'm looking for Joe Riddle.'
> 'Next door,' said the man. 'Help yourself.'

Nichol Fleming, *Counter Paradise*, 1968:

> 'I'd like to check that car of yours.'
> 'Help yourself.'

Hartley Howard, *Million Dollar Snapshot*, 1971:

> 'Before you ask your questions, is it all right for me to ask one of mine?'
> Terrel shrugged and said, 'Help yourself. I'm in no hurry.'

Cf **be my guest!**

hemp is growing for the villain – the; also **hemp is grown for you**. Applied to a rogue 'born to be hanged' with a hempen rope: late C18–19 (JB; Ware.)

hence the pyramids. This c.p. is either applied to an unintentional *non sequitur* or deliberately said as an ironically jocular *non sequitur:* late C19–20. but not much used since WW2. It derives from a passage in the very rude, very droll recitation known to the earthy as *The Showman* and recorded in B & P, 1931.

her clothes sit on her like a saddle on a sow's back. Applied to an ill-dressed woman, this c.p. – recorded by BE – belongs to the very approximate period 1660–1750.

her country cousins (or **her relations**) **have come**. She is having her period; lower-middle classes': *c.* 1850–1940. (Manchon.) The latter form euphemizes the former, which puns in precisely the same way as Shakespeare's '*country* matters' – see my *Shakespeare's Bawdy*.

her face would stop a clock is derisively applied to the battle-axe or rear-end-of-a-bus sort of face: since *c.* 1890; 'still heard' in 1974, Mr A. B. Petch assures me and as I have, myself, noticed.

her knitting's out is a naval c.p. that, in WW2, was applied to a minesweeper that has her gear over the side. (PGR.)

her relations have come. See **her country cousins....**

herbs (or **'erbs**), **good** or **sweet**. See **good** (or **sweet**) **herbs!**

[**here am I, slaving over a hot stove all day (while all you do is** (e.g.) **sit at a desk)**. Used literally, i.e. seriously and aggrievedly, it is manifestly not a c.p. But, as Paul Beale, on 11 August 1975, points out, it is often employed jocularly: and then it is incipiently one: '*The* [utterance] of the hard-pressed housewife'.]

here come de jedge (or **judge**). 'A laughter-producing gag from one of our popular TV shows. One hears it frequently' (W. J. Burke, 9 April 1975): US: since early 1970s.

here comes the bride! is a jocular c.p., used – in the girl's presence – when an engagement is announced: since *c.* 1920.

here comes the gorblimey. A Cockney soldiers' derisive comment, addressed either directly to or in the hearing of such or such a battalion or to a section thereof: Regular Army: since the 1890s, but little heard since WW2. (B & P.)

here endeth the first lesson is a Protestant c.p., employed by the bored after a long speech or lecture or gratuitous exposition: since *c.* 1870; by 1960, slightly obsolescent. A dependable criterion of a bore is that he explains, at length, something nobody has asked him to explain.

here goes! See **here we go!**

here they come – mooching along, all of a bloody heap. B & P say: 'If one saw one's own or preferably another unit arriving in billets after a long march, one shouted:

Here they come
Mooching along
All of a bloody heap.'

A WW1 British army chanting c.p. Note *mooching* instead of *marching*.

here they come smoking their pipes! This c.p. of the Billingsgate fish-buyers was shouted when, at auctions, the bids were rapid and high: *c.* 1870–1940. Ware remarks that the c.p. probably signified 'independence and determination' – and he's probably right.

here we are again! At first (*c.* 1880) a form of greeting, it has, in C20 been very much a c.p. It was probably originated by Harry Paine. that clown, who in the 1870s and 1880s, at Drury Lane, began the Boxing Night harlequinade with a somersault and a cheerful 'Here we are again!' The late Frank Shaw writing to me, early in November 1968, remarked that it was 'still used, by, e.g., seaside pierrots' – a statement reinforced by Mr Vernon Noble's comment in a letter written on 11 December 1973: 'Joey the Clown in the old Harlequinade – forerunner and for many years an essential ingredient of pantomime – introduced the c.p. "Here we are again!" – which people are still saying without knowing how it originated.'

The phrase had been revitalized by the WW1 soldiers' song:

We're here because we're here,
Because we're here, because we're here,
Oh, here we are, oh, here we are,
Oh, here we are again –

recorded in Benham, 1948, and there glossed as 'Soldiers' Song. *c.* 1916'. But that song merges

We're here
Because we're here;
We're here
Because we're here,
Because we're here

with

Here we are,
Here we are,
Here we are again –

repeated *ad nauseam*. And even that combined version gave way to a music-hall 'prettying', which began with

Here we are, here we are,
Here we are again!

and ended with the lines

Hullo! Hullo!
Here we are again!

(See B & P, 1931, or that reconstruction, which, planned by EP and edited by John Brophy, appeared in 1965 as *The Long Trail*: What the Soldier Said and Sang in 1914–1918.)

Allan Monkhouse's *The Ray*, 1928, has, in Act III, this passage:

BRANSOME: How d'y' do? (*He bows to Robert*.)
ROBERT: This is unexpected, Mr Bransome.
BRANSOME: Yes, here we are again.

Bransome is a businessman of the theatre; the phrase has, for him, a reminiscence of the old song.

here we come, mum – dad's on the axle was a schoolboys' c.p., dating since *c.* 1910 and expressing satisfaction and delight at speed on bicycle or scooter, hence, among young men, at the happy or successful completion of some other activity.

here we go! (or, implying repetition, **here we go again**) arose, I think, *c.* 1850 or 1860, but I lack any early printed record; I remember it from *c.* 1902. Cf the longer-lived **here goes!**, used by J. H. Newman in a letter dated 1829, as the *OED* tells us, and approximately meaning 'There's not much chance, but I'll *try*' or, often, 'Now for it!'

here you are then! 'A quip at the time of the First World War, 1914–18, with indelicacy in the innuendo and embellished in a drone: "You can have it all/Up against the wall!" and developed into scabrous verse' (Laurie Atkinson, 18 July 1975). Cf **it's only human nature, after all.**

here's a belly never reared a bastard. This Anglo-Irish c.p. of mid C19–early C20 designates a boaster, whether female or, derivatively, who has 'suited action to the words. Obsolete' (Frank Shaw, November 1968).

here's a couple of matchsticks. A mostly workman's jocularity addressed to someone sleepy early in the day and accompanied by a gesture of handing him two so that he may prop his eyes open: late C19–20.

here's a fiver (or **a five-pound note**) **for you** is addressed to one who has received mail consisting wholly or mainly of bills and perhaps circulars: C20.

here's a ha'penny (or **a penny**) **– don't spend it all at one shop** (or **all at once**) is a jocularity accompanying the munificent gift to a (young) child: late C19–20; by 1960, obsolescent; by 1970, virtually obsolete.

[**here's fluff in your latch-key!** could, I suppose, be called 'a drinking c.p.' – current during WW2 among RAF officers and occurring in, e.g., Terence Rattigan's *Flare Path*, 1942, and enduring for several years after the war. But, predominantly a toast and nothing more, it is ineligible.]

[**here's hair on your chest!** and **here's how!**, being toasts, are not genuine c.pp.]

here's how!, by itself, is ineligible, for it's a mere drinking conventionalism. It has, however, prompted the elaboration: **here's how! I don't mean 'how'; I mean 'when'. I know how.** A correspondent from Highworth, Wiltshire, mentions having heard it in 1944.

here's incident! In *The Dramatist*, 1793, Frederick Reynolds causes his unsuccessful playwright, Vapid, who extols the virtues of theatrical incident, to use it several times; for instance, early in Act II, Vapid, realizing that he has just made a tremendous *faux pas* with Lady Waitfor't, exclaims, 'Mercy on me: – here's incident!' In a University of London MA thesis, Miss Madge Collins, writing about Reynolds, mentions that *here's incident!* became a c.p.

In the same scene, when the irate Lady, in departing, declares, 'Oh! I'll be revenged, I'm determined', Vapid *solus* remarks, 'What a great exit! very well! – I've got an incident, however.' A little later, Marianne bids him hide behind a sofa; he comments, 'Behind this sopha! here's an incident!' And in Act V:

MARIANNE: Did you really love me, Mr Vapid?
VAPID: Hey day! recovered! – here's incident!
MARIANNE: But did you really love me, Mr Vapid?
VAPID: Yes I did – here's stage effect!

With thanks to Miss Patricia Sigl.

here's me head – me arse is comin'! (or **here's my head – my arse is coming!**) A workmen's c.p., dating since *c.* 1895, but not much used since *c.* 1940, the female type having become much less frequent. It refers to a girl, or woman, wearing high heels and walking with head and shoulders well forward and with posterior, esp. shapely or buxom, well behind. It derives from the mostly Midlands description of a forward-sloping

person, as in 'Oh, he's all *here's me head, me arse is comin''* (which I owe to Mr Richard Merry).

[**here's mud in your eye!** is a very famous army officers' toast of WW1, *not* a c.p.]

here's Peter the Painter, a jocular c.p. of *c.* 1910–20, derives from the legendary figure supposed to have taken a leading part in 'the battle of Sidney Street' (London) in 1910.

here's the back of my hand to you! At the end of Dialogue I in S, Miss Notable says, 'Well, Mr *Neverout*; here's the Back of my Hand to you' – which is a flippant and probably challenging goodbye of late C17–mid C18.

[**here's to crime!**, being a toast, however common, is ineligible.]

here's where you want it! – accompanied by the speaker's touching or clearly indicating his own head, e.g. by a tap on his own forehead, means 'You must use your intelligence': since *c.* 1890. Cf the very closely related C20 c.p., **he's got it up there** – he's very intelligent indeed.

here's yer back! See LIVERPOOL CATCH PHRASES.

here's yer hat – what's yer 'urry? and **here's your hat – what's your hurry?** The late Frank Shaw, in a letter written in November 1968, thought that this was the original British form: and he should have known. In a letter written two months later, he described it as a 'graceless farewell to visitor. North Country.' He dated it as 'since *c.* 1920', but intimated that it had perhaps arisen ten or even twenty years earlier.

Mr W. J. Burke, in December 1968, informed me that the US version is *here's your hat – don't rush!* On the other hand, Colonel Albert Moe, on 30 June 1975, unequivocally and unquestioningly presents *here's your hat – what's your hurry?* as the US form.

I'd hate to be compelled to decide the priority: and, anyway, I lack the evidence to do so.

he's a cunt and a half is applied to any extremely objectionable fellow; as a c.p., dates from the middle or late 1950s; and derives from the low slang *cunt*, anybody one intensely dislikes. (See esp. *DSUE* Supplement.)

he's a fine fellow but his muck (or **shit**) **stinks.** He *is* a fine fellow, but, after all, he's only human: proletarian: C20. Cf **they think their shit doesn't stink.**

he's a Mr Nonesuch. See **Nonesuch.**

he's a poet . . . . See **that's a rhyme.**

he's a regular Indian and **he's on the Indian list.** These Canadian c.pp., dating since *c.* 1925, are applied to an habitual drunkard, esp. to one to whom it is illegal to sell liquor. It is illegal to sell liquor to Indians coming from any of their Settlements or reserves. (Professor F. E. L. Priestley.)

he's a whole team and a horse to spare, often elaborated by the addition of **and a (big) dog under the wagon** – and even more often shortened to **he's** – or come to that, **she's – a whole team.** He's a very fine and capable fellow, or she's a very fine woman: US, originally and chiefly New England. Farmer records the shortest form and the longest. The predominant form occurs in T. C. Haliburton, *The Clockmaker*, in all three Series (1837, 1838, 1840) and in its sequel, *The Attaché*, 1843–4, e.g. in Series II, vol. 1, p. 8, thus: '. . . It does one good to look at her. She is a whole team and a horse to spare, that gal, – that's a fact.' Apparently, this c.p. was current during the approximate period *c.* 1830–1900.

he's been looking in your paybook! is an Armed Forces' c.p. of 1939–45 in reference to a third person's imputation of illegitimacy or other sexual irregularity, a Serviceman's paybook recording many intimate details: and therefore it should be compared with the Australian soldiers' c.p. of 1914–18: **you've been reading my letters.**

he's been to Whitehall. He's looking very cheerful: an army officers' c.p. of *c.* 1860–1905. From an extension of leave obtained from the War Office. (Ware.)

he's built like a brick shit-house. See **built ....**

he's done so much bird is an underworld, esp. a convicts' c.p. dating from *c.* 1945. It occurs in Tony Parker and Robert Allerton, *The Courage of His Convictions*, 1962. A pun on the twittering of a bird and on cant *bird* imprisonment.

he's gone north about. A nautical c.p. that, dating *c.* 1860–1900, refers to a sailor that has died by other than drowning (B & L).

he's got it up there. See **this is where you want it.**

he's got ten bob each way on himself. See **get you!**

he's had a smell (occasionally **a sniff**) **of the barman's apron.** This c.p. refers to one who very easily gets drunk: since *c.* 1910.

he's in the catbird seat. W. J. Burke, 28 January 1969, writes:

> If some player, let us say a pitcher, was in complete command of the game and was moving along to a sure victory, [Walter] 'Red' [Barber] would say to him 'He's in the catbird seat!' I do not know how this phrase started.... In 1968 Doubleday in New York published a book entitled *Rhubarb in the Catbird Seat*, by Red Barber and Robert Creamer. I have glanced through this, did find a few of the [baseball] phrases, but no explanation as to their origins, etc.

Webster's Third International Dictionary, 3rd edn, does not include it. The phrase flourished *c.* 1945–55: cf **tearing up the pea-patch**. Literally, a *catbird* is the black-eyed thrush, a US song-bird.

he's making his will. See **making his will.**

he's not so well since he fell off the organ. This jocular c.p. – often a communal jest – has, throughout the C20, been addressed, not always unkindly, to a member of the company. The allusion is to an organ-grinder's monkey.

he's not tight, but he's taken up a lot of slack is a Canadian c.p. – 'recent', says Douglas Leechman, January 1969, and meaning 'He's not tight-fisted, but he *is* very careful with his money.'

he's one of us. This imputation of homosexuality may originally have been euphemistic, was prompted by the certainly euphemistic *one of those*, a homosexual, dates from *c.* 1910, and is a homosexual c.p.

he's playing hell with himself applies to a man conspicuously grumbling and muttering to himself: since *c.* 1950 or a few years earlier.

he's saving them all for Liza has, since before 1909, been applied by the lower and lower-middle classes to 'a good young man who will not use oaths or strike blows' (Ware).

It derives from that mythical youth who wouldn't give a beggar a penny because he was saving all his money for his girl.

he's saying something! See **talk to me!**

he's so tight he squeaks. See **tight as ....**

he's the whole show. He's the important man – or thinks he is – in the matter concerned: since *c.* 1912. Originally from 'showbiz', it is American and cited in 'Straight Talk', by S. R. Strait, in the *Boston Globe* of *c.* 1917. By *c.* 1945, obsolete (W. J. Burke.)

hey, Abbott! is recorded in W & F's list of seven 'Synthetic Fad Expressions' – without explanation or date. One can only deduce that it was ephemeral and apparently belongs to the late 1940s and early 1950s. They do, however, state that it was coined and popularized by a comedian. Cf **hi ho Silver**.

[**hey, damme!** (See the Gifford quotation at **what's to pay?**) Although a comic actor's 'gag' in a well-known, minor late C18 play, it cannot, any more than any other 'oathy' exclamation, be called a c.p.]

hey, Johnny! You like my sister? She outside, all black; inside, all cherry-red, just like Queen Victoria – bloody good bloke! 'A soldier's parody of the sales talk of any Oriental pimp' (Paul Beale, 12 June 1974): since the middle 1940s.

hey, lass, let's be .... See **hay, lass ....**

hey, mudder, give my brudder the udder udder! 'This Canadian c.p., used almost as a tongue-twister and clearly [originating] from one, has been current since *c.* 1930, although never – for rather obvious reasons – very general' (*DSUE* Supplement). This kind of brutally and brutishly callous insensitivity is particularly repellent and probably issues from an almost animal rebellion against the restraints of decent society.

hi, ho! Let her go, Gallagher! is an American c.p., dating from 1887, the years of William Delaney's song thus titled. (W. J. Burke.)

hi ho, Silver! – cf **hey, Abbott!** above – is one of the seven 'Synthetic Fad Expressions' listed by W & F (p. 655) in 1960, yet known to have existed as early as 1945, as Englishman Peter Sanders, 28 April 1975, assures me; he adds that he thinks it comes from a US cowboy film and that *Silver* is the name of a horse. (Peter Sanders spells it *hey ho* or *heighho*.) Almost meaningless. And Englishman Paul Beale, on 7 May 1975, confirms this supposition, thus: '"The Lone Ranger", masked cowboy hero of comic strip, film and TV, to his faithful steed. A sort of *giddy-yup*, for chasing villains, or [for] riding off into the sunset on completion of the week's good deed.' Cf the Seven Dwarfs' song, 'Hi ho, hi ho, and off to work we go' – as Ramsey Spencer suggests.

An American, Professor Harold Shapiro (13 May 1975), confirms and reinforces thus:

> One of the most popular radio serials of the 1930s and 1940s was 'The Lone Ranger'. Some Lone Ranger movie serials were also made. The Lone Ranger was a sort of cowboy Robin Hood, who wore a mask, used silver bullets (sparingly), rode a white horse named Silver, and had an Indian sidekick named Tonto, who in turn rode a horse named Paint (to urge his horse on, he said: 'Gettum up, Paint!'). Every week for a half-hour, 'the masked rider of

the Plains, with his great horse Silver, and his faithful Indian companion Tonto,' righted wrongs, – to the accompaniment, at the beginning and end of the program, of the anapaestic melody of the William Tell Overture. Well, at the beginning and end of the program the Lone Ranger urged his horse on with a great call of 'Hi ho, Silver, awa-a-ay!' In the middle of the program he merely said 'Hi ho, Silver!' As a c.p., *Hi Ho, Silver* could be used in an endless variety of (jocular) ways (e.g., 'Let's go!' or to signify something grand, as in 'Who does he think he is, Hi Ho, Silver?'); but, however used, it always referred to that radio serial. I recall a joke on Fred Allen's radio comedy show of the early 1940s which illustrated the universal knowledge of the Lone Ranger's call. [The Mrs Nussbaum one.]

high cost of dying – the, originally and still US, was adopted in Britain *c.* 1942, but confined to the middle and higher reaches of society. Clearly it puns that constant topic of conversation, *the high cost of living*.

high, low, jack and the game (where Jack is the knave in a pack of cards): US, either entirely or predominantly: John W. Clark, 28 October 1968, says:

Announcement by the decisive complete winner of a card game.... As a c.p., spoken by, or of, the unquestioned winner of any contest.... Mark Twain uses the term, though I don't remember where. Probably no longer universally or even commonly understood, but it certainly was in the latter half of the 19th century.

It derives from the card game known as All Fours or Seven Up or Old-Sledge or High-Low-Jack. 'As a c.p., now obsolete,' writes John W. Clark on 24 July 1975, 'except, like Euchre, in rural hinterlands, but it was certainly common in my childhood (oh, say, *c.* 1910–20).' He adds: 'Literally, the announcement of the highest possible hand; as a c.p., the crowing proclamation of complete victory in any contest.' To which he subjoins '[My wife] remembers a variant, "High, low, Jack, and win" – which I have never heard.'

hills are closing in on him – the. He's become very odd – beginning to go mad: among the United Nations troops in Korea: *c.* 1953–5. From the forbidding hills and mountains of Korea. (Anon., 'Slanguage', in *Iddiwah*, the New Zealand soldiers' periodical of 1953–4.)

hip, Michael, your head's on fire! A street c.p. addressed to a red-haired man: mid C18–mid C19. (Grose, 1785.)

hire a horse! See **get a horse!**

his death-warrant is out. See **death-warrant** ....

his gall is not yet broken. See **gall not yet broken.**

his grandmother and mine had four elbows. See **grandmother and mine** ....

his hair grows through his head. He is on the road to ruin: mid C16–early C18. Apperson cites Skelton, Deloney, Motteux. Hair instead of brains.

His horse's head is swollen so big that he cannot come out of his stables. He owes a great deal of money to the ostler: C17.

his legs grew in the night. See **legs grew in the night** ....

his master's voice comes from that famous picture advertisement in which the faithful dog listens wistfully to a record of his dead master's beloved voice; these words capitalized form the trade name of HMV records and record-players.

The c.p. arose early in C20 and is extant, although rather less used after than before WW2. In *The Curious Crime of Miss Julia Blossom*, 1970, by Laurence Meynell, a novelist exceptionally sensitive to dialogue, we read:

'If you don't realize that [the end of the affair between her husband and his secretary], Miss Vavasour, I am sure my husband will when he and I have talked together. Good night.'

'His Master's Voice,' Selina had said.... It hadn't been much of a retort but it was the best she could think of.

Every record issued by HMV bears a trademark reproducing the advertisement.

his means are two pops and a galloper is an underworld c.p. of *c.* 1740–1830; it means that he's a highwayman, his two main needs being a brace of pistols and a fast horse; and it appears in the 2nd edn of Grose.

his mother never raised a squib. He's a very brave fellow: Australian: C20. (Baker, 1959.) In Australian slang, a *squib* is a faintheart, one who tends to back out of an undertaking.

his mouth is full of pap. See **mouth is full** ....

his nose is always brown. 'He's a sycophant of the lowest order' – and so is the c.p.: C20.

his stockings are of (later **belong to**) **two parishes.** He is wearing stockings that don't match: *c.* 1770–1850. (Grose, 1796.)

his tail will catch the chin-cough. See **tail will catch** ....

hist! we are observed is a jocularly ironic C20 c.p., burlesqued by Hilaire Belloc in his 'spy' novel, *But Soft – We Are Observed*, 1928, and obsolete by 1940. It satirizes the language of spy melodramas.

An odd adumbration occurs in Thomas Morton's famous comedy, *Speed the Plough*, 1796. In Act I, Scene i, Gerald says 'Hush! Conceal yourself; we are observed; [come] this way.'

hit the road, Jack! 'A command to someone to leave' (CM): a US Negro c.p., dating since *c.* 1950.

[**hoist him in!** is a mid C19–20 nautical order, not – as I was at first tempted to suppose – a nautical c.p.]

hokey-pokey, penny a lump – the more you eat, the more you pump 'is often chanted derisively at children who have some ice cream, bought in the streets, by those who have none' (A. B. Petch, 31 October 1946): working-class children's: since *c.* 1902.

hold 'em and squeeze 'em, a C20 US c.p., derives from the instructors' advice on the rifle range: after sighting and aligning one's rifle on the target, to squeeze the trigger gently: all literal and technical. Its derivative, c.p. sense was 'Do it carefully, patiently, thoroughly!' Colonel Albert Moe (15 June 1975) thinks it to be 'obsolescent or even obsolete at this time'.

hold everything! See **hold your horses!**

hold her, Newt – she's a-rarin'. W. J. Burke, 28 January 1969, writes:

Goes back to the early '20's or earlier than that: I suspect it started in a comic strip or an early movie. A country bumpkin, presumably named Newt [for Newton], trying to hold a fractious horse or mare as she rears and stands on her hind feet, is the picture I conjure up, but the phrase itself can mean any number of things.

McKnight records it as being used by US university students in 1920.

Note that in general US slang, *newt* is 'a stupid person. *Some use since c. 1925*' (W & F) – perhaps from *neuter*, as in 'a neuter cat'.

It was adopted, *c.* 1948, in Canada: 'pseudo-rural, with a touch of contempt for the rustics' (Douglas Leechman).

hold my hand and call me Charlie! goes back to *c.* 1930, but was, by 1960, obsolescent and by 1970 obsolete. Mostly derisive; addressed by youth to girl.

hold up your head: there's money bid for you. Don't be so modest: people think well of you: a semi-proverbial c.p. of mid C17–mid C19. Apperson cites S, who uses the full saying, and Marryat, who uses the shorter, i.e. *there's money bid for you*. Perhaps from slave markets.

hold yer 'ush and watch thi cutlery! Shut up – and watch your property, especially your household goods!: North Country: since *c.* 1920 (? a decade earlier). 'First heard in Sheffield at a dinner in October 1938. Very dialect[al], this one!' (Lawrence Smith, 15 January 1975).

hold your horses! Hold the job up until further orders!: since *c.* 1890; originally, the Royal Artillery, but since *c.* 1930 heard frequently in also the RAF and even in the Royal Navy. (H & P.) The RAF used, from 1940, a variant: *hold everything!*, which, however, had, by 1944, become jargon or, if you prefer, a virtually official order.

holding the line with a man and a boy. 'The silence and inertia in the German trenches were a puzzle, and the old remark about "holding the line with a man and a boy" was passed round among us' (Edmund Blunden, *Undertones of War*, 1928): among British soldiers during WW1; applied to any thinly held line or trench and probably going back to *c.* 1895.

[**holiday at Peckham** (or, derivatively, **holiday with him**) – **it is all**. It is all over with him: late C18–early C20. There is a pun on *peck*, food, and *peckish*, hungry. Perhaps, rather, a proverbial saying.]

home, James, and don't spare the horses! dates from *c.* 1870 – if not earlier; originally addressed, esp. by a man about town, a clubman, to his private coachman, and then, when the motor car gained the ascendancy, to his chauffeur. Until *c.* 1925, the full wording was general; after that date – and increasingly – it has often been shortened to *home, James!*; since *c.* 1945, often spoken to a friend giving one a lift home by car.

Always good-tempered and humorous, this c.p. has become so thoroughly and intimately incorporated into the language that it can be employed as allusively, and even subtly, as this: '"Yes, sir; no, sir; three bags full, sir." Which just about summed it up. Bags full, and home, John. And don't spare Alitalia' (Manning O'Brine's espionage 'thriller', *Mills*, 1969, chapter 39). On the other hand, Catherine Aird's police 'thriller' of the same year, *The Complete Steel*, has this passage:

Detective Constable Crosby turned the police car. ...
'Home James, and don't spare the horses,' commanded Sloan, climbing in.
'Beg pardon, sir?'
Sloan sighed. 'Headquarters, Crosby, please.'
But then, the constable *was* a rather dull fellow.

Adopted in US, but no one seems to know, even roughly, when. My old friend (much younger than I), John W. Clark, writes, on 17 February 1975, 'Less common than it once was'; he also notes that, in US, the two members of the phrase – that is, *home James*, and *don't spare the horses* – have long become discrete and that the former is 'even more hackneyed than' the latter.

home on the pig's back is used either adjectivally or adverbially: 'very successful!' – 'easily and thoroughly': mostly among New Zealanders and Australians; since *c.* 1910; perhaps prompted by such idiomatic phrases as *to save one's bacon* and *bring home the bacon*.

home was never like this! expresses deep satisfaction and content at pleasure and comfort experienced in a home other than one's own. I never heard it before WW2, when, indeed, it may well have arisen.

hook at the end – a. See **with a hook ....**

Hooky Walker! – often shortened to **Hooky!** or to **Walker!** This phrase signifies either that something is not true or that it will not occur: C19–20, but little heard since WW2. (*LB* – in effect, the 4th edn of Grose).

Also, 'Be off!': since *c.* 1830. Soon *Walker!*, as in Dickens's *Christmas Carol*, 1843:

'Buy it,' said Scrooge.
'Walker!' said the boy.

According to JB, the phrase originated in one John Walker, a prevaricating, hook-nosed spy – which is perhaps true, but is probably a felicitous piece of folk-etymology – an elaboration of *Walker!*, Walk off, Oh, run away.

As so often with c.pp. of the 1820s and 1830s, the *locus classicus* occurs in Mackay

Hookey Walker, derived from the chorus of a popular ballad, was also [like *what a shocking bad hat!*] high in favour at one time, and served, like its predecessor *Quoz*, to answer all questions. In the course of time the latter word [i.e. (*Hooky*) *Walker!*] alone became the favourite, and was uttered with a peculiar drawl upon the first syllable, a sharp turn upon the last. If a lively servant girl was importuned for a kiss by a fellow she did not care about, she cocked her little nose, and cried '*Walker!*' If a dustman asked his friend for the loan of a shilling, and his friend was either unable or unwilling to accommodate him, the probable answer he would receive was '*Walker!*' If a drunken man was reeling about the streets, and a boy pulled his coat-tails, or a man knocked his hat over his eyes to make fun of him, the joke was always accompanied by the same exclamation. This lasted for two or three months, and '*Walker!*' walked off the stage, never more to be revived.

This may have been partly, yet certainly was far from being wholly, true. It recurred both in Dickens, as above, and in the Surtees novel *Hillingdon Hall*, 1845, chapter XXXVIII:

'Mrs Flather won't hear of it unless they are agreeable.'
''Ookey Walker!' grunted Mr Jorrocks [a true Cockney].

A C20 variant – obsolete by 1950 – was *that's a Walker!*, That's untrue.

hoot him! This derisively contemptuous Australian juvenile c.p. of *c.* 1910–40 means either 'Look at him!' or 'Hark at him!' according to the circumstances. It occurs frequently in Norman Lindsay's novel about boys, *Saturdee*, 1933.

hop along, Sister Mary, hop along! 'When the yobbos ogled the girls in the local "monkey run" [at York, *c*. 1919] and the girls passed by, the yobs used to sing, or call, after them, "Hop along, Sister Mary, hop along". I do not know the origin' (Wilfred Granville, 18 June 1973). Apparently North Country and *c*. 1910–30; probably from some local character – or piece of folklore.

hop and hang all summer on the white spruce is a Canadian lumbermen's c.p. and probably dates since late C19. It occurs in, e.g., the novels of John Beames.

hope – or **I hope** – **it keeps fine for you.** A military c.p., often ironic or derisive, of WW1, than which it was also both a little earlier and later. (Ernest Raymond, *The Jesting Army*, 1930.) It was, originally, a parting phrase; but it is often a passing comment upon a project – e.g., an important journey – mentioned by the second party. Wilfred Granville, 16 May 1969, pointed out to me that sometimes it is 'directed against one who is seen to take risks, whether in drink or in any other hazardous indulgence. "I think I'll have another gin." – "O.K., but I hope it keeps fine for you!"'

A fairly frequent variation is *hope you have a fine day for it*.

This c.p., in its predominant form, has become so imbedded in colloquial usage that it can be employed allusively, as in Adam Hall, *The Tango Briefing*, 1973: 'Of course he'd go straight into signals with London and ten minutes from now they'd have an emergency meeting at the Bureau and I hoped it'd keep fine for them.'

hope (or **I hope**) **your rabbit dies!** A jocular imprecation current, throughout C20. It occurs in, e.g., Dorothy L. Sayers's 'thriller', *Have His Carcase*, 1932. It originated as a curse, 'I hope you lose your virility!' – cf the eroticism of **pop goes the weasel!** Well, that's one theory; my own is that it originated as one child's threat to another.

hope you've got! – **what a**; also **some hope!** (or **hopes!**) and **what a hope!** (or **what hopes!**) All these forms bear only one meaning: that of a discouraging c.p. reply, or remark, to one who is confident of obtaining some privilege or other. Current throughout C20 (and probably from *c*. 1890) in the lower reaches of Society but esp. widespread during WW1 and WW2, notably among the soldiery in the former and in all three Services in the latter.

horse, a horse, my kingdom for a horse! – a. In *The Life and Times of Shakespeare*, 1968, by Maria Pia Rosignolo, occurs this statement: 'Richard III's cry of "A horse, a horse, my kingdom for a horse" immediately became a popular expression' – that is, a c.p. – still current today, esp. among actors and even, one hears, among disappointed punters at the racecourses. The phrase is in *King Richard III*, at Act V, Scène iv, line 7.

Horse-Marines! – tell that to the. See **tell that to the Horse-Marines!**

horse of another colour – a; usually preceded by **that's**. That's quite another matter: originally (1790s) US; anglicized *c*. 1840 by Barham's *Ingoldsby Legends*. Very probably suggested by Shakespeare's 'My purpose is indeed a horse of that colour' in *Twelfth Night* at Act II, Scene iii, line 181. (*OED* and Supplement.)

horses for courses originated, not unnaturally, in horse-racing circles perhaps as early as 1860, and then, *c*. 1890, became an upper-middle-class and upper-class c.p., applied to suitable marriages as opposed to *mésalliances*, but since *c*. 1945 applied mostly – and throughout a wider social range – to the potentialities of all kinds of competitions. By a rudimentary process of rhyming.

horse's head is swollen so big .... See **his horse's head ....**

horses sweat, men perspire, (and) ladies only glow is directed, in mild and often humorous reproof, at a man saying that he sweats and esp. at a man saying that a woman does: C20; by 1960, slightly obsolescent; since that date, many women have preferred to *sweat*.

hot and strong – I like my (or **he likes his**) **women.** This Australian c.p., dating from *c*. 1945, derives from 'I like my coffee – and my women – hot and strong' or some variant thereof and has probably been influenced by the prescription 'Coffee should be as *hot* as hell, as *sweet* as love and as *black* as night.' Cf:

[**hot, sweet and filthy** was, among prisoners of war in the Far East, 1943–5, a canteen name – not a c.p. – for, an allusion to, coffee.]

hot time in the old town tonight – a, often – indeed predominantly – preceded by **there'll be.** The shorter form, the earlier version, formed the title of an American song, words by Metz and music by Hayden, published in 1896. 'This was the song sung in Cuba during the Spanish American War [1898] and has become a part of our language. Popular with college students after a football victory.' (W. J. Burke, 23 September 1975.) Current also in Britain and the Commonwealth since early in C20. Less heard since WW2.

house broke up is a military (Other Ranks') c.p., indicating utter despair: *c*. 1870–1940. (Ware.)

[**housey housey!** The traditional cry that summons players of House: mostly military: C20. On the borderline of c.p., yet never quite achieving that status.]

how about that, with emphasis on *'bout*, is a US c.p. that, dating from the 1930s, became, early in the 1960s, very general indeed. 'Not a question, but an expression of surprise at what one has [just] heard' (Joseph T. Shipley, 16 August 1975). Noted by Professor S. I. Hayakawa in an American newspaper article, 'Language Changes. Slang is Imaginative, Picturesque', appearing late in 1973. Equivalent to **what do you know?** and adopted in Britain in the late 1960s.

See the following in Mickey Spillane, *The Erection Set*, 1972:

'There were incidents in New York, there were incidents here.... All checked with the police,' Lagen said. 'The handiwork of an expert.'

'How about that?'

how am I doin'? What do you think of that?: US: since *c*. 1935. (Berrey.)

how are the bots biting? How are you?: a New Zealand medical c.p., since *c*. 1929; by 1970, rather outmoded. Here, *bot* is short for *bot flies*, which afflict horses.

how are the troops treating you? is an Australian (not, one suspects, entirely respectable, nor obsessively virtuous) women's c.p. of 1939–45, then merely allusive, finally historical.

how are we? A jocular c.p., addressed to someone just met: C20. Cf the next three entries.

how are you going? An Australian c.p. of greeting; since *c.* 1920. How are you faring? How *are* you? (Barry Prentice.) Cf **'ow you going, mate?** and **:'**

how are you off for soap? was, *c.* 1830–1920, an urban c.p. It means no more than 'How are you doing?' – 'How are you?' and occurs in Frederick Marryat, *Peter Simple*, 1834, 'Well, Reefer, how are you off for soap?' (*OED*.) The late Frank Shaw, 1 September 1969, cites the *Comic Calendar* of 1841: 'If it has any meaning, [that meaning would be] "If you're not well off, off!"' If you're not rich, run away!

how are you popping? or **how yer poppin'?** How are you?: Australian, mostly juvenile: *c.* 1910–65. Norman Lindsay, *Saturdee*, 1933, '"How yer poppin' s'mornin'?"'

how *can* you? is elliptical for 'How can you be so foolish *or* stupid?' or 'How can you behave so?', or esp. 'How *can* you bear to make such a feeble pun or joke?': since at least as early as *c.* 1910.

how can you just be so? was an ephemeral (*c.* 1919–22) US university students' variation of **how did you get that way?** (McKnight.)

how daft can we (or **they**) **get?** 'Used in reference to the way we – or they – allow ourselves to be humbugged by advertisers and politicians' (A. B. Petch, 16 September 1974): since *c.* 1950. Cf **I'm not as daft as I look.**

how did (occasionally **how do**) **you get that way?** How did you come to get into that condition! – whatever the condition implied: US: from before 1922; anglicized by 1930. (*OED* Supp.)

It was recorded in HLM, and in the definitive edn of 1936, on p. 566, occurs a valuable footnote; McKnight mentions it in 1923, and, in the same year, Robert Benchley uses it in *Love Conquers All*; Berrey includes it in a group of expressions glossed as 'Don't be ridiculous!'

Cf **don't be that way!** (its origin?) and **oh, is that so?** Its popularity and its longevity probably result from its forcible and apposite sense and wording.

how *did* you guess? See **you have hit it.**

how do we go? What chance is there 'of obtaining something unspecified yet known to the person questioned'? (B & P): an army c.p. of 1915–18, then rather more general; obsolescent by 1937 and obsolete by 1940. Probably elliptical for 'How do we go about getting it?'

how do you get that way? See **how did you...?**

how do you like them apples? What do you think of *that*? – equivalent to **how am I doin'?**: since (early ?) 1930s. (Berrey.) In *The American Dream*, produced and published in 1961, Edward Albee writes:

> GRANDMA: They wanted satisfaction; they wanted their money back. That's what they wanted.
> MRS BARKER: My, my, my.
> GRANDMA: How do you like *them* apples?
> MRS BARKER: My, my, my.

how do you like your eggs cooked or **done?** An Australian c.p., dating from *c.* 1908, very common among the soldiery of 1914–18, and not yet obsolete, it is usually a malicious

comment upon another's misfortune. By 1915, a c.p. reply had been evolved: **scrambled, like your brains, you** (or **yer**) **bastard!**

how do you sell your string? Do you take me for a fool? I see through your planned swindle, hoax, etc.: underworld c.p.: C19. It occurs in H. D. Miles, *Dick Turpin*, 1841. Probably suggested by the underworld *get* (someone) *into a line*, to set him up for a swindle or to engage his attention while a robbery is being effected near by.

how do you work? is another underworld c.p.: How do you make a living now?: *c.* 1770–1840. (George Parker, *Life's Painter*, 1789.) Cf the modern police sense of *modus operandi* or manner of committing a crime.

how does that grab you? What do you think of that? Does that interest, or very much interest, you? Does that excite you?: Canadian, Australian, English, adopted *c.* 1970 from US, where current since the mid 1960s. (Cyril Whelan, 14 January 1975.) It was recorded in *DCCU*.

how does your body politic? In S, Dialogue I, Lord Sparkish says to the maid, 'Mrs *Betty*, how does your Body politick?' – which prompts the gallant Colonel to remonstrate, '*Fye*, my Lord, you'll make Mrs *Betty* blush.' Apparently this was a rude c.p. of *c.* 1700–60, probably with a pun on a now long obsolete sense of *body*: belly. Perhaps cf the C20 c.p., **how's your belly off for spots?**

how fares your old trunk? is a jeer at a large-nosed man: *c.* 1680–1850. (BE; Grose.) The reference is to an elephant's trunk.

how goes the enemy? What's the time?: Frederic Reynolds (1765–1841), one of the most prolific of all British minor playwrights causes Mr Ennui ('the time-killer') to say it in Act I, Scene i, of *The Will*, 1797. It almost immediately became a – usually somewhat facetious – c.p. and it has remained one, although it hasn't been much employed since 1939. I used to hear it occasionally from my father (1863–1952), from childhood into early manhood: and I suspect that he no more thought of it as being a c.p. than, at the age of (say) six, I did: which rather tends to show how a quotation held worthy of record by Benham, Stevenson, the *ODQ*, can also have become engrained in the very texture of colloquial English. See also **what says the enemy?**

how high is a Chinaman? A reply to, or a comment, in kind, to a question either stupid or unanswerable: since *c.* 1950. Punning on the pseudo-Chinese personal name *How Hi*.

how high is up? A retort to an unanswerable question: US: since *c.* 1920. (Edward Hodnett, 18 August 1975.) Cf **how old is Ann(e)?** and **which would you rather – or go fishing?** and **why is a mouse when it spins?**

how is (or **how's**) **that for high?** 'An enquiry often made a few years ago on all occasions, but now out of date. Meaning, it has none' (M): US. But a few pages later, Maitland glosses the c.p. thus, 'An enquiry often made nowadays in regard to practically any happening': so perhaps we had better assign it to the very approximate period 1876–95; its British currency to *c.* 1885–1900.

Two years earlier than Maitland, Farmer, in 1889, had dealt with it rather more spaciously:

A modern slang expression, which has to a large extent

taken the place of *bully* [excellent] ... borrowed from a low game, known as Old Sledge, where the high depends, not on the card itself, but on the adversary's hand. Hence, the phrase means, 'What kind of attempt is that at a great achievement?' It is of Western origin, having made its appearance in some of the Northwestern journals, but has spread, as words do, rapidly all over the Union [Schele de Vere, 1871] and has found its way to England also. A familiar nursery-rhyme has been altered to 'suit the times':

> Mary had a little lamb,
> It jumped up to the sky,
> And when it landed on its feet,
> Cried, *'How is that for high?'*

It appears also in Bartlett, 4th edn, 1877, and is there glossed, 'What do you think of it?'

how lies the land? and **who has any land(s) in Appleby?** Grose, 1785, has this entry: 'LAND, as, how lies the land, how stands the reckoning; who has any land in Appleby, a question asked the man at whose door the glass stands long, or who does not circulate it in due time' – an amplification of the entry in BE '"Who has any lands in Appleby?" a question askt the man at whose door the glass stands long.' Current *c.* 1670–1830. The English place-name *Appleby*, the county town of Westmorland, may originally have referred to cider (made from *apples*) – by a pun, for that county is not particularly noted for its fruit.

how long have you been in this regiment, chum? How long have *you* been in the Navy?: naval lower-deck: C20. (Wilfred Granville.)

[**how many beans make five?** securely occupies an indeterminate point on the no-man's-land between 'catch' question and c.p. I first heard it as a schoolboy (say 1900–10), but it probably goes back to the ludicrously – and unashamedly – palmiest days of Victorian wit and humour, approximately 1870–95.]

how many times? 'I heard this on and off during the First World War. When a Tommy had got married while on leave, his chums would generally pull his leg and ask "How many times?" when he got back. They meant how many times had he made love to his bride on the first night' (A. B. Petch): 1914–18.

how much? What did you say? What do you mean?: since *c.* 1845; slightly obsolescent by 1914, but not yet obsolete. In 1852, F. Smedley employed it thus:

> 'Then my answer must ... depend on the ...'
> 'On the how much?' inquired Frere, considerably mystified.

how nice and what a lot! This facetious c.p., dating since *c.* 1930 but obsolescent by *c.* 1960, expresses a profound gratification. Applied to, e.g., a very generous helping of cream.

how old is Ann(e)? is a US c.p. that had a vogue in (?)late C19–early C20 and nostalgically lingers on, as Colonel Albert Moe tells me (14 July 1975). A trick, almost meaningless, query; possibly prompted by *'anno* domini' in its colloquial sense '(old) age', and (1 August 1975) Professor John W. Clark writes:

> I have heard it all my life (though *very* rarely since [the early 1920s]. It is – or rather was – a mocking sequel to some utterly unanswerable question, or at least a question

abstruse or unintelligible to the user of the phrase, e.g. 'Do you suppose it will be raining like this a year from today?' (unanswerable by anybody) and 'Are Bolyai's and Lobachevski's geometries both hyperbolic, or is one of them elliptic or spherical like Riesmann's?' (hopelessly beyond the scope of the user of the phrase). It is (was) *always* a sequel to someone else's question – never an introductory utterance. It commonly had an undertone of derision (of a silly question) or inverted snobbery (of an abstruse one). Cf, therefore, **how high is up?**, **why is a mouse when it spins?** and **which would you rather ... ?**

how right you are!, late C19–20, almost certainly occasioned **I couldn't agree with you more**, which, in its turn, prompted **I couldn't care less**.

how strong are you? How are you off for money?: US tramps': C20. In *The Milk and Honey Route*, 1931, 'Dean Stiff' remarks, 'If you have a *pile* you answer, "So strong, I stink."'

[**how stupid can you get?** is merely one of a number of such questions, e.g. *how mean can you get? how low ...?* or *how 'square' ...?*]

[**how the other half lives** is not a c.p. but, by its very nature, a cliché – and it is not, as a c.p. must be, autonomous.]

how to do it and not get it – occasionally with the addition, **by one who did it and got it**. An Australian c.p. that, dating since *c.* 1950, refers to books that purport to be guides to marriage. 'Those who can, do; those who can't, talk about it.'

how to win (loosely, **make**) **friends and influence people**, originally a business *quasi*-slogan, had, by *c.* 1935, at latest, in US and by *c.* 1945 in Britain become a c.p. – often ironic and derisive. It has, since *c.* 1960, been so incorporated into both US and British English that it can be employed allusively and flexibly, as in Alistair MacLean's novel, *Ice Station Zebra*, 1963 (at p. 189):

> 'In this line of business I never tell anyone anything unless I think he can help me by having that knowledge.'
> 'You must win an awful lot of friends and influence an awful lot of people,' Swanson said dryly.
> 'It gets embarrassing.'

Cf also Desmond Bagley, *Landslide*, 1967, a novel with a Canadian 'hero' and setting:

> He was another of those cracker-barrel characters who think they've got the franchise on wisecracks – small towns are full of them. I was in no mood for making friends, although I would have to try to influence people pretty soon.

Then, in 1970, we find Val Gielgud, in his adult 'thriller', *The Candle-Holders*, presenting us with a hypothetical play and a witty title, thus: 'When I told her that a play called, *How to Make Beds and Influence People* was bound to fail ...'

It became established by the book, so titled, written by Dale Carnegie (1885–1955) and published in 1936, but the c.p. had arisen two or three years earlier: Dale Carnegie had, after all – for many years before 1936 – run a school for public speaking, toast-making, personal relationships in business. (With thanks to W. J. Burke.)

how we apples swim! How we enjoy ourselves – what a good time we have!: C16–20, but obsolescent by 1920, and by 1970 virtually obsolete. Often enlarged by **quoth the horse-turd**, which occurs in Ray, 1670; the longer form is probably the original, for it shows that there is a precise application to a *parvenu*, a pretender, a person socially out of his depth. In his *Works*, vol. III, William Hogarth writes, 'He assumes a consequential air ... and strutting among the historical artists cries, how we apples swim.' As horse-turds floating down a stream pretend to be apples, so ...: cf that other proverbial c.p. of *c*. 1650–1800: '**a bumble-bee in a cow-turd thinks himself a king**' (likewise listed by the admirable Apperson). Apperson cites such other authorities as Clark, 1639, and Edward Fitz-Gerald, 1852.

[**how will** (or **how'll**) **you have it?**, an invitation to drink, lies between cliché and c.p.: and is, I believe, the former rather than the latter.]

how would you be? is an Australian c.p. form of the greeting 'How do you do?' and differs from it by requiring an answer: since early 1950s. Its secondary sense is synonymous with **how's your dirty rotten form?** (Barry Prentice, 13 June 1975.)

how yer poppin'? See **how are you popping?**

[**how you doing?** is a colloquial US greeting and obviously elliptical for *how are you doing?* No less obviously, however, it cannot justifiably be classified as a c.p. And cf the entry at **another day, another dollar!**]

how'd you like to be the ice-man? was an ephemeral US c.p. included by HLM, 1936, in a group of phrases that he has attacked for 'sheer silliness' (p. 566, footnote 1).

how's battle? (or, less general, **how's the battle?**) was, in 1934–6, a greeting current among the cultured. Elliptical for *the battle of life* and referring to the mid-1930s Crisis.

how's biz? How is business?: Australian: since *c*. 1945. (Barry Prentice.) Cf **there's no business like show business**.

how's chances? What are the opportunities – for, e.g., doing business?: US: since *c*. 1930. (Berrey.)

how's crops? A US, originally and mainly Western, c.p. of greeting: C20. (Berrey.) Of entirely natural origin in agricultural areas.

how's it? How are you?: South African: since *c*. 1920 (Ashley Cooper Partridge, 13 August 1974). Either short for 'how's it with *you*?' or short for 'how's it going?' or, less probably, influenced by Ger. *wie geht's?* how goes it?

how's it all going to end? A jocular c.p. that, current *c*. 1906–10, arose from a popular song of *c*. 1906: 'Little Winston, little friend,' with the refrain, 'How's it all going to end?'

how's it goin'? (US) (or **...going?**) (British) is an 'extremely common greeting' (John W. Clark, 28 October 1968): certainly since 1920 and probably ever since late C19. Related to **how's things?**

how's pickin's? How are you doing? – How are you? – Howdy?: US underworld: C20. In a letter dated 9 March 1938, Godfrey Irwin wrote, 'Without any definite indication that stealing is on'. Cf Shakespeare's Autolycus, picker-up of unconsidered trifles.

how's that for high? See **how is that for high?**

how's that, umpire? What have you to say about that? How about that? What price – ?: since *c*. 1880: very English, as one would expect from its origin in cricket.

how's the body? How do you feel? Mostly, How are you?: Anglo-Irish: late C19–20. In, e.g., Brendan Behan, *Borstal Boy*, 1958.

how's the fag trade? A polite request for a cigarette: esp. in Suffolk: since *c*. 1910. *Fag*, a cigarette.

how's the weather up there? 'An almost obsolete hackneyed "how do you do?" (introductory, not daily) to a very tall person' (John W. Clark, 17 February 1975): US: C20.

how's the world treating (or **been treating**) **you?** A very popular form of greeting, esp. to one not seen for a long time: C20.

how's things? An extremely popular c.p., current throughout C20.

how's tricks? How are things going? How are you?: a US friendly greeting: C20; by 1920, also British. (From card games.) Probably from nautical *trick*, a turn at the wheel. In, e.g.: George Ade, *True Bills*, 1904; Maurice Lincoln, *I, Said the Sparrow*, 1925 (US speaker); H. M. Harwood, *So Far and No Father*, 1932; Michael Harrison, 1935; Terence Rattigan, *The Deep Blue Sea*, 1952; Jean Potts, *An Affair of the Heart*, 1970.

how's your belly (off) for spots? How are you faring? How are you?: a proletarian c.p. of *c*. 1900–25. Cf **how does your body politic?** and:

how's your dandruff? A vulgar, mostly lower-middle-class greeting: since *c*. 1950; by 1965, obsolescent; by 1975, obsolete.

how's your dirty rotten form?; sometimes *dirty* is omitted; often shortened to **how's your form?** 'This c.p. is not really a question, but is used when someone wins a lottery, passes an exam or gets a promotion. It is sometimes elaborated to *... dirty, rotten, stinking form?*' (Barry Prentice): Australian: since the early 1950s.

how's your father? John Brophy, in the 'Chants and Sayings' section of B & P, says:

> When the War [WW1] broke out, the new armies subsisted for a time on what catch phrases the music-halls produced. 'How's your father?' was one of the most popular, turned to all sorts of ribald, ridiculous and heroic uses. This was the last utterance of at least one dandified but efficient subaltern, dying of stomach wounds.

See also Stuart Cloete's *How Young They Died* (a novel about WW1), 1969:

> Jim went to the Empire.... Vaudeville. Variety. Dancers, trick cyclists, Harry Lauder, Marie Lloyd. Stars. Harry Tate, with his 'How's your father?' gag. Chorus girls in uniform, drilling. Spangles, tights and music with emphasis on the brass. War songs ...

That the c.p. survived, even if only as an historical and perhaps nostalgic memory, until well after WW2, appears from the fact that in 1967, Ruth Rendell, in *Wolf to the Slaughter*, could write: '"How's your father?" he said and when he said it he realized it was a foolish catch-phrase', and that on the front page of the *Daily Mail*, 23 April 1969, Miss Bernadette Devlin was reported as saying after her maiden speech in the House of Commons: 'It is the ritual which gets you over being nervous. All this stand up, sit down, kneel and hows-your-father was so funny', where *hows-your-father* means nonsense. Note that, on 1 April 1969, the acute observer of the vernacular, the late Frank Shaw, wrote: 'Supposed

Masonic secret phase. Cockney uses [it] for "thingummy" – often rather vulgarly. "He's been getting his 'ow's-yer-father off her." Other usages.'

It figures in the excellent representation of c.pp. in Benham, 1948 – its first appearance in a famous (and first-class) work of reference.

how's your love life? dates c. 1950; **how's your sex life?** from c. 1960. A 'catch-phrase question addressed to a girl or girls by youth(s) wanting to "get off"' (Wilfred Granville, 19 February 1969).

how's your poor (often **pore**) **feet?** was a c.p. 'rampant' in 1862, very popular until 1870, revived c. 1889, but obsolescent again by c. 1895 – and obsolete by 1910. It occurs in G. A. Sala's *Breakfast in Bed*, 1863.

It arose from some social occasion: and there are two or three anecdotes to support this, two of them referring to the presence of Royalty. Benham 1948, proposes an earlier date: 'This is alleged to have been a jocular saying in allusion to the fatigue resulting from visiting the Great Exhibition of 1851. (A retort, which also came into vogue, was, "Better since you licked them".)'

Clearly, the Great Exhibition version would rule out the presence of Royalty. No less clearly, the exact social occasion originating the phrase was soon forgotten and the phrase became senseless: HLM selected it as one of the stupider c.pp. This one seems to have reached the US.

how's your sex life? See **how's your love life?**

how's your sister? is a rather pointless c.p., dating from c. 1910, but by 1970 rarely heard. A friend writes, 'I believe this to be based on an anecdote. A punter, colliding with a barge, complained: "See what you've done? Broke one of my oars." "Did I, lovey? Speakin' of oars, how's your sister?" This may be in [Robert Graves's] *Lars Porsena*, 1927.' *Si non è vero* ...

There is a French vulgar riposte – 'Et ta soeur!' – which I heard before WW2 and may now be obsolescent (Camilla Raab, 1976). It goes back to before WW1.

[**hubba! hubba!** was, in the 1940s (? also the 1950s), 'an expression of approval' (CM) among US Negroes and occasionally among whites. But also an Australian cry of approval, dating since c. 1930 and used either by teenagers in reference – or addressed – to a pretty girl, or domestically and conventionally, as, for instance, when a young husband admires his wife's new gown, as Mr Barry Prentice tells me; the Australian expression could, just possibly, be related to the Cornish *hubba*, a fishing cry. But mere animal noises – cf the approbatory *yum-yum* – hardly qualify as true c.pp.]

hullo, baby – how's nurse? See **hallo, baby ....**

hullo, beautiful! A male 'getting-off' gambit addressed to a pretty girl and current since c. 1935; by c. 1970, virtually obsolete. The corresponding girl-to-boy gambit is *hullo, handsome!*, current since c. 1940 and not yet (1975) obsolete.

hullo, features! A satirical and quizzical, yet friendly, form of address: c. 1900–14. (Ware, who classifies it as proletarian.)

hullo, handsome! See **hullo, beautiful!**

hullo! hullo! hullo! – occasional variant **hallo**.... The traditional, British policeman's monitory comment upon an untoward incident or situation – becomes a c.p. when it's employed allusively, as it has been since c. 1960 at the latest

and probably since c. 1945 or 1946, and as in the story of that young police officer who, on returning home unexpectedly early, finds his wife in bed with three men, mildly exclaims, 'Hullo, hullo, hull*o*!', thus causing her to burst into tears and sobbingly reproach the clumsy inadvertent fellow with the classic words, 'Darling, you didn't say hullo to *me!*'

hullo! (or **what cheer!**) (if pronounced **whatcher!**) **my old brown son, how are you** (or **'ow are yer?**) was a well-known WW1 (soldiers') greeting, promptly taken into civilian life. The 'brown' refers to the khaki uniform. (Julian Franklyn; Laurie Atkinson; inter-confirmatory information.)

hullo, playmates! See **hello, playmates!**

hullo yourself (or **your own self**) **and see how you like it!** was a proletarian c.p. of c. 1910. It occurs in W. Pett Ridge's *Minor Dialogues*, 1895.

humble-bee in a cow-turd thinks himself a king – a. See **how we apples swim!**

hungry dog will eat a dirty pudding – a. This c.p. borders on the proverbial saying, deprecates fastidiousness and dates from c. 1850. Laurie Atkinson – to whom I owe it – compares that other virtual proverbial saying, *you don't look at the mantelpiece while you're poking the fire*, which, belonging to late C19–20, has a sexual connotation.

Hunt's dog, (which) will neither go to church nor stay at home – like. A semi-proverbial c.p., applied to a most unreasonably discontented person: mid C17–20. (Apperson.) Grose explains it anecdotally by reference to a certain labourer's mastiff. Attributed to – or claimed by – various English counties. (Apperson.)

hurrah for Casey! That's excellent – splendid – fine!: Australian: C20. (Baker.) From a famous political election.

hurry no man's cattle – you may keep a donkey yourself some day was a C19 hunting c.p., quoted thus by R. S. Surtees, *Handley Cross: or, Mr Jorrock's Hunt*, 1854, vol. I, in the chapter titled 'Another Sporting Lector' (Lecture): '"Hurry no man's cattle! you may keep ..." is the answer to the last' – i.e., to 'Over you go; the longer you look the less you'll like it.'

hurry up and get born! Wake up – you're years behind the times! Be your age!: US: since c. 1910. 'Our American visitors', said an English writer at the end of the war [in *English*, March 1919] 'are startling London with vivid phrases. Some of them are well known by now. "Hurry up and get born" is one of them'; so wrote HLM, 1922. Berrey lists it in a synonymy for 'Don't be ridiculous!' Not much heard since c. 1960.

hurry up the cakes! Farmer, 1889, writes: 'Look sharp! Be quick! Buckwheat and other hot cakes form a staple dish at many American tables, and the phrase is one often heard in this connection. It has now become pure slang – an injunction to expedite movement': as a c.p., it dates since c. 1830–1910.

An early recording is that in *Am*. Bartlett says that the phrase 'originated in the common New York eating-houses, where it is the custom for the waiters to bawl out the name of each dish as fast as ordered, that the person who serves up may get it ready without delay'.

I always do my best for all my gentlemen. See **can I do you now, sir?**, third paragraph.

I am becalmed – the sail sticks to the mast. 'My shirt sticks to my back' – says Grose, 1785; he adds, 'a piece of sea wit sported in hot weather'; a nautical c.p. of mid C18-late C19.

I am here to tell you! I tell you emphatically: a c.p. of affirmation: since *c.* 1945; by 1975, slightly obsolescent. In his *Pretty Polly Barlow*, 1964, Noël Coward, at the story titled 'Me and the Girls', writes: 'George Banks [the narrator] and his six Bombshells I am here to tell you began their merry career by opening a brand new night spot in Montevideo.'

I am (or **I'm**) **not here.** I don't feel inclined to work; or, I wish to be left alone: tailors': since *c.* 1870. (B & L.) Cf **I want to be alone.**

I apprehend you without a constable. Recorded in the Dialogue I of S, this smart c.p. of *c.* 1700-60, signifying 'I take your meaning', contains a pun on *apprehend* – to seize, hence to arrest – and *apprehend* – to understand.

I ask you! – often preceded by **well.** It is an intensive of the statement to which it is appended. It is characteristically C20, but may have arisen in the late 1880s; there seems to be an allusion in F. Anstey's *Voces Populi*, 1890 – a collection of 'sketches' that had appeared in *Punch*, in the piece entitled 'Sunday Afternoon in Hyde Park', where a well-educated, well-dressed demagogue harangues the crowd: 'But, I ask you – (*he drops all playfulness and becomes sinister*) if we – the down-trodden slaves of the aristocracy – were to go to them.' The tone of voice is usually derisive. It implies 'That's ridiculous, don't you think?' In *Letter to a Dead Girl*, 1971, Selwyn Jepson provides an excellent example:

'How can my finances be involved because I met Mrs Kinnon once in my life for a couple of minutes? I ask you!'

Harry begged not to be asked.

Cf this from Anne Morice's *Death of a Gay Dog*, 1971: 'My dear, you must be joking! When did you ever see anything so pretentious? ... I ask you! Just look at the way he's tarted it up!'

It occurs, as one would expect, in comedies of the 1920s and 1930s (and after). Miles Malleson, in *The Fanatics*, published 1924, has an opening scene with parents talking about their son:

MRS FREEMAN: He came home.

MR FREEMAN: Eh? What excuse did he give?

MRS FREEMAN: I only heard him upstairs in his attic ... playing the piano.

MR FREEMAN: *Playing the piano*!!! I ask you ... a grown man ... what is 'e? Twenty-six.

And in H. M. Harwood's *The Old Folks at Home*, played in 1933 and published in 1934, the opening scene contains the lines:

LIZA: You needn't have bothered with lizards, darling.

JANE: (*warningly*) Now, Liza!

LIZA: Well, I ask you. He's been simply living with these lizards for months, and all he's found out is that males can behave like females. I could have shown him that in half an hour, anywhere in London.

Somewhere about 1930, the phrase was established in the US; Berrey includes it in a synonymy for 'I don't believe it!'.

I asked for that! – and got it! Since *c.* 1930. Cited in the *Daily Mail* book page on 15 May 1975.

I been there before. Yes, I know all about that – 'I've had some!' American: since the 1930s, or a little earlier.

I believe yer, my boy. See **I believe you, my boy.**

I believe you. See **I believe you** (or **yer**), **my boy.**

I believe you – (but) thousands wouldn't is a late C19-20 c.p. indicative either of friendship victorious over incredulity or tactfully implying that the addressee is a liar. There is a variant, as in R. H. Mottram, *The Spanish Farm* (a WW1 novel), 1927:

'I did twelve months in the line as a platoon commander. How long did you do that?'

'Twelve months about!'

'I believe you where thousands wouldn't ...'

In *Billy Borker Yarns Again*, 1967, Frank Hardy uses the predominant form. Perhaps an elaboration of:

I believe you (or **yer**), **my boy.** Of this c.p., which fell a victim to WW2, *The Referee*, on 18 October 1885, wrote, ''Tis forty years since Buckstone's drama, *The Green Bushes*, was first played at the Adelphi, and since Paul Bedford's [that most popular actor's] "I believe yer, my boy!" found its way on to tongues of the multitude.'

Clearly, however, the theatrical reference was forgotten by myriads ignorant of the play: with the result that *my boy* soon came to be omitted.

Perhaps even more clearly, a reading of C19 plays reveals that the satirical *I believe you* had existed before John Buckstone's play was produced in 1845. In George Dibdin Pitt's *Susan Hopley; or, the Vicissitudes of a Servant Girl: A Domestic Drama*, performed 1841, Act III, Scene ii, contains a passage between ladies' maid Gimp and Dicky Dean the Cockney. Gimp says, 'What a fascinating fellow! Does he dance too?' and Dicky replies, 'I believe you; cuts capers, and goes through his steps. ... All the managers run arter him.' ('Him' is a donkey and Dicky is teasing the girl.)

A rather more serious reference occurs in Dion Boucicault's play, *Mercy Dodd; or, Presumptive Evidence*, performed in London, 1869, and in Philadelphia, 1874; it is cited as evidence of the early use of the simple *I believe you!* – not the literal but the ironic – thus, in Act I, Scene i, where, in reply to Mercy Dodd's 'Do you mean that you have ever been confined in prison?' Will Coveney says, 'Portland Bill. Off and on all my life!' and, at her further query, 'What for?', exclaims, 'Trespass! As I grow'd up I found the world belonged to other people, and I'd no business anywhere in it. Prison! I believe you! What d'ye call living outside in the streets of London?'

And an example from a better playwright: Henry Arthur Jones, in *An Old Master*, performed 1880, has this passage:

MATT[HEW]: ... Is she kind and good-natured?

SIMP[KIN]: Well, between you and me, she's a fire-eating old cat.

MATT: Is she though? What, proud and ill-tempered?

SIMP: I believe you.

Conclusion: Buckstone's *I believe yer, my boy* – often misquoted as *I believe you ...* – sprang from the generic irony, *I believe you*: and *I believe you*, although less used after WW2 than before it, was, as late as 1976, still far from moribund.

I bet! and **I'll bet!** are elliptical for 'I bet you did *or* do *or* will!' and have been current since *c.* 1870 at latest. A good example of the *I'll bet!* form occurs in Terence Rattigan, *After the Dance*, performed and published in 1939; in Act III, Scene i, we find one character saying, 'I've been reading Gibbon', and his interlocutor derisively exclaiming, 'I'll bet you have.'

I bet you say that to all the girls, originally and still frequently a feminine defensive conventionalism, has been also used, since the mid 1930s (if not earlier), as a derisive counterattack: and when thus used, it is a c.p.

I can always open me legs and make a bit (can't I?) has, I'm told, been a prostitutes' self-consolatory c.p., dating since *c.* 1930. It has, however, become, since *c.* 1940, rather more widely used.

I can hardly wait! See **I can't wait!**

I can't go faster than my legs will carry me. This C18–mid C19 c.p. occurs in S, in the opening dialogue:

LADY SM[ART]: Come, get ready my Things, where has the Wench been these three Hours?

BETTY [A MAID]: Madam, I can't go faster than my legs will carry me.

The saying would seem to have belonged to the lower-middle class.

I can't shit miracles. See **miracles ....**

I can't *think!* is uttered in a tone of disgust or amazement; is elliptical for 'I can't think, or imagine, what you mean *or* suppose you're doing' – and then the speaker almost always proceeds to tell the addressee his or, more often, her unfavourable opinion; is lower and lower-middle class; and is certainly at least late C19–20, but probably goes back to (say) 1800 – cf **you can't think**, which, I'd say, prototyped it.

I can't wait (or **I can hardly wait** – the former British, the latter both British and US) is an ironic c.p., applied to an imminent and undesired encounter or other occurrence: since *c.* 1930. In *Present Laughter*, published in 1943, Noël Coward, in Act II, writes:

FRED: ... She's coming to the station to-morrow morning to see us off, you don't mind, do you?

GARRY: I can't wait.

It recurs in *South Sea Bubble*, performed and published in 1956, Act II, Scene i, and in *Nude with Violin*, likewise produced and published in 1956, Act III, Scene ii.

In Norman F. Simpson's truly remarkable *One Way Pendulum: A Farce in a New Dimension*, produced in 1959 and published in 1960, we read:

MRS G.: (*off*) It's only until he gets them all trained, Sylvia.

SYLVIA: ... Gets them trained! I can't wait!

In *The Allingham Case-Book*, 1969, Margery Allingham, who had died in 1966, wrote:

'She'll be delighted to see you, Campion.'

'I can hardly wait.'

'You'll have to,' said Oates grimly.

Ross Macdonald, in *The Goodbye Look*, 1969, has:

'Dr Smitherham ... will introduce you to the parents when it's convenient.'

'I can hardly wait,' Maclennan said under his breath.

In 1971, the same novelist, in *The Underground Man:*

'Have you ever been arrested?' I said.

'No. I can hardly wait.'

'It isn't funny. If the authorities wanted to throw the book at you, they could be rough...'

Frank Norman, in *Much Ado about Nuffink*, 1974, also uses it:

'And what's so special about you?'

'I might tell you one of these fine days,' I winked at her. 'That is, if you play your cards right.'

'I can hardly wait,' she parried.

I could do it (or that) before breakfast. That's easy: C20: perhaps originally and mainly Australian.

I could do that a (or a real) favour is 'a tribute to the charms of an attractive woman, or a picture of one' (Laurie Atkinson): since *c.* 1945.

I could do you a favour. As from one man to another, it menacingly intimates a show of physical strength; it is either jocular in a healthy way or implicative of a contemptuous claim for animal superiority: since *c.* 1930. (Laurie Atkinson, November 1969.)

I could eat that without salt. A would-be smart youths' c.p. applicable to a pretty girl happening to pass by: not in polite society: since *c.* 1945. Often *without salt* is omitted: cf its opposite, *I couldn't eat that*, applicable to a very unattractive girl. Pamela Branch, *The Wooden Overcoat*, 1951, 'I couldn't eat the last one' (a lodger).

The complementary girls' c.p. is *he could eat me without salt*, he loves me madly; I suspect that this c.p. may go back to C18.

I could go for you in a big way, if used among men, imputes effeminacy or softness: since *c.* 1942. If by men to women, it implies male desire manifested in the usual way.

I could shit through the eye of a needle is a low c.p. uttered 'on the morning after': C20.

I could take up the slack of my belly .... See **belly and wipe ....**

I couldn't agree with you more – usually shortened to **I couldn't agree more** – is the prompter of **I couldn't care less**; it dates since *c.* 1936, was at first a Society c.p. that, by 1940, was very common among Service officers, and is still heard often enough, even though it has never been nearly so popular as its junior; on the other hand, it has always remained a civilised, urbane, cultured – or, at the least, an educated – c.p. So very English, it yet became, by the late 1950s, also US, as in Edward Albee, *Who's Afraid of Virginia Woolf?*, 1962, in Act I:

NICK: I was going to say ... why give it up until you have to?

MARTHA: I couldn't agree with you more. (*They both smile, and there is a rapport established.*) I couldn't agree with you more.

And as in Amanda Cross, *The James Joyce Murder*, 1967.

'That woman again? It seems scarcely believable.'

'I couldn't agree more.'

Although less general in the 1970s than in the 1930s and 1940s, it is only a little less so: and a pleasant example occurs in Laurence Meynell, *The Curious Crime*, 1970:

'What's the use of being paid good money if you don't spend it?'

'I couldn't agree more,' Colin said gratefully.

There is also a very good one in Michael Innes's contribution to *Winter's Crimes*, edited by George Hardinge, 1972:

'Then the trustees ought to have done that job themselves.'

'I couldn't agree more. But they're lazy bastards.'

Very naturally, this c.p. appears in comedy, for instance Noël Coward's *Present Laughter*, 1943, Act II in which Joanna says: '... It's an adult point of view and I salute it. I couldn't agree with you more.'

In Coward's *Relative Values*, performed 1951, at Act I, Scene ii, the following occurs:

FELICITY: There's nothing inferior about her, social or otherwise.

PETER: All right, all right – I couldn't agree with you more.

His *South Sea Bubble*, performed and published in 1956 has, at Act III, Scene i:

BOFFIN: Perhaps she didn't drive very well. Or perhaps she was drunk – what do you think?

SANDRA: I couldn't agree with you more.

I couldn't care fewer was, *c.* 1959–62, an occasional variant of the next. Such inanity couldn't last very long; it did last longer than it deserved to do.

I couldn't care less. I'm entirely indifferent – it really doesn't matter either way: prompted by **I couldn't agree (with you) more**: arose *c.* 1940, originally among the upper-middle class, but by 1945 fairly general socially and extremely popular among those who did use it; by the late 1940s, almost everybody was doing so. Since *c.* 1945, also Australian, as in Alexander Buzo's *Rooted* (performed in 1969 and published in 1973), Act I, Scene iii. In 1952, Sydney Moseley, *God Help America!*, could write, 'Ordinary citizens "couldn't have cared less!" – to use a cant post-war phrase current in England'; clearly he couldn't have heard it before 1945, but that misfortune doesn't invalidate the main point of his statement.

The phrase migrated to the US and, well before 1970, it had become so thoroughly naturalized there that it could be employed allusively, as in Stanley Ellin, *The Man from Nowhere*, 1970:

'How did she react?.... Did it seem to hit a nerve?'

Elinor shook her head. 'She couldn't have cared less.'

Cf John D. Macdonald, *Dress Her in Indigo*, 1969, ' "I haven't any idea where Rocko went, and I couldn't care less." ' And Helen Nielsen, *Shot on Location*, 1971,

'Koumaris won't like it.'

'I couldn't care less.'

Dr Douglas Leechman, of its Canadian currency, says (January 1969): 'Perhaps 25 years old, in my experience.'

I didn't ask what keeps your ears apart. This low, very witty c.p., dating since *c.* 1949, is the devastating counter to the low comment, or rejoinder, *balls!* or *ballocks!*, nonsense! Probably suggested by to *have more brawn* (or *balls*) than brains.

I didn't blow it out of my nose. A Canadian c.p., dating from the late 1950s, meaning 'I didn't do it offhand or easily'. Dr Douglas Leechman, in April 1967, wrote to me: 'Ex a French c.p., I believe. Heard in the last few years.'

I didn't come up in the last bucket (or **with the last boat**); **I didn't fall off a Christmas tree.** The first, C20, is naval; the second and third are more recent, arising in the middle 1940s and commoner in the Services than among civilians. All three mean 'I know my way about – I'm not to be fooled'. (The first: Wilfred Granville; the other two, Laurie Atkinson, 11 September 1967.)

I didn't get a sausage (or **so much as a tickle**). I got nothing for my pains, esp. I got no money: since *c.* 1945.

I didn't know that. On 4 December 1974, my late friend Norris M. Davidson, of Gwynedd, Pennsylvania, wrote:

We have a new Catch Phrase over here. It is 'I didn't know that!' About a year ago, the Ford Motor Company introduced a series of radio and TV commercials in which their 'salesman' extolled some of the superior points of the new Ford car – or truck [lorry]. His prospective customer then said: 'I didn't know that!' The phrase is now being echoed by comedians, radio announcers, and the like – upon the slightest provocation. The phrase is stated in 3 descending notes on the first 3 words – and 'that', the 4th word, is accented and returns to the original note used on 'I'. Silly, isn't it? But there you are!

I didn't know (or **know that**) **you cared.** See **this is so sudden**, near beginning and near end. Note that it is usually spoken gushingly and simperingly, in reference to a gift made, not to the speaker but to a third person. Current in Britain and Australia, and probably elsewhere, since *c.* 1945.

I didn't raise my boy to be a soldier was, *c.* 1914–19, an American c.p., generated by the song so titled, with words by Bryan, music by Piantadosi, rendition by Ed Morton. (W. J. Burke.)

I didn't think that was sun-tan on your nose is a C20 – and esp. Suffolk – c.p., implying that the addressee is a 'creeper', a toady.

I do not wish to know that! See **I say! I say! I say!**

I don't care if I do! and **I don't mind if I do!** I am disposed, I should rather like, to do something. Yes, please!: the former since *c.* 1700, the latter since *c.* 1910. The latter became 'the rage' and by 1946 almost a public nuisance; but then, it had been a Tommy Handley 'gag' in the famous WW2 'ITMA' show. (EP, 'Those Radio Catch Phrases', in the *Radio Times*, 6 December 1946.) It occurs, for instance, in Australian Frank Hardy's *Billy Borker Yarns Again*, 1967. The former, on the other hand, had, by far, the greater impact in the US, where it has been recorded over a long span of time, for instance in T. C. Haliburton's *The Clockmaker*, 2nd Series, 1838, 'Won't you join us? Well, said I, I don't care if I do.' Also in Farmer, 1889, and in Berrey, 1942. But the US usage was anticipated by, e.g., Henry Carey in *The Contrivances*, 1715:

ARG[US]: ...But woulds't drink, honest friend?

ROB[IN]: I don't care an [= if] I do, a bit or so; for to say truth, I'm mortal dry.

Cf Joseph Elsworth, *The Rival Valets: A Farce*, performed in 1825; in Act I, Scene i, the housekeeper says to valet Frank, 'Will you come in and have a little refreshment', to which he replies, 'Why, I don't care if I do.'

The later phrase appeared in print very soon after it began to be used in 'ITMA' and, by 1948, it had become so embedded in everyday speech that it could be employed in an allusive pun: on the back of Frank Worsley's *Itma*, published in 1948, was an advertisement for Croid Glue, with the letterpress: '"A tube of CROID, Colonel?" – "I don't mind if I GLUE, Sir!"' Colonel Chinstrap, played by Jack Train, first appeared in 'ITMA' during the autumn of 1940, the famous words being, on the very first occasion, in a rather different form:

> VOICE: Father's a fool, by Gad, and if he'd been in my regiment in India, I'd have had him drummed out.
> TOM: Didn't I meet you in Rumbellipoor, sir?
> VOICE: You did not, sir. I was never there.
> TOM: Then you must have a double.
> VOICE: Thanks, I will.

The c.p., *I don't mind if I do*, had its adumbrations; and my own impression – no more than an impression – is that it arose, *c*. 1860, among the upper-middle class. If so, it gradually achieved a much wider currency; and, thanks to 'ITMA', by the end of 1940, a classless currency. I notice that 'Taffrail' – Henry Taprell Dorling – in *Pincher Martin, O.D.*, 1915, mentions a shy youth using the jocular variation, **I don't mind if I does**. In John Boland's novel, *Kidnap*, 1970, in a lower-middle-class setting:

> 'Another cake, Mrs Thomson?'. ...
> 'Thanks, love, I don't mind if I do.'

The phrase was inevitably taken up by the theatre. Noël Coward's *Peace in Our Time*, 1947, Act II, Scene iv (a public house) has the following dialogue:

> PHYLLIS: Anyone want another drop before closing? There's still some left in the bottle.
> ALMA: You have it, Phyllis.
> PHYLLIS: I don't mind if I do. (*She pours the remains of the champagne*.) Here's how!

Coward uses it again in *Relative Values*, produced in 1951, at the end, and yet again in *South Sea Bubble*, 1956.

In short, *I don't mind if I do* could almost be said to belong to the social structure of Britain. Yet it has, I suspect, established its predominance in the US too. In *The American Dream*, 1961, Edward Albee uses it thus:

> MOMMY: ...Won't you come in?
> MRS BARKER: I don't mind if I do.

Its social acceptability in Britain is questioned in Michael Innes's *The Mysterious Commission*, 1974:

> 'May I offer you a glass of sherry?' he asked. 'It seems a reasonable hour for something of the sort.'
> 'I don't mind if I do,' Mr Peach (although back with another wholly inadmissible locution) made a small gesture which was entirely a gentleman's.

I don't care (occasionally **worry**) **two tin fucks about it!** A low C20 c.p.; 'I couldn't care less!'

I don't fink! See **I don't think!**

I don't go much on it. I don't much care for it; usually I dislike it: since *c*. 1925.

I don't have to! was, *c*. 1920-5, current among US university students.

I don't know! – often spoken in a tone of exasperation and, late C19–20, belonging to those strata of society which once would have been classified as lower class and lower-middle class. On Saturday, 3 July 1971, I overheard in Holborn, London, a woman exclaim to her husband, less helpful than he might have been with their over-tired fretful two-year-old child, 'Reely, Bill! *I* don't know!' Elliptical for 'I don't know what to say' (or 'think').

[**I don't know much about Art, but I know what I like** ranks as No. 1 in Gelett Burgess's list of 'bromides' (i.e., boring and too often repeated remarks) on pp. 24–32 of his witty monograph, *Are You a Bromide?*, 1906. It lies on the border between c.p. and cliché: both British and US, and dating, I'd say, since the middle or later 1890s: still with us.]

I don't know whether I'm Angus or Agnes is a 'Men Only' c.p., 'used in very cold weather or after swimming in cold water.... "I'm so cold I don't know...."' (Leechman): Canadian: since *c*. 1930. Cf the Australian *not to know whether one's Arthur or Martha*, dating since *c*. 1920, but hardly achieving the status of c.p. It can be used by men or women about themselves or another, meaning 'coming or going' or a general state of muddle – no overt sexual overtones. In general use in Australia since at least the 1950s. (Camilla Raab.)

I don't lie – I sit. S, Dialogue I, has:

> COL[ONEL]: Indeed, Madam, that's a Lye.
> LADY ANSW[ERALL]: Well, 'tis better I should lye, than you should lose your Manners. Besides, I don't lye, I sit.

Whether this punning retort ever became a full c.p., I lack the evidence to decide.]

I don't mean maybe! See **and I don't mean maybe!**

I don't mind if I do! See **I don't care if I do!**

I don't see it – often shortened to **don't see it!** The 4th edn of *Am* has both forms: 'A very common expression, equivalent to dissent': since *c*. 1860 or perhaps a decade earlier. Adopted in Britain *c*. 1890.

I don't see the Joe Miller of it. I don't see the joke; I don't see any fun in doing this: *c*. 1810–95. Here, a *Joe Miller* is a jest, from the sense 'a jest book', originally a specific jest book that, published in 1739, was identified with, although not written by, the famous comedian, Joseph Miller (1684–1738).

I *don't* think! reverses the ironical statement it follows: mainly proletarian: since *c*. 1880 (Cf the slangy *not half!*, most decidedly so!) The *OED* adduces this effective example from Dickens, 1837: '"Amiably disposed ..., I don't think," resumed Mr Weller, in a tone of moral reproof.' In the late C19–20, it often elicits the retort, *you don't look as if you do* or *I didn't suppose you did*, and in C20 – at least up to *c*. 1950 – one often, Cockney fashion, substitutes *fink* for *think*.

In 1927, Collinson wrote:

> The frivolous use of the vulgar I don't think or fink in emphatic refutation of a foregoing statement. Thus [H. G. Wells, *Christina Albert's Father*, 1925] has 'as for bringing a contrite heart ... I don't fink'. This expression was much used in the early years of the century, but always with an awareness of its vulgar origin.

Since *c*. 1960, mostly *I don't think!*

A few years earlier, Noël Coward had, in his (I think) first published, although not first written, play, *'I'll Leave it to You.' A Light Comedy in Three Acts*, performed on 21 July 1920 at the New Theatre, London, and published two or three months later, in Act I, soon after Uncle Daniel arrives:

DANIEL: Don't leave me all alone. I'm a timid creature.

SYLVIA: (*turns*) After all that broncho busting! I don't think!

Miles Malleson had forestalled Coward when, late in 1914, he wrote *'D' Company*, published in 1916, only to see all copies soon destroyed by public prosecution; there:

ALF: You're a liar. An' I tell yer why.... We're goin' ter Africa.

TILLEY: Africa. I don't fink.

This play was reprinted in 1925. A year earlier, Malleson in *The Fanatics*, Act II, has a chorus girl remarking: 'That man gave her another ring yesterday ... must of cost *hundreds*. She says there is nothing in it ... I *don't* think.'

The phrase travelled to the US. In HLM, 1922: '*Shoo-fly* afflicted the American people for at least two years, and "I *don't* think" ... quite as long.' In the definitive edn, 1936, Mencken altered 'two years' to 'four or five years' and said that *I don't think* was 'scarcely less long-lived'.

I don't want to be a sergeant-pilot, anyway is, since *c.* 1935, a jocular RAF c.p., alluding to masturbation, which has so long been reputed to impair one's mental and physical powers.

I don't want to play in your yard. A mock-childish American c.p. of *c.* 1894–1929; adopted in Britain *c.* 1895, and in the Commonwealth *c.* 1896. Occasioned by the song so titled, published in 1894, words by Philip Wingate, music by H. W. Petrie, sung by the Lynon sisters. (Edward B. Marks, *They All Sang*, 1934.)

I don't worry two tin fucks about it! See **I don't care two ....**

I dood it, i.e. **I doed** or **do'd it**, I did it, is a US c.p. – W & F call it a 'fad expression' – of *c.* 1945–55. Either mock-puerile or mock-illiterate. They attribute it to some popular comedian.

I dreamt I met you – unfortunately! A humorous greeting: C20. 'An often used c.p., and still' (Frank Shaw, November 1968).

I drew a lemon. See **answer is a lemon** – – latter half of entry.

I feel an awful heel is spoken to the accompaniment of a hand placed upon the addressee's back or shoulder: Australian juvenile: since *c.* 1930. (Barry Prentice.)

I feel for you but I can't reach you! is a US c.p. of sympathy: *c.* 1930–50. (Berrey.)

I get you, Steve! I understand: US: C20; by 1915, also Australian. This is the version cited by S. R. Strait in 'Straight Talk', published by the *Boston Globe* in *c.* 1917. (W. J. Burke.) Cf and see **got me, Steve?**

I give up! is both British and US (in, e.g., Berrey) and it dates since *c.* 1890 in Britain and perhaps a little later in US. It expresses a comic or rueful sense of futility or even despair.

I go – I come back. This WW2 c.p. began with 'ITMA' as produced at Bangor in mid-1940. Frank Worsley, in *Itma*, published in 1948, writes: 'During this series [of six shows, ending on 24 July 1940] many of the famous crop of ITMA characters made their first bow, the first one to do so being

Ali Oop, the saucy postcard-vendor (played by Horace Percival).' Later in the book, as he reviews ITMA's run of over three hundred performances, he says, 'People still remember *Ali Oop*, with his hoarse whisper, "I go, I come back"'; but by 1950 it had, except reminiscently, become obsolescent – and by 1960, virtually obsolete. Cf the entry at TOMMY HANDLEY CATCH PHRASES.

I got ears for what you're saying. Now you're really talking sensibly – or very pertinently indeed: US Negroes': since *c.* 1940, although esp. in the 1940s. CM remarks that it 'sometimes implies approval of what is being heard'.

I got (or **had**) **'em** (or esp. **her**) **on the five-yard line** is applied when something untoward and frustrating has occurred: US: since *c.* 1930. It comes from US football. A US correspondent says, in 1968:

When the attacking team gets as near to the goal as five yards (the field being 100 yards long), it is very likely to make a touch-down. As a catch phrase, used, e.g., by an almost but not quite successful seducer: 'I had her on the five-yard line – and just then the God-damned doorbell rung!'.

I got mine, how are you making out? – with *I* and *you* emphasized. A rather cynical, utterly self-centred American Navy c.p., dating from at least as early as 1930. Colonel Albert Moe, United States Marine Corps, ret., on 30 September 1975 compared it to the USMC's c.p. usage of *semper fi*, short for *semper fidelis*, always faithful. (Cf also the British **fuck you, Jack, I'm all right.**)

Colonel Moe also notes that *semper fi* has been employed as a c.p. since not later than 1920 and that it is not merely cynical but often callous. He had, two days earlier, cited pp. 40, 301, 302 of Anton Myrer's *The Big War* (WW2), 1957, as closely showing that *semper fi* is semantically synonymous with the almost too famous British **fuck you, Jack ....**

I got news for you. See **I've got news for you.**

I got your number; American: since *c.* 1912. Cited by S. R. Strait in his merry verses ('Straight Talk') in the *Boston Globe* in *c.* 1917, it means 'I see what you mean – or are up to' and was, by 1960, almost obsolete.

I gotta million of 'em was the original property of Jimmy 'Schnozzle' Durante (middle and late 1940s and the 1950s): and, by its popularity, the tag became a c.p., often used with no very precise application or meaning. (W. J. Burke.) It was adopted in Britain as **I've got a million of them**, q.v.

I grow while I'm standing is, in Australia, a C20 c.p. used in declining a proffered seat. (Barry Prentice, 15 December 1974.)

I had a shit, shave, shower .... See **I've had a shit ....**

I had 'em (or **her**) **on the five-yard line.** See **I got 'em ....**

I had 'em rolling in the aisles; *rolling* often omitted. Spoken by a comedian successful in making his audience laugh uproariously: music-hall and theatre: since *c.* 1920. Wilfred Granville cites the shorter form and glosses it thus: 'A comedian's boast that his gags so reduced the audience to helplessness through laughter that the people at the end seats fell into the aisles.' Cf **not a dry seat in the house.**

I have a bone in my leg, C18–20, not much used after *c.* 1940; **... in my arm**, C17–18; **... in my throat**, the predominant form of C16. A humorous excuse for a feigned inability to walk. S, Dialogue III, has:

NEV[EROUT]: Miss come be kind for once, and order me a Dish of Coffee.

MISS: Pray, go yourself; let us wear out the oldest first. Besides, I can't go, for I have a Bone in my Leg.

I have (or I've) a picture of Lord Roberts. 'A c.p. rejoinder to someone asking for something' (Laurie Atkinson): mostly army and RAF: since *c.* 1918, by which time it would no longer have much 'trading' value.

I have a visitor (or visitors). A Victorian and Edwardian euphemistic c.p., 'I have a flea – or fleas – on me or in my bed or...': during WW1, *I have visitors* meant 'I have body lice.'

I have friends to stay. See **friend has come**....

I have had my moments. This unmarried women's c.p., dating since *c.* 1950, means 'I've had sexual experience.'

I have influence in the right quarter. See **influence**....

I have made up my mind – don't confuse me with the facts. 'A U.S. Admiral quite recently. Seems to be gaining currency in the Royal Navy' (Rear-Admiral P. W. Brock, in letter dated 1 January 1969).

I have my agents. I'm well informed in the matter, I have private sources of information: among army and air force officers and NCOs: since 1939. (Rohan D. Rivett, *Behind Bamboo*, 1946, concerning prisoners-of-war in Japan.) In jocular allusion to 'secret agents'.

I have news for you! 'Well, let *me* tell *you* something!' or 'That's what *you* think'. This is a c.p. that either modifies or contradicts. Since the late 1940s. On 1 September 1975 I saw a *Daily Mail* poster that read, 'We have news for you': clear evidence of establishment.

I have no pain, dear Mother, now,/But oh! I am so dry, is a famous quotation from a poem by Edward Farmer (1809–76), *The Collier's Dying Child*. In a shanty parody, this became 'I feel no pain, dear Mother, now,/But oh! I am so dry' – with the ribald addition, 'Please lead me to a brewery/And leave me there to die' (the invaluable Cohen).

Mr Laurie Atkinson, late in 1974, justly remarked that the first two lines were 'often quoted with dramatic emphasis when the speaker had nothing better to say.' (Early 1900s – mid C20.) To which I should, I fear, add the precautionary gloss, 'That's a pun on a speaker, or an actor, *drying up*'.

I have to hand it to you! 'I must say – you're very good at it indeed.' 'I recognize your superiority.': US: C20. (Berrey.)

I have to see a man about a dog is often offered as an explanation of – a reply to – someone's awkward question about one's destination; more often, simply 'Excuse me – I must leave you now': British and US: late C19–20. Also, in C20, a casual remark that one has to go to the lavatory. In the US of *c.* 1920, it meant particularly 'I must go out and buy some liquor' (W & F).

A humorous variant that never became very general: *I have to see a dog about a man.*

I haven't a thing to wear. Of specifically feminine c.pp., this is the most commonly used; even more widely used than **you know what men are**. It dates from at least as early as 1890 – and probably goes further back by a generation.

What she means is, 'For this very special occasion, I haven't a dress, a gown, a robe, that I haven't already worn at least once': and men should, ostensibly, sympathize, for, after all, it's a damnably awkward situation.

I haven't laughed so hard (or **so much**) **since my mother caught her (left) tit in the wringer.** I haven't laughed so much for years: non-cultured Canadian: C20. A 'sick joke' current many years before 'sick' humour became a fashion.

It has the variant: *... since grandma caught her tits....*

Cf also the English c.p., *I haven't laughed so much since father died*, described by the late Wilfred Granville on 13 January 1969, as 'a light-hearted comment on hearing about a mishap to someone who is unpopular': which sets things in a rather clearer light.

I hear you is a Scottish c.p., dating since *c.* 1905. Early in August 1970, the late Lord Reith was interviewed by Mr Malcolm Muggeridge; in the course of the interview, the following bit of dialogue occurred:

REITH: I hear you.

MUGGERIDGE: Going back –

REITH: Did you get what I said just now?

MUGGERIDGE: You said *I hear you.*

REITH: That's a Scots expression.

MUGGERIDGE: What does it signify?

REITH: I hear you – that the remark is not worth answering or that the remark you made was untrue.

Contrast **you heard!**

I heard the voice of Moses say. See **roll on, my bloody twelve!**

I hope it keeps fine for you. See **hope it**....

I hope to tell you! A US c.p. of affirmation: since *c.* 1925; by 1960, virtually obsolete. (Berrey.)

I hope we shall meet in heaven. S, opens in St James's Park with the following:

COLONEL: Well met, my Lord.

LORD SP[ARKISH]: Thank you, Colonel; a Parson would have said, I hope we shall meet in Heaven.

This originated as a pious ecclesiastical convention of C17–20; it soon gained a much wider currency, as the quotation shows.

I hope your rabbit dies! See **hope your**....

I kid you not. 'No kidding' – I mean it, I'm being serious: since the middle 1950s; by 1970, slightly obsolescent. In Francis Clifford, *The Hunting-Ground*, 1964, an English journalist uses it on several occasions: and I suspect that it was originally – and that it remained predominantly – journalistic. Note that in the *Sunday Times*, 5 November 1972, Alan Brien writes,

Argued last night at a *Time* magazine party with Kingsley Amis....

'I kid you not,' said Kingsley.

'By the way, does he [a character in a Kingsley Amis novel] say "I kid you not"?' 'No! But then neither do I.'

'Popularized by the film [1954] of Herman Wouk's *The "Caine" Mutiny* [1951], a novel in which it was the deposed Captain Queeg's "trademark". It lingers still in some people's speech' (Paul Beale, 11 August 1975). By *c.* 1960, also Australian; it occurs in Alexander Buzo's *The Roy Murphy Show*, performed in 1971.

On the analogy of the archaic Standard English *I like you not, I love you not*, etc.

I knew it in the bath is a theatrical c.p. of C20: 'an actor's jocular lament when he dries up at rehearsals. Like so many stage catch-phrases, it is probably true' (Granville).

I know and you know, but it (or the thing) doesn't know, where *it* or *the thing* is usually a machine or a mechanical device: mainly Australian: since the late 1940s. Used esp. by workmen to justify, or partly justify, some malpractice. (Barry Prentice.)

I know one thing and that ain't (occasionally **isn't**) **two**. I know this certainly and emphatically, as in 'But one thing I do know, and that ain't two; he used to be very dirty' – which occurs in one of the novels, and collections of stories, written, *c.* 1895–1925, by Edwin Pugh: predominantly Cockney: since *c.* 1880.

I left you in this position. Paul Beale, 18 July 1974, writes:
   Army c.p. from the manual of Drill Instruction, chapter 2 onwards. After the introduction, every subsequent lesson begins thus, and as all senior NCOs have to teach a drill lesson as part of their promotion qualifying course, all are familiar with the phrase. As you can imagine, it lays itself open to all sorts of parody and abuse.
Since, at latest, 1945. Cf the navy's **it should not be possible**.

I lift up my finger and I say tweet tweet, hush hush, but now, come come enjoyed a brief popularity as a c.p. in the 1930s. From the lyric of a Leslie Sarony song of the period. (Vernon Noble, 10 May 1976.)

I like Ike, which began as a political campaign slogan for Dwight (popularly Ike) Eisenhower, came to mean ' "I don't know why but I just like it", referring to anything from apple pie to Zen Buddhism' (W & F, in the Introduction to the Appendix); but by 1970, it was, as a c.p., virtually obsolete. Main factors in the popularity of the phrase were Eisenhower's own vast popularity and the effectiveness of the long *i* used thrice, the rhyme *like – Ike*, the three successive monosyllables, as Farb points out.

I like it but it doesn't like me. This semi-jocular, ruefully serious, c.p. of C19–20, refers to food or drink, or even work, that one likes but that disagrees with one. This is, in fact, the modern form of a c.p. that goes back to *c.* 1700 or perhaps a little earlier, *I love it …*, as in Dialogue I of S:
   LADY SM[ART]: Madam, do you love Bohea tea?
   LADY ANSW[ERALL]: Why really, Madam, I must confess, I do love it; but it does not love me.

I like me – who do you like? 'Retort called forth by anyone displaying an unseemly high opinion of himself. General' (Paul Beale, 28 January 1975). Since *c.* 1950.

I like my women hot and strong. See **hot and strong** ….

I like that! See **well, I like that!**

I like work: I could watch it all day is a witty Australian c.p., dating from *c.* 1950. (Barry Prentice.) But the Australian usage stems from the very much older British usage. My very old friend, Oliver Stonor, says that the latter was sparked off by Jerome K. Jerome, *Three Men in a Boat*, which in chapter XV, p. 18, has: 'I like work: it fascinates me. I can sit and look at it for hours. I love to keep it by me; the idea of getting rid of it nearly breaks my heart.'

I like your nerve! See **of all the nerve!**

I live at the sign of the cock's tooth and headache was, in late C18–early C19, a tart reply to an impertinent and inquisitive 'Where do you live?' (Grose, 1796.)

I look like the wreck of the *Hesperus*. A c.p. used by 'a compliment-seeking woman' (Frank Shaw, November 1968) and also ruefully: C20. In reference to a famous shipwreck, celebrated in prose and, esp., verse.

[**I looks towards you** and its response, **I catches your eye**, are drinking conventions rather than true c.pp. Both of them occur in Nevil Shute's novel, *Pastoral*, 1944, as Peter Sanders has reminded me, as he has reminded me of so much else. They are probably Cockney in origin and may go back as far as 1850 or even earlier.]

I love it but it doesn't love me. See **I like it** ….

I love my jest an the ship were sinking, where *an* was already archaic for 'if' or, better, 'even if': apparently *c.* 1660–1720; at first and always predominantly a nautical c.p. In *Love for Love* (at Act III, Scene iii), 1795, William Congreve has Ben ('half home-bred and half sea-bred') exclaim, 'Handsome! he! he! he! nay, forsooth, an you be for joking, I'll joke with you; for I love my jest, an the Ship were sinking, as we say'n at sea.'

I love my wife – but oh, you kid! was a US c.p. of *c.* 1916–40. The 'kid', it seems, was the usual sexy little bit of 'sucker bait'. Recorded in HLM, second edn, at p. 424.

I married him for better or for worse – but not for lunch is an Australian 'c.p. used by a woman whose husband has retired, works at home or comes home for his midday meal' (Barry Prentice, 1 May 1975): since the 1940s. A pun on the words in the Anglican marriage service.

I may be crazy but I ain't no fool dates from 1904, and, although not much used since *c.* 1950, is not yet (1976) obsolete. American, it became almost immediately a c.p. when Bart Williams introduced it by singing, in 1904, the song thus titled, words by Rogers and music by Williams. (W. J. Burke cites Edward B. Marks's *They All Sang*, 1934.)

I might as well plough with dogs! All this is most ineffectual: C17–20; a c.p. that, by *c.* 1700, had become semi-proverbial and was, by *c.* 1860, used only in dialect. (Apperson.)

I must have killed a Chinaman is, in Australia, applied to a run of bad luck: C20. It derives from a widespread belief held there. I remember hearing it among 'the Aussies' of WW1.

I must have notice of that question. I don't wish to reply, or to answer; you're being difficult or awkward: since the early 1950s. 'From parliamentary procedure' (Frank Shaw). Often spoken with a smile.

I must (or **I really must**) **have one of those** was an ephemeral c.p. of the early 1880s – *c.* 1880–3, to be delusorily precise – deriving from a comic song and therefore, not at all surprisingly, non-aristocratic. (Ware.)

I must love and leave you – but, rather more usual, **I must love you and leave you** dates from *c.* 1890 – perhaps from a decade earlier – and probably comes from dialect; apparently the Cheshire dialect – see Dr Bridges's *Cheshire Proverbs*, 1917. Outside of dialect, *I must love you …* is, I think, not proverbial but a genuine c.p., as its occurrence in H. V. Esmond's *The Law Divine*, performed on 29 August 1918 (and published in 1922) makes clear in Act II:

EDIE: (*going to door*) Well, after this little social intercourse, I must love you and leave you.

In short, when used literally, it is semi-proverbial; but when, as in that quotation, it means no more than 'Very sorry, but I *must* go', it is a c.p. There is a variant: *I'll love you and leave you....*

Mr Laurie Atkinson has pertinently remarked, 'As sailors do their wives': and (18 July 1975) he makes it clear that this afterthought often forms part of the c.p.

NB. Mr Atkinson has noted that the c.p. is used 'especially between women at the end of a chat when taking leave'.

I must or I'll bust. 'I simply must go the w.c.' – the toilet – the loo – the john – or whatever the predominant term may be: a mainly Australian c.p.: since *c.* 1925.

I must ring up the Duchess. See **Duchess** ....

I need (or **want**) **a piss so bad, my back teeth are floating** or **I can taste it; I want a shit so bad, my eyes are brown.** These are Canadian – need I say, decidedly low Canadian – c.pp. of C20. Cf **I must or I'll bust.**

I need that like I need a hole in the (or **my**) **head!** I don't need it at all – indeed, it would be hateful, or disastrous, or ludicrous: adopted in Britain *c.* 1950, from US, where it was extremely popular *c.* 1948. W & F, 1960, remark that it was 'popularized by comedians' and 'contains elements of Jewish wit': but was it not, in origin, entirely Jewish?

I never liked it, anyway! 'Of something broken, lost, mock-resignedly; can be sour grapes meant to amuse, show you're a philosophical type' (Frank Shaw, 25 February 1969); 'If a housewife breaks something, she tends to declare, "I never liked it, anyway", often in a resigned tone of voice' (Shaw, later in same year). The late Frank Shaw dated it as arising in the late 1940s.

Contrast **it come off in me 'and, mum** (or **ma'am**).

I never remember a name and (or **but**) **I always forget a face** is 'a c.p. when people are discussing their inability to remember names and faces' (Barry Prentice): Australian: since the late 1940s. Prompted by the cliché, 'I never remember a name but I always remember' – or 'I never forget' – 'a face.'

I only do it for (occasionally **for the**) **kicks.** I shouldn't do it at all if I didn't get a thrill out of it: since the 1950s. (Fernley O. Pascoe, 15 January 1975.)

I only work here (emphasis on *work*). I am not responsible for my employer's policy or methods: since the late 1940s. (Barry Prentice.)

I owe you one 'means that I will retaliate for some advantage which another has obtained, or for an injury done' (*Am*, 1877): US: only very approximately, *c.* 1840–1900. The expression seems to have migrated from England, for George Colman the Younger, in *The Poor Gentleman: A Comedy*, published 1802, in Act I, Scene ii, uses it to mean 'I am very much obliged to you' – esp. for a witticism, a jest, a pun:

OLL: I am now Cornet Ollapod ... at your service.

SIR C: I wish you joy of your appointment. You may now distil water for the shop from the laurels you gather in the field.

OLL: Water for – Oh! laurel-water. He! he! Come, that's very well, indeed! Thank you, good sir – I owe you one!

Perhaps elliptical for 'I owe you a drink for that', because in Act II, Scene i, Ollapod says, 'Come, that's very well! very well indeed, for a bumpkin! Thank you, good Stephen, I owe you half a one.'

I prefer your room to your company is a middle-middle-class hint, containing a middling pun and probably dating from *c.* 1880.

I quite agree with you. See **what do you think?**

I really dig it! I understand it thoroughly and enjoy it immensely: US: since *c.* 1960; and among young Britons since *c.* 1962. A specializing of the generic *dig it*, to understand, hence to understand and enjoy something.

I'd exile on the farthest frigate
Those who claim they 'really dig it' –

says Sydney J. Harris, in *This Cat Doesn't Dig All That Groovy Talk* (see **right on!**).

I really must have one of those. See **I must have** ....

I refer you to Smith! imputes a lie or a boast: 1897–*c.* 1899. As Ware tells us, it comes 'from a character named Smith with an affliction of lying in *The Prodigal Father* (Strand Theatre, 1897)'. Redding Ware had an enviable knowledge of the theatre, to which he had contributed several light comedies of some merit; he was also a close observer of the vogues and eccentricities of everyday colloquial English.

I resemble that remark; with *remark* often omitted. A waggish c.p. retort to any jocular insult: since the 1920s. Originally a juvenile pun on 'I *resent* that remark'; I first heard it in *c.* 1930 and last heard it on 22 November 1974.

[**I say!** Whether as a means of obtaining attention or in admiration or astonishment, it cannot, strictly, be called a c.p. Both US, as in *Am*, 1877, and British, as in Ware. Contrast:]

I say! I say! I say! On 6 November 1968, the late Wilfred Granville wrote to me as follows about this c.p. and about **I do not wish to know that** and **kindly leave the stage:**

Kindly Leave the Stage is the title of a recent TV programme that is said to contain the corniest gag in the history of the music-hall. ... This programme was on BBC1 this autumn. Some of the old-timers were roped in to give the authentic touch.

A character, mid-stage, is interrupted by a 'comic' rushing up to him yelling 'I say, I say, I say'. First character shushes him off with 'Kindly leave the stage'; intruder persists with some fatuous question, such as 'Why do chickens lay eggs?' First gent irritably, 'Why *do* chickens lay eggs?' Intruder, 'Because they can't lay bricks.' That sort of feeble stuff! Years old in the music-halls, e.g. the Metropolitan, Edgware Road, in the 1890s, or the old Bedford, Camden Town, and suchlike houses in that era of entertainment. Sometimes a number of so-called 'comics' would come on the stage in succession to harass the lone lead with the bloody 'I say, I say, I say' thing until it became irritating.

For some years after it had died in the music-halls, 'comics' used it in touring musicals (known as 'E-flat Revues') or in concert parties at the seaside. A lull followed this in the 1929–1939 period until, with the formation of ENSA, during WW2, when many 'comics' who had not had a job for many years reintroduced this 'I say ...' business with the fatuous question thing. But it used to be a feature in the old times when variety bills catered for unsophisticated audiences upon whom subtler comedy would have been wasted. So you could fairly say the 1890s, as a date for the period [of its heyday].

He goes on to say: '"I don't wish to know that" is a brush-off when the "I say, I say, I say" fellow tries to interrupt the lead's patter. I asked my wife if, in her young days, she had personally heard this "I say ..." business; she remembers it clearly in a concert party while she was on holiday. It was usually a "second comic's" technique.'

Support comes from Frederick Lonsdale's *The High Road*, performed in 1927, and rewritten as an acting edn, and copyrighted, in 1928, near the end of Act II:

> LORD TRENCH: (*turning to* LADY TRENCH) Let me catch you in your bath, that's all!
>
> HILARY: (*... jovially*) I say! I say! I say!

Hilary, by the way, is a good, rather vulgar, little man. Cf the next two entries.

I say – what a smasher! dates from late 1945 and comes from the BBC radio programme, 'Stand Easy' – a post-war version or reshaping of 'Merry-Go-Round'. Perhaps first written *about* by myself in 'Those Radio Phrases', printed in the *Radio Times* of 6 December 1946 – an article I was invited to contribute but could not have written without the material generously supplied by Mr Campbell Nairne, who, at the time Deputy Editor, became Editor.

Mrs Shirley M. Pearce, on 12 January 1975, in reference to the years 1939–50, when she was a child and then a young girl, supplied the following 'From a well-known toothpaste advertisement of WW2':

> On seeing a good-looking girl, [one would say]:
> 'I say, what a smasher –
> Two fried eggs and a bacon rasher!'
> On seeing a plain girl:
> 'Spotlight on charm!' (Sarcastically.)

I say, you fellows! is a schoolboys' c.p., dating since *c.* 1940 but, by 1970, somewhat less popular in those discriminating circles. In Frank Richards's Greyfriars School stories, the long-famous character, Billy Bunter, is constantly using these hallowed words. The author's real name was Charles Hamilton.

I see, said the blind man is originally and predominantly US: since *c.* 1930. An elaborate and humorous way of saying 'I understand'. (Berrey.)

I shall fall into the ragman's hands. See **my rents** ....

I shall see you dangle in the sheriff's picture-frame. 'I shall see you hanging on the gallows' (Grose, 1785): underworld: *c.* 1750–1830.

I sha'n't play! I don't like it at all; I'm annoyed: Australian: since *c.* 1885; by 1935, obsolescent: by 1965, virtually obsolete. From the peevish childishness expectable in children; half-jocular, in origin at least.

I should coco! 'I should say so!' – indicating emphatic agreement: 'Bare agreement (like *I should shay so*); almost in code; sly doubt, caustic comment being held in reserve, but implied': Cockney: C20. (Laurie Atkinson, late 1974.) *Coco* = imperfect rhyming slang for *say so*.

I should fret! *I* should worry! – It's no business of mine: US: C20; by 1970, outdated. (Berrey.) Cf **I should worry!**

I should have (better, **of**) **stood in bed!** is US and it implies that one has had so unhappy or frustrating or unsuccessful a day that one might just as well have *stayed* in bed: since *c.* 1935 (W & F).

In *Strong Cigars and Lovely Women*, 1951, John Lardner, that talented son of a talented father who died untimely, as charming as he was able (I had an hour's chat with him while he was *en route* to report the Olympic Games about to be held, 1952, in Melbourne), wrote:

> It may well be that Mr [Joe] Jacobs is the first fight manager in history to be tapped for [Bartlett's] *Familiar Quotations* ... No quotation book that calls itself a quotation book can look you in the eye these days unless it includes 'I should of stood in bed'.

This department notes that the book has been further enlarged to accommodate the second of Joe's great coinages: 'We wuz robbed!' The phrase is attributed by some scholars to Anon. and by others to Ibid., but it was the work of Jacobs. It was uttered after that Schmeling and Mr Jacobs had licked the stuffing out of Jack Sharkey, only to hear the verdict go against them. [In Bartlett, given as 'we *was* robbed'.]

According to the poet [Uncle Daniel] Parker [the New York *Daily Mirror* poet] ... the origin of 'I should of stood in bed' is wrongly described in the book. It seems there is a nonsensical footnote to the effect that Jacobs gave birth to the words after losing a bet on the World Series of 1934.

As it happens, the great man coined them 2 feet from your correspondent. It was the only time I heard a famous quotation in the making ... On this occasion – 1935, it was – he was seeing his first and last ball game. Mr Jacobs had the seat behind me in the press box at Detroit for the opening game of the World Series, though Lonnie Warneke was pitching very nifty ball for the Cubs, Mr Jacobs did not like it. An icy wind was curdling his blood, along with everyone else's. It was the coldest ball game I can remember.

A neighbor asked Joe what he thought of baseball, and Joe to him, these deathless words did speak: 'I should of stood in bed' .... So now Joe, in the heavenly meadows, has a piece of Bartlett's *Familiar Quotations*. It is a nice break for both sides.

The edn of Bartlett must have been that of 1948, where, incidentally, the date is *not* given as 1934, but correctly as 1935.

(With thanks to *Newsweek*, for the International Editorial service, for their generous and valued permission to quote this passage.)

[I should live so long! I'll be very lucky indeed to be still alive at the period – or the date – you've just mentioned: US; esp., US Jews, this being an entirely Yiddish idiom: since *c.* 1920, if not much earlier. The great authority on Yiddish, Leo Rosten, firmly holds (9 June 1975) that it is neither c.p. nor cliché and notes that '*you* should live so long' also is very common.]

I should murmur. See **I should smile.**

I should of stood in bed. See **I should have stood in bed.**

I should say! 'Hearty enthusiasm in youth finds an expression such as *yes, indeed*, a dead form of the language. *I should say* soon proves inadequate, and the conditional future changes to the active future, *I'll say*. The process once started runs to the limit, *I'll tell the world*' (McKnight): US university students': *c.* 1920–2.

I should smile! I shall – with pleasure! The *OED* gives the earliest British example as at 1891. It came from the US. Charles H. Hoyt (1859–99), in *A Bunch of Keys; or, The Hotel*, performed in 1883, wrote in Act III,

SNAG: ... Do you require a room?

P.F.: You bet.

SNAG: Single room?

P.F.: Well, I should smile.

John Kendrick Bangs, famous for his *Houseboat on the Styx*, wrote *Katharine: A Travesty*, 1888, and in it occurs the passage:

TRANIO: Well, sirrah, what news is't thou hast brought? Is the wedding finished? Are the cuckoos caught?

GREMIO: Well, I should smile. That wedding was unique.

In *The Pedagogical Seminary*, March 1912, A. H. Melville, in an article titled 'An Investigation of the Function and Use of Slang', based upon a test paper answered by boys and girls of four grades, presumably in 1911, classed *I should smile* as 'temporary' and, concerning this and seven or eight others current at this particular seat of learning, wrote: 'Most of these expressions drop out of usage as soon as the time or occurrence which recalls or represents them is forgotten.' But this particular c.p. had already been in use for almost thirty years at least: even such so-called ephemeralities tend to be far more widely distributed and longer-lived than the user or even the recorder tends to think.

Clearly Mr Melville had failed to consult M, who says:

I should smile or *snicker* or *murmur*, vulgarisms much in use to signify acquiescence with a statement made. 'Are you going to the picnic?' 'Well, I should smile.' A little of this goes a long way, but scores of expressions of this character are in use, so some reference to them is necessary. The variants *snicker* and *murmur* were not adopted in Britain, and did not, I believe, last very long in US.

I should smile is recorded, 1942, by Berrey: but this fact does not necessarily mean that it was still, at that date, extant in the US.

In England, I occasionally heard it during the period 1921–39. Cf:

I should worry! I'm certainly not worrying about that!: since *c.* 1910 in Britain and the Commonwealth. A modern example occurs in Jack Ripley, *Davis Doesn't Live Here Any More*, 1971, ' "I should worry! I have already broken so many rules, an extra breakage will go unnoticed." ' It is sometimes linked with a following **it'll all be the same in a hundred years**.

It was borrowed from the US. Mencken states that *I should worry* ('probably borrowed, in turn, from the Yiddish' – 'From the Yiddish' unequivocally, says Joseph T. Shipley, 16 August 1975) was, by Britons, 'absurdly changed ... into *I should not worry*': presumably he had heard it so misused or, more likely, taken a correspondent's word for it that they did: but I myself never heard the misuse. Berrey lists it as a synonym of 'It's not my concern'. W & F includes it – and regards it as a synonym of 'I don't care' or 'I have no reason for alarm or concern'. Its US currency seems not to have preceded the C20; my earliest record rather indicates 'since *c.* 1910', the phrase being memorialized in S. R. Strait's 'Straight Talk', published in the *Boston Globe*, in *c.* 1917. (W. J. Burke.)

I thank you! See **ay thang yew!**

I think you are a witch. Thomas Heywood, in Act I of 'The Second Part' (1631) of *The Fair Maid of the West*, causes Toota, Queen of Fesse, to say to Clem, the Clown:

Now, sir, you are of England?

CLEM: And I think you are a witch.

QUEEN: How, sirrah?

CLEM: A foolish proverb we use in our country, which to give you in other words, is as much as to say, You have hit the nail on the head.

At a rough guess, it was current *c.* 1605–55; and probably it lent itself to irony. Cf **you have hit it** ....

I think your policemen are wonderful has, by newspapermen, been credibly attributed to celebrities, not unnaturally female, visiting Britain: since the 1930s. From being a visitors' cliché it rapidly became a British c.p., usually jocular and occasionally ironic.

[**I used your soap two years ago; since then I have used no other** was the caption to a drawing (of a tramp) by Harry Furniss in *Punch*, 1884 (vol. LXXXVI, p. 197): and has, ever since, teetered on the borderline between an extremely popular quotation and a c.p., without quite 'making the grade' of c.p.]

I want a piss so bad .... See **I need a** ....

I want to be alone is reputed to have been a plea made frequently by Greta Garbo at the height of her fame. Certainly she either originated it, or popularized it, as a c.p. – cf the US slang, *do a Garbo*, to evade publicity. (Berrey; W & F.) No less certainly, Greta Garbo was not a solitary: she merely insisted on privacy. With her friends at Hollywood, as the late Lothar Mendes once told me, she was warm-hearted and delightful. It became also British and was, as late as 22 April 1974, used in the ITV 'Coronation Street' series (as Mr A. B. Petch has reminded me).

I want to go places and see things (US) is a c.p. only when used derisively – since *c.* 1930. (John W. Clark, 17 February 1975.)

I want to know! In *Am.* 1859, J. R. Bartlett quotes this passage from Sir Charles Lyell (the famous British geologist), *A Second Visit to the United States of North America*, 1849:

Among the most common singularities of expression are the following: 'I should admire to see him' for 'I should like to see him'; 'I want to know!' and 'Do tell!' both exclamations of surprise, answering to our 'Dear me!' These last, however, are rarely heard in society above the middling class.

Apparently current *c.* 1800–90.

In John Neal, *The Down-Easters*, 1833, at chapter I, p. 45, the following occurs:

How? – *snacks* [shares] – hey? I don't understand you – I never heard of this before. I *want* to know! exclaimed the other down-easter [i.e. New Englander]. Well, you *do* know, replied the southerner, in perfect good faith, mistaking a northern exclamation for a formal interrogatory.

In short, the meaning is 'What you've just told me is remarkable *or* exciting *or* exceptionally interesting.'

In T. C. Haliburton, *The Clockmaker*, 3rd Series, 1848, concerning a young US girl being flattered by means of phrenology, Sam Slick of Connecticut remarks, 'And she keeps a-saying – "Well, he's a witch! well, how strange! lawful heart! Well, I want to know! – now I never! do tell!" – as pleased all the time as anything.'

A C20 example occurs in Gelett Burgess, *Love in a Hurry*, 1913, '"I want to know!" said Rosamund, with lively sarcasm' and indignation at a studied insult.

The phrase is recorded by Berrey, 1942, as an exclamation of 'surprise or astonishment'.

I was doing it when you were running up and down your father's backbone was a Services', esp. the British Army's, c.p. of WW1 and WW2; a WW1 variant of **before you came** (or **come**) **up**. The *it* is any activity whatsoever.

The civilian version is *when you were a gleam in your father's eye*, which occurs allusively in Harold Pinter's *The Homecoming*, 1965, 'That night ... you know ... the night you got me ... what was it like? Eh! When I was just a glint in your eye.'

I wasn't born yesterday. I'm not a fool: C19–20. It lies on the border between c.p. and proverbial saying: *ODEP* cites from Marriott, 1837, 'The widow read the letter and tossed it into the fire with a "Pish! I was not born yesterday, as the saying is."' It passed into US usage.

I weep for you! is a variant, more US than British, of the satirical **my heart bleeds for you**.

I will be hang'd, and my horse too. See the quotation from S at **at a church with a chimney in it**.

I will knock out two of your eight eyes is a mid C18–early C19 Billingsgate (London) fishwives' c.p. The other six, as Grose, 1788, enumerates them, are the b*ubies*' (nipples, 'eyes' of the breasts) – the naval ('eye' of the belly) 'two pope's eyes' (? the anal and urinal orifices) – and '*** eye', presumably the sexual aperture.

I will not make a lobster-kettle of my cunt. 'A reply frequently made by the nymphs of the Point at Portsmouth, when requested by a soldier to grant him a favour' (Grose, 1788): c. 1750–1850. Cf the slang *lobster*, or *boiled lobster*, a soldier, from his red coat (or jacket).

I will pay you as Paul did the Ephesians is a raffish c.p. of c. 1750–1850. (Grose.) The explanation lies in the words usually added: **over the face and eyes and all the damned jaws**. An elaboration of *pay*, to beat, to punish – cf the later form of the phrase, *I will pay you over face and eyes*.

I will work for my living. An underworld c.p., expressing the ultimate in improbability: since c. 1950 or a few years earlier. In effect, a preliminary *when* that happens has been implied.

I wish I had a man – I wouldn't half love him! A Servicewomen's declaration of amorous longing: WW2.

I wish I had as many shillings! Frank Worsley, in *Itma*, 1948, says:

> Tommy's [i.e., Tommy Handley's] remark, 'I wish I had as many shillings!', for instance, became quite a rage apart from Funf's incursion into the language, and 'I always do my best for all my gentlemen' was soon heard on all sides. They were the first of the many ['ITMA' 'gags'] to be adopted as part of everyday conversation.

And not only during ITMA days (1939–48) but for some years afterwards.

I wish I may die!, a c.p. of emphatic assertion, seems to have covered most of C18, as well as C19–20. It occurs in, e.g., George Colman, *The Jealous Wife*, at Act V, Scene ii, where

Toilet, a lady's maid, says to her mistress, 'I wish I may die, Ma'am, upon my honour, and I protest to your ladyship, I knew nothing in the world of the matter, no more than a child unborn.' As that quotation implies, it is predominantly a lower- and lower-middle-class expression.

I wish I may never hear worse news! S, Second Conversation, has the following:

> FOOTMAN: Madam, Dinner's upon the Table.
> ....
> NEV[EROUT]: I wish I may never hear worse News.

Partly a c.p., not quite obsolete; in C18, partly a conventional courtesy – as it presumably was at first.

I wish my head will never ache till that day. See S, First Conversation:

> LADY ANSW[ERALL]. Why, you must know, Miss is in Love.
> MISS: I wish my Head will never ache till that Day. [i.e. I'll be lucky if my first headache doesn't come before that.]

It seems to have fallen out of, at least, frequent use by the end of C18.

I wonder what they will (or **they'll**) **think of next!** See **what will they** ....

I wonder who's kissing her now was originally the title of a song that was sung, 1909, in a very popular play, *Prince of Thought*, as W. J. Burke, citing Edward B. Marks, tells me. The song became 'the rage' all over the English-speaking world and, in the US at least, gained some sort of currency as a c.p.

I won't be shat upon! I will *not* be 'squashed' or browbeaten or silenced: raffish: since c. 1930. By a punning blend of *sat upon* and *shit upon*.

I won't eat you! See **we won't eat you!**

I won't put a churl upon a gentleman. S, Third Conversation has:

> LORD SM[ART]: Tom Neverout, will you taste a Glass of the *October*?
> NEV: No, my Lord, I like your Wine; and I won't put a Churl upon a Gentleman: Your Honour's Claret is good enough for me.

This c.p., c. 1550–1850, means 'I won't drink ale or beer immediately after wine' – the implication being that whereas wine is a gentleman's drink, beer or ale is a yokel's; but that didn't prevent the gentlemen from drinking the latter.

I won't say I will, but I won't say I won't, mostly American, dates from 1923, when Irene Bordoni sang it in *Little Miss Bluebeard*; words by De Sylva and music by Gershwin. Noted by Edward B. Marks, *They All Sang*, 1934. (W. J. Burke.)

I won't – slightly. I certainly shall!: a military c.p. of c. 1925–39. It may have lasted a little longer, but I never heard it during my army service (September 1940–January 1942): but this sort of feeble jocularity does tend to have a short life.

I won't take me coat off – I'm not stopping is a music-hall 'gag' become a general-public c.p.: 'North of England comedian Ken Platt in radio comedy shows, post-WW2' (Vernon Noble, 8 February 1975). Cyril Whelan, 17 February 1975, says that Platt

enjoyed a short flurry of success in the mid 1950s; he's

remembered only for this tag, belongs to the world of 'Workers' Playtime' and 'Come friendly bombs and drop on Slough', and was a paler image of Al Reed, a phlegmatic Northern comedian who enjoyed quite wide popularity for 'Right, monkey' and 'Give over'.

I won't wear it! I won't tolerate, or put up with, it: Cockneys': since *c.* 1930. The slang *wear it* = to accept, to tolerate, something. (C. H. Ward Jackson, *It's a Piece of Cake*, 1943.)

I won't work has, since *c.* 1912, been applied to a member, or members, or the corporate body, of the *I*ndustrial *W*orkers of the *W*orld.

I work like a horse – (so) I may as well hang my prick out to dry! is a good-humoured excuse for – or palliation of – either an accidental or a ribald exposure: late C19–20.

I wouldn't be found dead in it! I certainly shan't wear that hat or that dress or skirt 'or whatever': feminine: C20.

I wouldn't bet a pound to a pinch of shit. This low c.p. expresses a complete lack of confidence: late C19–20. Cf **I wouldn't give you ….**

I wouldn't bet on it! You would be foolishly rash to count on it: late C19–20. Originally among (horse-) racing men.

I wouldn't give you the sweat off my balls or the steam off my shit. This disagreeably low Canadian c.p., belonging to C20, expresses a pretty thorough detestation.

I wouldn't kick *her* out of bed. A normal healthy male's comment on seeing the photograph or a picture of an attractive female: since *c.* 1920.

I wouldn't know! Originally – ?*c.* 1925 – a US c.p., it came to Britain in the late 1930s, the migration being a natural one, for the phrase means 'I couldn't say' or simply 'I don't know'. In a British film of 1940, *Pimpernel Smith*, Leslie Howard remarked, 'In the deplorable argot of the modern generation, "I wouldn't know".'

The phrase has been much used ever since. Foster thinks that it is a translation of *ich wässte nicht*, taken to US by Germans settling there.

Often it implies 'It's outside my territory – not my subject'. Not merely a disclaimer of competence but a proud claim to ignorance of a subject that doesn't interest one. Occasionally a 'brush-off' or a 'get-out' or a facile avoidance of a necessarily long or tedious explanation.

The nuance 'I'm in no position to know' or 'I can't be expected to know' is appositely exemplified by that master of colloquial English, Denis Mackail, in *Where Am I?*, 1948: 'Perhaps this accounts for the weather that we have been having lately. Well, *I* – to use the modern, familiar, and rather desperate phrase – wouldn't know.' (The essay in which the c.p. occurs is titled 'The Word for It'.)

I wouldn't like to meet him in the dark is, in general, applied to any formidable or dangerous or sinister man and, among the womenfolk, a probably rather too venturesome fellow: C20.

I wouldn't say No! Yes, *please!*: since *c.* 1920. 'He said, "I suspect you might find a drink helpful." – "I wouldn't say no."' Rather coy.

I wouldn't stick (or put) my walking-stick where you stick (or put) your prick (or you stick … where I wouldn't ….) A medical c.p. addressed by physicians to men going to them with venereal disease; or by Services' medical officers to servicemen assembled to listen to a brutally, yet salutarily, frank talk upon the dangers of consorting with either prostitutes or 'enthusiastic amateurs'; commoner in WW1 than in WW2 – I myself heard it at such a gathering in Egypt very soon after we arrived there in 1915.

It probably dates from late C19. In 1959 John Winton, in *We Joined the Navy*, records it as having been used by a MO addressing a group of midshipmen and saying, 'Tomorrow we'll be getting to Gibraltar … and I've no doubt that some of you'll be putting your private parts where I wouldn't be putting my walking-stick' – for fear of rapid corrosion.

I wouldn't trust him (or, the occasion demanding, her) as far as I could throw him (or her). This c.p., applied to a spectacularly unreliable person, dates from *c.* 1870. In April 1967, Dr Douglas Leechman told me, 'I recently encountered "I wouldn't trust him as far as I could throw an anvil in a swamp"' – a Canadian variant. Then there's the South African *I trust him as far as I could throw a piano*, 'which I heard from a Springbok in the Western Desert in 1942' (Yehudi Mindel, 5 May 1975).

Cf two further variants: *I wouldn't trust him with a kid's money-box* (specifically, utterly dishonest), C20; and *I wouldn't trust him with our cat* (of a man with an unsavoury sexual record): C20.

I'd hate to cough! is, with wry humour, said by one who is suffering from acute diarrhoea: late C19–20. (I heard this, several times, on Gallipoli, 1915: both diarrhoea and dysentery were distressingly common – and severe.) It springs from the marked effect coughing has, as an aid – among the constipated – to defecation.

I'd have to be lifted on (and off). 'Worldly weariness of old, or older, man at unfledged youth's enthusiasm for a girl's charms' (Laurie Atkinson, late 1974): C20.

I'd have you to know! Let me tell you!: US: C20. Berrey, 1942, classifies it as an 'expression of affirmation – decidedly emphatic. By *c.* 1945, very common also in Britain.

I'd like a pup off that indicates a male's sexually covetous approbation of an attractive female: Services': since *c.* 1930. That is, out of that bitch.

I'd like to get you on a slow boat to China (*from England* understood). I'd like to have enough time with you to influence you slowly and gradually: a nautical c.p., mostly jocular: C20.

I'd love to be a fly on the wall. I should very much like to see and hear what is going on without being seen: mostly Australian, yet also common in Britain: C20. (Barry Prentice, 15 December 1974.)

I'd rather keep you a week than a fortnight is directed at a consistently hearty – or, a greedy – eater: in the main, Australian: since *c.* 1870; by 1976, slightly obsolescent.

I'd rather you than me! – with *I'd* often omitted. Dating from *c.* 1930, it predicts – as *the best of British luck!* predicts – the possibility – even the probability – of failure.

I'd watch it! I certainly won't! Certainly not! According to Manchon, this is a low c.p.: ? *c.* 1910–40. But also, since *c.* 1930 at latest, a menacing 'Look out!' or 'Be very careful!'

idea is cold, the – 'it is of no further use' (Berrey, 1942): US: *c.* 1920–50.

if – a big if supplies a cold *douche* to a very improbable, and startling, supposition or hypothesis: C20; by 1976, slightly outmoded.

if ever! See **well, if ever!**

if he doesn't like it he may do the other thing! 'The other thing' is 'lump it' – put up with it. Recorded by Baumann, it belongs to the approximate period, 1860–1914. Cf **if you don't like it, you can lump it.**

if he fell in the shit, he'd come up smelling of violets is applied to a man exceptionally fortunate: late C19–20. I first heard it in 1912.

if he had the 'flu, he wouldn't give you a sneeze has, since *c.* 1920, imputed extreme meannesss. Probably occasioned by the great influenza epidemic of 1918–19.

if he's not careful he'll shit himself. See **shot himself!**

if I am a dog, shake hands, brother! S, Dialogue III, has:

NEV[EROUT]: ... Why, Miss, if I spoil the Colonel, I hope you will use him as you do me; for, you know, love me, love my Dog.

COL: How's that, *Tom*? say that again. Why, if I am a dog, shake Hands, Brother.

Belonging to C18, this is 'one of the animal–human group of witticisms patterned by the Classical retort of old woman herding asses to pert youth, "Good morning, mother of *asses*. – Good morning, my *son*."'

if I die for it, short for **even if I die for it**, was current *c.* 1660–1760. In the final scene of Act III of Susannah Centlivre, *Marplot in Lisbon*, 1711, the egregious Marplot exclaims, 'Egad I'll not tell where Charles lives, if I die for it.'

if I disremember correctly is a US c.p., glossed by Berrey, 1942, as meaning 'if I have not forgotten'; probably since *c.* 1920; by 1975, somewhat outmoded.

if I had a dog with no more wit, I would hang him occurs in the opening Dialogue of S, and can probably be dated C18– early C19:

NEV[EROUT]: Alack a day, poor Miss, methinks it grieves me to pity you.

MISS: What, you think you said a fine thing now; well, if I had a Dog with no more Wit, I would hang him.

if I have breath is a c.p. of asseveration, synonymous with **as I live and breathe**: current *c.* 1660–1750. Thomas Shadwell, in *The Lancashire Witches*, 1680, at Act II, Scene i, causes the love-sick maid Susan to exclaim, 'Mother *Demdike* shall help me to Morrow: I'll to her, and discourse her about it: if I have breath, I cannot live without him.'

if I have the name, I may as well have the game, late C19– 20, is a feminine c.p., used by a woman unjustly accused of promiscuity. Contrast **that's the name of the game.**

if I hit you, it's the graveyard – if I miss, it's pneumonia is a picturesque comic US threat: *c.* 1910–60. (Berrey.)

if I live and breathe. See **as I live and breathe.**

if I lose my stick, I must have a shy for it. 'I will have a fight before I give up my right' (Egan's Grose, 1823): underworld and near-underworld: *c.* 1810–50.

if I stick a broom up my arse, I can sweep the hangar at the same time. This RAF c.p., dating since *c.* 1925, is uttered, with a bitter humour, by one who has been assigned a string of tasks that will keep him busy for hours.

if I was as big as you, I'd challenge Dempsey. A US c.p. of the 1920s. Ring W. Lardner, *What of It?*, 1925, article titled 'Lay Off the Thyroid'. Jack Dempsey won the world heavy-weight championship on 4 July 1919 and lost it to Gene Tunney on 23 September 1926.

if I were near you, I wouldn't be far from you. If I were near you, I'd deal with you vigorously; if near at all, very near indeed: C18. In S, Dialogue I, Miss says this to a screaming child.

if in danger or in doubt – run in circles, scream and shout! Since *c.* 1925. Used as in Roger Busby, *A Reasonable Man*, 1972, 'The incident room was now buzzing with activity, detectives from all over the city frantically trying to look busy, fearful of the wrath of the CID chief. What was that old Navy saying? "If in danger or in doubt ... shout!"' Cf **when in danger ... .**

if in doubt, toss it out! See **when in doubt ... .**

if it had been a bear ... . See **if it were a bear ... .**

if it had teeth ... . See **it's staring you in the face.**

if it isn't one thing it's another! often preceded by **well** – is a C20 c.p., both US and British. In *Blue Goops and Red*, 1909, Gelett Burgess writes:

When Aunt Ethel and Mr Jack called to take Alonzo and Peter and Bessyrose out to ride in the automobile, you would have thought that they would behave nicely. But they didn't.... That rather frightened Peter and Alonzo and Bessyrose, so after that they kept very quiet and still and began to enjoy the ride.... All the same, pretty soon a tire was punctured, and Mr Jack said, 'Well, if it isn't one thing, it's another!'

if it moves, salute it – if it don't, paint (occasionally **whitewash**) **it!** was the army's and RAF's advice to recruits and, in a way, motto: middle and late 1940s and 1950s.

Professor John W. Clark, in a letter dated 28 October 1968, writes: 'It was certainly common in the U.S. Armed Forces in 1944–46, and still understood, but I question whether it's a c.p. outside of military circles.' Correct! Never a c.p. outside of the British and US fighting Services.

There is, however, an Australian derivative variation: *if it moves, shoot it – if it doesn't, chop it down*, a c.p. used to satirize 'the philosophy of those who are trigger-happy and axe-happy' (Barry Prentice, 1 May 1975).

Cf **if it's too big to shift ... .**

if it takes a leg! 'Threat of a desperado, in search of revenge' (George P. Burnham, *Memoirs of the United States Secret Service*, 1872): US underworld: *c.* 1850–1910. Even at the cost of a leg.

if it were a bear, it would bite you; also **if it had been a bear, it would have bit you.** A semi-proverbial c.p., applied, C17– 18, to 'him that makes a close search after what lies just under his Nose' (BE, 1698). It occurs also in Draxe, 1633, and in S, as Apperson tells us. And see **it's staring you in the face.**

if it were a black snake, you'd be dead. See **it's staring you in the face.**

if it's too big to shift – paint it! is the navy's lower-deck c.p. 'used when any awkward job confronts the men, or when taking heavy stores on board' (*Sailors' Slang*): C20. Cf **if it moves** ....

if my aunt had been a man, she'd have been my uncle; also **if my aunt had been an uncle, she'd have been a man**. A mid C17–mid 20 semi-proverbial c.p., applied derisively to one who has, at length and most tediously, explained the obvious. It also, in C19–20, rebukes someone who has used a most unrealistic conditional, e.g. 'I could have done it if ...' (Apperson.) A scabrous late C19–20 variant is *if my aunt had been a man* or *if my aunt had been an uncle – she'd have had a pair of balls under her arse.*

if not pleased, put your hand in your pocket and please yourself! is a mid C17–18 c.p. retort to a grumbler. Like the preceding phrase, it occurs in Ray.

if only I had some eggs, I'd make (occasionally **cook**) **eggs and bacon – if I had the bacon**, with several slight variations, is an army c.p. of WW1: wistful if applied to oneself, mildly satirical if to another.

if that don't pass! See **well, if that don't pass!**

if that's nonsense, I'd like some of it! retorts upon one who has just reproved a man for talking smut: since *c.* 1925.

if the devil cast his net is a probably mid C19–20 c.p. sent to me by the late Frank Shaw, 4 January 1969, with this comment:

> The jovial fellow suddenly coming on a group of jolly, half-drunk fellows like himself comes out with it as if nobody had ever said it before; he makes them feel very devils themselves and they receive the witticism, as if it was new [to them] also. 'What a capture he'd have!' understood. I just don't, at the moment, know how old; I definitely suspect Irish origin; origin, anyhow, in old folk yarn.

Mr Shaw added, 'We see the devil as a diabolical fisherman.'

if they're big enough – they're old enough is a callous and cynical masculine c.p., referring to the nubility of *young* teenage girls: C20. With an allusion to the age of consent.

if wet – in the vicarage is 'facetiously used when making any arrangement' other than church arrangements; the ecclesiastical usage obviously originated the profane: C20. (Frank Shaw, 1 September 1969.) For origin, cf **good time was had by all – a.**

if you are angry, you may turn the buckle of your girdle behind you. Addressed to 'one Angry for a small Matter, and whose Anger is as little valued' (BE, 1698): late C16–mid 18. Merely signifying '... for all it matters and if *that*'ll help you'.

[**if you blind me, you must lead me** is perhaps not a proverbial saying but a c.p.: C18. S, near end of Dialogue I has:

> MISS: Poh; you are so robustious: You had like to put out my Eye: I assure you, if you blind me, you must lead me.]

if you call yourself a soldier, I'm a bloody Army Corps! This was a WW1 military c.p., virtually extinct by 1940. It implied a vastly superior soldierliness in the speaker. (B & P, 1931.)

if you can name it (or **tell what it is**) **you can have it** refers to an odd-looking person or thing: C20.

if you can't beat (or, US and Australian, **lick**) **'em** (or **them**), **join 'em** (or **them**)! 'Since the early 1940s in Britain' (Frank Shaw) – or was it not rather the mid 1950s? It seems to have originated in the US: in the poem 'Laments for a dying language', forming part of *Everyone but Thee and Me*, 1962, the lamented Ogden Nash writes

> We're in an if-you-cannot-lick-'em-join-'em age,
> A slovenliness-provides-its-own-excuse age,

It is also recorded by Safire. It could, I suppose, have arisen in politics and been applied to areas where one party is crushingly predominant.

An excellent English example occurs in Nicholas Freeling's *Over the High Side*, 1971:

> He buzzed round to Belgrave Square, but none of the lovely ladies were in: pity, that – he wondered whether they knew all about Stasie's little ways. If you can't beat them, join them. If you can't join them, there are even simpler verbs. He wasn't altogether happy about all these Anglo-Saxon monosyllables.

Cf Derek Robinson, *Rotten with Honour*, 1973:

> 'It wouldn't do any good.'
> 'Then what would?'
> 'Avoiding the whole smaller issue.' He turned smartly down a side street. 'If you can't beat 'em, don't join 'em.'

if you can't get a girl, get —— [a named] school. Australian schoolboys': since *c.* 1930. The implication being that, at the rival school particularized, many of the boys were homosexual.

if you can't stand the heat, get (loosely, **keep**) **out of the kitchen.** If you can't stand the pace or the strain, don't get involved! US, since *c.* 1950; British, since *c.* 1970. Political in origin. Indeed it was Harry S. Truman (born 1884) who originated the saying; he used it frequently in public speech and in conversation – and in print, e.g. in his *Mr Citizen*, 1960. (Bartlett.) An indication of British usage occurs in Julian Symons, *A Three Pipe Problem*, 1975:

> Val spoke without looking up from her paper. 'If you don't like the heat you should get out of the kitchen.'
> 'I don't know what you mean.'...
> 'I think you do.... If you don't like the noise, why come and live here [in Baker Street, London].'

if you can't take a joke, you shouldn't have joined. 'Addressed to anyone temporarily dissatisfied with Service life; e.g., after having his weekend leave cancelled' (Paul Beale, 1 October 1974): perhaps since *c.* 1930; certainly since *c.* 1950. Also used to a complaining fellow-workman.

if you don't like it, you can lump it (or **... you may do the other thing**) and one or two other variants, but these are or have been insufficiently general for them to rank as c.pp. 'If you don't like it, you'll just have to put up with it.' The two recorded forms date from at least as early as *c.* 1860; Hotten, 1864, records the derivative ... *you may do the other thing*, which seems to have fallen into disuse by 1914 at latest. Dickens, 1864, 'If you don't like it, it's open to you to lump it.' The *lump it* version was adopted from the US, where it had been current for at least a generation.

if you don't want the goods, don't muck 'em about! originated among Cockney stall-holders, apparently in latter half of C19, and came to be transferred to other activities; extant. (With thanks to Cyril Whelan, 14 January 1975.)

if you feel froggish (or **froggy**) **leap!** (or **take a leap!**) This is an urban Negro challenge to fight: 'If you think you can beat me, come ahead' (CM).

if you had as much brains as guts, usually followed by **what a clever fellow you would be!** was, *c.* 1760–1820, addressed to a man both fat and stupid. (Grose, 1788.)

if you know what I mean is a c.p. only when it is used ironically, as in Noël Coward, *South Sea Bubble*, performed and published in 1956, at Act I, Scene i:

> CHRISTOPHER: And sometimes, some of the things he says, sort of shakes 'em up a bit. If you know what I mean.
> BOFFIN: I do, I do, indeed, I do.

It seems to have arisen early in C20.

Edward Albee, *Quotations from Chairman Mao Tse-Tung*, performed in 1968: When, in her third speech, the Long-Winded Lady uses it, *she* is manifestly using a cliché, but the dramatist is, I think, suggesting to the audience that *he* is using it as a c.p.: 'I try to imagine what it would have been like – *sounded* like – had I not been ... well, so involved, if you know what I mean.'

if you like it – you may! is a c.p. of late C16–mid 17. In James Shirley's *The Witty Fair One*, performed in 1628 and published in 1632, we hear, in Act II, Scene ii, Worthy saying of a witty poem by the ineffable Sir Nicholas Treedle: 'Ay, marry, sir' – to which Treedle replies, 'Now, if you lik't you may.' Edmund Gosse, in the Mermaid edn, remarks, 'This is from the prologue to Ben Jonson's *Cynthia's Revels*, and was popular as a playful defiance.' The full title of the Jonson piece was *Cynthia's Revels; The Fountain of Self-Love. Or Cynthia's Revels. A Comedy*, 1601.

if you looked at him sideways, you wouldn't see him refers to a very thin man: C20; but little used after WW2.

if you say so. If you *say* so, it must *be* so: since *c.* 1950, as an established c.p.; often heard well before that date.

if you see anything that God didn't make, throw your hat at it! 'This c.p., current since *c.* 1930, deprecates undue modesty' (Laurie Atkinson, 1967).

if you vant to buy a vatch, buy a vatch – (but) if you don't vant to buy a vatch, keep your snotty nose off my clean window! A semi-jocular Jew-baiting c.p., sometimes shouted by (mostly London) boys outside a jeweller's shop: C20. Cf **if you're going to buy ....**

[**if you want anything – just whistle.** Apparently US, but not, perhaps, a genuine c.p. The late Norris M. Davidson wrote, 13 February 1975: 'I think this is the last line of a dirty joke. One of those Abie and Becky stories.' Joseph T. Shipley remembers that in the first Humphrey Bogart–Lauren Bacall film, Bogart hands her a silver whistle and the comment, 'If you want me, whistle', which Dr Shipley thinks an allusion. Yet again there's dissent, for another correspondent (Mr D. R. Bartlett, FLA) thinks that it comes 'from the Bogart–Bacall film, *To Have and Have Not* and is spoken by Lauren Bacall ... "If you need me, all you have to do is whistle. You know how to whistle, don't you?" – or words to that effect.']

if you want to get ahead, get a hat! seems to have arisen in the 1930s; it has been remembered either as an Underground advertisement for a hatter or as a slogan used by the hat manufacturers when hat-wearing began to decline: but apparently it went out of fashion during WW2. (Based on

Ramsey Spencer, 16 February 1975, and others.) Clearly it owed much of its popularity to the neat pun.

if you will pardon my French. See **pardon my French!**

if your aunt had balls, she'd be your uncle! See **if my aunt ....**

if your head was loose, you'd lose that too. Addressed to a very forgetful person, esp. a child: late C19–20.

if you're going to buy, buy; if not, would you kindly take the baby's bottom off the counter! A Canadian c.p., addressed by butchers to customers: since *c.* 1920. (Douglas Leechman.) Cf **if you vant to buy a vatch ....**

if you've got the money derives from a popular song (? late 1940s), 'If you've got the money, Honey, I've got the time'. Now heard sometimes as a facetious reply in either direction, i.e. in reply to 'Have you got the time?' (What is the time?), 'Yes, if you've got the money!' Or, less commonly, in reply to 'Have you got the money?' 'Yes, if you've got the time.' (Paul Beale, 12 September 1975.)

I'll 'ave to ask me dad. Concerning 'ITMA' in late 1944, Francis Worsley, *Itma*, 1948, writes:

> Practically the only person untouched by her [Miss Hotchkiss's] domineering ways was the Ancient Mark Time, who, when taxed with any question, invariably replied: 'I'll 'ave to ask me dad!' This saying caught on with the public, and was being heard on all sides in a very short time. Sometimes ... it caused some embarrassment, one such case being, I'm told, at the General Election [of 1945] when Randolph Churchill, being heckled by his audience, was asked a question and, before he could reply, was greeted with loud yells of 'He'll have to ask *his* Dad!'

This c.p. prospered from November 1944 until the end of 1945, and was still heard occasionally until at least 1950; twice or thrice since (*c.* 1955 and *c.* 1967) I have heard it.

I'll be a monkey's uncle! – often preceded by **well** – expresses astonishment: Canadian: since *c.* 1945; adopted from US, where current since the 1930s, if not considerably earlier. Cf the entry **cut off my legs ...**, near end.

I'll be hanged! An exclamation of either severe reprobation or profound astonishment: C16–20. Nathaniel Field, *Amends for Ladies*, written *c.* 1612, but not published until 1618, at Act IV, Scene ii has, 'I'll be hanged, if you were not busy too soon.' The *OED* cites an example from Addison, 1711.

But strictly, and to prevent a misapprehension, the construction *I'll be hanged if ...* is a cliché; it is the elliptical *I'll be hanged!* which is a c.p.

I'll be laughing haversacks indicates an anticipated pleasure that will ensue upon the fulfilment of certain conditions: the three Services': since *c.* 1930. (Laurie Atkinson.)

I'll be one (or **a marble**) **upon your taw.** I'll pay you out!: respectively from *c.* 1770 and *c.* 1780; obsolete by 1890, except among schoolboys. (Grose, 2nd edn, 1788; Vaux, 1812 – published 1818.) It derives from the game of marbles, a *taw* being the large and usually superior marble with which one shoots.

I'll be seeing you, often shortened to *be seeing you!* – in US, often *be seein' yuh!* – or even *seeing you!* or *see you!* A very common valediction since the middle 1930s; it has been punningly distorted to *Abyssinia!*, clearly a phonetic 'telescoping' or conflation of *I'll be seeing you.*

[**I'll believe it when I see it**, 'a c.p. used by a doubting Thomas' (Barry Prentice, 1 May 1975), stands on the vague border separating some proverbial sayings from c.pp.: it certainly goes back as far as late C19 – and perhaps very much farther.]

I'll bet! A variant of **I bet!**

I'll bite (or **I'll buy**) **it** (or **that**); **no! I'm not selling – serious!** 'All right! Tell me what the answer – esp. what the catch – is'; also, just plain 'I'll accept, *or* I accept, that': C20. Clearly *I'll buy it* (or *that*) was prompted by *I'll bite*: of the C18 *bite!*, 'caught you or tricked you'. *I bite*, when understood as meaning, or when misunderstood for, *I'll buy it*, generated the further c.p., *no! I'm not selling – serious* (for *seriously*) – itself hardly before 1930. In *The Judas Mandate*, 1972, Clive Egleton exemplifies the fact that *I'll buy it* is often used as a c.p. reply to 'Have you heard the story about — —', thus: 'His face broke into a beaming smile. "At least we shan't be able to offer little Willie's excuse." Garnett said patiently, "Go on, I'll buy it."' Cf **I'll pay you that one!**

It is also US. In E. V. Cunningham, *Millie*, 1973, we read:
'And I am afraid. There's something ignominious about being afraid.'
'There's also something ignominious about the way you were before.'
'I'll buy that. If I can stay alive without being this nervous, well, it might work.'

I'll cut you off with a shilling. See **I'll strike you out of my will.**

I'll dance at your funeral. See **dance at ....**

I'll do Justice Child. I'll turn King's Evidence: an underworld c.p. of late C17–earlyish C18. 'I'll ... Impeach or Discover the whole gang, and so save my own Bacon' (BE). The reference is to Sir Francis Child the Elder (1642–1713), who became High Sheriff, and later the Lord Mayor, of London.

I'll do (or **fix**) **you!** I'll settle your hash! Often jocular: ... **do** ..., since *c.* 1910; ... **fix** ..., since *c.* 1920. Spoken to a girl, it carries a playful sexual threat.

I'll draw you off a goffer. A naval c.p., challenging an angry man: *c.* 1910–40. From *goffer*, a bottle of aerated water, tending to bubble – hence, a man bubbling up into a bad temper, hence becoming angry. (F & G.)

I'll drink to that! – indicating a genially hearty assent – is an alternative of **you can say that again**, dates from *c.* 1950, and was originally US but by 1955, also Canadian; not unknown in Britain, yet hardly a c.p. there. Mr Ben Traver calls it 'a celebration image' – cites *Addiction*, a monthly newsletter, February 1975, and adds that it 'may be one of the most powerful phrases in the language' (early 1976).

I'll eat my hat! is not a c.p. when it is followed by 'If I'll do this or that', it is a cliché. But it is a c.p. when, late C19–20, it expresses surprise at what *has* been done.

I'll expect you when I see you is addressed to one whose announcement of a visit or a meeting isn't to be depended upon: late C19–20. A late occurrence: the TV serial, 'Coronation Street', episode of 15 October 1973. (Thanks to Mr A. B. Petch.)

I'll first see thy neck as long as my arm! I'll see you hanged first: *c.* 1650–1750. (Ray, 1678; Apperson.)

I'll fix you! See **I'll do you!**

I'll give you Jim Smith! I'll give you a thrashing: proletarian; mostly London streets': 1887–*c.* 1890. Ware, 1909, tells us that a pugilist so named was prominent in 1887.

I'll give you my mother for a maid was, *c.* 1700–40, a c.p. used by London fashionable society. S, Dialogue I, has:
MISS: ... It is better to be an old Man's Darling, than a young Man's Warling' (despised person; later, ... *young man's slave*).
NEV[EROUT]: Faith, Miss, if you speak as you think, I'll give you my Mother for a Maid.
The implication being that Miss's continued spinsterhood is as wildly improbable as the speaker's mother's virginity.

I'll go he! is a New Zealand c.p. exclamation of surprise: since *c.* 1920. From those children's games in which one participant is either blindfolded or otherwise made the 'victim'. Cf:

I'll go hopping to hell! – esp. when preceded by **well,** an addition that affords a vigorous rhyme. Indicative of astonishment – or of profound admiration – or of both: C20.

I'll go out into the garden and eat worms. I'll now eat humble pie: often ironic. Probably rural in origin, it arose *c.* 1880. More a feminine than a masculine c.p.

I'll hand it to him! 'An idiomatic way of prefacing a compliment, often reluctantly. E.g., "I'll hand it to him, he is often generous." In use in New Zealand since about 1930' (Arthur Gray, of Auckland, on 29 March 1969). And not unknown in Britain.

I'll have a basinful of that! is applied to a new word or a long one: mostly lower and lower-middle classes': since the early 1930s. A synonym recorded in Michael Harrison's novel, *Spring in Tartarus*, 1935, and current since *c.* 1910, is *I'll have two of those;* the *basinful* version is still current in the 1970s, the other was obsolescent by *c.* 1970.

I'll have to ask me dad. See **I'll 'ave to ....**

I'll have two of those! See **I'll have a basinful of that!**

I'll have your gal! 'A cry raised by street boys or roughs when they see a fond couple together' (B & L): mostly Londoners': *c.* 1880–1914.

I'll have your guts for garters! A threat, originally serious, latterly humorous: mid C18–20. In C20, it has been a racecourse and low Cockney c.p. Cf Desmond Bagley, *Landslide*, 1967, '"Your father isn't going to like that. He'll have your guts for garters, Howard. I doubt if he ever ruined a deal by being too greedy."'

Yet, since WW2, the phrase has gradually mounted the social scale – not that it has yet (1976) become either aristocratic or cultured. In Tim Heald's engaging 'thriller', *Deadline*, 1975, we read of a journalist declaring, 'If this doesn't work, then I think Parkinson [his 'boss'] will, as they say, "have my guts for garters".'

But it must have gone underground for a century or more: Robert Greene, *James the Fourth*, at Act III, Scene ii: 'I'll make garters of thy guts, thou villain'; and Jack Lindsay found, in an early C17 parish register, *I'll have your guts for garter points.*

In November 1969, Laurie Atkinson glossed the present usage thus: 'The garters not so much historical as English homely phrasers' love of alliteration and assonance.'

I'll have your hat! was, *c.* 1870–1905, a street c.p. – a mild, semi-comical threat. (B & L.) Contrast:

I'll hold him. In a note from Laurie Atkinson (October 1969) occurs a salutary warning that certain apparently homosexual c.pp. are merely ironic or facetious, as when one man, angry and irritated, says to another, 'I'll fuck you!' he merely expresses mood; and a third man will interpose a mock-encouraging *I'll hold him* – a genuine male c.p. current throughout C20.

I'll knock seven kinds of shit out of you! A low naval threat: since *c.* 1920. The non-c.p. slang is *knock the shit out of* someone, to thrash him, of which the c.p. is patently an elaboration.

I'll lay you six to four. 'This improper fraction is often used to enforce argument by non-punters' (Shaw), esp. among would-be sporting characters, and implying a temperate degree of assurance: since middle 1940s and perhaps since as early as 1930.

I'll leave it all to the cook. I won't take that bet: a sporting c.p. of *c.* 1815–40. (Egan's Grose, 1823.) A cook is a good judge of meat, but it takes an experienced betting man to judge horseflesh on the hoof.

I'll leave it to you to choose, to decide, etc: C20. Noël Coward's earliest published, although not earliest written, play was called '*I'll Leave It to You.*' *A Light Comedy in Three Acts*, performed on 21 July 1920 at the New Theatre, London, and published two or three months later. Act I ends with the phrase being used literally.

> SYLVIA: What we want to know, uncle, is how on earth we are to start? (*They all nod.*)
> DANIEL: (*smiling benignly, arms outstretched*) I'll leave it to you!

I'll let you off this time, from being a teacher's condonation of a pupil's misdemeanour, has, since *c.* 1950, been a c.p., as employed – and in the *milieu* there indicated – in: 'Widely used by the boys my wife has to teach. "All right, Miss, let you off this time!" they say, to excuse some stupidity of their own' (Paul Beale, 23 March 1975).

I'll make (or **I think I'll make**) **a separate peace.** See **separate peace** ....

I'll make you sing 'O be joyful!' on the other side of your mouth – the original form; in C20, *O be joyful* has been omitted. A mid C18–early C19 threat. (Grose, 1788.)

I'll nark yer! This Australian, mainly urban, c.p., dating from *c.* 1905, combines the sense of slang *nark*, to annoy, and *nark*, to foil.

I'll pay you that one! I 'bought' that – I admit I've been 'had': Australian: since *c.* 1920. In, e.g., Kylie Tennant, *The Honey Flow*, 1956. Cf **I'll bite**. Hence, that's a good story – that's a very good joke: Australian: since *c.* 1945. (Barry Prentice.)

I'll push your face in and **I'll spit in your eye and choke you** are working-class threats, often used playfully: late C19–20. Cf:

I'll put you where the rooks won't shit on you. A jocular version of *I'll kill you* used humorously: army: since *c.* 1935. The implication is 'I'll put you underground'.

I'll saw your leg off! See **my word! if I catch you** ....

I'll say! An enthusiastic Australian affirmative: since *c.* 1930, but by 1965, slightly obsolescent; also British, since *c.* 1925. Adopted from the US: McKnight notes its US college use; Berrey records it as a general Americanism. A very neat US example occurs in Edward Albee, *The Sandbox*, written in 1959 and published in 1960:

> YOUNG MAN: (*Flexing his muscles.*) Isn't that something?
> GRANDMA: Boy, oh boy; I'll say. Pretty good.
> YOUNG MAN: (*Sweetly.*) I'll say.

A c.p. in the first line and two in the second, with the third c.p. ironically repeated and emphasized in the third line. A characteristically subtle, yet outright, example of Albee's utterly sincere, (here quietly) shattering satire.

As a Briticism, it is perhaps elliptical for 'I'll say it is!' rather than for *I'll say so!*

I'll say so! is, by H. L. Mencken, in 1922, included in a short list of US army c.pp. already falling into disuse. It passed into British slang. Dodie Smith's *Call It a Day*, performed in 1935 and published a year later, at Act II, Scene ii, has:

> DOROTHY: (*looking at the photograph*) Look at your superb waist-line.
> MURIEL: And was it agony? I'll say so ...

I'll see you further, with or without the addition of **first**. I certainly *won't*!: since *c.* 1840 – it occurs in, e.g., Mayhew's *London Labour and the London Poor* (at chapter I, p. 29), 1851. In C20, *first* is omitted.

I'll see you in church (or **in court**) or **in gaol (jail)** are humorous c.pp. used on parting from someone: mostly Australian: apparently dating from a little before WW1. (Barry Prentice.)

I'll shit! is an emphatic and vulgar expression of deeply felt indignation or contempt or disgust: American: since, I think, the 1940s. Recorded in *DCCU*.

I'll show you mine if you show me yours. 'A phrase used by children comparing genitals' (Barry Prentice, 15 December 1974): dating from at least as early as late C19, and probably from fifty – a hundred – years earlier. Only the most starry-eyed of parents believe in the innocence of children. Frederick Forsyth, *The Dogs of War*, 1974, has:

> 'Have you any scars from wounds?...'
> 'Some.'
> 'Show me,' she said. '... Go on, show me. Prove it.' ....
> 'I'll show you mine, if you'll show me yours,' he taunted,

mimicking the old kindergarten challenge.

I'll strike you out of my will; also, **I'll cut you off with a shilling**. 'Jocular use among workingmen who have little or nothing to leave' (A. B. Petch, 16 January 1974): since the middle or late 1940s.

I'll swing for you if you don't! – if you don't agree – if you don't do it – etc. A proletarian threat of *c.* 1820–90. (Hotten.) The implication, obviously, is 'I'll be hanged for murdering you.'

I'll take a rain check. I'll accept, another time, if I may: US: since late 1940s (it's not in, e.g., Berrey, 1942), W & F recording it in 1960 as, '... promise to accept an invitation at a later date'. A *rain check* is a ticket, or the stub of a ticket, valid for the replay of a game cancelled or abandoned because of bad weather, usually because of persistent rain.

I'll take vanilla is either an elaboration or the original of *vanilla!*, of which W & F, 1960, note that it is a usually jocular expression of disbelief, 'used when the lie or exaggeration is of no great consequence'.

On 11 July 1975, Colonel A. Moe wrote: 'The phrase is usually intended to convey an attitude of indifference or to exhibit a lack of concern ... The meaning = it makes no difference.' But he also quotes from Carl Sandburg, *The People, Yes*, 1936: 'The city editor managed to have the final words. "I'll take vanilla! horsefeathers!"' – that is, 'Nonsense!'

I'll tell it to nobody (or **no one**) **but friends and strangers** is a C18 c.p., at first of the fashionable world of London. S, in Dialogue I, has:

NEV[EROUT]: Miss. I'll tell you a Secret. if you'll promise never to tell it again.

MISS: No. to be sure. I'll tell it to no Body but Friends and Strangers.

That is, everybody.

I'll tell the cock-eyed world! and **I'll tell the world!** The former, an elaboration of the latter, is recorded by Berrey, and dates from *c.* 1930. The latter, anglicized in 1930 or 1931, goes back to *c.* 1917, occurs in HLM. who includes it as one of the favourite affirmations of the US Army in 1917–18; W & F describe it as 'now archaic'.

I'll tell you one thing – and that's not two; in C19–20. often **... and that ain't two**. The former, C18–20, appears in S. Dialogue I:

LADY SM[ART]: I'll tell you one thing, and that's not two; I'm afraid I shall get a Fit of the Head-ache To-day.

I heard it, in the street, so recently as 13 June 1972. It may last for years yet, for it's a pleasantly positive, without being too aggressive, way to emphasize one's point or statement.

I'll tell you those! is a US. notably a Chicagoan. emphatic variant of **I'm telling you**: *c.* 1890–1910. George Ade. *Artie*. 1896. '"Say. I like that church. and if they put in a punchin'-bag and a plunge they can have my game. I'll tell you those."' The phrase. which occurs several times in *Artie*, became so popular that it could be varied, thus: '"They've got me entered, but I don't know whether I'll start or not. I'm leary of it; I don't mind telling you those"' (ibid., p. 60). Elliptical for 'I'll tell you those things.'

I'll tell you what!: late C17–20; hence, **I tell you what!**: C19–20: hence, **tell you what!**: mid C19–20. I'll tell you something. The first occurs in Shakespeare and Tennyson; the second, in Violet Hunt, 'I tell you what, Janet, we must have a man down who doesn't shoot – to amuse us!'; the third, in Baumann. (With thanks to the *OED*.) It's an 'introducer': and it lies on the borderline between cliché and c.p.

But the best example I've found comes in Elizabeth Inchbald's *I'll Tell You What*, 1786. The Prologue, written by George Colman, begins:

Ladies and Gentlemen, *I'll tell you what!*

Yet not. like ancient Prologue. tell the Plot— and ends:

But hold—I say too much—I quite forgot— And so I'll tell you—NO—SHE'LL tell you what. It still prospers, as in

'Can you help me, George?'

'Don't think I can. Bill! No, wait a moment, I'll tell you what! Come and see me tomorrow – I may, by then, have news for you.'

I'll tell your mother is addressed to a young girl – or ironically to a girl not so young – out with a boyfriend: late C19–20.

I'll try anything once has, since *c.* 1925 in both Britain and the US, been affected by the adventurous and the experimental, sometimes jocularly or satirically. Frank Clune's very readable autobiography, published in 1933, bears the title *Try Anything Once*. The phrase was anticipated by Miles Malleson in *Conflict*, 1925, Act II, Scene iii:

DARE: He can't *eat* me.

MRS TREMAYNE: I'm not so sure of that.

DARE: I've never been eaten before; I'll do anything once. In some contexts, it is virutally synonymous with **there's always a first time**.

I'll venture it – as Johnson did his wife – and she did well. A semi-proverbial c.p., implying that sometimes it pays to take a risk: *c.* 1650–1800. Apperson cites Ray. 1678. and Fuller. but doesn't elucidate who Johnson was; nor can I.

illegitimis non carborundum! Literally. 'Let there not be a *carborundum*ing by the illegitimate!' – Don't let the bastards grind – hence, wear – finally, get – you down or break your spirit!: carborundum (silicon carbide). being extremely hard. is used in grinding and polishing: owing to its apparently having the form (*-undum*) of a L gerund. the word has prompted a piece of delightful mock-L. From being an army Intelligence c.p. of 1939–45. it became, as early as 1940. a more general army c.p.. chiefly among officers. I have often wondered which Classical scholar. irritated and exacerbated almost to desperation. coined this trenchancy; and I like to think it was my friend Stanley Casson. who. born in 1889. became Reader in Classical Archaeology at Oxford and who. after directing the army Intelligence School early in WW2. went to Greece to lead the resistance there and was killed mid-April 1944, a learned, witty, gallant scholar and man of action.

The phrase had by the late 1940s gained a fairly wide currency among the literate. In 1965. Mr Barry Prentice assured me that, in Australia, its use was by no means confined to those who had a little L.

In Martin Woodhouse's novel, *Rock Baby*, 1968. it occurs allusively thus: '*Nil carborundum* all right, I thought. Don't let the bastards grind you down. like it says in the book. but how was I to set about it?'

I'm a bit of a liar myself. This US c.p., probably dating from the 1880s or rather earlier. was, *c.* 1900, adopted in the British Empire.

I'm a Dutchman if I do!: since *c.* 1850; **I'm a Dutchman**: since *c.* 1830. I'm somebody else = disbelief; as in 'If there's anything there. I'm a Dutchman.' By 1940. obsolescent; by 1970. rare.

I'm a stranger here myself. This pellucid statement. which circumstances oblige us to make often enough, has, both in Britain and in US, become a c.p. either humorous or ironic or both: since *c.* 1950. Paul Kavanagh, *Such Men Are Dangerous*, 1969 in US and very early 1971 in Britain, has:

'Is it like this all vinter long?'

'I'm a stranger here myself.'

A pleasant British example occurs in Dorothy Halliday, *Dolly and the Cookie Bird*, 1970:

'Well done. I suppose you don't know where he's hidden the rubies?'

'I'm a stranger here myself,' said Derek, who still looked as if he had had four gins in a row. It was the first joke I had ever heard him make, which explains its unremarkable nature.

Connotation: 'I'm no more likely to know than you yourself are'; hence, 'I don't know what's going on and I shouldn't care to guess'. In short, from being a plea of specific ignorance, it has, as a c.p., become a sort of general excuse for inability, or unwillingness, to help.

I'm a tit man myself. I'm far more interested in a girl's breasts than in her legs: US: since the late (? middle) 1940s. Oddly, it hasn't become at all common in Britain – not, at least, up to 1976.

I'm a true dog of the game, or else take away my gun. I'm an honest fellow and I 'shoot straight' or 'play the game': a rural, sporting, upper-middle- and upper-class c.p. of c. 1670–1750, perhaps originally and predominantly in Ireland. See Charles Shadwell (a younger son of laureate Thomas) in his comedy, *Irish Hospitality; or, Virtue Rewarded*, published in *The Works*, 2 vols, 1720, at Act I, Scene i, where Sir Jowler Kennel, who thinks almost more highly of his dogs than of his neighbours, asks Sir Patrick Worthy to be allowed to pay court to one or other of his two daughters:

SIR PAT: I hope, Sir Jowler, you won't act like a *Poacher*, but give 'em – when married – Law enough.
SIR JOW[LER]: Pshaw, pshaw, no, no, I'm a true Dog of the Game, or else take away my Gun, as the saying is.
(Perhaps with the innuendo '... or may I be castrated!')

I'm always out of the picture – just clambering round the frame was 'current [among naval personnel] in the Indian Ocean c. 1942–1943' (Rear-Admiral P. W. Brock, 20 March 1975). A 'local catch phrase', yes; yet illustrative of the fact that a local, short-lived c.p. may be a good one; He adds: 'I believe someone, perhaps a Royal Marine, wrote a song with this motif.'

I'm all right, Jack! See **fuck you, Jack ....**

I'm as mild a villain as ever scuttled a ship is a c.p. applied to oneself in a tone of jocular reproach and not entirely condemnatory disapproval: C20; little heard since WW2, but not yet obsolete even by 1975. Probably based on – or prompted by – the literal *I'm a bit of a villain myself, but –*. Cf **I'm a bit of a liar myself.**

I'm fire-proof. Short for **fuck you, Jack, I'm fire-proof!** – the RAF's adaptation of **fuck you, Jack, I'm all right!**: since c. 1930. Cf the civilian pun on the RAF motto, *per ardua ad astra: per ardua ad aspidistra.*

I'm from Missouri. *D.Am.* at 'Missouri' states that the phrase, in full, is *I'm from Missouri [and] you'll have – or you have – to show me*; that it apparently dates from c. 1880 or a year or so earlier; that it occasionally has *I come* for *I'm*; and that a demonstration is necessary, the speaker being either extremely sceptical or extremely reluctant to believe, without it.

W. J. Burke, 28 January 1969, says:
'I'm from Missouri' and its corollary 'You'll have to show me' qualify for a c.p. tag. We call Missouri the 'Show Me State'. We Missourians (yes, I was born there) wish to have proof of something before we believe it. We are not easily fooled or taken in. 'I'm from Missouri' is now used by non-Missourians as an expression of skepticism.

A further variant is *I'm from Missouri, you've got to show me.* (Colonel Albert Moe, 28 June 1975.)

I'm going down now, sir. See **don't forget the diver!**

I'm going to die is 'said twice, plaintively, followed by a pause, and then resolutely, in a Cockney accent, **nah, fuck it! I'll go tomorrer**' (Paul Beale, 5 April 1976): since c. 1945.

I'm going to do a job no one else can do for me. Used among men when one of them excuses himself to go to the lavatory: since c. 1950. (A. B. Petch, 16 September 1974.)

I'm going to get my head sharpened. I'm going to get a haircut: RAF: c. 1950–70.

I'm Hawkshaw the detective, usually completed rather than elaborated by – **he took a sly glance at me**: c. 1864–1914. From melodrama and burlesque, notably of the Transpontine sort. 'He was a character in Tom Taylor's *The Ticket-of-Leave Man*' (1863) and the implication of the c.p. is that 'someone is behaving like a copper's nark' (Frank Shaw, 30 October and early November 1968).

Tom Taylor (1817–80) wrote many successful plays, of which *The Ticket-of-Leave Man* was perhaps the best and was spectacularly successful, and during his last six years he edited *Punch*.

I'm in condition to-night! I feel good tonight: c. 1955–70. Either from a 'quack' muscle-builder's advertisement or, as Paul Beale has suggested (23 March 1975), from 'a TV comedian of the early 1950s, as he flexed non-existent muscles'. Cf **you too can have a body like mine.**

I'm in the boat – push off! was used by the army in WW1 and up to c. 1939. (B & P.) The equivalent of **fuck you, Jack, I'm all right.** Cf:

I'm inboard – fuck you, Jack! The same sense as the preceding entry: naval: C20. Variant of ... *bugger you, Jack!*

I'm it is 'used in derision of the "Great I am" type of actor' or music-hall, or variety, performer: since c. 1920. (A. B. Petch, 4 January 1974.)

I'm Jolly Jack the Sailor just come home (or **in**) **from sea.** Of the approximate period 1880–1914, it originated in the music-halls. (Frank Shaw, 25 October 1968.) Probably connected with – perhaps even the predecessor of – **Ballocky Bill the Sailor.**

I'm like all fools – I love everything that's good belongs to C18 and occurs in both Dialogue I and Dialogue II of S, 1738; thus in the second:
LADY SM[ART]: Mr *Neverout*, do you love Pudden?
NEV: Madam, I'm like all Fools; I love every Thing that is good. But the Proof of the Pudden, is in the eating.

I'm nice. I feel very well: US negroes': since c. 1960. (CM, 1970.)

I'm not having any. See **I'm not taking any.**

I'm not here. See **I am not here.**

I'm not just a pretty face, often extended by **you know.** I'm not merely pretty (or occasionally, of men, handsome) – I do possess *some* intelligence. 'A feminine c.p. addressed to a crass male. "I have brains as well as looks"' (Wilfred Granville, late December 1968). Since c. 1965 or a very few years earlier. It occurs in Miles Tripp's psychological 'thriller', *Woman at*

Risk, 1974, thus: ' "She's not just a pretty face," Philpott went on, "she's clever too" ', which supports my own opinion that, strictly, the c.p. is *not just a pretty face*, and that this can be, and is, often preceded by *I'm* or *She's*.

But the c.p. is also used jocularly 'among men (from women's protest that they have ability, brains, as well as beauty) at proved acumen, handyman's help in the home, or when hunch is proved right' (Laurie Atkinson, 18 July 1975).

I'm not made of money. See **you must think ....**

I'm not out for chocolate – just had grapes! No, thank you!, used intensively and rather contemptuously: c.p. of *c.* 1905–14. It occurs in W. L. George's penetrating and perspicuous novel, *The Making of an Englishman*, 1914.

I'm not so green as I'm cabbage-looking. See **not so green ....**

I'm not taking (or **having**) **any.** Not for me: respectively since *c.* 1895 and since *c.* 1890; the latter occurs in J. Milne, *Epistles of Atkins*, 1902.

I'm off in a shower (or **cloud**) **of shit.** Good-bye!: Canadian Army c.p. of WW2 – and occasionally, among civilians, since 1945.

I'm on agen with Monaghan and off agen with you had a brief life (English), 1910–*c.* 1914, and was adopted from a song title that, in 1910, was sung by Maggie Cline. Edward B. Marks, *They All Sang*, 1934. (Thanks to W. J. Burke.)

I'm only asking. I'm merely asking a simple question, not expecting some benefit; I merely wish to know; I ask out of curiosity, nothing more: since *c.* 1910.

I'm only here for the beer. I've no right to be here – all I want is a bit of fun; I'm not a serious person: from late 1971 or very early 1972. From a beer advertisement – for Double Diamond – of 1971.

Often shortened to *only here for the beer*, which has become so widely accepted that, in the *Sunday Times* Magazine of September 1973, a summer-resort article can be headed 'Only Here For La Bière'.

I'm proper poorly is one of the scores of c.pp. either originated or popularized – often both – by the music-halls: this one arose, I think, in the 1930s. (Frank Shaw, 25 October 1968.)

I'm skinning this cat, often elaborated by the addition of **and you are not paid to hold the tail.** Mind your own business!: US: since *c.* 1920; by 1970, somewhat outdated. (Berrey.)

I'm so empty I can feel my (or **me**) **backbone touching my** (or **me**) **belly button.** An uncouth, undeniably humorous, c.p.: C20. In, e.g., Alexander Baron, *There's No Home*, 1950. Cf:

I'm so hungry I could eat a shit sandwich – only I don't like bread is 'a rather repugnant self-explanatory c.p., which is not used in vice-regal circles' (Barry Prentice): Australian: since *c.* 1950. Cf the preceding entry.

I'm sorry I came in! An ironic, almost resigned, c.p. 'spoken by one who, expecting quiet, enters a room where there's a lot of human noise' (Frank Shaw): since the late 1940s.

I'm speaking (or **talking**) **to the butcher – not to the block.** 'Putting 'em in their place! If the boy speaks up before the workman can frame a reply, or if Jack's missus joins in the (acrimonious) argument: but it *can* be used jocularly' (Julian Franklyn, 1962): Cockneys': C20.

I'm telling you indicates emphasis: adopted, in early 1920s, in Britain: from US, where used since *c.* 1910. Supp. 1 of HLM notes that it is one of 'a number of familiar American phrases': for which the erudite Dr Roback had argued a Yiddish origin; and Berrey includes it in a long list of 'expressions of affirmation'. Cf **I'll tell the (cock-eyed) world!**

I'm trying to give them up rapidly became an all-purpose reply to an offer of almost anything. Its origin, of course, was a rejoinder to the 'Goon Show' invitation of the 1950s – 'Have a gorilla?' (q.v.). (Camilla Raab, confirmed by Paul Beale.)

I'm willing – but Mary isn't, with *I* and *Mary* strongly emphasized. Used by a dyspeptic or other stomachic sufferer when some food is offered: C20. This is, of course, *little Mary*, the stomach.

I'm with you, pal – or with **pal** omitted – is a US c.p. of agreement, not, it is true, wildly enthusiastic, yet genuine: since *c.* 1920. (Berrey.)

in (whichever is, currently, the world's most unpopular country) **people are shot for less** is 'a c.p. (often jocular) implying that the hearer is living in such a tolerant country' (Barry Prentice): Australian: since the late 1940s. As in 'You're reading my book. In——, people are shot' – or 'being shot' – 'for less.'

[**in a pig's eye**, at first merely euphemistic for **in a pig's arse** or **arse-hole**, was, *c.* 1945, adopted in Britain from Canada, which took it from the US (*in a pig's ass*); the vulgar form came from a bawdy song current since long before 1940. This violent negative – as in 'In a pig's eye you will!' – is only very doubtfully a true c.p.]

in a while, crocodile. See **see you later, alligator!**

in Annie's room. See **Annie's room ....**

in everybody's mess but nobody's watch. Directed at a seaman both a cadger and chary of work: the Royal Navy: *c.* 1880–1914. (Bowen.) Also in the US Navy: C20. Berrey comments: 'said of a busybody'.

in her (or **his**) **skin** is a pert – originally a smart – evasive c.p. reply to 'Where is So-and-So?': C16–20. In George Gascoyne, *Supposes*, performed in 1566, Act I, Scene iv begins:

DULIPPO: Ho, Jack Pack, where is Erostrato?
CRAPENO: Erostrato? Marry, he is in his skin.

In S, Dialogue I, 1738, we find:

COL[ONEL]: Pray, Miss, where is your old Acquaintance Mrs *Wayward*?
MISS: Why, where should she be? If you must know, she's in her Skin.

In C19–20, it has largely been one of the domestic c.pp.

in inverted commas (or **in quotes**) simply means either 'emphatically' or 'I'm quoting —— for emphasis'. 'I didn't hear it until *c.* 1972. Often accompanied by the speaker's sketching quotation marks in the air with the forefinger of one or both hands.' (Paul Beale, 12 September 1975.)

in the words of the Chinese poet expresses disgust on hearing bad news or on receiving unpleasant instructions: Canadian: since *c.* 1910. If a friend hears one say this, he is expected to ask, 'What Chinese poet?' and thus to afford the opportunity of replying, 'Ah Shit, the Chinese poet'; *c.* 1919, also current in England, with the variant name, 'Hoo (or Who) Flung Dung'.

Prompted by **Confucius he say**.

[**in your dipper!** is a defiant New Zealand expression that, used *c.* 1920–40, lies midway between a c.p. and a piece of slangy violence.]

in your hat! Nothing doing! I shall certainly do no such thing: a US c.p. of *c.* 1920–40. Clarence B. Kelland, *Speak Easily, c.* 1935, says: 'I found it impossible to make my way, though I requested sundry persons to let me pass. One gentleman thus addressed replied, cryptically, with the following sentence: "In your hat!"' Later in the same novel: 'To my letter the editor replied with a terse note, which read: "In your hat! You're getting off easy ..."'.

Professor Paul Korshin, in private conversation with me on 14 July 1972, dated the phrase as 'since *c.* 1890; by 1970, obsolescent'; he defined it as 'indicating a derisive refusal or rebuttal or general negative' and explained the semantics thus: 'You can put that in your hat and *wear* it!'

include me out! Leave me out – of the discussion or plan: US: since the late 1940s; by 1950, also British. One of the few genuine Goldwynisms; 'Most of the zany cracks attributed to Sam Goldwyn are the work of Hollywood gagmen', as A. B. Petch has remarked.

Indian .... See **he's a regular Indian**.

Indians about! Beware! – presumably of detectives or of rivals: US professional gamblers': *c.* 1830–1900. (Matsell.) Semantically cf **the natives are hostile**.

infirmary – my (or **the**) **answer's in the**. My answer is Yes: late C19–20; obsolescent by 1937, virtually obsolete by 1945. A pun on *in the affirmative*. Hence, 'My answer's unfavourable' or 'The news is bad': since *c.* 1910 and, immediately after, much more general than the earlier sense, but itself obsolete by 1950.

influence in the right quarter, usually preceded by **he has**. An ironic c.p., applied by New Zealand soldiers during WW1, to a comrade landed with a menial or distasteful job, e.g. cleaning out the latrines.

International FYB Week. See **what *is* this? International ....**

iron's down – the. Granville comments: 'Becoming obsolete, this catch-phrase means a bad or unresponsive audience. When the *iron* safety curtain is lowered the audience cannot be heard on the stage.'

is everybody happy? As a c.p., it means 'Is everybody satisfied? Comfortable?' Since the late 1940s and throughout the 1950s. Ramsey Spencer associates it with such morale-boosting radio programmes (in WW2) as 'Workers' Playtime' (4 February 1975).

On the other hand, Cyril Whelan (17 February 1975) thinks that, 'since long before WW2, it has been the traditional cry of the red-nosed comedian using an excuse to get some audience participation working, [in readiness] for the raucous chorus guaranteed to come rolling back at him from the stalls .... The general area of my guess would be pantomime' – or perhaps rather pantomime and music-hall reacting upon each other. It seems that Mr Whelan is right about the date: in 1905 came a popular American song, words by Williams, music by Ernest Hoyan. (Edward B. Marks, *They*

All Sang, 1934. With thanks to W.J.B.) The English vogue probably derived from the American.

Also, not altogether independently, it is the boisterously hearty query of the hosts at holiday camps, both over the microphone and personally to groups: and this usage has helped to promote the c.p. (Paul Beale, 5 February 1975.)

is he with you? – No! I thought he was with you. An 'exchange between any two members of a party, *à propos* – and across the face of – a third friend, who has just made an exhibition of himself in some way; e.g., by making a foolish (or too clever) remark, breaking wind, etc.' (Paul Beale, 11 December 1974): since 1950. Cf **excuse my pig ...** and **you can't take him anywhere**.

is it cold up there? is jocularly addressed to a very tall person: late C19–20; not much heard since *c.* 1960. Frank Shaw's comment, made on 1 April 1969, was: 'To tall man by purveyor of stale wit.'

is it my turn to utter? is 'an exaggeratedly comical catch-phrase meaning "Do I speak next?" ... usually said of one who has not been paying attention at rehearsals and is caught "off"' (Granville): *c.* 1920–60.

is it possible (**!** rather than **?**); often shortened to **possible!** A US c.p., expressing amazement or admonition or consternation: C19–20. It occurs more than once in John Neal's *Errata; or, The Works of Will Adams*, 1823; his *Brother Jonathan*, 1825, has, at Act II, Scene 114;
'Nathan Hale! – is that you?'
'Is is possible?' said Hale, coming forward, with great eagerness.
And at Act II, Scene 352, he has:
'To be sure! – we were at school together.'
'Possible! – why have I never heard of it?'
It also occurs in T. C. Haliburton, *The Clockmaker*, all three series, 1837, 1838, 1840.

is (or **was**) **my face red!** and **was his face red!** are exclamations of acute embarrassment. US since *c.* 1930 (recorded by, e.g., Berrey, 1942); adopted in Britain, in the early 1950s.

is my hat on straight? How do I look? Vernon Noble, on 29 April 1975, told me:
In *Fifty Great Years*, a booklet published by Kemsley Newspapers to mark the Golden Jubilee, 1947, of the *Evening Chronicle*, Manchester, I came across the following paragraph in reference to the female fashions of the early years of the century (1907 to 1914, it seems):
Hats were, at first, enormous. Their wearers had to sidle like crabs to get on trams. 'Is my hat on straight?' became a catch phrase.
I was born in 1908, but my recollection is of the First World War period when women's hats were considerably reduced in size, but the phrase remained in currency for 'How do I look?'

is that a catch or a have? is a low and raffish admission that the speaker has been fooled: *c.* 1880–1910. Should the fooler attempt a definition, the victim turns the tables by exclaiming **then you catch** (or **have**) **your nose up my arse!**

is that a promise? and **that's a promise!** and – the most general – **is that a threat or a promise?** The traditionally licentious soldiery's stock retort to *fuck you!*: WW1 (and doubtless during the Boer War); and later. The currency has very probably been much wider than merely in the army – in, e.g., the navy.

Of the three, the third has, throughout the C20, also been applied other than sexually: as Wilfred Granville noted (19 February 1969), it is 'a question asked when a doubtful proposition has been made'. And in *A Three Pipe Problem*, 1975, Julian Symons exemplifies its usage, neatly, thus:

'Goodbye. I advise you to keep out of my way.'

... She smelt of cigarette smoke and gin. 'Next time, Mr Holmes? Is that a threat or a promise?'

Cf **promises, promises!**

is that all? An ironic c.p., uttered exclamatorily in reference to high prices or charges: C20. (A. B. Petch, in letter dated May 1966: 'Still heard'.)

is that good? A question intended to disconcert one's interlocutor by its unexpectedness and by its at least partial air of a *non sequitur*: mostly among men of the law and among those who well could have been lawyers or barristers. I first heard it in the late 1920s, but suspect that it may already have been current for a generation. As in, e.g.:

'I won a hundred pounds on the Derby!'

'Is that good?'

is that so? See **oh, is that so?** It might be as appropriate here as anywhere else in the dictionary to quote Professor Emeritus F. E. L. Priestley's comment (September 1975), 'What an enormous number of c.pp. there are, expressing agreement or disagreement, and nothing else!'

is that the way to London? See **that's the way to London?**

is there a doctor in the house? is sometimes used jocularly and non-literally and therefore as a c.p. (as Mr A. B. Petch reminds me on 4 January 1974): since the late 1950s. It owes something to a most amusing film so titled.

is there any other kind? is the c.p. comment upon, or reply to, 'It's a dodgy business': since *c.* 1950.

is there room for a little (or **small**) **one?** – often shortened to **any room...?** or even to **room...?** – is addressed collectively – and either humbly or hopefully – to the occupants of a crowded vehicle: C20. Often ironic, as when the suppliant is anything but small.

is this a proposal or a proposition? Canadian: since *c.* 1940; English and Australian since *c.* 1943. Cf 'to *proposition* a girl' – to suggest sexual intimacy to her.

is you *is* or is you *ain't*? Well, *are* you or *aren't* you, e.g. sure?: US: originally negroes': since the middle 1940s; by *c.* 1970, obsolescent. From the immensely popular song and gramophone record, *Is You Is or Is You Ain't My Baby* [my girl]?, written by Billy Austin and Louis Jourdan, in very close collaboration in words and music, and published in 1944. (With thanks to the Music Room of the British Library.)

Hence such allusive variants as *am I is or am I ain't?* and *are we is or are we ain't?* – as in Clarence B. Kelland, *No Escape*, 1951:

'What for do you want to know?' Pazzy asked.

'Curiosity.'

'Look,' said Pazzy, 'are we is or are we ain't pals?'

'We are,' Jonathan told him.

is your father a glazier? See **glazier ....**

is your journey really necessary? was a WW2 slogan (1940–5); since as early as 1944 it has been used as a jocular c.p., by 1960 slightly, and by 1970, very, obsolescent. An excellent example occurs in Wolf Rilla, *The Dispensable Man*, 1973:

'I have no intention of returning [to England], either myself or the money.'

Smith nodded, a little sadly it seemed. 'No, I suppose not.'

'In that case, was your journey really necessary?'

Smith's melancholy eyes suddenly lit up. 'You remember the war, then, do you? Is Your Journey Really Necessary? Careless Talk Costs Lives?'

is your rhubarb up (, old woman)? or **how's your rhubarb, missis?** Do you feel inclined to make love?: low: *c.* 1830–1900. Without the female vocatives, it can also apply to a man. Perhaps, as Dr Douglas Leechman has suggested, from a catch line in a comic song, and he cites the Canadian variant, *say, old woman, is your rhubarb up?*, which he calls 'another old timer'. Benham dates it as having arisen *c.* 1835, without giving any evidence: but, as Sir Gurney Benham was a conscientious as well as an excellent scholar, I accept the date. The form he quotes is simply *is your rhubarb up?*

is zat so? is a jocular US variant of *is thasso?*, a slovenly form of **is that so?** Cf the *howzat?*, How's that?, of cricket. It occurs in Berrey and in, e.g., Clarence Budington Kelland's *Speak Easily*, *c.* 1935:

'G'wan,' said Sam.

'Is zat so?' said Sim.

'Yes, zat's so,' said Sam.

ish ka bibble! (or as one word) *I should worry!* In the US it had a tremendous vogue *c.* 1913 and, via Canada, reached England *c.* 1925 and lasted perhaps a decade. Probably adopted from the Yiddish, with *ish* representing Ger. *Ich*, I, and the rest of the phrase a distortion. Berrey, 1942, records it without date or comment; HLM had briefly noticed it in 1922; W & F after stating the sense to be 'I'm not worrying' or 'I don't care', adduce two examples and then sum up by saying, 'A popular *c.* 1925 rejoinder' – even though HLM has implied a vogue beginning some five years earlier.

isn't that just dandy? can – of course – be literal and approbatory, but mostly it's ironic; sometimes bitterly ironic: US: since *c.* 1910. (Recorded by Berrey.)

isn't that just like a man! and **isn't that just like a woman!** are the interlocking female and male comments upon the crassness and unpredictability of the opposite sex. Also, though perhaps less frequently: *oh, well! you know what men* (or *women*) *are!* A further US modification, applied to women, is *oh, well! you know how women are!*

In 1920, Irvin S. Cobb published a book titled *Oh, Well! You Know How Women Are!* And in the same volume appeared Mary Roberts Rinehart's article, 'Isn't That Just Like a Man!' Within the volume occurs this passage:

'Kin you beat 'um?' says the conductor. 'I ast you – kin you beat 'um?' The man to whom he has put the question is a married man .... Speaking, therefore, from the heights of his superior understanding, he says in reply: 'Oh, well, you know how women are!' We know how they are. But nobody knows why they are as they are.

Harold Pinter's *The Collection*, a TV play produced in 1961, a stage play of 1962 and a publication of 1963 has, at p. 31 of the Methuen edn:

JAMES: Mmm. Only thing ... he rather implied that you led him on. Typical masculine thing to say, of course.

STELLA: That's a lie.

JAMES: You know what men are.

How far the c.p. goes back, I should not care to hazard anything more than: probably since c. 1850. It seems to have been US before it became also British; yet it could easily, except for the *how* form, have been the other way around.

isn't that just too ducky! is, by Berrey, 1942, recorded as a US ironic c.p.; and by W & F, 1960, as *isn't that just ducky!*: apparently since c. 1930 and c. 1945 respectively. It reached Britain by 1950 at the latest.

isn't that something (**?** or **!** or both) was adopted by Britain from US c. 1945. An expression of emphatic admiration, it means 'You must, like me, admire that – it's unique!' (Frank Shaw, 1 September 1969) or '... find it remarkable' (W & F at *something*). A good US example occurs in the Albee quotation at **I'll say!**

it adds up and **doesn't add up**. 'It makes sense' and 'It makes nonsense' – It fails to make sense: although occasionally heard earlier, it was only in the late 1950s that the phrase became a genuine and general c.p. (Laurie Atkinson). Either elliptical for *it adds up* (or *doesn't add up*) *correctly* or an extension of the colloquial *add*, to yield the right answer.

it ain't all honey. It isn't all pleasure, or fun: c. 1904–14. Cf 'It ain't all honey and it ain't all jam,/Wheelin' round the 'ouses at a three-wheeled pram' – words adorning a music-hall song of Vesta Victoria's, c. 1905. Cf:

it ain't gonna rain no more likewise comes from a popular song: it dates from c. 1935, and is prompted either by a downpour or by steady rain. At another level of usage, it was, for some years, also a popular jingle.

it ain't hay! See the more usual **that ain't hay!**

[**it ain't the 'untin' 'urts the 'orses' 'ooves – it's the 'ammer, 'ammer, 'ammer on the 'ard 'igh roads** (or **'ighroads**). 'First heard in Norfolk or Suffolk c. 1900' (Douglas Leechman, December 1968). Not, I think, East Anglian dialectal, but hunting folk's exaggeration and elaboration of rural poetry, becoming a hunting c.p., dating from (?)c. 1870. Paul Beale ran it to earth in an early *Punch* cartoon.]

it all depends on what you mean! is a derisive or a smilingly jocular, often temporizing, c.p.: since 1941. The reference is to Dr Cyril Joad (1891–1953), who, on the BBC 'Brains Trust', nearly always made this sapient remark, tantamount to a request for definition, no matter how simple the question. As Vernon Noble remarked on 18 January 1974, 'Older people still use it in conversation, as it's lingered in their minds.'

it all rubs off when it's dry. Don't take harsh words or summary punishment too hard: naval: late (?mid) C19–20. Rear-Admiral P. W. Brock adds, 'I've read this in the memoirs of some Victorian admiral who said it was about the best advice he ever had, and I found it so.' The mud that sticks – but not for very long.

it bangs Banagher. See **bangs Banagher**.

it came from a hot place belongs to C18. In Dialogue I of S, 1738, we see:

LORD SP[ARKISH]: This Tea's very hot.

LADY ANSW[ERALL]: Why, it came from a hot Place, my Lord.

A particularity that became a generality; roughly = 'And for a very obvious reason'.

it can't be did! A jocular perversion of 'It can't be done': late C19–20; obsolescent by 1940, virtually obsolete by 1960.

it can't happen here. This bitterly satirical c.p., dating from c. 1936, was promoted from the status of age-old occasional comment, complacently uttered by self-deluding optimists, into a ruefully aware irony; suddenly thus promoted by the success, the bite, of Sinclair Lewis's novel, *It Can't Happen Here*, which, appearing in 1935, both in US and in Britain, 'dramatized the dangers of the Nazi technique as it might be applied in the United States' (*Encyclopedia Britannica*). It is extant as a c.p. – and still heard as a solemnly pompous statement. Cf **famous last words**.

it come off in me 'and, ma'am (or **mum**) – less frequent, yet common enough, **it was broke already, mum**. Domestic servants' c.p., dating from mid C19, perhaps earlier. Frank Shaw, writing in February 1969, says: 'If a housewife breaks something, she has, since the late 1940s, tended to declare, **I never liked it anyway**' [which see separately].

it comes from a hot place. See **it came from a hot place**.

it couldn't happen to a nicer chap and **it couldn't have happened to a nicer guy**. Generously congratulatory, whether in address or in reference: the former, British, arose in the late 1940s; the latter, US, arose, I believe, during WW2. The fame of incorporation into a free syntax is exemplified in Mickey Spillane, *The Erection Set*, 1972, thus: 'A financial whiz kid. He parlayed a small bundle into a fat fortune and it couldn't have happened to a nicer guy.'

it curdles one's milk. See **curdles one's milk**.

it didn't fizz on me. This affair, this action, etc., had no effect on me: Canadian c.p., since c. 1945. (Douglas Leechman.) From soft drinks: 'It fell flat'.

it didn't go into his boots. There was an effect, inevitable yet not immediately obvious: mostly Cockney: C20. It did at least go *some*where.

it does your eyesight good. See **it will do your eyesight good**.

it doesn't add up. See **it adds up**.

it doesn't grow on trees (or, of currency and bank notes, **they don't ....**) Directed at those who think that money is easily obtained: late C19–20.

it doesn't stand up and **it won't get off the ground** are c.pp. applied to a plan, a scheme, an experiment, that has nothing to commend it: the former, since c. 1940, the latter, since 1942 – and originating in prototype aircraft that don't achieve flight.

it dries me up. It angers or exasperates me beyond words – deprives me of speech; as in 'It *dries me up* when I think of the terms he offered for the part': theatrical: C20. (Granville.)

it fell off the back of a lorry is an underworld and fringe-of-the-underworld c.p., now (1976) rather more widely known; dating since soon after WW2, and used as in John Wainwright, *Cause for a Killing*, 1974, where a shady character, standing at a window and looking down at a busy London street, says:

They are not thieves. [*This is bitterly ironical.*] They use a phrase. 'It fell off the back of a lorry.' That's the expression, friend. It covers everything from transistors to three-piece suites. From fountain pens to fur coats. They all 'fall off the back of a lorry'. And those mugs down there buy them at give-away prices. And don't ask awkward questions.

Barry Prentice (1 May 1975) notes that in Australia it's a *truck*.

it figures! That makes good sense; but, in many contexts, it is equivalent to 'Well, what would you expect?'. US and dating since, I'd guess, the middle 1940s. (It was John W. Clark who, on 17 February 1975, reminded me of it.) It has, since *c.* 1955, had some slight British currency.

it fits where it touches; of trousers, **they fit where they touch.** This jocular c.p. is applied to loose, very ill-fitting clothes: latish C19–20. (Jack Lawson, *A Man's Life*, 1932.) Since *c.* 1960, to suggestively tight clothes, especially trousers.

it had my name (or **number**) **on it** was, in WW1, applied by a soldier to the bullet that wounded him. (F & G.) Revived in WW2. (PGR.)

it happens all the time, which is equivalent to **it's just one of those things**, q.v., dates from *c.* 1925. The easy philosophy of the (for *some*) lighthearted 1920s.

[**it is a fine moon, God bless her!** stands midway between proverbial saying and c.p.; well, perhaps nearer the former than the latter: mid C17–20; obsolescent by 1930. Apperson.]

it is as good to be in the dark as without light is a semi-nonsensical c.p. that, occurring in Ray, 1670, recurs in Dialogue III of S, 1738:

LADY SM[ART]: It is as good to be in the Dark, as without Light; therefore, pray bring in Candles. They say, Women, and Linnen, shew best by Candle-Light.

It is easy to dismiss this kind of wit as childish: examined, it emerges as proto-Learish and almost Lewis-Carrollish.

it is sitting up and begging. See **he can make it sit up and beg.**

it just goes to show. See **that just goes to show.**

it must be the landlady. An ironical c.p. used by actors (esp. in touring companies) 'receiving faint applause on a line that usually gets a good hand. Cf **God bless you both!**' (Granville). Complimentary tickets have always been freely distributed among theatrical landladies.

it only wanted a man on the job. A jocular c.p. uttered by a willing helper as devoid of modesty as he is rich in kindliness: late C19–20.

it puts years on me is a late C19–20 c.p. of rueful disparagement.

it rattles like two skeletons .... See **noise like ....**

it rots battleships (or **your socks**). Water, as opposed to beer, is harmful: public-house c.pp.: C20. (Laurie Atkinson.)

it shouldn't happen to a dog! It's too unjust or disagreeable to be wished on even a dog; occasionally, however, applied to persons, as in 'He's one of those unpleasant fellows who shouldn't happen to a dog' (Wilfred Granville, letter of 19 February 1969).

it sits up and begs. See **he can make it sit up and beg.**

it smells. See **it stinks.**

it snowed! is lower- and lower-middle-class c.p. indicative of misery or even of disaster; adopted, before 1909, from the US. (Ware.)

it stinks is the intensive of – and much commoner than – **it smells**; adopted, *c.* 1945, from US, where, recorded by Berrey in 1942 and by W & F in 1960, it arose *c.* 1930; applied in general to anything offending one's intelligence, honesty, sense of taste and, in particular, to inferior entertainment, e.g. a film.

it takes all sorts is the c.p. form of the proverbial *it takes all sorts to make a world*: late C19–20. A good example occurs in Peter Driscoll's novel, *The White Lie Assignment*, 1971: 'I paid the driver and he swung away, shaking his head. It takes all sorts, he'd be thinking, and I suppose it does.'

it takes one to know one. You're as bad as the person you're criticizing: late (?mid) C19–20. ' "He's a thief." – "It takes one to know one." ' (Barry Prentice, 15 December 1974). Probably suggested by the proverb, *it takes a thief to catch a thief.*

it takes two to tango. Premarital coition, like the begetting of large families, requires active co-operation between the sexes: a mainly feminine c.p., implying that either of these two activities is not operated only by selfish males: mostly Australian: since *c.* 1935. 'From a popular song thus named' (Barry Prentice); *DSUE* Supplement. By 1974, slightly outmoded.

it turned out a lemon. See **answer is a lemon ....**

it turns me on. It gives me a thrill: general US, yet predominantly teenagers', since *c.* 1967, but at first (the 1950s) drug (esp. marijuana) addicts', as recorded by W & F, the reference being, as in the slangy *switch on*, to 'turning on the light'.

In a Philadelphia newspaper of late May or early June 1970, Sidney J. Harris, in a witty poem entitled 'This Cat Doesn't Dig All That Groovy Talk', declares that, in the scale of condign punishment, he would reserve

The royal dungeon for the peon
Who dared exclaim 'it turns me on'.

it was broke already. See **it come off in me 'and.**

it was one of those days. See **it's not my day.**

it wasn't there is a C20 theatrical 'reproof addressed to a stage manager who *pinches* a curtain call on a dead house. The applause wasn't there' (Granville).

it went like a bomb. It was a tremendous success. It began, in the late 1940s, with cars possessing an extremely rapid acceleration and a fine turn of speed; by the early 1950s, it had been taken over by the world of entertainment; by the late 1950s it was being applied to parties, love affairs, what-have-you, as in Mary Stewart, *The Gabriel Hounds*, 1967:

'A sort of Grand Tour, wasn't it, with Robbie?'
'Sort of. Seeing the world and brushing up my Arabic ... Oh, it all went like a bomb.'

Obviously from the explosion of large bombs.

it will (or **it'll**) **all be put down in evidence against you** is jocular, dating since *c.* 1935. Obviously from police procedure.

it will all come right on the night. See **all right on the night.**

it will be long enough is one of the comparatively few c.pp. that contain a genuinely clever pun: C18–20; by 1940 obsolete. As in S, Dialogue I:

LADY SM[ART]: Colonel, methinks your Coat is too short.
COL: It will be long enough, before I get another, Madam.

it will be (or **it's**) **(either) Sydney or the bush**. A momentous choice or a final decision: Australian: late C19–20. Edward Shann, *An Economic History of Australia*, 1930 has, ' "Sydney or the bush!" cries the Australian when he gambles against odds.' Cf the US **that's strictly bush**.

it will be there. For sure – you can *count* on it!: underworld, esp. among convicts: since *c.* 1940.

it will do your eyesight good is applied to something well worth seeing: late C19–20; by 1950, virtually obsolete.

it will (or **it'll** or **'twill**) **last as many nights as days** is a pert answer or comment upon durability: C18–20, although seldom heard in C20, and obsolete by 1950. It occurs in Dialogue I of S, and, on the ladder of wit, it stands alongside **as old as my tongue and a little older than my teeth**.

it won't do! is the signal for desisting from a burglary: underworld, esp. burglars': *c.* 1800–80. It occurs in, e.g. the anonymous book *The London Guide*, 1818.

it won't get off the ground. See **it doesn't stand up**.

it won't wash. See **that won't wash**.

it would make a cat laugh. See **cat laugh**.

it would make a man piss. Esp. of a person's lies and effrontery: it revolts me; it fills me with contempt. In, e.g. Pepys's Diary, 15 November 1667. (With thanks to Ramsey Spencer.) Apparently since (say) 1640; at some time, it became *it would* (or *it'd*) *make a man piss blood*, which is extant. Very much a male c.p.

it'll all be put down in evidence .... See **it will all** ....

it'll all be the same in a hundred years is a consolatory c.p., probably dating from the 1890s and, by 1940, verging on the status of an accepted proverb. Partly an elaboration of 'Why worry?' but strictly the c.p. form of the proverbial *it will all be the same a hundred years hence* (C19–20; by 1970, obsolescent). Earlier forms of the proverb itself are *'twill be all one a thousand years hence* (S, 1738) and *all will be one at the latter day* (Day of Judgement). With thanks to *ODEP*.

it'll all come out in the wash. It'll all be discovered eventually; *hence*, It'll all be settled eventually; *hence*, Never mind – or don't worry – it doesn't matter: C20. It is recorded by that acute observer of everyday speech. W. L. George, in his best novel, *The Making of an Englishman*, 1914.
By 1920 or so, it had become also US. (Berrey.)

it'll last my (or **our**) **time**, the cautious person warily – or perhaps wearily – adding, **I hope**. A 'famous last words' c.p., dating since *c.* 1945 but general only since *c.* 1948, it is less cynical than nostalgic, and therefore not to be treated as exactly equivalent to *après moi le déluge*.

it'll look well on the train call is a theatrical c.p., dating *c.* 1890–1940 and then becoming more and more obsolescent. Granville, a book that has unfortunately been allowed to go out of print, says:

In the days when the Sunday trains were full of touring companies and the changes *en route* were frequent, the parading of golf clubs, the carrying of fur-collared overcoats, etc., gave an air of opulence to the company, and a harp, displayed on the station platform, ... set a hall-

mark on a musical comedy troupe. This catch phrase greeted any request to tour an awkward piece of luggage. 'It'll look all right on the train call, I suppose' (the reference being to the informal roll-call a little before the train left).

it'll pass with a push. An Australian c.p. that, indicating a somewhat grudging approval, dates from *c.* 1950. (Barry Prentice.)

it'll put hair on your chest. See **that'll grow more hair on your chest**.

'ITMA'. See **it's that man again!** and also TOMMY HANDLEY CATCH PHRASES.

it's a bastard (often **a proper bastard** or, Australian, **a fair bastard**) is very common among both working men and servicemen for anything very difficult or extremely exasperating: C20. Cf the Australian *it's a fair cow*, late C19–20.

it's a breeze is an Australian c.p., applied to anything easy: since before 1945. (Barry Prentice.) From sailing.

it's a deal. Agreed!: late C19–20. ' "Come to dinner tomorrow night." – "Love to, it's a deal!" ' – an example of post-WW2 usage sent to me on 7 January 1969. Prompted by 'We've made a deal', an agreement.

it's a different ball game. ' "Different rules apply." An American c.p., which is very common in Australia' (Barry Prentice, 1 May 1975): as US, since the 1930s (?earlier); as Australian, since the middle 1940s and probably occasioned by US servicemen. Literally, 'not *base*ball, but, e.g., basketball or handball'

it's a dog's life is 'said of a rotten job, or life on the breadline, the dole, etc. A life you wouldn't wish on a dog.' (Wilfred Granville, in a letter of 19 February 1969.) Despite the violent change of sense, this c.p. probably derives from – or, at the least, was prompted by – the C17–19 proverb, *it's a dog's life, hunger and ease*. Cf **it shouldn't happen to a dog!**

it's a fair cop was originally an underworld c.p., addressed to a policeman: since *c.* 1880. (Ware.) Hence, since *c.* 1920, a general humorous c.p., equivalent to 'All right! you've caught me *or* caught me out'. See, in E. H. Hornung's famous *Raffles*, 1899, ' "All right, guv'nor," drawled Raffles, "don't excite. It's a fair cop." ' Frank Shaw has noted its prevalence in Edwardian English comics. And in *Cecilia*, 1932, Allan Monkhouse writes in Act II:

CECILIA: And yet you'd reckon me pretty good at asserting myself.
DAN: Before a sympathetic audience – yes.
CECILIA: You think I'm caught?
DAN: Fair cop, as the criminals say.

it's a fair cow. See **it's a bastard!**

it's a freak country and **it's a free country**. Of the former, Mr A. B. Petch, in March 1966, wrote thus: 'Sometimes heard in respect of the "sights" we see nowadays, like the dirty, long-haired teenagers. From the other expression, *it's a free country*': the former, since *c.* 1960, the latter since late C19, as a characteristically British expression of tolerance.

it's a game! It doesn't make sense: a British Army c.p. of 1915–18, 'applied to the war and to the military machine' (B & P).

[**it's a gas** (or **a gasser** or **a gig** or **a giggle**). It's very funny indeed: the first two, Australian: since *c.* 1961, Mr Barry Prentice tells me. The latter pair British: since *c.* 1945, at first, as in Frank Norman, *Bang to Rights*, 1958, low slang, then, *c.* 1955, the smart young set, then general. What causes giggling; *gig* shortens *giggle*. But, like *it's a doddle*, it's very easy to do, it's a walk-over, these potential c.pp. depend far less on their popularity as c.pp. than on the wax-and-wane of the nouns *doddle, gas, gasser, gig, giggle*, and so they hardly qualify.]

it's a gift! Well, that has been very easily obtained, *or* That presented no difficulty – as easy to accept as a gift: late C19–20; by 1950, slightly obsolescent.

it's a go! Agreed!: mostly US, since *c.* 1890 (Berrey records it), and Australian and New Zealand since some years before 1914.

it's a good flat that's never down. Even the biggest fool or dupe (a flat) finally has his eyes opened: *c.* 1790–1870. (Vaux, writing in 1812, calls it 'a proverb among *flash* people' – the underworld.)

it's a good game – (if) played slow or **slowly** is an 'ironic c.p., evoked by repeated manual maladroitness, repeated inconvenience, idling, or imposed tedium of waiting, etc.' (Laurie Atkinson, 1959): fighting Services': WW2.

it's a great life if you don't weaken. See **great life** ....

it's a great war was an often jocular but usually ironic c.p. of WW1, although not before 1915; as used by the army, it could be extremely bitter.

it's a hard life! Used literally, it is clearly *not* a c.p.; but it's often used jocularly or ironically, and then it is a c.p.: late C19–20. In *The Law Divine*, performed on 29 August 1918 and published in 1922, H. V. Esmond writes in Act II:

EDIE (*going to door*): Well, after this little social intercourse, I must love you and leave you.
JACK: Upstairs again?
EDIE: Upstairs again. (*She laughs.*) It's a hard life.

it's a lemon. See **answer is a lemon** ....

it's a little bit over is an Australian butchers' c.p. of late C19–20. Butchers in Australia always try to sell you more meat than you asked for, and apprentices are taught to use the phrase as an excuse for an apparent mistake. (A valued correspondent.)

it's a long lane that has no pub is a jovial, even a jocular, c.p. that twists the old proverb '... that has no turning': C20. (Frank Shaw.)

it's a long time between drinks. Bartlett tells us (p. 824 *b*, footnote) that the most reasonable tradition is that John Motley Morehead, Governor of North Carolina in 1841–5, was visited by James H. Hammond, Governor of South Carolina in 1842–4. When in a discussion the latter grew heated, Morehead exclaimed, 'It's a long time between drinks', and thus restored amity and calm.

From being a famous quotation, as indeed it still is, it became also a c.p. But don't expect me to tell you when – at a very rough guess, I'd say *c.* 1880 or 1890; but at least I can state that, already by 1908, it had become so well established that it could be employed allusively thus, in Chapter IV ('He Discusses Finance') of *The Genial Idiot* by John Kendrick Bangs (1862–1922), the US humorist and wit, better known as the author of *A House Boat on the Styx*:

I honestly don't like to lend money, believing with Polonius that it's a bad thing to do. As the Governor of North Carolina said to the Governor of South Carolina, who owed him a hundred dollars, 'It's a long time between payments on account', and that sort of thing breaks up families, not to mention friendships.

The c.p. came to Britain and, among the educated and the well-read, has been widely understood although not widely used. I occasionally try it out on writer friends and acquaintances afflicted with a literary conscience and say, 'The only adverse criticism I have to make of your books is that "it's a long time between drinks".' Sometimes I'm treated to a blank and glassy stare, sometimes to an appreciative grin.

A link between quotation and phrase is provided by James Maitland, *The American Slang Dictionary*, 1891: he cites *between drinks, a long time*, as a slangy synonym of 'a long time'.

it's a lulu! It's a beauty, a 'humdinger': US: since *c.* 1890. Perhaps from the font-name *Lulu*, a reduplication of the *Lou* of both *Louis* and *Louisa* or *Louise*. (Based partly on my *U* and partly on W & F.)

it's a monkey's wedding is a C20 South African c.p., 'applied to weather characterized by a drizzling rain accompanied by a shining sun' (Professor A. C. Partridge, 18 November 1968).

it's a new ball-game (or **ballgame**). Whatever has gone before doesn't count – we start again: US: since *c.* 1940. Edward Hodnett, in a letter dated 18 August 1975, says that, applied originally, in baseball, to a game where the score is tied, particularly if late in the game; it passed to negotiations and, in passing, became a c.p.

On the same day I received a letter from W. J. Burke, who notes the variant, *it's a brand-new ball game*, which he says means 'Something had suddenly happened to change ... the outcome – what seemed like a loss may now result in victory'.

it's a new one on me. See **new one** ....

it's a nice place to live out of. See **nice place to live out of**.

it's a nice place to visit but I wouldn't want to live there. 'A c.p. often used of "perfect" cities like Canberra' (Barry Prentice, 15 December 1974): Australian: since *c.* 1955.

it's a nice place you have here. See **nice place you have here**.

it's a piece of cake. It is, was, will be something very easy to do, a 'snip'; occasionally. It's a wonderful opportunity: RAF: since *c.* 1938; by 1946, widely used by civilians. It is recorded by W-J, and by EP in *A Glossary of RAF Slang*, 1945, as well as by PGR. Origin: 'as easy to dispose of as a piece of cake'.

it's a poor arse that never rejoices. A C20 c.p. uttered, when someone breaks wind, by a member of one of those 'gangs' or cliques or fraternities of would-be wits in which public-houses abound. Cf Grose's *ars musica*, dog L for *ars musicalis*. Based on the proverb, 'It's a poor heart that never rejoices'. Cf:

it's a poor soldier who can't stand his comrade's breath is an army – originally the Regular Army – c.p. dating from late C19 and defiantly offered by the culprit when his companions complain of an offensive fart. Cf the preceding entry.

it's a rumour! (often **'s a rumour!**), an army c.p. of 1915–18, was a retort on 'an opinion expressing a very well known fact or [on] a statement emphatically (and usually disagreeably) true' (B & P).

[**it's a screech** falls into the same category as **it's a gas**, q.v.]

it's a shame! was, in WW2, an Australian variation of **it's a rumour!**

it's a small world, British and US, dates since *c.* 1890 and is brightly proclaimed at an unexpected meeting either between two persons belonging to widely separated countries or between two compatriots meeting far from their own country.

George Ade, *In Pastures New*, 1906, writes:

'It's a small world.' This is one of the overworked phrases of the globe-trotter. It is used most frequently by those who follow the beaten paths. In other words, we find it difficult to get away from our acquaintances.... To the ordinary traveller it is always a glad surprise to find a friend coming right out of the ground in a corner of the world supposed to be given over to strangers.

Thus begins the amusing chapter XI, titled 'Cairo as the Annual Stamping Ground for Americans and Why they Make the Trip'.

it's a snice mince-pie. This c.p. arose *c.* 1916, was obsolescent by 1937 and obsolete by 1945. It was suggested by the sibilance of the words *a nice mince pie*, esp. when preceded by *it's*. Weekley once noted: 'As I write [1917] there is a slang tendency to say *snice* for *nice*, etc.'

it's a state secret has, since *c.* 1933, been, though rarely since *c.* 1950, either pompously or jocularly used by someone who refuses to disclose information no matter how trivial. Cf **don't make a Federal case out of it!**

it's a term of endearment among sailors. See **term of endearment**.

it's a way they have in the army was, in 1915–18, an army, mostly officers', c.p. But even then it was a revival of a c.p. current since *c.* 1880 or even earlier and deriving from a popular song that, *c.* 1880, opens thus. But I never heard it used during my army service in 1940-early 1942 and I doubt whether it was used at all during WW2; certainly not since.

it's a wonder that didn't choke you! See **choke you ....**

it's agony, Ivy! comes from the music-halls; was apparently current during the 1930s; and Frank Shaw passed it to me on 25 October 1968. It 'was said by Bob Pearson as "Mrs Hoskins" in "Ray's a Laugh", 1949–54' (BBC Written Archives Centre, Caversham Park, Reading). Cf **ee, it was agony, Ivy!**

it's all bob. See **Bob's your uncle**.

it's all go. Paul Beale writing in 1975, says:

A neutral c.p. indicating that life is a constant round of activity, which may be pleasant or otherwise. 'There's a dinner in the mess Friday, drinks with the other lot Saturday lunchtime, off to Dave's in the evening, down to the coast Sunday ... cor, it's all bloody go, I tell you.' Or conversely: ''Ere I was on guard Monday night, then again We'nsday and Sat'day, and now the bastards've got me for bleedin' fire picket. It's all go in this lousy outfit – and no mistake.'

it's all good clean fun. 'Palliation of making a butt of a person, or persons, in a group – or when fun has been fast at others' expense; not necessarily free from impurity' (Laurie Atkinson, late 1974): since *c.* 1945.

it's all good for trade, often preceded by **ah, well!** A 'concluding conversational phrase [– a gambit –] when options are best left open; what the boss said, what she said; the final (? bathetic) outcome. (I always felt some trade between the sexes was [sometimes] hinted at. [I first heard it in an] officers' mess, 1943–4.)' (Laurie Atkinson, 18 July 1974.) In October 1969, either L.A. or another friend, Ramsey Spencer, had written: 'The opting-out rejoinder. Your friend or his wife has paid too much, or another friend has been unfairly used. Best sum it up, [for] regret won't alter it: "It's all good for trade!"'

It goes back, I think, to commerce during the 1920s or, at latest, the 1930s.

it's all happening is hard to nail down, its senses ranging from '(But) it all *is* happening, you know' to '(But) it really *is* so, whatever you may think' and to 'Wake up and face the reality!' Patricia Newnham, in March 1976, writes, 'I have heard this as a semi-laconic response to someone marvelling at an event or [at] a display of some kind'. Since at least as early as 1939 in Britain and late 1941 in the US. Contrast – and cf – **it can't happen here**. (A reminder, 22 April 1975, from Fernley O. Pascoe.)

it's all in a lifetime. Why grumble? It's no use doing so: late – ?rather mid – C19–20.

[**it's all in the day's work** is far more a cliché than a c.p.]

it's all (or **it all comes**) **in the seven.** That's to be expected; it's a matter of course: army: (?late C19–20). 'In allusion to the soldier's term of service with the colours' (F & G) – that is, on continuous service.

it's all in the twelve is a 'remark levelled against any sailor who bemoans his lot or grumbles at Service conditions. It means that "he shouldn't have joined if he couldn't take a joke"' (*Sailors' Slang*). Cf the preceding c.p. entry and **if you can't take a joke ....**

it's all money dates since *c.* 1945 and serves as a c.p. reply to one who apologizes for paying in small coins or in more coins than are either necessary or sensible.

it's all over bar the shouting. See **all over bar the shouting**.

it's all right by me. I agree: a US c.p., perhaps of Yiddish origin, as mentioned in HLM, Supp. 1. Mencken cites an article published in 1941 by Dr A. Roback, the predecessor of Mr Leo Rosten in the field of Yiddishisms, and mentions that 'a Yiddish popular song often sung in 1938 was "Bei Mir Bist Da Scheen" (By Me You Are Beautiful)' – that is, in my opinion. By 1945, heard occasionally among Britons; by 1950, heard frequently.

it's all right for some (or **you**). This C20 c.p., 'deprecates another's "sitting pretty"' (Laurie Atkinson).

it's all right if it comes off. This mainly Australian c.p. dates from *c.* 1930 and applies to an apparent attempt at a swindle. (Barry Prentice.)

it's all Sir Garnet. See **all Sir Garnet!**

it's all systems go. See **all systems go**.

it's (or **that's**) **all very fine and large**. See **all very large and fine**.

it's always jam tomorrow (but) never jam today dates, as a mainly civilian c.p., since *c*. 1917. The immediate occasion was probably the sugar shortage experienced during WW1, but its ultimate source was 'Jam yesterday and jam tomorrow, but never jam today' in Lewis Carroll's *Through the Looking Glass*, 1871. It should be compared with **pie in the sky when you die**.

it's an old army game. 'And don't let anybody tell you that the expressions, "It's an old army game" and "Go away, boy, you're bothering me" belonged to W. C. Fields. It was Charles Kenna who used both these expressions in his act many many years before Fields even walked on the stage' (Joe Laurie, Jr, *Vaudeville from the Honky-Tonks to the Palace*, 1953; with thanks to my friend, Mr W. J. Burke, 9 April 1975). Therefore *it's an old army game* is a US c.p. and can be said to date from early in C20.

Yet another US friend, Colonel Albert Moe, says, in a letter dated 5 June 1975, that the meaning 'It's the system and therefore hard to beat or circumvent'(my own definition)'does not seem to go back any further than WW2, and, chronologically, seems to be the last of several meanings that are associated with the phrase'. He continues: 'Prior to WW2, I had heard it used ranging from a major swindle to a minor deceit, i.e. to take advantage of someone's trust or gullibility. It was used to explain or justify the manipulating of any situation to the advantage of the manipulator, whether it be fleecing a lamb (pigeon) or finding a scapegoat.' Moreover, he has found that the earliest recorded evidence – John Quinn's *Fools of Fortune*, 1890, and Herbert Ashery's *Sucker's Progress*, 1938 – refers to such gambling games as chuck-a-luck and stud poker; both games are either 'designated' or 'called' not *a*, but '*the* old army game'.

Paul Beale, writing on 1 May 1975, says:

My friend Mary Priebe from Seattle. ... Her interpretation is that it can be heard to excuse some crafty wangle; one, usually, that has been successful, or to describe any slightly devious ploy.... I recall that there was a British TV comedy series a few years ago ... called 'The Army Game'.

And then, on 2 May 1975, Professor Harold Shapiro tells me that *he* has always heard it as *it's the old army game* and that it's still in use, although he'd be surprised to hear it from someone under say thirty-five.

It always seems to imply 'the system' – either as it affects someone or as someone attempts to beat the system, and always seems to imply the usual foul-up (on the part of the system), or a 'con' or dodge (on the part of the system or the part of the individual).

On 17 May 1975, John W. Clark confirms *the*. See also **old army game** .... and, at the end of that entry, the reason why I've allowed two entries for what, to some, will be one c.p.

it's an old Southern custom. See **custom** ....

it's as cheap sitting as standing. Why stand when you can sit?: C17–20. S, Dialogue I, has:

LADY ANSW[ERALL]: Well, but sit while you stay; 'tis as cheap sitting as standing.

One of the domestic c.pp., which tend to wear so well.

it's 'as I roved out'. It's 'of no consequence, no more than those songs so often starting "as I roved out"' (Frank Shaw, November 1968): C20. Perhaps these *roved out* songs were supplemented by the carols beginning 'As I rode out'.

[**it's as simple as that!** 'As you see, it's really very simple': since *c*. 1944. Originally, I think, an Armed Forces', mostly an instructors', c.p., from a blackboard, or a mechanical, demonstration. (With thanks to Professor T. B. W. Reid, letter of 1 January 1972; the fact, not the theorizing, is his.)

It went to Australia in, I think, the latish 1940s; on 1 May 1975, Barry Prentice commented thus: 'A c.p. that some people introduce into every conversation'.

Clearly, however, it is, esp. when used literally, also a cliché.]

it's bad manners to speak when your arse is full. A C20 proletarian c.p., addressed to someone who farts noisily in company. An earthily humorous reference to the domestic adage, 'It's bad manners to speak when your mouth is full'.

it's baloney .... See **it's boloney** ....

it's been a very good year for girls has, since *c*. 1960, been a presentable young males' c.p. of gratification at the constant compliance of presentable young women. (Fernley O. Pascoe, 15 January 1975.) In jesting allusion to good years for wines.

it's been known. It's not unknown: often ironic: since the middle 1940s. Elliptical for 'It *has* been known to happen'.

it's been real is a US 'expression said on leave-taking ... indicating the speaker's enjoyment of the time spent together or at a social function. *Orig. from* "it's been *real fun*"' (W & F, 1960) – or perhaps 'a real pleasure'. *DCCU*. derives it from 'It's been real nice' (enjoyable). Hence. ironically, 'It's been real dull' or 'very boring'. Both sets of US editors supply no date, however roughly approximate, so I'll hazard the guess that the earlier sense arose *c*. 1945–6, as a result of WW2's impact upon the national consciousness, and that the derivative sense arose *c*. 1955.

it's being so cheerful as keeps me going. In his book *Itma*, 1948, Frank Worsley mentions that a great success of 'ITMA' in 1946 was Joan Harben playing the part of

Mona Lott [punning *moan a lot*], the depressed laundry-woman, with her incredibly unlucky family always involved in some fearful disaster or other.... But, with true British grit, poor Mona sticks it out, for 'it's being so cheerful as keeps her going'. This type of unhappy comedy has always been popular in this country.... Mona Lott appealed to everyone's sympathy, but especially to that of woman listeners.

it's boloney (or **bologny** or **baloney**) – **no matter how thin you slice it**. It's utter nonsense. no matter how hard you try to prove the opposite. US. dating since the middle or late 1930s and recorded by Berrey. 1942. Originally an illiterate pronunciation of Italian *bologna*. the sausage so named. as W & F have noted.

it's brutal! and **it's murder!** are both US in origin: and the former immediately, the latter soon, became also British. The former was suggested by the latter: and the latter, dating from *c*. 1910 or earlier, was anglicized by 1920. The application ranges from brutally hard ('murderous') work to harsh treatment, to extortionate prices.

In Britain, there exists the variant, *it's sheer murder*.

it's cheap at half the price. See **cheap at half the price.**

it's dead, a theatrical c.p. of C20, means 'The applause has died down' (Granville).

it's for the birds. See **that's strictly for the birds.**

it's Friday – so keep your nose tidy is a non-cultured, non-educated, late C19–20 c.p. (but obsolete by 1970), uttered only on a Friday, a day that, in folklore, is – or was – thought to be unlucky; it means 'Keep out of trouble' and implies 'Mind your own business!'

it's getting deep in here. The company's deteriorating, the conversation's becoming more and more affected or insincere: US, and rather low: since c. 1945. *It* = 'the shit'. (Professor John T. Fain, 25 April 1969.)

it's gone over Borough Hill after Jackson's pig. It is lost: a rural, esp. Northamptonshire, c.p. of mid C19–20; obsolescent by 1930 and by 1970 rarely used. (Apperson.)

it's good enough for *Punch* (for inclusion in that very English periodical with its very high standards): since, I'd guess, late C19 and certainly not later than c. 1908, when I first heard it used. (Reminder, 22 April 1975, by Fernley O. Pascoe.)

it's got a back to it. I'm lending, not giving, it to you: Londoners': C20. A pun on 'You must give it *back*'.

it's got bells on. That's a *very* old story! I don't remember having heard it before 1930, but I suspect that it goes back to c. 1920 – or even to c. 1900. Perhaps a reference to the 'chestnuts' told by medieval, notably the court, jesters, who wore cap and bells; or perhaps to the bell of a town crier. Cf **tell me the old, old story.** (Owed, in part, to Frank Shaw, letter written in November 1968.)

it's half-past kissing time and time to kiss again. See **kissing time** ....

it's in your eye! is an exclamation uttered 'when an opponent's bowl comes to rest in the line of draw to your jack': South African bowls players': C20. (Professor Ashley Cooper Partridge, in a letter dated 18 November 1968.)

it's (or **it was**) **just one of those things** is applied to something inexplicable, esp. if that something simply has (or had) to happen: since the middle 1930s. Nevil Shute, *The Chequer Board*, 1947, 'It wasn't his fault he got taken by the Japs. It was just one of those things.' Popularized by an extremely popular Cole Porter song of the 1930s thus titled. In Act II, Scene i, of *Relative Values*, performed in 1951 and published in 1952, Noël Coward writes:

NIGEL: But he was such a mild, inoffensive little chap. What on earth did he do?

FELICITY: We have no proof that he actually did anything. It – it was just one of those things.

it's kissing time. See **kissing time** ....

it's like a nigger girl's left tit – neither right nor fair. A Canadian c.p., apparently in the main, feminine rather than masculine: since the middle or early 1960s. A correspondent tells me he heard it in 1968.

it's like that, is it? and **so that's the way it is** are almost exactly synonymous c.pp. dating from very soon after WW2. Slightly cynical, more than slightly resigned yet ruefully humorous, acceptances of fate.

it's money for jam and **it's money for old rope.** Both refer especially to payment for work done, but they are not perfectly synonymous, the former being applied to money very easily earned, the latter to money paid for nothing or almost nothing; the former arose c. 1900, and its derivative sense, 'It's too easy!' arose c. 1910 and was very common in the army of WW1 (see, e.g., B & P), and the latter, originally low, c. 1905, occurring in, e.g., James Curtis, *The Gilt Kid*, 1936. By c. 1950, however, these two c.pp. were virtually interchangeable – and were possessed of the same social status; to Wilfred Granville, writing on 6 November 1968, they were indistinguishable, one from the other. And then, on 18 July 1975, Laurie Atkinson supplied this gloss: '(Mainly Services) of favourable duties, especially those which earn privilege; also of winning streak at, e.g., card games.'

it's murder! See **it's brutal!**

it's my story. See **that's my story.**

it's naughty! It's dangerous: an underworld c.p., dating since c. 1920. (*U*.)

it's naughty but it's nice refers to sexual intercourse. In the US, some time in the 1890s, Minnie Schult sang – and popularized – the song so titled; the c.p. arose therefrom and reached Britain by c. 1900. Cf Marie Lloyd's song, 'A little of what you fancy does you good' – which likewise generated a c.p.

it's nice to get up in the morning, with its rider, **but it's nicer to lie in bed,** understood, comes from an old song, and as a c.p. dates since c. 1900; by 1960, obsolescent – except when used ironically.

it's nice to have a peg to hang things on! has, in C20 although not much since c. 1960, been the natural plaint of one who, in business, has to pay the penalty of a superior's mistakes.

[**it's no go.** It's no use – a waste of time. Current in Britain since c. 1820 or a little earlier, and in US, less commonly, since c. 1900, it does not fully qualify: it's a piece of straightforward slang, with no derivative and deviant meaning.]

it's no skin off my nose! See **no skin off my nose.**

it's not cricket means 'It's unfair!' and was adumbrated in 1867 (see W. J. Lewis, *The Language of Cricket*, 1934) but did not become a widely accepted c.p. until the very early 1900s. In Act III of *The Partners*, performed in 1913 and published in 1914, Stanley Houghton wrote: 'It may even enable you to take high place in the ranks of the emancipated – but it is not playing the game. In other words, Cynthia, it is not cricket.' This phrase has always puzzled Americans and foreigners: and has delighted the few it no longer puzzles. In one of his *Inside* ... books, John Gunther wrote a perceptive paragraph about it: clearly he had 'done his homework'.

Mr John Morris, CBE, formerly Director of the BBC's Third Programme and the author of several notable books, tells an amusing story concerning an incident, c. 1950, at the Lawn Tennis Championships at Wimbledon. When a very fine player, afflicted by a diabetic seizure of cramp, lay writhing on the ground, an irate English colonel exclaimed, 'Oh, I say! It just isn't cricket!'.

it's not done and **it isn't done** date, the latter since c. 1870 (see the *OED*), the former since the 1880s, and mean 'It is bad form' or behaviour unacceptable in good society. It could be described as an upper-class counter. Collinson writes, 'To reprobate unseemly conduct we now currently employ the expression "it's not done" ... with the jocular variant "it's not a done thing".' He supports *it's not done* by references to John Galsworthy's *The White Monkey*, 1924, and H. G. Wells's *Christine Albert's Father*, 1925.

it's not much if (occasionally **when**) **you say it quick** or **quickly.** Applied to a large sum of money or a very high price or charge: since *c.* 1910 or perhaps a decade earlier.

[**it's not my bag.** It's not my concern or 'line' or current interest: not a c.p., for it can be *any*one's 'bag' in any tense or number.]

it's not (or **it just isn't**) **my day.** A philosophical acceptance – arising in, I seem to remember, the late 1940s – of a day when things persist, or have persisted, in going wrong. On the very day it first occurred to me as a candidate for inclusion, I was reminded of it in a Bloomsbury 'pub': 1 March 1969. Cf the past-tense counterpart, *it was* (*just*) *one of those days.*

it's not my end. The sailor's way of disclaiming responsibility: 'It's not my end, chum, I'm not carrying that can back': lower-deck naval: since *c.* 1925. (PGR.) Cf the underworld *end*, share of the loot.

it's not my scene. Sometimes 'It's no concern of mine' 'I'm both disinterested and uninterested in the whole business' – but more often 'It doesn't attract me' or 'It's not the sort of thing I'm interested in'. Adopted, *c.* 1972, in Britain from the US, where widespread by 1970. Originally, *scene* was used by US negroes in the 1940s–50s for 'the main area of popular group activity, such as a street corner, a bar, a poolroom' (CM, 1970). The variants, *it's not me* and *it's just not me*, indicate that it is not something I would do, or wear.

it's not on. It's extremely inadvisable; it's impossible: since *c.* 1964, as a c.p., although one had heard it being used as early as *c.* 1960. In its May 1971 issue, the *Spectator* noted it as the average Briton's reaction to the Common Market. Short for *it's not on the cards.* There are two variations: *it's just not on* and *it's simply not on*, both with *on* emphasized.

it's not right – it's not fair is a derisive c.p. addressed to a complainant and applied to his complaint: mainly the Armed Forces': since *c.* 1905.

it's not so much the cross we have to bear – it's the flaming splinters on it! It's the *little* things we find the hardest to bear: mostly, perhaps originally, naval: C20. (Rear-Admiral P. W. Brock in late 1968.)

it's not the bull they're afraid of – it's the calf is an Australian c.p., applied to girls and implying that they fear not the loss of virginity, but pregnancy: C20.

it's not the end of the world is 'said of some minor mishaps or disappointment. "Even if the book is rejected, it's not the end of the world"' (Wilfred Granville, 6 February 1969); 'A consolatory expression heard today' (A. B. Petch, 4 January 1974): since *c.* 1945.

[**it's not the money – it's the principle.** 'Is this a proverbial saying or a c.p.?' asks Barry Prentice, 9 June 1975. Well, in the fact it's neither: it's a (very often hypocritical) cliché.]

it's not what you know but who you know is sometimes a merely cynical, but usually a 'sour grapes', c.p., dating since *c.* 1945. 'Speaker, hopeless, anyhow. Equally hopeless hearer

nods solemn assent' (Frank Shaw, November 1968). Current in Australia as well as in Britain: 'Influence is more important than ability' (Barry Prentice, *c.* 6 March 1975).

it's OK by me! See **okay by me!**

it's old hat, often shortened to **old hat!** A condemnation of something very much outmoded: late C19–20. I heard it used in 1973 by a distinguished Professor of English Language. Decreasingly employed since *c.* 1955. (A reminder by Fernley O. Pascoe, 22 April 1975.)

it's on us. The police – or, in prison, the warders – are here, i.e. at the scene of the crime or the trouble: underworld: since *c.* 1920.

it's only human nature, after all! Laurie Atkinson, writing on 18 July 1975, says:

[A] Palliation of 'youthful indiscretion' or [of] coarseness in social context. [Perhaps] from well-known verse:
It's only human nature, after all,
For a boy to take a girl against the wall,
And increase the population
Of the rising generation –
It's only human nature, after all.

I can vouch for [its currency during] the 1920s; and in all probability going back to [late] Victorian times.

For the period, cf **here you are then!**, and for semantics, cf **man can't 'elp 'is feelings, can 'e?**

it's only lent. 'A nonchalant acceptance of defeat, either physical or moral. It is sometimes embellished with the addition, "I'll get my own back"' (Julian Franklyn, 1962): mostly Cockney: since *c.* 1920. Semantically cf **it's got a back to it.** 'Said to a reluctant spender or party-sharer' (Leechman): originally (?*c.* 1945) Canadian; by 1955, also current in Britain. Also a Canadian, hence also British, c.p. 'addressed to one [including oneself] suddenly confronted with an unexpected expenditure': since the latish 1940s.

it's polite to wait until you are asked. See **don't say No ....**

it's pretty soft. That's very foolish; that's crazy: American: since *c.* 1912; obsolescent by 1945. Cited by S. R. Strait in 'Straight Talk' in the *Boston Globe* of *c.* 1917. (W. J. Burke.)

it's rabbits out of the wood. See **rabbits ....**

it's raining in London. 'And, speaking of affecting British mannerisms and habits, who remembers when cuffs on a man's trousers brought down the jibe: "It's raining in London"?' (Robert Benchley, *My Ten Years in Quandary*, 1936, in the article headed 'As They Say in French'): US: ?*c.* 1920–9.

it's rough on rats. See **rough on rats.**

it's sheer murder! See **it's brutal!**

it's showery! See **what a shower!**

it's snowing down south is an Australian feminine c.p. addressed to one whose slip is showing: during the late 1940s and the 1950s, but rapidly less since then. Perhaps it was suggested by the English schoolchildren's **it's snowing in Paris**, current since *c.* 1919 and recorded by Mr and Mrs Peter Opie in *The Lore and Language of Schoolchildren*, 1959; on the other hand, it may have gone to Australia from the US (Berrey).

[**it's so blunt that it wouldn't cut butter**, applied to a blunt knife, is not a c.p. but a cliché.]

it's so cold it would (or **it'd**) **freeze the balls off a brass monkey** dates since *c.* 1870 or 1880 and is common throughout the Commonwealth. (Australians even speak of *brass-monkey weather*.)

it's staring you in the face; if it had teeth it would bite you; if it were a black snake, you'd be dead. 'The three phrases are used when a person is looking for an object in plain view' (Barry Prentice): C20. The first, going back, I suspect, to mid C19, is English; the third is Australian; the second is fairly general – and should be compared with **if it were a bear, it would bite you**, recorded separately.

it's that man again! was, during the late 1930s, frequently applied to the machinations of Hitler, the *Daily Express* always referring to him as *that man*: and when Tommy Handley, aided by his brilliant script-writer, Ted Kavanagh, and the equally brilliant producer, Frank Worsley, inaugurated his radio show under the title of 'ITMA' ('It's That Man Again') these words immediately achieved national fame – and the linguistic status of Catch Phrase; the radio show ran from 19 September 1939 until Handley's death in latish 1949. See esp. Ted Kavanagh's biography, *Tommy Handley*, 1948, and Frank Worsley's *Itma*, 1948; and cf the entry TOMMY HANDLEY CATCH PHRASES.

it's the beer speaking is C20 public-house wit addressed not only to one who breaks wind in public-house company but also to one who speaks boastfully or extravagantly. Cf **it's a poor arse that never rejoices**.

it's the berries. It's superlative or remarkable: US, 'common *c.* 1920–*c.* 1930 student use.... Archaic' (W & F). It passed to Canada, where apparently extant: 'By no means recent' (Douglas Leechman, December 1968). Perhaps from the attractive colour of many berries.

it's the change before death. 'Very ironical. Someone has acted out of character, e.g. a mean man generously. A Liverpool usage still' (Frank Shaw, November 1968): C20. A play on 'the change of life'.

it's the greatest thing since sliced bread. A 'c.p. to describe any useful novelty. Current and widespread in the army (? and beyond) for at least fifteen years' (Paul Beale, 22 August 1974): yes, beyond, although never very widespread: since, I think, *c.* 1950.

it's the poor as 'elps the poor is a Cockney c.p. that, probably dating from *c.* 1850, became, *c.* 1920, a Cockney proverb – though I shouldn't swear to it that it has yet been enshrined in the dictionaries of proverbs. Cf the Japanese proverb, 'It's the poor who give alms to the poor'.

it's the same difference, often shortened to **same difference!** and even to **same diff!** There *is* no difference – it's precisely the same thing!: the long forms are Canadian and date from *c.* 1940, the shortest are Australian, since *c.* 1945. (The first, Douglas Leechman, the latter, Barry Prentice.)

[**it's the thought that counts**, said when a gift is of very little value, is a conventional cliché that, by the late 1960s, was fast becoming a satirical cliché.]

it's turned out nice again 'was popularized by English stage and film comedian George Formby' (Vernon Noble, 14 January 1975): since *c.* 1930.

it's up there you want it. See **that's where you want it**.

it's what your right arm's for is addressed to someone raising a flagon or a large glass (a 'jar') of a 'long' drink, notably beer: since, if I remember rightly, the 1920s. (Mrs Shirley M. Pearce, 23 January 1975.)

it's winning the war, often preceded by **anyway**, is an ironic, usually cynical, often bitter c.p. applied to anything, esp. an order or a task, disliked intensely: army: 1915–18. (F & G.)

it's wonderful how they make guns, let alone touch-holes. 'A c.p. used by women ... to deflate male superiority, especially about sex' (Laurie Atkinson, 11 September 1967): mostly in naval and military circles: late C19–20. The erotic imagery of gunnery (as, e.g., in the WW2 film, *Target for Tonight*) is involved: *gun*, penis, and *touch-hole*, vulva.

it's your ball. The initiative lies with you: Canadian: since *c.* 1946. From ball games: 'The ball's in your court, so play it.' (Douglas Leechman.)

it's your funeral. The result, the consequence, will be *your* concern, not mine: originally – *c.* 1850 – US, and in the negative; but, by *c.* 1890, mostly affirmative; anglicized *c.* 1860, mainly in the affirmative – and in C20 almost always so. Cf the quotation at **believe it or not**.

Gelett Burgess, *Love in a Hurry*, 1913, has: 'Flodie nodded, with a hard look in her eyes. "All right," she said slowly, and gulped something down. "It's *your* funeral."'

it's your pal you have to watch is applied to the act, or the words, of a friend: since the late 1940s. Frank Shaw, 1 September 1969, compares Richard Crossman's remark, made in that year, about Labour MPs: 'With friends like mine, you don't need enemies' – itself an allusion to the proverb, 'With a Hungarian for a friend, who needs an enemy?'.

it's your pigeon! It's your concern: late C19–20. Hence also, in C20, throughout Commonwealth. This is the *pigeon* that means 'business' in Anglo-Chinese, where it is usually spelt *pidgin*.

I've arrived – and to prove it, I'm 'ere (or **here**). Cyril Whelan, writing to me on 17 February 1975, says:

> Despite much raiding of the memory banks and a fairly rigorous inquisition of friends, I'm afraid I'm unable to remember the origin of [this]. It was certainly a comedian of the 50s: and I think the fact that the tag is remembered independently of the individual makes quite a pertinent point. This kind of expression becomes popular and is used *ad nauseam* within groups of friends, newspaper headlines, etc., for a short, intense period while the radio or television show retains popularity or novelty. The impetus then seems to wear off, but the phrase is retained in the lower strata of the collective memory for use at much later dates and often quite far removed from the original context.

Which, you'll admit, is subtly and pellucidly expressed. 'I wish I had said that,' remarked Wilde. 'You will, Oscar, you will,' retorted Whistler.

Well, since then I've been told that the c.p. was originated by that accomplished entertainer, Max Bygraves, in 'Educating Archie', a radio show based on the ventriloquist's doll Archie Andrews, which ran from 1950 to 1953 (BBC Written Archives Centre, Caversham Park, Reading).

I've been poorly – proper poorly is a c.p. reply to the query, 'How have you been?': since the late 1940s. Based on a 'radio comic's opening phrase of the 1940's (Frank Shaw, January 1969); by 1970, obsolescent.

I've been through the mill – ground and bolted. I'm much too experienced to believe, or to do, that: nautical mid C19–early C20. (B & L.)

I've been swaying with an old mess-mate. See **swaying** ....

I've done (or **had**) **more sea miles than you've had** (or **eaten**) **pusser's peas** is a naval boast, dating since *c.* 1917 and claiming a comparatively long service at sea. (A *pusser* is, of course, a purser.) Cf **get some service in!**

I've eaten a hundred like you for breakfast and had a dozen more as afters is a c.p. boast so exaggerated as to be genuinely funny and comical: rare, I believe, before 1950 and not very widespread until *c.* 1955. (A. B. Petch, 16 January 1974.)

I've got (or **I've**) **a bit of string with a hole in it** is a facetious would-be witty reply to a request for something-or-other quite different: C20.

I've got a feeling in my water, with **I've** often omitted, is used as a c.p. reply to, e.g., 'Well, what makes you think it'll be all right this time?'. It means 'I can't give you a precise reason, yet I strongly feel that it *is* so': C20 and probably back to 1850, if not further. (Paul Beale, 17 February 1975.)

I've got a million of 'em seems to have been one of Max Miller's 'gags': 1940s and 1950s. (Vernon Noble, 8 February 1975.) See **I gotta million of them**. But the precise interrelationship is obscure.

I've got (illiterately **I got**) **news for you**. I have something important – *or* startling *or* contradicting what you've just said – to tell you: US: since early 1950s. In *The Zoo Story*, performed in Berlin 1959, in New York 1960 (which was also the year in which it was published), Edward Albee causes Jerry to remark to Peter: 'Hey, I got news for you, as they say.'

I've got the time if you've got the inclination. Besides the ordinary usage, i.e. of sexual innuendo, which, clearly, is not a c.p., there exists a derivate sense, current since *c.* 1950: a 'retort to ejaculations of surprise or indignation (e.g. *bugger me!* or *fuck me!*) A gently pink' – suggestive – 'contrast between impulse and sobriety' or caution. (Laurie Atkinson, late 1974.)

[**I've got to do my thing** – 'very recent hippy talk, "I must express myself"' (Douglas Leechman, January 1969) – is not a c.p., but a cliché: every 'hippy' has to do this and insists on telling you so, in any grammatical tense and number.]

I've had (or **I had**) **a shit, shave, shower, shoe-shine and shampoo**. See **shave, a shilling** ....

I've had more sea miles .... See **I've done more sea miles** ....

I've had more women than you've had hot breakfasts or **dinners** is an older man's cynically jocular boast to a younger, clearly much less experienced, man: C20. The female counterpart, from 'knowing' woman to comparatively inexperienced girl is ... *more men than* ....

I've had more women ... has become so incorporated into the language that there can naturally occur such allusions as this in Act I of John Osborne's *Inadmissible Evidence*, produced in 1964 and published in 1965:

BILL [speaking of a typist]: She looks as though she could do with a bit [of fornication]. She's got the galloping cutes all right. Joy. *She*'s had more joy sticks than hot dinners.

I've heard that one before. Noël Coward, *Waiting in the Wings*, performed and published in 1960, has at Act II, Scene i:

PERRY: There's no need to get into such a fizz. She's promised to let me see whatever she writes before it goes in.

MISS ARCHIE: I've heard that one before.

To attempt to date a c.p. of this sort would be to attempt the impossible. At a guess – a wild, wild guess – I'd hazard 'Since the 1890s, perhaps the 1880s, possibly the 1870s': and then, as likely as not, be a generation astray.

I've not seen you since last year, 'a tiresome "gag" many use on January the 1st each year' was recorded, as Frank Shaw informed me on 1 September 1969, as far back as the *Comic Calendar*, 1841.

I've seen 'em come and I've seen 'em go. 'Said of those (manager, n.c.o., officer) who start new job like a whirlwind and end with over-zealous mistake, hoped for by staff' (Laurie Atkinson, 18 July 1975): dating since the 1920s. A cynicism prompted by the proverbial 'A new broom sweeps clean'.

I've seen 'em grow and **I've shit 'em!** are army c.pp. used in WW1, the former indicating contempt for someone's rapid promotion, esp. a junior's; the latter scorn for soldiers of another regiment. The polite one appears in F & G, the rude one in B & P. Cf **scraped 'em off me puttees**.

I've something to do (that) nobody else can do for me. I must pay a visit to the lavatory: never euphemistic; always – rather laboriously – jocular: C20. (In April 1966. Mr A. B. Petch reminded me of this.)

J

Jack disregarded, as in **fuck you, Jack**, and **I'm all right, Jack**. See **fuck you, Jack!**

Jack doesn't care and **Jack loves a fight** are C20, mostly naval, c.pp., referring, the former to the seaman's infectious insouciance, the latter to his love of a scrap, esp. fisticuffs.

jack-knife carpenter! is 'a cry of derision hurled at a man, especially a carpenter, who uses a pocket knife in an emergency. Legend has it that all jack-knife carpenters end up in hell' (Douglas Leechman): Canadian: since *c.* 1910; by 1960, obsolescent.

Jack loves a fight. See **Jack doesn't care.**

Jack's come home is a theatrical c.p., applied to a happy-go-lucky, slapdash hotel or boarding house: C20. It occurs in, e.g. Ngaio Marsh, *Vintage Murder*, 1938.

jam on both sides. See **d'you want jam on both sides?**

jam tomorrow. See **it's always jam....**

jammed like Jackson. A late C19–20 naval c.p., used when something leads to disaster or goes less, although still, seriously wrong; rather less common since *c.* 1945. From one John Jackson who, in 1787, refused to listen to his pilot and consequently went close to wrecking his ship. (F & G.) The earliest record of the c.p. I have occurs in W. N. Glascock, *Naval Sketch-Book* (chapter II, p. 136), 1826, 'Jackson's story is elaborated in the *Letters and Papers of Admiral of the Fleet Sir Thomas Byam Martin GCB* (Navy Records Society, 1903, pp. 106–7):–as Rear-Admiral P. W. Brock informs me.

jig is up – the. The game is up – All is discovered: US: *c.* 1860–1920. George P. Barnham, in his very readable *Memoirs*, 1872.

jobs for the boys has become a lighthearted c.p., synonymous with 'nepotism'. But originally it was a political, hence soon a semi-political, c.p., that was current while Leslie Hore-Belisha was Minister of Transport (1934–7); it could, however, have arisen early, for every Minister and every Government is, by the nature of things, wide open to such charges; some, admittedly, more than others. (David Hardman, 1974.)

'A c.p. that is used by and of members of the Australian Labor Party'–as Barry Prentice told me on May Day, 1975.

job's jobbed – that. See **that job's jobbed.**

Joe Miller. See **I don't see the Joe Miller of it.**

John Hughes won't save yer! See LIVERPOOL CATCH PHRASES.

John Orderly! (or **Audley!**) is a US circus people's command to hurry: C20. (Recorded in Berrey and elsewhere.) By a sort of hasty or slapdash disguising of *order!* – i.e., come to order, and get moving!

Johnny Walker. See **still going strong like....**

join the army and see the world – the next world! A ruefully jocular gibe uttered by disgruntled soldiers: since *c.* 1948. Poking fun at the recruiting slogan, 'Join the army and see the world'.

join the back of the queue! is addressed to someone slow – esp. if exceedingly slow – in the uptake: since *c.* 1948; by 1970 obsolescent. (A. B. Petch, March 1966.) Exactly synonymous is **go to the back of the class!** Probably since the 1920s and certainly possessing greater vitality.

join up! Get some service in!: fighting Services: since *c.* 1925. An elaboration of the simple synonymous injunction, *join!* (H & P.)

join? when I get out of this (lot), they won't get me to join a Christmas club! Forces': WW2.

joined the club or **the family – she's** (occasionally preceded by **that girl's**). See **she's joined....**

joint is jumping – the. The place – the building or the hall – is very lively: among US 'pop' music lovers, esp. teenagers: late 1930s–40s. (Berrey.)

joke (or **joke's**) **over!** This and **when do we laugh?** are sarcastic c.pp. addressed to the maker of a feeble witticism: since *c.* 1925. The former is sometimes said by the joker himself when he sees that his wit has misfired.

joking – you have to be (or **you must be**). See **you're joking.**

jolly hockey sticks! Mr Peter Sanders, in a letter dated 21 October 1968, says:

> One c.p., a great favourite in the family, is 'Jolly hockey-sticks!' – our 16-year-old daughter's riposte to anything smacking of tradition or convention. She picked it up last year at her school. Dartington Hall. 'Jolly-hockeysticks' was recently used as an adjective 'The jolly-hockeysticks image ...' (of compulsory games) in the *Sunday Times*, 13 October 1968.

The phrase is mildly derisive of the jolly, hearty, games-loving atmosphere encouraged in many British girls' Public Schools: and it provided the title of a 'middle' in the *Evening News* of 7 May 1973. Cf Paul Beale's gloss, dated 15 April 1975: 'This exclamation came, I think, from the film based on Ronald Searle's "St Trinian's" cartoons of appalling schoolgirls. Now used to parody the girls' public-school accent and hearty games attitude.'

Joseph – not for. See **not for Joseph!**

Josephus Rex. See **you are Josephus Rex.**

Judy Fitzsimmons. See **don't make a Judy Fitzsimmons of yourself.**

jump, Jim Crow! arose, says Benham, from the popular song, 'Jim Crow', recorded in the *Song Index* Supplement, ed. by Minnie Sears, 1934, with the gloss, 'T. D. Rice (music and words)' – but no date. The British Museum's *Modern Music Catalogue*, however, dates it at 1839 and refers to it thus: ' "I come from ole Kentucky." *Jim Crow*, arranged with an accompaniment, for the Spanish guitar. *London*, [1839] fol' (i.e., folio).

Jim Crow became – perhaps already was – a vaguely generic name for a negro; long disused. Semantically from 'as black as a crow'.

June too-too belongs to the year 1897 only: 22 June was the sixtieth anniversary of Queen Victoria's reign: a non-aristocratic, would-be smart-set c.p., punning '22' and satirizing the 'too-too' vogue initiated by the Aesthetes and promptly aped by social aspirants. (Ware.)

Jupiter Pluvius has got out (or **put on** or **turned on**) **his water-can** is a c.p. circumlocution for 'It is raining', applied mostly to a heavy shower: since *c.* 1870; obsolescent by 1920 and obsolete by 1940.

[**jury – hang half and save half**. The jury may be **a Kentish** – or **a London** – or **a Middlesex** jury: respectively C18–19, late C18–mid C19, C17–19. The implication, as dramatist Middleton suggested of the prototypal third form is: 'Thou … will make haste to give up thy verdict, because thou will not lose thy dinner.' Recorded by Apperson, it is either a semi-proverbial c.p. or originally a proverbial saying that became also a c.p.]

just a crazy mixed-up kid. See **crazy mixed-up kid**.

just fancy (or **just fancy that!**) A c.p. either indicating one's own astonishment or admiration or inviting one's interlocutor to admire or to be astonished by something or other: C20. In either sort, it is sometimes very ironical.

In *Design for Living*, written *c.* 1932 and published 1933, Noël Coward, in Act III, Scene i, has:

HELEN [*social poise well to the fore*]: It's funny how people alter; only the other day in the Colony a boy that I used to know when he was at Yale walked up to my table, and I didn't recognize him!

LEO: Just fancy!

Helen is American, and Leo maliciously ironic. A c.p. dating from *c.* 1880 – or perhaps much earlier. Both forms are elaborations of the exclamatory *fancy!*

just for the hell of it. See **for the hell of it**.

just for the record. Let me make – *or* thereby to make – my position clear; Let's get things straight!: since *c.* 1955 in Britain. Cf the Standard US 'I wish to go on record as saying…'; but the probable genesis is this: *to keep the record straight*; then more colloquially, *just to keep the record straight*; whence the entirely colloquial *just for the record*.

just in time – or born in the vestry! is, obviously, applied to a wedding held only just in time to prevent the coming child from being adjudged illegitimate: C20. It 'has lost some of its sting now that legitimacy no longer depends on being born in wedlock' (Peter Sanders, 27 November 1968).

just like a midshipman's chest: everything on top and nothing handy is the full, original version of **everything on top and nothing handy**: naval, mostly officers': since *c.* 1890. Recorded in *SS*, the shorter form; the full form was communicated to me, late in 1968, by Rear-Admiral P. W. Brock.

just like Roger was a short-lived voguish c.p. of the 1870s. Benham glosses it thus: 'In reference to the Tichborne trial, 1972'. A famous trial, spectacularly notorious.

just my handwriting! I can do that with the utmost ease; but also 'That's right up my street' and, indeed, 'just my cuppa'; since *c.* 1930.

just one of those things. See **it's just one of those things**.

just part of the Austin Reed service, I suppose? was current in the 1930s: and it arose in, as well as partly making good-natured fun of, Messrs Austin Reed's advertising slogan. Since *c.* 1950, the predominant form has been **it's all** (or **just**) **part of the service**.

just start something! That is, 'If you're looking for trouble': American: C20; adopted in Britain *c.* 1944. Cited by S. R. Strait in 'Straight Talk' in the *Boston Globe* of *c.* 1917. (W. J. Burke.)

just tell 'em Joe sent you. A US c.p. of the early 1920s. 'Probably an instruction on how to get into a speakeasy during Prohibition' (John T. Fain, 2 April 1969).

just the job! That, or this, is exactly what I need (or needed) *or* want (or wanted): fighting Services: since *c.* 1935; by 1950, in fairly general civilian use. (H & P.)

just the job for my brother from Gozo. Try to get someone else – Not for *me*!: naval: *c.* 1860–1914. Gozo is one of the Maltese islands – and many Maltese were, until *c.* 1970, employed by the navy. Cf **not me, Sare**….

just the ticket. A variant of **that's the ticket**.

just what the doctor ordered is a c.p. of unqualified approval, applied to anything particularly suitable or relevant, or to anything exceptionally good or unexpectedly agreeable: C20.

In his *Itma*, 1948, Francis Worsley wrote, concerning 'ITMA''s visit to Scapa Flow in January 1944, 'Everything we did on the spur of the moment seemed to be just what the doctor ordered, and from then on we knew we had the best audience in the world': a quotation that, better than any generalization, exemplifies how very much part of the language this particular c.p. had become.

A US example occurs in Jean Potts, *An Affair of the Heart*, 1970: '"Thanks for everything, Gene. You're just what the doctor ordered."' And on 26 February 1972, it figures in an advertisement in the *New Yorker*.

[**kamerad!** See the ONE-WORD 'PHRASES']

keep a cow. See **as long as I can buy milk....**

keep him (or **it**) **in – he'll get pecking if let out** is a low, mostly North Country c.p. addressed to a man with his flies open: late C19–20. A pun on *cock*; cf the US sense of *pecker*.

keep it clean! and, later, **keep the party clean!** The former, since the early 1920s and obsolescent by 1960; the latter, since *c.* 1930. Don't talk smut or tell dirty stories; don't act loosely or indelicately. A correspondent, *c.* 1965, commented thus: 'But the speaker often does not quite mean it. "Give me my hat and knickers," she said. "I thought you were going to keep the party clean."'

keep it dark! Keep it secret: underworld: *c.* 1830–70. Cited by 'Ducange Anglicus', i.e. John Camden Hotten, in 1857; this little-known work amounted to a 'trial run' for *The Slang Dictionary*, 1859.

keep it on the deck! and **keep it on the Island** (or, later, **island**) are synonymous, the former naval only, the latter naval in origin and general in usage. The former, C20; the latter, since *c.* 1895. 'Naval football supporters' cry when the ball goes too often into touch' (Granville, for *deck*); and for *Island*, Granville remarks that 'When football matches were played on Whale Island, Portsmouth, in the old days, the ball occasionally went into the water when it found touch.' On 17 January 1944, Frank Butler, in the *Daily Express*, spoke feelingly of 'That monotonous "Keep it on the island" when the ball is banged into the grandstand to clear a dangerous position'.

keep moving! See **push on – keep moving.**

keep off the grass! Be careful!; Be cautious! – often in playful sexual reference to a male paying attention to a girl regarded by the speaker as his own property: late C19–20; by 1960, obsolescent; and by 1970, virtually obsolete. Originally it was proletarian. It derives from notices in parks and elsewhere.

keep on smiling! See **keep smiling!**

keep on truckin'! As the Salvation Army puts it, 'Keep *on* keeping on': since the 1930s. Basically 'Keep moving!' Ben Grauer, on Christmas Day 1975, explained it as 'Keep on doing what you're doing; especially, encouraging or approving a vigorous or self-assertive action; he adds, 'Originated by Negro dancers and spread to Whites.' US: it derives from the name of a dance popular in the 1930s. Writing to me in 1974 and 1975, Norris M. Davidson and Joseph T. Shipley say it is an obsolete phrase. 'Comes from the great marathon dance contests that were a part of our 1930s scene, when all the partners clung to one another, half-asleep, but on and on moving around the dance hall through the night, like the great trucks that go endlessly across our continent through the dark hours, as they "keep on truckin'" for the prize' (Joseph T. Shipley, 7 March 1975).

'Little used by educated people, even in their relaxed moments; I think they merely regard it as vulgar and tiresome ... I should classify it as merely (voguish and probably evanescent) slang. ... Current among the vulgar and the young' (John W. Clark, 17 February 1975). And on 19 May 1975, John Browning, US citizen, London bookseller, two-worlds poet, classified it as (having become) a hippies', as well as a teenagers', c.p.

keep (or **keep on**) **smiling!** was a sort of morale-boosting slogan during WW1, but some of us got a little tired of it and used it, either ironically or bitterly, in direct allusion to the slogan, with the implication 'That's kids' stuff!'. Rather like being expected to *grin and bear it* (cliché) – as if, often, it's more than enough, just having to experience and suffer it.

keep taking the tablets! Apparently from either a radio or a TV show: 'The Goon Show' or Morecambe and Wise: ?late 1960s or early 1970s.

keep that in ... and at the matinée! That's worth repeating: theatrical: since *c.* 1910. 'This greets the introduction of any felicitous gag, or business that amused the company at rehearsals or was tried out during a performance'; *and at the matinée* is 'employed if the gag is exceptionally brilliant' (Granville).

keep that under your hat! That's strictly confidential: late C19–20; by 1975, slightly obsolescent – like hats.

keep the change! You're welcome! *or* Not at all!: US: since *c.* 1920. (Berrey.)

keep the party clean! See **keep it clean!**

keep the tambourine a-rolling! Keep things moving and lively: Londoners': *c.* 1830–70. See the Surtees quotation (*Handley Cross*, 1854) at **all round my hat!**

keep up, old queen! was, in late C19–mid C20, but obsolescent by 1930 and obsolete by 1940, a c.p. of farewell 'addressed by common women to a sister being escorted into a prison van' (Ware.)

keep yer 'earts up, lads! As an expression of civilian goodwill shouted to soldiers on leave in 1914–18, it clearly isn't eligible; but abused, among soldiers, by the soldiers themselves, it does qualify, for it was then ironic and was often accompanied by a muttered *if yer belly trails the ground*.

keep your eye on the sparrow! A 'new c.p. from America. Presumably something to do with being aware of the evil things life and men do' (Gareth Murshallsea, assistant editor of *Books and Bookmen*, in a private communication, March 1976): since 1975 or, at earliest, 1974. Clearly an allusion to bird-droppings at awkward moments – a splendid deflater of pomposity.

keep your eye on uncle and **watch your uncle**, where *uncle* = me. Uttered by the leader of a group, either in banter or as a leg-pull: since *c.* 1930; by 1970, rather 'old hat'.

keep your fingers crossed! dates from *c*. 1920 in Britain, where it means Pray for me! *or* wish me luck, for I'll badly need it, and from *c*. 1930 in US, where – whether 'lighthearted or serious' – it means Wish me luck! (as Edward Hodnett tells me on 18 August 1975). Probably it was originally prompted by *make the sign of the Cross* in order to ward off bad luck.

keep your hair on! was, *c*. 1867–1913 (to judge from the evidence afforded by Benham, by Ware, and by B & P), a c.p. applied, sometimes with ludicrous incongruity to any mishap. Cf **keep your wool on!**

keep your legs together! is a C20 Australian c.p., 'used to a girl. It is equivalent to "Be good!"' (Barry Prentice.)

keep your nose clean, originally proletarian and not unknown among criminals, was also an army c.p., with the special sense, 'Avoid strong drink – it gets you into trouble': late C19–20. But, by *c*. 1920, the army nuance had become simply 'Keep out of trouble!' – often, with an undertone of 'Mind your own business!'. All, however, are predominantly valedictory.

keep your shirt on! Don't lose your temper!: an Australian and New Zealand c.p. of late C19–20. It is also US of probably the same period; John W. Clark (on 2 June 1975) attests its existence since early C20 and in the same, the earliest and basic, sense of 'Don't get over-angry', with deriving nuances, 'Don't get over-perturbed' and 'Don't be over-hasty'. And on 18 August 1975 Edward Hodnett glosses it as '*c*. 1900. Don't be impatient!'

keep your thanks to feed your chickens! I neither need nor want your thanks: C17–mid C18. Semi-proverbial. (Apperson.)

keep your wool on! Don't get, or be, angry: *c*. 1880–1914. (B & L.) Cf **keep your hair on**, much the commoner, more lasting, expression.

keep yourself good all through! Be – in *every* way – good: a society c.p. of 1882–*c*. 1890. (Ware.)

keeping up with the Joneses arose very soon after WW2 and signalized, as well as characterizing, the rapid revival of snobbery. On the marriage of Mr Anthony Armstrong-Jones, in 1960, to HRH Princess Margaret, it almost immediately, from being a cliché, became a c.p., the process accelerating on his elevation, in 1961, to the peerage.

It is perhaps the stupidest of all the stupid aspects of the social scene, this fear of possessing fewer 'status symbols' (esp. motor cars) and of otherwise appearing to be less well-off, less important, less smart, than one's neighbours and associates.

Kemp's shoes. See **would that I had Kemp's shoes to throw after you!**

keystone under the hearth (, **keystone under the horse's belly**) – the second part often omitted – was a C19 smugglers' c.p. that became proverbial, the reference being to the concealment of contraband spirits below the fireplace or in the stable. (Apperson.)

kick, bollock and bite! 'A character in Bethnal Green when in his cups and immediately prior to falling down the stairs at Liverpool Street Station used to holler "Kick, bollock and bite" as a warning *cum* battle cry. He was renowned for this, and the phrase attained a moderate currency in the building

trade' (C. A. Worth, 28 January 1975): Londoners': C20 – probably *c*. 1925–50.

kick for touch! is an intimation that 'Here's a tricky situation' and a warning that 'You had better try to extricate yourself from it as soon as possible': a c.p. among Public School men and the young people moving in smart sets: since *c*. 1920; by 1970, slightly obsolescent. From Rugby football. (Communicated by Wilfred Granville, letter of 19 November 1968.)

kill that baby! Switch off the spotlight: film industry: since *c*. 1930. A *baby* because it's only a small light.

kill who? was, *c*. 1870–1914, a proletarian 'satirical protest against a threat' (Ware.). Semantically of the same order as **you and who else?**

killing a snake? is a Canadian golfing c.p., jocularly addressed to a player taking many strokes in a sand-trap: since *c*. 1930.

Kilroy was here was at first a US WW2 c.p., recorded in HLM, Supp. 2; Mencken mentions that he knows of three theories of origin, but wisely hazards none of his own. W & F comment that it arose in 1940 and was in wide use immediately before the US entered WW2, the phrase coming to mean 'the US Army, or a soldier, was here' and it could be applied to any place anywhere. It caught on in Britain and spread rapidly; by 1942, it was written on walls or other convenient places by British and US troops, no matter where they were stationed or fighting. For a tolerably credible theory, see the Supplement to *DSUE*.

kindly leave the stage! See **I say, I say, I say!**

King of the Road! See **get off and milk it!**

King's horse – you shall have the. A c.p. directed at a liar: *c*. 1660–1840. (Apperson.) Implying that a statement, especially a claim, was either grossly exaggerated or utterly false.

kiss me, Hardy! is a jocular c.p. of late C19–20. Although indubitably a c.p., it has never been wildly popular. From Nelson's dying words, which certain historians suppose to have been '*Kismet, Hardy*', which I find most improbable.

On 21 October 1968, Mr Peter Sanders, who served in North Africa and elsewhere, wrote thus to me: 'How about counter catch phrases, if such beasts exist? I know one – the rude soldiery's counter c.p. to "Kiss me, Hardy!" which is "Kiss my arse, I'm next for admiral!" Fairly common in WW2, but I suspect it is much older' – so do I, but cannot, at present, prove it.

kiss me, sergeant! was, in the British Army during WW1, 'a common piece of facetiousness, uttered after a sergeant had been more than usually officious; and often in camps, to the orderly sergeant after he had commanded "Lights out!"' (John Brophy in B & P).

In 1974, Michael Page published a collection of WW2 songs under the title *Kiss Me Good-Night, Sergeant-Major*; this helps to establish the variant ...*sergeant-major*.

In the post-WW2 army, since *c*. 1948, it has been used to satirize the mollycoddling of recruits.

kiss my arse! – American and Canadian **kiss my ass** – has been a c.p. either of entire incredulity or of profound contempt or, more generally, an intensified negative: British, mid C19–20, the others since *c*. 1860: but all three perhaps a half-century earlier. Often shortened to *my arse!* as in Ernest Raymond, *A Song of the Tide*, 1940:

'More like ten past [eight o'clock].'

'Ten past, my arse.'

Cf **kiss my Parliament!**: the 1660s. This rude c.p. was based on the *Rump* Parliament. Ernest Weekley once quoted Pepys's *Diary* for February 1660, 'Boys do now cry, "Kiss my Parliament."'

Also cf **kiss my tail!**: a violently contemptuous retort of C18–20; by 1930, obsolescent, and by 1960, virtually obsolete.

Also, **so is my arse!** and **ask my arse!**, both to be seen under *A*. Cf also:

· **kiss my foot!** Rubbish: mostly Australian and Canadian: latish C19–20. But much less common than the c.p. preceding this. Also *my foot!*: late C19–20.

kiss of death – the, has, since *c*. 1950 in Britain and since *c*. 1945, in US, been applied to a fatal – or, at the mildest, an extremely dangerous contact. Foster quotes *The Observer*, 18 September 1966, as saying, 'Allying with Churchill was regarded as the political kiss of death even in 1939'; and Safire defines it as 'unwelcome support from an unpopular source'.

The earliest literary source I've happened on is 'Stop Me if You've Heard it' in Noël Coward's *Star Quality*, 1951: '"Poor Budge," they would be saying, "the kiss of death on every party – he never knows when to stop."'

Obviously from Judas Iscariot's kissing of Christ, in the great betrayal scene; thence to any other callous betrayal; and perhaps with a famous US thriller, *The Kiss of Death*, intervening.

kissing time – it's or **it's half-past kissing time and time to kiss again.** The former is a shortened version of the latter, and the latter must date from at least as early as *c*. 1850; during the approximate period 1870–1914, it was, mostly among Londoners, a low c.p. reply to a woman asking a man the time, and said to derive from a very popular ballad; the longer form has also, like the shorter, been, in C20, addressed to children continually asking one the time, as HLM records in 1922.

Cf the C18 **an hour past hanging time** and **half-past....**

Kitchener wants you was, during WW1 – more precisely, in 1915–18 – an army c.p., addressed to any man selected for a filthy job or for very arduous, or perilous, work. It was prompted by a very famous enlistment poster, showing a sternly pointing Lord Kitchener captioned with these words, a poster frequently reproduced ever since. In Alec Waugh's famous novel, *Jill Somerset*, 1936, we read that 'All those [men] who had attested under the Derby Scheme should wear khaki armlets; there'd be no more embarrassments; no more soldiers jeering their "Kitchener wants you".' (B & P.)

kneeling on it. See **you're kneeling on it.**

knitting's out. See **her knitting's out.**

knob of a chair and a pump handle – a. A lower-middle class reply to the enquiry 'What is there to eat?': since *c*. 1890; by 1975, decidedly obsolescent.

knock! knock! dates from mid-November 1936, and derives, in Britain, from its effective use by Wee Georgie Wood in a radio music-hall programme on the night of Saturday 14 November 1936. Originally, it has been said, it was a US c.p. It is used by someone about to tell a smutty story or, esp., to make a pun in dubious taste. In this sense, obsolescent by 1975. A correspondent, Mr Alan Smith, wrote on 7 June 1939: 'It is possible that this derives from the Porter's scene in *Macbeth*, Act II, Scene iii.' But from *c*. 1960 onwards it has also been used by a person knocking on a door, saying *knock! knock!* and, without further ceremony, entering the room.

knock three times and ask for Alice is 'a jocular c.p. – used, for example, to short-circuit someone else's long-drawn-out directions as to location' (Laurie Atkinson): C20; originally, Cockneys', but since 1939, mostly the Armed Forces'.

knocked-knees and silly and can't hold his water. A Public Schools' pejorative c.p. of late C19–20.

know it – not if I. See **not if I know it.**

know of – not that you. See **not that you know of.**

know whether I'm Angus or Agnes (or **Arthur or Martha**) – **I don't.** See **I don't know....**

Kruschen feeling. See **that Kruschen feeling.**

L

la! la! See oh! la! la!

ladies of Barking Creek – the. See like the ladies....

Lammie Todd! I would – if I got half a chance!: tailors': *c.* 1860–1940. Probably from the name of a well-known tailor.

lareovers for meddlers was, late C18–early C19, 'an answer frequently given to children or young people, as a rebuke for their impertinent curiosity' (Grose); the earliest recording comes in BE underworld glossary, *c.* 1698; then dialectal usually as *layers for meddlers*, or even, occasionally, *lay horses for meddlers*, a piece of folklore that seems to belong esp. to Westmorland, as Mr Allan R. Whittaker informs me. Nevertheless *lareovers* ... has survived in the form *lay-overs for meddlers*. *Lareovers* is 'a contraction of *lay-overs*, i.e. things laid over, covered up, or protected from meddlers' (Apperson).

large mouth, large cunt; occasionally big for *large*. An example of not entirely scientific male folklore: ?mid C19–20; certainly C20.

larks in the night – the. A 'jocular c.p. for birds which are regarded as responsible for more births than the stork' (Barry Prentice): Australian: since *c.* 1930. A pun on a *lark* or a bit of fun, and *bird*, a girl.

[lass in the red petticoat shall pay (or piece up) all – the. Dating *c.* 1660–1800 and occurring in, e.g., J. Wilson, *The Cheats*, 1664, and recorded by Apperson, it is probably to be classified rather as proverbial than as c.p.]

last of the big spenders – the, is an Australian c.p., current since *c.* 1960 and applied, with caustic irony, to one who is extremely mean; whether in direct address or in reference. (Barry Prentice, 1 May 1975.)

last of the Mohicans – the, and, derivatively, the last of its tribe, applied to the last of a series, a packet, etc., as, e.g. the last cigarette in a packet: C20; the former, in the US and then in Britain, the latter in Australia. From James Fenimore Cooper's most famous novel, *The Last of the Mohicans*, 1836; but in Britain, the former, as Frank Shaw once remarked, is often used by people who've never heard of Fenimore Cooper's book, and, in the US, it is used of 'any sole survivor in any group, or any vanishing group ... and everyone gets the point, for Cooper's book is universally known. I have heard the expression all my life' (W. J. Burke, 9 April 1975 – and that would literally mean since, say, 1915). It has been a c.p. – well, probably since latish C19.

[last one home is a cissy is an English schoolchildren's taunt, and, like last out, lousy! – a children's late C19–20 c.p., applied, esp. in Australia, to games – is traditional: therefore, not a c.p. The same applies to last one in is the cow's tail, applied, as Douglas Leechman reminds me, to a bathing scene.]

laugh? I thought I should have died dates from *c.* 1880; originally, general, but by *c.* 1930, the standard of syntactical literacy having deteriorated, it was, in the lower and lower-middle class, superseded by *laugh? I thought I'd die!*

An excellent example occurs in Miles Malleson's play, *Black 'Ell*, written and published in 1916, but the first edn copies were promptly seized by the police on the grounds that it was subversive, and the second edn was not published until 1925; a housemaid says, 'There was a young chap on the platform makin' a speech or somethink ... they pulled 'im orf ... and 'is glasses fell orf an' 'e trod on 'em 'isself ... LARF! ! ! ! I thought I should er died.'

laughing haversacks. See I'll be laughing haversacks.

lawyer must be a good liar – a good. See good lawyer....

lay of the last minstrel – the. A cultured Canadian c.p., dating from *c.* 1860 and applied to a particularly unattractive girl. (Douglas Leechman.) In allusion to Sir Walter Scott's famous poem and with a pun on the slangy US-become-also-English *lay*, a partner in sexual intercourse.

lay off the comedy! Stop trying to be funny!; Be serious!: US: since *c.* 1930. In Noël Coward's *Relative Values*, produced 1951 and published 1952, at Act II, Scene ii, Don Lucas, a film star, irritably exclaims, 'Lay off the comedy a minute, will you? This means the hell of a lot to me.'

layers (or layovers) for meddlers. See lareovers for meddlers.

lead me to it! With pleasure!; That'll be easy, or a great pleasure: C20. Dorothy L. Sayers's *The Nine Tailors*, 1934, has:

'Can you ride a motor-bike?'
'Lead me to it, guv'nor!'

lead on, Macduff! is a late C19–20 c.p., based upon the very frequent misquotation of 'Lay on, Macduff' in Shakespeare's *Macbeth*, Act V, Scene vii, line 62. The c.p. occurs in, e.g. Edward Burke, *Bachelor's Buttons*, 1912.

Douglas Leechman (early 1969) defines its Canadian nuance as 'All right, let's go, get started, etc.'.

lean on your chin-straps! was, 1915–18, heard in the army when the troops were either marching up a very steep hill or finishing a long and arduous route march. (F & G; B & P.)

leave it all to the cook – I'll. See I'll leave....

leave it for the cleaners! 'A c.p. often heard when someone drops small change on the floor' (Barry Prentice): Australian: since the late 1940s.

leave me alone for that! See let me alone for that!

leave the deck to the last! is an ironic shout, greeting 'that hapless rating working aloft who has spilled paint on to the deck' (Sailors' Slang): naval: C20.

leave the sea and go into steam! Transfer to a steam-driven ship!: sailing-men's c.p. of *c.* 1860–1900. (Bowen.)

left her purse on the piano! was, late C19–early C20, a 'satirical hit at self-sufficiency' (Ware). Non-aristocratic, non-upper-middle class, it implied that a woman visitor, boasting of her efficiency and excellent memory, departs without her purse.

legs grew in the night, therefore he could not see to grow straight, usually preceded by his. A jeering c.p., addressed to a bandy-legged man: c. 1760–1820. (Grose, 1796.)

legs up to her bum. See **she has legs....**

lemon.... See **answer is a lemon – the.**

lend us your breath to kill Jumbo! A proletarian c.p. of 1882– c. 1910, it was a 'protest against the odour of bad breath' (Ware). 'Chiefly in allusion to a famous elephant at [the London] Zoo (d. 1885)', says Ware at *Jumbo*.

lend us your pound! Pull your weight on the rope: jocular nautical, esp. naval: late C19–mid C20. (Bowen.)

Les be friends! 'A mixture of a bad joke [a pun on *Les*, a Lesbian, and *le's*, illiterate for *let's*] and a catch phrase ... more generally used than one would expect' (a correspondent, 25 March 1965): since the early 1960s.

let 'em all come! arose in 1896, was at first proletarian, but by 1912, general; and it expressed a cheeky defiance. Ware attributes its origin to the way in which Britons received the following trio of setbacks in world popularity: the German emperor's congratulatory message to Kruger on the Boers' repulse of the Jameson Raid; the USA's communication about the British boundary dispute with Venezuela; and the shortly ensuing tricolor'd agitation in the Fr. press. The c.p. was noted by Collinson and recorded by Benham.

let 'em trundle! Clear out! *or* Run away!: apparently c. 1695–1730; occurs in Congreve, *The Way of the World*, 1700 (cited by McKnight). Presumably a reference to the game of bowls.

let 'er go, Deacon! (or **Gallagher!**) See **let her go....**

let 'er rip. See **let her rip!**

let George do it! – roughly, Let someone else do it!. A journalistic c.p., dating from c. 1910 and applied to the enlistment of an unnamed expert or authority and the putting of the writer's own words into his mouth, and probably, as HLM pointed out in 1922, deriving from the synonymous Fr. *laissez faire à Georges*, which goes back a long way, had an historical source, but 'later became common slang, was translated into English, had a revival during the early days of David Lloyd George's career, was adopted into American without any comprehension of either its first or its latest significance, and enjoyed the brief popularity of a year'. W & F pinpoint it to c. 1920 and note that it was popular during WW2, when it 'implied a lack of responsibility in helping the war effort': clearly the phrase was general enough during all the intervening US years. Moreover, as Professor John T. Fain wrote to me, on 25 April 1969, it 'can still be heard' in the US. In Britain, it had, by 1950, become very obsolescent – and by 1970, I'd say, obsolete. ·

let her cry – she'll piss the less was a semi-consolatory c.p. of mid C18–early C20, supposed to have been originally addressed, as *the more you cry the less you'll piss*, by sailors to their whores – or so Grose, 1796, tells us. The third-person form verges on the proverbial.

let her (or 'er) go, Deacon (, she's headed for the barn)! and **let her (or, better, 'er) go Gallagher!** are Western US 'calls

to a "bronco-buster"' (Berrey): the former of C20 and perhaps a little earlier; the latter, recorded by HLM in 1922, is far the more general and has long had a much wider application, with the predominant sense, 'Let's begin!' – and dating from c. 1880, for it occurs in, e.g., James A Herne, *Mary the Fisherman's Child*, performed in 1888 and later called *Drifting Apart*, near end of Act II:

> HESTER: Ready, Mary.
> MARY: All ready?
> SI[LAS]: Let 'er go, Gallagher. [*Song and dance.*]

In Gene Fowler, *Timber Line, A Story of Bonfils and Tammen*, 1938, we read that Bonfils sometimes visited prize fights. 'He frequently attended the Coliseum, a temple of fistiana presided over by Reddy Gallagher, a quondam athlete of Cincinnati, and of whose right fist the saying originated: "Let 'er go, Gallagher".' Mr W. J. Burke tells me that Bonfils and Tammen ran the newspaper the *Denver Post* and Gallagher was in Denver around the 1890s:

> I have known the expression all my life.... If someone gives vent to emotions, makes a verbal attack against some person or thing, becomes exercised over an injustice and speaks out with force, we are likely to exclaim in a humorous and approving manner, 'Let 'er go, Gallagher!' [20 June 1975.]

let her (or 'er) rip! Let her go freely! Damn the consequences!: mid C19–20. Probably US in origin, as both Ware and Thornton believe.

let her went! Let it go! – 'a slang expression indicative of surrender and abandonment' (Farmer, 1889): c. 1885–90. This kind of facetious c.p., based upon a deliberate grammatical solecism, is usually shortlived; cf such slang inanities as *used to was*, used to be, and (the originally negro) **is you is or is you ain't?**, are you or aren't you?

let him alone until he weighs his weight! is a Bow Street Runners' c.p., to the effect that a criminal is not yet worth arresting, his offences being so small that no reward attaches to his apprehension, whereas a capital crime will produce a large reward: c. 1770–1830. Vaux notes that if a criminal *weighs forty*, there is a reward of £40 attached to his capture.

let him pick the bones out of that! See **pick the bones....**

let it all hang out! Originally a US negroes' c.p. of the 1960s–70s, according to CM and meaning 'Be free!' or 'Be uninhibited!' – it gradually gained a much wider acceptance; in Canada, a rapid acceptance. I notice that Donald MacKenzie uses it in *The Spreewald Collection*, 1975. On 17 March 1974, Mr W. J. Burke wrote to me thus:

> We have a phrase going in the US that has caught on and is used widely. 'Let it all hang out.' It has had wide media exposure during the past two years. How it started, I do not know.... The meaning is: Make a full confession, don't hide anything, be nakedly frank and honest. Come clean. Tell the truth. I suspect it had some reference to the male sexual organ to begin with.

That and shirt-tails too, I'd say. In a later letter (12 May 1974), Mr Burke informed me that his friend Martin Goldman, editor of *Intellectual Digest* magazine, had written to him: '*Let it all hang out* may have dirty-linen connotations, but that may be a matter of laundering the language. Methinks the phrasing has sexual origins.' Glossed in *DCCU* as 'Tell the truth, the whole truth, and nothing but the truth.'

let it spread! – usually preceded by **aw**. 'Abandon care about over-eating and one's spreading waist-line'. (Laurie Atkinson, late 1974.) American and British: since the middle or late 1960s. In the *Observer* Review, 7 May 1971, Katherine Whitehorn asks, 'And what about the "Aw, let it spread" attitude to fat?'

let it sweat! Let things now take their usual course – don't interfere any more!: since *c.* 1920; by 1970, slightly obsolescent. Perhaps suggested by the army's WW1 expression, *sweat on the top line*, to be in eager anticipation, esp. if one is about to obtain something very much desired or needed.

let me alone for that! – often shortened to **let me alone!** Take my word for it!; You can depend upon me for that!; You don't need to worry about *me*, I'll manage: very common in Restoration Comedy and, indeed, until *c.* 1880.

Thomas Shadwell's *Bury Fair*, performed and published in 1689, at Act II, Scene i, has the pretended Fr. count say, 'Is ver well: lette me alone for dat' – and this from a man whose English is, in general, very faulty, yet retentive of a phrase he must often have heard.

In his *Squire of Alsatia*, 1688, Act V, in the setting of Mrs Termagant's fine lodgings, we find:

CHEAT[LY]: Madam, you must carry yourself somewhat stately, but courteously to the Bubble [i.e. the dupe].

SHAM[WELL]: Somewhat reservedly, and yet so as to give him Hopes.

TERM[AGANT]: I warrant you, let me alone; and if I effect this Business, you are the best Friends.

A rather earlier example had occurred in Edward Ravenscroft, *The London Cuckolds*, performed in 1681 and published in 1682, at Act II, Scene iii:

JANE: You must not stay long; therefore who you do, do quickly.

TOWN[LY]: Let me alone.

Still earlier was George Villiers, Duke of Buckingham, who, in *The Rehearsal*, produced in 1671 and published in 1672, a play of which 'the first draft ... was written and ready for the boards in the summer of 1665' (Montague Summers, editor), has at Act I, Scene ii:

SMI[TH]: This is one of the richest stories, Mr *Bayes*, that ever I heard of.

BAYES: I [= ay], let me alone, I gad [= begad], when I get to 'em; I'll nick 'em, I warrant you.

At this point, it might be noted that during the Restoration period of this c.p., it sometimes bore the connotations, 'Oh, stop fussing! *I* can attend to this' and 'Don't be so concerned, so anxious – I'm not the fool you seem to think me' and 'Don't worry – *I* know what I'm doing'.

In William Burnaby, *The Modish Husband*, performed and published in 1702, at Act V, Scene ii (p. 337, lines 18–21, in F. E. Budd's edn, 1931, of Burnaby's plays), we find:

LIO[NEL]: But where is the Person; mustn't I know her before I marry her?

CAM[ILLA]: No, nor after neither, I'll pass my Word.

LADY R: O! let me alone for that –.

Susannah Centlivre's *The Man's Bewitched*, 1710, has at Act I, the scene in the churchyard:

SLOUCH: Ay, and his Man *Staytape*, too; and he works like a Dragon – My Master will soon be fit [i.e., fitted] Forsooth.

MARIA: Fit, quotha! For what? ha, ha.

NUM: For what! Nay, nay, let me alone for that, an [= if] I don't show her for what, when I have her once, I'll be flea'd [i.e., flayed].

And in the next Act, scene 'the outside of Trusty's House', has:

MANAGE: Well, Sir, what am I to do now?

CONSTANT: Why, go watch about *Sir David*'s Door, and as you see occasion, employ your Wits.

MANAGE: Very well, Sir, let me alone for that; your humble Servant, Gentlemen. [*Exit.*]

In *The Drummer*, 1716, Act IV begins:

VEL[LUM]: John, I have certain orders to give you – and therefore to be attentive.

BUT[LER]: Attentive! Ay, let me alone for that.

Isaac Bickerstaffe, in *The Maid of the Mill*, 1765, uses the shorter form, and his collaboration with Samuel Foote, *Dr Last in His Chariot*, 1769, Act II has:

AIL[WOULD]: But, Prudence, art thou not afraid, that her very thinking me dead will break her heart?

PRU[DENCE]: To be sure, sir, if you should keep her in her fright too long.

AIL[WOULD]: O, let me alone for that....

The c.p. occurs as late as David Garrick and G. Colman's *The Clandestine Marriage*, 1766, at Act III, Scene i:

STERL[ING]: But, Sir John! one thing more. [Sir John *returns*.] My lord must know nothing of this stroke of friendship between us.

SIR JOHN: Not for the world. – Let me alone! Let me alone. [*Exit hastily.*]

And later still in Richard Brinsley Sheridan, *St Patrick's Day: or, The Scheming Lieutenant*, produced in 1775 and published in 1778, where Act I, Scene i, has:

THIRD SOLDIER: ... If we be to have a spokesman, there's the corporal is the lieutenant's countryman, and knows his humour.

FLINT: Let me alone for that, I served three years, within a bit, under his honour, in the Royal Inniskillions.

Mrs Hannah Cowley, in *Which Is the Man?*, 1783, uses the occasional late variant *leave me alone for that* – which occurs also in Prince Hoare's *Lock and Key*, 1791.

Mrs Elizabeth Inchbald (1753–1821), actress, novelist, playwright, also uses it, in *Such Things Are*, 1788, at Act II, Scene i:

MEAN[RIGHT]: Yet do it nicely – oblique touches, rather than open explanations.

TWINE[ALL]: Let me alone for that.

Even later comes Arthur Murphy, *The Way to Keep Him*, 1794, at Act II, Scene ii:

LOVE[MORE]: Sly, sly. – You know what you are about.

SIR BASH[FUL]: Ay, let me alone. – [*Laughs with* Lovemore.]

In *The Marriage Promise: A Comedy*, 1803, John Till Allingham, at Act I, end of Scene i, makes Tandem, steward to a country estate, boast:

I put some brandy into his beer ... and then won all his money from him at cribbage – that's the way to get on.

Oh, let me alone – I am a man of business.

In 1808, George Colman the Younger, in *The Review, or the Wags of Windsor*, at Act II, Scene i, writes:

BEAUGARD: Zounds! get along; and come with the chaise, as you will.

LOONEY: Let me alone for that. (Going.)

In the astonishing late source, Benjamin Webster's *A Bird of Passage: A Farce*, performed in 1849, the admittedly late form *leave me alone for that* appears in its short form, thus:

MRS R: Not a word of what we've been talking about, or he'll imagine — —

CHICK: Leave me alone!

A year later, Morris Barrett and Charles Mathews, *Serve Him Right! A Comic Drama*, early in Act I, repeat the *leave* form, Harry Bellamy exclaiming, 'Suspect? Of course she does – but not *me* – no, no, leave me alone for that.

And the latest instance I've found: Richard Jones, *The Green Man: A Comedy* – adapted from the Fr. of MM. D'Aubigny and Funjol – 1862, where, in Act II, Scene iii, we find:

GREEN: What, you are already provided with a writ.

CLOSE: Let me alone for that, and it shall be put in force, too.

Clearly, *let me alone for that* merits the comment, 'One of the two or three most widely used and longest-lived c.pp. in the language'. (Nor did I watch for it, much less seek it out. Its ubiquity spoke for itself.)

let me be hanged! is an occasional Restoration variant of **let me die!** It occurs in, e.g., *The Braggadoccio*, 1691, 'By a Person of Quality', at Act III, Scene i:

CAROL: I am sorry for your misfortune.

BRAV: Let me be hang'd, if I was not baited by a pack o' slaves.

In the same play, at Act I, Scene iii, there is another occasional Restoration variant, **let me die in a ditch!**

let me chat yer (or you). Let me tell you! An Australian and New Zealand soldiers' c.p. of WW1; at least, from 1915 (Recorded by Baker; also in his *NZS*.)

let me die! belongs to two widely separated periods and has two distinct senses: the earlier, *c.* 1660–1850, is a c.p. of asseveration, roughly 'Let me die if I lie', hence 'I assure you'; the later, *c.* 1860–1914, means 'You'll cause me to die laughing' – cf **you'll be the death of me!** and **carry me out!**

In Thomas Shadwell, *The Volunteers*, produced in 1692 and published in 1693, at Act I, Scene ii (lines 491–2 of the D. M. Walmsley edn), we find:

WIN[IFRED TO THE DANCING MASTER]: Go, go, get you gone, let me dye, you have the Charmingest way with you.

Used also by men, as for instance, by Sir Nicholas Dainty in Act II, Scene ii (lines 68–9): 'Yes, Puppy and Fool, and Impudence, are familiar Names: let me die.' It may also occur at the beginning of a sentence, as when, in Act III, Scene i (lines 191–2), Teresia exclaims, 'Let me die, I never saw anything so fine.'

Cf Colley Cibber, *The Comical Lovers*, produced *c.* 1707, in Act I:

PHILOTIS: Count Rhodophil's a fine gentleman indeed, madam; and, I think, deserves your affection.

MELANTHA: Let me die but he's a fine man; he sings and dances, *en Français*, and writes the *billets-doux* to a miracle [i.e., miraculously].

She repeats the phrase on several occasions within this one scene.

And at Act V, Scene i, Melantha, again speaking, says: 'O, here's her highness! Now is my time to introduce myself, and to make my court to her; in my new French phrases. Stay, let me read my catalogue – *Suite, figure, chagrin, naïveté*, and *let me die*, for the parenthesis of all.'

A decade earlier, Colley Cibber, in *Women's Wit: or, The Lady in Fashion*, 1697, had written (Act II, the scene between Lenora and Longville, the former speaking): 'Let me die, but you are a second *Phaeton*! This equipage and chariot were enough to set the whole beau-monde on fire.'

Arthur Murphy, in *The Upholsterer* (1758), a brisk farce, opens thus: 'BRISK: Mr Belmour! – Let me die, sir – as I hope to be saved, sir.'

In 1762, George Colman's *The Musical Lady*, in Act II, opening scene, has:

SOPHY: Nay, now, I'm sure you flatter me! Is my style so purely Italian? have I quite got rid of that horrid English cadence?

MASK: Let me die, madam, if your whole conversation and behaviour do not make me fancy myself in Italy; Signora Lorenza at Florence was the very type of you.

David Garrick, in *Neck or Nothing*, 1766, at Act I, Scene ii, writes thus: 'MARTIN: A fine creature! [*Salutes her.*] Madam, I have seen the world! and from all the world, here would I chuse a wife, and a mistress – a family of beauties; let me die!'

In *The Sultan*, 1784, Isaac Bickerstaffe, at Act II, Scene i, has Roxalana say: 'What, do they think we are going to prayers? Let me die, but I believe it is their dinner.'

The 'catalogue' in *Woman's Wit* suggests that the origin may lie in the Fr., *que je meure, si.…*

let me die in a ditch! A variant of the preceding. See **let me be hanged!**

let me out – I'm not barmy; also **let me out – I'm barmy**. An Armed Forces' pantomimic c.p., expressing a lively desire to be rid of Service restrictions: 1939–45.

let me perish! is synonymous with **let me die!**: *c.* 1660–1710. In Act II, Scene i, of *Love in a Wood*, performed in 1671 and published in 1672, William Wycherley writes: 'DAPPERWIT: 'Tis no fault of mine, let me perish!'

And in *The Double-Dealer*, produced and published in 1694, William Congreve, at Act II, Scene i, has:

LADY FROTH: … Mr Brisk, you're a judge; was ever anything so well bred as my lord?

BRISK: Never anything but your ladyship, let me perish!

let me shake the hand that shook the hand of Sullivan! had a brief vogue (from 1898, when Johnny Carroll sang it, until, say 1905). The reference is to John L. Sullivan, who held the world heavyweight championship from 1882 to 1892, and who died, aged seventy, in 1918. But a c.p. only when *not* used literally; it connoted a derisive irony. (W. J. Burke, 23 September 1975.)

let me tell you! – recorded, as a British c.p., by HLM, Supp. 2, – has existed, as an emphatic tag, probably since *c.* 1700, but, as a c.p., only since 1944. The radio programme, *Happidrome*, popularized it: in every instalment, Enoch says, at least once, 'Let me tell you, Mr Lovejoy', with every word emphasized.

let the dog see the rabbit! Get out of the way! Get out of the light!: common among dog-track frequenters of *c.* 1938–50; but also common in the fighting Services, 'in reference to one who wishes to do or see something' (Laurie Atkinson).

A good example occurs in Angus Ross, *The London Assignment*, 1972:

> This [room] was locked, and this time Billie had no key. She swore violently.
>
> 'Just step aside, love,' I said. 'Let the dog see the rabbit.'

Loosely, **show the dog the rabbit!**

let the good times roll! (1900s–1920s) a cry for enjoyment: music, talk, drinking, etc.' (CM); US negroes'.

let you off this time! See **I'll let you off**....

let your braces dangle, usually completed by **and let yourself go** and often preceded by **you want to** (i.e., need to). Relax and enjoy yourself: since *c.* 1945.

let's appeal against the light. Let's object, just for the hell of it: Australian: since *c.* 1950. Satirizes the gamesmanship of batsmen appealing unnecessarily at cricket.

let's be having you! See **let's have you!**

[**let's call it a day!** is almost certainly a cliché, not a c.p.]

let's call it eight bells is a naval officers' excuse for drinking before noon, 'the conventional time; i.e. any time after 11 a.m., when the sun is said to be *over the foreyard*. Eight bells are sounded at noon' (*Sailors' Slang*).

let's face it was originally – '*c*., I believe, 1957', Mr A. L. Hart, Jr, tells me on 18 February 1972: US; it became also British, Australian, New Zealand, within a year or two. Here, 'it' is the current situation, whether international or national or local, and whether collective or individual. Predominant meaning: Let's be *honest* about it! Late in 1974, Laurie Atkinson glossed the c.p. as a 'palliation of introducing an aspect or topic hitherto avoided out of tact'.

let's feel your pulse is a jocular c.p., vague in sense and application: late C19–20; by 1945, very obsolescent, and by 1975, virtually obsolete.

let's get down to the nitty gritty. Let's get to the nub of the conversation: a very slangy US c.p., dating since *c.* 1965, Mr Norris M. Davidson tells me. It was indicated by Sydney J. Harris – see **right on!** By *c.* 1972, adopted in Britain.

let's get the show on the road! A US c.p., dating from perhaps as early as *c.* 1910 and certainly very common since *c.* 1930, and originating as a theatrical or other show-business, esp. touring companies', exhortation to stop wasting time and to 'get moving'; by *c.* 1940, also British.

Ellery Queen, *Cop Out*, 1969, has the following: '"Okay, okay," Furia said. Malone could have sworn he was grinning under the mask. "Let's get the show on the road, as they say."' In the very next year, Stanley Ellin uses it in *The Man from Nowhere*. Cf its allusive employment in Michael Butterworth's English novel, *The Black Look*, 1972: '" Never mind about the slim quarto volume of arty pictures that's going to win you immortality, love," said Sonia Hammersley. "Let's get this bloody show on the road."' Allusive also is the following example from Thomas Patrick McMahon's very American novel, *The Issue of the Bishop's Blood*, 1972:

> 'It won't get you in trouble?'
>
> 'What doesn't?' he said cheerfully. 'Let's get the show on the road.'

let's go back to square one. See **back to square one!**

let's go home! is a US negro c.p. of *c.* 1920–40: 'an agreement among jazzmen to do the final chorus of a number'. A blend of two ideas: the joy of going home and the relief of finishing something. (CM.)

[**let's have one!** At **how will** (mostly **how'll**) **you have it?**. Lyell gives, as the commonest colloquial invitations to take a drink, the following, all of late C19–20, except the last two (rarely heard before *c.* 1910): *what'll you have?* and *what's yours?* and *what is it? – how'll you have it?* and *let's have one! – name yours – what about a small spot?* and *d'you feel like a small spot?* Cf **name your poison!**

But I feel that full c.p. status should be denied to these drinking terms.]

let's have some light on the subject! Turn on the lights!: C20 (I can remember it from at least as early as 1910). An example of an uncommon sense-development: that from the figurative to the literal instead of the other way about.

let's have you! and **let's hear from you!** are non-commissioned officers' c.p. calls, the former to men due to turn out for a parade or a fatigue, and dating from *c.* 1910; the latter – 'Hurry up!' or 'Look lively!' – dates from late C19, was esp. common in WW1, and derives from the vocal numbering of a rank of soldiers. (F & G for the latter.)

The former may well have come from *let's be having you!* – a foreman's summons to his gang or party to start work.

let's make the scene! Let's share in what's going on: US: since *c.* 1965. Originally, hippy talk. Indicted by Sydney J. Harris in the poem quoted at **right on!**

let's play silly buggers! Let's pretend we're mad *or*, playfully, Let's do something silly: a proletarian c.p., dating from early in C20 and, by late 1914, adopted by the British army. B & P have suggested that this c.p. was prompted by a lot of wistful and, from the angle of reality or even of realism, rather silly talk about the possibility of being released from service.

let's see the color of your dough! Let's see your money! – either to ascertain whether one can pay or to demand immediate payment: US: C20. (Berrey.)

letter in the post office – a (in full, **there is a letter ...**). Refers to the monthly period: late C19–20; obsolescent by 1935 and obsolete by 1945.

[**lice will become nits**: proverb rather than c.p.]

lid on it – that's put the. See **that's put**....

lie back and enjoy it! 'A c.p. allegedly used as advice to a girl when escape from rape is impossible' (Barry Prentice, 15 December 1974): since *c.* 1950.

lie down and I'll fan you! is a reply to any such request for service as the addressee feels to be unjustifiable: RAF, esp. among NCO Regular Servicemen: since *c.* 1925. With an allusion to the ministrations of punkah-wallahs in India and with an implication that the requester must be either feverish or distraught to have made the request at all. (PGR.)

lieutenants might marry, captains may marry ... occurs in full in Gavin Lyall's 'thriller', *Blame the Dead*, 1972, where one WW2 'type' says to another, '"Lieutenants might marry, captains may marry, majors should marry, colonels must marry," he quoted': army officers': since *c.* 1930. (I have to admit that as a GSO 3 (Education) in 1941 I never heard it.)

life begins at forty (or **40**) was generated in the 1940s by a much-read book so titled – and by a popular song.

life is just a bowl of cherries has been an American c.p. since 1931, when the song so titled was sung by Ethel Merman in *Scandals*; words by Brown, music by Henderson, as Edward B. Marks tells us in *They All Sang*, 1934; 'Marks sometimes omitted first names' (W. J. Burke, 23 September 1975). Pearl Harbor bombing, 7 December 1941, rather jolted this rosy view of life: after that date, it tended to be ironical and to become obsolescent. Introduced to me by Mr Ben Grauer during a long chat in 1974.

life's *like* that! belongs to the 1920s and 1930s, although it's still heard occasionally – hardly as a c.p. A Noël Coward sketch titled *Travelling Light*, written in 1924, ends thus:

> ATTENDANT: You rang, Madame?
> WOMAN: Shh! He's asleep.
> ATTENDANT: Very human, Madame. Life's like that.

lights of Piccadilly Circus shining out of his (or **your**) **arse-hole – he thinks he's (got)** (or **you think you've got**) **the**. A low c.p., dating since *c.* 1920, used mostly by the Services, and applied to someone's somewhat noticeable self-esteem. It adapts and elaborates the older and much more widely used *she thinks the sun shines out of his arse* or *arse-hole*, she regards him almost idolatrously: late C19–20, for certain, but perhaps dating since late C16, for it's the earthy sort of c.p. one could expect to have existed for centuries without getting into print or, at the least, into respectable print.

lights up! was, *c.* 1900–14, a playgoers' way of intimating their condemnation. (Ware.)

like a barber's cat – all wind and piss. See **like a snob's cat**....

like a fart in a windstorm. See **as much chance as a**....

like a one-armed paperhanger with crabs is a low c.p., descriptive of someone moving about restlessly: mostly Servicemen and ex-Servicemen: C20. The reference is to crab lice, which, infesting the pubic region and the arm pits cause intense itching. (An anonymous contributor, 14 January 1975.)

like a sheep's head – all jaw. Belonging to mid C18–20, although slightly obsolescent by *c.* 1935 and almost obsolete by *c.* 1970, it has been scathingly applied to an excessively talkative person. (Grose 1788.)

like a snob's cat – all piss and tantrums was a low c.p. of *c.* 1820–50. (JB.) This snob is a cobbler or shoemaker. Extant is *like a barber's cat – all wind and piss*, applied, late C19–20, to a man all talk and no performance.

like a spare prick at a wedding, often preceded by **standing about**. Unwanted, useless, idle, esp. with a hint of painfully embarrassed superfluity: low: since, at latest, 1920, when I first heard it, but probably dating since *c.* 1880 or 1890.

In Act I (p. 40 of the Faber edn) of John Osborne's *West of Suez*, produced and published in 1971, we find:

> EVANGIE: Besides, you do, at least, seem to enjoy everything...
> ROBERT: Instead of looking like a professional spare prick at a wedding.

like all fools I love everything that's good, late C17–20, occurs in, e.g., S, 1738, Dialogue I:

> LADY SM[ART]: ... Colonel, do you like this Bisket?
> COL[ONEL]: I'm like all fools, I love every thing that's good.

The *ODEP* classifies it as a proverb in the form. 'I am a fool: I love anything (*or* everything) that is good.'

like Aunt Fanny, often preceded by **you're**, is disparagingly addressed to someone either inexperienced or very clumsy with tools: workmen's: C20. Contrast **my Aunt Fanny!**

like Barney's bull is, esp. among Australians, a low c.p. of late C19–20, notably in the two combinations, *like Barney's bull – hitched, buggered and bewildered* and *like Barney's bull – (well) fucked and far from home*: these two 'addenda' sometimes stand by themselves.

Also cf **all behind – like Barney's bull**.

like hell I will! An intensive refusal. 'I certainly sha'n't!': since the middle 1940s. (A. B. Petch, 31 October 1974, says: 'Heard on and off.')

like Jack the Bear – just ain't nowhere. A US negroes' c.p. of *c.* 1930–50, indicating extreme disappointment or frustration or wounded vanity. (CM.)

like MacArthur I shall return. This mainly Australian c.p. dates from 1942 and denotes that 'one's absence will only be temporary, especially if it is suspected that one is trying to escape hard work'. It derives from General Douglas MacArthur's famous promise to the Filipinos 'to return and liberate them from the Japanese'. (Barry Prentice.)

like something the cat's brought in or, in Australia, **like something the cat brings in of a wet night**. Applied to one who looks utterly bedraggled or very disreputable: since *c.* 1920. Also **look what the cat's brought in!** As e.g., a young bird, rain-heavy.

like the butcher's daughter – dripping for it is self-explanatory in its application to a liquescent woman: perhaps mostly, yet far from being only, Australian: C20.

like the ladies of Barking Creek. Of women (esp. of girls still virgin) excusing themselves from intercourse on the grounds of having their period: since *c.* 1910; by 1920, also Australian. From the well-known limerick about the ladies of Barking Creek – who have their periods three times a week.

[**like the man said**. 'No particular man, any man. A throwaway introduction to a remark' (Vernon Noble, 9 December 1974): US: less of a c.p. than a cliché, it dates from the 1950s.]

like the man who fell out of the balloon: he wasn't in it refers to one who stood no chance whatsoever, as in an undertaking, an adventure, a boxing match, an athletic event: C20. (The *Humorist*, 28 July 1934.)

like the story of Pharaoh's daughter, who, you may recall, found the infant Moses in a basket: 'a well-known Australian c.p.', Barry Prentice tells me, of C20. For its dry scepticism, cf **you'll be telling me**....

like to bet on it? Are you absolutely sure it won't happen?: C20. (Wilfred Granville, 7 January 1969.) Probably elliptical for 'Are you so sure it won't happen that you'll bet on it?'

like Tom Trot's dog – he'd go a bit of the road with (Anglo-Irish **wid**) **anyone**. 'He's too easy-going, anxious to please, of no fixed principles' (Frank Shaw, November, 1968): Anglo-Irish: ?mid C19–20; then, by 1900 or a little earlier, also English. The *Trot* is not merely alliterative, but also allusive to such a phrase as *always on the trot*, restlessly active and busy.

lines like a butter-box, often preceded by **she has**, is a nautical c.p. that has, in latish C19–20, been applied to 'a clumsy, full-bodied ship' (Bowen). Since it refers mostly to sailing-ships, it became, c. 1930, obsolescent, and by c. 1950, obsolete.

lips hang in your light – **your**. See **your lips**....

listen (sometimes **look**) **who's talking!** is addressed derisively to one who, in the circumstances, really shouldn't be talking at all, esp. in such a censorious way: lower and lower-middle class: C20. (A. B. Petch, 4 January 1974.)

The US form is **look**..., vouched for by Colonel Albert Moe in letter dated 15 June 1975.

[**little bird told me** – **a**. A semi-proverbial c.p.: C18–20. It replies to the (not necessarily expressed) query, 'Who told you?' Rather more of a proverbial saying than of a c.p.]

little bit of all right – **a**, often with *little* omitted. Something excellent or unexpectedly pleasant; an attractive, esp. if compliant, female: late C19–20. (Manchon.) It occurs, e.g., in Freeman Wills Crofts, *Mystery in the Channel*, 1931: 'This looked a bit of all right.' In c. 1919–30, often Anglo-Frenchified to *a bit of tout droit*, itself from the bogus Fr. *un petit morceau de tout droit*.

little bullshit goes a long way – **a**. It pays to flatter – to boast – to 'con' people: Australian: since 1919. (Barry Prentice.)

little – **but, oh my!**; usually preceded by **he is** or **he was**. In *Mr Bonaparte of Corsica*, 1895, John Kendrick Bangs says, ' "Did you ever hear that little slang phrase so much in vogue in America," queried Napoleon, coldly fixing his eye on Barras – "a phrase which in French runs, '*Petit, mais O Moi*' – or, as they have it, 'Little, but O My'? Well, that is me." ' Apparently it was current in the US in the 1890s and early 1900s, for witness also Guy Wetmore Carryl, *Grimm Tales Made Easy*, 1902, in the poem titled 'How Hop O' My Thumb Got Rid of an Onus':

The youngest of the urchins heard,
And winked the other eye;
His height was only two feet three.
(I might remark, in passing, he
Was little, but O My!)
He added: 'I'd better keep mum.'
(He was foxy, was Hop O' My Thumb!)

The phrase travelled to Britain and to Australia; I heard it in the latter country in 1912 or 1913. Nor is it yet defunct.

What does need to be added is that this c.p. was mostly employed with a waggish imputation of sexual prowess and mischief.

[**little fields have big gates**. Is this a c.p., originally rural, or an unrecorded rural proverb of (?)C19–20? It refers to the fact that many small women bear many big children, the reason pretty clearly being that they possess an invincible vitality.]

[**little fish are sweet** is probably a proverb in the making: C20. (A. B. Petch, January 1974)]

little green men is a Canadian c.p., alluding to mysterious beings reported to have been seen emerging from flying saucers: since 1957. (Douglas Leechman.) Influenced by 'horror comics' with their pictures of little men from outer space.

little less off and a little more on – **a**, is the 'sarcastic injunction to a "dressing-room" star who is full of facetiousness and arrogance, but has no marked talent to justify the attitude' (Granville): theatrical: C20.

little of what you fancy does you good – **a**. In *Waiting in the Wings*, produced and published in 1960, Noël Coward has at Act III, Scene i:

MAY: Only a very little. (*He goes round filling glasses*.)
ALMINA: Oh no, I daren't, really I daren't.
PERRY: Come on – a little of what you fancy does you good. 'Marie Lloyd sang and winked as she sang it, and it was for long a c.p.' (Vernon Noble, 11 December 1973): C20 – and extant! Cf **it's naughty but it's nice**.

little old ladies in tennis shoes. This US c.p., says Professor John W. Clark on 22 October 1968, is applied to

bourgeois beldames – fussy, prim, self-important, naïve, ignorant, self-confident, self-righteous, gullible, conventional, conservative, old-fashioned, prudish, unfashionable, and typical rural or small-town. They wear tennis shoes because their feet hurt and they don't care how they look.

Apparently since c. 1920.

little rabbits have big ears. A C20 Australian warning to speak more quietly or less frankly in front of children. Partly a c.p., but partly also a mere modification of the proverb, *little pitchers have big ears*. (Barry Prentice.)

[**live and let live!** is a proverb or, at the least, a proverbial saying, *not* a c.p.]

LIVERPOOL CATCH PHRASES. On 25 October 1968, the late Frank Shaw wrote to me thus:

'**There's hair** [pronounced *durs ur*] **on baldy!**' – shouted derisively by Liverpool street girls c. 1924.

'**John Hughes won't save yer!**' – shouted after eligible-for-Service types c. 1917. A shopkeeper named John Hughes was alleged, in a court case, to have found ways of getting exemption from conscription for young men (often Irish) in his employ. Lasted, with origin forgotten, into the 1920s.

Buy a book (prounounced *bewk*), **Where's yer white stick?** (suggesting blindness), and other taunts to unpopular soccer refs, I quote in *Lern Yourself Scouse*. Used for decades to a defective kicker. **Here's yer bewk**. [i.e. Book of Rules.]

There he is – **wheel him in. There he is** – **bail him out**. The girls again won't let the boys alone. 1920–30? Or just *Bail him out* – shouted after any unpopular person.

A month later, Mr Shaw told me the Liverpool equivalent of **Bob's your uncle** has, since c. 1920, been **you're laffin bags**, where *bags* = 'very much'.

Note also **make yer name Walker** and **muck in! yer at your granny's**.

living bloody wonder – **a**. An Australian c.p. of ironic appreciation: since c. 1930. (Barry Prentice.)

living in seduced circumstances is a raffishly jocular c.p., applied to a pregnant unmarried girl or woman: since c. 1920.

living with mother now is addressed by females to a man either proposing or 'propositioning': 1881 – c. 1914. Ware noted that, originally, these words formed the refrain of a rather doubtful song.

load of old cobblers – **a**. See **that's a load**....

Lombard Street.... See **all Lombard Street**....

long and slender like a cat's elbow. A C18–mid C19 saying, midway between c.p. and proverb. (Fuller.)

long as a piece of string. often preceded by *as.* 'A teasing reply (mainly) to questions about length of time, e.g. "How long will you be?"' (Laurie Atkinson, late 1974.)

long nose is a lady's liking – a. A low c.p. of C19–early C20. In a male, a long nose is, in popular mythology, said to denote a long penis. Cf **large mouth....**

long short'uns or short long'uns? is an Australian c.p. addressed to a male wearing trousers that fail to cover his ankles: since *c.* 1930. (Barry Prentice.)

long-tailed bear – a, often preceded by **that's.** You're lying: not used in the more cultured circles: late C19–early C20. Ware gives, 'Bears have no tails.'

long time no see! I haven't seen you for ages: British and US: since the early 1900s. In British usage, it derives from Far East, specifically Chinese, pidgin; it came to Britain by way of the Merchant Service, reinforced by the Royal Navy; Wilfred Granville (5 November 1967) says that it is a 'China-side locution akin to such phrases as *no can do, chop chop, no wanchee,* etc. Naval officers used to greet "old ships" who'd been on China Station with "Hullo, old boy, long time no see."'

The US and Canadian use of the phrase probably comes from the same source but has been strongly influenced by two or three very widely distributed popular anecdotes. Dr Douglas Leechman (18 November 1967) writes: 'I first heard it about 1910.... Very common out here' (British Columbia). Berrey, 1942, lists it as a greeting. W & F gloss it as 'A common student and young adult greeting *c.* 1940–*c.* 1945'. but it's very much older than that; and in the British Commonwealth it is still going strong, as indeed it is in the US – witness the allusion in Jack D. Hunter, *Spies, Inc.,* 1970: '"Well, well, well," Carson beamed. "Long time no behold. How are you, Mr Fitch?"' Rather oddly, the oldest printed record I have of it is afforded by Harry C. Witwer's *Love and Learn,* 1924 (p. 73). Perhaps slightly on the wane since *c.* 1972. Nevertheless, this is one of the most widely used of all c.pp. whatsoever, despite the fact that many of us find it tiresome. Whence:

long time no see – short time buckshee (i.e. free): 'Services', Far East. Wishful thinking for a prostitute's greeting' (Paul Beale, 28 January 1975). Since *c.* 1950.

look! do me a favour, will you? – with *look!* or *will you?* or both often omitted; sometimes **look here....** Run away! Stop talking!: since the late 1940s. Basically equivalent to 'Please!', but it has several nuances – esp. minatory or expostulatory or derisive. as in Ngaio Marsh. *Clutch of Constables,* 1968:

'But your wife ——'
'Wife? Do me a favour! She's my mum!'

Cf Jack Ripley. *Davis Doesn't Live Here Any More,* 1971. '"Do me a favour." I snap. "Keep your nose out of my affairs."' And there are many examples in later novels.

It derives from and modifies and extends the sense and application of an underworld c.p. that, dating from the early 1940s, conveys a warning: *do yourself a favour.*

look – no hands! is often applied to something done cleverly, yet not conspicuously, if indeed at all, useful: since *c.* 1910. From the proud, showy claims of a child riding a bicycle

with no hands on the bars. A good example occurs in Lesley Storm's comedy. *Look, No Hands!* which opened at the Fortune Theatre. London, on 19 July 1971; and a significant allusion had occurred in Peter O'Donnell. *A Taste of Death,* 1969: 'This is vox-operated transmission ... the set automatically switches to send when ... and to receive when ... No hands.'

But perhaps the best example of all is the allusion in Terence Rattigan. *Variation on a Theme,* produced and published in 1958, at Act I. Scene ii. where Ron, a ballet dancer, rehearses teenaged Fiona, who's not very good, in a ballet routine.

He lifts her on to his shoulder with practised ease. Still giggling, she clutches first at his neck. Then she removes her hands precariously and waves her arms triumphantly in the air.

FIONA: No hands!

look on the wall and it will not bite you was. *c.* 1660–1914. addressed derisively to a person 'bitten with mustard' (Ray).

look (occasionally **see**) **what the cat's brought in!** See **like something the cat's brought in!**

look what the wind has – or **the wind's** – **blown in!** See **who's arrived!:** jocular: C20. Cf **like something the cat's brought in!**

look who's talking! See **listen who's talking!**

look you! is applied to Welshmen by all other nationals when they wish to allude to, or to impute or imply, any decidedly Welsh characteristic: C19–20. It is a Cymricism well known since C16 at latest; so much so that it occurs frequently in the plays by James Shirley (1596–1666). as. e.g.. in Act V. Scene iii. of *Love Tricks, or, The School of Compliment.* where Welshman Jenkin says. 'Hark you, is there another Selinas? Bless us awl, here is very prave Love-tricks, look you.'

look you there now! You surprise me! Colloquially: Well, I never!: late C17–mid C18. Sir John Vanbrugh, in *The Confederacy,* produced and published in 1705, at Act I. Scene i. where Mrs Cloggit, a woman of the people, uses it twice.

MRS AMLET: ... Would you believe it, Mrs Cloggit, I have worn out four pairs of pattens with following my old lady Youthful, for one pair of false teeth, and but three pots of paint.

MRS CLOGGIT: Look you there now!

looking for maidenheads is a c.p. directed at someone looking for something either unprocurable or, at the least, exceedingly scarce: since *c.* 1890; since WW2 becoming increasingly difficult to find, hence the phrase is now somewhat nostalgic and obsolescent.

looks as if he has lost a pound and found sixpence. See **he looks....**

looks good to me. elliptical for 'It *or* that looks good to me'. is American, dating since *c.* 1910 and mentioned in 'Straight Talk'. by S. R. Strait in the *Boston Globe* of *c.* 1917. (W. J. Burke.)

looks like a wet weekend. often preceded by **it.** This Australian c.p., dating since *c.* 1930, has been used both by girls menstruating at the weekend and, since *c.* 1940, addressed by males, most of them expectably teenaged, to a girl carrying a packet that, to judge by its size, may well contain a carton of tampons or sanitary pads.

looks (or **it looks**) **like rain** refers to the probability of an imminent arrest: US tramps': C20. (*U.*)

looks towards you. See **I looks....**

loss is (sometimes **was**) **ours – the.** In S. 1738. Dialogue II opens thus:

> LORD SM[ART]: I'm sorry I was not at home this Morning. when you all did us the Honour to call here. But I went to the Levee To-Day.
>
> LORD SP[ARKISH]: O. my Lord; I'm sure the Loss was ours.

This courteous c.p.. perhaps originally a witty convention. has survived from late C17 to the present.

lost a pound and found sixpence. See **looks as if he has....**

lost the key of the 'angar door. An RAF c.p. dating from the 1920s or the early 1930s. From a topicality explained in Flying Officer B. J. Hurren's *Stand Easy.* 1934.

lovely bit of boy – a. is a Servicewomen's c.p.. applied – since 1939 and esp. throughout WW2 – to a man of whom they physically approve. Cf the next two entries.

lovely grub! is another WW2 (and after) c.p.. meaning 'Very nice indeed!' and applied to anything – from tasty food (*grub*) to a furlough or any other agreeable experience. Contrast:

lower than a snake's hips (occasionally **belly**). Despicable: mostly Armed Forces': after 1939. Hence, since *c.* 1945, the shortened *lower than a snake* and. since *c.* 1947. *he'd* (or *he could*) *crawl under a snake's belly with a top hat on.* (Laurie Atkinson. 1959.)

[**luck to him! – bad** (or **good**). A pejorative or an approving c.p.. which can. on occasion. be meant either ironically or jocularly congratulatory: C19–20. On the borderline between c.p. and cliché. but rather the latter than the former.]

lucky one – aren't I the (but also **aren't you ...** and **isn't (s)he ...**). 'Congratulations, either sincere or sarcastically meant' (Paul Beale, 11 August 1975) – or, of course, ironic: although I heard it during the 1920s. I rather think that it didn't become very widely spread before the 1930s. 'Non-U'. Cf:

lucky you! – often **lucky old you! –** is. C20. used in admiration or in envy – or both. (A. B. Petch. 4 January 1974; Mrs Margaret Thomson. 29 January 1975.)

Lushington. See **Alderman Lushington.**

lying in bed barefoot. See **you must have been ....**

lyonch.... See **gone to lyonch.**

M.F.U. See the **snafu** group of WW2 military c.pp.

Macready pauses is, in theatrical circles, applied to an actor who, either on this one occasion or habitually, pauses too long after a telling speech or line or witticism: since c. 1855. William Macready (1793–1873), the great mid C19 actor, had a bad habit of pausing inordinately long in any dramatic or emphatic or unusually eloquent speech. (With thanks to the late Wilfred Granville.)

mademoiselle, I love you well (rhyme: *selle* – *well*) was in late Victorian and Edwardian times – say, rather, c. 1880–1914 – 'verse of courtly gallantry, which, however, continued: "Pray, let me kiss your toe"/"No, no, monsieur (pronounced m'seer)./My bum's too near/If you should stoop so low." Older ladies could quote the first two lines at parties' (Laurie Atkinson, late 1974).

Madras for health, Bengal for wealth. George Colman's *The Man of Business* performed and published in 1774, shows Tropick, a ship's husband back from India, and Fable, a businessman, after greeting each other, early in Act III talking thus:

FABLE: Excellent! – And his elder brother, that was placed at Madras, is he removed to Bengal yet, as he proposed?
TROP: He is, he is: but ——
FABLE: That's right: Madras for health, Bengal for wealth – that's the maxim there, you know. ['There' being India.]
TROP: Very true, very true; but ——.

Whence it appears that *Madras for health, Bengal for wealth* was a c.p. in the East India Company among the merchants and bankers dealing with the merchandise of India: c. 1740–1820.

Mafeking is (or **has been**) **relieved.** The former is an Australian c.p., in use among shift workers on being relieved and, vulgarly, among workmen, after defecation: C20. (Barry Prentice.) Norman Franklin, in March 1976, says that in 1940, he heard 'Buller, the relief of Ladysmith; cascara, the relief of Mrs Smith'; the reference being to the Boer War and to the laxative.

The latter is a British sarcastic reply to someone, 'usually a gossiping busybody who says "Have you heard the latest?"' He adds that, on 23 October 1969, he heard the shortened *the relief of Mafeking* employed by Jimmy Jewel in an episode of TV's 'Nearest and Dearest'. This reference to a highlight of the Boer War (1899–1902) implies 'That's stale news' – in the comic mode of the proverb 'Queen Anne's dead'.

make money of that! S, in Dialogue III, causes Miss to say, 'Well, but I was assured from a good Hand, that she lost at one Sitting, to the Tune of a hundred Guineas, make Money of that.' General sense: 'That's a lot of money' – 'That isn't chicken feed' – 'And that ain't hay'. Apparently late C17–18.

make no mistake! In Act III of Leonard Grover's US comedy, *Our Boarding House*, produced 1877, although not published until 1940, Colonel Elevator on several occasions uses this predominantly US c.p. as in, e.g.: 'Colonel M. T. Elevator is always the highest-toned gentleman, make no mistake' (and, make no mistake, 'M.T.' *is* a pun on 'empty'): since c. 1850.

make way for a naval officer! is a WW1 army c.p. which survived among ex-Servicemen right up to WW2. Cf **gangway for a naval officer!**

make way for Woolwich Arsenal! – often shortened to **Woolwich Arsenal!** – was, in WW1, applied by satirical, not unkindly, onlookers, to 'the Poor Bloody Infantry', more heavily laden than a Christmas tree – cf the slang *in Christmas-tree order*, in full marching order.

make yer name Walker! Run away! Go away. A Merseyside c.p., dating from the early 1920s. (Frank Shaw, November 1968.) Cf **my name's Walker** and **Walker, London**.

makes you see double and feel single is a US c.p., applied to strong drink: since c. 1925. (Berrey.)

makes you shit through the eye of a needle, with it understood and with **without splashing the sides** often added. A vulgar, originally and mostly Cockney, c.p. applied to any substance that causes diarrhoea: late C19–20.

makes you think, doesn't it (or – often jocularly – **makes you think, don't it?**) A humorous c.p., dating from the 1930s in the Armed Forces (H & P) but general since the 1920s, and, as *makes yer think, don't it?*, current among Cockneys much earlier – probably since the 1870s or 1880s. A late example occurs in Philip Gleife, *The Pinchbeck Masterpiece*, 1970: 'Then she looked at me, solemn and round-eyed like a beautiful owl. "Makes you think, don't it?" Her enunciation was still clear but she spoke slowly.' But a better example occurs in another novel published in the same year, John and Emert Bonett's *The Sound of Murder*. They describe the usual courtroom ghouls thus:

As he came level with the group, a shrill, grinding voice, redolent of malice and marital infelicity, was saying, 'And, mark you, *she* was in the flat when *'e* fell out of the winder.'

Her listeners nodded in venomous concert. 'Makes you *think*, don't it?' came the comment, and the vulture heads nodded again.

make yourself at our house! Make yourself at home: jocular: C20; by 1945, slightly – and by 1970, very – obsolescent.

making a trundle for a goose's eye. See **weaving**....

making dolls' eyes and **putting spots on dominoes** and the obsolete **putting holes in pikelets** (muffins or crumpets) are evasively pert answers to a query as to what one does for a living: C20.

making his (or **her**) **will** – he (or **she**) is; also **he's** (**she's**)....
Jocularly applied to one who is writing a letter or making notes or merely filling in a form: C20. (A. B. Petch, March 1966.)

Malley's cow is an Australian c.p., used of someone who has departed and left no indication of his present whereabouts. From a piece of Australian folklore. (Baker.)

malt's above the water – the. He is drunk: a semi-proverbial c.p. of *c.* 1670–1770. (Apperson.) Cf the equivalent proverbial *the malt is above wheat with him* of mid C16–early C19.

man about a dog. See *going to see* . . . .

man can't 'elp 'is feelings, can 'e? 'Proletarian: C19–20' (Laurie Atkinson, 18 July 1975): perhaps, rather, C18–20. Clichéd 'wisdom of the simple' (usually not so simple), not a c.p. Cf **it's only human nature, after all!**

man robbed himself – the. 'Someone in the house assisted the thieves' (Matsell): an ironic US c.p. of *c.* 1840–1900.

man the pumps! 'Bear a hand!' *or* 'Help! Help!': rather more general in the US than in the British Commonwealth: C20. Clearly from the literal nautical sense. (John W. Clark, 11 October 1968.)

man wasn't meant to sleep at home every night – a: 'Applied to men (as sex) credited with roving eye. [E.g. on p. 100 of] *God Stand up for Bastards.* [by] David Leitch, 1973' (Laurie Atkinson, late 1974): certainly since not later than *c.* 1910 and probably current since late C19.

man's gotta do what a man's gotta do – a. US: since *c.* 1945. As a piece of homespun philosophy, spoken 'straight', it is merely that: homespun philosophy. But when it is 'guyed' or 'sent up', it becomes a jocular c.p., sometimes applied to the most trivial occasions.

[**many a good tune played on an old fiddle**, usually preceded by **there's**. Rather a proverb than a c.p. The reference is sexual.]

many are called lies midway between allusive cliché and, when used playfully, genuine c.p.: C20. (Frank Shaw, November 1968.) Elliptical for the famous Biblical quotation, 'For many are called, but few are chosen' at St Matthew, xxii, 14.

Marines have landed – the, often completed by **and the situation is well in hand**: Help is coming *or* Help has arrived: US: C20. Cf Britain's **cavalry are coming** (or **are here**).

It has become so well known in the US that it can be – and often is – employed allusively, as in Clarence B. Kelland, *Speak Easily*, 1935:

I . . . gave her the number.

'Keep on being compromised until I get there,' she said, 'but let it go at that. The marines are about to land.'

The c.p. comes from the (in the US) famous quotation, 'The Marines have landed, and the situation is well in hand': commonly said to have been originated by Richard Harding Davis, in a cable sent from Panama in 1885. But Colonel Albert Moe, who had always been sceptical of this origination, went into the matter and discovered that 'Davis was in college in 1885. He had no connection with the landing at Guantanamo in 1898 (it was unopposed) – he was observing the Rough Riders at San Juan' (Letter of 30 June 1975).
Cf **the navy's here**.

[**mark my words!** is rather a cliché than a c.p.]

[**married but not churched**, late C19–20, is almost a c.p. Cf the next.]

married on the carpet and the banns up the chimney. Living together as if man and wife: C19–20; by 1930, somewhat obsolescent; by 1950, obsolete. Cf the preceding entry.

marry, come up, my dirty cousin! Addressed to one who affects an excessive modesty: mid C17–18; then dialectal. (Apperson.)

[**m'as tu vu?** 'A common French-Canadian expression used by one proud of his performance, and who hopes it was noticed. Such a one is often referred to as a *m'as-tu-vu?* [or 'Hast thou seen me?'] (Douglas Leechman, either in December 1968 or in January 1969). For the formation, cf the derivation of the Fr. (and English) *vasistas* from Ger. *was ist das?* – 'What is that?'.]

mashed the potatoes for the Last Supper – he (or **she**). This Canadian c.p. dates from *c.* 1940 and is used thus: '*Know* him? He helped me mash the potatoes for the Last Supper! Known him for years' (Douglas Leechman).

match me, big boy! A request for a match: since *c.* 1930: US become, *c.* 1940, also British. (Berrey.) Obsolescent by 1960, obsolete by 1970.

match! quoth Hatch (or **Jack** or **John**) **when he got his wife by the breech** (or **when he kissed his dame**) – **a**. This c.p., recorded by Ray and 'Proverbial' Fuller, was current *c.* 1660–1750. (Apperson.)

maturing in the wood. This jocular c.p., dating since *c.* 1950, is applied 'to men whose heads are full of ideas that never get any further than their heads' (A. B. Petch, April 1966). With a pun on liquor maturing in the cask – and a slyly humorous allusion to wooden heads.

may all your kids be acrobats! A theatrical 'trouper's expression of provocation' (Berrey): US world of entertainment: since *c.* 1920.

May bees don't fly now (or **all the year long**). Addressed to one who begins his sentences with 'It may be': the former, late C17–18; the latter, mid C18–20. The latter occurs in Grose, 1788; the former occurs in S. 1738, in the Dialogue I, thus:

MISS: May be there is, Colonel.

COL[ONEL]: But *May-bees* don't fly now, Miss.
Perhaps the commonest form is *May bees don't fly this month*. Not often heard since *c.* 1914, it is extant.

There is a pun on *maybe*, perhaps, and a *May bee*. The Scots form is *mayhes* – or *May-bees* – *are no aye honey-bees*. (Apperson.)

may he dance at his death! 'May he be hanged!' (Matsell): *c.* 1840–1914. That is, at the end of a rope.

may I die! is a C18 c.p. used either in vehement protestation or in vigorous asseveration. In Act I of Charles Macklin's lively *Love à la Mode*, produced 1759 but not published until 1782, Mordecai – concerning Sir Archy Macsarcasm – says,

The man indeed has something droll – something ridiculous in him . . . his strange inhuman laugh, his tremendous periwig, and his manners altogether, indeed, has something so caricaturely risible in it, that – ha, ha, ha! may I die, madam, if I don't always take him for a mountebank doctor at a Dutch fair.

may I have the touring rights? 'If anyone makes a good joke, or tells an original story, the hearer might say: 'I like that, it's good. May I have the touring rights?"'(Granville).

Jocular on the literal sense – 'the rights to tour a version of a London show': theatrical: C20.

may I never do an ill turn! A C18'c.p. of emphasis, as in Isaac Bickerstaffe, *Love in a Village*, 1763, at Act III, Scene i, where Sir William says: 'May I never do an ill turn if I knew what to make on't' and, later, 'And, may I never do an ill turn, but I am very glad to see you too.'

may I pee in your cap? (or **hat?**) is a North Country working men's c.p., addressed to someone taken short: C20; by 1975, obsolescent.

may you live all the days of your life! In Dialogue II of S, 1738, the Colonel, drinking to Miss Notable, says, '"Miss, your Health; may you live all the Days of your Life"' – which, not a mere, somewhat elementary jocularity, connotes 'Live fully, not merely exist!'

[**may your prick and your purse never fail you!** is half a toast, half a c.p., of C18–mid C19. James Dalton, *A Narrative*, 1728, has: 'They bid the Coachman drive on, and civilly saluted the Player, wishing *his —— and Purse might never fail him.*']

May your rabbits die! See **hope your rabbit** ....

me and you! is a US negroes' c.p. dating since *c.* 1950. One negro writer, CM, glosses it thus: 'Short for: "It's going to be me and you" – a way of saying, we're going to fight'; and another, Edith A. Farb, in a cyclostyled thesis, 1972: 'A challenge to fight: "there's just me and you, so let's fight".'

mean to do without 'em, usually preceded by I. Elliptical for ... *without women*, this c.p. was popularized on the music-halls by Arthur Roberts in 1882 and went out of use *c.* 1910. (Ware.)

medal showing! and **you're wearing your medal** (one button) – or **medals** (plural) – **today**. Addressed to a man whose fly is undone. with one or more buttons showing: mid C19–20. A jocular c.p. that was. at first. a euphemism.

men are interested in only one thing. (i.e. Sexual intercourse.) A cynical feminine c.p.. dating from *c.* 1920; or. rather. that was when I first heard it – but it probably goes back to *c.* 1880 or perhaps even earlier. And so are women. But neither sex to the extent the c.p. implies. Cf **it takes two to tango**.

men over forty don't double is a naval c.p. – 'a sneering remark addressed to a youngster with a tendency to skulking and slackness' (*Sailors' Slang*): C20.

meow-meow! See **miaouw-miaouw!**

Meredith, we're in! A c.p. uttered when one succeeds in getting into a place. e.g. a tea-shop. just before closing time: since *c.* 1910. It occurs in. for instance. C. F. Gregg. *Tragedy and Wembley*. 1936. Said to have come from a music-hall song. but. according to Frank Shaw (30 October 1968). from a music-hall sketch by Fred Kitchen.

message received loud and clear (often shortened to **message received**). I understand what you're getting at; I get the point – there's no need to go on and on about it!: since the middle 1940s. From the literal phrase much used by the Services. esp. the RAF, during WW2.

mew! mew! Tell that to the Marines!: tailors': *c.* 1860–1940. Contrast **miaouw! miaouw!**

miaouw! miaouw! has, since the early 1920s, been addressed either by a third party to two persons engaged in malicious gossip or by one party reproving another for such gossip. The remarks are *catty* and the claws are out. Indeed it was probably prompted by 'Don't be so *catty!*'

Also. since *c.* 1945. US. (W & F. who list it on p. 605. as *meow* (*-meow*).)

midshipmen have guts, ward-room officers have stomachs, and flag officers (have) palates is a naval c.p., dating since *c.* 1860; by 1965, obsolescent. (Bowen: *Sailors' Slang*.) Cf **horses sweat** ....

miles and miles and bloody miles of sweet fuck-all or. more politely. **of bugger all**. jocularly and ruefully describes either the African desert or the Canadian prairies: the former is a soldiers' description. WW1 and again in WW2; the latter a Canadian civilian description, since *c.* 1919. (The latter comes from Dr Douglas Leechman; the former from my own experience.)

Miles's boy is spotted. We know all about *that!*: addressed to anyone who, in a printing office, begins to spin a yarn: since *c.* 1830. From Miles. a Hampstead coach-boy. 'celebrated for his faculty of diverting the passengers with anecdotes and tales' (B & L). By 1970. obsolescent.

milk in the coconut. See **that accounts for the** ....

miller's waistcoat. See **stout** ....

mind boggles – the. A c.p. comment upon any marked absurdity: since the late 1950s but had been occasionally heard for at least a decade longer. 'Popularized. and possibly even originated. in the strip cartoon "The Perishers". written by Maurice Dodd and drawn by Dennis Collins, which has appeared in the *Daily Mirror* since the late 1950s' (Paul Beale, 11 December 1974). Nichol Fleming, *Hash*, 1971, has:

> 'I believe the old buffer was ... cashiered for some kind of behaviour unbecoming to an officer.'
> 'The mind boggles.'

mind how you go! A c.p.. common only since *c.* 1942. bearing the general meaning 'Look after – take care of – yourself'. and addressed also to someone either caught in traffic or slipping on. e.g.. a banana skin. or indeed to someone setting forth on a journey. e.g. to a distant country; hence. since *c.* 1945. also psychologically or morally. In V. C. Clinton-Baddeley. *To Study a Long Silence*. 1972. occurs this fragment of dialogue:

> 'Good night.' said Davies.
> 'Good night. guv.' said the bus conductor. 'Mind how you go.'

And it may have been originally a bus conductors' warning to passengers as they step off a bus.

The variant *watch how you go* has been common in the Services since *c.* 1935 and became general a decade later. although little used since the late 1960s.

mind my bike! 'A c.p. from a popular war-time radio programme; often heard at the time. but obsolete by 1950. Used simply for the sake of saying something' (Ramsey Spencer. 10 May 1969); the speaker was the actor and radio and TV star. Jack Warner. who used it in the show 'Garrison Theatre'. Aspic'd in amber by Stephen Potter in his *The Sense of Humour*. 1954.

mind the barrow! In *The Spanish Farm Trilogy*, 1924, R. H. Mottram wrote:

> Outside, the NCOs were 'falling-in' the men under the shelter of the embankment, in the gathering dusk. From without came a North-country voice growling: 'If A catches them, A'll slog 'em, bah gum!' and a Cockney: 'Mind the barrow, please! The Sergeant said I was to have my little spade, but 'e won't let me take my little pail....'

The Cockney catchword he had heard in the dusk had caught on, and all about him, shopmen and clerks, labourers, mill hands, miners were bellowing at the top of their voices, 'Mind the barrow, please!' as they skidded and waded, fell and died.

Apparently only during WW1 – and afterwards, for a while, among ex-Servicemen. (The quotation, I owe to Mr A. B. Petch.)

mind the Brussels! See – at **did you enjoy your trip?** – the note on *mind the Brussels*; and add these details. The phrase may go back beyond 1900. On 19 December 1974, Christopher Fry provided me with evidence that this c.p. was still current at that date, and commented thus: 'The humour of it, of course, is in giving a cheap floor-covering the grandeur of a Brussels carpet.'

mind the (or your) step! Look after yourself: the former addressed to a departing visitor, and dating from *c.* 1880, and recorded by Ware in 1909, soon developed a non-literal application, but obsolete by 1960; perhaps originally an admonition to a drunkard. The C20 *mind your step* has always been predominantly metaphorical and, by *c.* 1930, it had almost entirely ousted *the*. Cf **mind how you go!**

mind you – I've said nothing. Perhaps I shouldn't have said that, so don't quote me: Anglo-Irish: C20. This is the title of a book by Honor Tracy sub-titled 'Forays in the Irish Republic' and published in 1953.

mind your eye! Be careful: C18–20. The *OED* quotes a passage belonging to 1727. By 100 years or so later, it had become also US. In 1844, T. C. Haliburton, in *The Attaché* (one of the Sam Slick stories) in the 2nd Series, vol. I, p. 64, writes, '"Mind your eye" is the maxim you may depend, either with man or woman', and then, at p. 77, 'It's the language of natur', and the language of natur' is the voice of Providence. Dogs and children can learn it, and half the time know it better nor man; and one of the first lessons and plainest laws of natur' is, *" to mind the eye".'*

Cf **mind how you go!** and:

mind your helm! Take care!: nautical: C19–20. Cf the preceding entry.

mind your own interferences! Mind your own business!: jocular: since *c.* 1910 or perhaps four or five years earlier; by 1960, slightly obsolescent, and by 1970, virtually obsolete. Cf:

mind (occasionally **tend to** or **stick to**) **your own potatoes!** Mind your own business!: US: C20. (Berrey.)

mind your three S's! Bowen records this as a simple naval rule for promotion: Be *sober*, *silly* (simple – not offensively intelligent), *civil*: mid C19–20.

mind your worm – here comes a blackbird. Addressed to boys fishing with a line baited with a worm; but also, sexually, by a group of much older girls coming upon a group of young boys bathing naked: proletarian, esp. Londoners': late C19–20. It occurs in e.g. Alfred Draper, *Swansong for a Rare Bird* (1970, at chapter V).

mine's up! I've a 'cushy' job (e.g., administration rather than labour): among prisoners of war in the Far East during the years 1942–45. From '*I'm all right, Jack!*'

miraculous pitcher that holds water downwards – the is a conundrum c.p. ('What is the miraculous pitcher...?') – the answer being the female pudendum – of mid C18–19. (Grose, 1788.)

Miss Otis regrets has been turning up, over and over again, in my post-1934 reading of American novels, short stories, humorous sketches, light-hearted plays, clearly used as a catch phrase. I thought from a play or a film, but no! as since Christmas 1975 I've surmised, from a song. No less clearly, it never gained a very wide acceptance: not one of half a dozen well-educated and cultured Americans could tell me the source. Only a week ago, I went to the wonderful British Library catalogue of modern music: the *Miss...* volume had gone to the binders for repair: so I asked at the Enquiry Desk, and their 'musical expert' immediately said, 'It *may* have come from a play or a film; all *I* know is that it's the title of a song'. Then, yesterday morning, I was shown the score; the song begins, 'Miss Otis regrets she's unable to lunch today'. That score forms part of Messrs Chappell & Co's series, *Melodies Made Famous by the Years*, London, 1962. Forefronting the score itself was the information 'copyrighted 1934' – words and music by Cole Porter. The amiable fellow added, 'It has been revived by a "pop" singer.' The very next day – this morning in short, I received an air letter, dated 14 April 1976, from Dr Joseph T. Shipley, who, after confirming the British Library's information, reported thus, 'Written not for one of his musical comedies, but for the private entertainment of his friends. Monty Woolley (well-known play-director [and actor]) dressed up as a butler, and while Cole played the piano, Monty sang it. For a year or more, Monty delighted in dressing as a butler and singing the song at parties.

'The song was included in the "hit" film biography of Cole Porter, *Night and Day* [the title of one of the best-known of C.P.'s songs], 1946, and became widely known. [C.P., 1893–1964.]

'*Miss Otis regrets* was a humorous way of expressing one's distaste, or refusal to accept unwanted overtures, invitations, and the like.'

In other words, Dr Shipley implied that, as a c.p., it was obsolete. But is it? In a novel by Hugh Pentecost, *Girl Watcher's Funeral*, 1969 (US) and 1970 (Britain), occurs this passage:

> 'Good evening, Captain Pappas,' Pierre Chambrun said. He looked at what must have been my pea-green face and smiled. 'Miss Otis regrets –' he said.

I think that this c.p. has reached a state of advanced obsolescence, but that it lingers in the memories of all Cole Porter lovers and that the 'pop' singer's revival of it may considerably delay its passage to obsoleteness.

(Written during the early afternoon of 21 April 1976. I admit to a small, unsquashable self-congratulation on my persistence – call it obstinacy if you wish 'and see if I care'.)

And then, on 26 April, I received, from Miss Katherine Hartley of CBS News the information that the song was dedicated to Miss Elsa Maxwell, the famous columnist, and that it was sung publicly in England before it was thus treated in America – by the once well-known Douglas Byng in the revue *Hi Diddle Diddle*, 1934. On 28 April the aforementioned musical authority at the enquiry desk told me that this information about the British performance is included in the Modern Music Catalogue entry 'To coin a phrase' – such is life!

The song *was* originally a 'private' or party piece, but it was first sung publicly in the US in the same year as in London: 1934.

In America, it formed part of the musical comedy, *Anything Goes*. In Britain, by the way, *Hi Diddle Diddle* was performed at the Comedy Theatre on 3 October (1934).

Therefore **anything goes** should be American – dated 'at least as early as 1934, when the musical comedy so titled first appeared'.

mission accomplished. The job has been done; or, the purpose has been fulfilled. US, since 1942; adopted, although less generally, in Britain, 1944. Originally a military formula. Jean Potts, *An Affair of the Heart*, 1970, has, 'Mission accomplished, and very neatly too.'

Mister and Mrs Wood in front. It's a nearly empty house: theatrical: C20. Plenty of seats, few people. In *Showman Looks On*, 1945, C. B. Cochran (remember Mr Cochran's young ladies) has the variant *Wood family in front*. From the wooden seats or wooden parts thereof.

Mister Nash.... See **Nash is concerned.**

Mister Nonesuch. See **Non such ....**

Mister Palmer. See **Palmer is concerned.**

Mister to you! See **ne'er an M under your girdle?**

Mistress Kell(e)y .... See **you must know Mistress Kell(e)y.**

Mistress Kell(e)y – but in the form **Mrs Kell(e)y – won't let young Edward play with you** is a derogatory c.p. addressed to a child either ill-behaved or dirty: Australian: since *c.* 1925. The allusion is to bushranger Ned Kelly, as much a folk-hero in Australia as, say, Jesse James is in the US. (Barry Prentice.)

mix me a hike! Pay me off, *or* Give it to me: US tramps': since *c.* 1920. (See 'Dean Stiff's' *The Milk and Honey Route*, 1931.) This is the 'walking' sense of *hike*, noun and verb.

mixing the breed! is uttered by someone using another's hairbrush and comb or by another (whether owner or not) watching him: non-U, non-cultured, non-tactful: late C19–20.

mixture as before – the. Originally and still 'the same again' – a drinking c.p. in reply to 'What'll you have?' Hence applied to acceptance of the offer of anything already had; hence, 'the same old ingredients, the same old features, the same old programme as before – as, e.g., in an electoral campaign: since *c.* 1920, British and, since *c.* 1930, by adoption US ('Not common in this country,' says John W. Clark, 28 October 1968). Probably from the phrase used literally on a chemist's or druggist's bottle of, e.g., cough mixture.

molasses won't run down his legs is a US c.p., 'said of a lazy person' (Berrey): since *c.* 1920; by 1970, somewhat obsolescent.

money for jam or **old rope.** See **it's money for jam.**

money talks is a semi-proverb and a semi-c.p., but perhaps justifiably classified as a c.p. based on, or arising from, such adages as Torriano's 'Man prates, but gold speaks' in 1666. In 1915 P. G. Wodehouse wrote, 'The whole story took on a different complexion for John. Money talks' – cf also A. Palmer in *The Sphere*, 1925, 'Money talks.... So why not listen to it?' (Partly Apperson.)

Also cf the US c.p. extension, *money talks turkey even in Greece*, with a pun on *Turkey*, on *talk turkey*, to talk good, hard commonsense, and in the grease used in, or caused by cooking.

Monkey Brand, as Collinson remarks, is 'often applied derisively to an ugly face'. It derives from the well-known advertisement of a Lever Brothers' kitchen soap: a monkey gazing at itself in a frying-pan. As a c.p.: the 1920s–30s.

monkey on horseback.... See **who put that monkey....**

monkey see – monkey do! A Canadian and US c.p. 'addressed to one who imitates the actions of another, or as warning not to do such and such because someone (usually a child) might follow suit' (Douglas Leechman): since *c.* 1925. By *c.* 1950, also English, but, according to Paul Beale in a letter dated 11 December 1974, rather to describe the learning of a process, which, although performed thereafter with reasonable competence, is never actually understood. 'They're trying to teach us computer programming. I can write it out OK, but really it's "monkey see, monkey do": I haven't a clue what's actually happening inside the bloody machine or what I'm really doing it for.'

Mons – gassed at and **on the wire at Mons** are WW1 soldiers' replies to enquiries about someone's whereabouts: both 1916–18. There was, of course, no gas used at Mons; nor, come to that, any barbed-wire entanglements during the Retreat from Mons. F & G record the latter, B & P both. Cf the more general **hanging on the (old) barbed wire.**

[**moon ....** See **it is a fine moon ....**]

more beef! A c.p. cry for the help of one or two more men when a heavy load or a very hard task demands it: Canadian: since *c.* 1910. (Douglas Leechman.)

more curtains! 'Shouted by leary Cockney girls when a person clad in an evening frock passes by' (Julian Franklyn, Feburary 1939): since *c.* 1910; by 1950, obsolescent, and by 1970, obsolete.

more dirt, the less hurt. In *Handley Cross; or, Mr Jorrock's Hunt*, 2 vols, 1854, in the chapter entitled 'Another Sporting Lector' (lecture), during a disquisition on the c.pp. of the sporting set at that time, the jovial lecturer tells us that '"More dirt the less hurt!" is a pleasant piece o' consolation for a friend with a mud mask' (from a fall on the hunting field). A year earlier, in chapter XXIII ('The Great Run') of *Mr Sponge's Sporting Tour*, 1853, occurs this brief exchange:

'You're not hurt. I hope?' exclaimed Mr Puffington....

'Oh no!' replied Sponge. 'Oh no – fell soft – fell soft. More dirt less hurt – more dirt, less hurt.'

This is a C19 fox-hunting c.p.

more firma, the less terra – the. 'A c.p. used by those who distrust air travel' (Barry Prentice): mostly Australian: since *c.* 1950. A pun on *terra firma*, land as opposed to sea, and on *terra*, land, and *terror*.

more hair on your chest! See **that'll grow more hair on your chest!**

more hair there than anywhere. Itself a c.p.. it evokes the c.p. response. **on a cat's back.** but the implication is 'around a girl's pudendum': mostly Canadian: since the late 1940s.

more holy than righteous is a domestic c.p.. dating from late (?mid) C19 and applied to a very *holey* pair of socks – socks rather than stockings; nor is the phrase solely feminine. Not much used since *c.* 1960.

more in anger than in sorrow is a 'cynical. or humorously grim. reversal' of the cliché *more in sorrow than in anger*: US: since *c.* 1950. In a letter of mid-March 1975. John W. Clark notes also the 'closely parallel reversal. "Mother is not hurt; she is just frightfully. frightfully angry."'

more kid in him than a goat in the family way. Incurably addicted to 'kidding': Australian: since *c.* 1930. (Baker. 1959.)

more money than I could poke a stick at. See **has more money** ....

more power to your elbow! expresses encouragement: late (?mid) C19–20. Anglo-Irish in origin. it is both British and US: recorded by M.

more R than F was. *c.* 1860–1910. a c.p. directed at someone more rogue than fool; esp. at a servant appearing much more foolish than he is.

more than somewhat. literally 'more than rather much'. seems to have. *c.* 1925. become a US c.p. – meaning 'very much' or 'decidedly' – as a result of Damon Runyon's frequent and effective use of it. during the 1920s and early 1930s. in his newspaper columns; and to have become an English c.p. in 1932, from its occurrences in the book that made him internationally famous in 1932. *Guys and Dolls.* as. e.g.. in 'Social Error': '[Handsome Jack] is sored up more than somewhat when he finds Miss Harriet Mackle does not give him much of a tumble.' And in 'Butch Minds the Baby': 'I am now more nervous than somewhat.' And in 'Romance in the Roaring Forties': 'Dave somehow thinks more than somewhat of his dolls.' The impact was reinforced by Runyon's *More than Somewhat*. 1937. but the war of 1939–45. esp. America's entry in December 1942. deadened the impact; yet the c.p. was. in (say) 1950. no more than moribund; by 1955. however. it was generally regarded as an antique.

more than that! This lower-deck naval c.p.. dating from *c.* 1930. emphasizes that one's job or pay or whatever exceeds anything that can be opposed to it. In short. 'a fabulous amount'. says Granville. who. in a letter. cites a derivative in 'Some lovely dames at the dance last night. lusher than that'.

[**more there's in it, the more there's on it – the.** In the Dialogue II of S. 1738. occurs this example:
NE[VEROUT]: Why then. here's some Dirt in my Tea-Cup.
MISS: Come. come; the more there's in't. the more there's on't.
A 'lost' saying. of which the sense is obscure. Perhaps it is a proverb. perhaps a c.p.]

more war! was. seemingly in 1898 only. or maybe for a year or so longer. a Cockney c.p. applied to a quarrel. esp. among women. Ware says that it referred to the Spanish-American War.

more wind in your jib! Used by the sailors in a ship in foul wind on meeting a ship in a fair wind: mid C19–early 1920.

The wishers' ship hopes that thus she will gain a fair wind. (Bowen.)

morning after the night before – the. is applied to the effects of a drinking-bout or to the person showing those effects: C20. Very common in Australia; almost equally common elsewhere.

Moss. See as Moss ....

mother, is it worth it? A 'women's c.p.. when anything goes wrong. particularly sex-wise. From the agonies of childbirth. Used ironically of things that go wrong in domestic life' (Wilfred Granville in a letter): C20. And cf **oh mother** ....

mother of that was a whisker – the. That's a most improbable story!: *c.* 1850–1900. Cf the mainly dialectal synonymous *the dam of that was a whisker.* which was. however. applied to a big lie.

mouth is full of pap – his. Applied to one who is still childish: mid C18–early C19 (Grose. 1788). *Pap.* babies' food.

Mr .... See **Mister** .... **Mrs** .... See **Mistress** ....

much wit as three folk – as. See **as much wit** ....

muck in! yer at yer granny's. You're welcome: Liverpool: C20. From. of course. the literal sense: 'Eat up after all. you're at your grandmother's'. (Frank Shaw. 1 April 1969.)

muckhill on my trencher. See **you make a muckhill** ....

Mudros. Chios – and chaos was a 1915 Services' c.p.. satirizing the fact that the Mediterranean Expeditionary Force at that time had three separate authorities (or commands) and bases. Mudros and Chios were Gr. islands not very far from the Turkish coast (and Gallipoli).

mum, me bum's numb is a c.p. originally *c.* 1910 North Country. but by 1920 very widely distributed. It humorously alludes both to childish frankness and to dialectal pronunciation.

[**mum's the word!** Don't say a word. keep it secret!: this borderlines cliché and c.p. and is. I think. rather the former than the latter. Originally. a literal warning.]

murder is out – the. The mystery has been solved: C20; by 1970. obsolescent. From the proverbial *murder will out.*

'murder!' she cried was. *c.* 1910–30. the c.p. of any girl luckless enough. at a dance. to encounter a clumsy. heavy-footed. partner.

music as a wheelbarrow – as good. See **you make as good** ....

music's paid – the. 'The Watch-word among Highway-men. to let the Company they were to rob. alone. in return for some Courtesy' (BE): late C17–early C19. From the harp on the reverse of an Irish farthing or halfpenny.

[**must be hurt for certain, for you see her** (or **his**) **head is all of a lump.** usually preceded by (**he or**) **she.** as in S. 1738. It may be an ostensibly callous c.p.. but is more probably an integral part of a normal conversation. The words are spoken. of Miss Notable. by the gallant old colonel.]

must have been drinking out of a damp glass (or **mug** or **pot**). usually preceded by **you** or **he.** A jocular c.p. either addressed or referring to someone who has caught a cold or is afflicted with rheumatism: C20.

must have worms – he (or **she**). is applied to a fidgety. restless child: mid C19–20. (A. B. Petch. 9 January 1974.)

must I spell it out for you? See **spell it out for you?**

[*must* **is for the King**. S, 1738, near the beginning has:
COL[ONEL]: *Tom*, you must go with us to Lady *Smart*'s to Breakfast.
NEV[EROUT]: Must! why Colonel, *Must* is for the King.
Only kings have the right and the privilege to be so peremptory. C17–18 as a c.p., rather longer as a proverb. (*ODEP.*)]

must you put in your two cents' worth? See **two cents' worth.**

must you stay? can't you go? appeared in *Punch* on 18 January 1905 and has certainly been a c.p. ever since. 'Referring to the prolonged stay of the Russian Admiral Rodjestvensky, at Madagascar on his way to meet the Japanese Fleet' (Benham). But I suspect that this caption merely exemplifies a c.p. that had existed from a few years earlier: and *ODQ* has a record of it as having been used before 1897. the year in which its originator. schoolmaster Charles John Vaughan. died: it was his customary speeding-up of departure to boys 'too shy to go' after a 'guest' breakfast. although in the form 'Can't you go? Must you stay?' – as recorded by G. W. E. Russell in *Collections and Recollections*, 1898, 2nd Series, 1895.

mutton dressed (or **dressed up) as lamb** has, since latish C19, been directed at middle-aged and elderly women dressing in an unbecomingly youthful fashion. Drawn from the terminology of the butcher's shop.

my answer's in the infirmary. See **infirmary....**

my arse and your face. See **yes, my arse ....**

my arse is dragging. I can hardly walk; indeed. I'm completely exhausted: Canadian: since *c.* 1915. (Douglas Leechman.)

my Aunt Fanny! expresses incredulity: C20. Contrast **like Aunt Fanny!**

my belly button's playing hell with my backbone. I'm damned hungry: mostly lower-middle class: C20. Cf **my guts ...** and **my stomach ...** and:

my belly thinks my throat is cut. See **my stomach ....**

my brother from Gozo. See **just the job for....**

my eye and Betty Martin. See **all my eye and ....**

my feet are killing me. A mostly feminine c.p., dating since *c.* 1890 in Britain, it became, *c.* 1900, also US: it occurs in, e.g. Damon Runyon, *Take It Easy*, 1938. The dictionaries of (British) English language and quotations are singularly reticent about this phrase, but at least we may compare the c.p. **how's your poor feet?**
In the title story of Noël Coward's *Pretty Polly Barlow*. 1964, a British sailor speaks up for one of his four parrots: '"Gladys don't swear," said the giant defensively. "She only says 'Action Stations' and 'My feet are killing me'."' As so often, Noël Coward supplies a very neat example.

my friend (or **little friend) has come.** See **friend has come....**

my gate's shut. See **gate's shut.**

my goodness is coming out. In Dialogue I of S. 1738, occurs this passage:
[*Miss feels a Pimple on her Face.*]
MISS: Lord, I think my Goodness is coming out: Madam, will your Ladyship please to lend me a Patch?
She implies that she is pimply – or more precisely, pimply *because* she is chaste.

This c.p. was. I think. current throughout C18–19 and early C20; I first heard it just before WW1 but have not heard it since WW2.

my guts begin (or **are beginning) to think my throat's cut** is a (low) c.p. of *c.* 1750–1914. (See esp. *DSUE* at p. 363.) The predominant C20 form is, among men. *my belly thinks...* and, among women and 'old women'. *my stomach.....* q.v.

my heart bleeds for you. Despite its 'My withers are wrung' overtone, it is often ironic – often bitterly so: since the late 1940s. 'Probably by a wincing reaction against that gushing sympathy which is insincere and, indeed, hypocritical – and wouldn't part with a penny. A variant c.p., more US than British, is *I weep for you*' (*DSUE*). In *Samantha*, 1968 (British edn), E. V. Cunningham makes his very likable Japanese detective say to his chief: '"With all respects to my esteemed boss ... I am aware of his financial difficulties. My heart bleeds for the poverty of those who guard the wealthiest city in the world."' In the same novel occurs the further variant. *you're breaking my heart.*

my hero! is. Wilfred Granville told me. in a letter dated 11 March 1964. a c.p. 'that greets a diver who breaks surface with small green crabs or perfectly useless fish. such as wrasse': since the late 1950s. It probably derives from the ironic use of the phrase by girls satirizing the mushier sort of film. Cf this passage in P. G. Wodehouse's *Aunts Aren't Gentlemen*. 1975. in which the immortal Bertie Wooster offers to do something brave for his hard-bitten. sharp-tongued. bullying Aunt Dahlia:
'It will merely be one more grave among the bulls. What did you say?'
'Just "My Hero",' said the aged relative.

my life. The unnamed witty author of 'Complete Vocabulary of Spoken English' in *Punch*. 10 October 1973, has this entry: 'My life = *I am about to tell a Jewish joke*': since the late 1960s, when Yiddish humour, slang. c.pp. began to hit the Gentile headlines.

my lips are sealed. A statement made, more than once, by Prime Minister Stanley Baldwin during the abdication days of late 1936–early 1937; upon King Edward VIII's abdication, feeling ran high for a period of some months. The first such statement was: 'My lips are sealed. I am bound to keep silence.'
Occasionally it is impossible to distinguish between overworked quotation – outright cliché – and polite c.p. But in its wider application, this is a genuine c.p.; that is, when it substitutes for 'I'd rather not say' or 'I shan't answer *that* one', uttered with a smile that does duty for 'if you don't mind' or 'with respect': usually humorous or wryly ironic or both.

my long-lost che-ild. 'Theatrical rant is commonly burlesqued by such phrases as "my long lost che-ild" (Collinson): *c.* 1890–1914. Like **dead and she never called me mother.** it satirized the Surrey-side or Transpontine melodrama of *c.* 1860–1914.

my mother sews too. 'Heard on 21 February 1969. First pupil: "So?" [= so what?] Second pupil: "*My* mother sews too."' (Mr D. J. Barr, schoolmaster): Canadian schools' punning retort to someone saying *So?*: since *c.* 1965. But I suspect that it has a far wider distribution and that it goes back to late C19 – if not, indeed, to C17.

my mother told me there'd be days like this, but she didn't say there'd be so many. Applied to a 'tough' time. esp. in the army: Canadian soldiers': 1939–45. An oblique reference to menstruation. (Douglas Leechman.)

my name is Benjamin Brown, Ben Brown. 'Bend down, a formula pleasantry when there is no inspiration and meant to be outrageous. but is merely tedious' (a correspondent): since c. 1950 – perhaps much earlier.

my name is Haines! Farmer writes: 'A slang intimation of an intention to depart quickly.... This expression is similar in character to "There's the door, and your *name* is Walker!" It is said to have originated in an incident in the life of President Jefferson.' Therefore C19. Cf **my name's Walker!**
This US c.p. has been recorded earlier in V.

my name is Twyford. I know nothing about it: semi-proverbial c.p. of c. 1680–1830. Used by Peter Motteux in 1694 in his completion of Urquhart's translation of Rabelais and recorded by 'Proverbs' Fuller in 1732 and referred to by Charles Whibley in his essay on Rabelais: all cited by Apperson. In the *New Statesman* of 20 February 1937. David Garnett writes: 'Josiah Twyford. 1640–1729, learned a secret process in the manufacture of glaze by persistently feigning stupidity and was thus ... able to lay the foundation of the famous firm of sanitary potters.' So apparently not *all* 'don't-knows' are stupid.

my name is 'Unt not cunt. I'm nobody's fool or dupe: mostly RAF: since the middle 1940s. An elaboration of the slangy *Joe Hunt*. that man who, in the Services, gets all the dirty work.

my name's Simpson – not Samson is a workmen's c.p., uttered when one is confronted by work too heavy for one person: C20. It was either originated by some humorist named *Simpson* or derived from a scabrously witty limerick concerning a young woman named Ransom.

my name's Walker! I'm off: mid C19–20; by 1975, obsolescent. Cf the variant noted at **my name is Haines.** There are several explanations about the origin of *Walker*; my favourite is that it's merely a pun on *walker*, one who walks, hence esp. one who walks off.

my nose itches is a C18–20 invitation to kiss. the dovetailed reply being as in S. 'I knew I should drink wine. or kiss a fool'; or, C18–20. 'I knew I would shake hands with a fool'; or. in C19–20. 'I knew I was going to sneeze *or* to be cursed. *or* kissed. by a fool'. But by c. 1945, obsolescent.

my oath, Miss Weston! On my honour *or* Cross my heart!: naval (lower-deck): C20. but little used after the 1930s. 'An expression originating in the lifetime of Dame Agnes Weston. the widely known and honoured foundress of hostels for bluejackets at the naval ports, in connection with temperance pledges' (F & G). Noted by John Laffin in his *Jack Tar*. 1969.

my part! Ironic for '*I* should worry!': since c. 1926. Perhaps elliptical for 'It's *not* my part – share – duty – to look after that'.

my rents are coming in. 'I have torn my Pettycoat with your odious romping; my Rents are coming in; I'm afraid I shall fall into the Ragman's Hands': thus exclaims Miss Notable in Dialogue I of S: C18. Puns on rents in one's clothing and the old-clothes-man.

[**my son the doctor.** John W. Clark has, in a letter of mid-March 1975. suggested that this phrase originated as a cliché. based on Yiddish and first used by proud Jewish mothers. but is now used by others; and that it has come to be employed humorously and derisively and. by being so used. has taken on the status of a c.p., with the users' full knowledge that it originated as a cliché. I'm not entirely convinced. but I'm perhaps being a foolish 'doubting Thomas', for John Clark very, very seldom errs in such delicate discriminations.]

my stomach thinks my throat is cut. 'I have the very devil of an appetite' or 'I'm perishing of hunger': a semi-proverbial c.p.: C16–20. Recorded as early as 1540 by Palsgrave. (Apperson.) In late C19–20. mainly rural. Two frequent variants are **my belly thinks my throat is cut.** C18–20, and **my guts ...,** c. 1750–1914.

my troubles! is the Australian version of '*I* should worry!': since c. 1910. (Baker.) Cf **my part!** Perhaps elliptical for 'That's not one of my troubles'.

my watch runs upon wheels was a c.p. of very late C17–late C18. In S. near the end of the Dialogue I. we find:
COL[ONEL]: Pray. my Lord; what's a Clock by your Oracle? [What time is it?]
LORD SP[ARKISH]: Faith, I can't tell; I think my Watch runs upon Wheels.

my wife (less commonly. **husband) doesn't understand me** is used repeatedly by men – or women – seeking sympathy and. sooner or later, sexual relations outside marriage: probably almost immemorial. both in Britain and in the US.
What are *they* complaining about? It would be damned awkward for the speakers if they *were* understood!

my word – if I catch you bending! In the London streets of c. 1895–1914. it was a semi-sexual c.p.; but then it became much more general in use and bore an additional meaning – 'The answer is, "I'll saw your leg off" (all from a song)', as Julian Franklyn once phrased it: a humorous threat. Cf the next – by which it was. I'd say. prompted.

my word – if you're not off! is a c.p. of either dismissal or deterrence and was current c. 1890–1914; during its last four or five years. it was, like the c.p. preceding this. often augmented thus: *if you're not off. I'll saw your leg off.*

N.A.B.U. See **T.A.B.U.**

N.B.G. No bloody good: C20. This affords a useful example of that phenomenon whereby, although the full phrase has not achieved the status of c.p., the abbreviation has done so.

N.C.D. See **no can do**.

name and the game – the. See **if I have the name....**

name is mud. See **and his name ....**

name of the game – the. implies 'the precise meaning of which is——' and 'not to beat about the bush, the word is——': originally American. but not at all general before c. 1965; Dr Douglas Leechman in late 1968 glossed its Canadian usage thus: 'The name of the game is murder – for instance. Very recent.' It did not become British until 1973. In American fiction. I have noticed that Stanley Elliot uses it in *Stronghold*. 1974. In the *Daily Telegraph*. 7 August 1975. David Holloway. reviewing Edwin Newman's *Strictly Speaking*. says. 'Mr Newman protests properly about the use of "the name of the game"'; and. one day earlier. Paul Beale had written. 'I feel that it's a newish c.p.. probably originating in sports journalism. It annoys me because it's one of the smug and "knowing" ones.'

The particular sense noted above has widened to 'the predominant factor – the true purpose, the plan, the crux' and various nuances thereof, e.g. 'what is really, not what is apparently, happening'.

Cf **that's the name of the game**.

name your poison! What are you drinking?: 'a dated (?25 years ago) invitation'. says Paul Beale. Dated. certainly! By 1977. virtually obsolete. British. it goes back. however. to the 1920s. Note also:

name yours! and **give it a name!** What'll you drink? (Water is honourably excluded.) Both: late C19–20; but rare after 1940. (See Lyell. a too little known book. published in the Far East.)

Talking of *what'll* .... when I was a post-graduate at Oxford in 1921–3. my College had a small drinking club. which called itself 'the *What'lling* Club'.

Napoleon's greeting to his troops – Good morning. troops. John Brophy. in 'Chants and Sayings'. Appendix A of B & P. 1930. says: 'The headlong descent from the heroic strain was another form of stock humour. As. imitating a reciter's announcement of the title of his "piece":

Napoleon's Greeting to his Troops –
"Good morning. troops."'

The c.p. apparently dates from late C19 and became obsolete c. 1940.

napoo finee. No more – finished!: army: 1914–18. A tautological elaboration of *napoo*. nothing more. no more. and *finee*. finished: Fr. *il n'y en a plus. fini*. literally 'there's no more of it. finished'. The British soldier dealt no less heroically with foreign languages than he did with the enemy.

Of *napoo*. B & P write: 'The word came to be used for all the destructions. obliterations and disappointments of war. e.g. "The bread's napoo"; "The S.M.'s [Sergeant-Major's] napoo"; "Napoo rum".'

napping – as Moss caught his mare. See **as Moss....**

Nash (usually **Mr Nash**) **is concerned** was an underworld c.p. of late C18–mid C19 and it meant that So-and-So had departed. or. as Vaux. professional criminal sent to Australia for his country's good. wrote as an exiled convict 'Speaking of a person who is gone. they [his underworld companions] say. he is nashed.' Here. *Nash* or *nash* derives from the Romany *nash. nasher*. to run.

natives are restless (to-night) – the. See the second paragraph of:

natives were hostile – the; occasionally **are** for **were**. and **pretty** (or if the flak had been very heavy and severe. **bloody) hostile** for the unmodified **hostile**. 'Anti-aircraft fire was heavy': RAF aircrews. reporting a raid over Germany: 1940–5. (PGR.) A characteristic meiosis, based on 'The natives were hostile', occurring so frequently in books of travel and exploration. esp. of Africa. The c.p. passed. c. 1945. into civilian and general use. Cf John Mortimer's moving play. *The Judge*. 1967, at Act II, Scene viii.:

SERENA: You did that to me! Picked me up out of the cold hotel ... and dumped me into *this!*
JUDGE: To make it up to you.
SERENA: This outpost! This desert! This frontier! Alone! With the natives hostile!

Since c. 1945. there has been a derivative variant: *the natives are restless*. often with *tonight* added. This c.p. vaguely alludes to the unrest of the emergent African and Asian peoples. but is also used in reference to unfriendly audiences. whether of theatre or vaudeville. of radio or TV – or of political gatherings. It has spread to the US. In John Crosby. *The White Telephone*. 1974. we see: 'He [a not entirely apocryphal President] picked up the phone. "The natives are getting restless," said Miss Doll' [about some second-echelon Federal men].

Perhaps from the restless natives of the North-West Frontier of India during British rule; perhaps. too. it owes something to Rudyard Kipling's tales of India.

navy's here – the. ' – and all is well. for we've been rescued'. This became a c.p. almost immediately after the press and radio reported the freeing of 299 British seamen from the Ger. supply ship *Altmark* in Jossing Fjord. Norway. by the Royal Navy's destroyer *Cossack*. whose boarding party was led by Lieutenant Bradwell Turner. who shouted these reassuring words to the prisoners. The *Cossack* was commanded by the intrepid Philip Vian. who described the incident in his stirring memoirs. *Action This Day*. and who died with the rank of Sir Philip Vian. Admiral of the Fleet.

Cf **Marines have landed.**

nay, nay, Pauline! In Act III of *Father and the Boys* (A Comedy-Drama), 1924, the inimitable George Ade has:

LEMUEL [the father]: What's the kick? Everybody told me, 'Take a vacation – circulate – have some fun – cut loose –.' ... I've got out and cut loose – and now you're trying to head me off. Nay, nay, Pauline!

General sense: 'certainly not!' or 'nothing doing!' In 1946, Peter Tamony traced *Nay, Nay, Pauline* to J. S. Wood's *Yale Yarns*, 1895; and HLM, Supp. 2, lists it among US c.pp. derived from songs.

Cf **not to-night, Josephine**, which may, I suspect, have prompted the US song and saying.

'nay, nay!' quoth Stringer, when his neck was in the halter was, *c.* 1660–1750, a semi-proverbial c.p., applied to one speaking too late. It occurs in Ray's and Fuller's books of proverbs and has been included in Apperson.

Probably from a topical instance, perhaps of an innocent man, but possibly suggested by to *string up*, to hang someone.

near enough is good enough has, since *c.* 1945, been an Australian c.p. 'applied to a very common attitude' (Barry Prentice, *c* 6 March 1975). This might easily become a proverb.

near the foreman, near the door is a tailors' c.p., dating from *c.* 1850 and implying that it is best to keep as far away from the foreman as possible; by 1940, virtually obsolete. (B & L.)

neat but not gaudy, originally serious, and Standard English, *c.* 1800 took an ironical turn and had, by 1838, when Ruskin, in the *Architectural Magazine* for November, could write, 'That admiration of the "neat but not gaudy", which is commonly reported to have influenced the devil when he painted his tail pea green' (Apperson) become a c.p. A variant by elaboration, current by 1860, is *neat, but not gaudy, as the monkey said, when he painted his tail sky-blue*, with the final clause often omitted. (F & H.) A further variant is *neat but not gaudy, as the monkey said when he painted his bottom pink and tied up his tail with pea-green*, not much used after *c.* 1900, but in the latter half of C19 was often applied to old ladies – and to some not so old – dressed flamboyantly. A C20 variant, rare after *c.* 1960 and obsolete by 1970, is *neat but not gaudy, chic but not bizarre*.

But this note merely touches the surface of a c.p. that merits an article or even an essay.

neck as long as my arm .... See **I'll first see thy neck** ....

Ned Kelly was hung – literately **hanged – for less**. This Australian c.p., a mildly jocular reproof or complaint (e.g., of excessive taxation), has been current since the 1930s, as Barry Prentice tells me. The reference is to the famous bushranger, who has become something of a hero to many Australians.

ne'er an M under your girdle? Have you no manners? – *esp.*, Haven't you the politeness to say 'Master' (or 'Mistress' or 'Miss'): *c.* 1540–1850. Apperson cites Udall's comedy, *Ralph Roister Doister*, Swift, and Scott. In the Dialogue I of S. we read:

NEV[EROUT]: Come then, Miss, e'en make a Die of it; and then we shall have a burying of our own.

MISS: The Devil take you, *Neverout*, besides all small Curses.

LADY ANSW[ERALL]: Marry come up: What, plain *Neverout*, methinks you might have an M under your Girdle, Miss. Cf the C20 '*Mister* to you!'

ne'er stir! See **never stir!**

Nellie's room. See **Annie's room** ....

never a dull moment! This naval c.p., dating since 1939, is used ironically in moments of excitement or danger, but also in moments of personal, incidental, stress, as when one's leave has been cancelled for some usually unexplained reason. From *c.* 1945 onwards, it has been widely used among civilians too – usually on much less exciting or dangerous occasions.

never be rude to the stage carpenter – he might be your manager next week. In a letter dated 19 February 1968, William Granville says:

Dating from the fit-up times [the period of the portable theatres], when the carpenter seemed to be the only one with any money and could be relied upon to weigh in with a few quid when the company was at dry-up (closure stage) point for lack of funds.

c. 1880–1920.

[**never change a winning team**, like **never change a winning game**, is a sporting cliché.]

[**never explain and never apologize**, the maxim of the Royal Navy's officers, is said to have been originated and 'promoted' by Admiral 'Jacky' Fisher: C20. (*Sailors' Slang*.) Almost a c.p.]

never fear: [the speaker's name] **is here**. Sometimes this is a cheerful greeting, at other times a jovial and friendly reassurance: since the middle 1940s, perhaps much earlier (say *c.* 1920). Paul Beale, 12 December 1975, reminds me that the lure of rhyme or, rather, of a jingle has always been current among those who would never dream of reading poetry; nor only among the youthful.

never give a sucker an even break! (See the Carl Sandburg and the Fredenburgh quotations in the latter paragraphs of **old army game**.) This is a famous quotation become, by 1920 at latest, a c.p. Although 'often attributed to W. C. Fields [1879–1946]' – as Bartlett informs us – it is more credibly attributed to a remark made by Edward Francis Albee (1857–1930). From the US it went to Australia in the mid-1940s and it occurs in, e.g., Frank Hardy's *Billy Barker Yarns Again*, 1967, early in the story, 'Cheats Never Prosper – If They Have Principles'. It had reached Britain by 1944 – *via* the American Army.

never had it so good, usually preceded by **you've** (less often by **they've** or **we've**); in US usage, **never had it so good – you** (or **we** or **they**). So far as Britain and Northern Ireland, then the Commonwealth, are concerned, it was 'sparked off' by Prime Minister Harold Macmillan (1957–63): 'Our people have never had it so good', which, by the educated and the cultured, is occasionally rendered into L: *nunquam id habuistis tam bonum*. (For the Latinity, cf *excrementum tauri* and, as a c.p., **non illegitimis carborundum**.)

But 'the Americans were using this idiom by the end of the Second World War, and possibly long before that. In German it is old established, while in modern German it is heard a dozen times a day': and this, adds Foster, seems to indicate that 'we are dealing with an idiom carried over into American English by the speech habits of German immigrants'. (Cf **I wouldn't know**.)

never let it be said was originally a lower-class genteelism, and as such it was used by W. L. George in *The Making of an Englishman*. 1914: C20. By *c.* 1920, it had, socially, become much more general and no longer regarded as a genteelism. Its meaning. 'I feel so discouraged that I could give up'; 'Never let it be said'. Semantically cf **never say die**.

never mind buying the bye – buy the bleedin' beer! was, *c.* 1890–1914, a mainly Cockney c.p., uttered as a comment when someone had remarked 'Oh, by the bye'. Dr Douglas Leechman, an Englishman by birth, has (early 1969) noted: 'Heard in England before 1904.'

never no more! Never again: humorously emphatic: late C19–20. Occurs in, e.g., Somerset Maugham, *The Casuarina Tree*. 1926.

never say die! From being a motto, it has, since *c.* 1915 – esp. when used humorously – become also a c.p., as in the final speech of Terence Rattigan's *Who Is Sylvia?*, performed in 1950 and published in 1951; Mark, after half a lifetime of 'leading two lives' and being routed by his wife, says, 'Pity. It was fun. Oh, well, never say die, I suppose. (*They move towards doors. Oscar turns off lights.*) Come on, Oscar. (*They go out into the hall together.*)'

never stir!; in C17, **ne'er ...!** A c.p. of emphasis or confidence; of assurance or reassurance: *c.* 1660–1785; it is equivalent to 'Let me never stir again if I lie to you or mislead you!' In Act III, Scene i, of Thomas Shadwell's *Epsom Wells*, performed in 1672 and published in 1673, Bisket, a comfitmaker, to Tribble, a haberdasher, says: 'I vow she has had more temptations than any Woman in *Cheapside*, ne're [*sic*] stir' (lines 457–9 of D. M. Walmsley's edn); and in *The Miser*, 1672, and in *The Volunteers*, Act IV, Scene ii, performed 1672, published 1673, he employs a variant: Sir Timothy Kestril exclaims, 'Oh, what a Devil ailes you, Let me never stir I meant her no more hurt than my own soul.' And also in *The Virtuoso*, produced and published in 1676; and yet again in *The Scowrers*, 1691.

   William Wycherley, in *The Country Wife*, performed *c.* 1672, published in 1675, has:

HARCOURT: ...I would be contented she should enjoy you a-nights, but I would have you to myself a-days, as I have had, dear friend.

SPARKISH: And thou shalt enjoy me a-days, dear dear friend, never stir.

In the same year, he uses it again – in *The Plain Dealer*, at Act II, Scene i.

   The phrase was, indeed, much favoured in Restoration comedy. For instance, we find William Congreve, in *Love for Love*, performed and published in 1695, at Scene ii of Act II, having Mrs Frail say of Miss Prue, '... She's very pretty! Lord, what pure red and white! – she looks so wholesome; – ne'er stir, I don't know, but I fancy, if I were a man——.'

   And here are several examples from the next century. In 1763, Isaac Bickerstaffe, in *Love in a Village*, at Act III, Scene iii, causes Hodge to exclaim, 'Know you! ecod I don't know whether I do or not; never stir, if I did not think it was some lady belonging to the strange gentlefolks.'

   In 1770, Samuel Foote, *The Lame Lover: A Farce*, at Act III, Scene i, final grouping, Jack says: 'Father, never stir if he did not make me the proof ... of a new pair of silk stockings.' But eighteen years earlier, Foote had shown that the phrase was so general, so very familiar, that it could already

be incorporated into the very syntax of colloquial English; in *Taste*, at Act II, Caleb, a boy, excited by cries, says: 'Mother! – father! never stir if that gentleman ben't the same that **we** see'd at the printing-man's, that was so civil to mother': a quotation that shows how far down the social scale the phrase had slipped. The fashionable world had long ago discarded it. Foote uses it again in *A Trip to Calais*, 1778.

   Like so many other Restoration comedy c.pp., it owed its long life mainly to its neatness and compactness.

never tell me! See **don't tell me!**

never the better for you. See **better for your asking....**

never trust me! A c.p. of asseveration, roughly equivalent to 'Never trust me again if this doesn't happen as I say it will': lower and lower-middle class: late C19–20; somewhat obsolescent by *c.* 1935; by 1970, more than somewhat.

never up, never in! A US golfing c.p., indicative of pessimism: since *c.* 1920. Literally, never up to the hole with the first putt, nor into it with the second. Hence, almost immediately, a scabrous c.p. 'with sexual side-glance' (John T. Fain, 25 April 1969).

new one on me – a (usually preceded by **it's** or **that's**). This is the first time I've heard of, or seen, *that* being done: since *c.* 1920.

Newgate – he that is at a low ebb.... See **he that is at a low ebb at Newgate....**

[**Newgate seize me!** Objurgatory cliché, not c.p.]

Newmarket Heath. See **fine morning....**

Newton got (or **took**) **him.** See **old Newton....**

next time you make a pie, will you give me a piece? is a male hint to a girl that she should sexually co-operate with him: Canadian: *c.* 1895–1914.

next time you see me, (I hope) you will know me – the. In T. C. Haliburton's *The Clockmaker*, 3rd Series, 1840, we find:

At last one of the dancin' girls came a-figerin' up to me ... and dropt me a low curtshee.

Well, my old rooster, said she, the next time you see me, I hope you will know me; where did you learn manners, starin' so like all possest.

Originally US and dating from *c.* 1820, it had, by *c.* 1850, become also British, often in the variant form, *well, the next time you see me, you'll know me, won't you?* Cf **do you think you'll know me again?**

next way, round about, is at the far door – the. You're going a long way round: C17 semi-proverbial c.p. Recorded in *P. Here. next* = nearest, i.e. shortest.

nice going! An interjection of approval, approbation, congratulation: US, since *c.* 1910; British, since *c.* 1920. (Berrey.) Originally applied to athletics, hence to games, it soon came to be applied also to artistic or musical or literary or theatrical performance.

nice guys finish last is a US c.p. dating since *c.* 1955: originated by Leo Durocher (born 1906) during his management. 1951–4, of the Brooklyn Dodgers baseball team. (Owed to Dr Edward Hodnett, 18 August 1975.) Used originally among baseball players and 'fans', it caught on, has been widely employed ever since, and has been canonized by inclusion in Bartlett.

nice one, Cyril! That's neat or brilliant or most effectual. It arose either from the slogan for Wonderloaf bread, as one correspondent claims, or, as seems to be the predominant opinion, in the world of entertainment, in a gramophone record made early in 1973 by Tottenham Hotspur Football Club in appreciation of a player's – *Cyril* Knowles's – footballing ability, the full version being:

Nice one, Cyril.
Nice one, son!
Nice one, Cyril.
Let's have another one!

From being local, it rapidly became a national c.p. (With thanks to the Rev. Christian Bester of Cotton College, Staffordshire, which is where I first heard it used.) The *Evening News* of 17 July 1975 has: 'Knowles – the song Nice One Cyril was dedicated to him – would welcome a transfer back to his native Yorkshire.'

The wording of the full version has, perhaps inevitably, acquired an indelicate meaning.

nice pair of eyes. See **she has a . . . .**

nice place to live out of – a. often preceded by *it's*. Indicating unpleasantness, it was current *c.* 1890–1940. (Ware.)

nice place (but esp. **nice little place**) **you have here** (or **you've got here**); often introduced by *it's*. Applied literally, it clearly isn't a c.p. – and nobody would suggest that it was – but applied ironically either to a dead-beat hovel or room or, more often, to a very grand place, it is certainly one: and, as such, it dates from *c.* 1942. In his book *Itma*, 1948, Frank Worsley recalls how, when Itma performed at Windsor Castle on 21 April 1942, lunch was served in the apartment of the Gentlemen of the Household, with the gentlemen waiting to welcome the players. 'The ice was broken at once by Tommy [Handley] who looked round and remarked "H'm, nice little place you've got here!" Everybody laughed.' The remark caught on almost immediately.

It soon became familiar in the US, where, as in the British Commonwealth of Nations, it has remained so. In *Spies, Inc.*, 1969, Jack D. Hunter writes, 'I folded myself into a big Dixie cup I assumed to be a chair and said, "Nice place you have here." . . . His handsome face registered undisguised satisfaction. "Yeah," he said. "Not bad for a South Philly [Philadelphia] paisan, eh?" ' Cf Ed McBain, *Hail, Hail, the Gang's All Here*, 1971: 'A criminal bargain basement, awaiting only the services of a good fence. "Nice little place you've got here," Carella said, and then handcuffed Gross to Goldenthal and Goldenthal to the radiator.'

An apposite English example occurs in Catherine Aird's *The Complete Steel*, 1969, a police photographer saying to his superior, in a room at a Stately Home, ' "Nice little place you have here, sir." "And a nice little mystery," rejoined Sloan tartly.'

An occasional variant is *quite a place you have* – or *you've got – here*, as in Philip Quaife's speech-alert, speech-sensitive novel, *The Slick and the Dead*, 1972, 'I . . . looked around at the soft, black-velvety comfort . . . "Quite a place you've got here," I remarked.'

One of the most successful and urbane c.pp. existing in and since 1942.

[**nice weather for ducks!** is applied humorously to wet weather – the wetter, the likelier. In his novel, *Experiment at Proto*, 1973, Philip Oakes writes:

'Right you are,' said Mark. Another formula uttered, he thought. Conversation on this level was like swapping coloured tokens, a kind of linguistic barter. At first he had been derisive, but lately he had found himself collecting banalities to trade. 'Nice weather for ducks' and 'it'll get worse before it gets better'; he was becoming used to serving them with a flourish.

It arose probably fairly late in C19. But rather, I think, a c.p. than a cliché.]

nice work! and **nice work if you can get it!** Expression of warm approval of a good piece of work or of a very favourable and agreeable arrangement: the former, since *c.* 1930; the latter, an obvious extension, since *c.* 1942. I remember that, very soon after WW2, the radio commentator Ronnie Waldron, in judging a beauty contest, remarked 'Nice work – if you can get it!'

The latter was promptly adopted in the US where it is still used frequently. Clarence Budington Kelland, *Stolen Goods*, 1951, has:

'What's an assistant buyer?'

'A cross,' said Roger, 'between a whipping boy and a doormat.'

'Nice work if you can get it,' the pudgy young man said.

He grinned again. 'That,' he explained, 'is a cliché. Make the most of it, you intellectuals.'

The earliest printed record I've found of the longer form occurs in Noël Coward's *Peace in Our Time*, 1947, at Act I, Scene ii:

GEORGE: Good for you – nice work if you can get it.

niet dobra! 'No good!': current at the latter end of WW1 among members of the North Russian Expeditionary Force; 'usually with an intermediate English expletive' (F & G), as in *niet bloody dobra*. Adapted from Russian.

nigger in the woodpile – a (or **the**). See the inevitably obsolescent **there's a nigger . . . .**

[**ninepence for fourpence.** According to Collinson, this was a political c.p. of 1908–9. From national health insurance. But surely a slogan?]

nineteen bits of a bilberry. See **he'll make nineteen . . . .**

ninety-nine, a hundred, change hands! is a Royal Navy (lower-deck, of course) c.p., scurrilously imputing self-abuse: C20.

ninety-nine and forty-four hundredths per cent pure. often written **99 and 44/100ths % pure.** US. 'Much less common since Ivory Soap no longer uses it in its advertisements, where it started, probably some 50 years ago' (John W. Clark, 17 February 1975).

nit! nit! – in the language of convicts in British prisons – means 'Stop talking, someone's listening!' and it dates from *c.* 1930 or a little earlier. Literally 'nothing! nothing!'; *nit* being a variant of *nix*, nothing.

no back talk! Farmer says of it: 'A slang catch phrase indicating that the matter in question is closed to discussion: there's nothing more to be said': *c.* 1880–1910.

no better for your asking. See **better for your asking . . . .**

no, but I'm breathing hard or, with a slightly different implication, **no, just breathing hard.** 'A common Service reply to the innocent question, "Are you coming?" is likely to be "no: just breathing hard" or "no: but I'm breathing hard" ' (Paul

Beale, 30 September 1975): the Services in general, although especially the army: since *c.* 1950. A sexual pun.

no! but you hum it and I'll pick up the tune. A c.p. originally and still addressed by a public-house. or a smoking-concert. pianist to a member of the audience asking 'Do you know such-and-such song or tune?'; hence, by anyone asked to the person asking, 'Do you know whatever-it-happens-to-be?': late C19–20. A good example occurs in chapter VI of Alfred Draper's *Swansong for a Rare Bird*, 1970, concerning a 'pub' pianist:

'Do you know the arse is hanging out of your trousers?' Well. we all knew what was coming because it happened every Saturday night. Gloria [a queer] swung around on the stool and said. 'No. but you hum it and I'll pick up the tune.' Naturally. everyone laughed like a drain. Even me. though I'd fallen out of the cradle laughing at the joke. There's a slightly shorter form often preferred: *you hum it and I'll pick up the tune.*

no can do. I can't do it *or* That's impossible – no means of doing it: originally. at least since *c.* 1850. but probably *c.* 1830. pidgin English of the Chinese ports; by *c.* 1890. *passepartout* English and by *c.* 1900. a c.p.. whence the Royal Navy's refusal. at the officer level. of an invitation: *NCD*.

Collinson said that the c.p. *no can do* was created 'in imitation of Pidgin'. but *no can do* certainly was – it still is – genuine pidgin and is simply the negative of *can do* and perhaps earlier than *can do* itself.

A fairly early printed record of the negative occurs in Charles R. Benstead's *Retreat: A Story of 1918*. published in 1930.

[**no carrion will kill a crow**. applied in C17–18 to gross eaters. is a proverbial saying rather than a c.p.]

no comment! I have no comment to make: a suave and elegant snub. this is 'a jocular catch phrase in imitation of politicians and prominent people who often say this when they are being pestered by reporters and TV interviewers' (A. B. Petch): since *c.* 1950 as a c.p. Barry Prentice. on May Day 1975. comments thus: 'It is unfair. but true. to suggest that this c.p. usually means, "Your allegations are correct. but I am not going to admit it yet".'

It may well have arisen in diplomatic circles before passing to the politicians. radio and TV. film stars and other such 'personalities'.

Jon Cleary. *Man's Estate*. 1972. has:

'But you still haven't told me what you're here for. Or is that an undiplomatic question?'

'No comment.' said Roth. with his gentle smile. 'Another cliché.' [But c.p.. not cliché.]

no complaints! See **can't complain**.

no compree! I don't understand: a military c.p. of 1914–19. A sort of Hobson-Jobson for the Fr. *je n'ai pas compris.* (F & G). Hence. 'No thanks – I don't want any': likewise military: 1915–19. (*Ibid.*)

no dice! Not a chance!; No luck!; *or* It won't work: US and Canadian: since *c.* 1925 (? much earlier). Recorded by Berrey. 1942. and by W & F. 1960. Obviously from gambling.

no difference! It doesn't matter which – or. come to that. who or when or why: US: since *c.* 1945 – perhaps very much earlier. Elliptical for *it makes no difference.*

John Godey. in his magnificent novel. *The Taking of Pelham One Two Three*. 1973. has:

'I want two policemen to walk down the track. One to carry the bag with the money. the other to carry a lit flashlight. Acknowledge.'

'Two cops. one with the money. one with a flashlight. What kind of cops – Transit or NYPD?' [New York Police Department.]

'No difference.'

no! don't tell me – let me guess. occasionally **I'll guess.** Dating since *c.* 1941. it allows for two further variations: *no* omitted; and *now* instead of *no.*

no error! An occasional variant of *and no error.* q.v. at **and no mistake.**

no flies on him occurs in **there are no flies on him** or **me** or **you.** etc.: in combinations. none of which can fairly be classified as a c.p. But there's an extended form with variable *him* or. less often. *her:* and that elaborated form is clearly a c.p.: *there are no flies on him – but you can see where they've been.* which goes back at least to *c.* 1920 and probably to Edwardian or even very late Victorian days. Worth noting also is *no flies on me!:* current in US since *c.* 1910. Recorded by S. R. Strait in 'Straight Talk' (the *Boston Globe. c.* 1917).

no flowers – by request! This jocular c.p. means 'no complaints. *please!*': C20; by 1945. slightly obsolescent. and by 1975 virtually obsolete. From a frequent enjoinder in funeral notices.

no fooling or **no foolin'** is a humorous US way of affirming something: since *c.* 1910. (Berrey.)

no future at all (or simply **no future**) **in it.** either form is often preceded by **there's.** These are fighting Services. esp. RAF. c.pp.. dating since 1939. Whereas the former implies danger in the raid or sortie concerned. the latter either does the same or merely hints that the task is a thankless one. (*The Observer.* 4 October 1942. both phrases; and in H & P and C. H. Ward Jackson's *It's a Piece of Cake.* 1943.) Deriving from earlier familiar Standard English. *there's no future in it (at all).* as applied to a hopeless love affair. it naturally became also a civilian c.p. as early as 1944 – and it still is.

no go; often preceded by **it's** – and when it is. a c.p.: it's no use; it's impracticable; it's impossible: since *c.* 1820; by 1940. somewhat outmoded; by 1975. decidedly obsolescent. (Moncrieff. the playwright. 1830.)

no good for the white man is a 'generally disparaging remark about any uncongenial situation. as in "Hell! It's taters this morning – no good for the white man. old boy!": since *c.* 1945: notably. although not exclusively. army and probably mostly officers' (Paul Beale. 23 June 1974).

no good to Gundy. Very unsatisfactory: Australian: C20. It is recorded by Baker who in the 1959 edition notes the variant *no good to gundybluey.* which looks like an elaboration.

But who was this Gundy? My loyal and learned contributor Ramsey Spencer wrote to me on 31 January 1973: 'Could this character be related to that Solomon Grundy who, in the rhyming tag. was born on Monday. passed through the vicissitudes of a lifetime in six days. and was buried on Sunday?' Well. stranger things have happened.

no good to me! That won't satisfy me – by a long way! Since *c.* 1880; by 1940. slightly obsolescent. and by 1970 very much so. An early example occurs in F. Anstey's entertaining and valuable dialogues. *Voces Populi.* vol. I. 1890.

no grease! is an engineers' c.p.. imputing a lack of *polish* or of good manners: *c.* 1880–1914. (Ware.)

no harm in looking. As Mr Barry Prentice once remarked. this is 'the motto of husbands and boy friends whose eyes wander': perhaps esp. Australian: since late C19. But, as used by window shoppers. it is common in Britain.

no harm in trying; often preceded by **there's**. and followed by **that's how *I* got it!**; illiterate and pseudo-illiterate variants are **no 'arm in tryin'** and **that's 'ow *I* got it.** To which should be added **God loves a trier**. with the proviso that the third lies on the borderline between c.p. and not yet fully accredited proverb; it is also sarcastic. as indeed are the other two. All three are applied to petty theft or to the giving of wrong change. or to a perhaps accidental or absent-minded pocketing of something merely lent. as a lighter or a box of matches; all three are almost as often used defensively by the offender as accusingly by either the victim or an observer; and all three go back at least as far as 1900 – *God loves a trier*. probably much farther and the other two. perhaps a little farther. (An amplification and elaboration of a note sent to me. in November 1968. by the late Frank Shaw.)

no heart to appeal to and no arse to kick. 'A committee may have. as they say. no heart to appeal to and no arse to kick' (Katharine Whitehorn in the *Observer*. 5 November 1967): since the middle or late 1950s. Laurie Atkinson. who sent me the quotation. commented in November 1969. 'Deplores the impersonal in shared authority in specific instance'.

no hide. no Christmas box is an Australian c.p.. dating since *c.* 1930 and referring to a specific instance of 'hide' (brazen impudence or aureate self-confidence) and meaning 'I certainly won't!' or 'No hope of that'. Presumably a pun – a rural pun. at that.

no hits. no runs. no errors. from being a literal statement in baseball. has – because of the varying situations in that game – acquired three different shades of meaning. always clear in the context. in C20 US c.p. usage. as Colonel Albert Moe points out in a letter dated 11 July 1975:

(1) failure. bad job. strike-out. fizzle. no go; or decisive defeat ... (2) uneventful. in which everything went like clockwork. no hitches developed. and no mistakes were made ... (3) perfection. overwhelming success; or ... satisfying accomplishment. As an example of (2). this quotation from *The New York Times* of Sunday. 2 September 1945. Rear-Admiral Oscar C. Badger reporting to Admiral Halsey on the uneventful passage of fleet units (Task Force 31) into Tokyo Bay (after the Japanese surrender): 'No runs. no hits. no errors' [*sic*].

To Professor John W. Clark. the predominant c.p. sense is: 'a perfect performance' (24 July 1975).

Berrey lists it as *no hits. no runs and no errors* and equates it to 'failure' and 'decisive defeat'.

no. I'm not selling – serious. See **I'll bite.**

no. I'm Reddy's brother is the stock response – the c.p. reply – to 'Are you ready?': 'not rare in Canada. Since about 1910 in my experience' (Douglas Leechman. January 1969).

no, just breathing hard! See **no, but I'm breathing hard.**

no kidding! Truly! Honestly! I'm not fooling: US (latish C19–20); then. *c.* 1910. to Canada (as Douglas Leechman tells me). whence. by *c.* 1920. also to the British Isles. whence the rest of the Commonwealth. (Berrey.) W & F note that. used interrogatively. it forms 'a somewhat doubting response to a statement that seems not entirely credible'.

In Edward Albee's *Who's Afraid of Virginia Woolf?*, 1962, Act I has:

NICK: It was probably more in the principle of the thing.
MARTHA: No kidding. Anyway ...

An excellent late US example comes in John Lange's novel. *Binary*. 1972:

She stopped when she saw them.
'I took the wrong turnoff. Can I give you fellows a lift?'
'We're going to Phoenix.' Peters said.
'No kidding.' the woman said. 'That's my home town.'
'No kidding.' Peters said. 'Which part?'
'The right part.' she said.

no matter for that. you shall carry the rake. 'If you tax a Girl with playing the loose [i.e.. being unfaithful]. she shall immediately reply. *No matter ...*'. as we read in Anon.. *Tyburn's Worthies*. 1722: an Essex c.p. of *c.* 1710–50. An example of rural imagery: 'You shall have the raking. the harrowing. even though you "missed out" on the ploughing' (cf the Lucretian metaphor. *to plough the fields of woman*).

no matter how thin you slice it .... See **it's boloney ....**

no more chance than a cat in hell without claws and **no more chance than a snowball – or snowflake – in hell.** No chance whatsoever: the latter. late C19–20; the former. *c.* 1750–1850. and Grose. 1796. says of it that it was applied to one 'who enters into a dispute or quarrel with one greatly above his match'.

[**no more to be said!** – elliptical for 'There's no more to be said' – seems to have. *c.* 1660–1750. been a c.p. It occurs frequently in the comedies of 1660–70. and later; for example. in those of Thomas Shadwell. e.g. *The Scowrers*. 1691. Act V. has the following in the final scene:

SIR WILL[IAM]: Sirrah. Coxcomb. if you speak one Word. I'll slit your Wind-pipe.
WHACH[UM]: Very well. very well! no more to be said.]

no more use than a sick headache. See **headache ....**

no name – no pull. If I don't mention names. there should be no offence taken. hence. e.g. no action for libel or for slander: tailors': *c.* 1870–1914. Cf:

no names – no pack drill. Use no names and you'll be all right!: the British Army: since *c.* 1890. In B & P. 1930. its WW1 use is glossed thus: 'Used by a soldier relating something and wishing not to involve another by mentioning his name; it was taken over from the Regular Army.'

It recurred. although rather less frequently. among the army's Other Ranks in WW2. Moreover. it has been used fairly often by civilians from 1919 onwards; it has achieved print. as in Kenneth Giles. *Death and Mr Prettyman*. 1967. a crook speaking: 'Orright I'm giving it to you straight. There's a boy I know. No names. no pack drill. It was on the night of September eight – remember. she done a bloke in outside a station?'

It occurs also in, e.g., Laurence Meynell, *The End of the Long Hot Summer*. 1972. Indeed. it is extant and not even

(1976) obsolescent, although the young might declare it to be slightly archaic.

In WW1 (and before), drill with a heavy pack 'up' was a common military punishment.

no percentage is elliptical for 'There's no percentage in it' – no profit, no advantage: US: dating since *c.* 1945 and adopted *c.* 1960 in Britain, as in Tom Barling's dangerously readable underworld-and-police 'thriller', *Bergman's Blitz*, 1973, where the speaker, a London professional criminal, remarks, 'You'd have me back inside whatever I said. So why say anything? No percentage.'

no poes emptied, no babies scraped. (Here, *poes* is the plural of *po*, a chamber pot, French *pot de chambre*.) See **eleven o'clock** ....

no possible probable shadow of doubt, no possible doubt whatever, taken from Gilbert and Sullivan, is a cultured c.p. of late C19–20; it is either independent of, or in retort on, or confirmation, perhaps rather an elaboration, of Standard English *of that there is no possible doubt*.

no problem. 'Not a c.p. in its literal sense, but is one, I think, as a recently (the last two or three years) frequent euphemism for "no offense" ' (John W. Clark, 4 March 1975).

no rats! A proletarian c.p. of *c.* 1890–1930, it means 'He (or, of course, she) is Scottish'. Ware remarks, 'A Scot is always associated with bagpipes, and ... no rat can bear ... that musical instrument.'

no rest for the wicked! – occasionally preceded by **there's**. Uttered either by or about a person not wicked at all but kept extremely busy: late C19–20. Partly in humorous irony and partly in reference to several Biblical passages.

no return ticket. He's – or she's – mad. This lower-class c.p. of late C19–20, although little used since *c.* 1940, shortens *He's going to Harwell* [a lunatic asylum] *and has no return ticket*, itself a c.p. no longer used after *c.* 1910. (Ware.)

no second prize! is an Australian c.p., dating since the late 1930s and 'used when someone makes an unoriginal suggestion' (Barry Prentice).

no shit!; also **that's no shit!** The commoner form means 'That's the truth'; *no shit!* means 'Is that truly so?' This US c.p. apparently dates from the 1930s. (W & F.)

no show without Punch, often preceded by **there's**. Applied to a person who is constantly popping up, no matter where you are: late C19–20. A reference to the 'Punch and Judy Show'.

no sir! and **no sir(r)ee!** – with emphasis on *-ree*. This emphatic US negative, recorded in Thornton for 1847 and probably going back at least a decade, became, *c.* 1920, an English c.p., still used occasionally.

In Edward Albee's disturbing, salutary, deeply moving play, *Who's Afraid of Virginia Woolf?*, produced and published in 1962, George – quietly the pivot and pilot of the entire play – remarks to Nick: 'I don't mean to suggest that I'm hip-happy ... I'm not one of those thirty-six, twenty-two, seventy-eight men. No-siree ... Not me. Everything in proportion.'

no skin off my nose, often preceded by **it's** or **that's**. It's not my responsibility that this should have happened *or* It doesn't affect me adversely *or* It doesn't harm me in any way –

financially, morally, physically: since *c.* 1925, at the latest; I remember it from well before WW2 but neither before nor during WW1. It had become also US some years before WW2: *teste* Berrey. It almost certainly comes from boxing or, anyway, fisticuffs. Ramsey Spencer (25 March 1975) relates it to the toast, 'Here's to the skin off your nose!'

no soap! The deal's off!; Not a hope!; You're wasting your time: since *c.* 1945; adopted from US, where current since *c.* 1930 and where it also bears the meaning, 'I don't know' – esp. when this is an evasive answer. The US usage is recorded by Berrey and by W & F; the British is exemplified – as Frank Shaw once told me – in a short story ('Wedlock') by 'George Egerton'. A rhyme on *no hope*. Cf **no dice!**

no speaka da English. 'A phrase that is often used about foreigners' (Barry Prentice): Australian: since *c.* 1920, although occasionally heard earlier; and occasionally heard elsewhere.

no sweat! It is – or it was or it will be – no trouble: US: dating since *c.* 1935, if not a lustrum or even a decade earlier; during the 1960s, much favoured by 'hippies'. Elliptical for 'It causes (*or* caused, *or* will cause) me (or you) no sweat – no undue exertion'. (John T. Fain, 25 April 1969.)

no tell is a frequent reassurance made by someone asked to keep a secret: since *c.* 1945. Perhaps a jocular imitation of pidgin.

no thank you – I've had some! I don't believe what you've just said: US: since *c.* 1925. (Berrey.) From 'No thank you – I've been caught before, but never again.' Cf:

no thanks! You don't catch me in that way: society: *c.* 1885–1905. (Ware.) Cf the preceding entry. But, in C20, this c.p. meant something very different: like **not now** or **not now – later**, it is, among the raffish, a standard retort to a man saying *fuck me!*

no, thanks – I bruise easily. Since *c.* 1920: Michael Warwick says, in 'Theatrical Jargon of the Old Days', *The Stage*, 3 October 1968:

> 'Come into the office, darling', once the approach of amorous theatrical agents, is succeeded by the more modern references to 'casting couch', a rather abused term, and the astute reply of one old-time actress, 'No, thanks – I bruise easily', is often joked about.

no Tich! No talk, *please*, about the Tichborne case!: society: the 1870s. The notorious Roger Tichborne case of fraudulent claim was perhaps the best-known *cause célèbre* of the era. (Ware, at *pas de Lafarge*.)

no tickee, no washee. Literally, 'No ticket – no laundry', a Chinese laundry's refusal to work without being paid, but soon came to be applied to any situation where credit is unjustifiably asked for or even expected: US: late C19–20. (Colonel Albert Moe, 15 June 1975.)

no wanchee! 'Pidgin English for "I don't want it, thank you" ' (Granville in a letter): much used in the Royal Navy, esp. on 'China side' or the China Station: late C19–20. Rather less used since *c.* 1945.

[**no way!** It's impossible – can't be done! US: since *c.* 1969. (Not in W & F, enlarged edn. 1967.) Elliptical for 'There's no way to get out of it or avoid it'. By 1974, adopted in Britain.

(Cyril Whelan, 14 January 1975, in a letter; Philip Stahl of Bronxville, over lunch, 28 January 1975.)

John W. Clark, however, on 17 February 1975, convincingly writes: 'Hardly a c.p., I think, any more than "Hell, no!" (which means no more and no less). I should call it nothing but a tiresome vogue slang phrase. Seldom heard among the educated, except in mockery.' He adds: 'I first heard it in California three or four years ago; within the last year or so it has begun to be heard in the Middle West.' (John Clark lives in Minneapolis.)]

nobody asked you, sir, she said is taken from the old comic song, 'Where Are You Going To, My Pretty Maid?', published in 1878. It became a c.p. late in C19. Harold Brighouse, *The Game: A Comedy in Three Acts*, one of *Three Lancashire Plays*, published in 1920, presents, in Act II, uncle and niece:

EDMUND: You needn't flatter yourself you've talked me into consenting to this marriage.

ELSIE: Nobody asked you, sir, she said.

nobody can say black's my eye occurs in S. 1738, where, in the Dialogue I, occurs this passage:

NEV[EROUT]: Oh, Miss! I have heard a sad Story of you.

MISS: I defy you, Mr *Neverout*; no Body can say, black's my Eye.

A proverbial saying of C15–19; in C18–mid C19, also a c.p. Elliptical for '... black is the white of my eye'. Cf **black's your eye**.

nobody is going to sell me wooden nutmegs. This is a North Country, esp. Yorkshire, boast of one's own alertness and freedom from gullibility: since *c.* 1830. Joan Fleming, *Screams from a Penny Dreadful*, 1971, has this passage: 'Better, I thought, take him home and introduce him first to Nanny whose boast always was that "Nobody is going to sell *me* wooden nutmegs".' For both the sentiment and the form, cf the US c.p., **don't let anyone sell you a wooden dime** (or **don't take any wooden dimes**), perhaps prompted by the British c.p.

noise like two (or **a pair of**) **skeletons fucking on a tin roof – a**; also, **it rattles like two** (or **a pair of**) **skeletons....** This c.p. arose *c.* 1920 at latest, perhaps *c.* 1900, in the US, passed rapidly to Canada, whence, *c.* 1940, to the British Isles and other members of the British Commonwealth.

none of your fancy fours and fives. In 1952, Granville wrote, 'It is now a catch-phrase in the provincial theatre' and cautiously notes that this was originally a 'remark alleged to have been made by an agent to a leading touring actor being offered a part in a play, and meaning "You can have the part, providing you'll accept a reasonable [*sic*] salary – no four or five pounds a week".' The c.p. itself has existed since WW1; the alleged incident must date from a little before it.

none the better for your asking. See **better for your asking**.

Nonesuch, he's a Mr. He's very conceited: *c.* 1870–1914. (Recorded by Baumann in 1887.)

noose is hanging – the. Everything is ready and everyone expectant: US: 'Some far-out and beat use since *c.* 1955' (W & F). A cool reference to the ghoulish eagerness of crowds awaiting a hanging.

nose is bleeding. See **your nose....**

not a bad drop this! This is excellent liquor: an Australian drinking c.p.: C20. In, e.g., Frank Hardy, *Billy Borker Yarns Again*, 1967.

[**not a bit of it!** Not a true c.p.: merely a verbose colloquial synonym of *not at all!*]

not a dry seat in the house is 'an indelicate catch-phrase, meaning that the scene, or [the] comedian, was so funny that the audience was utterly helpless with laughter' (Granville): theatrical: since *c.* 1930. The c.p. plays on the cliché of dramatic critics, 'There wasn't a dry eye in the house' and was presumably suggested by the vulgarism, 'I pissed myself laughing.'

not a heel! Nobody: Cockneys': *c.* 1880–1920. Edwin Pugh, *Harry the Cockney*, 1912, has this exchange:

'Seen anybody?'

'Not a soul. And you?'

'Not a 'eel.'

'That's odd.'

not a word of the pudding! Say nothing about it!: late C17–mid C18. (BE, at *mum-for-that*.) Why *pudding*? Cf the next two entries.

not a word to Bessie about this! This phrase began as a 'gag' of Kenneth Horne's in the radio programme 'Much Binding in the Marsh', which adorned the war years of 1939–45, and quickly spread to the general public as a humorously monitory c.p., not yet (1976) quite extinct. (Paul Beale's reminder.) Cf the preceding c.p. and the one following this.

not a word to the vicar! Mum's the word! *or* Keep it dark!: since *c.* 1925; by 1965, slightly obsolescent. (With thanks to Richard Merry.) The now obscure reference being to some such enormity as brandy on the plum duff or rum in the coffee. Cf the preceding two entries.

not 'alf (pronounced *arf*)! See **not half!**

not bloody likely! and **not Pygmalion likely!** The latter is a cultured variant of the former and, with the Cockney girl Eliza Doolittle's startling use of the phrase, it arose when G. B. Shaw's *Pygmalion* appeared and rendered popular the late C19–20 existing Cockney c.p. *not bloody likely*, emphatic for the simple 'not likely'.

'Eliza Doolittle's "Not bloody likely" is very common in US among sophisticated people – only among those of them who know its literary source, and know their hearers know it' (John W. Clark, 17 February 1975).

A modern US example of *not bloody likely* occurs in Joseph Hansen's novel, *Fadeout*, 1970:

'Do you know these lines, Madge? "The weight of the world is love. Under the burden of solitude, under the burden of dissatisfaction, the weight, the weight we carry is love ...".'

'I wanted to set the weight down,' she said.

He shook his head and gave her a small regretful smile. 'Not bloody likely,' he said.

not for Joseph; not for Joe. The former, which appears in C. Selby's *London by Night*, 1844, was current *c.* 1830–1920; it gradually gave way to the latter form, recorded in 1867 and current since *c.* 1860 – a form worthily 'enshrined' in Galsworthy's *Swan Song*, 1928, thus: 'Not if he knew it – not for Joe!' and honoured by a place in Benham. Why *Joseph*? Perhaps in reference to the famed Joseph of the Old Testament. Cf the next.

not for this child. Not for me: since *c.* 1890; obsolescent since *c.* 1940, but not yet obsolete. Collinson records this c.p.; and *this child* (I or me) was adopted, *c.* 1890 or a little earlier, from the US.

not guilty, my lord. Not *my* fault! *or* No, not *I*! A c.p. current since *c.* 1890, but just beginning to become obsolescent as early as *c.* 1945, and by 1970 very much so. In *What's Bred in the Bone*, produced in 1927 and published in 1928, Harold Brighouse, in the second act, writes:

LEONARD (*close to her*): Have you been pawed by a nigger?
AUDREY: Not guilty, my lord.

Clearly taken from the law courts.

not half! is an exclamation of emphatic assent: originally (*c.* 1905) and still mainly Cockney; very common in the British Army of WW1. '"Did you like it?"–"Not half!"' It has gained a place both in B & P and in Lyell's glossary of roughly the same period; also in Benham. A good example of Cockneys' ironic meiosis.

not if I am in orders for it! is a military c.p. of refusal, dating since *c.* 1930 (if not very much earlier), but little used since *c.* 1950. Literally, 'I sha'n't [or 'wouldn't'] do it even if I were, in Daily Orders, instructed to do so.'

not if I can help it. You certainly *won't* – not if *I* can do anything to prevent it: C20. A clear allusion occurs in John Osborne's *A Sense of Detachment*, produced late in 1972 and published in 1973, in Act I (on p. 23 of the Faber edn):

GIRL: Don't tell me. I'll guess. Not that *you* could, anyway.
BOX MAN: I'll see you later.
GIRL: Not if I can help it.

not if I know it! 'I certainly sha'n't be *or* do it – at least, not if I'm conscious'; 'Not if I can avoid it': since *c.* 1860. (The *OED* quotes Thomas Hardy, 1874.)

not if I see you first. See **see you!**

not if *you* don't is the c.p. rejoinder to **do you mind?** (which see!) and it dates from within a year of the latter's promotion to c.p. status. It is used as, e.g., in James Barlow's *In All Good Faith*, 1971:

Eithne was standing in her pants in the dirty bathroom. She was plucking her eyebrows or something. She objected, 'Do you mind?'
'Not if you don't,' he countered, equally automatic.

not in (all) your puff! Synonymous with the originating **not on your life!** and comparable with **not on your Nellie!**, it arose, if my memory serves me faithfully, during the 1930s.

not in front of the children! When used literally, it is not – obviously – a c.p. But it has, since *c.* 1920, often been used either ironically or jocularly. In *I'll Leave It to You*, performed on 21 July 1920 at the New Theatre, London, and published two or three months later, Noël Coward, in this, his earliest performed comedy, has, in the opening scene, where the young people of a family chat and chaff, employed a variant:

SYLVIA: Knowing you for what you are – lazy, luxurious—
BOBBIE (*pained*): Please, please, please, not in front of the child. (*Joyce kicks.*) It's demoralizing for her to hear her idolized brother held up to ridicule.

not in these boots (or, more often, **trousers**)! Jocularly 'Cer-

tainly not!': respectively, *c.* 1869–1900, and recorded by Benham; and, arising *c.* 1920 but obsolescent since *c.* 1960, and recorded by Collinson, and glossed thus by Julian Franklyn (31 January 1969): '*not in these trousers*. Since *c.* 1920. Expressive of unwillingness to perform some action: make a journey; become involved in a scheme; etc. Used both seriously and jocularly; often reduced to *not in these*, deliberately, saucily, by women.' He thought that the phrase originated in some music-hall comedian's gag.

not just a pretty face. See **I'm not just a pretty face**.

not me, Chief, I'm radar (or **asdic** or **gunnery** or ...) is a c.p. 'used by a rating when given an order to do something not connected with his usual job, or if volunteers are asked for' (Wilfred Granville, in letter dated 22 November 1962): Royal Navy: since *c.* 1946. The specialist's revolt against generality. This 'Chief' is the Chief Petty Officer.

not me, Sare (or **Senew**) – **my brother from Gozo** is 'supposed to be the standard Maltese alibi against any charge. "Sare" and "Senew" were, of course, phonetic for "Sir", "Señor", and Gozo is the second largest island of the Malta group' (Rear-Admiral P. W. Brock, 1 January 1969): late C19–20. Cf **two other fellows from Poona** and Kipling's variant, *me, sar? not me, sar*. *My brother Manuel, sar*, in *A Fleet in Being*, 1898, and **just the job for my brother from Gozo**.

not much! dates, in Britain, from *c.* 1885 and means 'Not likely!' or 'Certainly not!' – a sense obsolete by 1940 at latest. It was adopted from the US: Farmer writes: 'Not at all. A common colloquialism': dating since the 1860s and obsolete by *c.* 1920. From before WW2, it has predominantly meant 'You certainly *did* (or *were*) – or *do* (or *are*) – or *will!*' and was, in the Services during WW2, used with heavy irony. Cf the next.

not much you didn't (or **don't**, or **wouldn't**)! The first two (*didn't*, *don't*) are clearly a mere extension of **not much**; the one – meaning 'You certainly *would!*' – more strongly and worthily carries the escutcheon of catch-phrasery and may have been US and Canadian before it was British. Of the basic and originating *not much*, a splendid – almost a 'splendiferous' – example occurs in the verse of that delightful, often exquisite, US author of light verse (and prose) and artist Oliver Herford; in *The Bashful Earthquake and Other Fables and Verses*, both written and illustrated by him, and published in 1899, there is a poem titled 'The Silver Lining' containing these lines:

I too found refuge from Despair
  In sonnets to Amanda's fair
White brow or Nell's complexion rare
  Or Titian hair –

Which, when she scorned, did I resign
  To flames, and go into decline?
Not much! When sonnets fetched per line
  Enough to dine.

not now – later. See **no thanks!**

not on your life! Certainly not! Since the late 1880s, or perhaps a few, or not so few, years earlier. It seems to have become, *c.* 1900, also US: I've noticed it recorded in, e.g., A. H. Melville's article, 'An Investigation of the Function and Use of Slang' in *The Pedagogical Seminar*, March 1912; in HLM, 2nd edn, 1922; in Berrey; W & F; and, indeed, Edward

Albee uses it in Act II of *Who's Afraid of Virginia Woolf?*, 1962:

MARTA: (*Loud: a pronouncement.*) And Daddy said ... Look here, kid, you don't think for a second I'm going to let you publish this crap. Not on your life, baby ... not while you're teaching here.

But why *life*? Simply, I'd suppose, because it is one's most notable possession. Cf the Fr. intensive *jamais de la vie!* Contrast the triviality of **not on your tin-type!** More influential, probably, was the cliché 'not even if your life depended on it!' Cf the next five entries.

not on your life, boy! is a Canadian – apparently only Canadian – intensive of the preceding: c. 1920–30. 'With a pun on *Lifebuoy* Soap' (Professor F. E. L. Priestley, in letter dated 19 August 1975).

not on your Nannie! (or **Nanny!**) is an occasional variant of **not on your Nellie**, which is a development from **not on your life!** Anglo-Irish and dating since c. 1950. Professor Alan Bliss tells me, 'A very common expression in Dublin is "not on your Nannie!" Has this the same origin as "not on your Nellie"?' (Letter of 8 December 1961). Julian Franklyn thought *Nannie* a mere arbitrary alteration of *Nellie*. So do I. Cf also:

not on your natural! Certainly not! C20. That is, 'Not on your natural life'. There may be an allusion to imprisonment 'for the term of his natural life'. Cf the preceding two, and the following two, entries.

not on your Nellie! (or **Nelly!**) **Not on your life!** An intensive tag, dating since the late 1930s. Used by, e.g., Frank Norman in his very readable *Bang to Rights*, 1958. Short for *not on your Nellie Duff!*; and *Nellie Duff* rhymes on *puff*, breath, breath of life, life itself. Therefore cf **not on your life!**

In 'Me and the Girls', one of the stories in Noël Coward's *Pretty Polly Barlow*, 1964, occurs this passage: '"None of those pony-tails and tatty slacks for George Banks Esq. Not on your Nelly. My girls have got to look dignified whether they like it or not."'

Cf the preceding three entries and also:

not on your tin-type! (also written *tintype*). Certainly not!: US and Australian: c. 1880–1925, but surviving for another (say) fifteen years; it occurs in, e.g., Christina Stead's *Seven Poor Men of Sydney*, 1930. The reference is to an old-fashioned type of photograph and there seems to be a feeble pun on **not on your life!**

not Pygmalion likely! See **not bloody likely!**

not so as (or **so's**) **you would** (or **you'd**) **notice** (it); variant, **not that you would** (or **you'd**) **notice** (it). Well, not noticeably; or I'd hardly have said (or thought) so: since the late 1920s.

In his earliest play to be produced and published, '*I'll Leave It to You*', A Light Comedy, 1920, Noël Coward writes, at Act II:

MRS CROMBIE: I take it that yours is a gold mine.
DANIEL: Not so that you'd notice it.

not so daft as I'm cabbage-looking. A North Country variant of **not so green** ... (Frank Shaw, 1 April 1969.)

not so green as I'm cabbage-looking, often preceded by **I'm.** I'm not such a fool – such a simpleton – as I look (or as I seem): mid C19–20. In 1853 appeared a novel of English undergraduate life: Cuthbert Bede's *The Adventures of Mr*

Verdant Green. Some years ago, I noticed its use by Ernest Raymond in his novel, *Mary Leith* (1931). From the entirely natural and proper equation of immaturity, hence daftness, with the colour green; one of the world's oldest metaphors. Cf **not so daft** ....

not so old nor yet so cold. S, 1738, in Dialogue I, has:
NEV[EROUT]: Miss, what do you mean? you'll spoil the Colonel's Marriage if you call him old.
COL[ONEL]: Not so old nor yet so cold—— You know the rest, Miss.

An already long-established proverb had, it seems, become something of a c.p. by c. 1700; but apparently, as a c.p., obsolete before the end of C18. Not so old as to be impotent nor yet so unloving as to fail to keep his wife warm in bed.

not so scarce as all that! See S, 1738, in Dialogue I:
NEV[EROUT]: Come, come, Miss, make much of naught, good Folks are scarce.

Young Neverout implies that good *men* are scarce: and 'Good folks are scarce' is a C17–20 proverb. The women, so admonished, reply 'But not so scarce as all *that!*'; which is a late C19–20 c.p., not very much used since c. 1945.

not so you'd notice it! The American form – employed by, e.g., S. R. Strait in 'Straight Talk' (the *Boston Globe*) c. 1917 – cf **not so as you would notice** (it).

not that you know of is defiantly addressed to one who has referred to something he either proposes, or is about, to do: c. 1740–1820. The *OED* cites novelist Samuel Richardson's 'As Mr B. offer'd to take his Hand, he put 'em both behind him. – "Not that you know of, Sir!"' Cf **not today, baker!**

not that you'd (or **you would**) **notice** (it). See **not so as you would notice** (it).

not to worry! Don't worry – there's nothing to worry about: current, since the middle 1930s, in the Services, and then, suddenly, in 1957–8, it began to be generally and very widely used; Mr Paul Beale (28 January 1975) remarks that it 'was often qualified by "unduly"; and *not to worry unduly, old boy* was a common Services' phrase in the ten years or so around 1960'. Dr Douglas Leechman thinks it goes back to c. 1935; it may well have done so, and has certainly been current in the Services since the middle and probably the early 1940s. Mr Peter Sanders tells me that the phrase was current in the War Office and the Ministry of Defence at the time of the Korean War (1951); on 5 November 1967, Mr Wilfred Granville writes: 'It is old hat. I first heard it, *ad nauseam*, in Admiralty about ten or twelve years ago, when I was researching the RNVR book'; and, late in 1968, Mr Barry Prentice informs me that it is also Australian.

The Services used to base it upon a Maltese analogy; Italian scholars compare *non tormentarsi!* and suggest that British officers returning from the Italian campaign and from the British occupation of Italy in 1944–5, brought it to England; Colonel Archie White, VC, suggests that it may, in form, have been influenced by such locutions as *ce n'est pas* – colloquially *c'est pas* – *à refuser*, but, more pertinently, why not by *ce n'est pas* – or *c'est pas* – *à s'en faire?* Those analogies may have intervened, it is true; yet I prefer my own theory – that *not to worry!* merely truncates, or is elliptical for, *you are not to worry*, there's nothing to worry about.

To quote two examples from among so many. John Arden, in *Wet Fish: A Professional Reminiscence for Television*,

written 1960. produced 1961. published 1967. gives this one:
GARNISH: Miss Walters? No panic after all. dear. Not to worry.

Alistair Mair. *Where the East Wind Blows*. 1972. has:

'Oh. I say! I'm terribly sorry——'

'Not to worry.'

not today, baker! refuses an offer or a suggestion: Canadian: since *c*. 1945. Connoting (Dr Douglas Leechman tells me) 'Oh. no! You don't catch me like that!' Cf **not that you know of.**

But Douglas Leechman. in December 1968. says: 'In England. used by my mother. say 1895. Meaning "Not this time. thank you!"' Moreover. in the England of 1885 (and probably for some years longer). *not to-day. Baker* was being addressed to any young man paying. to a young woman. court obviously undesired by her: and. according to Ware. the reference was to a thus surnamed military man 'given into custody for pressing his attentions upon a young lady travelling by accident alone with him'.

Benham offers rather different evidence.

not tonight, Josephine is a c.p. used by husbands. lovers. boy friends. to wife or mistress or girl friend. in refusal of a nudge. a hint. even a virtual request for sexual intercourse: always humorous or. at least. semi-humorous: late C19–20. Apocryphally attributed to Napoleon Bonaparte. said to have been given to decline Josephine's expressed desire. Hence, since *c*. 1970. it has been used in other and often trivial circumstances and without regard to sex. as in the loose variant exemplified by 'Care for a drink?'–'Not today. Josephine.' This last (supplied by Mr Barry Prentice) seems to be confined to Australia.

Of **not tonight, Josephine**. Vernon Noble (12 March 1974) remarks that it 'originated from music-hall fun based on romanticizing of Napoleon's relationship with Josephine. the widowed Viscountess de Beauharnais. whom he married and divorced. The legend of Josephine's sexual appetite produced the catch-phrase current in England'–and. in C20. elsewhere. Mr Noble suggests that George Robey may have done something to increase the popularity of the phrase.

Mostly – and. I'd suppose. firmly – ignored by the editors of dictionaries of quotations. it has nevertheless got itself into J. M. Cohen's alert and catholic *Penguin Book of Quotations*. 1960. Mr Cohen quoting the pseudonymous Colin Curzon's infinitely moving verses:

I'll tell you in a phrase. my sweet. exactly what I mean ...

Not tonight. Josephine. [In a poem thus titled.]

Napoleon's name is also enshrined in **Napoleon's greeting to his troops.**

not waving but drowning. In a letter dated 10 April 1970. the late Miss Stevie Smith. author of *A Good Time Was Had by All*. 1937. wrote to me: 'One of my later titles – "Not Waving but Drowning". published about 1958 – does seem to have passed into a sort of general use. at least I have heard people using it and have even seen it used as a column heading (with acknowledgements to me) in the *Evening Standard*.' But this phrase. as opposed to **a good time was had by all**. never attained a general currency. Perhaps. however. one might go so far as to say that. in literate and cultured. certainly in literary. circles. it was a c.p. of *c*. 1958–70.

not what it's cracked up to be. often preceded by **it's**. It falls

short of its reputation: since *c*. 1910. Often applied to copulation.

not yet dead. a theatrical c.p. of 1883–*c*. 1920. was applied to 'an antique fairy' in pantomime. (Ware.)

not you by your asking. A c.p. reply to 'Who owns this?': late C18–early C19. Cf the far better known **none the better for your asking**.

not you. Momma – siddown! 'A c.p. from the Ben Lyons. Bebe Daniels. Vic Oliver wartime [WW2] radio comedy show. "Hi. Gang!"' (Paul Beale. 11 August 1975). Not yet (1975) entirely dead.

nothing below the waist is a tailors' c.p. dating from before 1928 and meaning 'no fool'. *The Tailor and Cutter*. 29 November 1928. has: 'Took me for a josser [a simpleton]. Nothing below the waist. me. I'm not to be rubbed about.' From a process in tailoring.

nothing but. 'Used to emphasize or conclude a preceding remark' (Berrey.) US: since the 1920s. Cf **and how!**

nothing but up and ride? Is that the end?; Is there nothing else?; Why! Is it all over?: a semi-proverbial c.p. of *c*. 1620–1750. Recorded by Clarke. 1639; Ray; Fuller. 1732. (Apperson.) From horse-racing?

nothing doing! Certainly not! – in retort upon an invitation to amorous dalliance or to an unattractive or shady offer or suggestion: since the 1890s. In 1927. a schoolgirl. writing about Elizabeth I. evolved this masterpiece: 'Philip of Spain asked her hand in marriage. but she replied. "Nothing doing!"' Probably developed from the colloquial *there's nothing doing*. there's no business being done.

In Act II of Alfred Sutro's *Living Together*. performed and published in 1929. the following occurs:

JULIA: I don't walk off with another girl's chap ...

TONY: We're free. aren't we?

JULIA: [*Shaking her head*.] Nothing doing. Tony.

TONY: This is ridiculous ...

JULIA: I've told you. nothing doing.

The phrase had reached the US by the late 1920s; Berrey records it in 1942.

nothing for nothing – and very little for tuppence-ha'penny. often preceded by **you get**. A c.p. dating since *c*. 1910 and originated by George Bernard Shaw. 'Shaw's coinage.' writes Mr Ramsey Spencer on 17 July 1974. 'is reminiscent of *Punch's* "Nothink for nothink 'ere. and precious little for sixpence" (vol. LVII. 1869). also used by Kipling (nautically adjusted) in *The Ship That Found Herself* (1895).'

nothing happening is a US negroes' c.p. of *c*. 1940–60. Clarence Major glosses it thus: 'Often a response to "What's happening?" The implication is that things are more than simply slow'–in short. 'dead'.

nothing in my young life. usually preceded by **he's** or **she's**. He means nothing to me: since *c*. 1930. Originally among the youthful and concerning a member of the opposite sex. It occurred. for instance. in a story by Achmed Abdullah in *Nash's Magazine*. February 1935.

nothing like leather is applied to anything that recalls and emphasizes. esp. if one-sidedly or tendentially. the doer's – or the speaker's – trade (originally. of course. that of a currier): since *c*. 1670. as. e.g. in L'Estrange. 1692. and Mrs

Gaskell. 1855. (Apperson.) Since the late 1920s, the phrase has been a leathersellers' and shoemakers' slogan: and the slogan has repopularized the c.p. Folk-etymologically, the saying originated in an anecdote about a certain cobbler's praise of his own wares.

nothing that you oughtn't answers the question. 'what shall I do?' and has, at the lower social levels, been current throughout C20. (A. B. Petch. 30 March 1976.)

nothing to cable home about. It's – or that's – ordinary, usual, unremarkable, unexciting: Australian: since c. 1914 or 1915. It arose. I believe, in the Australian expeditionary force during WW1.

More widely used is *nothing to write home about*, which dates from late C19 and is common to all English-speaking peoples, including – by c. 1918 – the US; Berrey records it and notes the (US) variant, *nothing to wire home about*. Cf **nothing to make a song about.**

nothing to do with the case! is often a polite way of saying 'That's a lie' and it dates from Gilbert and Sullivan's *The Mikado*, first produced on 14 March 1884. By 1935, a trifle obsolescent, but not yet obsolete. We still, even although only occasionally, hear the words from which the c.p. has been distilled: 'The flowers that bloom in the spring, tra-la, have nothing to do with the case', sung, as Ware tells us, with an alluring liveliness by the inimitable George Grossmith. From the phraseology of the law-courts – cf **not guilty, my Lord.**

nothing to make a song about. Nothing to make a fuss about; nothing in the least important: mid C19–20. Cf **nothing to cable home about.**

nothing to wire (or write) home about. See **nothing to cable home about,** second paragraph.

now can you? 'From c. 1914 divorce case in which a witness had overheard these words issuing from the bedroom, "Now can you (get in)?" It became a c.p. among youths who called after girls thus to cause a few giggles or, more hopefully, dates. Mostly working-class' (Wilfred Granville, 14 January 1969).

now don't that beat the band! See **don't that beat the band!**

now **he tells me!** On 30 March 1969. Mr D. J. Barr, a Canadian schoolteacher (of Hillsport, Ontario), wrote to me: 'One student used it after a spelling test, as if he [had] expected me to tell him his mistakes during the test.'

It had travelled, during the 1950s, to both Canada and Britain as a US export: in the US, it began as a Hebraism and, among Gentiles, became a c.p., with the general sense 'And he thinks of telling me – when it's too late to be of use'. In Gavin Lyall's 'thriller'. *Blame the Dead*. 1972. occurs this piece of dialogue:

He'd heard that Pat Kavanagh was last heard of working for Dave Danner.

'Now he tells me.'

Expectedly and predictably, it has – or could be said to have – the variant, '*now* you tell me!'. It occurs in, e.g., Blaine Littell. *The Dolorosa Deal*. 1973:

'Forget it! It happened in Bangkok. You're going to Jerusalem.'

'When did it happen?'

'Two weeks ago.'

'*Now* you tell me?'

Mason heard Webster's familiar chuckle at the other end of the line. 'Mazel tov! You're off to a good start. You even sound Jewish.'

now I'll tell you one (emphasis on *you*) expresses 'incredulity at telling of scandalous, titillating, but unbelievable episode, or news in one's circle' (Laurie Atkinson, 4 June 1975): since c. 1932. Earlier (December 1974) L.A. had commented thus: 'In response to a witticism, tall or funny story, boast, etc. since early 1930s: adopted from US via "talkies", where informed incredulity was a mark of wise-guy sophistication'.

now I've heard (or seen) everything! is an ironical, yet usually good-natured, c.p., expressing a mock admiration or wonderment: since the middle 1940s. An Australian example (*heard*) comes in Frank Hardy. *Billy Borker Yarns Again*. 1967. Cf **this I must hear (or see).**

now, Mrs Rowbottom, *if* you please! I'm ready when *you* are: Canadian: since c. 1930. (Douglas Leechman, who adds: 'Of anecdotal origin'.)

now she bumps. See **bumps....**

now she knows (all about it)! (or **she knows all about it now!**) is, not unexpectedly, applied to a bride any time shortly after the bridal night: C20. but not much used since c. 1950, virginity being no longer regarded – by most females – as advisable or even desirable.

now she's talking! is a nautical, esp. a naval, c.p., 'said of a ship's boat as she begins to move through the water which begins to slap her strakes' (*Sailors' Slang*): late C19–20.

now tell me another! See **now you tell me one.**

now then, me lucky lads! is a workmen's ironic c.p., applied, since c. 1910, to work and deriving from showmen's and three-card tricksters' and racing tipsters' invitation to the 'mugs' to enter or to participate. Cf Tommy Trinder's gag, **You lucky people!**

now then, only another nineteen shillings and elevenpence three farthings to make up the pound before I begin the service. A military c.p., dating since c. 1908 and used by someone desirous of raising a loan or of starting a 'bank'. (B & P.)

now then, shoot those arms out! You couldn't knock the skin off a rice pudding! has, since c. 1910 or a little earlier, been used by drill sergeants and physical-training instructors, at first in the army (see esp. B & P) and then, after WW1, also in the RAF.

now, there's a funny thing – there *is* a funny thing is one of far too few domestic c.pp., and even this one verges on the potential proverbial saying, belonging. I'd guess, to late C19–20. I cannot do better than to quote Ramsey Spencer, who, on 4 February 1975 and in answer to a query, writes: 'I remember from my earliest days (putting my perceptive memory as starting c. 1910), as indicating that my mother's suspicions were beginning to be awakened by some unlikely coincidence or circumstance. So it must have been current then' – to judge by at least two other correspondents, early 1975, it still is. 'The meaning *funny-peculiar*, rather than *funny-haha*.'

But it was also – or, rather, it became – one of Max Miller's gags, as Vernon Noble tells me 8 February 1975. And nine days later Cyril Whelan amplifies it by writing: '[This] was the "filler" used between shots by Max Miller, the celebrated Cockney comedian who pushed open vulgarity to the limit before it was modish to do so.'

Oddly enough, Sir John Betjeman – on Radio 4, 12 April 1975 – played a Max Miller record that, in the 1920s, included the phrase. (Thanks again to Mr Spencer.)

There exists no contradiction here. Max Miller didn't just 'pluck it out of the air': perhaps quite unconsciously, he probably drew on a childhood memory – what we used to call the tribal memory – and utilized it, revived it, popularized it.

now we shall be sha'n't. This jocular, non-cultured perversion of **now we sha'n't be long** arose in December 1896 and was probably dead by 1900. Ware notes that it is purposely meaningless. This meaningless type of c.p. is fortunately as short-lived as it is tedious.

now we sha'n't be long is an 'intimation of finality' – of obscure origin, although 'probably from railway travellers' phrase when near the end of a journey': 'people's, 1895 on'; obsolescent by c. 1915 and virtually obsolete by c. 1930. (Ware.) It occurred in the *Daily Telegraph* of 8 September 1896 and in Somerset Maugham's *Liza of Lambeth*, 1897.

now we're busy was, earliest, a c.p. implying action and dating from 1868, but – as a c.p. – obsolete by 1914. From the 1880s, it was also 'an evasive intimation that the person spoken of is no better for his liquor, and is about to be destructive' (Ware); obsolete by c. 1920.

now what have you (got) to say for yourself? was, c. 1920–60, a c.p. of humorous, semi-ironic greeting.

now you tell me! See **now he tells me!** – final paragraph.

now you tell one and **now tell me another** date from the early 1920s; Frank Shaw, in a letter dated 1 September 1969, derives it from 'a tearful 1920s "love" song'.

now you'll think I'm awful. 'A c.p. used by women after making an uncharitable remark or after spreading a rumour. It is also said to be used after a casual sexual encounter' (Barry Prentice, 15 December 1974): very widely employed, originally as a cliché: late C19–20; a c.p. by c. 1910, esp. if humorously rueful.

now you're asking! is a variant of **that's asking!** It dates from the late 1890s and occurs in, e.g., Leonard Merrick's once famous *Peggy Harper*, 1911. A better example comes in Francis Clifford's *Act of Mercy*, 1959: there the sense 'That's

a very difficult question' (cf **that's a good question**) emerges very clearly:

'What we can't grasp,' Susan said, 'is why there's been a revolution in the first place. I mean – what brought things to a head so suddenly?'

'Ah,' Swann sighed. 'Now you're asking.'

now you're cooking with gas. 'Now you are on the right track'; now you've got the right idea: American: probably since c. 1940, for it resulted from an intensive Radio and Press campaign, carried on by the gas industry during the middle and late 1930s to combat the rapidly increasing use of the electric range (stove): Ben Grauer, in letter written on Christmas Day 1975. He notes the intensive variant, *now you're cooking on the front burner* and the 'moderator', ... *on the back burner*. He further remarks that *now* is often omitted. Recorded by Berrey, 1942, and by W & F, who, in 1960, have glossed it thus: 'Originally swing ['pop' music, especially jazz] use. Fairly well known c. 1940, still some use.' It promptly travelled to Canada as Professor F. E. L. Priestley informed me on 19 August 1975.

now you're railroadin'! 'You speak truly' (Berrey, 1942); also a c.p. 'of approval and admiration' (*ibid.*) or 'an expression of commendation, no matter what one is doing' (*ibid.*): a US railway c.p. of C20.

now you're talking! Now you're saying something worth while (or arresting): since c. 1880, a date based upon the *OED*. Adopted c. 1900 by US; recorded by Berrey (as an interjection of 'approval and admiration'). In letter dated 19 August 1975, Professor Priestly tells me, it travelled early to Canada.

nowt so queer as folks. See **there's nowt....**

nuff said. A comic perversion (*nuff sed*) or variant of **enough said**: US origin, according to Ware, on whose evidence its British use could be dated as from c. 1870; but John Brougham, in his farce, *Po-Ca-Hon-Tas or, The Gentle Savage*, performed in New York, 1855, has this passage in Act I, Scene i:

COL: *Conclude* it done! The deadliest weapon I can find, I'll name.

OPO: Nuff said, old top. I'll go it blind!

nutted 'em! is an exclamatory c.p., uttered when the pennies turn up two heads at the gambling game of two-up: Australia and New Zealand: C20. From slang *nut*, the head.

O begga me! or **O Bergami!** is the way Ware presents these variants, but what he should, I think, have written was *O Bergami!* and its derivative *oh, beggar me!*, with *beggar* for *bugger*, naturally. Ware classifies it as 'London people's'–i.e., proletarian–and dates it at 1820; he adds: 'Still used in the streets as intimating that the person addressed is a liar, or worse. From one Bergami–a lying witness at the trial of Queen Caroline–whose denial of everything brought about this phrase, with his eternal "non mi ricordo" [I don't remember].' At *non me* in his very valuable book, Ware notes that the *non mi* of the It. *non mi ricordo* became, *c.* 1820–30, the London proletariat's synonym for a lie and was used thus: 'That's a *non me* for one'–'That's a lie, to start with'.

o bop she bam, also written **o-bop-she-bam**, is a US negro jazz phrase of release-of-tension excitement or exhilaration; it dates from *c.* 1960. Clarence Major 'jazzes it up' by describing it as existential–as perhaps an attempt to comment adequately upon the undefinable elements of *la condition humaine* of the negro in the US–or perhaps simply a way of communing with that 'mystery often referred to as God'.

OK entries. See **okay**....

obvious, my dear Watson! See **elementary** ....

of all the dumb tricks! is described by Berrey as an 'interjection of personal displeasure': US: since *c.* 1920 and probably earlier. The corresponding British exclamation would be 'Of all the bloody stupid things to do, *that* is the stupidest!'–which, however, doesn't qualify as a c.p.

of all the nerve!; **what a nerve!**; **you've got a nerve!**; **your nerve!**; **I like your nerve!**; also **of all the gall!** All were, originally, US; but, whereas the last has always been solely US, the others became, *c.* 1918, also British. As Americanisms, they are impossible to date with any accuracy; I'd hazard 'since the 1890s'.

off and on! See **off yer and on yer!**

off to Durban! 'A music-hall gag for any person going on a gallivanting holiday. Since *c.* 1920' (Professor A. C. Partridge, in letter dated 18 November 1968): South African.

off yer and on yer!–sometimes shortened to **off and on!**, and itself elliptical for **off yer** (or **your**) **fanny and on yer** (or **your**) **feet!** 'The limited use of the shortened phrase–i.e., *off and on!*–by Marines was as a command by the "non-com" to "turn-out"–or to resume activity after a rest period even though every individual was already standing' (Colonel Albert Moe, 15 June 1975). The two longer phrases were presumably current in both the navy and the army; and the longest passed into some general currency: late C19–20.

often trod but never laid. (Of women) often 'mauled' but never slept with: since the late 1940s. Here, *trod* = *trodden* on; and *laid* comes from 'to lay', to copulate with.

oh, after you! That'll do! *or* Stop talking!: tailors' c.p., dating since *c.* 1870 and always used ironically. (B & L.) Cf **after you, Claude**....

oh, baby! was current among US students esp. in 1920–2, and decreasingly throughout the remaining 1920s. (McKnight.) It was apparently influenced by the much-longer-lived and far more widely distributed **oh boy!**

oh, bishop. See **bishop.**

oh, bloody good, wacco, (or **whacko,**) **Pup!** 'And after shooting down a Jap plane: "Oh, bloody good, wacco, Pup!" which was a queer New Zealand whoop of triumph the squadron had adopted': Kenneth Hemingway, *Wings over Burma*, 1944,–as Paul Beale, 17 November 1975, describes it, 'an informal account of the author's experiences with 17 Squadron, RAF, during the retreat from Rangoon to Calcutta, February–April 1942.... Their "in" phrase was, wherever possible, "Have a snort!"–not necessarily of alcohol', but clearly a cliché, not a c.p.

oh, boy! and **boy, oh boy!** and **oh, boy–did I!** Very general among US soldiers in 1917–18; arose *c.* 1910, if not a little earlier; current in England during the 1920s and after, but virtually obsolete by *c.* 1970. Of its English use, Mr Ramsey Spencer has written (10 May 1969): '*boy!* or *oh boy!* Indicative of anticipation or satisfaction, as in "Boy! D'you see what I see?" or "What a party! Oh boy! Oh boy!"' Or, of course, you can trust the urbane P. G. Wodehouse, master of limpid, effortless English, to provide a satisfactory example. In *Aunts Aren't Gentlemen*, 1974: 'E. J. Murgatroyd [a Harley Street consultant] would have been all for it. "Oh, boy," I could hear him saying, "this is the stuff to give the typical young man about town." The air ... seemed to be about as pure as could be expected, and I looked forward to a healthy and invigorated stay.'

McKnight quotes from the *Kansas City Star* (date not given) this example of a returned US soldier's language:
'Did you git clean over, Pink?'
 'Oh, boy, did I?'
'Git sick on the ocean?'
 'Oh, boy, did I?'
'Didya go over the top, Pink?'
 'Oh, boy, did I?'
'How did it feel?'
 'Oh, boy, believe me.'
'Pink, didya kill any Germans?'
 'Oh, boy.'
In his *Hand-Made Fables*, 1920, George Ade writes:
 They began to make out the White Houses and the big Red Barns and the Fat Stock ...
 'How do they look to you?' asked the Conductor.
 'Oh, Boy!' was all that Eb could exclaim.
The phrase was still going strong in the middle 1930s, as in Clarence B. Kelland, *Speak Easily*, *c.* 1935: '"You mean," said Mr James, "that you hooked this yegg with your

umbrella and grabbed off the ruby. Oh, boy! Where's the photographers? Won't I do a job with this!"'

A year or so earlier, Alec Waugh, *Wheels within Wheels*, causes an American to exclaim, '"Oh, boy, if you could see the look on my mother's face at times! She thinks she's living in a fairy tale. And as for that girl, oh boy and how! You should just see her!"'

In Ed McBain's *Shotgun*, 1968, we find this lovers' tiff:

'... Go ahead, go home, what do I care?'

'Oh, boy,' he said.

'Sure, oh boy.'

And again in his *Jigsaw*, 1970, when still healthily extant.

The variant *boy! oh boy!* occurs in, e.g., Morris Farhi's novel, *The Pleasure of Your Death*, 1972:

'Did you know, in the summer, now, the sun shines twenty-four hours a day?'

'No kidding?'

'And that nobody goes to bed. At least, not to sleep.'

'Boy, oh, boy.'

Another 1972 instance is afforded by Martin Woodhouse's *Mama Doll*.

To emphasize the longevity – of, at the least, its extraordinarily widespread use – the *New Yorker* of 19 May 1973 presents an elderly man as employing it in addressing his elderly wife.

But the popularity of such homely, apparently very ordinary, c.pp. is impossible to explain: yet I do not doubt that some 'smart Alec' will, in a learned and unreadable thesis, think it necessary to go beyond the natural explanation that such popularity was rendered possible, and was perhaps in the fact caused, by the homeliness and ordinariness and artlessness of the phrase.

oh, brother! is an exclamatory c.p., indicative less often of surprise or astonishment or assent or relief, than of dismay or wry comment or rueful afterthought: US: C20. Apparently suggested by the more naïve, less intelligent, yet more popular **oh, boy!** A late example occurs in Judson Philips, *Nightmare at Dawn*, 1970:

'Jane!' he said softly.

'Oh, brother!' the girl said, 'I thought you'd gone away. Where are you?'

oh, calamity! 'Expression so often used by lugubrious characters in farce played by Robertson Hare (1930s on) that it became adopted in jocular conversation,' as Vernon Noble tells me on 14 January 1975; or, as Paul Beale puts it, on 6 August 1975: 'Robertson Hare's woeful c.p. from the pre-war Aldwych farces, e.g. when [he was] de-bagged once again.'

oh, chase me! A satirical – or ostensibly satirical – invitation, issued by a girl to a youth, to run after her and kiss her. It arose, in the streets (originally those of London) in 1898, but it had disappeared by the end of WW1.

oh, come on – be a devil! See **be a devil!**

oh, definitely! seems to have arisen *c.* 1919, and by the end of 1920 it had begun its inane yet spectacular career. It notably occurs in, e.g., Sutton Vane's play, *Outward Bound*, 1924; satirically in A. A. Milne's *Two People*, 1931, and, above all and *ad nauseam*, in Maurice Lincoln's novel about 'the smart young things', *Oh, Definitely!*, 1933. The following example comes from Lincoln's book:

'What do you think of her?'

Peter considered the question for a few moments. 'She's dumb,' he said at length.

'Dumb?'

'Dumbest thing I ever met. If you forbade that girl to say "marvellous", and then stopped her from saying "definitely", she couldn't speak at all.'

oh, Gertie, get off my neck! See **get off my back!**

oh, good night! (*Low English.*) Meaning, "This is too much – I think I must be going"' (Ware). By 'low' he means not 'coarse' but proletarian. Period: very approximately 1895–1915.

oh, is that so? Farmer writes:

This expression ... serves the true-born American as a pendant to whatever observations may be addressed to him. It is both affirmative and negative, according to the tone of the speaker's voice; in the former case it takes the place of 'indeed!' or 'really!'; in the latter it does duty for 'not really!', 'surely not!'

It is an educated c.p.; moreover, it is also British; and it must date – from *when*? 1850 at the latest, I'd say; and perhaps from very much earlier. Cf **you don't say so**.

As late as 1923, in Robert Benchley's *Love Conquers All*, occurs this gem:

Among the more popular nuggets of repartee, effective on all occasions, are the following:

'Oh, is that so?'

'Eugh?'

'How do you get that way?'

'Oh, is that so?'

'Aw, have your hair bobbed.'

'Oh, is that so?'

'Well, what are you going to do about it?'

'Who says so?'

'Eugh? Well, I'll Cincinnati you.'

'Oh, is that so?'

oh, jolly D! A gag uttered by the character 'Dudley Davenport' (played by Maurice Denham) in Kenneth Horne and Richard Murdoch's radio show, 'Much Binding in the Marsh' (*c.* 1944–5). The words represent a Public School version of *oh, jolly decent!* – and there's a double pun in the name of the show: on picturesque English place-names and on the WW2, esp. RAF, slang term *binding*, (constant) complaining or complaints.

oh, la! la! and Anglicized **oo-la-la!** During WW1, *oh, la! la!* was a military c.p., used far more by officers than by Other Ranks; it expressed either joviality or a delighted astonishment. (B & P.) In a way, it extends the *c.* 1590–1930 *la! la!*, which expressed derision. Cf the slangy 'a bit of *oo la la*', a leg-show.

oh, Miss Weston! is a naval c.p., expressing disapproval – usually a pretended disapproval – of strong language: since *c.* 1910. 'Dame Agnes Weston was a great stickler for propriety' (PGR). Cf **my oath, Miss Weston!**

oh, mother, is it worth it? – C20 and perhaps almost immemorial – originated and is extant, as a feminine *cri de coeur*, and, as such, obviously not a c.p. But it has, in C20, been used with rueful humour and irony, mostly (of course) by women, mostly young women and girls – and then it is, no less obviously, a c.p. Its c.p. status has probably been reinforced by Arnold Wesker's little pamphlet, *The Modern Playwright or 'Oh, Mother, is it worth it?'* – referring to his early uphill struggle to make a living with his plays, and published in 1960. Cf **mother, is it worth it?**

oh, mummy, buy me one of those! This c.p., mostly Canadian and dating since *c.* 1920, recalls the much older **I (really) must have one of those!**, q.v. at **I must have....**

oh, my achin' back! 'Poking fun at the Japanese: Second World War [mostly in 1944–5]: South Pacific and US' (Douglas Leechman, 1973). Allusive to an old British c.p., **every picture tells a story.**

Originally, it seems, US. According to Miss Mary Priebe of Seattle, who was in the American Red Cross with the US Army from early 1940s for the next eleven years, the phrase swept through the US forces like an epidemic. She doesn't know the origin, but explains it as a mild expletive of exasperation.... She says it was sometimes, later, elaborated to *oh, my achin' back, sack, company!* but can't explain the significance of this. (Paul Beale in a letter written in 1975.)

oh, my giddy aunt! 'I think from Brandon Thomas's long-running farcical comedy, "Charley's Aunt" (1,466 performances on its first production starting in December 1892); countless revivals since then – and the "Aunt" is still running' (Vernon Noble, 14 June 1974). Usually uttered with a ruefully humorous smile or laugh, it occurred very frequently in, e.g., schoolgirl stories of *c.* 1946.

oh, my leg! was, *c.* 1810–50, addressed to someone recently freed from gaol. (JB.) A gibe allusive to the ex-prisoner's gait, caused by long confinement in fetters.

oh, oh, Antonio! This almost meaningless c.p. of *c.* 1912–30 vaguely expresses excitement and owes its existence to the once extremely famous song so titled.

oh, Pollacky! (stressed on the second syllable) – often shortened to **Pollacky!** or **pollacky!** – was, *c.* 1870–1900, an 'exclamation of protest against too urgent enquiries' (Ware). From the advertisements of a 'foreign' detective resident at Paddington Green, Ignatius Paul Pollacky, by birth an Australian, who established his agency in 1862. He achieved a fame embracing London as a whole: W. S. Gilbert's *Patience*, first performed on 23 April 1881, included among the qualities necessary to make a good heavy dragoon, that of 'the keen penetration of Paddington Pollacky'; he often advertised in the 'Agony Column' of *The Times* and when he died, aged ninety, that newspaper accorded him, on 28 February 1918, a well-deserved flattering obituary. (I owe most of this information to the staff of that courteous journal.)

oh, rather! is a variant – an elaboration – of *rather!*, meaning 'I should think so' (in reply to a question) and used by Dickens in 1836 (*OED*): late C19–20. Denis Mackail, *Greenery Street*, 1925, has '"Rather," said Ian enthusiastically. "Oh, rather!"'

Clearly not a c.p. when used as a conventionalism, a cliché; no less clearly and decidedly a c.p. when used ironically and satirically or when used in burlesque or 'send-up' or derision.

oh! sorry and all that! is a c.p. extension of the conventionalism *oh, sorry!* – itself an elaboration of *sorry!* Both British and Canadian ('Heard long ago, but can give no date': Douglas Leechman, December 1968) – and also, I believe, but do not assert, Australian and New Zealand. I heard it in England as long ago as the early 1920s.

oh, to be shot at dawn! 'A jesting colloquialism for anyone (including oneself) in trouble: ... shootings for desertion, cowardice, etc., taking place at that time' (B & P): military; Other Ranks': 1917–18.

oh, well! back to the grindstone! 'indicates that it's time to resume work after a break' (Mrs Shirley M. Pearce, 24 January 1975): C20 and perhaps since *c.* 1880. Cf **back to the drawing board!**

oh, well, it's a way they have in the army. See **it's a way....**

oh, well, you know how women (or, come to that, **men**) **are.** See **isn't that just like a man!**

oh, Willie! Willie! was, in 1898–*c.*1914, a c.p. of 'satiric reproach addressed to a taradiddler rather than a flat liar' (Ware). Cf **Willie, Willie – wicked, wicked!**

oh, Winifred! was, during the 1890s among the lower and lower-middle classes, a c.p. expressing scepticism and disbelief. Ware derives it from the reputedly miraculous cures effected by the water 'from St Winifred's Well, in Wales'.

oh, wouldn't it be loverlee! was, in 1958–9, a c.p. beloved by teenagers of both sexes and by shopgirls and office girls. It comes from the title of one of Eliza Doolittle's songs in *My Fair Lady*. (Michael Gilderdale in his valuable 'Glossary for Our Times' published in the *News Chronicle* on 22–3 May 1958.)

oh, yeah! Oh, no! *or* You think you know all about it. In *my* opinion, you don't. Adopted *c.* 1930, via 'the talkies', from the US; Brophy recorded it as a US c.p., but in the longer – perhaps the original – form, *oh, yeah! says you!*, and remarks 'An expression of scornful disbelief'. On 28 June 1934, the *Daily Mirror* headed an item 'Oh Yeah!'

HLM very briefly mentioned it in the definitive 4th edn, 1936; Berrey lists it thrice – once as synonymous with 'I don't believe it!', then includes it among 'disparaging and sarcastic flings', and finally as a threat; W & F, 1960, without dating it in any way other than by inclusion in their dictionary, gloss it as 'an expression of challenge, incredulity, or sarcasm'; early in 1969, Dr Douglas Leechman noted that in Canada it was 'very popular for a short time, *c.* 1940' and defined its Canadian usage as 'an expression of complete disbelief, uttered in an exaggerated tone'. In an article published late in 1972 and captioned 'Slang is Imaginative, Picturesque', Professor S. J. Hayakawa included it in a short list of 'counter-words' (*sic*) or 'repetitively-used expressions that are a substitute for thought. A few years ago it was "Oh, yeah!".'

But the US use goes, I think, back to the middle, or even the early, 1920s. A good, fairly early example occurs in Clarence B Kelland's novel, *Speak Easily*, *c.* 1935: 'It was magnificently absurd.... I said as much to Mrs Post. "Oh, yeah?" she responded.' Which further exemplifies the fact that the ironical usage is emphasized by casting *oh, yeah* in the interrogative.

oh, yeah! says (often written **sez**) **you!** See preceding entry, opening paragraph.

oh, yes, I've been there. I know what I'm about: 'a popular slang expression and usage' (Farmer): US: *c.* 1875–1914. Of women. 'sexually experienced'; of men. 'shrewd; much-experienced'. Adopted in Britain c. 1900; by c. 1940. obsolete.

oh, you are awful! See **you're awful, but I like you.**

oh, you beautiful doll! began, in the US. as a song title. words by Seymour Brown. music by Ayer (Oh. Edward B. Marks. why didn't *you*, in your valuable *They All Sang*. 1934. give all the names of composers. lyricists. singers in full?) and. as a c.p.. was still heard occasionally. even in Britain. where it was, although not very generally, current for 25 years or so.

oh, you kid! In HLM, Supp. 2, Mencken excoriates its users in the judgment.

the numerous catch phrases that have little if any precise meaning but simply delight the moron by letting him show that he knows the latest. *e.g.* 'How'd you like to be the iceman?' – 'Wouldn't that jar you?' – 'O you kid' – 'Tell it to Sweeney' – 'Yes, we have no bananas' – 'Ish ka bibble' (and its twin. 'I should worry') – and 'Shoo fly, don't bother me'.

Apparently c. 1925–35, although it lingered on for some years, to give way, briefly, to *oh, you kiddo!*, recorded by Berrey, 1942, in a long list of interjections 'of approval and admiration'.

oi, oi!, used in a particular tone of voice, interrupts or remonstrates with a speaker who is laying down the law. (Camilla Raab.)

oild, oild story – the, refers to the drivel drooled by the drunk: since c. 1950. This c.p. is at once a pun on 'the old, old story' and on the slang '(well) *oiled*', tipsy.

okay, baby! This US c.p., dating since at least as early as 1920, had become at least partly adopted in Britain by 1932 or 1933; there was, for instance, a letter published in the *Daily Mirror* of 7 November 1933, apparently indicating anglicization.

okay by me! – it's. Another US c.p. adopted in Britain at the same period as *okay, baby!* It had been adopted in Canada by c. 1930. The interrogative **okay by you?** might also be classified as a c.p.

okay, sheaf. An Australian pun on, and a synonym of, *okay, chief*: since c. 1930. Baker notes that it is a New South Wales 'advertising slogan that has won some currency. From Tooth's Sheaf Stout'. By 1970, very slightly obsolescent.

okey-doke! A teenagers' and semi-literates' reduplication of slang *oke*, itself a variant of *okay*, Originally (c. 1938) US, it reached Britain c. 1940. In Terence Rattigan's *Separate Tables*, 1955, in the section titled 'Table by the Window', when Doreen – a maid in service at Miss Cooper's Beauregard Private Hotel – enters the dining room, the following exchange takes place:

DOREEN: Yes. miss? (*Seeing John.*) Oh. you back? I suppose you think you can have breakfast at this time?
MISS COOPER: Just some tea. Doreen – that's all.
DOREEN: Okey doke.

old army game – it's an (or the). John W. Clark thinks it originated in the army and referred to some simple but tricky card game popular among soldiers. He also says: 'It became extended (in this country [i.e., the US]) to any unfairness or favouritism committed (often maliciously or venally) by military superiors. especially in the manipulation of red tape, and even to red tape … itself; then to any such thing, *not* military' (17 May 1975).

Through Colonel Albert Moe (in a letter dated 28 June 1975). Mr Jonathan Lighter quotes George William Small. *Story of the Forty-Seventh* (47th Coast Artillery. 1918). published in 1919: 'Name: Mech. Johnson. Nickname: Adley. Favorite Saying: "The Old Army Game".' And Carl Sandburg. *Good Morning, America.* 1928. has:

Since we have coined a slogan. Never give the sucker an even break and the Old Army Game goes ——
Let the dance go on …

It also occurs in Theodore Fredenburgh. *Soldiers March.* 1930:

'Do you get the idea?'
'Sure I get the idea. It's the old army game: first. pass the buck; second, never give a sucker an even break …'

And Leonard Hastings Nason. in *A Corporal Once*. 1930. uses the phrase *the old army game* at least three times.

Mr Lighter, by the way. says. 'As far as I know, it's always *the*, never *an*' – to which Colonel Moe rightly rejoins that he has, over many years, 'heard "an" as frequently as "the" in [this] phrase' and implies – what I'm pretty sure is the correct view – that, as is entirely expectable, whereas *the* is generic. *an* is particular.

But the whole matter is so complicated that this entry should be compared with **it's an old army game**.

old as my tongue and a little older than my teeth, usually preceded by **as**. A smart – originally a fashionable, evasive – reply to 'How old are you?': late C17–20; by c. 1930, slightly old-fashioned but far from obsolete. Recorded in Grose. 1788. it had already been aspic-in-amber'd by S. 1738. in the opening Dialogue. where the pertly charming Miss Notable uses it. Cf:

old enough to know better is a predominantly feminine reply to 'How old are you?': since late – ? rather. mid – C19–20. Cf the preceding entry.

old hat! See **it's old hat.**

old John – always on blob (or **ready to spit**; or **with a wet nose**): a low naval c.p.. directed at a mature rating of unhygienic habits.

old man must be working overtime – the. In reference to a man with a very large family: mostly lower-middle class: C20. Here, the *old man* is 'husband'.

old Mother Hubbard. See **that's old Mother Hubbard.**

old Newton got – or **took – him:** with *old* occasionally omitted. He crashed. esp. if fatally: RAF c.p. applied to a pilot suffering this fate: since c. 1925. Isaac Newton discovered the laws of gravity: and the pull of gravity is implacable.

old, old story. See **oild, oild story – the.**

old soldier – old shit; and **old soldiers – old cunts.** A Regular. then general, Army c.p.: since 1914. A gloss on the latter: an exacerbated sergeant or sergeant-major often adds, 'You ain't even that: a cunt *is* useful.' The former 'was the usual reply to a man who tried to claim superiority by reason of his long service' (Frank Roberts in PGR). Cf the second verse of the song in the next entry.

old soldiers never die: they simply fade away has been extracted from the British Army's C20 parody of the song 'Kind Thoughts Can Never Die' and the tune adopted from it:

Old soldiers never die,
Never die,
Never die,
Old soldiers never die –
They simply fade away.

Old soldiers never die,
Never die,
Never die,
Old soldiers never die –
Young ones wish they would.

This immortal ditty appeared in B & P and has been preserved in *The Long Trail*, lamentably out of print in Britain, but to be reprinted in the US.

old soldiers – old cunts. See **old soldier – old shit.**

olly, olly! was, among Cockney schoolchildren of *c.* 1870–1920, an invitation to a friend, or a companion, to play a game with, or to accompany, oneself; occasionally a farewell.

Hence, among all Cockneys, 'a shout of greeting or recognition, usually with a broad, rumbustious, freebooting leer to it' (Laurie Atkinson): C20.

Perhaps from *ho there!* or from Fr. *allez* (or even both) – rather than from Spanish *olé! olé!*

on a cat's back. See **more hair there than anywhere.**

on my shit list – he's (or occasionally **you're** or **they're**). 'Condemnation of fellow-worker or Serviceman who plays underhand trick on [one of] the group' (Laurie Atkinson, late 1974): since *c.* 1940. A pun on *be on the short list* for an appointment to a job or for promotion.

on parade, on parade – off parade, off parade, with *on* and *off* emphasized. A Regular, then a general, Army c.p. of late C19–20: 'or, in ordinary speech, "Keep your mind on your job"' (B & P).

on pleasure bent. A Canadian c.p. applied to a bandy-legged girl or young woman: since *c.* 1920. A crooked *gradus ad vulvam.*

on second thoughts I thought it best to put it in the old oak chest was 'heard during WW2 when the speaker was in danger of losing his temper or of over-hasty speech' (Peter Sanders, 21 May 1974).

It comes from the chant very popular with British soldiers during WW1 and dating back, I gathered during that war, some ten or twenty years earlier. Those words, however, formed only part of a mock-heroic chant that ran:

Today's my daughter's wedding day,
Ten thousand pounds I'll give away.
(*Three ironic cheers from the audience.*)
On second thoughts I think it best
To put it away in the old oak chest.
(*Audience*): *Yer mingy bastard! Chuck him aht!,* etc.

on the Erie. Shut up! Someone's listening: US underworld: since *c.* 1920. With a pun on Lake *Erie* and esp. on slang *eary,* with ears straining – usually applied to habitual eavesdroppers. The genesis may, by association both phonetic and semantic, have been *on the eary – eerie – Erie.* (For sources and quotations, see my *U.*)

on the stairs! was, *c.* 1860–1914, a tailors' c.p. in reply to a call for someone to do a particular job. Cf **up in Annie's room.**

on the wire at Mons or **Loos**; hence, **on the old barbed wire.** See **hanging on the barbed wire.**

on you! Hullo!: Australian: since *c.* 1925. As in
'Hiya, Curly. Hi, Ronnie,' I said ...
'On yuh, Terry,' said Curly.
Perhaps from *good on you!,* 'Well done!'

on your bike! Off you go! Run away!: since *c.* 1960. (Anthony Burgess in the *Listener,* 2 March 1967.) With an intimation that promptness and speed are advisable.

once a knight, always a knight – twice a night, dead at forty! A witty c.p., the 'twice a night' referring, of course, to sexual intercourse and the implication being 'as a regular thing'. Since *c.* 1950 at latest, but probably from at least fifty years earlier.

once aboard the lugger and the girl is mine. A male c.p., either joyous or derisively jocular, of late C19–20. It is based on a passage in Ben Landeck's melodrama, *My Jack and Dorothy,* which, produced at the Elephant and Castle theatre *c.* 1889–90, ran for many years, as the late Julian Franklyn, who knew a great deal about the 'Transpontine' or Surreyside theatres, once informed me. In 1908 A. S. M. Hutchinson's novel, *Once Aboard the Lugger – the History of George and Mary,* strengthened the impact made by the play. By 1970, very slightly obsolescent.

Cohen attributes it to John Benn Johnstone (1803–91) in *The Gipsy Farmer,* in the passage: 'I want you to assist me in forcing her on board the lugger; once there, I'll frighten her into marriage'; and says that this has since been quoted as 'Once aboard the lugger and the girl is mine.'

once before we fill and once before we light was a drinking c.p. of early C18. Ned Ward recorded it in *The London Spy,* 1709.

once is enough! has, throughout the C20, been applied by widowers, a few widows and divorced people – to marriage. It was canonized when, in 1938, one of Frederick Lonsdale's witty comedies was produced as *Once Is Enough.* (The year before, it had appeared in New York as *Half a Loaf.*)

once wounded, twice as windy was, in 1915–18, current among British soldiers, esp. the Other Ranks. This is the slang *windy,* 'having the wind up' (timorous, very much afraid), so widely used during, and for some years after, WW1.

once you've seen one, you've seen the lot. See **when you've seen one, you've seen the lot.**

one at a time. A (mostly fox-) hunting c.p. of *c.* 1820–70, if not much longer. In R. S. Surtees, *Handley Cross; or, Mr Jorrocks's Hunt,* 2 vols, 1854, we read, at the chapter titled 'Another Sporting Lector' (lecture): 'And "One at a time, and it will last the longer!" is a knowin' exclamation to make to a hundred and fifty friends waitin' for their turns at an 'unting wicket.' (A sort of turnstile.)

one consecutive night was, *c.* 1890–1915, a Society and theatrical c.p., meaning 'enough'. Ware cites the *Daily News* of 15 August 1890.

one flash and you're ash. 'A c.p. used about the atomic bomb and the hydrogen bomb' (Barry Prentice, 15 December 1974): Australian: since 1945.

one foot in the grave and the other on a banana skin. See **you've got one foot....**

one for the book, often preceded by **that's**. As an RAF c.p., it dates from the early 1920s and refers to *the lines*, or *line book*, which was kept in the Mess for the recording of gross exaggerations made by its members and was 'sometimes called a "Shooting Gallery"' (C. H. Ward-Jackson, *It's a Piece of Cake*, 1943); the latter name for the book derives from RAF slang *shoot a line*, to boast, to exaggerate shamelessly.

But much better known is the general c.p., *(that's) one for the book*, applied to 'a joke so funny or an event so extraordinary, that it deserves inclusion in "the book" – Joe Miller's Jest Book' (Douglas Leechman): originally US, Berrey recording it in 1942 as meaning 'that is something of account', it had, by the late 1950s, become popular in Canada and, by *c.* 1955, in Britain. In Clarence B. Kelland's amusing novel, *Speak Easily. c.* 1935, occurs this example:

'Sam slapped Sim on the back, and Sim countered by slapping Sam. 'That's one for the book!' said the latter.
'Ain't he the wise-crackin' kid!'

Since the late 1950s in Canada and by *c.* 1962 in Britain, the phrase had acquired the variant, *(that's) one for the record*, with reference to a book of records (in e.g. athletics).

Contrast **what a turn-up for the book!**

one for the gangway is the Royal Navy's C20 equivalent of the far better known **one for the road** and was probably suggested by it; it applies to a drink offered a guest just before he leaves the ship by the gangway. (Granville.)

For **one for the road**, see **and one for the road**.

one hand for the King (or **Queen**) **and one for oneself**; and **two hands for the King** (or **Queen**). These are C20 naval lower-deck mottoes. In late 1968, Rear-Admiral P. W. Brock wrote to tell me that he dated the two phrases as arising in mid C19; he added: 'In contrast to the maxim attributed to the Merchant Navy, "One hand for the ship and one for yourself", meaning that a man aloft should keep one hand on the jackstay for his own safety and use the other for handling the sail.' Of *two hands for the King* (or *Queen*), he remarked that it 'was used by a young officer or rating showing undue caution aloft'. The Merchant Navy's phrase appears in Bowen.

one hundred and twenty (usually written **120) in the water bag**. An Australian c.p. current in C20 and applied to an extremely hot day (120 degrees Fahrenheit).

one lordship is worth all his manners. 'His manners are perfect, but a lordship counts for more than manners.' An English c.p. of C17 – the pun clearly being on *manors*. It occurs in Ray.

one never knows, does one? You never can tell!: a playfully ironic c.p., dating from the late 1940s; slightly derisive of its literal, slightly pompous use.

[**one next door, it's number four – the**. One of the set phrases in the game of Bingo – not a c.p.]

one (or **two** or **three . . .**) **o'clock at the waterworks**. An Australian warning that one or more of one's fly buttons are undone: C20. Waterworks = one's urinary apparatus.

one of ours; and **put that light out!** From the WW2 remark and the WW2 order, came these two c.pp. uttered when a sudden, loud (esp. if very loud) noise is heard; but whereas the former fell into disuse *c.* 1960, the latter is still, in 1976,

no worse than obsolescent. Although *one of ours*, one of our heavy shells, had arisen in WW1, or one of our aircraft, or one of our bombs, arose in WW2, the phrase didn't – at least, so far as I remember – become a c.p. until *c.* 1944.

Of *one of ours*, it is to be noted that the phrase started during the Ger. air-raids on Britain during 1940–1, to be reinforced when well-meaning air-raid wardens reassured the timorous by suggesting that the crump of a bomb was merely the bark of an anti-aircraft gun – as if anyone but a fool could confuse the two sounds.

But *put that light out!* had enjoyed – and I mean *enjoyed* – an entirely independent existence and sense, usually as *put the light out!*, since late C19. When, at a private party or even a social gathering, a couple showed unmistakably that they wished they could be alone, some wag, usually male, cried, 'Put the light out!' – which became, in certain circumstances, rather a c.p. than either a cliché or a piece of low IQ'd traditional waggishness.

one of the mounted is a raffish c.p., dating from *c.* 1945 and applied to a female successful in 'getting her man'. Clearly a punning reference to the old saying – probably, at first, a proud claim – that 'the Mounties always get their man', the Mounties being the Royal Canadian Mounted Police.

one of these fine mornings you'll wake up and find yourself dead. An Anglo-Irish C20 c.p., either jocular or derisive – or both.

one of these odd-come-shortlies. In Dialogue I of S. 1738 we find:

COL[ONEL]: Miss, when will you be married?
MISS: One of these odd-come-shortlies, Colonel.

Current throughout C18–19 and, although obsolescent by 1920, not yet quite obsolete, the phrase means rather 'oh! some day. I suppose' than 'some day soon', even though, literally, it must originally have meant 'one of these odd days shortly to come'. It is applied to an event one cannot yet date.

one of those fine days, usually introduced by **it was** or **it has been** (or **it's been**) or **it is** (or **it's**). Elliptical for 'one of those days, when everything goes (or has gone) or went wrong'; or merely 'a hectic day': since the 'smart young things' of the 1920s. John Wainwright's exciting 'thriller', *Cause for a Killing*. 1974, begins thus: 'It was (as the saying goes) one of those days.'

one of those things. See **it's just one . . . .**

one of you two are both knaves. S, Dialogue III, 1738, has:
LORD SM[ART]: But, pray Gentlemen, why always so severe upon poor Miss. On my Conscience, Colonel, and *Tom Neverout*, one of you two are both Knaves.

That is, 'both of you are Knaves': a witticism of *c.* 1700–50. This c.p. belongs to those trenchantly illogical witticisms exemplified by 'There are two fools born every minute – and he is all three of them'.

one of your team is playing a man short, often introduced by **I see (that)**, has, since *c.* 1920, been jocularly addressed to a youth sporting an eleven [hairs]-a-side moustache. It derives rather from Association football than from cricket.

one squint is better than two finesses. This is, in the game of bridge (at not quite the highest levels), a c.p. warning one's partner that their opponents are trying to see his hand: mostly Anglo-Irish: since the early 1920s.

one star: one stunt was, in 1916–18, an extremely frequent c.p. of the entire British Army, but especially among officers: a newly promoted officer's uniform singled him out in any raid or attack. In WW2, the officer's battle-dress was the same as the Other Ranks'.

one that got away – the. At first, early in C20, derisive of anglers boasting about the fish that escaped and, oddly, remarkable for its size or its speed or its cunning; and then, since *c*. 1945, applied to someone who has providentially escaped some great danger, as, for instance, a bachelor from a female predator.

one that lives within a mile of an oak. Not far away. See S, 1738, towards the end of Dialogue I:

> MISS: Well, who was it?
> NEV[EROUT]: Why, one that lives within a Mile of an Oak.
> MISS: Well: go hang yourself in your own Garter ...

Current for a very long period: late C16–mid C19. The c.p. derives from the proverbial saying. (Apperson and others.)

one toot and you're oot. Not a word from *you*, please!: current in Britain since *c*. 1920 (as Ramsey Spencer assures me) and in Australia since *c*. 1950 (as Barry Prentice tells me). A jocularity based on Scottish dialect.

one-track mind. See **you've got a ...** .

[ONE-WORD CATCH PHRASES are not entirely a contradiction in terms, for usually they represent, either punningly or elliptically or formatively, a true phrase; or, expressed differently, when they stand, either phonetically or semantically, or both, for a true phrase.

Eleven that come immediately to mind are: *Abyssinia – Arbroath* (ephemeral) – *attaboy*, q.v. – *curtains!* (see **curtains for you!**) – *ishkabibble* (see **ish ka bibble**) – *period*, q.v. – *quoz*, q.v. – *Roger*, q.v. – *scrubbers*, q.v. – *snap*, q.v. – *wilco*, q.v.]

one word from you and he (or **she**) **does as he** (or **she**) **likes**. (Other pronominal variations are obviously possible – and no less obviously employed; but they're very much less employed.) He or she ignores your commands or orders or instructions: C20. Sarcastically derived from 'One word from me (etc.) is enough' or, less frequently, 'one word from me and he obeys'.

one you miss is the one you never get – the. A somewhat ambiguous, because slovenly, way of saying 'The one you regret is the one you missed' (failed to achieve, forwent) – or, as Barry Prentice has, 9 June 1975, neatly put it, 'A sexual opportunity neglected is gone for ever': C20: perhaps originally Australian.

only a little clean shit is derisively addressed to one who has been either bedaubed or self-fouled with excreta: C19–20. In Scotland, they understandably prefer ... *dirt*.

only a rumour! It's much worse than that! Australian: since *c*. 1919. (Baker.)

only another penny (needed) to make – or **make up – the shilling**. Used mostly by persons collecting money, esp. for a good cause: C20. With the advent of metrication, already 'on the way out' by 1974.

only asses make passes at lasses who wear glasses. Since *c*. 1960. An alteration and elaboration of Dorothy Parker's 'Men seldom make passes/At girls who wear glasses'. (A. B. Petch, 16 September 1974.)

only birds can fornicate and fly (with 'simultaneously' understood). 'Just an old saying the unromantic RAF had: "only birds can fornicate and fly. And birds don't booze"' (Gavin Lyall, *Shooting Script*, 1966): WW2 – and after.

only eating a good soldier's rations was, in 1914–18, applied by British, esp. English, soldiers to inferior soldiers; implying that that's all they were good for.

only here for the beer. See **I'm only here ...** .

only pretty Fanny's way. Characteristic: Parnell, *c*. 1718, has 'And all that's madly wild, or oddly gay,/We call it only pretty Fanny's way' (cited by the *OED*): C18–19. Probably a topical elaboration of 'only her (*or* his) way'.

only way to tell their sex is to get them in the dark – the. 'Heard today in reference to the difficulty in telling whether youngsters are male or female' (A. B. Petch, 16 September 1974): since the early 1960s.

only when I laugh (often written – heaven knows why! – **larf**). Elliptical for the literal 'It hurts only when I laugh'; but as a c.p., gaining a wider applicability, it has an overtone of irony: as a c.p., not much, if at all, before *c*. 1950. In 1968, Len Deighton increased the popularity of the phrase by titling one of his novels *Only When I Larf*.

oo-la-la! See **oh, la! la!**

ooh, an' 'e was strong! 'From a late '40's radio show, I think "Ray's a Laugh". A weekly "situation" was made to lead up to this c.p.' (Paul Beale, 6 August 1975); the 'gag' became – promptly became – a c.p.

oompah, oompah, stuff (or **stick**) **it up your jumper!** A jocularly derisive declaration of contempt or defiance or lighthearted dismissal: current since the 1930s – very common in 'the ranks' serving in WW2 (men and women) – and, by 1965 at latest, somewhat *démodé*.

[**oops-a-daisy!** A consolatory cliché, rather than a c.p., uttered as one picks up a child that has fallen: late (?mid) C19–20. A baby-talk alteration of *up-a-daisy* or *upsadaisy*.]

open the box! Make your mind up!: mostly lower and lower-middle classes': since *c*. 1920. (Frank Shaw, November 1968.)

open the door, Richard! is an Australian c.p., dating since *c*. 1930, and 'used when someone knocks on an unlocked door' (Barry Prentice).

'Not only Australian. I remember this as a song in this country [England],' says Ramsey Spencer, 3 March 1973; a few days later, he adds that 'the English song of this title dates from *c*. 1957'.

But it had probably come to England from the US: in HLM, Supp. 2, Mencken mentions it as having arisen during WW2 and become quickly defunct – yet not, apparently, quite so rapidly as he implies.

opportunity is (or **opportunity's**) **a fine thing, miss** (or **madam**). See **chance is a fine thing**.

or my prick's a bloater. 'A most unlikely alternative to the proposition just set out, which is by implication a dead certainty. "A fine pair o' knockers? Rubbish! Them's falsies, or my ..."' (Paul Beale, 18 July 1974).

or out goes the gas. A threat, current *c*. 1880–1905, 'to put an end to whatever is going on' (B & L).

[**or what have you?** lies midway between a c.p. and a cliché;

both British and US; it arose during the 1930s. I feel that it is very much rather cliché than c.p.]

or would you rather be a fish? 'A c.p. quip after proposed line of action (the more at the odds the better). To the response "Yes", the rejoinder is: "You haven't far to go"; rebutted by "No, it's too wet"' (Laurie Atkinson, March 1959). This set of witticisms – cf the 'chants' so popular among British soldiers in WW1 – dates from *c.* 1945 and springs from, indeed it forms an elaboration of, the c.p., **which would you rather – or go fishing**, which I remember as existing already in the late 1920s and which occurs in one of Dorothy L. Sayers's two or three best novels, *The Nine Tailors*, 1929. (Patricia Newham thinks that it comes from a famous song: that is true, in so far as the song reinforced the c.p. that prompted it.)

Cf *which would you rather be – or a wasp?*, current among London schoolchildren *c.* 1905–14, as Julian Franklyn once recalled; he added, 'So far as I remember, there was no standard reply.' Cf also such c.pp. as **how high is up?**, **how old is Ann(e)?**, **why is a mouse when it spins?**.

orchids to you, dear! was, *c.* 1935–55, a 'polite' variant of 'balls to you!' (*not* a c.p.). Based upon an etymological pun (someone with a curious mind really ought to collect such witty cerebrations) – of which most users of the c.p. were blissfully unaware.

order, counter-order, disorder. The late Colonel Archie White, VC, historian of the Royal Army Educational Corps, wrote to me, in a letter dated 30 June 1969, that it has been

a common saying amongst officers since long before my time – and that is now 60 years. The NCOs' more cynical version: 'Never obey an order: it will be cancelled before you finish it'.

I think I saw it in one of the Hornblower books [by C. S. Forester], and I've seen it a number of times in Victorian memoirs and in French military memoirs.

You would, I think, be accurate in saying that it is a sequence so inevitable where staff work is not of the best that it came to birth long ago in many armies and navies – and that the Air Forces of the world have doubtless heard of it.

The saying may also have sprung from the confusion that almost inevitably results from an excess of orders.

In Evelyn Waugh's satirical novel about army officers on Home Service, *Officers and Gentlemen*, 1945, we meet with this dialogue:

The Adjutant ... suddenly said; 'Sergeant-Major, couldn't we have recalled Mr Crouchback here and given him the address ourselves?'

'Sir.'

'Too late to change now. Order, counterorder, disorder, eh?'

'Sir.'

To indicate the degree to which this c.p. has become incorporated in the language, it will perhaps suffice to quote from the following passage on the opening page of Henry Cecil's novel, *The Wanted Men*, 1972: 'What they would have been like together in real war will never be known.... But if their behaviour at croquet is any guide, the proverbial order, counter-order and disorder might well have prevailed.' (But it never has been a proverb nor even a true proverbial saying.)

orders is orders. This jocular c.p., originally an army sergeants', became a general civilian c.p. very soon after WW1 – in 1919 or 1920. Like the preceding, it has been incorporated in colloquial English. Always with a humorous tone and undertone.

organize? you couldn't organize a piss-up in a brewery! See **couldn't organize ....**

our 'Arbour! and **our bridge!** These two gibes at Sydney-siders by those Australians who aren't, and esp. by Melbournites, have existed, the former since 1900 or even earlier; the latter, since *c.* 1925. It *is* a beautiful harbour; it's also a spectacular bridge over it. The retaliatory gibe is **stinking Yarra!**

out into the cold, cold snow lies half-way between a chant and a c.p. It has been current since very early in C20: and, as one might guess, it derives from the language of melodramatic and unblushingly sentimental ballads and plays. Probably quite wrongly, I've always supposed, heaven knows why, that there's a reference to *Uncle Tom's Cabin*.

out where the bull feeds. See **where the bull feeds.**

outside, Eliza (or **Liza**)! W are defines it as 'drunk again, Eliza' and says that it's 'applied to intoxicated, reeling women'; the implied meaning is 'Get out of this!' It is a low or streets' c.p. of mid C19–early C20. *Liza* is – or used to be – generic for 'females of the London proletariat': cf Somerset Maugham's title, *Liza of Lambeth*, his earliest and perhaps most compassionate novel.

over goes the show! This proletarian c.p. of *c.* 1870–1900, recorded by B & L, comments upon either a disaster or upon a sudden and dramatic change. It probably refers to the overturning of a Punch and Judy outfit.

over-paid, over-sexed – and over here was a fairly general c.p. applied by British Isles Britons, male and female, to the GIs stationed in Britain during 1943–5. Far more jocular than derogatory. (Mr Y. Mindel, 13 August 1972.) In Australia it was revived and applied to American forces personnel who spent 'rest and recreation' leave there during the Vietnam War.

over the left shoulder!, often shortened to **over the left!** (or even **over!**) This c.p. negatives one's own or another's statement and indicates derisive disbelief, the thumb being sometimes pointed over that shoulder. The full form is C17–20, but by 1930, slightly, and by 1970 very, obsolescent; *over the left!* is C18–20; *over!* is mid C19–20. Recorded at least as early as Cotgrave in his justly famous French–English dictionary, 1611. (Apperson.)

In 1870, H. D. Traill, 'Don't go? It's go and go over the left ... it's go with a hook at the end.' (F & H; *OED*.)

There is some reason to believe that it is, in Britain, a predominantly Cockney usage. Charles Smith Cheltnam, in *Mrs Green's Snug Little Business*, performed on 16 January 1865, has:

RAPPS: ...Never you take nothing upon your individual self, but just call for me *Joe*.

JOE: Oh, very well. (*Aside.*) Over the left!

The usage travelled to the US. Mencken records it in the definitive edn, 1936, of HLM, and again in Supp. 2, 1948; and so does Berrey in 1942.

Apparently from the centuries-old custom of throwing salt over one's left shoulder in order to avert bad luck.

over the top and the best of luck to you! – the last two words being usually omitted as grimly superfluous. An encouraging convention for the comfort of infantrymen about to leave the comparative shelter of a trench to deliver a frontal attack, the *top* being the parapet: it arose in July–August 1916, during the great Battle of the Somme – where one needed and occasionally met with good luck. The soldiers' song 'Over the Top', one of the 'Mademoiselle from Armenteers' group, begins thus:

Over the top with the best of luck,
    Parley-voo!
Over the top with the best of luck,
    Parley-voo!
Over the top with the best of luck,
Our number's up if we don't come back,
    Inky-pinky parley-voo!

It is recorded in B & P, 1931, a book that reappeared a generation later as *The Long Trail*.

In his novel, *Circle of Squares*, 1969, Bill Turner writes: 'I felt a sensation like cramp in my stomach as our car stopped, but there was no backing out now. Hirst opened the rear doors for us. "Over the top and the best of luck,"

Crossley muttered, getting out.' (Crossley was a veteran of WW2, not of WW1.)

There was a variant; F & G have this entry: 'OVER THE BAGS: Leaving the trenches to attack – going over the sandbags of the trench parapet. "Over the bags and the best of luck!" was a common phrase in this connection.'

John Gibbons, John Brophy, EP – these three knew all about it at first hand and on several occasions.

over you go: the longer you look, the less you'll like it! 'may be 'ollo'd to a friend looking long at a fence' – as Mr Jorrocks tells us in 'Another Sporting Lector' (lecture) in vol. I of R. S. Surtees, *Handley Cross; or, Mr Jorrocks's Hunt*, 1854, an expansion of *Handley Cross or The Spa Hunt*, 1843: a foxhunting c.p. of *c*. 1820–80, and perhaps very much longer.

'ow are yer? all right? 'of Wilfred Pickles' radio programme "Have a Go" with which the morale of the ageing was boosted in the late 1940s–50s' (Ramsey Spencer, 4 February 1975).

'ow you going, mate? How are you?: New Zealand: since *c*. 1920; also Australia, where it is usually followed by 'orright?'

p in swimming, silent – like the. See **silent** ....

[**paddle your own canoe!** – a song of *c.* 1875–1910 – became a cliché, not a c.p.]

paid out with spit is a c.p. reference to a small salary or low wages: US theatrical, since *c.* 1920; partially adopted, *c.* 1932, among English 'theatricals'.

pain in his little finger (occasionally **toe**) – a; often preceded by **he has**. Applied to a malingering Serviceman or workman: C20. One who runs to the medical officer or a civilian doctor on any excuse – or none.

pain in the arse (or **balls** or **penis**, etc.) – a. See **you give me** ... .

painters are in; or **have the painters in**. See **rags on** ....

Palmer is concerned – Mr. Applied, *c.* 1790–1850, to one who offers, or one who takes, a bribe: the underworld and its fringes. (Vaux.) A pun on *palmy* – to pass slyly.

panic stations! is a c.p. only when *not* used literally; esp. when employed humorously: since 1939 or 1940. From the navy's *be at panic stations* – to be prepared for the worst.

pap – his mouth is full of. See **mouth is full** ....

par for the course. See **that's about par** ....

pardon me for living! is 'an elaborate mock-apology, used by one checked for some minor error' (Douglas Leechman): Canadian: since *c.* 1945. It was very soon adopted in Britain; witness, in Noël Coward's 'A Richer Dust', one of the six stories comprising *Star Quality*, 1951, 'He jumped violently, and said in a voice of bored petulance, "Lay off me for one minute, can't you." Discouraged, she withdrew her hand as requested, muttered "Pardon me for living", and took a swig of tomato juice ...'

pardon (or **excuse**) **my** (or **the**) **French!** Please excuse the strong language! Dating from *c.* 1916, it was a non-cultured, non-Society c.p. A good example occurs in Michael Harrison's *All the Trees Were Green*, 1936, '"A bloody sight better (excuse the French!) than most."' Probably it was indebted to the British soldiers' experiences in the war-torn France of WW1, yet I cannot still an uneasy feeling that it arose during the Edwardian period.

The US form is either *excuse my French* (Colonel Albert Moe, 30 June 1975) or *if you will* (or *if you'll*) *pardon my French*, although *pardon my French* also exists in US, W & F citing Tennessee Williams, 1957. *If you will pardon my French* occurs in John Mortimer's *Collaborators*, produced and published in 1973, where Sam, an American, asks: 'Does she cut ball? – if you will pardon my French.'

parishes – his stockings are of two. See **his stockings** ....

[**parrot must have an almond** – the. This c.p. – very common *c.* 1520–1640 – was applied, whether equivocally or unequivocally, to incentive or reward or bribery. Bordering on a proverb, it is well covered by Apperson, who cites esp. Nashe's *Almond for a Parrot*, 1590. It alludes to a parrot's delight in almonds.]

Parson Mallum and **Parson Palmer**. See **remember Parson Mallum**.

parson would have said, I hope we shall meet in heaven – a. The opening dialogue of S. 1738, takes place in St James's Park, Lord Sparkish meeting Colonel Atwit:

COLONEL: Well met, my Lord.

LORD SP: Thank ye, Colonel; a Parson would have said, I hope we shall meet in Heaven.

Dating from late C17, it is still (1975) not quite extinct. Sometimes prefaced by *as* and sometimes modified to ... *would say* ....

party's over – the is 'often heard when something come to an end has been anything but a party' (A. B. Petch, 30 March 1976): since *c.* 1945.

pas ce soir, Josephine! is an English 'translation' into Fr. of **not tonight, Josephine!**, q.v. An embellishment and a politesse, it has been much less used than the English form; I doubt whether it has been used at all since 1960 or, at latest, 1970.

pas de Lafarge! Don't be a bore! Don't you know that's a forbidden subject – that everybody's sick of it?: a Society c.p., current, during the 1840s, in London, to which it came from Paris. It alludes to a notorious murder case: 'Did or did not Madame Lafarge murder her husband?' (Ware.)

past your heart: hold your hat on! is a coarse male exaggerative priapic boast to his female partner *in coitu*: raffish and 'pubby': the 1920s, says Laurie Atkinson; I remember hearing it used during the 1930s, but not since.

[**Patience is a virtue; virtue is a grace; Grace was a little girl who wouldn't wash her face**, the first line being a quotation, the second a naughty childish addition. 'This was certainly heard and said by us as children, in a sickeningly pious and provoking manner – guaranteed to needle even further anyone who was feeling rattled or impatient' (Miss Penny A. Cook in a letter dated 19 January 1975).

Yet clearly this is a chant, not a c.p., but it does show how thin, sometimes, is the borderline between the two.]

paws off, Pompey! Don't paw me about! A proletarian c.p. of *c.* 1910–40. (Manchon.) As if the girl were talking to the dog Pompey. Perhaps the sailors at 'Pompey' (Portsmouth) have had a say in the origination, as Patricia Newnham has suggested.

pay over face and eyes, as the cat did the monkey, slang for 'to give someone a terrible beating about the head', became a c.p. when, as so often it was, it occurred in the form, **he paid me** (or **you**) ... or **I paid him** (or **you**) .... Hotten records it in the 2nd edn, 1860, and it seems to have covered the very approximate period, 1840–1914.

Pearl Harbor. See **remember Pearl Harbor.**

peek-a-boo! originated in 1881, as an American song, sung by William Scanlon in *Friend and Foe*. It may have become a c.p. in the US, but not in Britain, where it has merely been a rather tiresome cliché.

peel me a grape, 'like *come up and see me sometime*, is owed to dear Mae West in *I'm No Angel* (? early 1930s). Coolly dismissive of a display of hysterical fuss. After a frantic and enraged admirer has slammed out, she turns to her Negro maid with a shrug and: "Beulah, peel me a grape"' (Ramsey Spencer, 4 February 1975).

Joseph T. Shipley – the eminent US historian of the US theatre – writing on 14 February 1975, modifies and amplifies thus: 'Apparently first spoken by Mae West in her play *Diamond Lil*, which opened in New York on April 9, 1928. ... Diamond Lil is a member of the demimonde who affects the manners (as she understands them) of the haut monde – the height of pseudo-sophistication.' And, by the way, Dr Shipley then mentions another line from the same play, the famous 'Come up and see me sometime', which was, as he puts it, to become her 'trademark'. And then, on 7 March 1975, he allowed me to quote from his *Guide to Great Plays*:

As actress and author, Mae West (b. 1892) occupies in the American theatre a special niche that she has carved for herself. She swaggers in it superbly, the tired businessman's bosom friend. To establish herself as prime exponent of one aspect of our life, she had not only to develop her special type of performance, but also to write the plays to which that performance added body and form. No picture of the American theatre would be complete without Mae West.

John W. Clark, however, in letter of 17 February 1975, writes: 'Perhaps rather a universally familiar quotation ... than a real c.p.; it is always, that is, allusive to her, and to her use of it, not applied to other situations.' Ben Grauer, however, writing on Christmas Day 1975, signalizes it as a c.p. encapsulating 'upstart insouciance and feigned elegance'.

Moreover, in the US there appeared, in 1967, Joseph Weintraub's anthology, *The Wit and Wisdom of Mae West*, which, in 1975, was published in Britain as *Peel Me a Grape*, thus placing the witticism high in the hierarchy of her sayings: there's canonization, almost a sanctification, of one of her wittiest and deftest c.pp.! (With thanks to John O'Riordan, March 1976.)

penny more and up goes the donkey – a. See **donkey!** ....

people are shot for less. See **in** (such or such a country) **people are shot** ....

[**period!** is that absurdity, a one-word c.p. Frank Shaw, writing on 1 April 1969, says that

finally; without extension or elaboration or modification, palliation or appeal: originally (*c.* 1945) typists', journalists', authors', broadcasters'; only since *c.* 1955 has it been at all general. 'Dead as a door-nail? Just dead. Period!' From a person dictating, and saying 'period' (full stop). Early BBC comic 'Stainless Stephen', ex-teacher, gave the whole idea of speaking punctuation signs a comic twist some imitated.

phoney as a three-dollar bill – as. See **queer as a three-dollar bill.**

pick a bloke from the Smoke! 'Cockneys' reminder to escape routine, gain reward. They have the gift of making little of obstacles' (Laurie Atkinson, late 1974): Londoners': since *c.* 1930, perhaps since as early as 1910 or even 1900.

pick a soft plank! Sleep easy: a nautical c.p., addressed to young seamen sleeping on deck for the first time (Bowen): mid C19–20; obsolescent by 1930 and obsolete by 1950.

pick him up and pipe-clay him and he'll do again was *c.* 1860–1910, a naval seamen's sarcastic remark directed at a Royal Marine fallen on the deck – esp. if he had fallen hard (Bowen).

pick on somebody your own size! British and – with *own* sometimes omitted – US: late C19–20. The general sense is 'Pick a quarrel with ...'.

In an article titled 'Lay Off the Thyroid' in *What of It?*, 1925, Ring W. Lardner mentioned 'the old stand-bys like pick somebody your size and you must be a good dancer, you are so tall, and if I was as big as you I would challenge Dempsey'.

pick the bones out of that! – let him (or **he can**). I'd like to see – or hear – him reply convincingly, or retaliate successfully, to that!: C20.

pie in the sky when you die. See **there'll be pie** ....

pig and goose – brandy is Latin for. See **brandy** ....

pig's arse and **pig's eye.** See **in a pig's arse.**

Pike's Peak or bust! (Rather similar to **California, here I come!**) The earliest record of the phrase occurs in the *Nebraska City News* of 28 May 1859, in reference to the gold discovered in the Cripple Creek – (now) Colorado Springs – area in that year; Pike's Peak was named after the explorer Zebulon L. Pike. In the gold rush, prospectors from the East and Middle West started across the Great Plains in their covered wagons, headed for the roadless, rugged and almost uninhabited foothills of the Rocky Mountains. See notably B. A. Botkin's, *A Treasury of American Folklore*, 1944, p. 310. Mr W. J. Burke, to whom I owe this information, on 22 May 1975, writes:

'Pike's Peak or bust' has become such a familiar expression no explanation is needed in the United States – everyone knows it means a determination to reach an objective, not necessarily a geographic one. It expresses hope, may imply difficulty of achievement; it always implies a buoyant, adventuresome, devil may care desire and determination to reach the top, to scale the mountain, to reach the decided-upon goal. The booming optimism of a young and cocky nation feeling its oats, tinged with braggadocio, chauvinistic.

pink pills for pale people. From the wording of a much-advertised remedy or tonic, comes this humorous c.p. interjected into talk about patent medicines: late C19–20; by 1940, obsolescent, and by 1950, obsolete.

pip, pip! arose either during or a few years before WW1 – perhaps from a musical comedy – and was, esp. during the 1920s, used – always trivially – both as cheerful greeting and more freely as a cheery 'Good-bye'! I remember hearing it during WW1, but never during WW2; and Douglas Leechman recalls it as having been also Canadian. Dead by 1950. Ramsey Spencer quotes from 'Bartimeus', *The Long Trip*, 1917, in which a young girl, asked how she'd reply to a rough calling *yah-boo!*, says, 'How thrilling! Why, I'd say "pip-pip".' It had become slightly obsolescent by *c.* 1925; yet Patricia Newnham 'when young' heard it during WW2–in the version *toodle-loo pip, pip!* 'jokingly said'. Camilla Raab remembers it as simply *toodle-pip!*

Mr Spencer (15 August 1975) adds that it was often used in reply to the farewell *tootle-oo* and thinks that it may have, ultimately, been 'based on early bulb-blown motor-horns, when the road-hogs deep *tootle-oo* was answered by the perky *pip-pip* of the smaller car'.

pipe and smoke it.... See **put that in your pipe....**

pissed in the sea.... See **every little helps....**

pisses more than he drinks–he. See **he pisses....**

pit-pat's the way! Don't stop! Go on! A proletarian c.p. of *c.* 1870–1914. (Recorded by B & L.)

pity about you! An almost hilariously derisive c.p. directed at a person either boastful or irritating or self-seeking–or to a person either constantly or excessively querulous: C20.

pity the poor sailor on a night like this! A semi-humorous, semi-compassionate c.p. that has, since the 1880s or 1890s, been uttered *à propos* of a stormy night. Perhaps prompted by *The Book of Common Prayer's* 'For Those in Peril on the Sea'.

place where the dogs don't bite–the. See **where the dogs....**

plant you now and see you later. I must–or I'll–leave you now and see you later: US underworld since *c.* 1930; by 1960, slang. (John Martin Murtagh and Sara Cowen Harris, *Who Live in Shadow*, 1960.)

play trains. See **run away and....**

play up, Nosey! A traditional London cry from 'the gods': late C18–early C20. From Cervette, that famous 'cellist of Drury Lane Theatre who, because of his very large nose, was called 'Nosey'. ('John o' London' in his *London Stories*, 1911–12.)

playing hell with himself. See **he's playing....**

playing it on the heart-strings, often preceded by *that's*, less often by *it's*. That's–or you're–being sentimental instead of realistic (Laurie Atkinson, late 1974): since *c.* 1920.

please, I want the cook-girl! was, *c.* 1895–1914, either directed at or 'said of a youth haunting the head of area steps' (Ware)–the household staff being 'below stairs'. Cf:

please, mother, open the door! was, *c.* 1900–14, a Cockney c.p., spoken admiringly to a pretty girl. They have winning ways, these Cockneys.

please, teacher! and **thank you, teacher!** The former indicates that the speaker wishes to make a remark (he requests permission to speak); the latter connotes irony or even derision towards someone who is either permitting condescendingly or explaining pompously or in excessive detail: C20. Both–obviously–from the schoolroom. To which should be subjoined the contemporaneous *please, teacher, may I leave the room?*, employed jocularly by adult humorists of retarded intelligence.

pleased.... See **he will be pleased!**

pleasure, Lady Agatha–a. Apparently a C20 Society c.p., but seldom heard since WW2. Perhaps from one of Oscar Wilde's comedies or from some other early C20 drawing-room piece. As Mr Brian Bliss has pointed out to me, it occurs in, e.g., Act II of Noël Coward's *Private Lives*, 1930:

AMANDA: Do you mind if I can come round and kiss you?
ELYOT: A pleasure, Lady Agatha.

[**pleasure to oblige a lady–it's a.** Not a c.p., but a workmen's conventionalism, often, says Laurie Atkinson, 18 July 1975, 'with gallant reference'.]

plough with dogs. See **I might as well....**

plus a little something some (loosely **the**) **others haven't got.** This jocular (and self-explanatory) c.p. dates from a motor-oil advertisement issued early in 1934 by the Shell-Mex and British Petroleum Company.

poet and didn't (occassionally **doesn't** or **don't**) **know it.** See **that's a rhyme.**

poke full of plums!–a. An impertinent reply to *which (is the) way to (such and such a place)?*: *c.* 1570–1680. It occurs in Brian Melbancke, *Philotimus*, 1583, and Giovanni Torriano, *A Dictionary of Italian and English*, 1609, and is treated by Apperson.

Pollacky! See **oh Pollacky!**

Polly put the kettle on and we'll all have tea comes from an old nursery rhyme, reinforced by Dickens's song 'Grip the Raven' and, as a c.p., dates from *c.* 1870. (Collinson.) Since WW2 it has become increasingly obsolescent.

poor blind Nell. See **and did he marry....**

poor chap, he hasn't got two yachts (or **Rolls-Royces**) **to rub together** is 'said of a rich man complaining of his poverty' (Peter Sanders, 21 May 1974): since the late 1960s. Cf the ironical 'Poor devil–down to his last million', which hasn't yet (15 March 1976) become a c.p., although it deserves to do so.

poor soldier–a. See **it's a poor soldier....**

pop goes the weasel!–occasionally preceded by **and**–has, since *c.* 1870, been regarded as a c.p.: originally proletarian, mostly Cockney. Ware remarks:

Activity is suggested by 'pop', and the little weasel is very active. Probably erotic origin. Chiefly associated with these lines–

Up and down the City Road,
In and out The Eagle,
That's the way the money goes,
Pop goes the weasel!

The City Road, a famous London street; The Eagle, a very well-known public-house in Shepherdess Walk. The *ODQ* attributes the song to W. R. Mandale and dates it 'Nineteenth Century'. In her *Song Index*, Minnie L. Sears classifies it as 'Children's Song'. The British Library's Music Index records *Pop Goes the Weasel* as 'an old English Dance', published in 1853. Perhaps, therefore, the song was composed to be sung to a dance that had existed long before, and continued to exist for some time after, 1853. Julian Franklyn (b. 1899) remembered it, as a Cockney c.p., at least as early as 1910; EP (b. 1894) remembers that the c.p. was freely used in New Zealand before 1910.

Very English.

pore ole thing–she'll 'ave ter go was a 'gag' employed by Frankie Howerd, in reference to his accompanist. It passed into general use to fit any vaguely similar circumstance or situation. (Paul Beale, 23 March 1975.) Perhaps it was reminiscent and even prompted by **don't shoot the pianist (he's doing his best)**.

pork chops are going to hang high. Very American, this c.p. predicts a hard winter. A Westernism. (Berrey.)

pot to piss (euphemistically **pee**) **in – he doesn't** (or **didn't**) **have a**. Indicates extreme poverty: mainly US and Canadian: dates since *c*. 1905. Often expanded by addition of **and not even a window to throw it out of**.

Potomac. See **all quiet on the Potomac**.

[**praise the Lord and pass the ammunition!** stands half-way between a cliché and a c.p. But it began as a famous quotation. 'Said at Pearl Harbor [7 December 1941]' by Howell M. Forgy (b. 1908), as Bartlett tells us.]

press on, regardless! – often shortened to **press on!** In Act II. Scene i. of *South Sea Bubble*, performed and published in 1956, Noël Coward uses the shorter form:

SANDRA: There are a million things I want to ask about – I don't know where to start.

GEORGE: Press on, my love. You're not doing badly.

As a c.p., it dates from the middle 1940s. Of its origin, Vernon Noble, a squadron-leader and one of the Air Ministry's four Official Observers (the other three were John Pudney, the late H. E. Bates, John Bentley) during WW2, has, in a letter written on 11 December 1973, recalled that the original form, *press on regardless*, 'was one of those joking phrases, defiant of all adversity, minimizing hardships, like "the gremlins have got into it", offered as an explanation for the inexplicable troubles with an aircraft'.

Common among flying, especially bomber, crews during the war, it refers to the determined prosecution of an air-raid over Germany, despite losses before the target was even reached.

See also **we must press on …**.

press the flesh! Shake hands!: *c*. 1910–40. It was recorded by A. E. W. Mason in his novel, *The Sapphire*, 1933.

pretend you're a bee – and buzz. This Australian c.p. of dismissal dates from *c*. 1950 and clearly puns on *buzz off*, run away. (Barry Prentice.)

pretty Fanny's way. See **only pretty Fanny's way**.

private peace – I'll make a. See **separate peace …**.

pro bono publico – no bloody panico! For the public's sake, no panic, please: originally and still, in the main, theatrical, used to prevent or to allay panic or alarm in an emergency, for instance, a fire or a sudden death at a public performance or even a minor emergency at rehearsal: C20. Note that the L. *pro bono publico*, in the public interest, is reinforced by the It. *panico* and perhaps also by the *-o* (a very, very common It. suffix) of English *no*.

In Laurence Meynell's *Die by the Book*, 1966, the actor 'hero' says: 'The taste of the tobacco steadied me. "Pro bono publico, no bloody panico." I reminded myself. The great thing was not to flap.' In a letter dated 19 November 1968, Wilfred Granville noted that, during the 1920s–40s, it was often used, jocularly, in the Royal Navy; he added that **'not to worry!'** (q.v.) would be the modern version.

promises, promises! Paul Beale, writing on 17 February 1975, says:

[A] c.p. within the past 2 or 3 years, used either sarcastically or jokingly (the soft answer turning away wrath); e.g., 'If I find this is a bum steer, I'll bloody well *do* you!' – 'Nyah, promises, promises!' The answer might as likely have been 'Is that a threat or a promise?' which is fairly common in Service circles still.

public enemy number one was originally applied to 'Kill Crazy Dillinger' – a once-famous Midwest US outlaw (as Berrey reminds us); it became a US c.p. It reached England after WW2. Mr A. B. Petch, in a communication dated 4 January 1974, reminds me that it is 'sometimes used for the Prime Minister in office' and that it was 'used by Jimmy Jewel in *Spring and Autumn*, a comedy series in 1973'.

pudding …. See **not a word of the pudding!**

pull a soldier off his mother – he wouldn't (occasionally preceded by **pull?**). Directed at a very lazy or slack man: originally (*c*. 1880) nautical, esp. naval, it became, *c*. 1900, also military.

pull down the blind! was, *c*. 1880–1940, a London lower classes' c.p. addressed to couples making love. (Ware.)

pull down your vest! In M, 1891, James Maitland scathingly glossed it as 'a stupid expression which originated a few years ago, became a catch phrase on the streets and then faded into deserved oblivion'.

Fourteen years earlier, in the 4th edn of *Am*, I see it glossed thus: 'A curious flash expression of recent origin, without meaning. It is heard on all occasions, coming alike from the lips of the street-boy, who would "shine your boots", and a fashionable attendant of the clubs [club member, not club servant]; yet no man can tell whence it came.' Bartlett quotes, from *Burton's Events of 1875–76*, published either very late in 1876 or, less probably, very early in 1877, the following verses written by H. G. Richmond.

Flash sayings, you know, now-a-days are the rage. –
They're heard in the parlor, the street, on the stage. –
'You're too fresh' and 'Swim out, you are over your head';
But a new one's been coined, and the old ones are dead.
'A Centennial crank' is one that is new,
And 'Crawl out of that hat' is quite recent too;
But the latest flash saying with which we are blest
Is to tell a man quietly, '*Pull down your vest*'.

John W. Clark, writing on 24 July 1975, says:

Common here as a c.p. up to, say, 20 or 30 years ago, when 'vests' (waistcoats, remember) 'went out'. Men's clothing makers have tried during the last 15 years or so to bring them back 'in', but with only very moderate success, and the phrase has never regained its wide currency. Its commonest – perhaps its only – use was as an irrelevant interruption, meant to be distracting and disconcerting, of a long-winded bore's tiresome discourse.

As it happens, Colonel Albert Moe had, only a week or thereabouts earlier, noticed what he judged to be a merely 'nostalgic', and predicted to be a brief, revival.

pull in your ears (– you're coming to a bridge)! occurs in a long list of 'disparaging and sarcastic flings' recorded by Berrey: US: since *c*. 1930; little used since *c*. 1960.

pull the chain! expresses the greatest contempt for a feeble joke or stupid remark: since *c*. 1960; by late 1965, already obsolescent – and by 1970, virtually obsolete. There is – obviously! – a withering cloacal reference.

pull the ladder up, Jack – I'm all right! is a late C19–20 variation of **fuck you, Jack....**

pull the other one – it's got bells on it! – with *it* often omitted. 'A rejoinder to a fanciful statement or a tall story. "We don't believe it. Pull the other leg, it has bells on it"' (Wilfred Granville, 13 January 1969).

Frank Shaw attributed it to the 1920s.

It has become so widely accepted that it sometimes occurs allusively, as in Karen Campbell's 'thriller', *Suddenly, in the Air*, 1969, 'Or was it my little joke! If so, I could pull the other one – it had bells on.' This shorter form recurs in the anonymous 'Complete Vocabulary of Spoken English' in *Punch*, 10 October 1973; the writer glosses it thus: 'There seem to be some flaws in your argument.'

Presumably from pictures of court jesters, wearing cap and bells.

A derivative variant is *pull the other leg!*, as in Robert Crawford, *Kiss the Boss Goodbye*, 1970:

'In the frames, you see, are jewels.'
'Go on,' I said, 'pull the other leg.'

Miles Tripp, *Five Minutes with a Stranger*, 1971, has:
'I'm on a research project,' I said.
She paused. 'Researching what?'
'Charitable deeds and the motives behind them. You almost qualified as a Good Samaritan.'
'Pull the other leg,' she said.

pull up your socks! '"Take heart, and try harder." Very common, and for at least 20 years,' writes John W. Clark, on 24 July 1975, of its US currency. Adopted from Britain, where it has been current since, I think, *c.* 1910, but where it has, since *c.* 1945, become increasingly outmoded.

pull your ear! Try to remember!: lower classes': *c.* 1860–1910. (Ware.)

pull your finger out! See **take your finger out!**

pull your head in! You're sticking your neck out – i.e., Be careful, you're talking foolishly or wildly: Australian: since *c.* 1930, often in the allusive variant, *pull it in!* An ephemeral Sydney version, *c.* 1948–51, was *pull your skull in!* (Sidney J. Baker, in a letter dated 7 August 1950; Kylie Tennant, *The Joyful Condemned*, 1953.) Probably, as Barry Prentice told me some years ago, 'from the habit of army men sticking their heads out of troop trains and making smart remarks: the origin was "Pull your head in, or people will think it's a cattle train."'

pulling the right string? See **are you pulling the right string?**

pump is good – your. See **your pump....**

punch a Pom a day! – i.e., a *Pommie*, i.e. an Englishman. A xenophobic c.p., used by New Zealanders and, I rather think, Australians: since *c.* 1950. 'It seems to owe something to slogans such as "Drinka pinta milk a day" and "Eat an extra egg a day"' (Barry Prentice, 9 June 1975).

Punch has done dancing. I can no longer dance to your tune – a tune of requests and solicitations: *c.* 1870–1910, perhaps with a decade added at either end. 'It was said with bitterness when good-natured helpfulness was felt to be taken as a matter of indifference over the years, and so, at another call, was brought to an end by the person concerned. It was used by my father, who was born in the early 1860s' (Laurie Atkinson, in letter of 6 August 1974). This was

the Punch both of Punch-and-Judy puppetry and of general folklore.

Punch's advice to those about to marry, as in 'Remember *Punch's* advice...: Don't!' This is the c.p. form of 'Advice to persons about to marry – Don't!' (*Punch*, 1845, VIII, 1). The witticism has been attributed to Henry Mayhew; and the c.p. has existed since very soon after 1845.

puns are punishable is a c.p. that – obviously – is itself a pun: mostly Australian: since *c.* 1930. The dovetail rejoinder is *there is no punishment when no pun is meant.* (Barry Prentice, 1 May 1975.)

push in the bush is worth two in the hand – a. A working-men's erotic parody – since *c.* 1925 – of the proverb, *a bird in the hand is worth two in the bush*, with a pun on *bird* and a reference to female pubic hair.

push on – keep moving! (See the Gifford quotation at **what's to pay.**) Originally a quotation from Thomas Morton's *A Cure for the Heart Ache*, 1797 (Act II, Scene i), it immediately 'caught on' with the public – in other words, became a c.p., but, to judge by the absence of other references, had, I'd say, a very short life, perhaps a mere two or three years and almost certainly not more than ten (1797–1806).

push the boat out! Go ahead – *I'm* all right!: military: WW1. Cf **pull the ladder up!**

put a cross (or **an X**) **on the wall!** 'Addressed to someone who has done something out of character, or when something strange or unexpected happens' (Barry Prentice): Australian: since the late 1940s. To mark – to record – the event.

put a galley down your back! Such-and-such a superior wishes to see you: printers': since *c.* 1860; obsolescent by 1930 and obsolete by 1950. A galley would serve as a screen – or, rather, as a protection against a metaphorical caning.

put a stone in the pot with 'em – and when it's soft, they're cooked! This C20 Australian c.p. is applied to food that remains tough, however long it's cooked. Jean Devanney, *By Tropic Sea and Jungle*, 1944, has, 'The old saying applied to them [galahs] ...'

'This c.p. is also British – a famous recipe for cooking porcupine. *In extenso*. When it's soft, throw the porcupine out and eat the stone' (Douglas Leechman): late C19–20 and apparently the originating c.p.

put an X on the wall! See **put a cross....**

put another record on! and **change the record!** A C20 c.p., addressed to one's wife, or to anyone else, 'going on about something'; 'Heard as "For God's sake, put another record on, will you?"' (A. B. Petch, April 1966). Socially, lower-middle class. A gramophone record, of course.

put crape on your nose – your brains are dead. Wake up!: US: from before 1919 and until *c.* 1940. HLM notes that a serious British periodical (*English*, 1919) recorded its impact upon London in 1918–19; despite its vividness and picturesqueness, that impact was very brief.

put her (or **him**) **down – you don't know where she's** (or **he's**) **been.** 'A jocular c.p., addressed to a friend who is demonstrating affection for a friend of the opposite sex, kissing, walking arm in arm, etc.' (Paul Beale, 23 March 1975): since the 1950s or a little earlier. From Mother's remark to thoughtless child, carrying or hugging, e.g., a doll or a ball picked up in the street: 'Put it down, darling, you don't know *where* it's been!'

put in a good word for me! Addressed facetiously by scoffers and agnostics to a person seen going to church on Sunday: since *c.* 1920 – if not twenty-or-so years earlier. (A. B. Petch, 10 January 1974.) A subconscious insurance against eternal punishment.

put (or **shove**) **it where the monkey put** (or **shoved**) **the nuts**; also **you can put** (or **shove**) **it**.... Go to blazes! *or* Go to hell! Or, more specifically, addressed to one who refuses to share, or to hand over, something expectantly requested by the speaker. In *Ulysses*, James Joyce has the variant ... *where Jacko put the nuts*, Jacko being a favourite name for a monkey. A low c.p. of late C19–20. Obviously the reference is anal, the vulgar equivalent being 'You can stick (or stuff) it!' and the polite, '**You know what you can do with it**', q.v. As Mr Y. Mindel reminds me, the phrase 'contains a physiological inexactitude: strictly the monkey puts his nuts in his cheek pouches'. He adds, 'The innuendo is probably intended, anyway.' What's a scientific inaccuracy to the coiners of graphic, earthy phrases?

Occasionally *nut-shells*, which perhaps makes better sense; also occasionally – but only very occasionally – *monkeys*; often ... *the monkey puts* (or *shoves*) *its* (or *his*) *nuts*; rarely, *that* for *it*. Cf:

put it where the sergeant put the pudding. You know what you can do with it. A low c.p. of late C19–20. The physiology of this phrase seems to be even more slapdash than that of the preceding phrase.

put me in! Let me join you!: prison cant: since *c.* 1925 – perhaps from a decade earlier. Literally, '*Include* me!'

put more water in it! – with *water* emphasized – has, since *c.* 1880 or so, been humorously addressed to someone tipsy or well on the way to becoming tipsy. (I was reminded of this one by the generous Mrs M. Thomson of Bray-on-Thames on 15 January 1975.) Probably from the, at first, serious advice tendered by teetotallers to those less total. Cf **take more water with it!**

put that in your mess kit! Think that over!: US Army: C20. (Berrey.) A deliberate variation of:

put that in your pipe and smoke it! Make what you can of what I've just said!; Digest that, if you can!; Put up with (*or* tolerate) that – if you *can*!: since early C19. Peake, 1824; Dickens in *Pickwick Papers*; 'Ingoldsby' Barham; Miss Mary Braddon (1837–1915), the now forgotten bestseller of late C19. (With thanks to *OED* and *ODEP*.)

It's a fact worth noting: that, despite its continuous currency and continual – indeed, constant – use, very little attention has been paid to this phrase, which is, I'd say, rather more of a c.p. than of a proverbial saying.

And, by the way, it derives from the very widely held, not entirely erroneous, belief that pipe-smoking and meditation go together.

put that light out! (occasionally **the** for **that**). See **one of ours**.

put the lights out! is perhaps more frequent than **put the light out**, q.v. at **one of ours**, third paragraph. Laurie Atkinson (20 March 1976) rightly points out that **put the lights out!** was usually completed by *they want to be alone*. He cites 'From the back of the hall a drunken voice shouted a favourite cliché

[read 'catch phrase']: "Put the lights out! They want to be alone." [J. A. Cuddon, *The Bride of Battersea*, 1967]: of two boxers hugging in a clinch'. I first heard it *c.* 1912; it probably goes back to the 1890s – perhaps to the 1880s.

put them in a field and let them fight it out! or, more colloquially, **put 'em in a field and let 'em fight it out**; there is also the more positive variant **... and make them** (or **force them to**) **fight it out**. Let the Heads of State fight out between (or among) themselves the wars they start, and thus prevent millions of innocent and rightly reluctant men and women and children from getting killed: Servicemen's (hence others') in WW1 and again in WW2. War is probably mankind's most spectacularly stupid folly: and one can only conclude that the age of miracles is *not* passed, the greatest, most mysterious miracle of all being that the human race has, so far, survived the human race.

put this reckoning up to the Dover waggoner! was, *c.* 1810–40, usually addressed to the landlord of an inn. JB says, 'The waggoner's name being Owen, pronounced *owing*.'

put up or shut up! Prove what you say or be silent: originally US: late C19–20. Back your assertion by putting up money – or shut up! (W & F; Berrey.)

Hence, in C20, also British but often apprehended as 'Put up your fists and fight, or shut up!' Desmond Bagley, in *Landslide* (set in Canada), 1967, has: 'Now, put up or shut up. Do you have anything to say? If not, you can get the hell out of here. ...'

put your money where your mouth is! Back your words with cash: Britain and Australia: since *c.* 1945. (Barry Prentice, *c.* 6 March 1973; John Braine, *The Pious Agent*, 1975, but ostensibly dated 1960.) Its complete incorporation into British speech-ways was, in September 1975, confirmed when a very widely displayed Government poster began to advise all good citizens, 'Put your money where your mouth is' above a smaller-lettered line advertising the National Savings Bank Accounts Department and, by so doing, forestalled the Trustee Savings Banks.

Adopted from US, where current since *c.* 1930, if not earlier. (Colonel Albert Moe, 28 June 1975.)

put your pudden up for treacle! 'Encouragement to be forthcoming; with a suggestive strain to give a double edge. Used, 1917–18, by officers in the Royal Naval Air Service' (Laurie Atkinson, late 1974).

puts years on me (usually preceded by **it**). See **it puts**....

putting spots on dominoes. See **making dolls' eyes**.

putting their things together or, in full, **they're** (occasionally **they are**) **putting** ... 'When a wedding reception is nearing the end, and the happy pair have gone to change before leaving on their honeymoon, [a male guest] may ask, "Where have they got to?" and another will likely reply, "They're upstairs, putting their things together" – which will probably encourage another male to say, "Have they started already?"' (A. B. Petch, 30 March 1976): lower-middle and middle-middle class: since early C20, I'd guess. A pun on the euphemistic *things*, sexual parts: cf the Shakespearian 'to *exchange flesh*'.

putting your two penn'orth in (Anglo-Irish); or **coming in** (or **you must come in**, or **must you come in?**) **with your two eggs a penny**. A scathing comment upon a paltry contribution to the conversation: respectively latish C19–20 and C18–early 20. In Dialogue I of S, 1738, Swift has:

NEV[EROUT]: Come, come, Miss, make much of naught, good Folks are scarce.

MISS: What, and you must come in with your two Eggs a Penny, and three of them rotten.

There is a C18–19 variant: '... *five eggs, and four of them rotten*'. Semantically cf the C20 'There are two fools born every minute' (or 'Two fools are born every minute') with its witty addition, 'and you are all three of them'.

Also cf the US **two cents' worth**.

putty won't stick. A US underworld c.p., applied, apparently *c.* 1850–1910, to 'any attempted deceit that miscarries'. George P. Burnham, *Memoirs of the United States Secret Service*, 1872, has, 'This kind of "putty won't stick" much with him' – This kind of trick won't fool him.

Q.E.D. *Quod erat demonstrandum*, which was, or had, to be shown or proved, and now *has* been: educational world: C19–20, although not much used since *c.* 1960. A tag of Euclidean geometry; a tag used humorously, often with a mock-pompous intonation.

Also, naturally, *quod erat demonstrandum* itself.

quarter flash and three parts foolish. A fool with a dangerous smattering of worldly knowledge: raffish, mostly London: *c.* 1810–50. (Pierce Egan, *London*, 1821.) Cf the obsolete slang *fly flat*, a would-be expert.

Queen, you've spoke a mouthful was a c.p. of 1929–30 and probably for a few years earlier and later. Harold Brighouse, *Safe amongst the Pigs*, performed 1929 and published 1930, has the following in Act II:

ROBERT: ... You may have uses for more money than you've got.

CELIA: Queen, you've spoke a mouthful.

ROBERT: This is serious, Celia.

Of anecdotal origin, apparently – but I do not recall the occasion.

queer as a three-dollar bill, the introductory **as** being usually omitted. Very odd, or strange, indeed: Canadian: late C19–20. There are no such bills (bank notes).

The US equivalent is (*as*) *phoney as a three-dollar bill*, recorded by W & F, 1960.

quick and dirty! Paul Beale, writing on 7 March 1975, says:

I heard it in 1973 from a retired colonel, talking about intelligence reports which were produced fast and without scrupulous accuracy. I heard it again recently, used by a computer expert to describe 'initial print-outs', before 'the program has been de-bugged'. One might use it as well to describe a first edition on which proof-reading has been skimped to meet a publishing deadline.

Probably since *c.* 1960.

quick and nimble: more like a bear than a squirrel was, C18–mid C19, addressed to, or directed at, someone moving slowly when speed was required. (Fuller; Grose, 1788.)

quid est hoc? – hoc est quid. A punning c.p. of mid C18–late C19. (Grose, 1796.) As Hotten explained, the question *quid est hoc?* – What's this? – is asked by one man tapping the bulging cheek of another, who, exhibiting a 'chaw' of tobacco, answers *hoc est quid* – 'This is what' – a *quid* of tobacco.

quiet as it's kept. 'Used prior to revealing what is assumed to be a secret' (CM, 1970): US negroes': since *c.* 1960.

quite a place you've got here. A variant of **nice place....**

quite a stranger, often preceded by **well!** Addressed to a person one hasn't seen for some time: C20. (R. Blaker's novel, *Night Shift*, 1934.)

quius kius! Hush! *or* Cease!: theatrical: *c.* 1875–1910. (B & L.) Mock L. for 'Quiet please!', the second element perhaps suggesting *please*, the first probably representing *quietus*.

quod erat demonstrandum. See the first Q entry.

quodding dues are concerned. This is gaol matter – i.e. an offence that, detected, involves imprisonment: *c.* 1780–1850. (Vaux.)

quoth the raven 'was the code sign for actors to beware of certain digs' or lodgings, as Michael Warwick tells us in his article 'Theatrical Jargon in the Old Days', in *The Stage*, 3 October 1968: in short, a theatrical c.p. of *c.* 1890–1940. From Edgar Allan Poe's famous line, 'Quoth the Raven, "Nevermore"', in that very famous poem, 'The Raven'.

[**quoz!** is that not entirely absurd contradiction in terms, a single-word c.p. It was included by Mackay in his wonderful pioneering article, 'Popular Follies of Great Cities' – in effect, London and its c.pp. It was employed to intimate incredulity; I suggest that, approximately, it synonymized **sez you!**]

R.C.s, Parsees, Pharisees and Buckshees indicates 'the Sergeant-Major's view of all those religious sects and oddities who do not conform to the Established Church and who can refuse to attend church parades, or could, when there were such things' (Paul Beale, 6 July 1974): army: since *c.* 1945. Cf **Sudanese, Siamese ....**

rabbits out of the wood, usually preceded by **it's**. It's splendid – sheer profit or a wonderful windfall: racing c.p., dating since *c.* 1920. Such rabbits cost nothing, whereas those in a butcher's shop *do.*

rag on every bush – (oh,) he has a. He is (or he's in the habit of) courting or 'chasing' more than one girl at a time: *c.* 1860–1914.

rags on – she has the; and **she's got the painters in** or **the painters are in**. She is having her period: mid C19–20, the first obsolete by 1940, the conjoined pair decidedly obsolescent by 1950. None could be called cultured or even tactful.

rarest thing in India – Guardsmen's shit, preceded by **the**. Originally, **what is the rarest thing in India? – Guardsmen's shit**, shouted by Regular Soldiers not Guardsmen at a Guards unit or section as it passed: late C19–20. In reference to the fact that Guards regiments never served in India in, at least, peacetime. (With thanks to Mr Y. Mindel.)

rarin' to go is a probably late C19–20, certainly C20, c.p. – US, of course, and originally Western – but only when it is used jocularly or ironically. It indicates an impatient eagerness to get started and, when used literally and therefore not as a c.p., it was applied to a high-spirited horse: dialectal for *rearing to go.*

[**rather!** See **oh, rather!**]

rather keep you for a week than a fortnight, the *you* often omitted. See **I'd rather keep you ....**

rather you than me! See **I'd rather you than me!**

rave on! Just go on talking nonsense! A US students' c.p. of the early 1920s (McKnight.) Cf the colloquial *raving mad*, very crazy indeed.

read (or **have you read**) **any good books lately?** goes back to at least as early as 1920. The stock reply, whether among authors anywhere or at literary cocktail parties, has, since the late 1940s, been, 'No! but I've written one'.

read 'em and weep! is, among US gamblers of C20, a dice-thrower's 'threat that he is going to throw a winning number' (Berrey). Not, since the middle 1940s, unknown among British gamblers.

read me and take me! was a Restoration Period c.p., used in reference to riddles and meaning, approximately, 'Get me?' *or* 'Get me!' It occurs in, e.g., Dryden's *Marriage à la Mode*, performed in 1672 and published in 1673.

ready whore, ready money. It's easy to find a prostitute if you

have the cash on you: raffish: *c.* 1660–1800. In Thomas Shadwell's *The Amorous Bigot*, 1690, at Act II, the scene in the Parks, Tope, a roistering adventurer, exclaims, 'These damn'd young Fellows ... will snap up all Adventures; they have the better of us at cruising, we have no Game to play at but ready Whore, ready Money.'

real money. See **that was real money.**

real nervous (or, more often, **'way out**), **dad**. A jazz-lovers' adjectivally admiring c.p., dating from *c.* 1950. (*Observer*, 16 September 1956.) Perhaps from 'It makes me real nervous [excited]' and *way out*, exceptionally good or unusual. Patricia Newnham, March 1976, writes, 'I think there is a link with drugs. Very much in use with teenagers today.'

red herring ne'er spake word but e'en, 'Broil my back, but not my weamb (or womb)'. A c.p. of *c.* 1650–1700: *womb* being belly, *weamb* a dialect version of that word. (Apperson.)

Red or dead. See **would you rather be ....**

Reds under the bed was of political origin and applied to excessive suspicion of Communist influence. It has been applied – as a c.p. – to any excessively or pathologically suspicious attitude. It arose in the US, during Senator McCarthy's Communist witch-hunt in the 1950s and soon reached Britain, where it has been very common indeed during the 1970s. (Ramsey Spencer, 4 February 1975.)

Relief of Mafeking – the. See **Mafeking ....**

remember Belgium! 'was heard with ironic and bitter intonations in the muddy wastes of the Salient' – the Ypres salient. 'And some literal-minded, painstaking individual, anxious that the point should be rubbed well in, would be sure to add: "As if I'm ever likely to forget the bloody place!"' (John Brophy in B & P).

remember I'm your mother and get up them (or **those**) **stairs!** was often used by the British soldier during WW1. A memory of childhood. (B & P.)

remember Parson Mallum! and **(remember) Parson Palmer!** Pray drink about, Sir!; Don't keep the bottle, or the decanter, in front of you! The former: late C16–18; the latter, C18–19. The latter carries the rather special sense of a reproach to 'one who stops the circulation of the glass by preaching over his liquor' (Grose). Both of these admonitions verge on the proverbial. (Apperson.)

remember Pearl Harbor! was, in WW2, an Australian c.p., often preceded by **don't panic** (jocularly **don't picnic**) and used in much the same way as the **remember Belgium!** of WW1. (Barry Prentice.)

Whether it has ever been a US c.p. seems open to question: some Americans say 'Yes, but only among Servicemen – and perhaps among journalists'; others hotly deny that it was ever a c.p. even in those two categories; a temperate US view is that it does figure prominently in the lectures, talks, seminars of staff instructors at Service colleges. On 17 February 1975, John W. Clark writes, '[Now] heard even less often than **remember the Alamo.**'

remember the Alamo! was occasioned by the massacre, in 1836, of a small US force by General Antonio Santa Ana, at that time President of the emergent independent Mexico: a warning, even if in jest. (Ramsey Spencer, 4 February 1975.)

I could hardly do better than to quote what Professor Emeritus John W. Clark wrote on 17 February 1975: 'A c.p., certainly **in US**, but now *never* used as a chauvinistic battle cry or with real reference to the Alamo, or otherwise than humorously. Universally understood, but not really very frequent.' Nor better than to add Mr W. J. Burke's comment, dated 25 March 1975: '"Remember the Alamo!" was the great-grandfather of "Remember the *Maine!*" and "Remember Pearl Harbor!" and could have gained currency any time [after 1836]. Even at this late date it is still in use, and heard more often than the other two exhortations.'

Cf the British **remember Belgium!** of WW1 and the Australian and perhaps US **remember Pearl Harbor!** of WW2.

remember the girl who went out to buy a knicknack and came back with a titbit. A low or, at best, a raffish Canadian c.p. of *c.* 1935–55. For the benefit of the innocent, *with a titbit* puns on *with a tit* (nipple) *bit* or *bitten*.

remember there's a war on! '"Don't waste time; don't be frivolous; let's get back to our real job." A popular admonition to "scroungers" and "gossips"' (John Brophy in B & P): WW1. Yet more frequently: **don't you know there's a war on?**

When used literally, it clearly isn't a c.p. – but it was very frequently employed with jocular irony, e.g. for 'Hurry up!' or as a palliative, 'After all, there is a war on'.

remember your next astern and **beware of your latter end** are Royal Navy c.pp.; the former, meaning 'Do unto others as you would have them do unto you', deriving from the literal advice to ships in station, 'Keep a good look-out both on the ship ahead and the ship astern ... and so avoid collision' (*Sailors' Slang*); and the latter, 'Watch your step!' – esp. towards the end of one's Service career' (*ibid.*): late C19–20.

result of a lark in the park after dark – the. Applied jocularly and insensitively to a pregnant girl: public-house and raffish wit: since *c.* 1930. (A. B. Petch, 14 January 1974.)

retreat? Hell, no! We just got here! has, from a famous quotation (the US Captain Lloyd S. William, at Belloar, on the Western Front, 5 June 1918, to the retreating French who advised him, just arrived, to turn back), become a c.p., 'used when someone may suggest that a task be abandoned before completion, or to give up or quit on some endeavor. It has been heard at athletic contests, even when it is late in the game and your team is hopelessly behind' (Colonel Albert Moe, 15 June 1975).

rhubarb. See **is your rhubarb up ... ?**

ribbin runs thick (or **thin**)–the. There is – or he has – much (or little) money: late C17–mid C19. (BE; Grose.) By itself *ribbin* or, later, *ribbon* was an underworld term for money.

rich get richer and the poor get poorer – the; with a jocular variant: **the rich get richer and the poor get children.** The former was originally (? late C19) a bitter cliché, which later

(?*c.* 1920) was employed humorously; the latter (C20) has always been humorous – admittedly somewhat wry-mouthed.

[**Richard's himself** (or, in Cockney, **hisself**) **again!** In Act III, Scene iii, of *Susan Hopley; or, The Vicissitudes of a Servant Girl: A Domestic Drama*, performed in 1841, George Dibdin Pitt writes:

GIMP: Poor young man! What an awful situation!
DICKY: No such thing – Richard's his-self again.

I cannot date the saying more closely than *c.* 1830–60. On maturer consideration I think that this is a cliché, enjoying a special popularity during that period – or perhaps merely a conventionalism.]

riding his low horse is a jocular c.p., dating since *c.* 1930; referring to a tipsy, or a half-tipsy, fool either boasting very rashly or otherwise acting foolishly; not very common. (A. B. Petch, 1966.)

right, monkey! 'Coined by North of England comedian [and monologuist] Al Read in radio series, 1950s on: "And I said, 'Right, monkey!'"' He reported domestic chatter' (Vernon Noble, 8 February 1975). See also the reference to him in **I won't take me coat off ...** and cf **you'll be lucky ....**

right old commercial going on – a. There's 'a right old brawl' or quarrel taking place: Suffolk: C20.

right on! 'has come to mean something like "you're on the right track" – "continue your present course" – or simply "OK"' (Norris M. Davidson, 15 June 1971): US – perhaps originally US negro – since *c.* 1960, in full force, yet already common enough during the 1950s.

In a Philadelphia newspaper of late May or early June 1970, Sidney J. Harrison, in a witty poem entitled 'This Cat Doesn't Dig All That Groovy Talk', declares that:

By fearful tax I'll put the bite on
All the squares who gargle 'right on!'

In the *New York Post* of 20 February 1976, Max Lerner, in a most entertaining and instructive article, wrote that 'A striking phrase emerged in the '60s: "Right on". Alas, it has all but disappeared. I am sorry to see it go. It had warmth, humor, camaraderie.'

By *c.* 1970 the phrase had been adopted in Canada; on 14 August 1974, Douglas Leechman defined its Canadian currency as 'precisely correct, exactly it'.

Cf the British **bang on!**

right you are! All right!; Certainly!; Agreed!: mid C19–20. (Hotten, 1864; Churchward, 1888.) 'Right you are; I don't think I'll go up,' is an example quoted by the *OED*. Apparently prompted by the colloquial *all right!* and the Standard English *you are right*.

ring up the Duchess! See **Duchess ....**

rise and shine (naval and hence also military) and **rouse and shine** (naval). An order (become a c.p.) to get out of bed: respectively late C19–20 and C19. F & G, give this definition for *rise* ...: 'A barrack-room orderly corporal's call, on reveille sounding for the men to rouse out'; Bowen at *rouse* ... cites the version, which John Brophy in B & P, 1931, glosses as follows:

the disagreeable or the amusing reality of the orderly-corporal's rousing cry in camp, billet or barracks:

Show a leg! show a leg!,

which dates from the early nineteenth-century Navy. Two popular variants were

Rise and shine,

and, no matter if the sun were not due to appear for some time,

The sun's scorching your eyes out (*or* burning a hole in your blanket).

An enlightening quotation is this from Douglas Reeman, *The Destroyers* (a naval story of WW2), 1974: '"Wakey, wakey, lash up an' stow. Rise an' shine, the sun's scorching your bleeding eyeballs out." The age-old joke at half-past five of a spring morning.'

road up for repairs! In society – a very long way from being Society – indicates that the female at whom the c.p. is directed is having her period: latish C19–20; by 1950, obsolescent, and by 1970, virtually obsolete. In long-outmoded unconventional English, *road* is the female pudendum.

Robinson Crusoe. See **you're not Robinson Crusoe.**

[**Roger!** – a one-word c.p. for 'That's understood and agreed' and 'That's OK' – was originally an RAF (*c.* 1937) then general Armed Forces' 'code word' of acknowledgment: British and by adoption, US. 'Considerable civilian use after WWII' (W & F).]

Roger the lodger is a c.p. that has, since *c.* 1925, been directed at, or in allusion to, a male lodger who makes love to the mistress of the house. *Roger*, not merely because it rhymes on *lodger* but also because it puns on *roger*, (of the male) to coit with, 'from the name of Roger, frequently given to a bull' (Grose).

roll on! is the very general shortened form, both of **roll on, duration!** (see next entry) and of **roll on, time!**, q.v.

roll on, big ship (or **that boat**) and **roll on, duration!** Military c.pp. of 1917–18, expressing a fervent wish that the war might end. The ship is, of course, that which will take the weary troops home. But the *that boat* c.p. came a little later – since *c.* 1925 – and belonged to the RAF. The commonest was *roll on, duration*, which derived from the fact that 'the volunteers of 1914–15 enlisted for three years or the duration of the war' (B & P).

roll on, Blighty! A military c.p. of 1915–18, equivalent to 'When this bloody war is over,/Oh, how happy I shall be!' *Blighty*, England, home, comes from Hindustani *bilayati*, foreign, esp. European.

roll on, cocoa! A prison c.p., expressing a desire for the evening meal to arrive with bedtime to follow: since *c.* 1918. (James Curtis, *The Gilt Kid*, 1936.) Imitative of **roll on, duration!**

roll on, death! May this monotony, this feeling of desperation, end! 'The cry of the "fed-up", or of the instructor whose pupils are slow in responding to his teaching' (PGR): mostly army: WW1 and WW2.

roll on, duration! See **roll on, big ship!**

roll on, my bloody twelve!; in full, **I heard the voice of Moses say, Roll on...!** A very common naval lower-deck c.p. of C20. 'Active service ratings are "in" for twelve years and as often as they are "chocker", they give vent to this expression' (Wilfred Granville in PGR).

roll on, pay-day! A workmen's c.p., uttered by those with

(almost) no money left: since *c.* 1919. Influenced by the Service c.pp. of WW1 – see **roll on, big ship!** Hence, since *c.* 1925, used by those who, weary of their present job, are looking for a better one.

roll on, that boat! See **roll on, big ship!**

roll on, time! May my sentence end!: a prison c.p., dating since *c.* 1880; not yet entirely obsolete. It occurs in, e.g., A. Griffiths, *Secrets of the Prison House*, 1894. Cf:

roll round!, with the year of release stated, is the US equivalent of **roll on, time!**: since *c.* 1880 at latest. An early example of its use occurs in Hutchins Hapgood, *The Autobiography of a Thief*, 1904.

rolling in the aisles – I had 'em. See **I had 'em (rolling) in the aisles.**

Rommel. See **that'll push Rommel back ....**

room for a little (or a small) one? See **is there room ...?**

root, hog, or die! Fend for yourself and earn your own living – or take the (dire) consequences: US: C19–20. In the chapter titled 'The Sixth Ward in the Old Days' (apparently the 1860s and 1870s), of *The Mulligans*, published in 1901 and written by Edward Harrigan (1845–1911), occurs this passage: '... Bimble's Band, that discoursed at intervals such airs as "The Solid Men to the Front!" "Root, Hog, or Die!" "Ham-Fat!" "When This Cruel War Is Over!" each selection, when finished, being cheered to the echo.' The *DAE* quotes the famous Davy Crockett as writing in 1834, 'We therefore determined to go on the old saying root, hog, or die', and an Iowa agricultural report, published in 1866 as stating, 'It has been a common practice with farmers ... to turn them [i.e., pigs] out into the woods or onto the prairies to get their own living.' Both a cowboy and later a minstrel song were thus titled: see Minnie Sears, *Song Index*, 1926, and its Supplement; and on 23 September 1975 W. J. Burke glossed it as an 'early Negro minstrel song'.

rosaries all the way. A Protestant c.p., slightly disparaging, to Catholic processions: C20. This, clearly, is a pun on the cliché, *roses all the way*, originally applied to the roses strewn on the road, the street, taken by a triumphal procession.

roses and raptures was, *c.* 1830–1900, a literary c.p., applied, Ware tells us in 1909, to the *Book of Beauty* kind of publication – what has, since *c.* 1960, become known as 'coffee-table books'. Very nice too, if you can afford them!

rot your socks? – wouldn't it. See **wouldn't it make you ....**

rough as bags and twice as dirty (or **nasty**). An Australian soldiers' c.p. of 1915–18, it was applied to the prostitutes frequenting the neighbourhood of Horseferry Road, London, where the AIF headquarters occupied a building. Cf the Australian simile (*as*) *rough as bags* and the English (*as*) *rough as a sandbag*, uncouth.

rough on rats – it's. That's tough luck!: since *c.* 1890; by 1960, obsolete. From, I vaguely remember, an advertisement for rat poison.

round the corner was, in WW1, 'the soldier's normal reply to "How far is it to ...?" It might be several miles' (B & P).

rous mit 'im! Throw him out!: US: *c.* 1920–50. Berrey says 'From German "*heraus mit ihm*".'

rouse and shine! See **rise and shine!**

Ruffians' Hall. See **he is only fit for ....**

ruffin cook ruffin, who scalded the devil in his feathers. A c.p. applied, *c.* 1750–1830, to a bad cook. (Grose, 1788.) *Ruffin* or *Ruffian* was, C13–early C16, the name of a fiend; hence, C16–early C19, the Devil.

Ruffin's Hall, a variant of *Ruffians' Hall*, q.v. at **he is only fit for ....**

rum, bum and bacca. See **beer, bum and bacca**.

rumour – it's a. See **it's a rumour**.

[**run away and play marbles**; and **run away and play trains** (with the variant **go and play trains**), signifying a contemptuous dismissal – the former, of late C19–early C20, and the latter, C20 – are not, I think, true c.pp.]

Run Away – Matron's Coming was, in WW1, an army c.p. directed at the *Royal Army Medical Corps*. Not very general. (F & G.)

run up a tack and sit on it until I call you! Oh, stop talking nonsense and be quiet for a while!: US students': early 1920s. (McKnight.)

S.A.B.U. See **T.A.B.U.**

S.N.A.F.U. and **S.N.E.F.U.** See **snafu.**

said he. In 1927 Collinson, in his invaluable book, recorded this example,

'Do you like that?'

'No, said he frowning.'

Current since the early 1920s and, although somewhat 'old hat', still far from having become obsolete. It derives, I'd say, from a novelists' trick that is also a journalists' mannerism.

sailors don't care – natural enough, with their girls in every port: latish C19–20. Canonized by inclusion in Benham. But Laurie Atkinson's gloss (18 July 1975) is valuable: 'Among soldiers, airmen and others, apt when what is in hand is not likely to be straightforward if niceties are allowed to get in the way; e.g., trespassers will be prosecuted, but if it's a short cut...' And, late in 1974, L.A. had glossed the c.p. thus: 'Quip to reject or mitigate undue caution'.

sailor's farewell – a, occasionally with **to you** added. A nautical, including naval, parting curse: late C19–20. Perhaps suggested by the apparently slightly earlier (and much sooner obsolete) nautical colloquialism, *sailor's blessing.* But the best comparison is that to be made with **soldier's farewell.** Cf also **the best of British luck (to you)!**

same diff is the Australian counterpart of the next: since *c.* 1945. (Barry Prentice.)

same difference. See **it's the same difference.**

same here! I agree: US: C20. (Berrey.) For 'It is the same here, i.e. with me'; 'I think the same as you do'. The drinking sense, 'I'll have the same [drink] as you' is hardly a c.p.

same in a hundred years. See **it'll all be the same....**

same OB. The usual price (for a ticket of entry): lower classes': *c.* 1880–1914. (Ware.) For *same old bob* (shilling), the usual entrance fee for most popular entertainments and pastimes during that period.

same old shit – but (or **only) more of it – the.** The Canadian Army's version of **snafu:** 1939–45.

same to you and many of them! – the, politely synonymous with the phrases immediately following this and is, so far as I've been able to ascertain, rather earlier, for it seems to have arisen *c.* 1880. In Act III of Stanley Houghton's *The Perfect Cure,* produced in 1913, we find:

CRAY: Confound Mrs Grundy! Confound Madge! Confound – yes, hang it, confound you, Martha.

MARTHA: The same to you, and many of them.

same to you with knobs on!; or the fairly common variant **... with brass fittings!** The same to you – only *more* so!: both belong to C20 and were prompted by – were, originally, perhaps euphemistic for – the low-slang expression, 'balls to you!' Clearly, however, there is reference to brass knobs on a bed, as Norman Franklin has reminded me.

The *knobs on* form was, at one time, very common in schools; it occurs in, e.g., Frank Richards, *Tom Merry & Co. of St Jim's,* as Mr Petch tells me. Cf the preceding phrase.

san fairy Ann (seldom **Anna**); occasionally **send for Mary Ann** (and **Aunt Mary Ann**). It doesn't matter, *or* It's all the same, *or* Why worry?: late 1914–18, then nostalgically; not, so far as I know, used during WW2, except among a few 'old soldiers'. B & P say:

An extremely popular phrase, approximated into English from the French *ça ne fait rien. ...* As the intelligence of the soldier penetrated year after year the infinite layers of bluff and pretentiousness with which military tradition enwrapped the conduct of the War, so his cynicism increased, became habitual.... Naturally he adopted a fatalism comparable to that of the Moslem murmuring his enervating '*Maalish*' – It does not *matter. ...* Let anything happen, the only appropriate comment was – *San Fairy Ann.*

Naturally, the phrase had its lighter uses, especially in defiance of the warnings of friends. It was so much used that variants were almost as popular – chiefly *San Fairy* and *San Fairy Anna.*

Hugh Kimber ends his war novel *San Fairy Ann,* 1927, thus: 'There is a magic charter. It runs, "San Fairy Ann".'

sandman (or **the dustman) is coming – the,** has, the latter since *c.* 1810, as in Egan's Grose, 1823 and the former (*teste OED*), since *c.* 1850, been either addressed to or directed at children beginning to rub their eyes and yawn. From their rubbing their eyes as if sand were in them; the same applies to dust in the eyes.

saucepan runs (or **boils) over.** See **your saucepan....**

save a sailor! is a Royal Naval officers' c.p., employed when, in the mess bar, a glass gives off a ringing sound: late C19–20. This sound is, in sailors' superstition, thought to augur a sailor's death by drowning. To prevent this misfortune, one places a finger on the glass, thus stops the ringing – and thus redeems the sailor. (*Sailors' Slang.*)

save the surface and you save all is a US 'sarcastic or cynical c.p. of general application' – derived from a varnish manufacturer's slogan; since the 1920s and 'still heard, though less than formerly' (John W. Clark, 17 May 1975).

saved by the bell. Saved, or spared, by a lucky accident or intervention: Britain and the Commonwealth: late C19–20. In boxing, the bell indicates the end of each round.

say anything but her prayers. See **she will say....**

say au revoir (also, slangily and facetiously, **au reservoir) but not goodbye!** We are not parting for ever – we'll see each other again: since *c.* 1910; the facetious form became obsolescent by 1930 and obsolete by 1950.

say, bo! A US form of address, probably at first (?*c.* 1880) among tramps and then more and more generally; by 1900 or very soon after, also British. For *bo*, see esp. Irwin, both at *bo* and at *hobo*.

say hey! is a US c.p. – and included in W & F's list of 'synthetic fad expressions', 1960.

say it again! I entirely agree with you: a tailors' c.p.: *c.* 1870–1920. (B & L.) A forerunner of **you can say that again!**

say it ain't so, Joe! W. J. Burke, writing on 25 March 1975, says:

[It] is a phrase that came out of a baseball scandal, 1920–21. The Chicago White Sox were bribed by gamblers to 'throw' a game in the World Series – or in a game leading up to that series. A small boy, who worshipped the team, is said to have approached one of the stars after the scandal broke and blurted tearfully, 'Say it ain't so, Joe', and from the sports pages to common speech was but a quick jump. When we face any situation with unbelief we say, 'Say it ain't so, Joe'.

From an academic angle, it may be suggested that this phrase merely extended the C20 synonym, not c.p., *say it ain't so!*: and the rhyming *Joe* – cf the British *have a go, Joe* – helped to perpetuate it.

say it – don't spray it. Don't spit while you're talking: Australian: since the late 1940s. (Barry Prentice, late 1968.)

say it with flowers! Send flowers!: originally (?*c.* 1920) US; by 1924 or 1925, also British. (Collinson.) Hence, 'Say it nicely!' – since *c.* 1925. The phrase owes some of its survival to its adoption by a well-known firm of florists.

say nothing when you are dead! Be silent!; Be quiet! A subtly trenchant c.p. of *c.* 1650–1750. (Ray.)

say, old woman, is your rhubarb up? See **is your rhubarb up?**

say one for me! Addressed to someone kneeling otherwise than in prayer: late C19–20. Perhaps mostly in Australia. (Barry Prentice, *c.* 15 December 1974.)

[**say 'uncle'!** A US formula, to which the required statement of surrender is *uncle!* A convention, not a c.p.]

[**say when!** has, since *c.* 1880 been a drinking cliché rather than a c.p. In *Modern Society*, 1889 (June 6):

'Say when,' said Bonko ... commencing to pour out the spirit into my glass.

'Bob!' replied I.

The 'dovetail' was outmoded by *c.* 1914.]

say when you're mad! Tell me when you're ready to lift: Canadian workmen's, one to another: since *c.* 1930. (Douglas Leechman.)

Says me! is the 'correct' reply to **says who?**: US: *c.* 1930–50. See the two quotations from Clarence B. Kelland at **says who?**

says what? is a variant of the contemporaneous **says which?**; and both forms were prompted by **says who?** In Clarence B. Kelland's *Dreamland*, 1938, we see:

'Yes, sir,' he said, 'I defy all of these personages and organizations and – and Mussolini.'

'Says what?' asked Algernon Swinburne's heavy, sleepy voice ... 'What's Mussolini done?'

says which? 'What did you say?': US: *c.* 1930–50. Clarence B. Kelland, in *Speak Easily*, *c.* 1935, writes:

'I trust,' said I ... 'that the studies you are undertaking

under Mr Greb are – ah! – proving of both interest and profit?'

'Says which?' she rejoined, and then very quickly she assumed a posture of elegant nonchalance.

Cf **says what?** and:

says who? Who says so? – addressed, in a truculent mode, usually to one's interlocutor: (W & F, without dating; Berrey roughly equating it to 'I don't believe it!' and, elsewhere, including it in a long list of 'disparaging and sarcastic flings'.) But two good – and earlier – references occur in a couple of Clarence B. Kelland's novels. *Speak Easily*, *c.* 1935:

'Alexander the Great'll see you through.'

'Says who?' asked Miss Espere.

'Says me, speaking up like a quartette.'

And *Dreamland*, 1938:

'Miss Higgs, you are guilty of reprehensible waste.'

'Says who?'

'Says me,' retorted Hadrian.

This c.p., dating since the early 1930s, is the progenitor of **says me!** and **says what?** and **says which?**

says you! See **sez you!**

schoolgirl complexion. See **that schoolgirl complexion.**

scraped 'em off me puttees! was, during WW1, a British soldiers' contemptuous reference to other soldiers; esp., perhaps, the Staff. (B & P.) Cf **I've seen 'em grow** and **they've opened another tin**, which are not at all points synonymous.

The allusion is to *shit*, whether literal or figurative.

scratch his arse with – he hasn't a sixpence to. A low c.p. of mid C19–20; obsolescent by 1930 and obsolete by 1950.

scratch my breech and I'll claw your elbow. Partly a proverb and partly a c.p.: C17–19. An earthy synonym of the entirely proverbial, and politer, *scratch me and I'll scratch thee* and, its modern form, *you scratch my back and I'll scratch yours.*

screams for later. See **cheers for now.**

[**scrubbers!** is a 'one-word c.p.', not a fully qualified c.p. It means 'That's finished' or 'That no longer exists': RAF: since *c.* 1930. (Examples can be found in, e.g., C. H. Ward Jackson, *It's a Piece of Cake*, 1943.) It may derive from the turf *scrub 'er*, to sponge off the big odds on one's (bookmaker's) board.]

seaman – if he carries a millstone – will have a quail out of it – a. A mid C18–mid C19 semi-proverbial c.p., alluding to seamen's traditional resourcefulness and ingenuity, esp. in the matter of acquiring food or drink. (Ray.)

search me! Also **you can** (or **may**) **search me!** Originally US (since *c.* 1900), it became, *c.* 1910, also British: 'But you won't find it' (a solution, an answer) is understood. The earliest reference I've discovered is in Gelett Burgess's essay, 'A Defence of Slang', in *The Romance of the Commonplace*, 1902. W & F cite a US book title, *You Can Search Me*, 1905; S. R. Strait, in 'Straight Talk' (*Boston Globe*, *c.* 1917), includes it in a list of c.pp. of the day; McKnight notes that it was very common among US students of *c.* 1920–2; George Ade uses it in his 'comedy-drama', *Father and the Boys*, 1924, in the form, *you can search me!*; Terence Rattigan, *While the Sun Shines*, performed on Christmas Eve 1943, and published in 1944, has in Act III, near end:

HORTON: Who is his lordship marrying in three minutes?

MULVANEY: Search me.

His distinguished contemporary, Noël Coward, in *Nude with Violin*, 1956, causes one of his characters to say, at Act II, Scene ii, 'In the idiom of our American cousins, Miss Jane – "search me!"'

The form *search me!* occurs in Hugh Pentecost's novel, *The Gilded Nightmare*, 1968, and in the *New Yorker*, 31 January 1970, where one of two visitors from outer space says to the other, 'Search me!'

An amusing 1960s British example of *search me!* comes in Ruth Rendell's novel, *Wolf to the Slaughter*, 1967:

'My daughter Sheila's having a jam session.'

'No,' said Burden with a smile, 'they don't call it that any more.'

Wexford said, belligerently from behind his beer, 'What do they call it, then?'

'Search me.'

see a dog about a man – I have to (or **I must**), recorded by Berrey, but also British, dates from the 1930s and is a jocular variant of:

see a man about a dog – I have to (or **I must**); also **I'm going (out) to see** ...; and the full, the original, form, **I have to** (or **I must**) **go to see a man about a dog**. I must visit a woman – sexually: late C19–20. Hence, I'm going out for a drink: late C19–20. In C20, often in answer to an inconvenient question about one's destination; I must go to the water-closet, usually to 'the gents', merely to urinate. Inevitably there arose the jocular variation, *going to see a dog about a man*.

see something new? is a C20 Suffolk c.p.: refers to someone who, usually pretty helpless and hopeless, has done something remarkable. (A Suffolk correspondent.)

see the chaplain! Turn to **go see the chaplain!**

see what I mean? is, naturally, a cliché when it is used literally, but a c.p. when it bears the sense, 'I told you what would happen. That's how it goes' (Wilfred Granville, letter of 23 January 1969): C20.

see what the cat's brought in! A variant of **look what the cat's brought in!**

see what the wind has blown in! See **look what the wind...!**

see ya! (or **see yer!**) is a post-1945 English, esp. Londoners', illiterate version of **see you!**

see yer at the Assizes! is (as Frank Shaw wrote to me on 25 February 1968) 'a lower-class facetious equivalent of **(I'll be) seeing you**': C20. But cf esp. **see you in court**.

see you! I'll be seeing you, *or* Au revoir: originally and mostly Australian: since *c.* 1930. (Baker.) By the late 1930s, also British (a good example occurring in Peter Dickinson's moving novel, *Sleep and His Brother*, 1971), the counter or 'dove-tail' being **not if I see you first**, as Peter Sanders has reminded me, in reference to the variant *see you soon*; and by the late 1940s – not necessarily independently of Australian or English usage – also US: W & F remark, 'Very common, esp. among students and younger people. Almost as common as "so long" or "good-by".'

I cannot resist an impulse to quote from Arnold Wesker's *I'm Talking about Jerusalem* (the new Jerusalem, a modern version of Utopia), produced and published in 1960, at Act II, Scene i, where Ada says to Dave about his friend Libby: 'He stood out here and he looked around and he said: "It's all sky, isn't it?" and then he stalked off with "see you".'

see you around! A valedictory c.p., dating since *c.* 1930, slightly more frequent ('Very common', says John W. Clark, 28 October 1968) in US than in the British Commonwealth. Cf **see you!** and:

see you bright and curly. 'I suspect a Canadian background for this farewell. *Curly* obviously change for *early*' (Paul Beale, 6 July 1974): since *c.* 1955.

see you (or **I'll see you**) **in church** is a 'common valedictory – always ironic' US phrase (John W. Clark, 28 October 1968): C20; but 'a good deal less often heard than, say, thirty years ago; seems to have come to be felt to be hackneyed and un-imaginative, and perhaps bucolic', he adds in mid-March 1975. Recorded by Berrey, 1942. Like the next, also – since *c.* 1910 – Australian.

see you (or **I'll see you**) **in court** (or, less frequently, **gaol, jail**) is another valedictory c.p., mostly Australian: since *c.* 1910. Humorous and occasionally ironic.

see you later, alligator! A US, Canadian and English c.p., to which the 'dovetail' or response is (**yeah, see you**) **in a while, crocodile**: *c.* 1950–60 and then derided as outmoded, yet still used. This sort of rhyming was, *c.* 1935–60, a vogue; a vogue that has left only a very small residue of phrases, which, after their vogue, strike me as being even more tedious and mono-tonously painful than one had felt them to be in their prime. On 9 April 1975, W. J. Burke described it as being, among teenagers, 'still heard'. Cf **what o'clock, cock?** and see the entry **don't knock the rock!**

see you soon! See **see you!**

see you under the clock! A lighthearted reference to an agreed meeting soon to take place, but not to any particular clock: since *c.* 1950. From meetings appointed to take place under a clock, e.g. at a railway station. (Wilfred Granville, late December 1968.)

seeing you! A shortening of **I'll be seeing you** and intimately comparable to **see you!** Extremely common since the middle 1940s, heard fairly often during the 1930s and even the 1920s.

seen something nasty in the woodshed. See **something nasty**.

sell the pig and buy me out! Often preceded by **dear Mother**. A naval c.p. of C20, perhaps also of late C19; 'used by anyone who is feeling "liverish" and "fed up" with the Service' (Wilfred Granville). Cf **who'd sell his farm and go to sea?** In B & P, 1931, in the section on 'Chants and Sayings', has the following:

Genuinely sympathetic... was the frequently heard say-ing:

Soldier on, chum!

Of which the next, also very common, reads like a parody:

Dear Mother, this war's a bugger,

sell the pig and buy me out, John.

——Dear John, pig's gone;

soldier on.

semper fi. See the second paragraph of **I got mine...** .

send for Gulliver! was, 1887–*c.* 1895, a Society c.p., referring to 'some affair not worth discussion. From a cascadescent incident' in Swift's Gulliver's Travels, Part I. (Ware, 1909.)

send for Mary Ann. See **san fairy Ann!**

send for the green van! 'Indicating that someone was going crazy or thought to be behaving strangely and requiring immediate removal to a mental hospital: 1950s' (Mrs Shirley M. Pearce, 24 January 1975).

send her down, Hughie! (and **..., Steve!**) This Australian – hence also New Zealand – c.p. of late C19–20, the *Steve* variant being used during WW1, expresses a fervent desire for rain. (*AS.*) Variations of the next, *her* for *it* being characteristically Australian.

send it down, David (with variant **Davy lad**)! The variant belongs to the Regular Army; and the basic *send it down, David* is often intensified by the addition of a repetitive *send it down*: late C19–20. In the army, esp. during WW1, it was used to implore David, the Welsh patron saint, to send a preferably very heavy shower, notably when it might cause a parade to be postponed or cancelled. Parts of Wales have a notoriously wet climate: and, what is more, Wales is 'the Land of *Leeks*' (leaks). Both F & G and B & P are eloquent about this c.p.

sent to dry us. 'Used to be said when prohibition was a leading topic' in Britain, esp. during the ten to fifteen years preceding WW1 and during the early 1920s. A pun on the cliché 'sent to try us.' (A. B. Petch, 10 January 1974.)

separate (or **private**) **peace – I'll make a**, occasionally preceded by **I think**. A wistful yet jocular, deeply felt yet lightly expressed, British soldiers' c.p., much used during the warweary years of 1917–18. (B & P.)

separate the men from the boys – that'll (or **this'll**). This crisis or national emergency will serve to determine who are the real men: much used by businessmen and orators: since *c.* 1930 in US and since the late 1930s in Britain; not much used since the 1960s. (Frank Shaw, letter of 1 September 1969.) A variant is *sort out the men from the boys*. And see **this is where the men are separated ....**

set 'em up in the other alley! This mostly printers' c.p. – mainly Canadian at that – has, in C20, been used 'when a task is accomplished. "O.K. So that's that. Now set 'em up in the other alley"' (Douglas Leechman). In other words, 'Well, *that's* done. What's next?' It's far from certain that there is a reference to ninepins.

seven and six – was she worth it? This is a Services' c.p., dating from WW2 players of housey-housey, which was retained in Bingo. (Mr R. Line, of Orpington.) In Great Britain, the sum of seven shillings and sixpence, was, for many years, the normal charge for many kinds of licences, including especially the marriage licence.

sex and beer soup are too good for the people indicates a 'mock-Marie Antoinette disdain for the senses of the people. Beer soup is a German dish made from beer, eggs and milk; of pleasing delicacy of flavour. Among a few of the British Forces in Germany' (Laurie Atkinson, late 1974): *c.* 1945–60.

sex rears its ugly head, very common in the late 1930s and throughout the 1940s, although used decreasingly since, was, when employed to mean 'Sex has (again) become operative', a cliché; but when – esp. perhaps in Australia – used as a synonym for *cherchez la femme*, it is a c.p., obsolete by 1970 at latest.

Sexton Blake! See **I'm Hawkshaw the detective.**

sez you! is that 'conventional' unconventional spelling of *says you* which assigns it to slangy usage. This derisive c.p., originally US, became also British *c.* 1930 and was signalized by Brophy; but in Britain, gradually – since *c.* 1950 – yet slowly, becoming more and more obsolescent. To paraphrase W & F, it arose in US 'since before *c.* 1925' and has been employed either to express a belligerent doubt of the addressee's knowledge or opinion or, at another level, authority or to indicate disbelief, esp. when the speaker does not wish to have to agree. It is also recorded by Berrey.

Noted in Benham and in other reference books, this snappy phrase has inevitably been used by hundreds of writers (the majority, very properly, US): for instance, Clarence Budington Kelland, who had a very sharp and sensitive ear for his compatriots' colloquial and slangy words and phrases; as in *Speak Easily* and *Spotlight*, both in the middle 1930s. The English novelist, Philip Macdonald, *RIP*, 1933, assigns it to an Englishman in the form *says you*, which recurs in, e.g., Selwyn Jepson's *The Angry Millionaire*, 1969.

shake the lead out of your ass! (or **arse!**) A US and Canadian, mostly workmen's, 'Get a move on!': since *c.* 1930. A US variant is *get the lead out*: W & F. Cf **get the lead out of your pants!**

shake your ears! – often preceded by **go**. A 'sick' joke of *c.* 1560–1790: advice to one who has lost his ears. It can be found in, e.g., Gabriel Harvey, 1573; Shakespeare: Mrs F. Sheridan, 1764. (Apperson.)

shall I put a bit of hair round it for you? is a crude question posed to a workman having trouble inserting something into something else, the 'dovetail' or usual response being, **yes, if you've got the right kind**: Canadian: C20. Analogous to **don't look down ....**

shall I spell it out for you? See **spell it out ....**

shall us? let's! Shall we do it? Let's!: Current, esp. among juveniles, *c.* 1895–1914. Probably suggested by Cockney *shall us?* for *shall we?*

shame on your shimmy! A partly facetious pun on 'Shame on you!': lower-middle class: since *c.* 1930. Here, *shimmy* is a slang form of *chemise*.

shame to take the money – a, sometimes preceded by **it's**. That's money very easily earned or otherwise received, esp. for work one has enjoyed doing: late C19–20.

shape up or ship out! Straighten up and fly right; snap out of it; get on the ball; a threat to get rid of the person so addressed unless he shows an improvement in the performance of his 'uties. Milieu: originally army usage during WW2 ... but not restricted to armed forces' usage (Arthur M. Z. Norman, 'Army Speech ...', in *American Speech*, May 1956): 'The soldier's language is cemented by more or less ephemeral idioms: *You've had it* (a promise of punishment); *Shape up or ship out* (start soldiering or be sent to a combat zone)' (Colonel Albert Moe, 14 July 1975). Note that Mr W. J. Burke, 18 August 1975, writes: 'Navy slang. Now used by any employer who warns employee to "get with it" ... or pick up his check.'

share that among you! was, during WW1 – or, at least, 1915–18 – a soldiers' c.p., uttered as one hurls a hand-grenade into an enemy trench or dug-out; 'he might be quite jovial about it' (B & P), for the action released him from tension and frustration.

sharp's the word and quick's the motion, often shortened to **sharp's the word**. A c.p. implying that a person is 'very attentive to his own interest' (Grose, 1788): since *c.* 1660; by 1930, slightly obsolescent, yet not, even in the 1970s, obsolete. An elaboration of *sharp's the word*, an enjoining of promptitude. In Sir John Vanbrugh's *The Mistake*, performed in December 1705 and published in 1706, Lopez speaking an aside to his master, Don Lorenzo, in Act III, says: 'Are you thereabouts [i.e., near the mark], i' faith? Then sharp's the word.'

In S, 1738 (but begun thirty years earlier), in Dialogue III, we see:

LADY ANS[WERALL]: Upon my Word, they must rise early that would cheat her of her Money. Sharp's the word with her: Diamonds cut Diamonds.

Here, *sharp* bears the two meanings, 'prompt' or 'very quick', and 'shrewd'.

In Richard Brinsley Peake, *Ten Thousand a Year: A Drama* (adapted from Samuel Warren's famous novel), performed in 1842, at Act I, Scene i, Titmouse, formerly a linen-draper's assistant, addresses his former close companion thus abruptly: 'What d'ye want with me, sir? Sharp's the word.'

When Sharp's Toffee launched their advertising campaign, many years ago, their publicity man brilliantly introduced the slogan, 'Sharp's a word for toffee'. Mr A. C. Drew of Trebor Sharps Ltd, as the old firm became during the 1960s, says that 'Sharp's a word for toffee', as a slogan, was first used in 1927, so far as he knows. Edward (later Sir Edward) Sharp began to manufacture this famous toffee in 1880, at Maidstone. The slogan did much to revive the c.p. *sharp's the word*.

shave, a shilling, (and) a shove ashore – a; also **shit, shave, shove ashore**. This naval (lower-deck) c.p. was applied to the procedure and priorities of short leave. The *shove* synonymizes 'a short time' or expeditious copulation. The variant *shit, shave, (and) shove ashore* likewise describes a matlow's evening-leave routine; and it has two elaborations: *I've had* – or *I had* – *a shit, shave, shower, shoeshine and shampoo*, a Canadian c.p. that, arising *c.* 1930, was very general among Canadian soldiers during WW2, implying as it did, a 'heavy date', and the British *shit, shine, shave, shampoo and shift*, where *shift* = a prompt and speedy departure. Lately, Paul Beale writes, *I've had* tends to be dropped, and the phrase starts simply *Time for a shit* ...

she carries the broom (at the masthead). She's a whore: a seaport c.p. of *c.* 1810–90. (JB.) The reference is to that broom which, attached to the masthead, indicated that the ship had been sold.

she couldn't cook hot water for a barber has, since *c.* 1880, been applied to an inferior housekeeper, esp. to a girl unlikely to be able to 'feed the brute' satisfactorily.

she didn't seem to mind it very much. A proletarian c.p., grimly ironic, implying considerable jealousy in the female concerned: *c.* 1880–1910. (Ware.)

she dunno where she are. See **'e dunno where 'e are**.

she goes as if she cracked nuts with her tail was, C19–early C20, directed at a woman with a provocative gait.

she had a hair across her arse is 'said of a perpetually bad-tempered woman, it being suggested that this minor irritation accounted for her evil temper. Recent' (Douglas Leechman, December 1968): a Canadian c.p.

she has a bun in the oven. See **she's joined the club**.

she has (or **she's got) a nice pair of** (pause) **eyes**. She has a very shapely figure: waggish: since *c.* 1960 or perhaps a decade earlier. The *eyes* euphemizes *breasts*.

she has (or **she's) been a good wife to him** is an ironic proletarian c.p. 'cast at a drunken woman rolling in the streets' (Ware): since *c.* 1905; by 1940, obsolescent; by 1975, virtually obsolete.

she has everything has, since *c.* 1945, been applied to an exceptionally – and, esp., physically – attractive girl or woman. Also **she has two of everything**; well, not quite everything.

she has (or **she's got) legs up to her bum**. A mid C19–20 c.p., slightly obsolescent by 1970, addressed by men to boys in order to imply a common humanity: 'She has legs too, you know; just like you, son.'

she has (or **she's got) round heels** is, in Canada, directed at a very accommodating female, her heels being so round that a mere nudge will put her on her back.

she has seen something nasty in the woodshed. See **something nasty ...**.

she has swallowed a stake and cannot stoop. See **swallowed ...**.

she has two of everything. See **she has everything**.

she hasn't had it so long, sometimes preceded by **but**. A reply to the oft-heard complaint, 'What has *she* got that I haven't (got)?' Since the 1940s.

'she' is a (or **the) cat's mother**. One of the two or three best-known of the domestic c.pp., this has, mid (?early) C19–20, been addressed, usually by a parent, to a child, whether very young or teenaged, referring thus to his or her mother. By 1960, slightly obsolescent.

There is a variant: *who is 'she'? the cat's grandmother?*: late C19–mid C20. (Professor T. B. W. Reid, letter of 1 January 1972.) In Dodie Smith's *Touch Wood*, performed and published in 1934; at Act II, Scene iv, there is the following exchange between Nonny, a little girl, and Elizabeth, a spinster, aged thirty-eight:

NONNY (*with a jerk towards Elizabeth*): Perhaps she'd play.

ELIZABETH: In my young days I was taught that 'she' was the cat's grandmother

– which exemplifies the entirely natural extension of the relationship.

she is in her skin. See **in his skin**.

she is so innocent that she thinks Fucking is a town in China; occasionally **she was...that she thought...was a town...**. This is a mostly Londoners' c.p., dating since *c.* 1940. The geographical reference is to Chinese *Fukien*, a south-eastern maritime province.

she knows about it now. See **now she knows about it**.

she looks as if she could eat me without salt. In S, 1738, Dialogue I, Neverout says: 'But. pray my Lady *Smart*, does not Miss look as if she could eat me without Salt?' – that is, finds me so delightful that she could eat me. A c.p. current throughout most of C18. Cf the C19–20 colloquialism: (a person) *good enough to eat*.

[**she rapes awful easy** is a jocularly sardonic US c.p., applied to girls not so very reluctantly admitting that they've been 'raped' once again: since the middle 1940s, if not a decade earlier. But 'this is just an example of a pattern; "I scare easy" is commoner' (John W. Clark, mid-March 1975). Not, therefore, a true c.p.]

she sails. A US underworld c.p., dating since the 1920s and applied to a compliant or accommodating girl or woman. (Berrey.) Cf the British tramps' **she's all right**.

she smokes and **she's a smoker**. She performs penilingism: low: C20.

she stacks up. See **she's class**.

she thinks she is wearing a white collar. She's putting on 'side': a Women's Army Auxiliary Corps c.p. of 1917–18. Among the 'Waacs' a white collar was worn by NCOs. (B & P.)

she walks like she's got a feather up her ass. This C20 Canadianism is applied to a woman noticeable for her self-conscious, mincing gait.

she was so innocent.... See **she is so innocent....**

she went out to buy a knickknack and came back with a titbit – is an occasional variant of **remember the girl**.

she will (or more commonly **she'll**) **die wondering**. An Australian C20 c.p., referring to a virgin spinster. Hence the c.p., *at least she won't die wondering*, applied, since c. 1920, to a spinster marrying late and badly. (Barry Prentice.)

she will go off in an aromatic faint was, in 1883–c. 1886, a Society gibe at 'a fantastical woman, meaning that her delicate nerves will surely be the death of her' (Ware).

she will say anything but her prayers – and those she whistles. She never says her prayers: current, late C17–mid C19, it was partly a proverbial saying and partly a c.p. S, 1738, Dialogue I, gives:

> LADY SM[ART]: Well said, Miss: I vow, Mr *Neverout*, the Girl is too hard for you.
> NEV[EROUT]: Ay, Miss will say anything but her prayers, and those she whistles.

(Apperson.)

she wobbles like a drunken tailor with two left legs was a late C19–mid C20 nautical c.p., applied to a ship that steers erratically. (Bowen.)

she would sell her hole for half a dollar is a contemptuous reference to a girl lacking in self-respect: C20.

she would take you in – and blow you out as bubbles. This 'men only' c.p. is, in C20, deflatingly directed at men addicted to amorous boasting.

she wouldn't know if someone was up her. A low, mostly Australian, c.p. referring to a remarkably stupid girl: since c. 1910.

she'll be apples (or **right**, or **sweet**). See **she's right**.

she'll be jake (or **right**) **Jack** (or **mate**). It'll work, *or* All will come right, be right, etc.: virtually the New Zealand national motto; known also in Australia, where used by, e.g., Nino Culotta; since c. 1920, *very* approximately. (Mrs Hazel Franklin, 13 February 1975.)

This use of *she* for *it* was originally Australian, but it soon found a home in New Zealand too.

she'll die wondering. See **she will die wondering**.

Sherlock Holmes! – often abbreviated to **Sherlock!** – has, since c. 1898, been ironically directed at detectors of the obvious; obsolescent since c. 1960, but not yet obsolete. Obviously in reference to Conan Doyle's detective, the most famous of all fictional sleuths. On 20 December 1968, Julian Franklyn told me that, because he smoked a bent meerschaum, he sometimes had *Sherlock!* or *Sherlock Holmes!* shouted at him by children in the street.

she's a hot member for a mile – she is and no mistake is a horse-racing c.p., dating from c. 1920 and obviously applied to a filly very fast indeed up to that distance. (Frank Shaw, 1 September 1969.)

she's a smoker. See **she smokes**.

she's all right is a British tramps' C20 c.p., applied to a female sexually willing. (Hippo Neville, *Sneak Thief on the Road*, 1935.) Cf **she sails**.

she's been a good wife to him. See **she has been....**

she's been fucked more times than she's had hot dinners. A low, proletarian c.p. of late C19–20. The male counterpart is **I've had more women than you've had hot dinners**, q.v.

she's class and **she stacks up** are synonymous US c.pp. applied to an attractive female, esp. if young; the latter implies an impressive mammary equipment: since c. 1920. (Berrey, 1942.)

she's good (or **very good**) **to the poor** has, since c. 1910, been a prostitutes' 'catty' c.p., applied to one who cuts her price, and thus lets the sisterhood down.

she's got...entries. See the **she has...** (or **she has got...**) entries.

she's got her run on. A Public School senior girls' statement of a menstrual period: C20.

she's had more fucks than you've had hot dinners. 'One of several similar expressions used to impress somebody' (A. B. Petch, 4 January 1974): C20. Cf **I've had more women....**

she's jake. See **she'll be jake** and **she's right**.

she's joined the club. She is pregnant – applied esp. to an unmarried girl: C20. This somewhat inexclusive club is *The Pudding* – or, in proletarian circles, *Pudden–Club*, which dates from latish C19. To *put in the pudden club*, to render pregnant, is extant; it was used in, e.g., James Curtis's remarkable novel of the underworld, *The Gilt Kid*, 1936. By itself, *pudden*, seminal fluid, which had, in C19–20 but obsolete by 1930, the synonym, *marrow pudding*, seems to have existed since Restoration times.

There is a variant, applicable to any pregnancy: *she has a bun in the oven*: C20.

she's making her will. See **making his** (or **her**) **will**.

she's right! That's *most* satisfactory!; *but also* That's all right, *or* Don't mention it!: both New Zealand and Australian: since c. 1925 or a little earlier. (J. H. Henderson, *Gunner Inglorious*, 1945, for New Zealand; Nino Culotta and, in sense 'All's well'. Alexander Buzo, *Norm and Ahmed*, performed in 1968, for Australia.) This colloquial *she* may stem from *she* for a ship.

Of the New Zealand use of *she's right*, Mr Arthur Gray of Auckland, New Zealand, wrote to me on 29 March 1969:

Sometimes *she's all right, Jack* [prompted, doubtless, by **I'm all right, Jack**] implies that all is well with the speaker, and others' interests can be disregarded. Often considered to be a comfortable cynicism on the part of New Zealanders, and increasingly quoted as a criticism of their attitude since the Second World War.

In Australia, *she's apples!* and *she's sweet!* are synonyms. *She'll be right!* is a common reassurance.

Cf the Australian **she'll be jake**.

she's very good to the poor. See **she's good ....**

ship is known by her boats – a. A naval c.p.: late C19–20. 'Emphasized by Lord Charles Beresford in his command in the early 1900s, but an unofficial c.p. before that' (Rear-Admiral P. W. Brock, 1 February 1969). Only as 'an unofficial c.p.' does it, of course, concern us: as an official one, it would be either a motto or a cliché or a sage piece of traditional advice. (Lord Charles Beresford lived 1846–1919.)

Shipka Pass. See **all quiet on the Potomac**.

shit (or **fuck**) **a day keeps the doctor away – a**, is an Australian c.p., dating from the mid 1920s: a jocular adaptation of the proverb *an apple a day keeps the doctor away*.

shit and sugar mixed is a vulgar reply to the query, 'What are the ingredients?' of this or that dish: C20. An offensive variation of an *ad hoc* 'That's none of your business'.

shit doesn't stink. See **they think their shit doesn't stink**.

shit – eh? (or **!**) Isn't that just too bad!: an Australianism, dating from *c.* 1945.

shit hits the fan .... See **when (the) shit hits the fan**.

shit, mother, I can't dance is a vulgar c.p., Canadian, and, as a distinguished correspondent puts it, used 'just for something to say': since *c.* 1920.

shit – or get off the pot! Get on with the job or let someone else do it or, at the least, try to do it!; Either do it or get out of the way and let someone else try!; *or*, simply, Make up your mind! (Robert Claiborne, 31 August 1966.) US: C20.

This homely and humorous c.p., which must verge upon being a US proverb, is so general that it can be employed elliptically and allusively, as where, in Robert Rostand's novel, *Viper's Game*, 1974, a frank secretary says to a dithering consul, 'Oh, come on, Walter. Let's get off the pot' – and make a decision. I notice that it has been enshrined in *DCCU*, 1971.

Adopted in Canada; during WW2, it was, in the army, directed at a player unable to 'crap out'. The c.p. became, *c.* 1944, also English (as Laurie Atkinson informed me on 11 September 1967) – thanks to the pervasive influence of the US Armed Forces.

Since *c.* 1940, there has been a 'refined' Canadian variant: *spit – or get off the cuspidor*.

shit! said the king – often elaborated to **... and all his loyal subjects strained in unison**, or **and ten thousand loyal subjects shat**. An Australian c.p. – of the same semantic order as **hell! said the duchess**.

shit, shave and shove ashore and **shit, shave, shower, shoeshine and shampoo** and **shit, shine, shave, shampoo and shift**. See **shave, a shilling, (and) a shove ashore**.

shit weighs heavy! A vulgar, either brutally sarcastic or jocularly ironic Canadian c.p., directed, since *c.* 1890, at a boaster.

shoe is on the mast – the. If you want to be generous, here's your opportunity: a C19 nautical become general proletarian c.p. Ware explains the origin thus: in C18, 'when near the end of a long voyage, the sailors nailed a shoe to the mast, the toe downward, that passengers might delicately bestow a parting gift' – something that, after so delicate a hint, they could hardly refrain from doing.

shoo, fly! or, in full, **shoo, fly – don't bother me!** This, one of the most famous of all US c.pp., seems to have first been reputably noticed by a famous man as early as 1893 – in the redoubtable Brander Matthews's article on slang in the July issue of *Harper's Magazine*, where he signally failed to foretell, and to estimate, its durability, for, as W & F remark in 1960, it 'has reappeared from time to time, usually without much specific meaning' – nevertheless, predominantly in the sense, 'Stop bothering me, and go away!' It kept on reappearing, too, in HLM, from the early edns until the definitive 4th in 1936, and again in Supp. 2, when he dealt with it at some length.

On 9 November 1968, Professor S. H. Monk wrote to me thus (alluding to **twenty-three, skiddoo**):

Another phrase for getting rid of small brothers who were bothering their elder sisters was 'Shoo, fly, don't bother me'. This I know definitely came from a soldiers' song in the Spanish–American War, when flies and the yellow fever mosquito were the serious enemy. The song is nonsense 'Shoo, fly, don't bother me' repeated three times and then the final line, 'For I belong to company G'.

That song revived and reinforced the popularity of a phrase noted as early as 1889 by Farmer: 'An exclamation of impatience.... *Fly* is not the insect as some have supposed, but simply a pleonastic addition to – *sh-sh-fly*, i.e. fly away! be off! The full phrase is now familiarily colloquial.' Farmer prints it as *shoo! fly! don't bother me*.

Yet *fly* is very probably the insect, after all.

But the phrase seems to have arisen much earlier than all those other historians and lexicographers had supposed, for Edward B. Marks, in *They All Sang*, 1934, records it had been sung by Bryant's Minstrels in 1869, with words by Billy Reeves and music by Frank Campbell; exactly a decade later, the same recorder, in *They All Had Glamour*, has this entry: '1869 Shoo Fly – Don't Bodder [*sic*] Me. Words – Billy Reeves, sung by Cool Burgess'. (I owe both of these references to my exceptionally well informed friend, W. J. Burke, who, moreover, has been indefatigable – and prompt – in his assistance to me.)

shoot it in the leg – your arm's full is recorded by HLM, 1922; but without comment. I make none myself, except to say that it sounds like either a 'smart Alec' nonsense c.p. or (Patricia Newnham, March 1976) a c.p. suggested by drug injections.

shoot that hat! and **I'll have your hat!** were, *c.* 1860–72, common, esp. in London, as derisive retorts. Cf **what a shocking bad hat** and **where did you get that hat?**

shore saints and sea devils was, mid C19–early C20, a nautical c.p., applied to those sailing-ship skippers as were lambs with their owners and lions with the crew.

short and thick – like a Welshman's prick. A vulgar saying applied, mid C19–20, to a short person, usually a male, very broad-bottomed. Yet another of those pieces of physiological folklore which are as inaccurate as they are earthy.

shot – that'll (or **that would**) **be the**; and **that's the shot.** That will – or would – be most satisfactory, *or* That's the idea!:

Australian: both since *c.* 1945, at latest; the former from Nino Culotta, the latter in A. M. Harris, *The Tall Man*, 1958. Semantics: that hits – will or would hit – the target; 'bang on'. Cf **shot to you!**

shot at dawn. See **you'll be shot at dawn.**

shot himself! If someone breaks wind in or near a group of men, it often elicits this comment, to which there is, from another member of that group, the 'dovetail' or response, **if he's not (bloody) careful, he'll shit himself:** late C19–20.

shot to you! You score there – a c.p. 'aimed at indifference or complacent cocksureness [occasioned by] a lucky chance or when sharp practice has triumphed' (Laurie Atkinson): in the Armed Forces: since 1939 or *c.* 1939. Cf the semantics of **that'll be the shot.**

should be sawn off at the waist has, since *c.* 1930 and in the RAF, been applied to a stupid girl.

shoving money upstairs is a mainly North Country c.p. of C20 and is used thus: 'When a man is worrying about going bald, someone tells him banteringly it must be with "shoving money upstairs"' (Albert B. Petch, 22 August 1946). The implication is that it would be much safer to put the money into a bank.

Julian Franklyn once told me that, among Londoners, it has, since *c.* 1920, been predominantly applied to 'spending money on useless "cures"' – esp., one would suppose, to the quack cures for baldness.

show a leg! Get out of the bed or hammock!: nautical, esp. naval, since early in C19; by early C20, also military. Literally, to show a leg from under the bedclothes. In his *The Conway*, 1933, John Masefield noted that on that training ship, from before 1891, the full call has been

Heave out, heave out, heave out! Away!
Come all you sleepers, hey!
Show a leg and put a stocking on it.

The earliest record I've come upon (and that was sent to me by Colonel Albert Moe) occurs in Alfred Burton's *Johnny Newcome*, 1818. Originally, the call was shouted in order to ascertain whether the occupant of the bed was male, not an unofficial bedwarmer. 'Short for *show a leg or a pusser's stocking*, a naval phrase dating from the time when women went to sea in HM ships, and a bare leg or a purser's stocking guaranteed a lie-in until "Guard and steerage" was called. Nowadays the cry means *hurry up; get a wriggle on*, etc.' (*Sailors' Slang*).

show must go on – the, has long been 'the traditional slogan [perhaps rather motto or c.p.] of the troupers'. Whatever misfortune or illness befalls, 'it is a point of honour not to let the other players down by deserting them when no understudy is available' (Granville.)

Common also in Australia and US.

show the dog the rabbit. See **let the dog see the rabbit!**

showing next week's washing. Your shirt is showing (at the flap): not entirely proletarian, nor in the least aristocratic or cultured: C20; by 1970, however, somewhat outmoded.

shrieks of hysterical laughter; and shrieks of silence was the stern reply. The former is mostly Australian and used when someone has advanced an untenable proposition or made a ludicrous suggestion, as in:

'I'm going to sell this car. Should get about eight hundred for it.'

'Shrieks of hysterical laughter.'

Clearly taken from dramatic and film critics' commentaries.

The latter, wholly Australian, provides an ironic synonym of 'No one replied, or said a word'.

Both date from *c.* 1950 and both were supplied to me by Mr Barry Prentice, whose ear for the Australian vernacular is exceptionally acute.

shrift.... See **he hath been at shrift.**

shut mouth never fills a black coffin – a. Keep your mouth shut and you'll never die untimely! Common among US gangsters since the early 1920s. Recorded in a very rare book, *Yankee Slang*, privately printed in London, 1932, by one who thought it best to use a pseudonym: 'Spindrift', whom the British Library catalogue reveals to be Ernest Tooné.

Beginning as an underworld c.p., it began also as a motto, a warning, and passed into the ranks of the very few underworld proverbs.

shut my mouf! Colonel Albert Moe, writing to me on 11 July 1975, says: 'When a person is astonished or surprised, he is very likely to allow his jaw to sag and to permit his mouth to be ... agape, e.g. to manifest open-mouth wonderment'. Harold Wentworth, *American Dialect Dictionary*, 1944: '1940 [from] *Negro*; Shut ma mouf.' Said by a negro (or, in imitation, a black-and-white minstrel) who realizes that he has said too much, or the worse thing. Meaning 'I should have kept my mouth shut.' (Dr Joseph T. Shipley, 16 August 1975.)

shut my mouth and call me Shorty! – often preceded by **well.** See **cut off my legs ...** near the end of the entry.

shut up and give your arse a chance. See **give your arse a chance!**

shut up, you little bastard. See **what did you do ....**

silence in the court – the cat is pissing (or **the monkey wants to talk**; or **the judge wants to spit**). These cogent enjoiners are addressed to anyone requiring or demanding or blatantly expecting silence: *c.* 1760–1850. Grose, 1785, for the first. The second is juvenile Australian: C20. (Barry Prentice.) The third is US: C20. (Berrey, 1942, includes in a list of slangy phrases synonymous with 'Be quiet' or, esp., 'Shut up!'.)

This is one of the more entertaining deflaters of pomposity.

silent – like the *p* in swimming. This fairly common c.p. has, since *c.* 1914, been used in less-than-academic exposition of a difficulty in pronunciation. 'Her name is Fenwick, where the *w* is silent – like the *p* in swimming.' To explain the obvious: there is a pun on *pee*, to urinate. Yet even in academic or, at lowest, scholastic circles, it occasionally serves to lighten the depressingly dogmatic assertions of manic phoneticians, who sometimes blindly and unsuspectingly, excel in a ludicrous putting of the cart before the horse.

[**silly old moo**; and **silly moo.** In the *Daily Mail* of 2 November 1968, at 'Comment', concerning the under twenty-fives, we read about what they, in their turn, 'will bore their children with': 'They'll recall old television programmes like ..., forgotten personalities like ..., try to remember catch-phrases from old comedy shows like "Sock it to me" and "Silly old moo".'

The phrase *silly old moo*, where *moo* is a euphemism for

the vulgar *cow*, was, as Vernon Noble, writing on 26 August 1974, says,

> applied by actor Warren Mitchell as the Cockney character Alf Garnett to his wife (played by Dandy Nichols) in long-running comedy series 'Till Death Us Do Part' (by Johnny Speight) on BBC television. Dandy Nichols said that the epithet was called to her affectionately in the streets when people recognized her.

But, strictly, this isn't a c.p. Those who need further information could do far worse than to consult the latest Addenda to *DSUE*. The same exclusion applies to *silly old mare*.]

Simpson. See **my name's Simpson ...** .

since AMOs were carved on stone. See **since Pontius was a pilot.**

since Auntie had her accident and **since Nellie had her operation.** For a very or a fairly long time: the former is Australian, as in 'I haven't been to Melbourne since Auntie had her accident', and it dates since *c.* 1920. (Barry Prentice.) The latter is English, dates since *c.* 1910, and is 'a burlesque c.p., marking banteringly a certain lapse of time' (Laurie Atkinson). Cf **since Willie died** and:

since Pontius was a pilot, as in 'He's been with that mob since Pontius was a pilot' (punning *Pontius Pilate*): RAF: since *c.* 1944. Belonging to the same semi-erudite – or, rather, mock-erudite – order, are, since *c.* 1946, *since the Air Ministry was a tent* and, referring to Air Ministry Orders, *since AMOs were carved on stone*, both of which, however, enjoyed only a very restricted currency, yet are perhaps worthy of inclusion as examples of what could be classified as armchair ingenuity rather than scene-of-action humour.

since when I have used no other has, since 1884 or 1885, been applied to any (usually domestic) article in common and frequent use. From the witty Pear's Soap advertisement showing an unmistakably grubby tramp, who says 'Two years ago I used your soap, since when I have used no other'. Cf **good morning! have you used Pear's Soap?**

The tramp advertisement dates from the 1890s and was based upon a commissioned painting of Phil May's. Intervening – probably originating – was *Punch*, 1884 (LXXXVII, p. 197), 'I used your soap two years ago; since then I have used no other.'

since Willie died is a C20 Canadian counterpart of **since Nellie had her operation**, q.v. at **since Auntie had her accident**. '"We haven't had so much fun since Willie died" – said in approbation of a good time' (Douglas Leechman).

sing, sing: or show your ring! 'Invitation to perform at an informal troop concert: the assembled company cheers at the victim, who either then does sing or drops his trousers' (Paul Beale, 30 September 1975): an Army c.p., probably throughout C20. The 'ring' is ('Well, naturally!') the anus.

sing us a song! This is 'a call from the gallery when an artiste is disapproved of': music-halls: late C19–20; by 1970, obsolescent. Granville adds that 'this exhortation is euphemistic for something grosser'.

sings more like a whore's bird than a canary bird, usually preceded by **he.** He has a strong, manly voice: *c.* 1760–1820. (Grose, 1788.) A *whore's bird* is a debauchee.

singular or plural? was, in late 1914–18, an army c.p.: a hospital enquiry when eggs appeared on the dietary. (B & P.)

sir, I see someone has offended you, for your back is up is one of the earliest 'sick' jokes: it was, *c.* 1750–1850, addressed to a humpbacked man. (Grose, 1785.)

'sir' to you. A c.p. of mock-offended dignity: probably since *c.* 1830. My earliest record (so far) occurs in R. H. Barham, *The Ingoldsby Legends*, Third Series, 1847, at the piece titled 'Jerry Jarvis's Wig':

> At this moment neighbour Jenkinson peeped over the hedge.
> 'Joe Washford!' said neighbour Jenkinson.
> 'Sir, to you,' was the reply.

Admittedly, however, the expression seems here to be literal and respectful. An unquestionable example, however, does appear in the inimitable P. G. Wodehouse's *The Pothunters*, 1902; a later example in H. A. Vachell, *Vicar's Walk*, 1933. By 1970, slightly obsolescent.

sir, you are speaking of the woman I love originated as a cliché in the 'Transpontine', or Surrey-side, drama during the 1880s and 1890s, and in corresponding US melodrama of the same period, as well as in Horner's Penny Novelettes, a genre enlarged and immensely improved in the novels by Charles Garvice, a man of culture and sensitivity; its pomposity rendered it a phrase of fun, used therefore as a c.p. from *c.* 1890 onwards in both countries.

Sirgarneo. See **all Sir Garnet!**

sit down – you're rocking the boat! Don't disturb the *status quo!* Both British and US: since *c.* 1920. Applied mostly to sociological or economic or political affairs. (For US use: Colonel Albert Moe, 15 June 1975.) Also **don't rock the boat!** – an 'exhortation to someone about to disturb a comfortable situation'. (Norman Franklin, March 1976.)

sit up and beg. See **he can make it sit up and beg.**

sit up and take notice! Wake up! American: since *c.* 1910. Recorded by S. R. Strait in 'Straight Talk' (*Boston Globe* of *c.* 1917); obsolete by 1942.

six foot of land – that's all the land you'll get has, in C20, been addressed to one who expresses a desire to 'own just a bit of land'. Cf the WW1 *become a landowner*, to die.

But usually either a threat ('You do that and I'll kill you', *six foot of land* for a grave) or a mostly well-intended warning – a pronouncement on a person's fate for continuing a present foolish activity or embarking on a foolish action or course of action. (With thanks to Mr Robin Leech of Edmonton, Canada.)

six hat and a fifty shirt – a. A US underworld c.p., dating from the 1920s and applied to one who, weak in the head, is strong in the back. (D. W. Maurer in *The Writer's Digest* of October 1931.) His hat is only a six-incher, but he needs a fifty-inch chest measurement in shirts.

six pips and all's well! Six o'clock and all's well: in, and since, 1933. There's a reference both to the BBC's radio time-signal and to the nautical *six bells and all's well.*

sixty-four, ninety-four was a WW1 army c.p., canonized in R. H. Mottram's *The Spanish Farm Trilogy*, 1927, thus:

> 'You see, I don't know the man's name. His number was given as 6494.'
> 'That's a joke, of course. It's the number that the cooks sing out, when we hold the last Sick Parade, before going up the line.'

'Of course it is. You're right. I ought to have remembered that, but I've been away from my regiment for some time.'

(With thanks to Mr A. B. Petch, August 1969.)

sixty-four-thousand-dollar question – the. See **that's the sixty-four-thousand-dollar question.**

sixty-nine! 'The shearers' code-warning that ladies or visitors are approaching and bad language is "out of order"' (*Straight Farrow*, a magazine, 21 February 1968): New Zealand: C20.

skid(d)oo! See **twenty-three, skid(d)oo!**

skin – in one's. See **in one's skin.**

[**skip it!** Don't bother with it! Forget it! A British and US borderliner between ordinary slang and c.p.: not, so far as I remember, common before *c*. 1930. Berrey, 1942, records it and Noël Coward, in *Peace in Our Time*, 1947, at Act II, Scene ii, has:

FRED: What a pity! He won't have much time to learn now, will he?

GLADYS: How do you mean?

FRED: Skip it.]

slanging dues concerned; in full, **there has** (or **have**) **been ....** In late C18–mid C19, this was an underworld-and-its-fringes c.p. uttered by one who felt that he had, esp. by his mates, been defrauded of his rights or of his fair share of the booty. (Vaux.) From *slang*, to cheat (someone); *dues* occurs in several underworld phrases of the same period.

sleep tight – mind the fleas don't bite. A children's goodnight to parents, brothers and sisters, friends: certainly of late C19–20, but perhaps existing very much longer: this is the sort of phrase that, naturally enough, escapes the attention of lexicographers, even the light-hearted.

sleeping near (or **next to**) **a crack.** See **you must have been lying ....**

slide, Kelly, slide! A short-lived American c.p., from the song, so titled, sung, and published, in 1889. It is recorded by Edward B. Marks in *They All Sang*, 1934, with the gloss, 'J. W. Kelly'.

sling 'em out! is the c.p. – almost the 'signature tune' – of *the dhobeying firm*, a partnership of two or more naval ratings undertaking to do their messmates' washing. 'An unofficial ship's laundry and a very lucrative business if the "firm" is an energetic one' (Wilfred Granville, in PGR, published in 1948). The '*em* refers to the dirty clothes.

slip me five! See **give me some skin!**

slow down a bit! Don't try quite so hard to do the right thing, *or* Don't be so very formal: since *c*. 1945. (Wilfred Granville, 13 January 1969.)

slower than the second coming of Christ. See **you are slower ... .**

smack it about! Get a move on!: naval: C20. 'From the vigorous smacking-about of brushes when painting the ship's side' (*SS*).

small contributions gratefully received is a British and US c.p. dating from *c*. 1900: it means what it says, but in an ironic tone of voice and often ludicrously applied to all contributions. In *The Heart Line*, 1908, Gelett Burgess writes:

'I believe that I might go so far as to imprint a salute upon your chaste brow!'

'I accept!' said Fancy Gray.

He stooped over and kissed her. She was graciously resigned.

'Thank you, Frank,' she said demurely. 'Small contributions gratefully received.'

From the advertisements of charitable societies.

[**small things amuse small** (or **little**) **minds** is, I should, unthinkingly perhaps, have said, is a proverb – or, if not a proverb, a cliché; yet several very intelligent friends of mine have proposed it as, unequivocally, a c.p. For instance, Mr Barry Prentice writes (May Day 1975): 'This is an extremely common c.p. in Australia. It is not unknown elsewhere, as it occurs in [e.g.] *A Woman on a Roof*, a short story by Doris Lessing ... reprinted in *A Man and Two Women* ... 1963. ... The c.p. is often used when a person is doing something that seems childish.' I've known it all my life, in New Zealand, in Australia, in England. The 'dovetail' reply is **and only small minds would notice!**]

small world! is, clearly, an ellipsis – it is also the quintessence of the cliché 'It's a small world', a greeting to an acquaintance met unexpectedly, esp. if after a long interval: since *c*. 1920.

smarter than the average bear, Booboo. Early 1970s: Paul Beale, writing on 17 February 1975, says:

[This is a] c.p. from the US cartoon series 'Yogi Bear' shown on TV in this country. Used by Yogi Bear (named presumably after the baseball star Yogi Berra) whenever he outwits any other character in the film. Booboo is his little satellite bear-friend. The phrase can be and is translated into all sorts of situations.

smear it with butter and get the cat to lick it off! A Cockneys' shattering deflation of the aspirations of youths desirous of growing a beard and signally failing to do so: late C19–20.

smell my finger! A vulgar male – youths' rather than men's – c.p. with an erotic implication: late C19–20.

smile! – I should. See **I should smile!**

smile, damn you, smile! Concerning such optimistic clichés as 'It won't hurt none to try', HLM, 1922, says, 'Naturally enough, a grotesque humor plays about this literature of hope; the folk, though it moves them, prefer it with a dash of salt. "Smile, damn you, smile!" is a typical specimen of this seasoned optimism.' So far as I've been able to discover, this US c.p. has been current throughout the century; Benham, 1948, glosses it as known in England since '*c*. 1907'. Cf:

smile when you say that, stranger is explained by a quotation from Desmond Bagley's novel, *Running Blind*, 1970:

'... I still love you, you silly bastard.'

'Smile when you say that, stranger.'

Originally and still predominantly referring to one man's calling another a *bastard*, and originally (?*c*. 1890) and predominantly still US, it occurs, if I remember rightly, in Owen Wister's romantic 'Western', *The Virginian* (1902), where those very words were used. Semantically related to the phrase preceding this.

Reinforced, *c*. 1920, when, in US, it was 'picked up in mock-solemn echo of Grade B Western movies' (Edward Hodnett, 18 August 1975).

smoke that in your pipe! The US form of **put that in your pipe**

and smoke it!: late C19–20. Recorded by Berrey, 1942, as a synonym of 'Think that over!' and attested to by Professor Emeritus John W. Clark and Mr W. J. Burke, late in 1968.

snafu phonetically shortens and typographically 'solidifies' *SNAFU*. There's an occasional variant, *SNEFU*; cf also *MFU*. The *FU* part is pronounced *foo*.

Snafu was, by HLM in Supp. 2, 1948, described as 'one of the few really good coinages of the war'; it represents 'Situation normal, all fucked up' (politely '... fouled up'); coined by British soldiers, it was, in 1943–5, well known, and used, in the US Army. The British variant *snefu (SNEFU)* = 'Situation normal, everything fucked up' – not very common, and mostly officers'; another British variant was *MFU*, a 'military fuck-up', indicating that someone has blundered, and this had its own modification: *Imfu (IMFU)*, when the blunder was on an 'imperial' scale – used only among officers.

From both the British and the US Army, *snafu* spread to the other Services.

snake in your pocket – a? or, in full, **have you got a...?**, often shortened to **got a...?** This Australian c.p. has, since *c.* 1920, been addressed to one who is reluctant (and very slow) to buy his friends a round of drinks, esp. when his turn to do so has come. The implication is that the snake will bite him when he puts his hand in his pocket to get at his money.

[**snap!** is – to be 'Irish' – a one-word c.p., deriving from the parlour game so named. It occurs frequently in N. F. Simpson's perturbing play, *The Hole*, performed in 1958.]

snice mince pie. See **it's a snice mince pie.**

snow again! – we didn't get your drift, often abbreviated to **snow again!**; variant: **snow again, kid! – I've lost your drift.** This US c.p., signifying 'Say that again! I didn't get your meaning' and punning on *snowdrift*, arose *c.* 1910 or a little earlier, to judge by the reference in HLM, 1922; it is recorded by Berrey, 1942, as *snow again, baby, I've lost your drift* and glossed as 'Explain yourself, I don't know what you're talking about'; and Douglas Leechman, early 1969, records its (derivative) Canadian currency as '*c.* 1910'.

[**snug as a bug in a rug – as.** A humorous c.p. elaboration of *snug*, comfortable: 'warm and cosy': since mid C18. (Apperson, who treats it as a proverbial saying: which, indeed, it partly *is*.) Cf:]

snug's the word! Say nothing about this! Let's keep things comfortable and say nothing about the matter: late C17–mid C19. The *OED* cites William Congreve and Maria Edgworth and Lover's *Handy Andy*, 1848. Cf preceding entry and also **mum's the word.**

so are you! – often so're you! This c.p., common all over the English-speaking world – and going back to heaven knows when – is used in defiance or bravado (or both). Robert Benchley, in *Love Conquers All*, 1923, includes it in the delightfully satirical list quoted at **oh, is that so?**

so busy I've had to put a man on (to help me). See **getting any?**

so crooked he couldn't lie straight in bed, usually preceded by **he's.** Directed at a thoroughly dishonest and unscrupulous fellow: Australian: since the early 1920s. (Barry Prentice.) It expectably occurs in Frank Hardy's *Billy Borker Yarns Again*, 1967 – with the frequent illiterate variant, *lay* for *lie*.

so dumb she thinks her bottom is just to sit on. This raffish,

mostly male, c.p. dates from when? I first heard it *c.* 1945, but suspect that it goes back to late C19.

so empty I can feel my backbone touching my belly-button. See **I'm so empty....**

so fast his feet won't touch. As Paul Beale has (1975) put it:

Army and possibly RAF. Always in connection with 'putting a man inside' for some misdemeanour. 'Cor, he'll need to watch it. If the RSM cops him at it, he'll have him inside so fast his feet won't touch!' (Deck, ground or floor understood.) Quite common. Current.

As an army c.p., with variations, it goes back to well before WW2 and was, if I remember correctly, often used during WW1; probably late C19–20.

so fools say! is a mostly Cockneys' retort to 'You're a fool': since *c.* 1880; by 1970, slightly obsolescent. It occurs *passim* in the novels and stories by Edwin Pugh.

This c.p. has an elaboration: *you ought to know – you work where they're made*; obsolescent by *c.* 1960.

so glad! – elliptical for 'I'm *so* glad' – arose in 1848 as an ephemeral London c.p. originated by the French King and revived by William Brough's *Field of the Cloth of Gold*, 1867, and still current in 1909, as Ware intimates.

[**so help me, Hannah!** A US c.p. of affirmation or asseveration: C20. (Norris M. Davidson, 3 November 1968.) Either an elaboration of *so help me!* or a euphemism for *so help me, God!* Hardly a true c.p.]

so is your old man, but usually **so's your old man!** Arising in Britain *c.* 1900, it was mildly obsolescent by 1935 and not yet entirely obsolete by 1976. The implication of impudent scepticism and, sometimes, a hearty derision, is well exemplified in Ngaio Marsh's novel, *Tied up in Tinsel*, 1972:

'... so I said: Do me a favour, chum. You call it what you like: for my book you're at the fiddle!'

'Distinguished and important collection!'

'Yeah! So's your old man!'

In the US, it arose *c.* 1915; 'Originally West Coast use' (W & F), and recorded by Berrey, 1942, as a slangy synonym of 'I don't believe it!' It passed to Canada early in the 1920s, as Douglas Leechman told me late in 1968.

On 25 April 1969, my friend Professor John T. Fain glossed the US use of the c.p., thus: '(*c.* 1920–*c.* 1940). "Your old man is a sonofabitch, too", or something like that. Typical expression when people sat around and "played dozens" – that is, tried to "put each other down" or get the better of, to silence, one another.'

In *Mr Deeds Goes to Town*, 1937, Clarence B. Kelland wrote:

'What's wrong with common people? That's what I want to know.'

'They are vulgar,' said Mr Bengold.

To this the only apt reply Longfellow could think of at the moment was to say, 'So is your old man,' but he did not feel that he knew his secretary well enough to make so flippant a rejoinder, so he kept silent.

Four years earlier, Philip Macdonald, in *RIP*, had put the phrase (*so's...*) into the mouth of a Canadian.

so lucky that if he fell into (or in) the river he'd only get dusty, usually preceded by **he's.** Attributing exceptionally good luck: C20.

But much commoner is *so lucky that if he fell in the shit, he'd come up smelling of violets*. See **if he fell in the shit ....**

so mean that he (or she) wouldn't give anyone a fright is a C20 c.p., with the variant (since *c.* 1915) **... wouldn't spit in your mouth if your throat was on fire**, applied to an exceptionally mean, close-fisted person. Cf:

so mean that he wouldn't give you his cold. See **he is so mean ....**

so my mother tells me, dating since *c.* 1700 or even a decade or two earlier, corresponds to the old proverb, 'Ask the mother if the child be like the father'; by 1950, slightly obsolescent. In Dialogue I of S, 1738, we find:

NEV[EROUT]: Pray, Mrs *Betty*, are you not *Tom Johnson's* daughter?

BETTY: So my Mother tells me, Sir.

so round, so firm, so fully packed. 'Originated in the advertising of a cigarette. ... Applied salaciously to women's figures. No longer used in advertising, and less heard now than twenty or thirty years ago' (John W. Clark, 4 March 1975): US: since (say) the middle or late 1940s.

so stupid that he (or she) can't chew gum and walk straight at the same time, usually preceded by *he's* or *she's*. Current since *c.* 1960, it occurs notably in John Braine, *The Pious Agent*, 1975: 'Not only is he so stupid that, to adopt a famous saying, he can't chew gum and walk straight at the same time, he's also illiterate.' Its American usage has been 'revived with President Ford' (Norman Franklin, March 1976).

so sue me! Then do something about it! Sometimes it means little more than 'So what?' This US c.p., dating from the early 1950s or a little earlier, occurs in, e.g., Jack D. Hunter, *One of Us Works for Them*, a US novel of espionage, 1967:

'That's one of the ritziest neighbourhoods this side of Chevy Chase.'

'So sue me.'

so that's the way it is. See **it's like that, is it?**

so they tell me is a c.p. only when used ironically or as a 'dry counter to a verbal "facer"; [made] to disarm malice and retain poise': heyday, 1930s; seldom heard before 1930; still heard occasionally among people aged 16 or over by *c.* 1940. (Laurie Atkinson, late 1974.)

so thin you can smell the shit through him, usually preceded by **he's**. This low, mostly Cockneys', c.p. dates from *c.* 1880 and is applied to an extremely thin man. (Julian Franklyn: communication.)

so well; and **so what?** The former, which had only a brief career (I myself never heard it), arose in or about 1936 and seems to have been a deliberate variation of the latter, which, in 1936, was adopted in Britain from the US: the former was Cockney, the latter (in Britain) at first Cockney but very soon general. Meaning either 'That doesn't impress me', or merely 'I'm simply not interested', **so what?** arose in US *c.* 1930 so far as I have, so far, discovered. W & F give no date, nor, of course, does Berrey, 1942; the latter synonymizes it with 'What does it matter?'.

In HLM, Supp. 1, Mencken notes that *So What?* was the title of a book by an Englishman, published in London in 1938; and 'So What?' is a chapter heading in Michael Burt's novel, *The Case of the Angels' Trumpets*, 1947. A good example occurs in Janet Green's remarkable novel, *My Turn Now*, 1971:

'You'll ruin me. Ruin my career.'

'So what? You've had your day. It's my turn now.'

But more effective is this, in Noël Coward's *Peace in Our Time*, 1947, at Act I, Scene iii:

ALBRECHT: I know that you are too stubborn to believe me, Mr Shattock, but I assure you that my intentions are friendly.

FRED: All right – so what?

so what does that make me? See **what does that make me?**

sock it to him! or **sock it to them!** but esp. **sock it to me!** (with or without **baby** added).

The first occurs as long ago as 1889, when, in chapter 33 of Mark Twain's *A Connecticut Yankee in the Court of King Arthur*, the Yankee, who is, naturally, the narrator, gets into a sociological argument with the smith and says:

'Well, observe the difference. You pay eight cents and four mills, we pay only four cents.'

I prepared, now, to sock it to him. I said: 'Look here, dear friend, *what's become of your high wages you were bragging about a few minutes ago?*' – and I looked round on the company with placid satisfaction.

Here, clearly, the sense of the phrase is 'to apply the *coup de grâce*, the final demolishing blow'. (I was alerted to this remarkable adumbration of the *sock it to ...* series by Mrs Barbara Lock Goodman, early in 1969.) Now it is worth noting that, in Mark Twain's *Life on the Mississippi*, 1883, appear these fateful words: 'A rich man won't have anything but your very best [coffins]; and you can just pile it [the price] on too, and sock it in to him – he won't ever holler.' Yet even earlier, *Am*, 1877, exemplifies *sock*, to strike, thus: 'Two loafers are fighting; one of the crowd calls out, "Sock it to him".' Can any origination be better supported than by this great scholar and that great writer?

The second occurs in Clarence B. Kelland's novel, *Spotlight*, 1937:

'People who work with me,' said Hadrian, 'need their health.'

'Boy, you had me fooled,' said Mr P[eak]. 'More power to you. Sock it to 'em, lad. I'll be getting along.'

Here clearly, the sense is, 'Give them hell!'

The third occurs, at first (I think), as either a 'teenybopper' (teenage hellion) cult expression of unpolarized violence and vague meaning: 'Liven things up!', or, as Mr W. J. Burke in December 1968 suggested, was 'originally a jazz term'; and, as he amplified on 28 January 1969, '"Sock it to me, now having a vogue in the Rowan & Martin hit "Laugh-In" (NBC), is a phrase borrowed from the vocabulary of Negro jazz musicians. "Laugh-In" started two years ago.'

Adopted from the US, in 1967 or 1968, it was propagated, to the limit of the ludicrous, by disc jockeys. On 28 October 1968, Dr Douglas Leechman of Victoria, British Columbia, Canada, wrote to me thus: 'To-day's c.p. here is "Sock it to me (or them ...)". It can be given a variety of implications, depending on who uses it and in what circumstances. Quite recent and heard often on the air.'

And then, on 3 November 1968, the late Norris M. Davidson, a US commentator (and another good friend), wrote:

There is a current revival of a phrase which, I am told, once had an obscene meaning. On our current 'most popular' TV comedy show – Rowan and Martin's 'Laugh-In' – the most repeated phrase is 'Sock it to me!'. And the one speaking the phrase always suffers instant retribution in the form of a clubbing, a bucket of water over the head, a drop through a trap door, etc.

Then, on 22 November 1968, Norris Davidson amplified further:

A column in the *Philadelphia Evening Bulletin* of November fourth by Merriman Smith, United States Press International Writer, is captioned: 'Sock it to 'em, Boys' and it turns out to be a rather lengthy treatise [*sic*] on the resurgence of that phrase. He cites the fact that the Rowan & Martin television show has given the phrase new life and that no less a person than Herbert Horatio Humphrey used it literally in several of his later campaign speeches and added the word *baby*, so that it came out 'Sock it to 'em, Baby!'. He cites the fact that Nixon also had used it at an earlier date in his speeches – without the *baby*. The column ends: 'Sadly, no one thought to say a kind word for Mark Twain in whose writings the phrase first appeared many years ago.' Unfortunately Mr Smith did not identify the precise work in which Mark Twain used the phrase.

Probably it was prompted by the basic (British and) US slang 'to *sock* (someone)', to punch or strike him hard. Note that both the Rowan and Martin show and the phrase 'became exceedingly popular here [Britain] too a few years ago' (Patricia Newnham, March 1976).

[**sod me up and down!** On the borderline between a picturesque oath and a c.p. of Cockney amazement, late C19–20; more the former than the latter. Contrast the next.]

sod you, Jack, I'm inboard! is a naval lower-deck variant of **fuck you, Jack, I'm inboard!** – than which it is felt to be slightly less coarse, slightly less offensive, and slightly more polite: C20.

[**Sod's Law,** like *Parkinson's Law*, is clearly not a c.p.; the former does, however, the more nearly approach the dividing line. In *The Times Literary Supplement* of 19 October 1973 there was a review of Richard Swinburne, *An Introduction to Confirmation Theory*. That review opened by saying, 'Philosophy, like life, is subject to what is vulgarly known as Sod's Law. In life, Sod's Law takes the form of doors opening the wrong way, love being unrequited, and so forth.' This provoked a correspondence; someone claimed to have written about Sod's Law in the *New Statesman* of October 1970.

My friend Paul Beale tells me that he first heard of it in mid 1972 and adds: 'Sod's Law is that which places mankind at the mercy of the small gods of minor misfortune and trivial annoyances. It decrees that if something *can* go wrong, it will.' Obviously the form *Sod's Law* was prompted by *God's Law*: and hardly less obviously the sense of the phrase owes much to the sense of 'It's a fair sod' – synonymous with 'It's a proper bastard'.]

soft as shit and twice as nasty. See **as soft as shit** ....

softly, softly, catchee monkey. 'Gently does it!': probably late C19–20. In Benham, 1948, it is given as a proverb, in the form '*Softly, softly' caught the monkey* and glossed as being of negro origin. But as *softly, softly, catchee monkey* it is a c.p. and used as in, e.g., Laurence Meynell's novel, *Die by the*

Book, 1966: 'In my time I had made one or two blunders by rushing my fences and I didn't propose to make the same mistake again. "Softlee, softlee, catchee monkey".'

On 16 May 1969, Wilfred Granville glossed it thus: 'Stalk your prey carefully; or, generally, to achieve an object by quiet application.'

In Michael Delving's novel, *The Devil Finds Work*, 1970, a detective says: 'I don't want to make him edgy.... I've got to be very careful. Softly, softly, catchee monkey, you know.'

This well-known phrase has, except for Benham, been neglected by the editors of the relevant works of reference; and I haven't been lucky enough to find an early quotation.

sold again and got the money was, *c.* 1840–80, a costermonger's c.p., uttered upon having bested someone in a bargain. (Hotten, 1859.) Cf the London simile current in late C18–mid C19: *sold like a bullock in Smithfield*, thoroughly duped or badly cheated.

soldier on, chum! was, during WW1, frequently heard among British, esp. English, soldiers, one to another. (See the entry at **sell the pig ...** .)

soldier's farewell (to you understood and occasionally expressed), usually preceded by **a.** Originally – from before 1909, when Ware recorded it – military and meaning 'Go to bed!', with various ribald, not to say bawdy, additions and ornamentations. But in WW1 and after, although still military, it meant 'Good-bye and bugger you!'. In *Oh! Definitely*, 1933, Maurice Lincoln writes: '"Good-bye ...!" he yelled.... "Soldier's farewell," he said amiably.' Synonymous is (*a*) *sailor's farewell*, a parting curse, both naval and, by adoption, military.

In B & P, John Brophy remarked that *a soldier's farewell* 'was originally invective.... But its chief use was as a jocular exclamation made very loudly for the benefit of others.'

soldiers? – I've shit 'em! 'An expression of contempt for another unit (esp. if slovenly)', as John Brophy explained in B & P, 1930: British soldiers': WW1 – and doubtless afterwards.

some children don't half have them (or **'em)!** See **some mothers ...!**

some hopes! It's *most* unlikely or improbable! This c.p. arose at the beginning of C20 and was very generally used in the British Army during WW1; far more so than the synonymous *what hopes!*; equally popular, however, was **what a hope!**

some like it hot became a c.p. somewhere about 1965. Its meaning, 'Some people like things, especially if sexual, to be hot.' Popularized by the world of entertainment; originally it was applied to fast-tempo'd, exciting, jazz music, now often described as 'cool', as Patricia Newnham reminded me in March 1976; see especially W & F at *hot*, sense 10, and *cool*, adjective, sense 3.

some mothers (or **movvers** pronounced and often written **muvvers) do have 'em!** is 'invariably Cockney, whether native or assumed' (Laurie Atkinson, 25 December 1974): since *c.* 1920. A BBC series in 1974 'Some Mothers ...' was for a wide audience: and it thoroughly popularized the c.p. The implication is that some children are either idiotic or thoroughly intolerable. But it also, e.g. among workmen, furnishes a jeer at clumsiness and among schoolboys and youths when someone has blundered.

In a letter dated 11 December 1973, Vernon Noble wrote:

[This] c.p. about difficult children [has] long been familiar in Lancashire and Yorkshire mill towns and [was] probably first popularized through his long-running radio series by Jimmy Clitheroe, Lancashire comedian famous for his naughty-boy parts. ... Other comics have since seized on the phrase.

Cf **some people rear awkward children.**

The popularity of this c.p. has generated the parody, *some children don't half have them,* 'used derisively of parents who are "squares"' (A. B. Petch, 4 January 1974).

some of my best friends are Jews (or, derivatively and far less commonly, almost any group or class or religion or race you happen to be prejudiced against) is 'a c.p. used just before making a disparaging remark about some segment of the human race' (Barry Prentice, 31 January 1969) – it is, therefore, employed to 'excuse bigotry' (Barry Prentice, 15 December 1974). Moreover, it is, of course, a Gentile c.p., current among those who secretly think – or, at any rate, feel – that Jews are not merely different, hopelessly different, from, but also socially inferior to, Gentiles. Common to the entire English-speaking world, it dates from not later than 1940 and has probably been current since the early 1930s, with equivalents in other European languages. It originated perhaps rather in US than in Britain. So enshrined is it in US folkways that it can be employed allusively, as in Alfred Marin, *Arise with the Wind,* 1969:

'I was never against those people [the Jews],' Weber said with feeling.

'Sure, some of your best friends were Jewish,' Clay said bitterly.

Indeed, as a friend of mine, a Gentile, once remarked, 'Makes you want to vomit, doesn't it?' Sometimes one wonders why, there being so much racial prejudice and even hatred about, there haven't been even more wars. The true miracle, the enduring miracle, the greatest miracle of all, is that, so far, the human race has succeeded in surviving the human race; clearly the age of miracles is *not* past.

Used as a plain statement, it is obviously not a c.p. But, esp. since the middle 1940s, it has been so derided, by both Jews and Gentiles, that it has come to be used jocularly – by, for instance, a Jew to a Gentile friend. It's rather like saying 'Some of my best friends are human beings – well, almost.'

some people (occasionally **parents**) **rear** (or **raise**) **awkward children**, with **do** sometimes inserted before *rear.* This c.p. dates, I'd say, since *c.* 1880, if not earlier, and is either addressed to or directed at someone who has been very clumsy. By *c.* 1960, it was showing signs of becoming a proverb, but it has not yet (1975) become one. Cf **some mothers do have 'em!**

some say 'Good old sergeant!' This military c.p., dating since *c.* 1890, perhaps earlier, was either spoken or shouted by privates within the sergeant's hearing. Of its use in the British army during WW1, John Brophy (in B & P) wrote,

There were thousands of really good sergeants, respected and liked. On the individual's conduct and character it depended whether the private shouted:

Some say 'Good old sergeant!'

Others say '— — [i.e., fuck] the old sergeant!'

with rancour or with quite affectionate jocularity.

This c.p. itself engendered, from *c.* 1919 onwards, the much more widely employed *some say 'Good old* [e.g., *Smith*]' – *some* (or *I*) *say 'Blast* (much more commonly '*Fuck*) *old* (Smith)'*!*

'Amongst children and young people it was also common to hear *but others tell the truth*' (Patricia Newnham, March 1976): *c.* 1920–60.

somebody's dropped his false teeth. Uttered apropos of a sudden noise, esp. a crash: since the early 1920s. In 1939–45, an Armed Forces' c.p. apropos of a bomb or a shell exploding some distance away.

someone forgot to pay the washerwoman and **someone's taken the water away.** These naval (lower-deck) c.pp. of C20 are applied thus: the former is a 'remark made on a wet day'; the latter, a 'self-conscious observation made by a member of a pulling-boat's crew when he misses the water and catches a crab' (*Sailors' Slang*).

someone's been looking in my pay-book! See **you've been reading my letters,** second paragraph.

something nasty in the woodshed – he (or **she**) **has seen.** Applied – in ironic derision of too many psychiatrists' too glib explanations – to 'a crazy, mixed-up kid': British and Australian: since the mid 1930s. Esp. in reference to one's mother (or, less violently, a dearly loved sister) making love, usually with 'the hired help', in a woodshed or other outhouse.

'This c.p. was originated by Stella Gibbons in her immortal *Cold Comfort Farm,* 1932, the satire that put an end to a vogue for novels of rural passions and dominant grandmothers' (Ramsey Spencer, 1959).

something the cat's brought in. See **like something** ....

something to hang things on. An infantryman's self-description, rueful yet humorous: WW1. As F & G phrase it: 'In allusion to the paraphernalia of his heavy marching order kit.' Whatever one looked like, one certainly did not feel in the least like a Christmas tree.

sometimes I wonder! Deriving from – and meaning – 'Sometimes I wonder whether you are entirely sane', *or* '... are right in the head': prompted by a stupid or very silly remark the addressee has just made; often delivered in a reflective tone and with a rather puzzled air: C20. (Barry Prentice.)

somewhere in France was, in 1915–18 and by the British army and by the Australians, Canadians, New Zealanders and others, put to jocular uses or arbitrarily, even senselessly, varied: and thus it became a c.p. (B & P.) From the heading of most Western Front letters home.

sooner you than me. See **I'd sooner you than me.**

sorry to keep you up. An Australian ironical c.p., addressed to someone who yawns: since *c.* 1920, if not since *c.* 1900. (Barry Prentice, 15 December 1974.)

sorry you spoke? – aren't you arose very early in C20 and occurred in, e.g., W. L. George, *The Making of an Englishman,* 1914; by 1950, obsolescent and by 1976 virtually obsolete. Addressed to someone who has spoken hastily and unjustly and who is clearly embarrassed at having done so.

sorry you've been troubled! This is the title of a Noël Coward sketch, written in 1923 and ending thus: '(*The telephone rings violently. POPPY snatches up the receiver, listens for a moment, then hurls the instrument to the floor.*) (Through clenched teeth.) Sorry you've been troubled!'. Dating from *c.* 1910, it obviously derives from telephone operators' often perfunctory apologies.

sort!–that's your. See **that's your sort!**

sort 'em out! A 'cry of derision evoked by a clumsy attempt at changing gear on a motor vehicle; sometimes extended to **sort 'em out–they're all there**. Another jeer at crashed gears is *d'you want/need a knife and fork?*' (Paul Beale, 11 June 1975). Since *c.* 1950.

so's your Aunt Susie! is classified by Berrey as one of the humorous 'disparaging and sarcastic flings' and is there synonymized with **so's your old man!** Very approximately 1930–50.

so's your grandmother! See **all my eye and my elbow!**

so's your old man! See **so is your old man!**

soul on! This US negro c.p. has been glossed by CM, 1970, as a 'phrase of encouragement to be authentic', i.e. sincere, to be a man of integrity, one of the *hommes de bonne volonté*: apparently since *c.* 1960.

sovereign's not in it–a. Applied to a person, esp. a sailor, suffering from jaundice: nautical, from before 1909 (Ware), and obsolescent by 1940, obsolete by 1950. In reference to the gold coin worth £1 sterling and to the patient's dark yellow complexion.

spare a rub? Let me have some, *or* After you with it!: tailors': *c.* 1880–1950 (very approximately). (B & L.)

spare my blushes! A c.p. response to an embarrassingly flattering statement or compliment: *c.* 1880–1940. In Arthur Wing Pinero's *Letty*, performed and published in 1903, we read, in Act II, where a photographer is posing a group:

PERRY: Ladies– Mr Ordish – Mr Neale – I have pleasure, and pride, in informing you that there is every prospect of my obtaining an effective picture, a strikingly beautiful picture –
NEALE: Spare my blushes!

(Neale is a commercial traveller, unlikely to blush.)

spare prick at a wedding–a. See **like a....**

speak up, Brown! is a Londoners' and Armed Forces' c.p., dating since *c.* 1930 (or a few years earlier) and addressed to one who has farted very noisily. I have also heard *did you speak?*, but rather doubt whether it ever became eligible.

speaking to the butcher, not to the block. See **I'm speaking....**

spell it out for you?–must (or **shall**) **I.** Surely it's clear (or obvious) enough?: since *c.* 1950. In late 1968, Wilfred Granville commented thus: 'Gives further emphasis to what now is already clear enough.'

spirit of the troops is excellent–the, was, in late 1916–18, a military c.p., 'taken from newspaper blather and used in jocular, and often in bitterly derisive, irony' (John Brophy, 3rd edn, of B & P).

spit and polish–no wonder we're winning the war! See **clean and polish....**

spit on the deck and call the cat a bastard! This British c.p. of the merchant marine belongs to C20 and is exemplified thus by my friend Paul Beale (28 July 1975):

In Richard Gordon's *Doctor at Sea*, 1953, chapter I,

occurs this phrase used by a crew member to welcome the new doctor aboard a merchant ship: '... Liberty Hall, this hooker. Make yourself at home. Spit on the deck and call the cat a bastard.' This vivid phrase ... has the ring, I feel, of genuine reported speech.

Not much doubt about that.

[Spital stands too nigh St Thomas à Waterings–the. A proverbial saying rather than a c.p. See *DSUE*, p. 941, at *Waterings.* ...]

spotlight on charm! See the second paragraph of entry at **I say–what a smasher!**

spring to it!, a military order, became, either in 1918 or certainly not later than 1919, esp. (of course!) among ex-Servicemen, a jocular, at first allusive, recommendation to 'Look lively!' Not quite obsolete, even by 1975.

square an' all! 'Of a truth; verily' (C. J. Dennis): Australian, originally proletarian: C20. An elaboration of the Standard English, then colloquial, *square*, 'straightforward'.

square one. See **back to square one.**

square your own yardarm! See **that's your worry!**

squattez-vous! Please sit down: late C19–20. It occurs in, e.g., Kipling's *Stalky & Co.,* 1899. Although obsolescent by 1950, it was still, as A. B. Petch remarked on 10 January 1974, 'sometimes heard for "Be seated" or "Take a pew"'. A blend of *squat* and *asseyez-vous.*

squeeze him and 'e'll fill a bucket is the c.p. equivalent of saying that he's as wet as a scrubber – a complete 'ullage', a thoroughly dim-witted, or useless, rating: the Royal Navy (lower-deck): C20. (Wilfred Granville, in letter dated 6 November 1968, but also in his *SS*.)

stab yourself and pass the bottle! Help yourself and pass the bottle: theatrical: *c.* 1850–1930. (Hotten, 1864.) From dagger-and-poison melodrama.

stag or shag? With or *without* a female companion? Australian: since the late 1940s. A pun on *a stag party*, males only, and *shag* (of the male), to copulate with, a copulation.

'stand always!'–as the girl said. A mid C19–early C20 c.p. with a punning reference to a physiological erection. This young woman seems to have belonged to the Ransom persuasion:

There was a young woman named Ransom
Who was screwed seven times in a hansom.
When she turned to her swain
And said, Let's do it again,
He said, My name's Simpson not Samson.

stand by your beds! This c.p. mimics and mocks self-importance, the speaker pretending that he is arousing the occupants of a room to activity – or to greater activity: Armed Forces': 1939–45. 'From disciplinary order of superior on entering a barrack room' (Laurie Atkinson).

[stand closer–it's shorter than you think. 'A non-cultured notice that is put near the WC in some homes ... to urge or shame males into standing closer so that they will not wet the floor. *Ladies, please remain seated during the entire performance* is much rarer' (Barry Prentice, 9 June 1975). The phrases occur together on printed cards to be bought in joke shops (Camilla Raab). This *might* some day rise from raffish witticism to raffish c.p.]

stand on a fag-paper! Advice to someone unable to reach up to something, esp. if he's rather short: mostly Londoners', and Cockneys' at that: since *c*. 1920.

stand on me for that! – often shortened to **stand on me!** You can take my word for it: sporting circles: since the 1920s, if not a decade or two earlier. The longer form is recorded in EP, *Slang Today and Yesterday*, 1933; the latter in Frank Norman's *Stand on Me*, 1959.

stand to, boys, the Jocks are going over! In B & P, 1930, John Brophy remarked that it 'belonged to the latter half of the war' – i.e. 1917–18. He added that it was 'a fairly kindly way of making fun of kilted soldiers and of the excessive popularity they enjoyed with journalists and women; spoken with exaggerated and comic respect on the advent of Highland troops – but without any mean feeling of jealousy'. The 'going over' refers to going over No-Man's-Land in an attack. Whereas on Gallipoli (and later) it was the 29th Division (English), on the Western Front it was the 51st Division (Scottish), which the very critical Australian infantrymen the most admired; not, however, that there weren't others.

stand up and be counted! Show your true political colours; hence also in other contexts: since *c*. 1920. (A. B. Petch, 4 January 1974.)

[**stand up, speak up – and shut up!** This famous advice to all post-luncheon and post-dinner speakers has become almost a c.p.; almost, not quite.]

[**standing prick has no conscience – a**; often elaborated with the complementary animadversion, **and an itching cunt feels no shame**. Probably mid C18–20; certainly at least mid C19–20. A low c.p. that, because of its verity and its force, had, by 1920 at latest, become a proverb – not, of course, to be found in the standard books of quotations and dictionaries of proverbs, yet none the less a proverb, for all that. Cf those other unrecorded proverbs, *Let your wind go free,/Where'er you may be*, with its variant *Let wind go free,/Where'er you be*, which, in its longer version, I heard from a septuagenarian parson excusing himself, somewhat perfunctorily I thought, to me after dinner one night in the summer of 1927; and *Short and thick/Does the trick*; *Long and thin/Goes right in*, which I heard from an Oxford don early in 1940; and **as soft as shit and twice as nasty** recorded separately in this dictionary. There are, I believe, two or three others, but if I ever heard them, I've unforgivably forgotten them.]

stands out like a shithouse in the fog, usually preceded by **it**: a low Canadian c.p.: C20.

stands Scotland where it did? This famous quotation from Shakespeare's *Macbeth*, Act IV, Scene iii, line 164, became a c.p. not later than, I think, the 1880s or 1890s. Cf S, Dialogue II:

COL[ONEL]: And, pray, Sir *John*, how do you like the Town? You have been absent a long time.

SIR JOHN: Why, I find little *London* stands just where it did when I saw it last.

(Thank God, he – this bluff Derbyshire squire – at least, didn't call it 'little old London'!) This quotation from Swift very clearly suggests that the phraseological pattern may have become general early in C17.

Starve 'em, Rot 'em and Cheat 'em is a naval (hence also military) c.p. of *c*. 1750–1880. Recorded at one end by Grose,

1785, and at the other by Hotten, 1864, it refers to the unfavourable reputation of the barracks, and the public-houses and brothels, at Strood, Rochester and Chatham.

In *Sailors' Slang*, 1962, Granville called it 'a good-natured libel' of these Medway towns.

state secret – a. See **it's a state secret**.

states can be saved without it was, according to Ware in 1909, a political, thence also an educated and cultured, c.p., expressive of ironic condemnation; current in the 1880s.

stay and be hanged! Oh, all right – if you must!: a mostly lower-middle-class c.p. of C19–early 20. (Ware.)

stay in your own backyard! was an American c.p., implying 'I don't want your company' and sometimes 'Mind your own business!' Period 1899–*c*. 1916. The song thus titled was published and first sung by J. P. Witmark in 1899; words by Kennett, music by Udall. (Edward B. Marks, 1934, cited by W.J.B.)

steady, Barker! was, *c*. 1941, adopted from the navy's version of the BBC radio programme 'Merry-Go-Round', as Campbell Nairne, formerly editor of the *Radio Times*, informed me while I was preparing 'Those Radio Catch Phrases', published in that weekly on 6 December 1946. *Steady, Barker!* was obviously prompted by steady, the Buffs! below.

steady, Jackson! 'Take it easy' (Berrey): US: C20; by 1960, somewhat obsolescent. I suspect that this c.p. may be ironic – prompted by the military tactics of General 'Stonewall' Jackson.

steady, the Buffs! A c.p. of self-admonition or self-adjuration or self-encouragement: late C19–20: military and – rather later, by adoption – naval; and finally among civilians. From an incident in the history of the East Kent Regiment, the nickname *the Buffs* perhaps originating in the fact that they were the first regiment to wear buff, or buffalo, leather accoutrements. (F & G.) Perhaps the c.p. arose when, in 1888, Kipling popularized the phrase in *Soldiers Three*.

Thus, a man aware that, tipsy, he is walking unsteadily, might say to himself, 'Steady, the Buffs!'

Steve. See **come on, Steve** and **got me, Steve?**

[**stewed, screwed and tattooed** – or sometimes **screwed, stewed and tattooed**. 'Strictly soldier–sailor lingo of the kind heard in dockside saloons the world over' (W. J. Burke, 18 August 1975): US: C20. Cf the British **bitched, buggered and bewildered (and far from home)**. But Mr Burke implies – and I rather agree with him – that *stew* ... is hardly a true c.p.]

stick around, fellers, maybe I'll use yer! 'Mae West's notable scripted line to extras who wanted to play in one of her films; said by that lady from her motion picture *persona*' (Laurie Atkinson, late 1974): American: (post-1932, when she went to Hollywood). A double-entendre that rapidly became a c.p.

stick it, Jerry! An army c.p. of *c*. 1914–18: and not necessarily nor probably in allusion to *Jerry*, a Ger. soldier: in the *Daily Express* of 6 November 1939, there is an 'item' pointing out that Lew Luke, a Cockney comedian, originated a sketch, 'The Bloomsbury Burglars', featuring Nobbler and Jerry; as Nobbler, Lew Luke would, as they hurled missiles at off-stage policemen, shout to his partner, 'Stick it, Jerry!'.

still (occasionally **all**) **alive and kissing – she's**. 'Used of a sexy girl' (A. B. Petch, 4 January 1974): since *c.* 1950. A pun on *all alive and kicking*, originally the street cry of a fishmonger.

still all in one piece. 'Used when someone has been in an accident and yet has sustained little, or no great harm: since *c.* 1919' (A. B. Petch, 10 January 1974).

still going strong – like Johnny Walker dates from *c.* 1924; by 1940, slightly obsolescent, yet, even by 1975, not obsolete. (Recorded by Collinson.) From a famous advertisement of a very famous whisky 'still going strong'. An elaboration of *to be going strong*, to be vigorous, to be (very) prosperous.

still he is not happy! Applied to one whom nothing satisfies and nothing pleases: *c.* 1870–5. Ware, following the *Daily Telegraph* article of 28 July 1894, attributes its popularity to a phrase uttered more than once, in a Gaiety Theatre burlesque in 1870.

still running – like Charley's Aunt is a C20 c.p. applied to plays and then also to films, implying a long 'life'; occasioned by the continuing popularity of that evergreen farce, *Charley's Aunt*. The c.p., however, has been comparatively little heard since *c.* 1960.

stinking Yarra! An insult hurled by Sydneyites at Melbournites: C20. The retort is **our 'Arbour!**, q.v. The allusion is to the myth that the Yarra is the only river that flows upside down – it is very muddy! Neither phrase has been very much used since the 1950s.

stir it up! – often accompanied by a mime of someone stirring a huge cauldron – is a third party's remark upon, and fomenting of, a quarrel either already in progress or clearly brewing: since *c.* 1955. (Laurie Atkinson.)

stockings are of two parishes. See **his stockings ....**

stomach thinks my throat is cut – my. See **my stomach ....**

stop it, Horace! Dating since *c.* 1930, this, as one of my most valued correspondents puts it, is 'shouted in a squeaky, semi-lisping, high-pitched voice after any refined-looking "delicate" young man: it does not mean Stop anything' – probably deriving from a George Robey 'gag'.

stop it – I like it! Mostly directed at giggling teenage girls pretending, neither very long nor very convincingly, that they dislike their boy friends' caresses: since *c.* 1920 or maybe a decade or two earlier. Cf Harry Lauder's famous song, 'Stop your tickling, Jock!'

stop laughing! Stop complaining! An Australian irony, dating since *c.* 1930, it is recorded by Baker; and it occurs in Jon Cleary's *Back of Sunset*, 1959.

stop me and buy one! belongs to 1934–9 and sprang from the very well known slogan used by Wall's Ice Cream.

stop me if you've (or **you have**) **heard it** (or **this one**) is the usually mock-considerate, certainly imminent, inveterate funny-storyteller's stock preamble: since the 1920s. If you try, it's at your own risk; if you succeed, you lose a friend.

In Noël Coward's *Star Quality*, 1951, one of the short stories is titled 'Stop Me If You've Heard It' and it contains this trenchant comment:

'Stop Me If You've Heard It.' That idiotic insincere phrase – that false, unconvincing opening gambit – as though people ever had the courage to stop anyone however many times they've heard it.

The sad, little story ends, '"I've got something to tell you," she said. "Stop me if you've heard it."'

[**stop spoofing me!** Stop trying to fool me: US students': 1920s. But, being entirely mutable, the expression isn't a true c.p.]

stop yer tickling, Jock! is a C20, non-aristocratic British c.p., current in and since 1904, but little heard after *c.* 1945. From Harry Lauder's song thus titled – published in that year – written by Lauder himself in collaboration with F. Folloy; technically, perhaps Lauder's cleverest and most exacting song. Cf **stop it – I like it!**

stout as a miller's waistcoat that takes a thief by the neck every day, usually preceded by **as**. This C18–early C19 c.p. glosses the proverb, *many a miller, many a thief*, and that other about a miller, a tailor, a weaver, in a bag. (Apperson.)

straighten up and fly right! Originally Marine Corps, since the early 1940s, and then Air Force, this US c.p. means 'Snap out of it – and get on the ball!'; hence, 'Act like a *true* Marine, or a *real* airman!' Synonymous with **shape up or ship out**, q.v. (Colonel Albert Moe, 14 July 1974.)

Basically an elaboration of the colloquial *straighten up* (both transitive and intransitive), to reform.

strictly for the birds. See **that's for the birds**.

strike – or give me the bill! Mind what you're doing!: *c.* 1660–1750. From an injunction to a man clumsy with this ancient military weapon, used later by the constabulary. (Apperson.)

strong, silent man, usually preceded by **a**. Originally a cliché of fiction, esp. among women novelists, e.g. Ethel M. Dell and Gertrude Page, it became, in the early 1920s, a mostly sarcastic c.p. By 1960, slightly – and by 1976, very – obsolescent.

stuff is here and it's really mellow – the. Among US 'pop' musicians and their devotees; this c.p. is glossed by Berrey, 1942, as 'likening "swing" to fine whiskey'; current, *c.* 1935–50 (*very* approximately).

stuff to give the troops. See **that's the stuff ....**

subject normal! refers to smutty talk or esp. to its resumption: Armed Forces', since *c.* 1939; by 1944 or 1945, it had become general. 'The lowest common denominator' – a mathematical term used derivatively for 'what is understood or accepted by the most people' – has also been called 'the one safe subject'.

such a dawg! was, in the theatrical circles of 1888–*c.* 1914, applied to a tremendous 'masher', as the knowledgeable Ware noted in 1909.

such a reason my goose pissed (or ... **pissed my goose**). This was, in latish C18–earlyish C19, the standard retort made to one who, as an excuse, gives some absurd or extremely feeble reason. (Grose, 1796.)

such is life without a wife! has developed from the world-old, world-wide, world-weary truism, 'Such is life', as an elaboration – and as a c.p. of late (?mid) C19–20. The addition, bearing little relation to the facts, has generated a serio-cynical rider, **and a thousand times worse with one**, current among those who believe not merely that you can't win 'em all but that you can't win, 'period'.

such (perhaps rather more often **these**) **things happen** (or, more usually, **will happen) in the best-regulated families**, sometimes with **even** inserted before *in*. One of the domestic c.pp., it is either apologetic or explanatory of a family quarrel or misfortune, esp. a little bastard. Probably dating since the 1870s or 1880s, these are variant forms of a genuine c.p.: but the c.p. itself represents, in one sense, a deformation, in another a natural and, indeed, expectable offshoot from a famous quotation: 'Accidents will occur in the best-regulated families,' opined the sapient Micawber in Dickens's *David Copperfield* (1849–50).

suck it and see! This derisive retort, current in the 1890s, apparently went underground for almost a generation, to be revived, *c.* 1945–60, by Australian children – and by English children in the late 1930s and until *c.* 1950. It arose from the habit of sucking sweets, esp. those as hard as a bullet or, at the least, as a rock.

Sudanese, Siamese, Breadancheese, Standatease. 'General round-up of all "the lesser breeds without the law"; our brown brothers' (Paul Beale, 12 June 1974): mostly army: since latish 1940s.

Sunday – *bloody* **Sunday!** has, probably since the 1880s or 1890s, so much been the cry of those stranded in a strange city or even in their own, therefore including all such as have no true home of their own, that it became a c.p. during the 1960s. The c.p. was not produced by the play and film of that title. The c.p. afforded the playwright a wonderful title.

sun's scorching your eyes out – the. 'A Service waking call [not official, but time-honoured] at reveille – regardless of the time of year – in winter long before sunrise. ... originally Navy, a Bo'sun's mate's expression in calling the hands – *e.g.*, "Heave out, heave out, heave out, show a leg there, show a leg, sun's a-scorching your eyes out!"' (F & G): late (?mid) C19–20; in C20, also army, with the variant, *the sun's burning a hole in your blanket* (B & P). It became a c.p. not later than 1919: applied by anyone awaking someone else, or, since *c.* 1945, as a mere adjuration to get up and go to work.

Cf **rise and shine**.

sup Simon: good broth! Dialogue II of S, 1738, has:

COL[ONEL]: O, my Lord, this is my sick Dish (the small quantity I eat when I'm feeling unwell): when I am well, I have a Bigger.

MISS: [*To Colonel.*] Sup *Simon*: good Broth.

An ironic c.p., current throughout C17–19, although in C19 mainly rural. (Apperson.)

sure as thou livest, then ... **you live**. A c.p. of assurance and especially of reassurance: late C16–mid C17. Thomas Middleton, *The Merry Devil of Edmonton*, 1608, at Act I, Scene i:

Nay, as sure as thou liv'st, the villainous Vicar is abroad at the chase this dark night.

This one I missed; I owe it to Colonel Albert Moe.

sure I'm sure! has, since not later than 1930, been the US c.p. reply to 'Are you sure?' Cf:

sure thing! Surely, *or* Certainly, in reply to either a direct question or an implied doubt: US (late C19–20), adopted in Britain by 1910 at latest. Cf the preceding entry and **that's for sure**.

surprise me! All right! Surprise me – show how intelligent, how original, you are! Both US, originally (I think), and

British by adoption: respectively since late 1940s and middle 1950s. A British example comes in John Mortimer's scathingly witty *Conference*, published 1960, in *Sketches from One to Another*, written by John Mortimer, N. F. Simpson, Harold Pinter. The neurotic US tycoon is interviewing Jones, who can't get a word in edgeways (or in any other way), and finally interrupts himself on the telephone to speak to Jones: 'Carry on, Jones. Surprise me!'

surprise! surprise! Either 'Here's a tremendous surprise for you', or, the surprised one speaking, 'Well! *What* a surprise!' Dating, I think, from the 1950s. Several examples: Noël Coward uses it in 'Me and the Girls', one of the stories comprising *Pretty Polly and Other Stories*, 1964. Dick Francis, in *Forfeit*, 1968, has:

'Try?' she said tentatively ...

'Surprise, surprise.' It sounded more flippant than I felt.

'I thought it might be you,' she said.

Also US, as in Edward Albee, *The American Dream*, 1961, near the end of the play, when Grandma says (to the audience), 'Shhhhhh! I want to watch this. [*The young man is framed in the doorway.*]' And Mrs Barker, the slightly sinister caller, says, 'Surprise! Surprise! Here we are!'

And as in Hillary Waugh, *Finish Me Off*, 1970: 'He sorted through the girl's items and found the injection paraphernalia in the kit. "A junkie," he said. "Surprise, surprise."' And also in Michael S. Lewin, *Ask the Right Question*, 1971:

'Oh,' she said ... 'Can I help you with anything else?'

'Yeah. A little information.'

'Surprise, surprise.'

By 1971, both in Britain and the Commonwealth and in US, the c.p. had become so embedded in colloquial usage that it was occasionally shortened to *surprise!*, as in John Godey's magnificent US novel, *The Taking of Pelham One Two Three* (1973), which ends with the sole survivor of the four 'takers' of a New York underground train jumping off a fire escape into the arms of a waiting detective: '"Surprise," Haskins said with a nice touch of irony.'

Of this c.p., one of the best and most widely used since *c.* 1950, Paul Beale has (17 February 1975) penetratingly written:

[A] c.p., occasionally as a genuine expression of astonishment and pleasure, but more often sarcastically and in disappointment; the expected worst has come to pass.

Wife, who didn't want to go out anyway: 'I'm awfully sorry, darling, but I've got this splitting headache.'

Husband, who has seen it coming [and] who very much wanted to go out, might respond in a deadened, unsympathetic and disenchanted tone: 'Surprise, surprise!'

surprised? you could have fucked (in polite company, **kissed**) **me through my oilskins** was current among undergraduates at the University of Oxford during the 1930s and then with a wide acceptance; slightly obsolescent by *c.* 1950 – rather more so by 1965 – yet still, in 1975, extant. A valued and frequent contributor glossed it thus on 7 August 1972: 'Meaning – if it means anything much – that the speaker is *not* surprised. (Suspect its origin was Royal Navy.)'

[**swallow a sovereign and shit it in silver**. This C19–20 vulgarism lies on the borderline between a proverbial saying and a c.p. It indicates the very acme of convenience.]

swallowed a stake and cannot stoop – he (occasionally **she**) **has** was, mid C17–mid C19, applied to an upright, stiff-mannered person. In C16–17 the form was *he has eaten a stake*. (Apperson.)

swaying with an old mess-mate; in full, **I've been ....** A naval (lower-deck) explanation of a boozy evening ashore: since *c.* 1860; by 1945, virtually obsolete. (F. Bowen, 1929.)

[**sweet damn' all** and all similar exclamatories are *not* c.pp., but mere violent asseveratives. The most famous of them is, I'd say, *sweet Fanny Adams*.]

swim out – you are over your head! was a US c.p. of the 1870s. *Am*, 1877, quotes, from *Burton's Events of 1875–76*, by H. G. Richmond's verses about 'flash sayings' that 'now-a-days are the rage,–/They're heard in the parlor, the street, on the stage,–/"You're too fresh" and "Swim out, you are over your head"', but does not gloss this saying, which sounds, to me anyway, like an early example of the 'sick' joke – a callous, a fiendishly insensitive, a macabre, joke or witticism.

swing it till Monday! – the motto of the Torpedo School, HMS Vernon – 'really meant "switch on and chance it"''

(Rear-Admiral P. W. Brock, 8 December 1973): late C19–early C20.

swing that lamp, Jack! is, in the Royal Navy (lower-deck), addressed to a 'line-shooter' (or teller of tall stories) and a hint that he is showing very bad form: since *c.* 1942. (Wilfred Granville in PGR.)

swoppin' sure for 'appen, exchanging 'certain' for 'perhaps'; 'forgoing certainty for a chance, from domestic affairs to political propositions. West Riding' (Vernon Noble, 11 September 1974): West Riding of Yorkshire: since *c.* 1930.

Sydney or the bush. See **it will be** (or **it's either**) **Sydney or the bush.**

'SYNTHETIC FAD EXPRESSIONS' is W & F's classification (and condemnation) of the more trivial and transient of c.pp. In 1960, they listed seven (all US, naturally): **coming, Mother!**; **Hey Abbott!**; **hi ho Silver!**; **I dood it**; **say hey!**; **what's up, Doc?**; **you're a good one!** (See the individual entries.) Such triviality and transitoriness are much less frequent than is generally supposed.

T

T.A.B.U.; N.A.B.U.; S.A.B.U.; also T.A.R.F.U. and T.C.C.F.U. Of these, the first four soon came to be written, and pronounced, 'solid' – that is, *Tabu, Nabu, Sabu, Tarfu*, with the *u* pronounced *oo*.

Respectively, a *typical army balls-up*: a *non*-adjustable *balls-up*; a *self* adjustable *balls-up*, where *balls-up* = confusion, 'mess': army, mostly officers', esp. in North Africa: 1940–5. *TARFU* is that state of confusion in which '*things are really fucked-up* (politely, *fouled-up*)'; *TCCFU* is a 'typical Coastal Command *fuck-up*' and was employed in the RAF, esp. in Coastal Command itself, 1941–4.

Cf **snafu**.

T.G.I.F. Among teachers in primary and secondary day schools, 'Thank God it's Friday!': C20.

T.T.F.N. See:

ta-ta for now! A c.p. form of 'Good-bye for the present!' – often 'initialled' to *T.T.F.N.*: esp. during the 1940s, it was instituted and popularized by the radio programme, 'ITMA': see TOMMY HANDLEY CATCH PHRASES below. In Frank Worsley's *Itma*, 1948, we read that Dorothy Summers first appeared in ITMA on 10 October 1940 and rapidly became famous in her role of Mrs Mopp and that, by mid-1943, 'Mrs Mopp's entrances and exits had become standardized. As she was going she bellowed "*T.T.F.N.*"'

tace is Latin for a candle. Be quiet *or* stop talking!: mid C17–mid C19, then only among a diminishing number of scholars. In Thomas Shadwell, *The Virtuoso*, performed and published in 1676, Act I, Scene i, has:

LONG[VIL]: A Wit! 'faith, he might as well have call'd thee a Dromedary.

SIR SAM[UEL HEARTY]: Peace, I say; *Tace* is Latin for a Candle.

It occurs in Swift, Fielding, Grose (1788), Scott; then in dialect. (Apperson.) The pun is double; *tace* in L. = be silent; a candle is snuffed out or otherwise extinguished. Cf **brandy is Latin for a goose**.

tact. See **that, Bill, is tack (or tact)**.

tail of my shirt looks like a french-polisher's apron – all brown, preceded by **the**. As a correspondent has phrased it, this c.p. is 'a would-be wicked pleasantry at the expense of a comrade': naval: since *c.* 1930. The imputation is one of sycophancy.

tail will catch the chin-cough, usually preceded by **his**. This mid C17–18 c.p. is applied to one who is sitting on wet ground. (Ray, 1678.)

take a bow! Congratulations!: US: since *c.* 1925; by 1975, obsolescent. (Berrey.) As if before a theatre audience calling 'Author! Author!'

take a carrot! A low, insulting c.p.: *c.* 1860–1940 (Hotten, 1874). Originally said to women and scabrously intended: cf **have a banana**, at first innocent, but soon, among the raffish, obscene. Cf the old Fr. *et ta soeur, aime-t-elle les radis?*

By *c.* 1880, it also, among men and without sexual innuendo, signified 'I don't care!' by 1940, obsolete. (Baumann.)

take a dagger and drown yourself! was, *c.* 1880–1910, a theatrical retort. From the old colloquial phrase, meaning 'to say one thing and mean another'. Cf **stab yourself and pass the bottle!**

take a red hot potato! was, *c.* 1840–60, a way of saying 'Be ιuiet!' – esp., 'Be silent!' (Duncombe, *Sinks of London*, 1848.) A very hot potato in the mouth is an effectual deterrent against talk, notably against loquacity.

[**take a running jump at yourself!** See **go and take...!** But not strictly a c.p.]

take all you want – take two! A US c.p., dating from at least as early as 1945 and applied to a qualified generosity. 'Originally, I am pretty sure, Yiddish – but used by Jews themselves in self-mockery – not anti-Semitic' (John W. Clark, 17 May 1975.)

take care! (or **take good care!**) This 'is now the fashionable last word on saying good-bye' (Douglas Leechman, 13 August 1974): Canadian: arising late in 1973 or very early in 1974. Cf the English **mind how you go!**

take eight! You've won, *or* I give in: a C20 military c.p. (F & G.) From points gained in some game or other.

But in Suffolk, since *c.* 1945, it has been addressed to someone breaking wind. Again: why, precisely?

[**take five!** See **take ten!**]

take good care! See **take care!**

take his name and number! – with **Sergeant** often added. 'This had a vogue as a popular catch phrase after the First World War' (A. B. Petch, April 1966): say 1919–25. Humorously nostalgic. Cf:

take his name, Sergeant-Major, take his name. An army c.p. of C20, but not very general before WW1. From the army order, issued by an officer, in precisely those words.

take in your washing! A nautical, esp. a naval, c.p. 'order to a careless boat's crew to bring fenders, rope's end, etc., inboard' (Bowen): late C19–20; by 1960, obsolescent.

take it away! Take the fellow away, he bores me with his nonsense: US, mostly students': 1920s. (McKnight.)

[**take it easy.** See **take it slow!**]

take it from here! Let's begin at this point and ignore what's been said or done or is past: since *c.* 1955. There was, in the 1950s, a radio show thus named.

take it from me. See **you can take it from me**.

take it off your back! Don't worry about it!: naval (lower-deck): C20. 'Borrowed from dock lumpers' (stevedores working at a fish dock), as Wilfred Granville tells us in 1962.

take it out of that! Fight away!: Londoners': *c*, 1815–60. JB adds: 'Accompanied by showing the elbow, and patting it.'

[**take it slow!** Variant, **take it easy!** The former is the US negro form of the latter. Not c.pp., although they might at first seem so.]

take me to your leader! is a world-wide c.p. used by the *little green men* – mysterious beings alleged, since *c.* 1950, to have been seen emerging from flying saucers: since the late 1950s. From comic cartoons about Martians landing on Earth and from Science Fiction. The linguistic lineage seems to have been: USA – Canada – Britain – Australia and New Zealand. (Frank Shaw; Barry Prentice; Douglas Leechman; and conversation.)

> June Drummond's novel, *Farewell Party*, 1971, has:
> 'Come too,' I said.
> 'And the host will clap hands when he sees me?'
> 'He won't mind...'
> 'Take me to your leader,' said Dave.

take me with you! In Beaumont and Fletcher's *The Noble Gentleman*, written not later that 1616, although not published until 1640, at Act III, Scene i, we see:

> SHATTILLION: ... Which we will likewise slip. [I.e., omit.]
> DUKE: But take me with you.

It had already occurred in Thomas Middleton's, *A Trick to Catch the Old One*, 1606, as Colonel Albert Moe has informed me. Meaning 'Please explain in detail', it belongs to the very approximate period, late C16–mid C17.

take more water with it! imputes clumsiness or incompetence or tipsiness, but mostly either of the first two as caused by the third: late C19–20. Originally and esp. a jocular c.p. addressed to a sober person happening to sway or to stumble.

[**take ten!**, like **take five!** – meaning 'Take a rest of ten, or five, minutes' – is clearly not a c.p. but an ordinary colloquialism.]

take that and see how you like it. Put that in your pipe and smoke it! Think that over: apparently US rapidly become also British: C20. (Berrey.)

take that fire-poker out of your spine and the (or those) **lazy-tongs out of your fish-hooks** (hands)! A nautical adjuration to rid oneself of laziness: late C19–early C20.

take the marbles out of your mouth! Speak more distinctly: an uncultured c.p. of late C19–C20.

take yer 'at orf in the 'ouse of God ... cunt! 'An army c.p., often attributed apocryphally to the fiercest RSM one has known. It is muttered *sotto voce* and then, after a slight pause, comes the viciously explosive epithet. Heard, of course, at church parade, but "for fun", anywhere. I first heard it in 1953.' (Paul Beale, 30 September 1975.)

take (or **pull**) **your finger out!** Get a move on! Get busy! Originally (*c.* 1930) RAF, as *take*...; adopted in either 1941 or 1942 by the army, where often *pull* was preferred. Officers' deliberately pompous variants: *dedigitate* and, among RAF officers, *remove the digit*. An alternative, since *c.* 1944, is *get your finger out!* A further RAF variant, WW2 and until 1950, was *he's got his finger wedged*. Wilfred Granville has noted the naval variant *take your fingers out*. (EP, *RAF Slang*, 1945; PGR.)

The semantics: 'Stop scratching your backside and get on with the job.'

take your pipe! Take it easy – have a rest!: among North Country miners and labourers: C20. 'Take your pipe out of your pocket and have a smoke.'

take your washing in, Ma: here comes the (whatever unit it may be). 'On the line of march, greetings were usually exchanged by meeting regiments' (B & P): military: late C19–20. No animosity felt and no malice intended.

talk about laugh! I, we, etc., really did laugh heartily! Belonging to the popular speech current throughout C20 and probably since *c.* 1860 or so, this is a non-cultured c.p., as can readily be perceived from the following piece of Services vernacular cited by a valued correspondent: 'Y'should've seen ol' Dodger; got half his pubes [i.e., pubic hairs] caught up in his [fly] zip. Talk about laugh!'

talk to me! is a US negroes' c.p. of the 1920s–1940s. 'When a jazzman is really communicating through his music, people often cry out "Talk to me!" Or they might say "He's saying something!"' (CM.)

talking to the butcher, not to the block. A variant of **speaking to...**, q.v. at **I'm speaking...**.

talks like a book with no leaves – i.e. pages – **in it**, usually preceded by **he** or **she**. 'An old expression used in reference to a person full of empty talk' (A. B. Petch, 30 March 1976): mostly lower-middle class and public-house: since *c.* 1920.

tall, dark and handsome, only when used derisively and ironically, since (perhaps) *c.* 1910: both British and US: from cheap romantic fiction, where the hero was so often described thus. John W. Clark (17 February 1975) notes that its formation resembles that of **fair, fat and forty**.

tall weed in the grass, bud! was, in the 1930s, an intimation to a fellow convict that a 'stool pigeon' was within earshot: at San Quentin. (Gladys Duffy, *Warden's Wife*, 1959.)

taller they are, the farther they fall, preceded by **the**. See **bigger they are...**.

tap run dry? (or **tap-water run out?**) A showmen's c.p., addressed to a quack doctor either unoccupied or idling while his fairground fellow workers are busy: since *c.* 1880. There is an implication that most of his medicines consist of (coloured) water. See Neil Bell, *Crocus* [quack doctor], 1936, for one example of this usage.

tap the Admiral. See **he would tap the Admiral**.

tata for now! See **ta-ta for now**.

tats and all! An underworld and fringe-of-the-underworld c.p. of *c.* 1780–1850. (Vaux.) It expresses incredulity at another's statement or, at the end of one's own, a contradiction of what has preceded the phrase, *Tats*, rags, small pieces of material; implication, 'worthless'.

tavern bitch has bit him in the head – **the**. He's drunk: late C16–mid C17. (Thomas Middleton, *A Trick to Catch the Old Ones* 1608; Apperson.) If ever you study the popular prints of C17–early C19, you'll notice how often a dog figures in the tavern scenes.

teacher! See **please, teacher!**

tearing up the pea-patch – he's (or **they're**). He is, or they are, ruining the game or contest or competition; hence, 'going on a rampage' (W & F) – applied originally to baseball: US: *c*. 1945–55, then decreasingly, although still heard at least as late as 1969. The expression was popularized by Walter Barber 'in his *c*. 1945–*c*. 1955 broadcasts of the old Brooklyn Dodgers baseball games' (W & F).

Thanks to the generosity of my old and learned friend, W. J. ('Jerry') Burke, I am able to amplify. In a letter dated 28 January 1969, he writes:

Sportscaster Walter 'Red' Barber began his Major League baseball broadcasting in Cincinnati, Ohio, in 1934. He was from the South, and most Southern boys lard their speech with homely colloquial phrases. Black-eyed peas are a favourite Southern dish, and almost everyone has a pea patch. If a stray dog or cow broke through the fence and got into one of these pea patches, a great deal of damage was done. One might hear such an expression as 'That critter is tearing up the pea patch!' It is an old expression down South and 'Red' Barber didn't create it. He popularized it. In describing a 'rhubarb' (baseball slang for a fight among players of opposing teams…) Barber would exclaim, 'They're tearing up the pea patch!' His listeners got the picture right away.

telegram from arsehole: 'shit expected' is a variation of the theme expressed by **it's a poor arse that never rejoices**: raffish: since *c*. 1910.

tell a green man! Please bring me up to date, *or* Put me wise!: among US jazz players and jazz devotees: since *c*. 1950. (W & F.) Here, *green man* may, rather vaguely, refer to the slang sense, 'a piece of paper money'.

But the c.p. also synonymizes **tell that to the Marines!**

tell it like it is! Tell it naturally without the slightest elaboration of style or withholding, or manipulation, of the truth: US, originally among negroes. CM (a negro author), 1970, inevitably includes it, but in this instance I find the explanation given by 'Whitey' the more valuable. On 3 December 1968, Professor John W. Clark wrote to me thus:

Hardly older than 1960, but very common now. Originally used by negro agitators with reference to giving what they regard as the real facts about the negro situation. Now generally used with regard to any situation in which it is supposed that the real facts have been suppressed: 'Let's be honest and factual' (as people have not commonly been hitherto).

On 25 April 1969, Professor John T. Fain classified it as 'a hippies' c.p.'

It reached Australia early in the 1970s. Mr Barry Prentice, *c*. 6 March 1975, writes, 'Our gutter press assures us that they "tell it like it is".'

A valuable allusive example occurs in Ross Macdonald's *The Goodbye Look*, 1969: 'The question made her· unhappy.... "You want me to tell it like it is, like the kids say?"' – which rather suggests that the c.p. had reached the juvenile public by (say) 1967.

The expression expectably corresponds to a human situation. In Irvin S. Cobb's *The Escape of Mr Trimm*, 1913, a poorly educated young woman says, '"I'm goin' to tell you the whole story, jest like it was," she went on in her flat drone.'

tell it not in Gath – when its meaning was, in late C19–early C20, being debased to 'Fancy *you* doing that!' or 'Fancy·you doing *that*!' – a c.p., drawn from the cliché, itself drawn from the *Bible* (2 Samuel, i, 20).

tell it to Sweeney received from HLM, Supp. 2, a contemptuous inclusion among 'the numerous catch-phrases that have little if any precise meaning but simply delight the moron by letting him know that he knows the latest'. Berrey, 1942, had included it in a long list of slangy and c.p. synonyms of 'I don't believe it!' W & F, 1960, date it from '*c*. 1920; now archaic' and gloss it as = 'Go tell it to Sweeney. He may believe you. I don't.' But it's older than 1920. In *The Pedagogical Seminary*, March 1912, A. H. Melville mentions it in his article 'An Investigation of the Function and Use of Slang' as being current among teenagers. The evidence tends to show that Mencken erred in dismissing the phrase so lightly. Perhaps originally a tribute to Irish eloquence and powers of improvisation. The British form was *tell that to Sweeney*: *c*. 1922–39.

tell it to the Marines! See **tell that to the Horse-Marines!**

tell me about me (or **myself**), often preceded by **now**. Not general before 1945, it is a courting c.p., reassuringly jocular, although it may have started off as a fatuously serious request.

tell me another! Tell me another story – I simply can't believe *that* one! *or* You don't (*or* you can't) expect me to credit *that*: C20. (W. L. George, *The Making of an Englishman*, 1914.)

It passed to US; Berrey, 1942, records it as 'I don't believe it!' Yet it had been used much earlier by Alfred Sutro in his comedy, *Rude Min and Christine*, 1915 (but clearly written before the outbreak of WW1 on 4 August 1914), near the end:

CLAUGHTON: ...I say, Minnie and I are going to get married.

GEORGE: [*Laughing.*] Go on! Tell me another!

tell me news!, often preceded by **that's ancient history**. A retort upon an old story or a stale jest: C18–20; by 1920, obsolescent; by 1945, obsolete. (S).

tell me the old, old story! comes from No 681 in *The Church of England Hymnary*, although the c.p. is also very popular among Nonconformists; often heard at, e.g., political meetings, where hecklers favour it; apparently since late C19. Among soldiers in the ranks, during WW1 (from late 1915 onwards), 'all rumours of good times to come and promises from authority would be met by the singing of the first line of a Nonconformist hymn – Tell Me the Old, Old Story' (John Brophy, in B & P).

Frank Shaw, in a letter written in 1969, curtly glossed the saying, thus: 'He's going to lie again. From hymn.'

In Scene ii of John Mortimer's witty comedy, *What Shall We Tell Caroline?*, performed and published in 1958, the following occurs:

TONY: ...But it's gone too far, you know – we should never have started it.

ARTHUR: Of course you shouldn't. Now there's a twinge of conscience.

TONY: You know as much as I do. There's never been a breath of anything amiss.

ARTHUR: (*singing bitterly*): 'Tell me the old, old story...'

tell that for a tale, often shortened to **that for a tale!** I don't believe that – it's too far-fetched altogether: an expression of utter incredulity: the former, *c*. 1870–1940; the latter, C20.

tell that to Sweeney! See **tell it to Sweeney!**

tell that to the Horse-Marines!; but predominantly **tell that to the Marines.** Don't be silly – do you think I'm a fool? *or* I don't believe it – someone else may: C19–20. John Davis, *The Post Captain*, 1806, has '*tell that to the Marines*'; in 1830, Moncrieff used the longer form – obsolete by *c.* 1900. An early variant was that employed by Byron in 1823: *that will do for the Marines, but the sailors won't believe it*. It was, in the form *tell it to the Marines*, very early adopted in the US. Sailors always did rather make fun of the credulity of the Marines. Cf:

tell that to the morons is a hecklers' c.p., current since *c.* 1950. Obviously a pun on **tell that to the Marines** (see the preceding entry).

tell the world. See **I'll tell the world.**

tell us something new! A retort upon a communication of stale news: late C19–20. (Lyell.)

tell you what. See **I'll tell you what.**

tell your mother ninepence!, sometimes preceded by a palliative **oh.** This c.p. expresses unwillingness to reply helpfully to a question requiring some thought, as in 'What a question! Tell your mother ninepence': mostly lower-middle and lower class: since *c.* 1917. Julian Franklyn, on 16 December 1968, opined that it arose soon after David Lloyd George introduced National Insurance in 1916, with employees paying fourpence, and employers fivepence, a week: the masses were already realizing that Lloyd George was a 'fast talker'.

tell your troubles to a policeman! was a cynical US c.p. of *c.* 1919–29. (HLM, 1922 edn.)

telling – that would be (or **that's**); also **that's tellings!** A reply to a question one does not, or should not, answer: since *c.* 1830. The *OED* cites Captain Marryat, 1837: '"Where is this ... and when?" "That's tellings," replied the man.' Often, in Australia, shortened to *tellings!* or *tellin's!*, as in Edward Dyson's *The Gold Reef*, 1901.

The form *that would be telling* seems to be C20 US.

Ten Sixty-Six and All That: 'One still hears this famous title in conversation' (Douglas Leechman, January 1969); and even now in 1976, although decreasingly since the very early 1930s. From W. C. Sellar and R. J. Yeatman, *1066 and All That*, an immensely popular comic 'potted' history of England. As a c.p., it lightly, yet rarely contemptuously, dismisses any event preceding the speaker's birth as unimportant – 'old hat' and all that – 'Queen Anne's dead!'.

ten up! is a stockbrokers' c.p., directed at a broker whose credit is either shaky or, at the least, suspect: since *c.* 1870. (B & L.) From the enforced deposit of 10 per cent obligatory in these conditions.

tend your own potatoes! See **mind ....**

tennis, anyone? and **who's for tennis?** These alternative c.pp. open a conversation or a flirtation: perhaps mostly Canadian: since *c.* 1950. But they come from the much older British usage: in Britain the c.p. goes back to *c.* 1910 and is 'the hall-mark of that so familiar species of English "social comedy" where there are French windows upstage centre' (Ramsey Spencer, March 1967).

The original form of the laconic *tennis, anyone?* was the slightly more formal *who's for tennis?*; and both have served

not only to initiate a conversation but also to comment, either ironically or enviously, upon the pastimes of the leisured (or the comparatively or apparently leisured) classes. It seems, indeed, to have arisen as a good-natured comment upon lawn tennis as an adjunct of tea-parties in the vicarage garden or at country-house weekends.

There has long existed the intermediate form, *anyone for tennis?* Jessica Mann, in her novel, *Mrs Knox's Profession*, 1972, treats us to this illuminating example:

> She had never seen a play where an actor sprang through French windows calling 'Anyone for tennis?' but she suddenly realised that this catchword, a shorthand joke to her for everything that was reactionary and moribund in England, represented something as real as a kitchen sink. In Orton, matinée land was still going strong.

And, with that sense of linguistic opportunism for which he was justly famous, Noël Coward, in the section 'Monday' or 'Me and the Girls' in *Pretty Polly Barlow and Other Stories*, 1964, shows us George Banks, actor, reminiscing thus: 'I had a bang at everything, Young Juveniles – "Anyone for tennis?" – old gentlemen, dope addicts, drunks.'

The c.p. passed to the US in the early or middle 1950s, so far as I have been able to ascertain. In the *New Yorker* of 20 September 1969, there was a wonderful 'picture' of a playhouse, the stage illuminating a small group of men and women in the nude, with one of the men brandishing a racket and addressing the drawing-room *ensemble*, 'Tennis, anyone?'

Tenth don't dance – the. An army officers' gibe at the 10th Hussars. It originated in 1823, when the officers, at a ball in Dublin and after long experience of London and Brighton society, declined to be introduced to the ladies on the unconvincing plea, 'The Tenth don't dance'. (F & G.) The saying probably lasted for twenty or thirty years.

term of endearment among sailors – (it's) a, is a palliative c.p., excusing the 'use of swear-word bugger. Unfair to the Navy, but sailors have had worse than that to bear; soldiers, airmen, and the French laugh it off too: *dirty bugger* is, however, meant to have a sting' (Laurie Atkinson, 11 September 1967). Current since 1890 or so. Jocular.

thank God we have (or **we've got**) **a navy!** A C20 c.p., muttered by the army when things were going very badly wrong; esp. during WW1. F & G remark: 'Said to have originated in a soldier's sarcastic comment when he saw a party of the old Volunteers marching by one Saturday night.' I suspect that it's far, far older. In his *Charles I*, 1933, Evan John suggested that it was originated by Sir John Norris in the days of that monarch. In a letter written on 22 October 1968, the late Colonel Archie White, says, 'I have seen examples of this disparagement of the Army as far back as the S. African War. I shouldn't be surprised if it were of Crimean origin. ... I think I have seen it in letters from the Crimea.'

Of its WW1 use, John Brophy writes, '"Thank Gawd, we've got a navy!" It was always "Gawd", even with north-country troops to indicate the burlesque of the original sentiment. This phrase was called into use whenever the incompetence of authority became more manifest than usual.'

Of its WW2 use, Laurie Atkinson writes (18 July 1975): 'Army and RAF NCOs' outburst of dismay when, e.g., a recruits' squad blunders out of formation in foot-drill; NCOs' exclamation when an "unbelievable" mistake or omission has been made in work or duty.'

thank God we have (or **we've got**) **an army!** An ephemeral and ironical army c.p., used when it heard the first official news of the Battle of Jutland on 31 May 1916. Obviously prompted by – and deliberately reminiscent of – the next.

[**thank heaven for little girls!** – a song sung by Maurice Chevalier in *Gigi* (1958), based on Colette's novel – has remained a popular quotation and has, I believe, failed to achieve the status of c.p.]

thank you and good night! Ramsey Spencer, writing on 4 February 1975, says:

> must surely come from the BBC Radio appeal programme 'The Week's Good Cause' (8.25 p.m. on Sundays) which ran for many years. It ended every appeal (except when rash innovators said: 'Good night and thank you for listening'); and as the majority of listeners' withers remained unwrung, is tantamount to 'Thank you for nothing' among the cynical.

thank you for nothing! I owe you no thanks for *that!*: C20. Frank Shaw, in letter of 25 February 1969, cites the variant *thanks for nothing!*, which he glosses thus: 'Ironic thanks for an unexpected rebuff or rejection or disservice, often preceded by "well"': since *c.* 1910.

thank you for those few kind words! is a semi-ironic c.p., recorded earliest, I believe, in my *Slang Today and Yesterday*, 1933, but going back, within my own memory, to *c.* 1910, at latest. A good example occurs in Alistair Mair's *Where the East Wind Blows*, 1972:

> 'But the thing that wrapped it up was the stuff you gave me, especially the photographs. They were, if I may say so, bloody good.'
> 'Thank you for those few kind words,' I said. 'Nice to know I've been useful.'

This c.p. occurs also in plays. In H. M. Harwood's *The Old Folks at Home*, performed in 1933 and published in 1934, I find, in the opening scene:

> LIZA: ... Professor – don't you think I should make a very nice Viceroy's wife?
> CHARLES: Well, if being ornamental is a qualification...
> LIZA: Of course it is, especially with Orientals.... And thank you for those few kind words.

thank you, ma'am. See **wham bang**....

thank you, teacher, and **please teacher!** belong to C20, and the latter is accompanied with the customary upraised hand. Whereas the latter indicates to his companions that the speaker wishes to interrupt the conversational free-for-all with a remark he supposes to be important or, at the least, timely, the former connotes either irony or derision towards someone condescendingly permitting something or explaining pompously.

thank you very much – the *very* heavily emphasized, and the phrase often preceded by **well** – is, clearly, a c.p. only when it's ironic: C20. Philip Purser, *The Holy Father's Navy*, 1971, has:

> 'My own view was that it was – shall we say a little unambitious for a Colin Panton special?' That was the flashing candour bit.
> 'Well, thank you very much.'

thank your mother for the rabbit was brought to my notice by the late Frank Shaw on 14 February 1969, but without definition, date, *milieu*. I suspect that it belongs to the same class of c.p. as **don't tear it, lady!**, i.e. street vendors' humour; that it is Cockney; and that it arose late in C19.

[**thanks a million!** Not a true c.p.]

thanks for having me, with ironic emphasis on *having*, is the c.p. uttered by a boarder to the landlady of the seaside boarding-house where he has been holidaying: C20. A pun on *having*, boarding, and *having*, befooling, swindling.

thanks for nothing! See **thank you for nothing!**

thanks for saving my life; or alternatively **thanks! you've saved my life.** A jocular c.p., addressed to one who has just 'stood' a drink: since *c.* 1919. An example of mildly ironic exaggeration. The phrase, however, is often used of thanks for almost any minor hospitality or kindness. Cf:

thanks for the buggy-ride! merely elaborates 'Thank you'; it is US in origin (recorded by Berrey, 1942): C20. It passed to Canada; Dr Douglas Leechman glosses it as 'a c.p. expressing thanks for some small service; often ironical'. Cf preceding entry.

that accounts for the milk in the coconut; US variant, **that explains....** That explains the puzzle or elucidates the mystery: US: mid C19–20. The *explains* form is recorded, 1912, by R. H. Thornton for 1853; James Maitland, 1891, 'When an explanation of something is given it is said "That explains the milk in the cocoa-nut" and it is sometimes added "But not the shaggy bark on the outside".'

This US c.p. passed, almost inevitably, to Canada. But it passed also – and very early – to Britain, Hotten recording it in his 4th edn, 1870; so far as I've ascertained, it seems to have been current there *c.* 1860–1910.

that adds up and **that figures.** That makes sense: the former, dating since *c.* 1950, is the British version of the US *that figures*, itself adopted, *c.* 1944, from US Servicemen.

that ain't hay. See **and that ain't hay.**

that ain't no lie. That's the literal – or the real – truth: US: *c.* 1880–1914. In the delectable George Ade's *Artie*, 1896, we read: '"You know you've got me right, don't you? And I guess you have, too. That ain't no lie."'

that allows me plenty of scope. See **that gives me....**

that bangs Banagher. See **bangs Banagher** ....

that beats creation. That's remarkable, even if only in effrontery: mid C19–20; obsolescent by 1930, obsolete by 1945. It had, *c.* 1905–40, some currency in Britain; noted by Weekley. Cf the next two entries. Cf:

that beats the band. Same sense as preceding entry: C20. The prototype of these phrases is, it seems, **that bangs Banagher**, q.v. at **bangs Banagher**. Cf also:

that beats the Dutch. That beats everything! – It's incredible – *or* That's the limit!: late C18–20. The *Dutch* simply because Britons are so ready to recognize the worth of their opponents: and in the latter half of C17, the Dutch navy was extremely hard to beat: *to beat the Dutch*, to do something remarkable, is recorded for 1775.

It was early adopted in US. M. includes it and adds that the superlative is *that beats the Dutch and the Dutch beat the*

Devil; and it had appeared two years earlier, in 1889, in Farmer.

that, Bill, is tack (or occasionally and schoolmarmishly **tact**); often preceded by **and**. This C20 c.p., somewhat outmoded by 1970, reposes on the chestnut of the plumber explaining to his assistant that 'tack is when you find her ladyship in the bath and you get away quickly, saying "Beg pardon, my lord!"' Variant: *and that is what they call tact*.

that cuts no ice. That makes no difference or has no importance or doesn't impress or influence me: US: late C19–20; anglicized just before WW1. A Canadian variant,? since *c.* 1910, is *that cuts no custard*. The American usage appears in, e.g., the witty S. R. Strait's 'Straight Talk' in the *Boston Globe c.* 1917, as W. J. Burke tells me.

that dame would make me a present of a parachute if she knew it wouldn't open. She hates me: US: 1920s. In Maurice Lincoln's *Oh! Definitely*, 1933, occurs (p. 216) this passage:
> '... Sally happens to be fond of you.'
> 'Fond of me, indeed,' said Peter scathingly, 'Why, as they used to say in the States, that dame would make me a present of a parachute if she knew it wouldn't open.'

that devil nobody is applied to the culprit when, in an accident or an error, no one will admit culpability: C20. (Probably I'm wrong to suppose that the originator of the c.p. was familiar with the C18 phrase *that devil Wilkes*.)

that explains the milk in the coconut. See **that accounts for ....**

that figures. See **that adds up**.

that for a tale! See **tell that for a tale!**

that gets me! is recorded in HLM, 1922, as a 'picturesque' phrase. Meaning: 'That annoys me': recorded by the *DAE* for 1867; current in Britain *c.* 1919–39.

that gives (occasionally **allows**) **me plenty of scope** is the counter to **don't do anything I wouldn't**.

that goes for me too. I agree entirely with what you say: since *c.* 1930. (Wilfred Granville, 11 January 1969.) Cf **them's my sentiments**.

that horse is troubled with corns, i.e., foundered: sporting world: C19–20; by 1930, obsolescent and by 1950, obsolete.

that is me all over. Just like me – to behave in such a way! A US c.p. of *c.* 1920–50. (Berrey.)

that is (or **that's**) **the object of the exercise.** That's precisely why we're doing it! That's the general or, come to that, the specific idea behind it all: originally army officers' in the 1930s and during WW1, but by the mid 1940s it had spread to civilians.

that job's jobbed. It's finished; it's all over: *c.* 1830–1960. The *OED* cites Marryat, 1840, 'That job's jobbed, as the saying is'. Laurie Atkinson recalls it as having been used by his mother, born in the 1860s, and glosses it thus: 'Used when the job had called for more than usual enterprise and determination, and it was good to know that it was behind one, for whatever reason; or when it was a little personal triumph' (16 July 1971).

that (or **it**) **just goes to show**, a C20 cliché has a jocular, deliberate, mostly Australian c.p. variant, **that just shows to go**, dating since *c.* 1930. (Barry Prentice.)

that kills it! That destroys my enthusiasm, interest, respect; that ruins it: US: since *c.* 1945. (W & F, 1960, 'Now fairly common.')

that Kruschen feeling. An allusion to vigour and energy and verve: *c.* 1925–40. (Collinson.) From a famous advertisement put out by Kruschen Salts.

that makes the cheese more binding. That improves matters. That's just what we need! A Canadian c.p. of *c.* 1945–55.

that makes two of us is addressed to someone who says that he doesn't understand what he has just heard or read: since *c.* 1940, or rather earlier.

that man wants burning! is a C20 British, esp. English, tramps' c.p. directed at anyone who has the audacity to disagree with one's own opinion.

that moan's soon made. That's a grief will soon be consoled: Scottish: since before 1885. (Ware.)

that must have been a butcher's horse by his carrying a calf so well was, mid C17–mid C19, a c.p. jest made at the expense of an awkward rider. (Ray, 1678; Grose, 1788.) There's a double pun: *calf*, a dull, oafish young fellow, and the calves of the legs.

that remains to be seen – as the monkey said when he shat in the sugar-bowl. Canadian: since *c.* 1930. A deliberately humorous elaboration of a cliché, a truism, that so irritated some wit that he vented his exasperation in scatology.

that rings a bell. That sounds familiar, *or* That vaguely reminds me of something relevant: since the middle, or maybe the early, 1920s. Perhaps from the ringing of a telephone bell or, less probably, the striking of a clock. (Not to be confused with the originally US *ring the bell*, to succeed – from one or other of several fairground devices.)

that schoolgirl complexion belongs to the approximate period 1923–39. From the inspired advertising poster of Palmolive Soap, as Collinson testified in 1927; the alert P. G. Wodehouse had mentioned the slogan in *Ukridge*, 1924; that slogan so captured the public fancy that it rapidly became also a c.p., among women and men alike.

that shook him; intensively, **that shook him rigid** or, less frequently, **that shook him, rotten**. That astounded or greatly startled or perplexed or perturbed or baffled him: originally WW2 Services', esp. the RAF; and then, by 1945, general. (H & P.) Literally caused him to shake with nerves.

that shouldn't happen to a dog. Terence Rattigan's *Variation on a Theme* performed and published in 1958, at Act I, Scene ii, has:
> FIONA: The last doctor's put her on a very strict régime. He even says she might have to ... go to Switzerland....
> MONA: Switzerland? That shouldn't happen to a dog.

This heart-felt, compassionate c.p. dates, I believe, from the early 1950s.

that takes me off! is a theatrical c.p., expressing either defeat (as in an argument) or sheer incredulity. '"*That took me off* (the stage), I couldn't argue any longer." A reference to an exit line' (Granville). British: C20.

that takes the cake! Literally 'That wins the prize', it came to mean 'Well, if that doesn't beat all!' – for, e.g., impudence, or wholly unexpected luck, good or bad, and simultaneously became a general US c.p. Of negro origin, it arose thus: 'At a cake-walk, a cake was given as a surprise to the one who could "shout his stuff" the best' (Holt); this cake-walk was not, of course, the dance but the contest popular at rural outdoor festivities. In 1891, M glosses the c.p. thus: 'Said of a tall fish story or of anything superlative'. From the negative evidence of its c.p. absence from *Am*, 1877, and from Farmer in 1889, I – perhaps rashly – deduce that it did not become an established c.p. until the late 1880s. On the other hand, it then passed very rapidly indeed to Britain, as early as 1895, that lively short-story writer, W. Pett Ridge, used in his *Minor Dialogues*, the derivative, allusive form *that takes it*.

that tore it! See **that's torn it!**

that was not very tasteful (i.e., that was in bad taste). On 21 April 1972, the *Australian Financial Review* reproduced a recent article published in the *Wall Street Journal* and quoted Lily Tomlin's 'running gag', 'That was not very tasteful', on the Rowan and Martin 'Laugh-In' show. This 'gag' can, I think, be said to qualify as a US cultured c.p. of 1972 *plus*. (With thanks to Mr Barry Prentice.)

that was real money – with **that was** occasionally added – is applied to the old £.s.d. coinage: 1973 onwards. (A. B. Petch, 4 January 1974.) But, as Norman Franklin reminds me, it applies, since *c.* 1975, to money before, say, 1970.

that went better in Wigan! A C20 British theatrical c.p. 'A music-hall comedian's *sotto voce* remark when a gag fails to get over. Wigan is a music-hall joke that has become a national one in England, though why this Lancashire town should be so treated is not known' (Wilfred Granville, 1952). Wigan, truly Lancastrian, is in fact rather charming.

that will (or **that'll**) **be the day**, with emphasis on *that*, and with a decidedly ironic inflection; also the humorous variant, **that'll be the bloody day, boy!** That's not very likely to happen: since late 1917, or early 1918. After a longish interval, it passed, during the 1930s, to New Zealand – witness *NZS* ('Expressing mild doubt following some boast or claim') – and, at the same period, to Australia, as in Eleanor Dark, *Lantana Lane*, 1959; Mr Arthur Gray of New Zealand has expressed himself rather more emphatically than Mr Baker, thus: 'A fervent denial of a suggestion, or an expression of complete incredulity. E.g., "You could be elected captain of the team yourself." – "That will be the day."' And Mrs Hazel Franklin has reminded me that New Zealand usage offers the variant, *that'll be the frosty Friday!* – which, if I remember correctly, dates from either 1915 or 1916. Deriving, I'd say, from army officers' 1915–18 *der Tag*, 'any much desired date or goal'; obviously satirical of Ger. *der Tag*, the day, historically 'the day when we Germans come into our own' – esp. 'the day we conquer Britain' (in WW1): cf the lively derision with which the ordinary soldier greeted Lissauer's *Song of Hate*, 'perpetrated (Aug. 1914) by one Lissauer' – as Weekley neatly and tartly put it.

Mr Dudley R. D. Ewes, formerly editor of the *Cape Times* tells me (17 December 1968) that, in South Africa, this c.p. has become so much a part of everyday speech that it's current also in Afrikaans as *dit sal die dag wees*. A South African example of the c.p. occurs in James McClure, *The Gooseberry Fool*, 1974.

The phrase is still very much alive: it occurred also in, e.g., Noël Coward's *Relative Values*, produced in 1951 and published in 1952, and in Terence Rattigan's *Variations on a Theme*, 1958.

In Britain, the c.p. has become so incorporated into the language that it can be employed allusively, as in Anthony Price, *The Alamut Ambush*, 1971: 'Roskill grinned at the incongruous idea of anyone outsmarting an alerted Shapiro. That, as old David was so fond of saying, would be the day!'

For a 'straight' example, cf this from C. P. Snow, *The Malcontents*, 1972:

'I thought you were going to cut the grass?' his wife said.

'I will,' he said, 'just let my lunch settle down.... You don't want to give me indigestion, do you?'

'Indigestion,' she said, 'that'll be the day.'

Moreover, it seems to have reached the US during the 1930s and to have been thoroughly acclimatized by the early 1940s. In Tucker Coe's 'thriller', *Wax Apple*, copyrighted in 1970, we read:

Bob said, 'Maybe the person who did it will confess. He didn't really want to kill anybody, he just wanted to hurt people. Maybe this will shake him up, and he'll confess.'

'That'll be the day,' Karter said.

It occurs with complete naturalness and no sense of adoption in the American Charles Williams's novel, *Man on a Leash*, 1973.

that will stop him laughing in church. That will take the smile off his face – That'll fix him: since *c.* 1930. Cf the (?mainly Public School) boys' version: *that will teach him to fart in chapel* or *that'll stop their farting in chapel*, 'That'll stop them from taking liberties.' All three: C20. The first is, I suspect, a euphemistic variant of the other two. (A combination of two contributions.)

that won't buy (the) baby a frock. See **this won't buy....**

that won't pay the old woman her ninepence, Ware (1909) tells us, was a Bow Street Police Court, London, c.p. condemning an evasive action: *c.* 1890–1914.

that won't wash! probably dates from *c.* 1840, to judge by Charlotte Brontë's 'That willn't wash, miss' (1849), quoted by the *OED*. The semantic clue: 'As good fabrics and fast dyes stand the operation of washing' (F & H).

Vernon Noble, writing on 14 January 1975, says:

Originally indicated unreliability (as of a statement) but by latter part of C19 had taken on the meaning of something not up to standard, not durable, unconvincing. In a letter by Charles Kingsley, referring to Browning, he wrote deprecatingly, 'He won't wash'.

The predominant C20 senses are 'It won't work' and 'It won't stand up to examination.'

The phrase duly passed to the US. Berrey, 1942, records it.

that would be telling! See **tellings...!**

that'll be the day! See **that will be...!**

that'll be the frosty Friday. See **that will be the day.**

that'll be the shot. See **shot – that'll be the.**

that'll grow (or **put**) **hair** (or **more hair**) **on your chest**; and **that'll put lead in your pencil.** That will render you potent *or* that will restore your virility: late C19–20. Both are applied to either food or liquor, the latter mostly to liquor; both are applicable at any time, but the latter esp. after illness or a sustained bout of lovemaking, even to a mere semblance of sexual fatigue; the former is used mostly by men, the latter by both sexes, among women not necessarily confined to what used to be called the lower and lower-middle classes.

The first is mainly Australian (Baker) and, as an invitation, or an encouragement to drink, it takes a shorter form, *more hair on your chest!* The second has been adopted in the US.

that'll larn (or **learn**) **you!** The former is US, the latter British: 'That'll teach you!': late C19–20. Although in form solecistic or entirely illiterate, neither indicates illiteracy in the users, the phrase having always been jocular, with occasionally a genuinely monitory undertone. Since *c.* 1919, *larn* has, even in Britain, predominated over *learn*.

A late example occurs in Len Deighton, *Yesterday's Spy*, 1975:

For a moment Ercole was taken aback. Then he roared, 'I hate you, I hate you,' and kissed Schlegel on the cheek. 'That'll learn you, Colonel,' I said softly.

that'll pin your ears back! That'll be a real set-back for you!: since *c.* 1940: mostly in the Armed Forces. (Laurie Atkinson.)

that'll push (or **that's pushed**) **Rommel back another ten miles** was an army c.p. of 1941–42. Gerald Kersh, in *Slightly Oiled*, 1946, says: 'When in North Africa there was some extra bit of red tape or regimental procedure, we always used to say: "And that's pushed Rommel back another ten miles." Everybody said ... "That'll push Rommel back another ten miles".'

that'll put (**more**) **hair on your chest**, or ... **lead in your pencil.** See **that'll grow hair** ....

that'll put your back up! That'll make you amorous: since *c.* 1920. From cats fighting; cf informal Standard English *fighting-fit*.

that's a bad cough you have! See **you've a bad cough.**

that's a bit hot! That's unreasonable or unjust: an Australian and New Zealand c.p.: since *c.* 1910.

that's a bit of all right. See **this is a bit** ....

that's a bit under is an office girls' and shop girls' c.p., prompted by a *risqué* joke or remark: since *c.* 1950; by 1970, obsolescent. 'Not infrequently the "under" is dropped in favour of a dipping action with the elbow' (Michael Gilderdale, 'A Glossary for Our Times' in the *News Chronicle*, 22 May 1958).

that's a cough lozenge for him! He's been punished or 'paid out' or beaten: proletarian: *c.* 1850–90. From an advertisement for cough lozenges. (Ware.)

that's a different story, and **that's something else again**, originally US (Berrey 1942, 'That's a different matter') and dating, the former since *c.* 1900, and the latter since *c.* 1930, became also British, the former *c.* 1918 and the latter not until *c.* 1944.

that's a good one. See **that's a good 'un.**

that's a good one (or **that's one**) **on me!** 'That's a joke on me' (Berrey, 1942): since *c.* 1920.

that's a good question, often altered to **a very good question** or shortened to **a good question!** or simply **good question!** That's a sensible or shrewd or very pertinent question; often as a time-gainer when one's seeking for an answer to an extremely difficult question; indeed, it often implies 'That's a question *I* can't solve'; since the middle or late 1940s, but not very common before *c.* 1955. From radio and TV 'panels'

and 'quizzes'. See also **good question** and cf **that's the sixty-four thousand dollar question.**

that's a good 'un (or **one**). What a fib! Occasionally, 'That's an *excellent* story!': late C19–20. But the original sense was 'That's very witty' or 'That's an excellent joke': since *c.* 1660. It occurs in, e.g., William Wycherley's *The Country Wife*, performed in 1672 and published in 1675, at Act III, Scene ii, thus:

ALITHEA: I hate him because he is your enemy; and you ought to hate him too, for making love to [in the old sense of 'paying court to'] me, if you love me.
SPARKISH: That's a good one! I hate a man for loving you! If he did love you, 'tis but what he can't help; and 'tis your fault, not his, if he admires you.

It occurs again in Joseph Addison's comedy, *The Drummer: or, The Haunted House*, 1716, at Act I, Scene i:

ABI[GAIL]: ... You first frightened yourselves, and then the neighbours.
GARD[NER]: Frightened! I scorn your words. Frightened, quotha!
ABI: What, you sot, are you grown pot-valiant!
GARD: Frightened with a drum! That's a good one!

And a final example: Joseph Ebsworth, in *The Rival Valets: A Farce*, performed in 1825, has, at Act I, Scene i, this dialogue, where the 'smart Alec' valet, Frank, says to the well-meaning, rather clumsy, very unlucky valet, Anthony: 'Besides, my figure and appearance are so superior to yours!' – to which Anthony indignantly replies: 'Come, damn it, that's a good one. You don't mean to say that you are more sightly than I am?'

that's a hell of a note! That's extremely and disagreeably surprising – extremely rude or impudent or insolent or insulting; 'What a plight or predicament!'; or, indeed, 'This is a very grave – even a disastrous – situation': US: since *c.* 1930. (Recorded by Berrey, 1942, and by W & F, 1960.) A (musical) note badly out of tune.

It spread, *c.* 1950, to Canada, where the predominant sense has been 'a grave situation' (Douglas Leechman), and, *c.* 1960, to Britain, where, however, it has not firmly established itself – up to 1975, at least.

that's a horse of another colour. See **horse of another colour.**

that's a laugh! That's ridiculous: since the 1920s. (Berrey.)

that's a load of old cobblers. That's utter nonsense: since the late 1950s. Often used by those who don't know that *cobblers* is rhyming slang, short for *cobbler's awls*, testicles.

that's a long-tailed bear. See **long-tailed bear.**

that's a promise! See **is that a promise?**

that's a rhyme if you take it in time; also **he's** (or **you're**) **a poet but doesn't** (or **don't**) **know it.** (A form that fits all persons and numbers is **a poet but don't** (or **doesn't**) **know it.**) The former is directed at one who rhymes accidentally and the reply is *yes, I'm a poet and didn't* ... ; the latter, in the *you're* ... form, elicits *yes, that's a rhyme* ...: mostly a lower-middle-class c.p.: since *c.* 1700. Cf **he's a poet**, directed – from *c.* 1850 until *c.* 1965 – at a long-haired male: and with this, cf *who robbed the barber?*, similarly directed, but dating since *c.* 1880 and not yet entirely obsolete.

In the Dialogue I of S, 1738, we find:

NEV[EROUT]: Well, Miss, I'll think of this.

MISS: That's Rhyme, if you take it in Time.

NEV: What! I see you are a poet.

MISS: Yes, if I had but Wit to shew it.

The *a poet but don't* (or *doesn't*) *know it* version has long been also US. In, e.g., Ring Lardner's *The Real Dope*, 1919, occurs this passage (sent to me by a correspondent on 13 February 1975): 'Well, Al, I wish you could of seen how surprised she was when she read [the verses] and she says "So you are a poet". So I said "Yes I am a poet and don't know it" so that made her laugh.' Note also Ellery Queen's *The Last Woman in His Life*, 1970: '"She can't hope to cope! I'm a poet and don't know it!"'

that's a sure card. That's a safe device or a shrewd expedient or one likely to succeed; and often applied to the person thinking of, or using, it: C16–20. (The anonymous *Thersites, an Interlude, c.* 1537; BE.) Manifestly from card-playing.

that's a very good idea, turn it round the other way. 'Workshop engineer's dirge on realization that the job can be better handled from the opposite angle: to the tune of a well-known ditty: "In the middle of the night/ When the bugs begin to bite,/ Scratch 'em out with all your might…"' (Laurie Atkinson, late 1974): since *c.* 1930, if not a generation earlier.

that's a very good question. See **very good question – a.**

[**that's about it**; and **that's about right**, with emphasis in each case on *about*. That's exactly right: Australian: since *c.* 1920. Clichés rather than c.pp.]

that's about (or **just about) par for the course.** That's pretty normal *or* That's what, after all, you can expect *or* might have expected: since *c.* 1920. From golf.

The predominant US form is (*that's*) *par for the course.* (John W. Clark, 24 July 1975.) The c.p., when applied to an individual, suggests that the standard – the criterion – is rather low.

[**that's about right.** See **that's about it.**]

[**that's about the size of it**, US (Berrey, 1942, 'That describes the state of affairs fairly well') – since *c.* 1910; hence British, since *c.* 1915. But – cf **that's about it** – cliché rather than c.p.]

that's all gay was, *c.* 1895–1915, a Cockney c.p., indicating a peaceable agreement. Used by, e.g., Edwin Pugh. But earlier, C19 underworld for 'The coast is clear'.

that's all I have (or **I've got) between me and the workhouse.** 'An old whine heard used by spongers and ear-biters' (persistent borrowers): late C19–20. (Albert B. Petch, 10 January 1975.)

that's all I need! Ironic for 'That's the last thing I needed or wanted'; 'That's the last straw!': since *c.* 1958; perhaps a lustrum or even a decade earlier.

that's all I wanted to know! The speaker bitterly confirms, and angrily resents, a thoroughly disagreeable fact or an exacerbating set of circumstances: since the middle 1930s. (Laurie Atkinson.) Cf the preceding entry.

that's all she wrote; and **that's what she wrote.** W & F, 1960, gloss this US c.p. thus: 'That's all there is … it's finished' and date it 'during and since WWII' and explain it as referring to a soldier's last letter from his sweetheart, telling him it's all over – what, in short, is known as a *dear John.* Cf:

that's all there is – there isn't (loosely **ain't) any more.** That's all: US: since *c.* 1900. (Berrey, 1942.) 'Said by Ethel Barrymore at the beginning, or near the beginning, of her theatrical career, in response to repeated curtain calls' (John W. Clark, 5 December 1968.) But, on 27 March 1975, Professor Clark tells me that Bartlett records *there's nothing more←that's all there is* as the correct form and as being a 'curtain line' contrived by Ethel Barrymore for the last act of Thomas Raceward's *Sunday* in 1906; he adds that he thinks the play was revived nearly thirty years later and that the c.p. arose then. With her first starring role, *c.* 1900, Ethel Barrymore (1879–1959) – who made her debut in 1894 – achieved fame in *Captain Jinks of the Horse Marines*; during the next five years, she appeared alongside Sir Henry Irving on one of his US tours – in 1905, in Ibsen's *The Doll's House* – and in 1906 in a Barrie play.

The variant *that's all there is – there is no more* was, on 20 August 1973, satirized in a caption that runs, 'This is your anchorman, John Moore, saying "That's all there is. There is no more." Until to-morrow at the same time, when there will be more.'

'Less common than formerly, but by no means extinct' (John W. Clark, 17 February 1975).

that's all very fine and large. See **it's all very large and fine.**

that's all we need! A natural variant of **that's all I need!**

that's as well done (or **said) as if I had done** (or **said) it myself** occurs in S, 1738. In Dialogue II Lady Smart speaks ill, and wittily, of oysters and Neverout remarks, 'Faith, that's as well said, as if I had said it myself.' They belong to C18–19. The C20 equivalent is 'I couldn't have done, or said, it better myself' – which, obviously, is not a c.p.

that's asking! You're asking when you shouldn't – *or* when I shouldn't answer: late C19–20. Cf **that's tellings** at **telling – that would be.**

that's before you bought your shovel. See **before you bought ….**

that's better out than in! An 'excuse for breaking wind in peer group; natural benefit justification of breach of social restraints' (Laurie Atkinson, 18 July 1975): C20, although perhaps not earlier than *c.* 1920.

[**that's chummy** (or **ducky**, or **just dandy**, or **(just) lovely**). That's the last straw! All are Australian, dating since *c.* 1946, except the third, dating since 1944 and adopted from US Servicemen. The second and fourth are common in England. (Barry Prentice.) But it's rather doubtful whether these ironic locutions can justifiably be classified as c.pp.]

that's decent of you is a c.p. only when it is spoken ironically: since *c.* 1910.

'D'you know, I believe you're almost honest.'

'That's decent of you.'

Variant: *that's damn'* (or *damned*) *decent of you!*

that's enough to make a cat laugh. See **enough to make ….**

that's fighting talk is a jocular retort upon a pretended affront: C20. (Laurie Atkinson.)

that's flat. See **and that's flat.**

that's for sure! Certainly; Surely: US, since *c.* 1925; adopted, during WW2, in Canada, Britain, Australia, New Zealand, and thoroughly naturalized by 1955 at latest.

that's for (or **strictly for**) **the birds**. Tell that to the Marines; but also – in Britain, at least – 'That's of no consequence'; in both countries, 'That's entirely unacceptable or utterly unwanted'; in US only, 'That's corny'. Adopted, *c*. 1955, from US, where current since the late 1940s. W & F, 1960, quotes, 'I won't buy it. Or any part of it. It's for the birds' (J. Crosby, in the *New York Herald Tribune* of 8 February 1952).

Canada often uses the variant *it's for the birds*. (Douglas Leechman, January 1969.)

From bread crumbs thrown to the birds in parks and other public places; insubstantial as opposed to good, solid food.

that's going some! indicates either approval or admiration – or 'That's going *too* far': US: C20. Recorded by S. R. Strait in 'Straight Talk', the *Boston Globe*, *c*. 1917, and by Berrey, 1942. Adopted in Britain and the Commonwealth by 1910 at latest.

that's gone – **as the girl said to the soldier in the park** was, in raffish circles, current *c*. 1890–1914. (Arthur Binstead.) Well, after all, there has to be a first time.

that's him with the hat on! This humorous c.p. indicates the whereabouts of a man standing near pigs, monkeys, scarecrows and other disparate creatures: originally farmers', then rapidly become general. An agreeable example of rustic wit.

that's how I got it. See **no harm in trying**.

that's how (or, more usually, **that's the way**) **the cookie crumbles**. 'There is a rather frequent expression here [in New York]: "That's the way the cookie crumbles" – meaning "That's how (this situation) has turned out" and there's nothing you can do about it' (Dr Joseph T. Shipley, 17 February 1974); but, only a week later, Dr Edward Hodnett declared it to be old-fashioned. It has been a frequent c.p. in the US since the 1950s and in Britain since the middle 1960s, the late Frank Shaw telling me on 1 September 1969: 'Recent'. British usage permits the very occasional *that's the way the cookie drops* or *falls* (Vernon Noble, 26 August 1974). It gained a wide currency also in Canada; on 19 August 1975, Professor Emeritus F. E. L. Priestley spoke of 'the now happily obsolete "that's the way the cookie crumbles"' and referred to 'the lovely take-off line in the movie *The Apartment* [1960] when Jack Lemmon says, "That's the way it crumbles cookie-wise"' – when he is also deriding 'the horrible "-wise" jargon of about ten years ago' (F.E.L.P.).

In *The Zoo Story*, produced in Berlin 1959, in New York 1960, and published in 1960, Edward Albee employs the more usual form thus:

JERRY: And you have children?
PETER: Yes; two.
JERRY: Boys?
PETER: No, girls .... both girls.
JERRY: But you wanted boys.
PETER: Well ... naturally, every man wants a son, but ...
JERRY: But that's the way the cookie crumbles?
PETER: (*Annoyed.*) I wasn't going to say that.

And Morris Farhi's *The Pleasure of Your Death*, 1972, has:

'I have no pals.'
'You poor bastard. Life's treated you pretty bad, huh?'
'That's how the cookie crumbles.'
'Ever ask yourself why?'
'No.'
'Time you did. Who'd trust you with a snake?'

'My mother.'

Cf **that's the way the ball bounces**.

that's just about par for the course. See **that's about par** ....

that's just about your size! is included by Berrey, 1942, in a long list of 'disparaging and sarcastic flings' and it means 'One would *expect* that of you': since *c*. 1930. Contrast **that's my size**.

that's just my handwriting; with waggish variant, **that's just my bloody** *écriture*. This c.p., dating since WW2 (apparently since *c*. 1950), 'accepts [a] manipulated disadvantage in arrangement and envisages resource that will turn discomfort against perpetrator' (Laurie Atkinson, 18 July 1975).

that's just too bad! This c.p., 'implying that an appeal to consideration or restraint has failed' (Laurie Atkinson), was adopted, *c*. 1937, from US, where it arose during the 1920s and was recorded by Berrey in 1942.

that's more like it! That's better – more acceptable or reasonable: C20. Both British (*DSUE*, 1937) and US (Berrey, 1942).

that's my boy! An occasional variant of **attaboy!** It occurs, e.g., in Act I of John Osborne's *Look Back in Anger*, produced in 1956.

that's my size! That suits me; I am agreeable; 'that's the ticket' (Farmer): *c*. 1880–1914.

that's my story and I'm stuck with it; or, in US, also ... **I'll stick to it**. Both forms are glossed by Berrey, 1942, as 'I mean it; I'm in earnest', but sometimes as indicating a stubborn unwillingness to retract. It came to Britain in the middle 1930s; and during WW2 the Royal Engineers had a variant: *that's my story and I'm stuck all round it*, that's my explanation and I'm standing by it.

In *Relative Values*, produced in 1951 and published in 1952, Noël Coward writes (at Act I, Scene i):

PETER: Is it?
FELICITY: Yes, Peter, it is and you needn't look quizzical either. That's my story and I'm sticking to it.

Australia has had its own version, dating since the mid 1940s and probably occasioned by US Servicemen there stationed during the latter half of WW2: *that's my story and I'm sticking to it*, is glossed (1 May 1975) by Barry Prentice thus: 'You can believe it or not'.

'Quite often heard turned the other way, i.e. "That's your story and you're stuck with it". In fact, this is perhaps the more common construction nowadays' (Paul Beale, 30 September 1975).

that's no lady – **that's my wife**, with occasional variant, **that wasn't a lady** – **that was my wife**. Probably it began as a music-hall joke (perhaps in a song) in the 1880s or 1890s. In Scene i, in the first dialogue (immediately after Refrain 1) of Noël Coward's *Red Peppers*, published in 1936 and written *c*. 1935, we read:

LILY: Who was that lady I saw you walking down the street with the other morning?
GEORGE: That wasn't a lady, that was my wife.

Later, Lily includes it in a list of 'hoary old chestnuts'.

[**that's not hay** and **that's not peanuts**. See **that ain't hay**.]

that's old Mother Hubbard. That's incredible: a non-aristocratic, non-cultured c.p. of *c*. 1880–1910. From the nursery rhyme. (Ware.)

that's one for the book. See one for the book.

that's one for you! That settles *you!* *or* Put that in your pipe and smoke it!: C20.

that's one on me! See that's a good one on me!

that's pushed Rommel back.... See that'll push....

that's put the lid (or tin lid) on it. Nothing more to be said, *or* That's done (or, finished) it: late C19–20, but obsolescent by 1945. A mainly Merseyside variant. C20, is *that's put the top-hat on it*. (Frank Shaw.)

that's show-biz for you! That's how it goes: originally applied to public entertainment, and US: C20. By the late 1930s, also British, and with a wider application, as in Laurence Meynell, *Death of a Philanderer*, 1968: '"Blue Plates" [an imaginary TV programme] finished, Pat[ricia] gone and my second novel the worst flop of all time. Which, as they say, is show-biz.'

[that's so! – a phrase of acquiescence – is not a c.p. but a cliché.]

that's something else – or, more emphatic, with again added. That's a (very) different matter: US: since the early 1930s; adopted in Britain during WW2. (Berrey.)

that's something like it! That's as it should be, *or* That's *far* more pleasant, *or* That's come closer to what I had expected: US: since the 1920s; adopted in Britain during the 1930s. (Berrey.)

that's strictly bush (or what a busher he is!) is applied to someone whose behaviour is unmannerly: perhaps since soon after 1905, for in that year *big time* and *small time* arose as complementary terms applied to show business, that being the date when *Variety* (the periodical) first appeared – and when *Variety* fathered those complementaries. My friend Mr W. J. Burke writes (13 May 1975):

> We also use 'Big League' to denote success, the term coming from Big League Baseball (The National League and The American League). Ball players who did not 'make' the Big League were said to be playing in the 'Bush League', and from that came the word 'busher', used to describe any person who had not made the grade, so to speak.... Bush is associated with backwoods, or rural fringes. Your Australian Bush may suggest parallels.

And it does, for cf it will be Sydney or the bush. He refers to Joe Laurie, Jr, *Vaudeville: From the Honky Tonk to the Palace*, 1953.

I'd say that whereas *that's strictly bush* is a c.p., *what a busher he is!* is not one.

that's strictly for the birds. See that's for the birds.

that's telling (or tellings). See telling – that would be.

that's telling 'em! – which in Britain would have been *that's tellin 'em where they get off!* US: since the 1920s. (Berrey.)

that's that. See and that's that.

that's the article is a variant of that's the ticket. That's the very thing we need: mid C19–20; obsolescent by 1940 and virtually obsolete by 1950. An article – or commodity – of commerce. Also, by *c.* 1900, US. (Berrey.)

that's the barber was, *c.* 1760–1830, an approbatory street saying. (George Parker, *A View of Society*, 1781; Grose, 1785.)

[that's the beauty of it: mid C18–20. Samuel Richardson, *Sir Charles Grandison*, 1753–4, has 'That's the beauty of it; to offend and make up at leisure'. The most agreeable or valuable or pleasurable part or aspect of anything. Also US: C20. (Berrey.) A 'borderliner' between cliché and c.p.]

[that's the bee's knees. See bee's knees.]

that's the cheese. That's the best, *or* the fashionable thing: since *c.* 1815, but general only since the 1830s or very early 1840s. Anon. (*The London Guide*, 1818; R. H. Barham, *The Ingoldsby Legends*, 1840; Charles Reade, *Hard Cash*, 1863); obsolete by *c.* 1920. Perhaps from the Urdu *chiz*, a thing (see esp. YB).

Adopted in US *c.* 1870. In Farmer it is glossed as signifying 'excellent performance' or 'quite the thing'. Obsolete by 1914.

that's the end! See that's the living end!

that's the end of the bobbin! That's the end of it – that's finished: mid C19–early C20. Mostly lower-middle class. B & L comment thus: 'When all the thread is wound off a bobbin or spool.... It rose from the refrain of a song which was popular in 1850.'

that's the give to stuff 'em. See that's the stuff to give the troops!

that's the living end! 'The utmost, in any situation. Recent' (Douglas Leechman, January 1969): Canadian. An extension of the never very general English that's the end, itself *c.* 1915–40.

that's the name of the game. Literally, that's what they call it; figuratively, that's what it's all about: since *c.* 1965. 'We [industrial psychologists] guarantee the objectivity. Personally. That's what makes us worth a lot of money to any modern and properly objective management. Ergonomics, baby. *That's the name of the game*' (Desmond Cory, *The Circe Complex*, 1975). Cf name of the game – the.

that's the object of the exercise. See that is the object....

that's the old Navy spirit. Colonel Albert Moe, in a letter dated 15 June 1975, writes:

> At one time, there was a great deal of animosity between Marines and sailors. A sailor could always count on the phrase 'Why is a Marine?' to get a rise out of a Marine. Or he might merely say 'Twenty-eighty' to get the same result. (This was during the time when a Marine private's pay was $21.00 per month, which was reduced to $20.80 after the 20-cent deduction for the 'hospital' fund.) This jibe is meaningless today under the present pay scale. There were many retorts by Marines, but one seems to have persisted and to have lingered on, i.e. 'That's the old navy spirit'. Just why [these phrases were so effectual] is something I have never understood. I only know that it worked. It was understood that 'the navy spirit' connoted 'I've got mine. How are *you* making out?'

I suggest that the sting in *why is a Marine?* lies in its literal meaning, i.e. 'Why does a Marine exist?' (at all).

that's the shot. See shot – that'll be the.

that's the sixty-four thousand dollar question! I find the question very difficult to answer: US, since the early 1950s and, by adoption, British since the late 1960s. From the US 'quiz game' – with a very much smaller top prize in Britain and the Commonwealth. (Frank Shaw, November 1968.)

But this is itself a development from and an elaboration

of the purely US *that's the sixty-four dollar question*, which, as a c.p., dates from *c.* 1942. Webster's *International Dictionary*, 1961, tells me that *the sixty-four dollar question wa* 'so called from the fact that $64 was the highest award in the CBS radio quiz show, "Take It or Leave It"' (1941–8). The meaning of both of these c.pp. is 'That is the crucial question – the most difficult one – a real puzzler.' It is still heard (27 January 1975) occasionally in Britain, whereas in US it was already, in 1969, passing into history, as Professor Emeritus S. H. Monk told me on 10 January of that year.

that's the snaffler! Well done! *or* Excellent!: naval, in the main: *c.* 1820–70. (Wm N. Glascock, *Sketch-Book*, 2nd Series, 1834.)

that's the sort of clothes-pin I am. That's my nature! That's *me!*: among men only: *c.* 1865–1914. One of the small group of domestic c.pp.

that's the stuff to give the troops! In B & P, 1930, John Brophy definitively wrote:

> *That's the stuff to give the troops* was heard whenever rations or billets, rum or any other creature comfort turned out better or more plentiful than might have been expected. It was varied into *That's the stuff to give 'em!* and *that's the give to stuff 'em!* and in this form would often be shouted approvingly to artillery in action.

It often became *that's the stuff!* – which, oddly enough, was current in the US as early as 1896 (*OED* Supplement).

Arising in 1915, the original form remained current among ex-Servicemen; the facetious form died with the war. In Britain, the c.p. probably (as Mr Laurie Atkinson has reminded me) originated in the old music-hall song (*c.* 1910–14):

That's the stuff for your Darby Kell!
Makes you fat and keeps you well,
Boiled beef and carrots!

that's the ticket! probably goes back to *c.* 1820; it occurs in, e.g., W. N. Glascock, *Sketch-Book*, 2nd Series, 1834, 'That's *you*, Ned – you has it – that's the ticket, bo.' It soon migrated to US, 'Sam Slick the Watchmaker' Haliburton using it in 1838 (*OED*); and it is recorded in *DCCU*.

In *Please Help Emily: A Flirtation in Three Acts*, performed in 1916 and published ten years later, H. M. Harwood writes, near end of Act I:

EMILY: We might send to Jessie to pack them. Couldn't you say I'd asked you to have them sent on?
TROTTER: That's the ticket. We'll do that. [The best idea or plan.]

The semantics are in dispute: either ticket is a corruption of Fr. *etiquette*, as Ware maintains, or it is a winning ticket in a lottery, or it's simply a ticket advertising the price of merchandise.

By 1940, slightly obsolescent: by 1976, somewhat obsolescent. For the US, W & F gloss it thus: 'In the phrase "That's the ticket", *ticket* = That's what I meant or wanted'; they offer no dating. Contrast:

that's the ticket for soup. You've got what you came for – so now be off!: from the late 1850s until a few years before WW1. Hotten, 1860, wrote that the c.p. came from 'the card given to beggars for immediate relief at soup kitchens'.

that's the tip. That's right – very much so, *or* That's the thing, *or* **that's the cheese**: *c.* 1860–1910. (Hotten, 1864.)

that's the tune the old cow died of. That's a damned unpleasant noise!: *c.* 1820–60. (Captain Frederick Marryat, *Mr Midshipman Easy*, 1836.) From an old ballad. (Apperson.) Hence, 'I asked for a loan or a small gift of money or provisions – not for a bloody sermon!': *c.* 1880–1940.

that's the way it goes is a c.p. of humorous resignation or of either rueful or defiant acceptance: mid or latish C19–20. It is probably the earliest of the derivatives from the cliché *that's how it is*.

that's the way the ball bounces is synonymous with **that's how** (or **the way**) **the cookie crumbles**. That's the way things go or turn out, *or* That's fate for you!: US: since *c.* 1954 (W & F) and adopted in both Canada and Australia very soon after. (Douglas Leechman; Barry Prentice.) In Canada, *that's how the ball bounces* is a frequent variant.

that's the way the cookie crumbles. See that's how....

that's (or that is) the way to London? (or **is that the way to London?**) A question disguising a nose-wiping on back of hand or on one's sleeve: mostly children's, but occasionally an adult jocularity, without the action; but always a vulgarity: C20.

that's too bad! – occasionally preceded by **well!** In Act III of Terence Rattigan's *Love in Idleness*, produced in 1944, published in 1945, we find:

MICHAEL: ... You dislike me, I dislike you. Well, that's too bad, but we needn't act like primeval apes about it.

I'd say that this characteristically British c.p., understated and ironic, goes back to *c.* 1880; but I've failed to record an early occurrence.

that's torn it. That has spoiled it. That's ruined everything: originally (*c.* 1905), low, but soon general, as in 'Ian Hay', 1909 (*OED* Supplement). A variant occurs in John Arden's *The Workhouse Donkey: A Vulgar Melo-Drama*, produced in 1963 and published in 1964, at Act I, Scene ix:

BUTTERTHWAITE: Afraid? You don't mean the police?
HOSTESS: That's right.
HARDNUTT: Oh, my Lord, no....
HOPEFAST: I say, Charlie, that's gone and torn it, hasn't it?

The US form – which neatly exemplifies the US preference of the Preterite to the Present Perfect tense – is *that tore it*. A US correspondent writes, 'I suggest that it was first applied to a coïtal stroke so violent as to tear the condom.' But if the origin is sexual, which I doubt, it may equally well have been feminine: the tearing of the hymen. Probably from a dress getting torn.

that's up against you! What do you say – what, indeed, *have* you to say – to that? Australian: late C19–mid C20.

that's up to you! caps a (most) convincing argument: C20. Often accompanied by a coarse gesture.

that's up your shirt. That's a puzzler for you: mid C19–early C20. (F & H.)

that's what gets me down! is a US expression of annoyance or irritation: C20. (Berrey.) Adopted in Britain *c.* 1918. Cf:

that's what gets my back up. That's what angers me: since the 1920s. Perhaps from cats fighting.

[**that's what *I* say** is a grossly overdone conversation tag, half way between cliché and c.p.: late C19–20.]

that's what she wrote. See **that's all she wrote**.

that's what *you* say! I simply don't believe it: US: C20. (Berrey.) Contrast **that's what *I* say.**

that's what *you* think! That's your opinion, but you're almost certainly wrong – badly wrong! : tone: scornful or, at the very least, derisive; period: C20. 'Derides ignorance of important factor [and implies] that projected action will be thwarted' (Laurie Atkinson, 18 July 1975).

that's where I am. 'That's what I enjoy, *or* believe, *or* do' – 'That's my thing' (*DCCU*): American: since *c.* 1960.

that's where it's at. That is a fair, a just, an accurate view of things: a somewhat illiterate, rather slangy, US c.p., dating since *c.* 1964 or 1965. (Norris M. Davidson, 19 July 1971.)

Adopted in Britain either in late 1972 or in early 1973: glossed by *Punch*, on 10 October 1973, as 'I think you're right'.

that's where the big nobs hang out is 'a jocular comment when a man expresses intention [to go to the urinal]. Certainly 1939–45 in the Services and later, offices and factories [and public houses]': Laurie Atkinson, November 1969: since *c.* 1935. Here *nob* is a pun on the slang senses 'important man' and 'prepuce'.

that's where you spoil yourself! was, in 1880–1, directed at a would-be smart, i.e. shrewd or crafty, person overreaching himself. (Ware.)

that's where you want it and **it's up there you want it**, with hand touching one's own forehead; *want* used in sense 'to lack'. You should use your brains! Lower and lower-middle class (since very early C20), become also WW1 military, and then civilian once more. In B & P, John Brophy comments: 'An expression of pride ... to indicate intellectual superiority after one had "wangled" extra leave or a "cushy" job or some such privilege.' Cf **this is where you want it.**

that's your best bet. That's your best way to do or achieve something, or to go somewhere: since the 1920s. From horse-racing.

that's your chicken and **that's your pigeon.** The former was a brief variation (*c.* 1920–35), recorded by Lyell, of the latter (C20).

The latter is better written *pidgin*, 'business'; *pidgin* is itself *pidgin*, pidgin English, for *business*.

that's *your* funeral! See **it's your funeral.**

that's *your* hard (British) (or **tough** (US)) **luck**. 'It's not my concern' (Berrey): C20.

that's your lot! 'is thought to come from [comedian] Jimmy Wheeler' (Vernon Noble, 8 February 1975); it means 'That's all you're going to get from me', or 'That's your share', since *c.* 1950. (Supporting evidence: Laurie Atkinson, November 1969.)

that's your pidgin. See **that's your chicken.**

that's your sort! indicated, *c.* 1785–1930, approval, usually of a specific action or method, only occasionally of some object. (Holcroft, the playwright, 1792; Hotten, 1864.) By ellipsis.

It is to be noted that the phrase seems to have been already well known by 1792, when Thomas Holcroft's *The Road to Ruin: A Comedy* was performed; the actor William Lewis, playing Goldfinch, a raffish, sporting, esp. a horsey man, so

popularized the saying that it enjoyed a furore *c.* 1792–1800 and remained very popular for a generation longer, partly because this comedy proved to be enormously successful and was revived at Drury Lane in 1824 and again in 1826 – and at both the Haymarket and Covent Garden in 1825. In Act II, Goldfinch signals his meeting with the amiable young spendthrift, Harry Dornton, thus:

GOL: Hah! my tight one!

HAR: [*Surveying him.*] Well, Charles?

GOL: How you stare! – an't I the go? That's your sort!

And a few lines further on:

HAR: You improve daily, Charles!

GOL: To be sure! that's your sort! An't I a genius? [*Strutting about.*]

HAR: Quite an original. – You may challenge the whole fraternity of the whip to match you!

GOL: Match me! Newmarket can't match me! – That's your sort!

In *Management*, 1793, Frederick Reynolds refers to Holcroft's phrase on three occasions.

The phrase, one perceives, is of vague sense – but tremendous significance. It's an intensive, with (apparently) the general meaning, 'I should *say* so!' It connotes an uncritical, warmhearted approval. Goldfinch's final words, in reply to a plea that he should now lead a sober life in trade, are: 'Damn trade! ... I'm for life and a curricle. A cut at the caster, and the long odds. Damn trade! The four aces, a back-hand, and a lucky nick! That's your sort!'

(I owe the Holcroft quotation to Miss Patricia Sigl.)

The phrase recurs in R. H. Barham, *The Ingoldsby Legends*, Third Series, 1847, and in Surtees's *Mr Sponge's Sporting Tour*, 1853.

It seems to have reached the US during the 1870s or 1880s. In 1891, M glossed it as 'A term of approbation or encouragement'.

that's your story and you're stuck with it. See **that's my story....**

that's *your* tough luck! See **that's *your* hard luck!** Cf:

that's *your* worry! It has (more colloquially, it's) nothing to do with me. 'A disclaimer of responsibility ("Who cares?") or, as the navy says "Square your own yardarm!"' (Wilfred Granville, 7 January 1969): C20.

thatta boy! is an occasional variant of **attaboy!** In Malcolm Bosse, *The Man Who Loved Zoos*, 1974, we read:

'Just so [i.e., provided] we don't lose it [i.e., confidence] in ourselves.'

'Thatta boy. What should I tell Hopkins?'

'Tell him ... I'm not up a blind alley yet.'

'Thatta boy.'

theirs not to reason why has, in C20, been used as a c.p. From Tennyson's 'The Charge of the Light Brigade'.

them as has – gits. 'Quite common in everyday speech. Refers to persons of great wealth.... Saying now applies to almost anybody better off than the speaker. Often a "sour grapes" expression' (W. J. Burke, 18 August 1975): US: C20.

them's fightin(g) words is probably the original form of, as it remains more common than, **that's fighting talk**: late C19–20. British; US (recorded by Berrey, 1942, *words*); Australian ('In my experience, jocular, rather than illiterate': Barry

Prentice, 31 January 1969); New Zealand – and elsewhere? Occasionally shorted to *fightin'* (or *fighting*) *words*, as in Alistair Mair, *Where the East Wind Blows*, 1972:

'Alive,' I said. 'Which is more than you'll be if you don't clear out.'

Berchard smiled ... 'Fighting words,' he said.

them's my sentiments! is a jocular c.p. of warmhearted agreement or approval: late C19–20. (John Galsworthy, *Swan Song*, 1928.) An excellent example of a famous quotation – from Thackeray's *Vanity Fair*, 1848 – that took some time to become a c.p.

them's shooting words! is 'a phrase going back to the days of cowboys and gunmen on the American frontier. People from our Western States still say, when they take their leave after a visit, "It's time to saddle up", a hangover from the Wild West days' (W. J. Burke, 25 March 1975). Cf the British **them's fightin(g) words!**

them's the jockeys for me! is a Canadian c.p., dating since *c.* 1950 and applied to anything delicious or very desirable. (Douglas Leechman.) Of anecdotal origin.

Early in 1969, Douglas Leechman wrote:

Have you heard of the dinner guest, venerable, white-haired, austere, silent, evidently a man of sense and dignity, perhaps wisdom, who remained silent throughout the conversation? When the dessert was brought in, and the silver cover lifted, he cried aloud: 'EEE! Lookee! Little mince poies. Them's the jockeys for me!'

then comes a pig to be killed! Expressing disbelief, used among the lower and lower-middle classes *c.* 1900–14. Ware says, 'Based upon the lines of Mrs Bond who would call to her poultry – "Come, chicks, come! Come to Mrs Bond and be killed!"'

then I will be hang'd, and my horse too. Equivalent to 'I'll be damned – *if* it's true': late C17–18. See the quotation from S at **at a church with a chimney in it.**

then the band began to play (or **played**), both often preceded by **and**. Then the fat was in the fire – then the trouble began: the longer version, *c.* 1880–1914; the shorter, C20. Kipling, 1892, 'It's "Thank you, Mister Atkins", when the band begins to play'; D. Coke, in *Wilson's* 1911, has 'then the band began to play'. Ware, 1909, adduces *then the band played*. Either from music played by a band at the end of a celebration or other public occasion, or, as Ware proposes, 'derived from the use of brass bands on the nomination day, which immediately sounded when the opponent of their employer attempted to address the people'.

Douglas Leechman, in January 1969, notes the Canadian variant or, rather, derivative, *and the band played on.*' "Things went on as usual" – or even more vague in meaning. Quite old.'

then the shit'll hit (or **then the shit hits**) **the fan!** See **when shit hits the fan.**

then the town bull is a bachelor! was, mid C17–mid C18, a semi-proverbial incredulous retort upon a woman's – or a man's – chastity (or other moral quality). (Ray, 1678.)

then you woke up! And then you came down to earth!: C20.

there ain't no more. See **that's all there is.**

there ain't no sech animal (or **animile**, or **animule**). I just don't

believe it!: US: perhaps since *c.* 1880; obsolescent by 1945, and obsolete by 1970. (Berrey.) Said to be of anecdotal origin: a rustic, seeing a giraffe for the first time, exclaimed 'There ain't no sech animal (or -ile or -ule)!' – and who could blame him?

I first heard the expression on Gallipoli in 1915, from an Englishman familiar with US speech.

there and back is a c.p. reply to the query, whether unwelcome or merely impertinent, 'Where are you going to?' Late C19–20 and always commoner among children than among adults; by 1950, obsolescent, yet not obsolete by 1975.

there are only a few of us left does not, of course, qualify when it is used literally. When used jocularly or ironically or 'deadpan', it became, *c.* 1965, a c.p. In Donald Mackenzie, *Postscript to a Dead Letter*, 1973, we encounter 'Jean Paul's one ... who knows that what he's done is good and doesn't bother to tell you. There are only a few of us left.'

This c.p. has the self-congratulatory variant *there aren't so many of us left, you know*, which, the earlier, may have arisen during the 1920s, in reference to survivors of Mons or The Somme or Passchendaele or any other sanguinary battle of WW1. (Fernley O. Pascoe, 15 January 1975.)

[**there are plenty more fish in the sea** (Australian) or **... pebbles on the beach** (British) lie at a point where proverb and cliché and c.p. meet. It has, throughout C20, been addressed to a girl when her romance comes to an end. (Barry Prentice, *c.* 6 March 1975.)]

there are two people I don't like and you're both of them. It arose early in the 1930s and may have been suggested by a silent-film subtitle. (Frank Shaw, 25 February 1969.) I don't recall hearing the c.p. before *c.* 1937. Cf the witticism, 'There are two fools born every minute and you're all three of them.'

there are worse in gaol (or **jail**). See **worse in gaol.**

there aren't so many of us left, you know. See **there are only a few....**

there, boys, there. There, lads, enjoy yourselves! There, lads, isn't that (or this) fine! Late C16–mid C17. In Beaumont and Fletcher's, *The Knight of the Burning Pestle*, performed in 1611 and published two years later, at Act III, Scene v, Merrythought sings:

If you will sing, and dance, and laugh,
    And hollow, and laugh again,
And then cry, 'there, boys, there!' why, then,
    One, two, three, and four,
We shall be merry within this hour.

there come de judge! A US c.p., adopted from a 'gag' in the television show 'Laugh-In', it belongs to the approximate period 1970–5. (Based on a communication from Professor Emeritus F. E. L. Priestley of Toronto, 15 August 1974.)

there goes his hotel! was, *c.* 1872–1920, a US professional gamblers' c.p., directed at one who goes on gambling until he loses even the money he had intended to reserve in order to pay his hotel bill. (*U.*)

there has to be a first time for everything. See **there's a first time for everything.**

there he goes with his eye out! In his remarkable essay Mackay, after discussing (*Hookey*) *Walker!*, writes:

The next phrase was a most preposterous one. Who introduced it, how it arose, or where it was first heard, are alike unknown. Nothing about it is certain, but that for months it was *the* slang *par excellence* of the Londoners, and afforded them a vast gratification. *'There he goes with his eye out!'* or *'There she goes with her eye out!'* ... was in the mouth of everybody who knew the town. The sober part of the community were as much puzzled by this unaccountable saying as the vulgar were delighted with it. The wise thought it very foolish, but the many thought it very funny, and the idle amused themselves by chalking it upon walls, or scribbling it upon monuments. But 'all that's bright must fade', even in slang. The people grew tired of their hobby, and *'There he goes with his eye out!'* was heard no more in its accustomed haunts.

The vogue of the phrase apparently belonged to the mid or latish 1830s. Note, however, that, early in chapter LIX of *Plain or Ringlets?*, 1860, Robert Surtees writes, concerning Mr Bunting: 'Four horses would be of no use to him with his mild style of riding, besides which he wouldn't like to go about with a man with one eye. The slang cry of "There you go with your eye out!" occurred to his recollection.'

I cannot avoid the *ignis fatuus* thought that perhaps this c.p. contains an allusion to some pertinent and widely quoted reference to the crowd's seeing, a generation earlier, Nelson pass with his one eye.

there he is – wheel him in! See LIVERPOOL CATCH PHRASES.

there I was on my ditty box saying nothing to nobody. A US navy and Marine Corps saying: C20. 'Not in the mainstream of American speech' (W. J. Burke, 18 August 1975).

there is a letter in the post office. See **letter** ....

[**there is more to this than meets the eye** is rather cliché than c.p.]

there is no punishment when no pun is meant. See **puns are punishable.**

there is the door the carpenter made, usually with *there* emphasized. You may go: lower-middle class: *c.* 1750–1800. It occurs in *Sessions Paper of the Central Criminal Court*, 1767, in the account of the trial of Rebecca Pearce. Cf **there's the door** ....

there is York Street concerned. See **York Street** ....

there must be an easier way (or **easier ways**) **of making a living** has, since the middle or late 1940s, been applied to difficult or dangerous, arduous or precarious, occupations, as in Brian Lecomber's exciting aviation 'thriller', *Turn Killer* (1975), where Ken Holland, stunt flyer, records, '... I was fighting down the hollow ball of fear in my stomach and listening to a still small voice somewhere in my head, saying for the thousandth time that there must be an easier way of making a living. I agreed with the voice ...'

there ought to be a law against it! is a (mainly Australian) expression of disgust: since *c.* 1960. (Barry Prentice, 15 December 1974; on 1 May 1975 he added, 'Self-evident in meaning, but very interesting sociologically.')

there she blows! is an impudent cry directed at a fat woman seen bathing: C20. From the whaler's cry upon sighting a whale.

there she goes with her eye out! See **there he goes** ....

there was a cow climbed up a hill. 'A retort, equivalent to tell-

ing a man that he is a liar' (F & G); John Brophy, in B & P, says:

If one were thought to be telling a lie, his mates either sang
     Comrades don't believe him (*ter*):
     He's such a bloody [or fucking] liar,
or chanted
     There was a cow
     Climbed up a tree:
     Oh, you bloody liar (*fortissimo*).
It is to be noted that many of the longer sayings were occasionally chanted.

In short, a C20 c.p., very popular in the British Army of WW1 – not much heard since *c.* 1950.

there were four turds for dinner – usually amplified, **stir turd, hold turd, tread turd and must turd.** 'To wit, a hog's face, feet, and chitterlings, with mustard' (Grose, 1796): a low rebus-c.p. of *c.* 1760–1830.

there you ain't was, *c.* 1870–1914, a proletarian, notably Cockney, declaration or imputation of failure. (B & L.) You're not on the spot when you're needed.

[**there you go!** Not a true c.p. – rather a cliché. US, it occurs in, e.g., Joseph C. Neal, *Peter Ploddy*, 1844, on p. 6.]

there'll be a hot time in the old town to-night. See **hot time** ....

there'll be blood for breakfast. See **blood for breakfast.**

there'll be pie in the sky when you die; more usually, **you'll get** .... A derisive and cynical US c.p. dating since *c.* 1907 and implying that a reward hereafter is an illusion and a delusion; apparently deriving immediately from the parody of a facilely promissory hymn and much influenced by the propaganda of the 1WW – industrial Workers of the World – movement. See esp. *Webster's New International Dictionary*, 3rd edn; and *DSUE* Supplement. Cf **there's a good time coming.**

there're gentlemen present, ladies! See **gentlemen present** ....

there's a blow in the bell. There's something wrong, something suspicious, somewhere: US underworld: *c.* 1920–60. (Herbert Corey, *Farewell, Mr Gangster*, 1936.) Something that fails to 'ring true'.

there's a blue shirt at the masthead. See **blue shirt** ....

there's a deal (or **a lot) of glass about.** It's a splendid, although somewhat vulgar, display; hence, a retort to a boast of achievement: both c.pp belong to the approximate period 1888–1910. From the glass cases – and perhaps mirrors – that characterize an exhibition of precious things (jewels, watches, gems, etc.).

there's a deal of weather about. See **deal of weather** ....

there's (or **there has to be) a first time for everything; also there's always a first time.** See Terence Rattigan, *Who Is Sylvia?*, performed in 1950 and published in 1951, in Act I:
     DAPHNE: Shall I let you into a little secret? This is my very first taste of caviare.
     MARK: Well, there has to be a first time for everything, doesn't there?
But *there's always a first time* is mostly a mocking, occasionally a consolatory, rejoinder to 'I've never done that before': it did not become general until *c.* 1945; it is both British and US; and it has, one surmises, a sexual origin. In the main, it is still (1975) a c.p., although it has, since

the late 1960s, snown unmistakable signs of becoming a proverb.

there's a good time coming is, used literally, a cliché; used ironically to one in trouble or danger – well and truly **up Shit Creek without a paddle** – it is, however, a c.p. – going back to when? I heard it, as a c.p., during WW1. Cf **there'll be pie in the sky when you die**.

there's a joke. See **joke over**.

there's a nigger in the woodpile is recorded by HLM, 1922; and in Supp. 1 he both notes that this characteristically US phrase has been 'traced by the *DAE* to 1861' – respectably old – and that it is, by that eminent dictionary, defined as a concealed or inconspicuous but highly important fact, factor or "catch" in an account, proposal, etc.' Berrey cites it as having the variant *on the fence* and as connoting suspicion.

there's a shape for you! referred, *c.* 1850–1910, to a person – or a quadruped – extremely thin.

there's a smell of gunpowder is an oblique, unexpectedly polite, reference to a breaking of wind: army: late C19–20.

there's a war on, occasionally preceded by **remember**, was current during the years 1915–18, among both soldiers, who used it with a sense of urgency, and civilians, who used it in apologizing for shortages and delays. Soldiers, moreover, used to say of civilians leading a safe and comfortable life, and, semi-jocularly of 'Base wallahs' that *they don't know there's a war on*.

And then it cropped up again in 1939–45, mostly in the form **don't you know there's a war on?**

there's 'air! See **there's hair!**

there's always a first time. See **there's a first time for everything**.

there's always something to inconvenience – or to disappoint – you: since the late 1940s.

there's an awful lot of coffee in Brazil! Since *c.* 1948. Perhaps from a song popular in the late 1940s and early 1950s. Only when it's *not* applied to coffee is it a c.p. It ironically and tactfully condemns the utterance of a truism by the addressee.

there's an 'oss a-layin' down the law. 'When you see a lawyer floored, sing out, "There's an 'oss a layin' down the law!"' (R. S. Surtees, *Handley Cross; or, Mr Jorrock's Hunt*, 2 vols, 1854, vol. 1, the chapter headed 'Another Sporting Lector', i.e. lecture): a fox-hunting c.p. of *c.* 1820–80. Here, 'floored' = thrown off his horse.

there's another show. A racecourse cry, meaning that a 'tic-tac' man has signalled fresh odds: C20. (The *Cornhill Magazine*, 1932, in an article by George Baker.) Another – a different – showing of the odds offered by bookmakers on the course.

there's blood for breakfast. See **blood for breakfast**.

there's eyesight in it. That's evident or obvious: since the early 1930s. Clear to the view.

there's gold in them thar hills is a US c.p. (recorded by Berrey, who glosses it as 'there is good profit in that enterprise'), current throughout C20 and probably also in latish C19, and deriving from the literal assertion dating, presumably, since the great gold rush of 1849; adopted in Britain, although not

very generally, during the 1930s and become fairly general during the late 1940s–50s.

Of its British use, Mr Ramsey Spencer remarked on 10 May 1969: 'A c.p. from the Frontier days in the US [and] anglicized by early Western films. Over here it was ironical, impugning the probability of some extravagant hope; by 1960, it was virtually obsolete' – true; but it has certainly been fairly popular in England during the 1970s. The c.p. is revealingly employed by Noël Coward, *Waiting in the Wings*, performed and published 1960, at Act II, Scene i, where Zelda, visiting a charity home for aged actresses, exclaims 'There's certainly gold in these yar hills.' Note, too, the significance of the fact that on the front page of the *Sunday Telegraph*, 7 April 1974, appeared a small cartoon of two miners looking at a couple of great slagheaps and one of them saying, 'I'm telling you – there's gold in them thar hills' – the reference being to a land-deal scandal relating to reclaimed land.

In respect of its US use, it is interesting to see how Clarence Budington Kelland, an immensely successful not-very-good novelist with an acute ear for easy colloquial everyday speech, uses it in *House of Cards*, 1941, in chapter XIV:

'If a bird from Chicago presents himself,' Ream said, please cherish him....'

She heard him chuckle. 'Thar's gold in them thar hills.' (The speaker is a contract bridge expert. He implies that there's a fortune to be made in that quarter.)

there's hair (occasionally **'air**)! There's a girl with a lot of hair!: London streets': *c.* 1900–10. (Ware.) Ware dates it at 1900 and refers it to the vogue that favoured 'packed masses, coming down over the forehead'; but the phrase lingered for perhaps a decade.

It developed into *there's (h)air – like wire!*, long and stiff: remembered by Colin Clair, the eminent biographer, and the historian of printing, as heard by him, at the mature age of six, in 1906, and recorded by Collinson in his alert, perceptive, shrewd book. Comparable is the Yorkshire, esp. the West Riding, simile applied to hair: *as straight as a yard of pump water*.

Cf the Liverpool c.p. *there's hair* – pronounced *durs ur – on baldy*, 'shouted by L'pool street girls *c.* 1924' (Frank Shaw, the great authority on Merseyside speech and folklore, in letter dated 25 October 1968).

there's life in the old dog (or **old girl**) **yet**. He or she is still very much alive, still capable of a love affair: late (? mid) C19–20. In H. V. Esmond, *The Law Divine*, performed on 29 August 1918 and published in 1922, in Act II we read:

BILL: ...He's much too old to go messing about with widows.

TED: (*chuckles*): There's life in the old dog yet.

And then Noël Coward wrote in 1923 a dramatic sketch titled 'There's Life in the Old Girl Yet' – included in *Collected Sketches and Lyrics*, 1931. Cf:

[**there's many a good tune played on an old fiddle** is not a c.p. but a proverb applied to an ageing sexual partner: *not* always, although male vanity would rather perversely have it so, by the man to the woman. (Apperson; *ODEP*.)]

there's money bid for you. See **hold up your head....**

there's more in that head than the comb'll ever take out. 'An ironic Anglo-Irish c.p. with the overt meaning, "You're clever"': C20. The reference to *comb* implies nits in the hair (Frank Shaw, January 1969).

there's no answer to that. See **well, there's no answer to that.**

there's no doubt about (significant pause) **you!** An Australian c.p., expressing admiration and dating since *c.* 1925.

there's no future in it. See **no future in it.**

there's no kick (or **squawk**) **coming.** That's satisfactory. That's O.K. by me – no complaints at all. US: since *c.* 1920. (Berrey.)

there's no 'must' about it, late (? mid) C19–20, is the c.p. that has emerged from a number of *there's no* (something or other) *about it,* which is a cliché pattern. Michael Arlen, *The Green Hat,* 1924, has for instance: '"You *must* do it." – "There's no must about it."' (cited by Collinson).

there's no show without Punch. See **no show....**

[**there's no snakes in Virginny** (Virginia). In full, if I don't do such or such a thing, there's no snakes in Virginny. I'll most certainly do it: American: very approximately 1800–90. 'I have encountered this expression, or a variant, at least half a dozen times in my readings in the nineteenth century' (Colonel Albert Moe, who then cites a passage from Matthew Edward Barker's anecdotes, about the Chelsea pensioners in the *London Literary Gazette* of 3 January 1824: 'Halloo!' –'I say ... if you ever send your Joey aboard of me again, and I don't break his neck, there's no snakes in Virginny.') Apparently it stands midway between c.p. and cliché, for it isn't entirely self-contained and free.]

there's no squawk coming. See **there's no kick coming.**

there's no two ways about it has, in C20, been a British c.p., but it came from the US, where it may have been current as early as 1840, to judge by the fact that, in his *Am,* Bartlett has the entry: 'THERE'S NO TWO WAYS ABOUT IT, *i.e.* the fact is just so and not otherwise. A vulgarism of recent origin, equivalent to the common phrase, *"there's no mistake about it"* or *"the fact is so and so and no mistake".'*

there's nothing like it is a C20 c.p. – as often as not used with little relevance or none.

there's nothing more – that's all there is is the textually correct form (as coined by Ethel Barrymore, 1879–1959, in 1906) of what has come to be rather more often used: *that's all there is – there isn't any more,* which see in its alphabetical order.

there's nothing spoiling. There's no hurry – no urgency: C20. Of domestic origin; and often domestic in application. (A. B. Petch, 4 January 1974.)

there's nowt so queer as folk. There's nothing so odd as people; It's a queer world!: mid C19–20. Originally and still a Yorkshire saying, verging on the proverbial: but since *c.* 1890, much used in other parts of England. The loose *there's nothing....* is to be deprecated.

Cf the witticism addressed to me in 1917 by a fellow Brigade Observer on the Western Front: 'There's an awful lot of human nature in men, women, and children.'

there's one born every minute, to which **they say** is sometimes appended. Elliptical for 'one fool'. This c.p. implies that either oneself or another has been duped: C20. By *c.* 1945, it had begun to acquire, yet by 1975 it had still not yet attained, the status of a proverbial saying. 'From a saying attributed

to P. T. Barnum (1810–91), the circus magnate, "There's a sucker born every minute"' (Douglas Leechman).

[**there's only one way to find out** – i.e., 'Try it!' – lies midway between cliché and c.p.: C20; ? rather late C19–20.]

there's shit not far behind is a late C19–20 workmen's c.p., evoked by a loud breaking of wind.

there's sorrow on the sea. 'Traditional warning to one *who'd sell his farm and go to sea*' (Wilfred Granville, 1962, but first recorded by him in 1949): probably from as early as mid C19. More poetical than most c.pp.

there's the door – and your name is Walker! See **my name is Haines.**

these sets take a long time to warm up. Originated with Kenneth Horne, in concert with Richard Murdoch, in the radio programme 'Much Binding in the Marsh' during WW2. The gag, with its sly dig (cf that *Binding = binding,* RAF slang for complaining), became a c.p., which endured to *c.* 1960 and then passed into the faëry realm of nostalgic memories.

these things will happen (even) in the best-regulated families. See **such things....**

they can do any bloody thing to you.... See **they can make you do....**

they can hear you – you needn't shout (or **there's no need to shout**). 'Sometimes said to big-mouthed Yorkshiremen and Lancashire people when they boast that all their relatives are living in the north' (A. B. Petch, 16 January 1974): C20.

they can make you do anything in the air force except have a baby. 'A c.p. tribute to authority and discipline' (Laurie Atkinson): RAF: since *c.* 1925. This is an adaptation of the army's (1914 onwards) c.p., which, obviously, substitutes *...in the army –* and which often adds and *they* (or *some of them*) *would have a bloody good try to do that!* Cf J. R. L. Anderson, *Death in the Thames,* 1974, 'The old saying that the army can do anything it likes with a man except put him in the family way expresses a pretty exact truth.' Among Australians, the predominant form was *they can do any bloody thing* (at all) *to you in the army except put you in the family way – and some of them would have a bloody good try to do that* (final word emphasized).

they don't grow on trees is a 'lament that few brilliant people or rare items are "in short supply" (few are in much demand)' (Wilfred Granville, late December 1968): since the late 1940s. This c.p. derives naturally, almost inevitably, from the much older *it doesn't grow on trees,* as applied to money.

they don't know there's a war on. See **there's a war on.**

they don't pipe dinner outside is a naval warning, whether to those who plan to desert ship or to those who, on completion of twelve years' service, rush unthinkingly into civilian life and thereby lose a number of benefits, such as duty-free tobacco and spirits: since *c.* 1930. (*Sailors' Slang;* 1962, and earlier Granville's book, *SS.*)

they don't yell, they don't tell – and they're very (very) grateful. A 'young men's tribute to love of good, mature women, and their supposed amorous response' (Laurie Atkinson, who, on 11 September 1969, records having heard it ten years earlier): since *c.* 1920.

they fit where they touch. See **it fits where it touches.**

they got (occasionally **they've got**) **me**; also **they got me, pal**. 'A trivial c.p., uttered when one hears a peal of thunder or a loud explosion' (Barry Prentice): mostly Australian: since the latish 1930s. From the 'traditional' cry of the mortally wounded – at least in stories and films.

The third version (*they got me, pal*) is the earliest and widest-spread, for it is 'a mock-heroic c.p., burlesquing the gangster films of the 1930s. Speaker staggers, clutching chest, at noise like gunfire' (Frank Shaw, January 1969).

they gotta quit kicking my dawg around is US, 'from an American song. Probably *c.* 1912. Was used as a [political] campaign song' (W. J. Burke, 18 August 1975): *c.* 1910–40, then less and less.

they hosed them out. Barry Prentice, writing on 1 May 1975, says:

> This grim [originally RAF] c.p. was used during WW2. The claim was made that there was so little left of the bodies of rear gunners on bombers that they had to hose out the remains. A book about 'Tail-End Charlies' entitled *They Hosed Them Out* was published in Australia in 1965 and in England in 1969. It was written by John Beede.

The c.p. had soon spread to the air forces of the Commonwealth.

they laughed when I sat down at the piano – but when I started to play!; emphasis on *play*. 'That old advertisement has crept into the language as a standard cliché' (Monica Dickens in *Woman's Own*): not a cliché but a c.p.: since the 1920s.

they must have captured a sugar-boat. See **captured**....

they sat on their hands is a C20 theatrical sarcasm, directed at an audience that has refused to clap. (Granville.)

they say the first hundred years are the hardest was a favourite, in 1917–18, among US soldiers on the Western Front (HLM, 1922), but not – although usually ... *the worst* – unheard among British soldiers in 1914–18 nor yet among both British and US in WW2. Also **the first hundred years are the hardest**.

they tame lions in the army was a Regular Army c.p. of *c.* 1890–1939. (Frank Richards, *Old Soldiers Never Die*, 1933.) The reference being – or had you guessed? – to military disciplinary measures. Cf **we'll soon lick you into shape.**

they that ride on a trotting horse will ne'er perceive it. S, 1738, in Dialogue I has:

> MISS: [To Lady Answerall.] Madam, one of your Ladyship's Lappets is longer than t'other.
> LADY ANS: Well, no Matter; they that ride on a trotting horse will ne'er perceive it.

The implication of this C18 c.p. is that only the idle notice trifles.

they think their shit doesn't stink; (he) thinks his shit doesn't stink. The former is applied to would-be superior girls: C20; the latter – in full, *he* (or *the sort of bloke who*) *thinks ... but it does, all the same, like any other bugger's* has, since *c.* 1870, been applied to any conceited fellow. In Canada the shorter form, *his shit doesn't stink*, is used. Not a c.p. much heard among the educated and the cultured.

they used to call him Robin Hood – now they call him robbin' bastard! 'A Services occasional c.p., particularly relevant in these days of leaping inflation, heard from time to time during the past couple of decades, *they used* ... of anyone suspected of overcharging' (Paul Beale, 21 April 1975).

they want to be alone. See **put the lights out.**

they're all in the box – just pick the right one. A Services' transport drivers' (esp. driving instructors') c.p., addressed to someone driving clumsily and chiefly if with a jarring of gears: probably since the middle 1930s. (Y. Mindel, July 1972.)

they're all up at (old) Harwich. They're in a nice old mess: late C19–early C20. (Manchon.) Why *Harwich*? Perhaps, folk-etymologically, from dialectal *harriage*, disorder, confusion.

they're better fuckers than fighters. See **better fuckers**....

they're eating nothing. They'll sell later, esp., their business: tradesmen's: C20; they are doing so badly that they cannot afford to eat. By 1970, obsolescent.

'they're off,' said the monkey, a proletarian c.p. of late C19–20, is applied to a race, notably a horserace just started, hence to something that has come loose. Often elaborated thus: *when he looked into the lawn-mower and carelessly lost his testicles.*

There exists a variant, *they're off, Mr Cutts.*

they're two a penny. 'Expendable; easy to come by; hardly worth notice. From a remark by Jesus (Matthew, 10) – "Are not sparrows two a penny. Yet without your Father's leave, not one of them can fall to the ground"' (Vernon Noble, 14 January 1975). Probably since latish C19; my own memory of it goes back to *c.* 1910.

they've opened another tin was current, among the army's Other Ranks, in 1915–18. 'An expression frequently heard ... in a depreciatory sense, with reference to some recently arrived draft, or officer' (F & G). Presumably a tin of sardines.

thin edge of nothing – the. Applied, during the 1920s and 1930s, 'when people are very crowded and there is hardly room to sit' (Lyell).

things are looking up! has, since *c.* 1925, been addressed to – or directed at – someone wearing a new suit or owning a new car. 'Jocular *double entendre* phrase: improvement in conditions; priapism' (Laurie Atkinson, 18 July 1975).

things I do for England! – preceded, of course, by **the**. Laurie Atkinson, writing on 18 July 1975, says:

> Self-congratulation on achievements unrealized or unsung by others. Current in 1930s; quoted from film *The Private Life of Henry the Eighth* .... script by Lajos Biro. Prompted by first marital felicity with one of his less attractive brides. – Apt when act of grace is duty rather than pleasure.

Cf **think of England!**

But it has been occasionally heard since the 1930s; it still is – I have myself heard it, more than once, during the 1970s.

things I do for you – the (exclamatory). Originally (*c.* 1955 as an established c.p.) and mainly British. Philip Purser, *The Holy Father's Navy*, 1971, has:

> Affection needs love as much as love needs affection.... I kissed her.
> She said, 'What are you thinking of?'
> 'Guess.'
> 'You must be joking.'

'I'm deadly earnest. And Deadly Ernest.'
Every couple has its private, awful jokes....
She relaxed. 'The things I do for you.'

things is crook in Muswellbrook; and **things is weak in Werris Creek**. Australian card-players' c.pp., applied to a poor hand; recorded by Baker: since *c.* 1920.

things you see when you haven't got your gun – the (exclamatory). For instance, an odd-looking man or an oddly dressed woman: probably late C19–20, although I myself don't remember hearing it before *c.* 1920; by 1971, slightly obsolescent, for, by that time, *not* to be oddly dressed was, in itself, almost an oddity.

think – I don't. See **I don't think**.

think I've just been dug up? See **do you think** ....

think nothing of it! This is both British and US, dating since the 1940s, meaning 'Oh, that's all right', *or* 'You're welcome'; 'It's a trifle – let's not exaggerate!'

In Terence Rattigan, *The Sleeping Prince*, performed 1953 and published in 1954; at Act I, Scene i, we read:

NICHOLAS:(*To* MARY.) I shall not soon forget your kindness in this matter, Miss Dagenham.
MARY: Think nothing of it.

Ellery Queen, *Cop Out*, 1969, has:

'Thanks a lot, Tru...'
Hyatt waved, 'Think nothing of it.'

Dominic Devine, *Illegal Tender*, 1970, also uses it:

'Thanks. I'm not holding you back?'
'Think nothing of it,' she said drily.

So does Val Gielgud, in *The Black Sambo Affair*, 1972:

'...No, Humphrey, you haven't wasted your time and effort.'
'Think nothing of it, Greg.'

It can also be found in Julian Symons, *The Players and the Game*, 1972, and Dick Francis, *Smokescreen*, 1972.

think of England! 'Occasional advice' – very little needed since 1945 – 'to a young bride ignorant about the facts of life. It is generally [rumoured] to have been said to Queen Victoria on her wedding night by her lady-in-waiting or some close relative who told her, "Close your eyes and think of England"' (Laurie Atkinson, late 1974): perhaps, therefore, dating since the late 1830s – but I'd have thought, since the late C19. Cf **things I do for England – the** and **close your eyes** ....

thinks he holds it. See **he thinks** ....

thinks his shit doesn't stink. See **they think** ....

thinks the sun shines out of her (or **his**) **arsehole** (or **arse**) – **he** (or **she**). He idolizes her, or she him: late C19–20 – and perhaps from very much earlier. The phrase has become so embedded in the language that it can, with perfect naturalness, appear in Julian Symons, *A Three Pipe Problem*, 1975, thus: 'And you said yourself that those two old people thought the sun shone out of Gledson's backside.'

[**thirty-four!** – 'Go away!' said by a salesman to another salesman, who is interfering – meant, *c.* 1930, 'Don't bother me'. (W & F.) So restricted, so almost technical, as to fail to rate as a genuine c.p.]

this has put the top-hat on it. See **that's put the lid on it**.

this hurts me more than it hurts you, a cliché – and usually a barefaced lie – used by parents administering corporal punishment to their offspring, has come, in C20 (I myself never heard it so used before *c.* 1920), to be a scathingly derisive c.p. reference to that very odd moral attitude which used to be taken by over-severe and, implicatively, sadistic, parents.

this **I** *must* **hear**, and *this* **I** *must* **see** express an amused intention, partly ironic and partly deprecatory: since the late, perhaps the middle 1940s. I can hardly do better than quote from a letter sent to me on 1 April 1969:

Based on 1930's joke, US–Yiddish origin. Eavesdropper by honeymoon bedroom.
'I'll get on top.'
'No, I'll get on top.'
'No, let's both get on top.'
Eavesdropper: '*This* I *must* see.'
Couple were trying to close suitcase. Collapse of stout eavesdropper.

'Widely current (and perhaps for twenty years) among all classes – perhaps especially the educated. A real c.p., I think, although only with the marked stresses' (John W. Clark, 17 February 1975).

By the 1960s, also British. Alistair MacLean has *this I must see* in his espionage 'thriller', *Circus*, 1975.

this is (or **that's**) **a bit** (or **a little bit**) **of all right!** That, or this, is excellent; also applied to a pretty and compliant female: originally and mainly Cockney: C20. An extension of the slang *a bit of all right*, something excellent or cosy or very welcome. The c.p. occurs in, e.g., Alexander Macdonald, *In the Land of Pearl and Gold*, 1907, '"That's a bit of all right," said the guard, cutting a piece of the stem and putting it into his mouth.'

Occasional variant, rare after *c.* 1930: ...*a bit of 'tout droit'*, from the mock or bogus Fr. *un morceau de tout droit*. (Manchon.)

this is *all* right! – meaning 'Things are all wrong', *or* 'Everything's wrong': *c.* 1896–1905. Ware quotes the *People*, 7 November 1897, 'This is *all* right, nothing to eat or drink, and no one to speak to.'

this is an orchestra – not an elastic band. 'The classic observation by an exasperated musical director after trying in vain to keep pace with the woman vocalist who was hopelessly out of tune and time' (Granville): C20.

this is better than a thump on the back with a stone. Said on 'giving anyone a drink of good liquor on a cold morning' (Grose, 1788): *c.* 1770–1850.

this is Funf speaking. See **Funf speaking** and TOMMY HANDLEY CATCH PHRASES.

this is it! and **this is mine!** are exclamations uttered when an approaching bomb or shell seems to portend one's imminent death: Armed Forces': 1940 onwards.

The former may have been adopted from US.

this is me and you! This is between me and you – and no one else is to know: convicts': C20. An example occurs in Jim Phelan, *Lifer*, 1938: '"This is me and you," Cobb went on, using the jail phrase demanding secrecy.'

this is mine! See **this is it!**

this is my day out is consecrated to those sacred occasions when one person 'stands treat' to a group in, or even to all the occupants of, a bar in a public-house: since *c.* 1930.

this is not (more emphatically; **definitely not) my day.** See **it's not my day.**

this is not only but also. In Dialogue I of S, 1738, Swift writes:

NEV[EROUT]: Miss, I want that Diamond Ring of Yours.
MISS: Why then, Want's like to be your Master.
[Neverout *looking at the Ring.*]
NEV: Ay marry, this is not only, but also; pray, where did you get it?

This is not only handsome but valuable is a C18 c.p. expressive of astonishment at, or admiration of, superlative quality. Characteristic of the polished eloquence of polite society in that century.

this is so sudden! is a C20 c.p., either jocular or ironic, and applied to any unexpected offer or, less often, gift. From the reputedly customary reply of a girl to an offer of marriage. (Collinson.)

US as well as British. See Clarence Budington Kelland, in *Dance Magic*, 1927:

'Petrie,' said Mrs Wilder, 'this is Jahala Chandler.... I'm going to make a team of you and Miss Chandler. Petrie and Chandler! How will that look in electric lights?'

Petrie turned to survey Jahala and his eyes twinkled. 'This is so sudden,' he cried, and compelled Jahala to smile back at him.

In Noël Coward's first-written play (1920), not performed (up to 1923, anyway), but published in 1925, Act III had contained this passage:

NAOMI: ... I want you to become a permanent member.
KELD: (*laughing*): This is very sudden.

And then in Act III of *This Was a Man*, published in 1928 after it had been 'hurriedly banned by the Lord Chamberlain and forbidden production in England', Coward employs another slight variation:

EDWARD: If I were free, Zoe, would you marry me?
ZOE: Edward!
EDWARD: I suddenly thought of it.
ZOE (*laughing*): This is terribly sudden.

As Barry Prentice remarks (1 May 1975): 'This c.p. is used in the same circumstances as "I didn't know (that) you cared"'; that is, as in the opening paragraph of this entry. He adds: 'It is also used when someone accidentally touches a person of the opposite sex, in such a way that it could be interpreted as an embrace.' This usage – not only Australian, by the way – is the later of the two; not, I think, earlier than *c.* 1950, but, to be scholarly-honest, I didn't hear it before the early 1960s.

this is something like! Richard Brome's *The Covent Garden Weekend ... A Facetious Comedy*, written *c.* 1642, published 1658, opens with Cockbrain – 'a Justice of Peace, the Weeder of the Garden' – saying to Rooksbill – 'a great Builder in Covent Garden'(a projector, a speculative builder): 'I Marry Sir [i.e., 'Aye, marry, sir!'] This is something like! These appear like Buildings! Here's Architecture exprest indeed! It is a most sightly situation and fit for Gentry and Nobility.' Rooksbill replies, 'When it is all finished, doubt-

lesse it will be handsome'; and Cockbrain asserts, 'It will be glorious.'

Probably this has been a c.p. since early C17. In mid C19–20, often preceded by *well.*

Clearly elliptical for 'This is something like what we want, *or* what is needed.'

this is the end! Not literally the end; merely intolerable or outrageous. Frank Worsley, in *Itma*, 1948, quotes part of a post-war, although still 1945, show:

TOMMY: Yes, she [Crafty Clara] sailed through the side of the tent, slap into the bearded man. He turned a somersault, so she saw the picture right through.
BRIGADIER (*furious*): This is the *end.*
TOMMY: That's what Clara said when the tattooed man put his shirt on.

This c.p. may have arisen on the outbreak of war in 1914.

this is the life! dates from *c.* 1910 and was popularized by British soldiers (with American following suit) in WW1, often with the ruefully humorous addition, *if you don't weaken.* Also *it's a great life,* q.v.

this is the way we exercise (and teacher says we may). 'A return [catch] phrase to a comment on [one's] activity, as much as to say "I'm working and there's not much more to be said about it". A phrase I knew as a child and thought it was meant to be suggestive' (Laurie Atkinson – b. 1904 – in a letter dated mid-December 1968): C20; by 1960, extremely obsolescent.

Perhaps popularized by the mnemonic quality of its metric form.

this is the weather we signed on for is a C20 merchant navy c.p., applied to agreeably warm, fine weather and a calm sea. (*Sailors' Slang.*)

this is too much! A retort or comment upon an excessive inconvenience or demand or effrontery: since the mid 1860s. (F & H suggests that it echoes *Artemus Ward among the Shakers, c.* 1862.)

this is where it's at and **this is where the action is.** This is where things – esp., notable things – are happening; this is the place you seek, if you want excitement: US: since the late 1950s; adopted in Britain in late 1960s. In the *New Yorker* of 17 April 1971, a C.E.M. drawing shows a mother hen addressing a just-hatched chick, 'Just take my word for it, kid. This is where it's at.'

Jonathan George, *The Kill Dog*, 1970, has the following exchange:

'I want to stay here.' She tried to laugh.... 'This is where the action is,' she said brashly.
'Please?'
...She translated:
'It's a phrase. A bit dated, but ... well ...'

this is where the men are separated from the boys (or ... **where they separate the men from the boys).** Now we'll see who the real men are; that is, where we can distinguish the genuine men from the 'phoneys': US: since before WW2, but I shouldn't care to guess how long before. (Colonel Albert Moe, 15 June 1975.) Dr Joseph T. Shipley, 16 August 1975, states that the former is the original shape and that it was coined by Mae West.

this is where we (hence also **I) came in.** We've come full circle, so we can leave now, cease now, etc.; I'm beginning to repeat myself, or someone else is doing so; I, we, have seen or heard all this before: US, then also British: since the 1920s.

'Unquestionably a c.p., and vigorously alive' (John W. Clark, 17 February 1975).

'It is, of course, in origin a remark made in the days of continuous showings of a film at motion-picture theatres, so that one went in at any stage of a film's progression – now used in any situation where something seems to repeat itself, and meaning "Let's go!"' (Joseph T. Shipley, letter dated 16 January 1975).

this is where you want it, the speaker pointing at, or rapping on, his forehead. You need to have brains: late C19–20. The same gesture accompanies the C20 c.p., *he's got it up there,* he's very intelligent.

this must be Philadelphia, Pennsylvania, seems to have been, *c.* 1898–1903 (perhaps rather longer), a US c.p., connoting sleepiness and a failure to keep up to date, for, in 'How a Beauty was Waked and her Suitor Suited', one of the poems in Guy Wetmore Carryl, *Grimm Tales Made Gay*, 1902, we read:

There were courtiers without number,
But they all were plunged in slumber,
The prince's ear delighting
By uniting
In a snore.
The prince remarked: 'This must be Phil
adelphia, Pennsylvania!'
(And so was born the jest that's still
The comic journal's mania!)

this should not be possible (or, more usually, **this should be impossible**). This quotation from the *Royal Navy Gunnery Manual* has become a naval c.p., 'employed sarcastically when something has gone wrong' (Wilfred Granville, 1962): *c.* 1910–35, and then used occasionally by the older men; by 1960, obsolete. It circulated only among officers.

That distinguished officer, Rear-Admiral P. W. Brock, in a letter dated 8 September 1971, writes:

It came from the gunnery drill books in force when I was a midshipman and acting sub-lieutenant, 1920–4. It concerned the tests of the safety arrangements that a gun's crew was expected to carry out on closing up at their quarters. There were various mechanical interlocks to prevent, for instance, closing the breech of a big gun before the power rammer was withdrawn, or firing with the breech not fully closed. The drill book instructed you to try to find a tube with the breech in this state, and went on to say 'This should be impossible'.

Sometimes *not* is changed to *no,* a change that invests the phrase with a pawky Scottish humour.

this training really toughens you: you get muscles in your shit. A WW2 c.p. employed by the Canadian Army.

this will give you the cock-stand is a male c.p., dating since *c.* 1910, and addressed to someone to whom one has offered a drink or a special dish.

this won't buy baby (or **the baby) a frock** (or **new dress**). But this won't do! I'm wasting my time (*or* being idle): C20. Leonard Merrick uses it, in, *Peggy Harper,* 1911: 'This won't buy baby a frock.' Although with increasing rarity heard in Britain since *c.* 1940, it remained popular in Australia, as

James Aldridge mentioned to me on 19 April 1969, in the form *this won't buy the baby a frock.*

thou shalt not be found out. 'This is known as the Eleventh Commandment. Another ten can be found in *The Latest Decalogue* by Arthur Hugh Clough' (Barry Prentice, 1 May 1975): C20; very common in Australia as well as in Britain. Clough lived 1819–61.

though I say it who shouldn't; and **though I says it as shouldn't.** See **although I say it** ....

thousand strokes and a rolling suck – a. A nautical c.p. of *c.* 1870–1930; applied to a leaky ship, the pumps requiring many strokes, and sucking – an indication that she is dry – only when the ship rolls. (Bowen.)

three acres and a cow satirized baseless or excessive optimism: Ware implies that it was current in 1887–*c.*1889; but Collinson notes that it was revived *c.* 1906. The late Alexander McQueen thought it directed ironically at Joseph Chamberlain's Jesse Collings, who proposed that every smallholder should possess them – he became known as *Three Acres and a Cow Collings.* The slogan had been coined by Chamberlain himself, who may have drawn the phrase from a song popular in the 1880s. Yet another theory appears in Brewer.

three hearty British cheers! Ironical or 'grudging praise for a minor accomplishment. "I passed that exam after three goes at it." – "Three hearty British cheers"' (Barry Prentice): British and Australian: since *c.* 1930.

three is an awkward number. An ephemeral c.p. of 1885–6, arising from Lord Durham's nullity-of-marriage lawsuit (Ware). It paraphrases 'two are company; three, not'; also it's an *odd* number. Cf **two's company** ....

three more and up goes the donkey. See **donkey – a penny** ....

three on the hook, three on the book is a dockers' c.p. for half a week's work: since the 1920s (perhaps earlier). The hook is a tool of the stevedore's trade; the *book* refers to the dole.

three turns (in late C19–20, less often **two) round the long-boat and a pull at the scuttle** is a nautical c.p. (obsolescent by 1910, obsolete by 1930) that, dating from before 1867, when recorded by Admiral Smyth in his dictionary of naval language, characterizes the (avoidance of) activities of an 'artful dodger' or skrimshanker. Bowen makes, 1929, the *two turns* phrase mean 'under sail, killing time'.

three weeks indicated, 1907–*c.* 1914, a sexual adventure either culminating within, or lasting, that time. It testified to the vast popularity of Elinor Glyn's novel, *Three Weeks,* published in 1907.

throw the baby out with the bath water. See **don't throw** ....

[**throw your rubbish where you throw your love** is a half-c.p., half-proverb of C19–20. Often applied, serio-comically, to an unwanted gift. I haven't heard it since *c.* 1930.]

throws (his) money around like a man with no arms (or **hands**), not necessarily with **he** preceding. He is as tight-fisted as can be: British and Australian: since *c.* 1930. (Baker, 1959; and Laurie Atkinson.)

thumb in bum and mind in neutral. See **with thumb in bum and mind in neutral.**

ticket – it's just the; and – which see also separately – **that's**

the ticket. That is exactly what is needed, or exactly right or fitting or suitable: C19–20. Christopher Fry, on 19 December 1974, remarked of both phrases: 'Often said to me in childhood.'

tie up your stocking! No heel-taps!: University of Oxford: late C19–20; obsolescent by 1930, obsolete by 1940; Ware limits the phrase to the drinking of champagne. The semantic origination is obscure.

[**tiger in the tank – a**, has since mid-1965, been progressing from potential to virtual c.p., thanks to the oil companies', hence the petrol stations', slogan; yet not, I think, quite succeeded.]

tight as a bull's arse in fly-time and **he's so tight he squeaks** (like a pair of tight shoes). He is incredibly mean with his money: Canadian (the former line): since the early 1930s. (Douglas Leechman.)

'til (or till) death do us part. 'Possibly a c.p. [in the US] rather than a cliché, in that it is indeed sometimes used, not with reference to marriage but a (usually irksome) responsibility, or what not, that one cannot hope to escape from – e.g., a burdensome … dependant, an unwelcome … office in a society, or, somewhat different, an unconquerable addiction to drugs or drink … !' (John W. Clark, 10 December 1975.) That convinces me that, so used, it *is* a c.p. in the US: perhaps – mere guesswork, this – since *c.* 1965.

'til (or till) hell freezes over is a c.p. letter-ending: ? originally Canadian: late C19–20; little used after *c.* 1940 and, by 1975, virtually obsolete. Cf – indeed, see – **yours to a cinder**.

time and tide wait for no man – neither do Beecham's pills. A jocular c.p. of C20, but very little used since *c.* 1940. A reference to a famous laxative.

time for a shit … See shave, a shilling ….

time for your O.B.E., Neddy. A 'Goon Show c.p. uttered every so often by the villainous Grytpype-Thynne to Neddy Seagoon, as one might say "Time for your medicine". Was quite popular in the army, where people are more noticeably awarded decorations' (Paul Beale, 25 May 1975).

time, gentlemen, please – haven't any of you got a home? is often heard in public-houses when the customers are unwilling to depart: since *c.* 1925. (A correspondent; name unfortunately lost.)

time I gave it the old one-two. In *The Sense of Humour*, 1954, Stephen Potter, the man who gave us the *-manship* books, writes, concerning the landlord of a public-house:

> Every now and then he utters some of the accepted comic phrases of our age, quite isolated, quite without reference. 'Mind my bike,' he will say. Then a little later: 'Time I gave it the old one-two.'

See also **don't forget the diver**.

time on that! 'Wait a while, sir; not so fast' (Matsell): US underworld and fringe of the underworld: *c.* 1840–80.

time you had a watch! 'Sharp reply to "What time is it?"' (Frank Shaw, November 1968): C20.

Tinker to Evers to Chance is the more usual form of **from Tinker to Evers to Chance**, which, however, see.

tintype… See **not on your tintype**.

Tippecanoe and Tyler too was selected by W & F as one of

two US political slogans that have taken on a 'generalized meaning and become popular … still heard = "this is even more wonderful than I expected" or more recently, since the slogan has become so old, to = "that's very old-fashioned".'

D.Am. makes it clear that originally the phrase was a rallying cry during the Log Cabin and Hard Cider presidential campaign of 1840 and that it promptly became the refrain of a popular song; also that John Tyler was a candidate.

Cf **I like Ike**.

'tis better than a worse. It might be worse: C18. In S, 1738, Dialogue I, see:

COL[ONEL]: I'm like all Fools, I love every Thing that's good.
LADY SM[ART]: Well and isn't it pure good?
COL: 'Tis better than a worse.

Cf the next.

'tis indifferent – as Doll danced. See **'twill last as many days as nights**.

'tis only I – be not afraid has, in C20, been 'an accusation of some (minor but impudent) trespass, in the form of an excuse; meant to discomfit intruder. For example, your neighbour is in your front doorway to look at a parcel left there in [your] absence' (Laurie Atkinson, December 1968). Apparently it derives from 'It is I, be not afraid' (The New Testament, Matthew, 14, 27; Mark, 6, 50; John, 6, 20).

titter that runs through the gallery – the. 'Example of party game to express a common phrase by mime for party to guess. One of the men who knew the game went from woman to woman, touching them on their [breasts]. Film studio staff. Early 1930s.' (Laurie Atkinson, 20 March 1976.) A pun on *tit*, nipple, breast.

to coin a phrase is used ironically, to excuse and apologize for either the immediately preceding or the immediately ensuing triteness, esp. if it's a cliché; or disarmingly equivalent to 'to use a familiar, a well-known, phrase': originally US: since *c.* 1945, yet not general in Britain until the middle 1950s.

Clarence B. Kelland uses it in *No Escape*, 1951 (British edn):

'Any port in a storm,' Jonathan said.
'To coin a phrase,' said Peggy.

Noël Coward, *South Sea Bubble*, performed and published in 1956, at Act III, Scene ii, has:

PUNALO(*inexorably*): … I will show your wife's clip to the Press and, to coin a phrase, bust the works wide open.

In Britain, the phrase became, as it were, canonized when, in 1973, RS appeared, a revision and enlargement of Edwin Radford's *Encyclopedia of Phrases and Origins*, 1945.

to -er is human. 'The slurred sound of dubiety punned with *to err is human* or, in Latin, *Humanum est errare*' (Laurie Atkinson, 20 March 1976): since *c.* 1960 – or perhaps much earlier.

to hell with you, Jack, I'm all right! is a euphemistic variation of **fuck you, Jack …**.

to make a fool ask – and you are the first. S, 1738, Dialogue I, has:

NEV[EROUT]: Pray, Miss, why do you sigh?
MISS: To make a Fool ask, and you are the first.

Probably current throughout C18.

toast your blooming eyebrows!, a proletarian c.p. of *c.* 1895–1915, synonymizes the slangy *go to blazes!* – itself, clearly, a euphemism of *go to hell!* (Ware.)

[TOASTS are not strictly c.pp. and therefore excluded.]

Tom Collins – whether or no. See **whether or no**....

Tom Mix in 'Cement' was, *c.* 1938–52, a retort to 'What's on at the pictures?' A pun '*to mix...*' and '*to mix* cement'.

Tom Tit on a round of beef. A children's c.p., shouted at someone wearing a hat, or a cap, too small; also 'used of anything small on anything big, e.g. of a lonely cottage on a hill' (Peter Ibbotson, letter of 9 February 1963): C20.

TOMMY HANDLEY CATCH PHRASES; that is, the c.pp. from 'ITMA', the most famous British radio show of them all, the show that did so much for morale, both at home and abroad, during the stressful years of WW2. In 1948, Frank Worsley could truthfully write,

Many of the 'ITMA' catch-phrases have passed into the English language. They reappear in advertisements, in pantomimes – always a sure sign of a successful saying – and even as captions for cartoons. There have been several series of comic postcards, and quite recently a progressive Brighton parson advertised as the subject of his Sunday Sermon: 'What *me*, in *my* state of health!'

They will be found, separately treated, in their alphabetical order. Perhaps the best known are **after you, Claude...**; **can I do you now, sir?**; **don't forget the diver**; **Funf speaking**; **I go – I come back**; **it's being so cheerful as keeps me going**; **it's that man again**; **ta-ta for now**; **what, *me* – in *my* condition** (or **in *my* state of health)?**

The famous radio comedian, Tommy Handley (1894–1949), is remembered chiefly for his radio show 'ITMA' – 'It's That Man Again' – which ran from 19 September 1939 until his death ten years later. ITMA owed much of its vast and enduring popularity to its script writer, Ted Kavanagh, and to its producer, Frank Worsley, and to the rest of Tommy Handley's cast. Kavanagh wrote Handley's biography and Worsley the story of 'ITMA'; and both of these books were rushed out before the end of 1949. The former remarked:

The show's catch-phrases were, of course, the trade mark with which Tommy was greeted wherever he went.... Writers had to be careful not to use parallel phrases, and worse than that was to give a cue which could expect an 'ITMA' answer.

Tommy make room for your uncle! was, from 1883 (*teste* Ware) until *c.* 1940, and then (*teste* Frank Shaw) among a few oldsters right up to *c.* 1970 addressed to the youngest man in a group or to the younger man of two. From a popular song.

[**ton for ton and man for man**, 'the fair division of prizes between two ships sailing in company' (Bowen), is naval jargon, not c.p., of C19.]

tongue is hinged in the middle and he (or **she**) **talks with both ends** – **his** (or **her**). Applied to an excessively loquacious person: late C19–20.

tonight's the night! indicates the imminence of something important. Since 1913, when Miss Iris Hoey starred in a musical comedy so named; for instance, the first night of a play. In Australia it has rather tended to prophesy a successful culmination to a sexual association.

too bloody Irish (or **right**) (or **true**)! are picturesque emphasizings of the colourless *of course*. All three have been widely used throughout the C20 and probably go back to *c.* 1870 or even earlier; the first two were favourites of English soldiers in WW1 and are duly recorded by B & P.

The late Gerald Bullett (in a letter written on 22 August 1950) suggested to me that *too bloody Irish* merely extends the synonymous *too Irish* and that *too Irish* is short for *too Irish stew*, rhyming slang for *too true*; he was probably right.

too damn' tooting! Certainly: C20. In Canada, **you're damn'** (or **darn'**) **tooting**, you're absolutely right. (Douglas Leechman.) Moreover, **you're darn' tooting** is also US.

There may be a pun on *Tooting Common*, London, and *common*, general or usual.

too late! too late! is a C20 military and, by 1930, general c.p., uttered in high falsetto and with a humorously derisive inflection. It derives from the story of that luckless fellow who lost his manhood in a shark-infested sea very soon after he had summoned help.

Also **help! sharks!**, the first word spoken in a normal voice, the second in falsetto. Clearly this secondary c.p. is spoken – or, like the first, chanted – with an impressive pause between the two words.

too old and too cold is either the 'traditional domestic excuse [made] by husbands for not being more demanding' (Barry Prentice) or the customary slighting reference made by chagrined and frustrated wives 'afflicted' with such husbands: C20 and perhaps much older. Probably suggested by **not so old nor yet so cold**.

too old at forty stands in a no-man's-land corner, contiguous to famous quotation and to cliché and to c.p. Attributed to Sir William Osler (1849–1919), the famous quotation was, in the fact, 'the uselessness of men above sixty years of age', which degenerated into *too old at forty*, which, by 1925 at latest, became a cliché, and, by 1930 at latest, also a c.p. – often used jocularly.

too rich for *my* blood! Too expensive for *me!*: C20. From the literal sense of the phrase (originally, I think, *too high...*): food (or wine) too rich for one's digestion.

too right! See **too bloody Irish**.

too short for Richard – too long for Dick is a 'Yorkshire expression for *N.B.G.* [no bloody good]; said to have reference to Richard III, who was known as Crookback' (Sir Archibald (later Lord) Wavell, 1 August 1939, in a letter). But how long it has been a c.p., I simply don't know. The saying, obviously, borders on the proverbial.

too thick to drink, too thin to plough was, *c.* 1900–50, although little after 1940, used by the inhabitants of New South Wales in derision of the Yarra River, which flows through Melbourne. Part of that not entirely humorous 'war' between Sydney and Melbourne which is characterized by the complementary c.pp., **stinking Yarra** and **our 'Arbour**.

too too (or **too-too**) and **too all but**; **too utterly too** and **too utterly utter**. The first is the oldest and the only one to have survived; the second, the shortest-lived, was described by Ware as 'resulting out of *Punch's* trouvaille "too-too"', which was 'first found in *Punch* in the height of the aesthetic craze' (1881).

The third, *too utterly too*, seems to have arisen in 1882;

it certainly went close to rivalling the second for its brevity of life.

The fourth, *too utterly utter*, arose in 1883, according to Ware, who says that it was the 'final phrase resulting from the satirical use of "too-too"'; it lasted far longer than the second, and third, which hardly outlived 1884 or 1885.

James Redding Ware, it may be added, was in an excellent position to observe the speech of fashionable Society: all four phrases were originated by Society: and only the first seeped down into the next stratum.

tootle-oo! See **pip pip!**

top-hat. See **that's put the top-hat on it.**

top mate before a mess mate, a mess mate before a ship mate, a ship mate before a station mate, and a station mate before a dog – a. This naval c.p., dating since *c.* 1860, was recorded by Captain George S. MacIlwaine, RN (a sub-lieutenant in 1865 and a commander in 1879), author of 'a random assembly of notes that appeared in the *Naval Review* in 1930,' says Rear-Admiral P. W. Brock, who goes on to say: 'One has seen this with *and a dog before a soldier* added'; he calls the whole 'a common saying'. It indicates the descending order of preference in a rating's choice of associates.

top your boom! Go away: a nautical c.p., addressed to one who has 'forced his company where he was not invited' (Bowen): *c.* 1810–1910. It occurs in W. N. Glascock's *Sailors and Saints*, 1829.

[**touch pot – touch penny** is half proverb and half c.p.: mid C17–very early C20. It means 'No credit allowed' and is clearly of public-house origin. (Apperson.)]

touch wood! When intended literally, it is a superstitious cliché; when used jocularly, a c.p. Or, expressed otherwise, the proverb is *Touch wood,/It's sure to come good*; and the c.p. is *touch wood*, which can, as proverb, be short for the full version, and which, as c.p., is derivative therefrom. Both are precautionary: uttered to avert bad luck in general or to avert a reversal of the good fortune of which one has, just this moment, boasted; as in 'I've been lucky, so far – touch wood!'

For the various origins proposed for this phrase, you must consult the folklorists; the more, the greater fun. As merest layman and not all that seriously, I suggest that it originates in some half-buried myth about 'the Great God Pan', haunter of woods and forests.

Americans say *knock wood*, as in Patrick Buchanan, *A Requiem of Sharks*, 1973, with reference to the probability of a bad hurricane, '"We're betting it doesn't happen. So far it hasn't. Knock wood."'

tough shit! Bad luck!; Hard luck!: a US c.p., indicating such indifference to the misfortunes and unhappiness of others as amounts to a callous denial of aid and comfort and an equally callous withholding of all sympathy or even ordinary human compassion. W & F and *DCCU* offer no dating, but the latter states that it indicates lack of interest and sympathy in and with the problems of the addressee. My guess is that, although probably used before 1940, it didn't become a widespread c.p. until during WW2. Cf:

tough titty! A Canadian and Australian c.p., synonymous with the preceding and dating since *c.* 1930. It also has some negro use in the US, as CM shows. Frequently used ironically. Semantics: a tough teat is hard on the baby.

tra la la! – Goodbye! – was a proletarian c.p., slightly contemptuous and not too polite, of *c.* 1880–90. Ware says that it 'took its rise with a comic singer named Henri Clarke, whose speciality was imitating Parisians.... he made a great hit with it as the burden of a chorus'. One must, I think, assume that Clarke was familiar with the Fr. slang sense of *tra-la-la*, i.e. the posterior, if that be so, then the phrase approximately signified 'Kiss my arse!'

trap for young players is applied to, e.g., marriage: mostly Australian: since *c.* 1955. (Barry Prentice.)

trap is down! – the. The trick – the attempt to cheat me – has failed; It's no go: *c.* 1870–1910. An allusion to the fallen door of a trap for birds.

tray bon for the troops. Excellent; (of a girl) attractive: British Army Other Ranks': 1914–18 and then nostalgically. (B & P.) Fr. *très bon.*

trooper's horse. See **you will die....**

trot the udyju Pope o' Rome! Ware says:

This is very enigmatic English, composed of rhyming and transposition styles, and is generally used by one man to another when he wants the wife, or other feminine person, out of the way. Udyju is judy (wife) transposed [strictly, back-slanged – judy being very common for wife or mistress equally]. Pope o' Rome is rhyming for home. Cockney: *c.* 1860–1920.

true for you! has, since *c.* 1830, been an Anglo-Irish c.p. of hearty agreement with another's statement. (*OED* Supp.)

truly as I live. See **as I am honest.**

trumpeter – he would make a good. See **he would make a....**

trumpeter is dead – his (or rarely **her**). This was *c.* 1720–1940, applied either to a person boasting on a particular occasion or to an habitual boaster. Benjamin Franklin, *The Busy Body*, 1729; Grose, 1788, in the original form, *his trumpeter is dead, he is therefore forced to sound his own trumpet; DNWP.* Cf *King of Spain's trumpeter*, a braying ass: a neat pun on the pun: *Don Key* = donkey.

Although it occasionally is *my* (or *your*) *trumpeter is dead*, the *his* form is that which has most securely attained the status of c.p.

trusted alone. See **he may be....**

try a piece of sandpaper! See **get the cat to lick it off!**

try back! was, *c.* 1810–60, addressed to a person boasting. (JB.)

try some horse-muck in your shoes! Workingmen's advice to undersized boys: late C19–20. Horse-dung, often used as manure, would cause them to grow.

try that on your piano! is US and recorded by Berrey as synonymous with 'Think that over!' – but also as 'Try that!' It seems to have been current *c.* 1930–50. Cf:

try this (occasionally **this on**) **for size!**, used in horseplay, often accompanies a playful punch, and has been current since *c.* 1930. It probably derives from either drapery or hattery or shoeshop salesmen's jargon. Hence, since perhaps a decade later, it is often applied to contexts remote from horseplay:

'See whether you like this drink or cigar or book or what-have-you'; as in Miles Tripp, *Five Minutes with a Stranger*, 1971: '"I simply supply the drinks." She came across. "Try this one for size," she said.'

In the first sense, it had, *c.* 1935–50, a variant: *how's that for centre?* – perhaps originally army and derived from marksmanship. Never very widespread. I cannot remember having heard it more than once.

tune the old cow died of – the. See **that's the tune . . . .**

turn it up at that! All right, you may knock off (work) now and call it a day: naval: since *c.* 1925. 'From the "turning up" of a rope when belaying' (PGR).

twelve o'clock! It's time to be moving: working classes': *c.* 1890–1914. (Ware.) Noon being break-off time.

twenty-eighty. See **that's the old navy spirit.**

twenty-three (written **23**), **skid(d)oo!** – the full expression is, in fact, an elaboration of **23**.

O'Malley's was a real drugstore. . . . It was devoted to the preparation and dispensation of prescription drugs and those few patent medicines that retained the stodgy respectability they had acquired in the days of twenty-three skiddoo [Jack D. Hunter, *Spies Inc.*, 1969].

This phrase has caused the recorders of US speech, beginning with HLM, and esp. the chroniclers of US slang (Berrey, 1942, onwards to W & F, 1960), much trouble and caused overmuch controversy.

To clear the ground a little, *skid(d)oo* derives from – and, in the imperative, synonymizes – *skedaddle*, to depart in haste or with at least an unseemly alacrity.

The earliest possible explanation I've seen is that advanced by Frank Parker Stockbridge (*teste* an editorial in the Louisville *Times* of 9 May 1929): that *twenty-three* or *23*

was launched by *The Only Way*, a dramatization of Dickens's *Tale of Two Cities*, presented by Henry Miller in New York in 1899. In the last act an old woman counted the victims of the guillotine, and Sydney Carton was the twenty-third. According to Stockbridge, her solemn 'Twenty-three!' was borrowed by Broadway, and quickly became popular. He says *skiddoo* . . . was 'added for the enlightenment of any who hadn't seen the play'. [HLM, definitive edn, 1936.]

W & F quote C. T. Ryan as writing in *American Speech*, 1926,

[Approximately twenty-five years ago] appeared in my vocabulary that effective but horrible '23-Skiddoo'. Pennants and arm bands at shore resorts, parks and county fairs, bore either [23] or the word 'Skiddoo'. In time the numerals became synonymous with and connotative of the whole expression.

W & F themselves define the full phrase as, on the one hand, 'a mild expression of recognition, incredulity, surprise, or pleasure, as at something remarkable or attractive'; and as, on the other, 'an expression of rejection or refusal' – or, of course, mere dismissal, whether literal ('Run away' – 'Beat it') or figurative ('I don't care').

W & F then supply an invaluable gloss: 'Like "shoo-fly", "twenty-three skiddoo" was often used without specific meaning. It was in male use *c.* 1900–*c.*1910, originally among students and sophisticated young adults. It was perhaps the first truly national fad expression and one of the most popu-

lar fad expressions to appear in the US.' They add that 'Ironically it is now associated with the 1920s and is frequently used to convey the spirit of the 1920s in novels and plays of the period'; they also note that, even in 1960, although no longer much used, it was still very widely remembered and understood.

Valuable as their entry is (what, indeed, should we in Britain do without it?), it can be enlarged and perhaps slightly modified.

Opinions, even among the at least apparently well-informed, differ. For instance, Joe Laurie, Jr, in *Vaudeville from the Honky-Tonks to the Palace*, 1953, writes: 'Tom Lewis, the man who originated the catchword "Twenty-three" (they added skiddoo to it later) in George M. Cohan's *Little Johnny Jones* [produced in 1904], was an old-time trouper from "Frisco".' (With thanks to W. J. Burke.)

The phrase, either in its full form or in one of its two shorter forms, remained popular until *c.* 1914 at least. In *The Pedagogical Seminary* of March 1912, A. H. Melville, analysing the slang expressions common at a school, finds that, there, *skiddoo* is very widely employed, but *twenty-three, skiddoo*, never.

In 1910, Oliver Herford and John Cecil Clay, in *Cupid's Cyclopedia*, have, under S, this passage: 'Poor Adam! (Poor Us!!!) There confronting him was this word in fresh bright paint, "SKYDDU". That night it rained. Oh, how it rained!'. (Here, painfully obvious, SKYDDU is a pun on *skiddoo* and *sky-dew*.)

In 1908, John Kendrick Bangs, author of that at one time world-famous *Houseboat on the Styx*, had written, in *Potted Fiction* (chapter VI, 'The Last Secret'): 'I am a Bravado, and our motto is "Sempre Bravado Sic Non Skiddoo".'

Still earlier, Bert Leston Taylor and W. C. Gibson had, in *Extra Dry*, 1906, in 'The Rime of the Water Wagon Mariner' (in part, a parody of Coleridge's poem), lyricized thus:

Hast thou the price, O Wedding Guest?
I know an onyx bar –
'Skiddoo!' replied the Wedding Guest,
And caught a Broadway car.

Much later than *c.* 1900–10 comes this illuminating example from Lyle Stuart, *The Secret Life of Walter Winchell*, 1953, in reference, it would seem, to the year 1923:

He was fast talking and persuasive. He snooped. He listened. But most of the time he talked.
'Listen, kiddo, how would you like to have your picture in *Vaudeville News*?' he would say.
'Twenty-three, skiddoo,' might be the response. [Here = run away and don't bother me.]

In 1958, Clarence Budington Kelland, in *Where There's Smoke*, writes, in a manner implying that the phrase now belonged only to the older generation: '"You will leave the dishes," her father said in a voice of command. And then with ill-simulated humour, "Twenty-three, skidoo with ye."'

In 1967, Jack D. Hunter – I can't resist quoting him again – writes in *One of Us Works for Them*: 'I would have been very angry if I hadn't felt the sudden, heady realization that today was someday, now was the hour, no time like the present, first things first, live today for today, and twenty-three skidoo. I quit.'

To serve as a comment on the mistaken belief that the phrase belonged peculiarly to the 1920s, the lively little book

EJ, published in the US in (note the date) 1972, begins the second chapter ('Some Words Die Young; Others Just Hang Around') thus: 'About fifty years ago the "in" groups frequently used such expressions as *twenty-three skiddoo* and *vo-dee-o-do*.... Expressions like *so's your old man* and *oh, you kid* lingered late into the thirties and died.'

It is, I think, relevant to quote from Dr Douglas Leechman, who, in January 1969, wrote: 'It was much used just before WW1, especially in US'– and thus he implied a limited Canadian currency. 'I believe it to be part of a long-forgotten telegraphic code, devised by one Phillips. Numbers took the place of frequently used phrases: thus, 30 meant "the end" and still appears on MSS; 23 meant "Away with you!" and 73, "best regards".' This code meaning of 23 could, just possibly, have been a contributory factor.

There are c.pp. serious; there are c.pp. semi-serious; there are c.pp. trivial; and there are c.pp. both trivial and either very silly or almost meaningless: proudly at the crest of the third group stands *twenty-three, skiddoo* as the finest of all US examples.

twice removed from Wigan is a disparaging c.p., used, since *c.* 1920, to describe Lancashire (hence, loosely, also Yorkshire) people living permanently in the south of England.

twiggez-vous? – also written **twiggy-vous** (or **voo**)? Do you 'twig' or understand?: *c.* 1892–1930. Kipling, in *Stalky & Co.*, 1899, has:

     'Twiggez-vous?'
     'Nous twiggons.'

(But *nous twiggons*, we twig, did not catch on.) From slang 'to *twig*'; on the analogy of Fr. *comprenez-vous*? For the form, cf **squattez-vous**; for the sense, cf the WW1 'Hobson-Jobson' *compree*?, do you understand?

But, in a letter dated 25 May 1949, Leslie Verrier, MRCS, wrote to me thus enlighteningly: 'I suspect that by the time it had filtered down to Kipling's schoolboys, it was rather *vieux jeu* in the metropolis. It may have originated in the song of Marie Lloyd by whom it was first popularized in 1892.'

'twill last as many days as nights is a characteristic C18 c.p., evasive and intentionally unhelpful; the vague general meaning is, 'for a (short) while', as in S, 1738, Dialogue I:

     MISS: See, Madam, how well I have mended it.
     LADY SM[ART]: 'Tis indifferent, as *Doll* danc'd.
     NEV[EROUT]: 'Twill last as many Days as Nights.

twinges round hinges through binges 'refers to "the screws" [rheumatism] – and one cause [thereof]' (A. B. Petch, 16 September 1974): since *c.* 1950.

two brothers alive and one married (as good as dead) was an ephemeral c.p., current in 1897 and adopted from a music-hall 'gag'. (Ware.)

two cents' worth – put in one's. One's opinion or advice, for what it's worth – the implication being that it's worth precisely that; whence, loosely, an idle remark, also an unasked comment: US, hence also, since *c.* 1945, Canadian. I have no earlier record than 1942, Berrey offering the variant *one's nickel's worth*, which doesn't seem to have lasted very well.

But clearly this is a c.p. only in the forms, *must you put in your two cents' worth?* or **who asked you to put in ...?**

two eyes upon ten fingers. See **two upon ten**.

two for the price of one is 'said when a man marries a fat girl or woman' (A. B. Petch, 30 March 1976): mostly lower-middle class and public house: C20.

two hands for the King (or **the Queen**). See **one hand for** ....

two heads are better than one – even if one is only a sheep's head. This c.p. is directed at or, usually, addressed to the second party to a plan or an undertaking; often in retort to the trite or proverbial *two heads are better than one*: C20, but perhaps going back to 1890 or even 1880.

two inches beyond upright was, *c.* 1900–14, applied to a hypocritical liar. Ware classifies it as 'People's' – that is, proletarian. He adds: 'Perversion of description of upright-standing man, who throws his head back beyond upright.'

two other fellows from Poona or, in full, **it must have been** .... A serio-comic denial of association, as, e.g., by one of two men seen drinking together or acting suspiciously: since *c.* 1910; but after *c.* 1960, *from Poona* has often been omitted. It occurs allusively in 'It Must Have Been Two Other Fellows' – the opening story in Len Deighton's *Declaration of War*, 1971, with its key passage: 'The Colonel still looked puzzled and Wool said, "Oh, well, it must have been two other fellows, eh?" He laughed and repeated his joke slowly.' The 'two other fellows' in this story were the two soldiers, Colonel and Lance-Corporal of twenty-five years earlier – so different, so (in some ways) superior to their present selves: in short, two other fellows.

Poona implies the old Regular Indian Army; a famous station.

two pun ten. See **two upon ten**.

two to one against you. The odds are very much against you getting your pledge back: a proletarian c.p. of *c.* 1890–1914 (Ware). A reference to the pawnbrokers' sign: two blue balls over one.

two upon ten, often corrupted to **two pun ten**; in full, **two eyes upon ten fingers**. A trade c.p., dating since *c.* 1850. Hotten, 1860, explains the saying thus: 'When a supposed thief is present, one shopman asks the other if that *two pun* (pound) *ten* matter was ever settled.' The full expression generated the short.

two white, two red, and after you with the blacking brush! Hence, **after you, miss, with the two two's and the two b's.** A London streets' c.p., addressed to a female excessively rouged and powdered: the 1860s. (Ware.) Two dabs of red, two of white, and a brush to tidy and heighten the eyebrows.

two with you! suggests a twopenny drink: common in taverns, inns, other drinkeries, of *c.* 1885–1914. (Ware, who intimately knew his London and its lighter side.)

[**two's company, but three's a crowd** is British, and Australian proverb (late C19–20) rather than a c.p.: it answers to the obsolete English proverb, *two is company, but three is none*, recorded by *ODEP*. (Barry Prentice, 1 May 1975.)]

Twyford. See **my name is Twyford**.

typical naval argument: assertion, flat contradiction, personal abuse – a. A naval officers' c.p. of Service, and self, criticism: since *c.* 1930. (Rear-Admiral P. W. Brock, in letter dated 1 February 1969. He queries the '*c.* 1930': the c.p. might, he thinks, have arisen a little earlier – or a trifle later.)

[**ugly as homemade sin**. CM says: 'An abusive remark' – without dating or gloss. A borderline case.]

umpah, umpah, stick it up your jumpah (or written as pronounced i.e. **oompah, oompah, stick it up your joompah**)!: q.v.

umpire .... See **how's that, umpire?**

unbounded assortment of gratuitous untruths – an, was a Parliamentary c.p. of late 1885–mid 1886. Ware glosses it as 'extensive systematic lying' and derives it 'from speech (11 November 1885) of Mr Gladstone's at Edinburgh'. Cf Lord Randolph Churchill's justly famous definition of a lie as a 'terminological inexactitude'.

uncle. See **he has gone to visit his uncle** and **keep your eye on uncle**.

Uncle Joe is much improved. He's – hence I'm – feeling much better, business or things are going much better: since *c.* 1930. Prompted by the 'improved' of an invalid's health and also by the second line of a raffish, once roguish, couplet, 'Since he had his balls removed'.

under the bunk! Shut up! (esp. at night): US convicts': since *c.* 1920. As if 'Get under your bunk and keep quiet!'

unrelieved holocaust – an, was a Society c.p. of 1883 and applied to even a minor accident. Ware tells us that it was occasioned by its use by a writer in *The Times* to describe the destruction (1882) of the Ring Theatre in Vienna and of a circus at Berditscheff in Russia, both fires being accompanied by a heavy loss of life.

up a — 's arse, and don't be (so bloody) nosey! 'A schoolboy's answer to the question, "Where is it?"' (Wilfred Granville, 7 January 1969): late C19–20. The juvenile version, which omits *so bloody*, derives from the male, adult, proletarian, mostly North Country version – the longer one; this latter version is also a reply to the more specific question, 'Where did you get that thing?'; neither has been much heard since *c.* 1960.

up a shade, Ada! has since *c.* 1950 in the RAF, espl while it was stationed in Malta, been an appeal for more room ('Move up a bit there!'). Hence, also applied to a noisy collision between two persons.

up against you. See **that's up** ....

up Alice's. A 'teasing evasion of questions such as "where did you get to last night?" – "You going out this evening?" Originally, and still mostly, North Country: since *c.* 1910, ?ten or twenty years earlier. (Laurie Atkinson, late 1974.) Not 'up at' nor 'along to', but 'up Alice's [vagina]'.

up and down like a fiddler's elbow is a lower-middle-class c.p. of late (? mid) C19–20 and applied to anyone very restless. Contrast the next two.

up and down like a shit-house seat was a Canadian Army c.p.

of WW2 and referred to a gambler's luck. (Douglas Leechman.) Contrast the preceding and the following c.p.

up and down like Tower Bridge is a Cockney c.p. of late C19–20. It has a 'scabrous innuendo' and is used 'in response to *How goes it?*' (Laurie Atkinson). Contrast the two c.pp. preceding this.

up and down – mind the dresser. A C20 Anglo-Irish c.p. employed of a party held at a farmer's house. (The dresser is, of course, the piece of furniture, not a person.)

up goes McGinty's goat. Things become exciting, e.g. as at a great explosion: ?originally Anglo-Irish: probably latish C19–mid C20. In William Guy Carr's *Brass Hats and Bell-Bottomed Trousers*, 1939, but valid for the Royal Navy throughout WW1, we read that an enemy shell lands 'kerplunk' among a cluster of British lyddite shells 'and up goes McGinty's goat'. Cf **down went McGinty**.

up, Guards, and at 'em! is a c.p. of light-hearted or, at the least, nonchalant defiance, virtually synonymous with **let 'em all come!**: late C19–20. Based upon a famous quotation that is almost certainly apocryphal: in 1852, when asked what he had, in the fact, said at the Battle of Waterloo (22 June 1815), the Duke of Wellington replied to the anecdotist J. W. Croker: 'What I must have said and possibly did say was, Stand up, Guards! and then gave the commanding officers the order to attack.' (*ODQ*.) By 'what I must have said', he clearly meant 'If I said anything, it would have been "Stand up, Guards!"' Nevertheless, there is no need to deny that *up, Guards, and at 'em* long ago achieved full c.p. status.

up, guards, and atap! According to H. W. Fowler and I. P. Watt, in an excellent article published in a ship's news-sheet of late 1945, among WW2 prisoners of war – in the Far East, 'Our officers spurred themselves to greater efforts in hut-building with the cry, "Up guards and atap!" [*Note*. All our huts were atap-roofed].' A debonair pun on **up, Guards, and at 'em!** Also note that *atap* is a Malayan word for thatch made from napa palm leaves.

up in Annie's room. An Army c.p., slightly preceding WW1, but at its height during it, in answer to 'Where's so-and-so?' – esp. to an enquiring sergeant or corporal. In contrast to the sombre **hanging on the (old) barbed wire** and – originally, at least – implying that the sought one was 'a bit of a lad with the girls'. Hence, a double in the game of darts.

Often shortened to *in Annie's room*, as F & G tell us. Occasional variant: **Nellie's**, as B & P inform us.

up she comes and the colour's red is an exclamation uttered at a favourable turn of events, notably if the opposition suddenly collapses or an obstacle is unexpectedly removed: since *c.* 1945 or perhaps ten years earlier. Presumably from gambling.

up Shit Creek (or, euphemistically, **up the creek**; or even, derivatively, **up the well-known creek**) **without a paddle**: after *c.*

1950, occasionally **... with a broken paddle**, which last I've never heard since *c.* 1960.

A C20 saying, perhaps originally naval; certainly, by *c.* 1920, RAF; and, by *c.* 1945, very widely used. Originally it denoted a being badly off course, with ne'er a paddle to steer by; hence, lost and in bad trouble; hence in bad trouble and no discernible or expectable relief at hand.

On 9 November 1969, concerning US usage, John W. Clark wrote to me: 'Sometimes, among people not acquainted with the full form, "up the creek".' In 1942, Berrey had listed *up salt creek* (but not *up Shit Creek*) and synonymized it with 'in a predicament'. In 1960, W & F remarked that 'Although the shortened form "up the creek" is common, the full original term is seldom heard now' and glossed it as 'Originally from homosexual usage' – which may or may not be true of US usage, but is not, I believe, true of British usage.

up there, Cazaly! was, *c.* 1930–50, an Australian, but esp. a Melbourne, cry of encouragement. Baker, 1943, writes: 'Cazaly was a noted South Melbourne footballer, whose speciality was high marking.' (Australian Rules Football, of course.)

[**up to you for the rent!**; **up you!** (Australian **upya!**); **up your** (this or that)! are not true c.pp. but mere verbal violences.]

up, up, up! See **get off and milk it!**

up with petticoats, down with drawers! It originated in a ribald couplet, dating since *c.* 1905. I first heard it, 1913, in Australia, but common in Britain too (*teste* Laurie Atkinson, late 1974). Often a 'dare' among mixed company friends in raffish or bibulous mood, often followed by the second line, 'you tickle mine and I'll tickle yours'.

up you go with the best of luck! 'The MO's benediction when sending you up the line after hospital' (B & P, 1931): British Army: WW1. Inevitably it incurred the odium of the soldier's derision.

upside down in cloud. 'Abbreviated version of "There we were, upside down in cloud, fuck-all on the clock, and still climbing" – commonly used to check line-shooters' (boasters): RAF operational: 1940–5. (Wing-Commander R. P. McDouall, in letter dated 12 April 1945, while I was on 'the Writers' Team' in Public Relations at the Air Ministry.)

[**use your loaf!** – Use your head (*loaf of bread*, rhyming slang) or intelligence – has, since the mid 1940s, been so common as to cause me to wonder: but no! However popular, it's still ordinary slang.]

[**used to was.** Used to be: mostly Australian: *c.* 1910–50. But mutable. Not a true c.p.]

usual speech not required was, *c.* 1870–1920, a British underworld c.p., tantamount to 'No bill!' in reference to the verdicts 'Guilty' or 'Not guilty'. (Clarkson and Hall, *Police!*, 1889.)

VR – VR – VR was, at the time of Queen Victoria's Diamond Jubilee, June 1897, a Cockney c.p. It punned on *ve are, ve are, ve are*, we are (thrice), and *VR*, Victoria Regina. (Ware.)

vas you dere, Sharlie? 'A radio comedian who called himself Baron Munchausen told tall stories to a "straight man" (Charlie), who expressed doubt. This was the gag line. It became popular for a while – if anyone expressed any doubt or scepticism, you said "Vas you dere, Sharlie?" in the 1930s' (Professor Emeritus F. E. L. Priestley, concerning its Canadian usage). Berrey records its American usage.

ve haf vays and means to make you talk, sometimes 'anglicized' – somewhat stupidly – **we have ways and means to make you talk**. 'Said always in a sinister mock-German accent to represent all the Gestapo films, Colditz, TV Series, etc. It gets misapplied and is quite general and popular' (Paul Beale, 7 May 1975). As a c.p. from (say) 1950 onwards. But note that 'it is also featured in the TV comedy show "Laugh-In" – as famous there [the US] as **very interesting**' (Patricia Newnham, March 1976).

veal will be cheap – calves fall. A jeering reference to a spindle-legged person: mid C16–18. (Ray, 1678; Apperson.)

venture it as Johnson did his wife. See **I'll venture it**.

very good question – a: See **that's a good question**, but add that in *The American Dream*, 1961, Edward Albee wrote thus:

MOMMY: Are you in the habit of receiving boxes?

DADDY: A very good question.

very identical thing – the! Just what I needed; exactly what I wanted; yes, *that's* what I asked for, or sought: c. 1830–90. J. E. Carpenter, *Love and Honour, or, Soldiers at Home – Heroes Abroad; an Original Domestic Drama*, performed in 1855, has at Act I, Scene i:

BOLUS: This, gentlemen, I assure you is –

BRIEF: [*Drinking.*] The very identical thing!

This c.p. occurs many times in the play; always used by lawyer Briefwit. To me, it sounds like an echo of Dickens – ?Sam Weller.

very interesting! 'A few years ago,' wrote Vernon Noble in a letter dated 18 January 1974,

an American comedy show – very successful on TV in the States – was shown weekly by BBC. It was called 'Rowan and Martin's Laugh-In'. A character in it, Arte [*sic*] Johnson (usually dressed incongruously as a German soldier) would exclaim 'Ver-rr-y interesting!' This became [in Britain] a catch-phrase introduced inconsequentially and [it] lingered for a few months after the series ended.

The pronunciation was *vairee* – with a Ger. accent.

very like a whale! was, in mid C19–early C20, applied to a very improbable, esp. to a preposterous, statement. Hotten recorded it in 1859 and, in his 2nd edn, 1860, noted the variant, *very like a whale in a tea-cup*, which seems to have lasted for no more than a decade. From Polonius's phrase uttered while doing his best (*Hamlet*, Act III, Scene ii, lines 392–8) to show a sycophantic approval of Hamlet's deliberately far-fetched similes.

very nice too! – often preceded by **and**; with emphasis on *too* and with the connotation, 'Well! Aren't you (isn't he, etc.) – *lucky!*' As in '"He's just come into a fortune." – "Very nice too!"' To a girl suddenly discovered in a state of entire or partial nudity, the polite man will say '(And) very nice too!': almost, in such contexts, a formula of courtesy. The phrase goes back to c. 1920 at least and probably much earlier.

very tasty – very succulent! was, c. 1948–57, an Australian c.p., popularized by the Australian comedian known as 'Mo'. (*AS*.) It elaborates:

very tasty – very sweet! was extremely popular in Britain during WW2, when precious things *were*! By 1965, obsolete – except as a rather self-conscious piece of nostalgia among older people. Yet it must be noted that as an erotic c.p., existing since c. 1900 (if not earlier), it is still very common.

villain. See **I am as mild a villain ....**

vim, vigor, and vitality. See the more usual form **wim ....**

Virgin for short but not for long is a humorous C20 c.p., applied, punningly, to girls forenamed *Virginia*.

vive la différence! 'A c.p. used when someone has just said that there is hardly any difference between men and women' (Barry Prentice): since 1919 or 1920. An adaptation rather than a simple adoption of the Ff. male toast.

To show how easy it is to err in 'coverage', another correspondent writes (4 January 1974): 'Heard when somebody mentions that women are [in temperament] different from men.'

vo-dee-o-do. See **twenty-three, skiddoo**, penultimate paragraph. Perhaps influenced by *vodudobo*, a curse, a word used in the Gullah – a negro – dialect of the Georgia and South Carolina coasts (Dr Lorenzo Turner, as glossed by HLM, Supp, 2, pp. 265–7); almost certainly, *vo-dee-o-do* (often written *vodeodo*) has been chosen for its abracadabraic qualities.

vote early and often. 'A c.p. used early in this century by political stalwarts. An indication that moral standards have risen in at least one area' (Barry Prentice, c. 15 December 1974): Australian.

vote for Boyle! According to PGR,

[A] catch phrase after the fall of Tunis [1943]. Hal Boyle, of the Associated Press, drove into Tunis chanting 'Vote for Boyle, son of the soil: Honest Hal, the Arabs' pal'. The Arabs, with their usual facility for picking up a phrase without knowing the meaning, puzzled the troops by greeting them with this cry, which they in turn adopted.

British Army in North Africa: 1943–4.

voulez-vous squattez-vous? Will you sit down?: since c. 1820;

by *c.* 1940, decidedly obsolescent; yet, even by 1975, not completely obsolete. 'Started by [the world-famous clown] Grimaldi,' says Ware. Not, you'll notice, *squatter*; and cf **squat-tez-vous!**

vy! vot a cake [= fool] **I've been!** appeared – Frank Shaw vouched on 1 September 1969 – in the Comic Calendar of 1841. Probably occasioned by some public event and probably ephemeral.

wait and see! Although probably used twenty or thirty years earlier, it became a general c.p. in March–April 1910 when Asquith employed it in reference to the date for the reintroduction of Lloyd George's rejected budget. Asquith was himself, 1910 onwards, called *Old Wait and See* and, on the Western Front, 1914–18, French matches, so often failing to ignite, were called *wait-and-sees*. (Eric Partridge, *A Covey of Partridge*, 1933.)

wait for it! – properly, the phrase is rapidly repeated, as in the Coward quotation below. If it derives from the army's *wait for it!*, wait for the word of command (e.g., to fix bayonets), it dates, as a c.p., since the latter part of WW1; if, however, it has a music-hall origin, the c.p. may go back to late C19.

In *Red Peppers*, written *c.*1935 and published in 1936, Noël Coward offers – immediately after 'Refrain 1' in the first dialogue, this vastly convenient example:

GEORGE: I saw a very strange thing the other day.
LILY: What was it?
GEORGE: Twelve men standing under one umbrella and they didn't get wet.
LILY: How's that?
GEORGE: It wasn't raining. (Wait for it – wait for it.)

That is, wait for the laughter to end before you resume the dialogue.

wait for your round! A theatrical c.p. of very approximately 1880–1940: Michael Warwick, in an article entitled 'Theatrical Jargon of the Old Days' in the *Stage*, 3 October 1968; says:

Actor-proof parts could always be recognized by the number of laughs or rounds of applause in any given scene, and the term 'wait for your round' is dated as the Dodo. But in the old days anyone killing a 'round' by coming in too quickly with their lines came in for some crushing criticism. The same principle applied to laughs.

wait till the clouds roll by! Inducive of optimism: 1884, Ware tells us; by 1915 it had become proverbial. Ware also tells us that it came 'from an American ballad'.

wake up and smell the coffee! Of this US c.p., Professor John W. Clark wrote, on 5 December 1968: 'Not, I think, in origin an advertising slogan. A derisive way of saying "You're dreaming" or "You're not facing the facts" or "You might as well be asleep". Fifteen or twenty years old, I should say, though possibly much older.' Perhaps, however, prompted by various aromatic-chromatic advertisements by coffee manufacturers.

wake up, England! is a 'c.p. used by anyone cross with himself for not seeing at once something fairly obvious. Variant: "Wake up [name], England needs you"' (Paul Beale, 6 July 1974): since *c.*1920.

wakey, wakey! Literally, as used in C20 by Services' noncoms, it obviously isn't a c.p.; but it inevitably became one. Deriving from the nursery, it was originally neither tender nor affectionate, despite its intentionally heavy irony when it was used by those good-humouredly bossy fellows.

Since *c.*1945, it has, partly because popularized by Billy Cotton, been very widely used figuratively in civilian contexts and not necessarily by ex-Servicemen: where the persons addressed merely seem to be asleep or are extremely slow in moving along or in getting something done. An elaborated version (I must admit that *I* never heard it in the army, 1940–2, nor in the RAF, 1942–5) was

Wakey, wakey, rise and shine!
Don't you know it's morning time?

walk, knave, walk! was, in C16–17, a c.p. taught to parrots – presumably in order to vex all who passed by. Apperson cites, e.g., 'Proverbs' Heywood, 1546; Lyly; 'Hudibras' Butler; The Roxburgh *Ballads*, *c.*1685.

Walker! See **Hooky Walker!** and **my name's Walker.**

Walker, London 'seems to have been a derisive street cry, like **get yer 'air cut**, of London street arabs; after, I think, a business's signpost. J. M. Barrie used it in *Walker, London*, "a farcical comedy in three acts", published in 1921. Could be associated with *make yer name Walker*, q.v.' (Frank Shaw, early November 1968).

walker – that's a. See **Hooky Walker!**

Walls have ices was, *c.*1930–45, a c.p. retort to *walls have ears* (very common as a government slogan in WW2), the reference being to the London firm of Walls, famous makers of sausages, and musically inclined vendors of ice-creams. Sometimes the c.p. ran: *walls have ears and sell ice-creams.* During the war years of 1942–5, there existed a jocular variation (still remembered, although hardly used, by a few): *walls have ears and ice cream*, which refers to a famous spy-slogan and puns on the firm's name. But all three forms were somewhat obsolescent by the late 1960s and virtually obsolete by the middle 1970s.

wanna buy a battleship? is a slovened version of **want to buy a battleship?**, q.v. at **do you want … ?**

wanna buy a duck? 'It was a catch phrase coined, *c.*1933, by a leading radio comedian named Joe Penner during the late 30s. Everyone [*c.*1933–5] repeated it, although I doubt if anybody ever attached meaning to the phrase. Does a catch phrase have to have precise meaning?' (Norris M. Davidson in letter dated 3 November 1968). The answer to his question is NO.

want to bet on it? (or **do you want … ?** or **you want … ?**) – with *bet* emphasized. Are you so sure that you'll bet on it?: since *c.*1945. See, e.g., Berkeley Mather, *The Terminators*, 1971: 'He was good, but not that damned good, I told him. "Does the sahib ever value his house, his cattle and his wife?" which is the Pathan way of saying, "You want to bet on it?"'

want to borrow something? A short form of **do you want to borrow something?**

want to buy a battleship? See **do you want to buy a battleship?**

want to make something of it? is a threatening response to criticism or insult: since *c.* 1925. Implying a readiness to punch the other fellow's nose. (Laurie Atkinson.) A neat example occurs early in Act II of John Mortimer's witty *Collaborators*, produced and published in 1973:

> SAM: All right, Hank. Where were you raised?
> HENRY: The rough end of Godalming. Want to make something of it?

wanted as much as a dog (or **a toad**) **wants a side-pocket** was, mid C18–early C20, applied to one who wants (desires) something he doesn't need. Grose, 1785, *toad*, and 2nd edn, 1788, *dog* and *as much need of a wife as a dog of a side-pocket*; Arthur Quiller-Couch ('Q'), 1888, has: 'A bull's got no more use for religion than a toad for side-pockets.' (Apperson.)

wants his liver scraping! – occasionally with **he** prefixed – has, by the army, been applied throughout C20 to a superior who's in a particularly vile temper. (B & P.)

[**'ware skins, quoth Grubber, when he flung the louse into the fire** lies on the border between proverbial saying and c.p.: mid C17–mid C18. (Apperson.)]

warm in winter and cool in summer is an Australian c.p., applied to women *qua* physical contacts: since *c.* 1940. (Barry Prentice.) The origin, as Norman Franklin has proposed, could reside in the Aertex slogan of the 1930s.

was my face red? See **is my face red?**

was your father a glazier (later, **glassmaker**)? See **glazier ... ?**

wash and brush-up tuppence was, *c.* 1885–1915, a humorously muttered lower-middle-class comment made by host to friend about to wash his hands in the former's house.

watch how you go! (Whence, at first loosely and then usually, the weaker **mind how you go!**) Look after yourself, be very careful: common in the Services since the earlyish 1930s, but not in widespread general use until the late 1940s.

watch it! Be careful you're running a risk: since the 1920s. (Peter Sanders, 27 November 1968.) Probably short for 'I'd watch it (*or* watch out) if I were you'. Cf:

watch my dust (or **smoke** or **speed**)! All three are US (Berrey records them as boasts): the first is the commonest; the third the least used, and rare since *c.* 1960; the second is also British – and seems to be of nautical origin, whereas the first seems to refer to the dust raised by the hooves of a galloping horse. Both the first and the second probably go back to late C19.

watch out for the golden rivet is a homosexual c.p. that has developed from *Go and find* (or *look for*) *the golden rivet*, 'an order given to a Merchant Navy first-voyager ... he'd be sent to more and more inaccessible places in search of this non-existent treasure' (Mr G. P. B. Naish, a noted naval historian, in a letter dated 12 March 1975 and written to Rear-Admiral P. W. Brock, who passed it on to me). Nobody seems to know quite when the c.p. arose.

But the phrase has other senses: and I cannot do better than to quote from Cyril Whelan's letter of 25 March 1975.

Seemingly it shows up most often as a jokey and tradi-tional valediction (*watch out for the golden rivet*) as the ship leaves the quay-side – but has a far wider allusive application.

My own suspicion is that reference to a golden rivet is sufficiently unexpected and bluntly esoteric to make it a powerful emblem of the user's length of service and knowledge of the ropes.... Because of this the phrase has, I suspect, acquired the real function of stamping the user as party to all the secrets and all the inner mysteries of life on board and is used literally self-consciously for that purpose.

watch the dicky bird! In Britain, Australia and New Zealand (I distinctly remember it being successfully addressed to my brothers and myself in 1901, in Gisborne, New Zealand) – since late C19–20 – a 'photographers' c.p. used when photographing children, so that they will be gazing at the camera lens with a bright, expectant look' (Barry Prentice).

watch your pockets, lads! is a humorous, unmalicious c.p., directed at any new arrival; mostly among workmen and WW1 British soldiers: C20.

watch your step! is an occasional variant of **mind the step!**, q.v.

watch your uncle! See **keep your eye on uncle.**

water's wet – **the**. A jocular, mock-helpful c.p., addressed to someone trying – at bath side or beach side – the temperature of the water with his toes: late C19–20. Probably to be included among the small stock of domestic phrases.

we aim to please, as in ' "That's very good of you, Bill." – "We aim to please," said I modestly', dates from the 1930s at the latest. From the newspaper advertisements and the brochures of travel agencies, employment bureaux, the great stores. In that slogan used jocularly as a c.p., the 'we' is humorously royal.

we ain't got much money, but we do see life! – often shortened to **we do see life!** and comparable with **this is the life!**: C20. In 1931, the Rev. Desmond Morse Boycott adopted it as the title for his book about tramps. Cf **we don't get much money ... and contrast:**

we are all born and we are none buried. ' "All right, you bas-tard, there's plenty of time to get my own back!" Used by Cockneys and others since before 1910.... I've seldom heard it since WW2, but when I was a kid [he was born in 1900] even schoolboys used it' (Julian Franklyn, 21 May 1968). I long wondered whether this were a proverb, but, all the appropriate dictionaries ignoring it, I've concluded that this was a true c.p. Not, I think, since *c.* 1970.

we are coming, Father Abraham, three hundred thousand more (or later, occasionally **strong**) 'During our Civil War, President [Abraham] Lincoln called for more volunteers for the Union Army after heavy losses to the Confederates at Bull Run and elsewhere. James Sloan Gibbins wrote a poem entitled "Three Hundred Thousand More", which was published in the *New York Evening Post* 18 July 1862. It began "We are coming, Father Abraham, three hundred thousand more". It passed into popular speech and was a morale builder, is still current in a situation calling for announced determination to support a person or a cause. Intended as a rallying slogan, it was to a considerable degree a c.p. and has remained one.' (W. J. Burke, 8 March 1976.)

we are just good friends. See **we're just ....**

we are not amused. Queen Victoria's famous snub has, in C20, been on the verge – has it not rather gone over it? – of becoming a c.p., as Vernon Noble reminded me on 12 February 1974. On the occasion of a private Palace soirée, when the Hon. Alexander Grantham Yorke, groom-in-waiting to Her Majesty, did an imitation of her. In imperial Russia he would soon have found himself banished to farthest Siberia.

we are the Ovaltineys was originally the title of a song that, on Radio Luxemburg (1930s), advertised Ovaltine. It became a c.p., mostly in the form of a chanting by children making fun of a noisy group: approximately 1936–40. (Frank Shaw, 25 October 1968.)

[**we breathe again** and, less commonly, **we live again** are partly clichés and partly c.pp. – the latter, only when used ironically and with a playful exaggeration: predominantly Australian and dating since *c.* 1920. (Barry Prentice, *c.* 15 December 1974.)]

we can (or **will**) **live with it.** See **we will live with it.**

we do get them! We *do* see some very odd people: since *c.* 1870 (mere guesswork). Cf **we've got a right 'un 'ere!**

we do see life! See **we don't get much money ....**

we don't get much money – but we do see life! 'First War [WW1] catch phrase meaning much the same as the Second War's [WW2's] *never a dull moment.* It was usually uttered in the middle of any form of panic or *flap* and was mainly of wardroom usage' (*Sailors' Slang*).

But, since the early 1930s, the predominant form has been *we haven't got much money, but we do see life!*: '[At first] said of jollification with "booze", piano and singing in poorer quarters of Edwardian London; almost certainly late Victorian [in origin]' (Laurie Atkinson, 18 July 1975).

we don't want to lose you – but we think you ought to go comes from a WW1 popular song, which faded out, even among civilians, soon after it and which, during it, had caused much ribaldry and – often bitter – irony among those who went, many of them never to return.

we had dozens of these, usually with an expletive preceding *dozens.* 'Like **who got yer** (or **you**) **ready?** and **does your mother know you're out?**, this is a deflating c.p.: C20' (Frank Shaw, November 1968). Cf:

we had one – and (or **but**) **the wheel came off.** See **had one ....**

we have a problem here seems to have gained ascendency over **I have** (**he** or **she has**; **you** or **they have**) **a problem** (**here**), which are natural mutations of the cliché *to have a problem*, to be confronted with a difficulty, a grave embarrassment, etc., whether personal or public, individual or collective, and by gaining ascendency, to have emerged from the vagueness and pedestrianism of cliché into the more luminous and particular world of the c.p. *We have a problem here* became, I'd surmise, a c.p. during the years 1970–1.

[**we have met the enemy – and they** (or **he**) **– is us.** Colonel Albert Moe writes on 14 July 1975:

Originally 'he' was used in lieu of 'they' and [it] appeared in a comic strip. In popular usage, I have heard only 'they'. Meaning: A person's or group's own faults [or failings] are responsible for lack of success ... one's own

worst enemy is oneself when one refuses to ... make any attempt to cope with [one's own shortcomings].

Walt Kelly's comic strip 'Pogo' began to appear nationally in May 1949; and in 1972 Kelly (1913–73) published his *Pogo: We Have Met the Enemy and He Is Us.* Pogo, by the way, is a possum, but a possum who constitutes a powerful 'satire on the unnatural behaviour of human beings, who live like marionettes – slaves to the repressions of their society': he had earlier satirized the Communist-hunting Senator Joseph McCarthy as 'Simple J. Malarkey'. (With further thanks to Colonel Moe.) But perhaps not a c.p., after all: Dr Joseph T. Shipley thinks not.

Mr W. J. Burke (18 August 1975) thinks it 'a corruption of "we have met the enemy and they are ours" [at our mercy], uttered by US naval hero Oliver Howard Perry at the Battle of Lake Erie, Sept. 10, 1813.']

we have ways and means to make you talk. See **ve haf vays ....**

we haven't got much money, but we do see life! See **we don't get much money ....**

we live again. See **we breathe again.**

we make 'em ourselves. Farmer says:

A street catch-phrase, which quickly spread throughout the Union, and was quickly supplanted by other slang expressions. [It] implies readiness to follow another's lead: or capacity to perform what others have done [usually the latter nuance].

Dates from the middle 1880s.

we must press on regardless is the c.p. crystallization of *to press on regardless* and it means 'We have urgent work to do – and must get it done as soon as possible' despite all the difficulties and dangers; RAF: 1941 onwards (by *c.* 1946, also civilian). Communicated by Squadron-Leader Vernon Noble to AC2 E. H. Partridge in February 1945.

[**we shall catch larks if and when the sky falls**, C16–20, is a proverbial saying rather than a c.p. (Apperson.)]

we sha'n't take salt! Our box-office returns will be very small: theatrical: late C19–20; obsolete by 1960. Ware glosses it as, 'We shall not take enough money to pay for salt, let alone bread'.

we want eight and we can't wait. This is an ephemeral c.p. of 1909 when eight dreadnoughts were demanded for the Royal Navy.

we want make-and-mends, not recommends. A C20 naval lower-deck c.p. *A make and mend* is a naval half-holiday, originally for attention to one's clothing; a *recommend* is a recommendation (for promotion) red-inked on to a sailor's Service Certificate.

we was (or **wuz**) **robbed** (or, in Australia, occasionally **rooked**). A jocular c.p. used when one has been either tricked or merely outsmarted: since the late 1940s. From the indignant and usually bogus claim of illiterate boxers when the referee has declared them defeated.

Cf the quotation at **I should of stood in bed.**

we will (or **we'll** – rather more often, perhaps, **we can**) **live with it.** A 'usually humorous acceptance of a minor nuisance or disruption of plan. "They're asking if they can send those blokes to-morrow, instead of Friday." – "Oh, well, tell 'em yes; we'll live with it"' (Paul Beale, 23 June 1974). Esp. army; since *c.* 1960, if not ten or fifteen years earlier.

we won't eat you! We're not dangerous – we sha'n't harm you: C18–20, but very little used since *c.* 1960. S, 1738, Dialogue II, has:

> SIR JOHN: What, you keep Court Hours I see. I'll be going...
> LADY SM[ART]: Why, we won't eat you, Sir *John.*

weak eyes – big tits summarizes a popular example of fallacious folklore: Australian: since *c.* 1920. (Barry Prentice, who comments: 'Often worded in other ways.') Cf **large mouth . . . .**

wear it in health is, when used by Jews, a conventionalism, a cliché, certainly not a c.p., which it becomes only when used jocosely by Gentiles in making a present of an article of clothing or a piece of jewellery: since *c.* 1950. (John W. Clark, 5 December 1968.)

weaving leather aprons was, *c.* 1840–1940, an evasive reply given to someone enquiring what one has been doing lately or what one does for a living. (Hotten, 1864.)

Variants: *I'm a doll's-eye weaver* (Hotten, 1874); *making a trundle for a goose's eye*; *making a whim-wham to bridle a goose* (both in Hotten, 1864). All were originally underworld phrases, which seem to have early become low slang. The insistence on *goose* may fairly be assumed to imply that the enquirer *is* a goose (a silly fellow) to be asking such a question.

wedding dues are concerned. They're about to get married, *and* It's time they got married: *c.* 1750–1840.

welcome aboard. In the US, this phrase is 'widely used as a greeting to a newcomer to an institution – or, for that matter, to a poker game. I found myself using it the other day in greeting a new English Department stenographer' (John W. Clark, 9 November 1968): since *c.* 1946. As it chances, I have no printed record earlier than 'He put Hubbard's material in the envelope, hesitated, then scrawled across the front of it, "Welcome aboard!!!!! Fred Frick"' (John D. Mac-Donald, *A Key to the Suite*, 1962). Perhaps less probably from the formal naval greeting than from the formal commercial-aircraft greeting, so rapidly popularized during the tremendous upsurge in civilian flying which took place very soon after WW2 ended in August 1945. Colonel Albert Moe, however, assumes it to have been naval in origin.

[**we'll just have to use brute force and ignorance on it** has not yet (April 1976) settled down to being definitely either a cliché or a c.p. On 1 October 1974, Paul Beale wrote:

> Usually in connection with things mechanical, to make them work, or to repair them, by 'shit or bust' methods. To force anything, e.g. a lock. 'So she won't ackle [work, act, perform], eh? All right, then, we'll just have to use brute force and ignorance on the bastard.'

Which way, I wonder, will the chips fall?]

we'll let you know. A synonym of **we'll write to you**.

we'll soon lick you into shape – we're lion tamers here. A sergeant-majors' and drill sergeants' pleasantry addressed to recruits undergoing their initial training, esp. in England: 1914–18. (Collinson.) Very seldom if ever (except with a nostalgic jocosity) used during 1939–45.

we'll write to you! – literally, 'the stock promise to an *un-*

promising applicant for an audition' – 'has become a theatrical catch-phrase, and is often directed at anyone singing out of tune in the dressing-room' (Granville). Cf **don't call us – we'll call you.**

well, ah'll go to Pudsey! is a late C19–20 Yorkshire, esp. West Riding, c.p. expressing astonishment 'and still used by old men in pubs', as Vernon Noble, in a letter dated 4 December 1973, tells me; he adds, 'Why Pudsey, cradle of Yorkshire cricket, I don't know.' Nor do I; nor even Joseph Wright in his vast *EDD.*

well – end it! (second word emphasized). A deflation of a poor storyteller, exhorted to finish his story when, in fact, he has already done so: since *c.* 1930. (Frank Shaw, November 1968.)

well, I ask you! See **I ask you!**

well, I declare!: occasional variant, **well, I'll declare!** A US c.p. of astonishment or shock: apparently since *c.* 1830; since *c.* 1920, very old-fashioned; by 1950, obsolete. The *OED* records it as occurring in Longfellow's *Kavanagh, A Tale*, 1849, thus: 'Well, I declare! If it is not Mr Kavanagh!' A more enlightening example comes in George Ade's *Doc Horne*, 1899:

> Suddenly Doc' straightened up in his chair and looked most intently at a passing man who carried a walking-stick and seemed to be in a hurry.
> 'Well, I'll declare!' he exclaimed.
> 'What's the matter, Doc'? asked the lush.
> Doc' continued to gaze at the pedestrian until he turned the corner.
> 'That's most extraordinary,' he said: 'I could have sworn that was Bridgeman.'

well, I like that! – often without *well*. An ironical c.p., meaning the exact opposite, 'often with the nuance, 'What cheek, you suggesting *that*!': late C19–20. (Wilfred Granville, 11 January 1969.) In short, a derisive, or an indignant, 'Certainly not!'

It may have come to Britain from US: See John Kendrick Bangs, *Toppleton's Client or A Spirit in Exile*, 1893:

> 'Don't look at me that way, I beg of you, Mr Toppleton,' said the spirit . . . 'I don't deserve all that your glance implies, and if you could only understand me, I think you would sympathize with me in my trials.'
> 'I? I sympathize with you? Well, I like that,' cried Mr Toppleton.

In a synonym of equivalents to 'the insolence of it!', Berrey lists (*well*) *I like that!*

Semantically, cf **not half!**

well, I never! See **you don't say!**

well, I should smile! is an extended form of **I should smile!**

well, I suppose it's winning (or **helping to win) the war**. See **clean and polish.**

well, if ever! was, *c.* 1810–60, a US c.p. of either astonishment or admiration. John Neal, *Brother Jonathan: or, The New Englander*, 3 vols, 1825, at chapter I, p. 150, has '"My stars!" cried Miriam, when she saw him in it [a calico waistcoat], first: "My stars! – well, if ever!"' – wiping her fat hands very carefully.'

Perhaps it is elliptical for 'Well, if ever I saw *or* heard such a thing!'

More usual is **if ever!**, as in *ibid.*, chapter II, p. 161: '"... Ruth Ashley – my own child; why Ruth, if ever! – what's the matter now, maiden – give the lad thy hand."' Neal uses it again in *The Down-Easters*, 2 vols, 1833 (at chapter I, p. 24).

well, if that don't pass! – with *well* only occasionally omitted. That's amazing!: US: *c.* 1820(? earlier)–1890. It occurs in, e.g., T. C. Haliburton's three-volume work *The Clockmaker*, 1837–40; and also in his *The Attaché*, 1843, Series I, vol. 2, pp. 136–7, thus:

'Not hear of *Bunkum?* why how you talk!'
'No, never.'
'Well, if that don't pass! I thought everybody know'd that word.'

Elliptical for 'Well, if that don't (or doesn't) pass understanding (*or* the imagination)!'

well, I'll be a monkey's uncle! See **I'll be a monkey's uncle.**

well, it seemed like a good idea at the time originated as a cliché: US; then, fairly soon, British. By being employed, humorously and ruefully, as a cliché, it has become, in the US at least, also a c.p., dating since the 1950s. John W. Clark, in mid March 1975, adds that it is applied to 'one's own impulsive or, rather impetuous actions, now recognized as foolish – as, one confesses, they should have been at the moment of action'.

well, lump it! See **do the other!**

well, that's that! See **and that's that!**

well, that's the bag. See **that's the bag.**

well, there's no answer to that. Miss Penny A. Cook, writing on 18 January 1975, says:

One punch line that seems to be catching on now is 'Well, there's no answer to *that!*' and there isn't – nor, of course, is there expected to be. It is the ultimate face-saver, leaving one with the last line, the last laugh, and without the necessity of having to think up an original retort to the preceding repartee.

Dating, I think, since late 1973 or early 1974. Supplementing that, is this: 'Eric Morecambe's catchphrase, meaning that the innuendo which can be read into the question makes an answer superfluous' (Mr D. R. Bartlett, FLA, in mid-March 1975). Paul Beale, on 5 February 1975, recalls 'the splendid Buckinghamshire dialect records of monologues by (Sir) Bernard Miles made before WW2, which used to end up with the discomfiture of "posh" village ladies, "...That 'ad 'er – unanswerable, that were."'

well, this is it. On 1 October 1974, Paul Beale writes:

Suddenly, within the last few months, this seems to be everybody's stock response to a statement with which they agree, where before they might merely have said 'Yes', 'Yes, isn't it?' or 'Too true', e.g. 'It seems to me there are too many layabouts sponging off the social services.' – 'Well, this is it! I mean, you know, honestly, let's face it ... etc. (ad nauseam).'

[**'well, well,' quoth she, 'many wells, many buckets'.** Half-proverb, half-c.p., of C16; recorded by Heywood, 1546. Cf the C20 'catch': '"Have you heard the story of the three wells?" – "No; what is it?" – "Well, well, well!"']

well, what do you know! expresses an incredulous or mildly ironic surprise: since *c.* 1920. (*NZS.*) Cf the Armed Forces' variation, 1939–45: *well, Joe, what do you know?*, derisively addressed to anyone named Joe; but the original form had become common in Britain by 1930 at latest and it occurred in, e.g., the film titled *Dunkirk*, 1958. As *well, what do you know*, it seems to have reached the US *c.* 1930, and Berrey, 1942, records the basic *what do you know?* – which arose in US *c.* 1910, S. R. Strait using it *c.* 1917 in 'Straight Talk' in the *Boston Globe.* In Ellery Queen's *The Blue Movie Murders*, 1973, we read: 'The eyes were at their widest when he opened the door of his flat and saw Hyde. "Well, what do you know?"'

More notably, Edward Albeë uses it in Act II of *Who's Afraid of Virginia Woolf?*, 1962.

well, you *said* you could do it! was, in 1914–18, an army officers' c.p. reply to, or comment on, a complaint: and it has, in much wider circles, endured, as Julian Franklyn testified on 14 January 1969.

[**well, you see, it was like this** is not a c.p. but a cliché.]

went over like a lead balloon, usually preceded by **it**. It was a 'flop' – a *rank* failure, as applied to a joke, a play, a film, a plan, an act or action either hoped or expected to succeed. American: *c.* 1950–8; it gave way to 'It was a lead balloon'. As you will have guessed, a lead balloon wouldn't even get off the ground. Attested by W & F and by *DCCU*, 1971.

went to night school and he (or **she**) **can't spell in the day time**, usually preceded by **he** or **she**, is a C20, esp. an Australian, c.p., directed at a bad speller. (Barry Prentice.)

we're all together – like Brown's cows. See **all together ....**

we're in business. According to Paul Beale, 6 August 1975,

Not necessarily commercially. A fairly common c.p., indicating that the first stage of any enterprise has been successfully accomplished; e.g., even looking up something in a dictionary that provides a lead to something else. General. I first heard it consciously about three years ago.

I myself first heard it *c.* 1960, and it may easily go back as far as 1950.

we're in, Meredith! See **Meredith, we're in!**

we're just good friends. Attributed, by newspapermen, to notorieties, usually filmstars, disclaiming that there's anything in a close association with a member of the opposite sex, esp. during a 'lull' between marriages. 'Since the 1930s. Hardly used seriously now, and used in mockery to enquiring friends with a "No comment – mind your own business" intent, usually by ordinary folk' (Frank Shaw, 1 April 1969); or, as A. B. Petch has put it (10 January 1974), 'Heard when a couple often seen about together are asked if there is anything in it.' Common throughout the British Commonwealth; for instance, Barry Prentice (1 May 1975): 'A c.p. that is used to kill rumours of romance.'

we're winning. Things are going well for us – or me: from 1942, the reference being to progress in the war, then quite general. Also 'an evasive stock answer to "How're we getting on?" or "How goes it?"' (Laurie Atkinson).

were you born in a barn? Addressed to one who leaves a door open, esp. when it's cold or windy outside: mid C19–20 – and, I suspect, fifty or more years earlier. Of the same order of enquiry as **is your father a glazier?**; in short, semi-proverbial. The Australian version is *were you born in a tent?* (Barry Prentice, 1 May 1975.)

wet arse and no fish – a. A fruitless quest or a sleeveless errand: late C19–20. Clearly originating either among trawlermen or among anglers.

we've got a right 'un 'ere! 'Usually A to B (official) about C' (Frank Shaw, November 1968): mainly Liverpool: since *c.* 1940. On the other hand, Vernon Noble writes (8 February 1975): 'Bruce Forsyth in BBC TV "The Generation Game" in which the public (related, e.g., father and daughter) participated in contests, 1970s.' There's probably no contradiction: the c.p. may have been a recurrent, for another reliable source (Cyril Whelan, 17 February 1975) states that this was an aside consistently and constantly used by the late Tony Hancock, who preceded Bruce Forsyth. Ironic. Implication: a fool or a very odd person indeed.

[**whacko!** That's splendid! A one-word c.p.]

whaddya want – eggs (or **an egg**) **in your beer?** See **what do you want – eggs ... ?**

wham, bang, thank you, madam! Since the early to middle 1940s, originally an Armed Forces' c.p.; applied to the rapidity of a male rabbit's breeding activities.

An adaptation of the US *wham, bam, thank you, ma'am!* – applied to hurried, almost mechanical, copulation with a strange woman: dated by W & F as 'since before *c.* 1895'. By itself, *wham-bam* means 'quickly and roughly' – brawnily, not brainily.

Cf the negro **bip bam, thank you, ma'am!**

what a beanfeast! '(*People's.*) Satirical exclamation in reference to a riot, [a] quarrel or [a] wretched meal; or other entertainment' (Ware): *c.* 1880–1914.

what! a bishop's wife? eat and drink in your gloves! A semi-proverbial c.p. of mid C17–mid C18. (Ray, 1678.) Apperson glosses it thus: 'This is a cryptic saying'. But probably it means 'You're quite the fine lady (now)!'

[**what a busher he is!** See **that's strictly bush.**]

what a drag! See **drag – it's a.**

what a dump! and **what a morgue!** What a dead-and-alive, or what a dull, place! The former arose *c.* 1919, the latter *c.* 1945, to die out by the early 1970s.

what a funny little place to have one! Dating since *c.* 1890 and slightly obsolescent by *c.* 1970. In reference to a mole; addressed to a woman; suggesting contiguity to *le petit coin.*

what a game it is! (often shortened to **what a game!**) A humorously, if wryly, resigned c.p., directed at life's little ironies and not quite so little vicissitudes: C20.

what a hope you've got! (often shortened to **what a hope!**); also **you've got a hope** (, *you* have)! and **what hopes!** This, in all its varieties, affords an excellent example of how very difficult it is to date such c.pp. as these. I can but hazard a guess that they go back to *c.* 1870 – and that, originally at least, they were Cockney. The first and the last seem to have been the most popular: cf John Brophy in B & P, 1930:

WHAT HOPES! – A retort expressing utter disbelief in some promise or prophecy of a future good (or not so bad as at present) time. A variation, addressed to a man confident of securing an advantage for himself, was *What a hope you've got!*

what a life! When used as a general animadversion on life as a whole, it is clearly not a c.p. but a cliché; when, however, it is applied to some trivial mishap or accident, esp. if in humorous disgust, it is no less clearly a c.p.; and it may go back to mid C19 or even fifty or, for that matter, a hundred years earlier.

In late C19–20, it has had the extension, *without a wife,* to which, in C20, the cynical add either *and even worse with one* or, more colloquially, *and a damned sight worse with one!* More common, however, is **such is life without a wife!** – q.v. Also US: Berrey synonymizes it with boredom.

what a load of rubbish! A modern c.p. chanted by spectators at football matches to show their disapproval of the players' performance; and thence, into all sorts of situations in "real life"' (Paul Beale, 17 February 1975).

what a long tail our cat's got! See **what a tail ... !**

what a lovely war! has been an army, hence – in due course – a civilian, c.p. ever since 1915. The army's irony was directed at conditions in general; its sarcasm, at profiteers and 'cushy'-jobbers and baseline troops. In the early 1960s, this was extended to the title of a revue dealing with WW1.

what a morgue! See **what a dump!**

what a nerve! See **of all the nerve!**

what a shocking bad hat! Mackay (1841), after noting that this succeeded *quoz!* as the phrase in vogue, remarked that

No sooner had it become universal, than thousands of idle but sharp eyes were on the watch for the passenger [i.e., passer-by] whose hat showed any signs, however slight, of ancient service. Immediately the cry arose, and, like the war-whoop of the Indians, was repeated by a hundred discordant throats. He was a wise man who, finding himself ... 'the observed of all observers', bore his honours meekly.... The obnoxious hat was often snatched from his head and thrown into the gutter ... and then raised, covered with mud, upon the end of a stick, for the admiration of the spectators, who held their sides with laughter, and exclaimed in the pauses of their mirth, *'Oh, what a shocking bad hat!' 'What a shocking bad hat!'....*

The origin of this singular saying, which made fun for the metropolis for months, is not involved in the same obscurity as ... *Quoz* and some others. There had been a hotly contested election for the borough of Southwark, and one of the candidates was an eminent hatter.... Whenever he called upon or met a voter whose hat was not of the best material, or being so, had seen its best days, he immediately said, *'What a shocking bad hat you have got; call at my warehouse, and you shall have a new one!'* Upon the day of election this circumstance was remembered, and his opponents made the most of it, by inciting the crowd to keep up an incessant cry of *'What a shocking bad hat!'* all the time the honourable candidate was addressing them. From Southwark the phrase spread all over London, and reigned for a time the supreme slang of the season.

The phrase, which seems to have arisen *c.* 1838 or 1839, soon became transferred to persons with a bad reputation or the most shocking manners. It was so used by John Surtees in a novel published in 1851–2 (see the quotation at **I don't think**); and then, in 1892, in *Vice-Versa* Anstey wrote, 'Regular bounder! Shocking bad hat!'

It survived well into C20; by 1930, it was outmoded and

by 1950, virtually obsolete except among people seventy or more years old.

Cf **where did you get that hat?**

what a shower! and **it's showery!** The latter derived from the former and was an air force saying, current during the approximate period mid 1930s to late 1940s.

But *what a shower!* arose, *c.* 1919, in the army, as an insult hurled at the members of another unit; later – in the RAF too – it would be directed at, e.g., an intake of recruits. In 1942, Gerald Kersh, in *Bill Nelson*, wrote, 'Some of the lousiest showers of rooks you ever saw': clearly *what a shower* was already being applied individually as well as collectively; for instance, it could be addressed to one who had made a bad mistake. It has survived among civilians, and indeed I heard it used so late as 26 February 1975.

The shower is popularly – and probably correctly – explained as elliptical for a *shower of shit*.

what a tail (often **what a long tail**) **our cat's got!** A mid C19–20 proletarian c.p. at a female 'flaunting in a new dress', the rear skirt of which she swings haughtily or provocatively. (Ware: the shorter, the original, form.)

Later it could be used of either sex and be addressed to – or at – a person boasting vaingloriously: usually in the longer form. Dr Douglas Leechman vouches for its Canadian usage.

what a turn-up for the book! has, since *c.* 1955 or a little earlier, expressed 'pleasure at the unexpected. (The book is, of course, the bookmakers)' (Peter Sanders, 7 August 1972). But it had originally been an underworld c.p., as in Arthur Gardner, *Tinker's Kitchen*, 1932.

what a way (occasionally **a hell of a way**) **to run a railway** (or **railroad)!** 'A c.p. directed at more or (mostly) less organized chaos: US, then Britain. From an American cartoon of the 1930s: signalman coolly surveying a number of trains colliding beneath his box' (the late Frank Shaw, January 1969).

On 8 December 1973, Rear-Admiral P. W. Brock wrote to me thus:

I have a cartoon from a frivolous American magazine called *Ballyhoo*, of 1932, showing an American railway signalman looking out of his signal box at two trains about to collide head on and saying 'Tch-tch – what a way to run a railway!'

A contemporary of my father said that it [this c.p.] was quite common in Canada at the turn of the century or thereabouts.

In *The General and the President* (MacArthur and Truman in opposition over Korea, 1951) the authors, Arthur Schlesinger, Jnr, and Richard Revere, remark – 'It is, *in the idiom of Missouri*, a hell of a way to run a railway'.

On *c.* 15 December 1974, Mr Barry Prentice quotes it as current in Australia in the form '… *railroad*', since *c.* 1950, if not seven or eight years earlier. In Alexander Buzo's *The Roy Murphy Show*, performed in 1971 and published in 1973, Roy, a TV compère with a tendency to pronounce *r* as *w*, speaking of Australian Rugby League football, says, 'City selection blunders like the shock omission of veteran Ken Irvine and the surprise inclusion of tyro Kel Brown. What a way to wun a wailwoad!'

what a wonderful (or **agreeable** or **pleasant** or the feeble **nice**) **way to die!** is a C20 'c.p. of consolation when someone has mentioned a death through drink, riotous living or other

cause due to debauchery' (Wilfred Granville, 13 January 1969). Whereas Wilfred Granville had always heard *nice*, I've always heard *wonderful*, as in

'Poor old man! He died, making love to his young wife.'
'Poor! What a *wonderful* way to go!'

[Which reminds me of one of the most remarkable pieces of plain and lucid English I've ever heard. *Scene:* a police court. The magistrate asks a middle-aged prostitute about a male death that has occurred in her room. 'Well, yeronner, we lay down on the bed and got on with it. After a while, he gave a great sigh. I thought he had come – but he was gone.' (Related to me by a Savile Club friend in, I suppose, 1972.)]

what about it? If you're ready, go ahead, *or* Let's go, let's get going (or busy): since *c.* 1914. In his *Carrying On*, 1917, Ian Hay (properly Ian Hay Beith) numbers it among the 'current catch-phrases'.

But in its perhaps predominant post-WW2 sense, 'Shall we make love?', it can hardly be called a c.p.

what am *I* supposed to do – cry? A US c.p., dating from *c.* 1930. Berrey treats it as a synonym of 'It's not *my* concern!' and '*I* should worry!'. Cf **what do you expect me to do – burst into flames?**

what are you going to make of it? is an Australian c.p., dating since *c.* 1930 and inviting the interlocutor to a bout of fisticuffs in order to settle the matter. (Barry Prentice.) Cf **want to make something of it?**

what can I – occasionally **we – do you for?** has, since the early 1920s (I remember hearing it *c.* 1925), been a jocular variation of *what can I* (or *we*) *do for you?* Based in British slang *do*, to cheat or to cheat out of.

what cheer, my old brown son – how are you? See **hullo, my old ….**

what did Gladstone say in (e.g., 1879)? A political hecklers' c.p.: late C19–20; not much heard since 1939. If the question were serious, it wouldn't be eligible; but usually it was either merely obstructive or goodhumouredly meaningless or, at the least, almost so. That great Gladstone scholar, Professor M. R. D. Foot, thinks that the c.p. could have arisen at any time after November 1879, when Mr Gladstone, as he was always known, conducted his famous Midlothian campaign. In a conversation on 1 March 1975, Professor Foot very properly reminded me that here, although indirect, is yet another tribute to the immense personal popularity of the GOM.

what did Horace say, Winnie? comes 'from Harry Hemsley's music-hall turn in the 1940s, in which he "did" the voices of a whole family of children, the youngest of whom, Horace, was quite unintelligible and had to be interpreted by an older sister, Winnie' (Paul Beale, 5 March 1976); it lasted into the 1950s. As a c.p. it was used in any vaguely similar situation.

what did thought do? was a C18 c.p., exemplified in S, 1738, Dialogue I:

LADY ANS[WERALL]: I thought you did just now.

LORD SP[ARKISH]: Pray, Madam, what did thought do?

The original form of the C19–20 **you know what thought did!** – often extended by **kissed another man's wife**, to quote the polite version.

what did you do in the Great War, daddy? was originally a recruiting poster of WW1. The British soldier seized upon it, derided it, repeated it 'scathingly in times of distress and misery' (John Brophy). In late 1917–18, 'there were many variations, some quite lengthy. We need cite but one reply: "Shut up, you little bastard! Get the Bluebell and go and clean my medals"' (EP, likewise in B & P). Poor daddy may have 'fought the war' at a base or been a general's batman.

what do I owe? See **do I owe you anything?**

what do you do for an encore? 'A question that is asked when somebody does something foolish or drops something' (Barry Prentice, 9 June 1975): Australian: post-WW2.

what do you expect (or **want**) **me to do – burst into flames?** An air force c.p. arising in 1940, but not much heard afterwards, it deprecates excitement. Obviously from aircraft catching fire after being hit by flak. (Laurie Atkinson.)

what do you hear from the mob? 'Common. Goes back to the Al Capone era of gangsterism, during Prohibition period. A familiar expression currently meaning, "What do you hear from our old gang of buddies?"' (W. J. Burke, 18 August 1975). Attested also by Colonel Albert Moe.

what do you know? is the more abrupt, probably also the original, form of **well, what do you know?** In 'Watching a Spring Planting', forming part of his *Love Conquers All*, 1923, Robert Benchley writes: 'Then you can laugh, and call out to a neighbour, or even to the man's wife: "Hey, what do you know? Steve here thinks he's going to get some corn up in this soil!"' Cf:

what do you know about that? A C20 expression of surprise, neither aristocratic nor upper-middle class, nor cultured, it could not fairly be called proletarian. It achieved a considerable popularity in the Services – esp. the army – during WW2. (PGR.)

Moreover, this c.p. had reached the US very soon after WW1, presumably via the returning US soldiers. In Robert Benchley's *Love Conquers All*, 1923, 'The Score in the Stands' offers this passage: 'SECOND INNING: Scanlon yelled to Bodie to whang out a double. Turtelot said that Bodie couldn't do it. Scanlon said "Oh, is that so?" Turtelot said "Yes, that's so and whad'yer know about that?"'

what do you mean, your bird won't sing? 'Indicative of disbelief. Dates from the 1920s. I believe there is a story behind this phrase. Perhaps even a *Punch* cartoon' (Peter Sanders, 21 May 1974).

what do you take me for? A usually indignant c.p., roughly equivalent to 'What sort of a person do you think I am?' Esp. 'What sort of a rogue or fool – or girl – do you think I am?' Current throughout C20 and perhaps going back some decades earlier. Denis Mackail, *Huddleston House*, 1945, has:

'Going out' means [for a girl in WW2 London] a night of Cimmerian darkness, partly, quite often, of considerable danger, partly of a plush *banquette* or a scrap of parquet in a cellar, partly of shouting for taxis, and partly of saying 'What do you take me for?' inside them.

what do *you* think? A late C19–20 c.p., implying 'You're too well informed, *or* too intelligent, not to know exactly what that, *or* this, means *or* meant.'

what do you think that is – Scotch mist? Variant: **what's that –**

Scotch mist? Occasional variant: **what's that – fog?** A sarcastic c.p. of the Services, notably the air force; dating from the mid 1920s; implying that the addressee is either 'seeing things' or, more usually, failing to see objects he ought to be able to see, 'Can't you see my tapes? What do you think they are – Scotch mist?' Hence, loosely, applied to noise. 'A bomb falls. "What was that?" – "Well, it wasn't Scotch mist."' (Wing-Commander R. P. McDouall, letter dated 17 March 1945.) For the pattern cf:

what do you think this is – Bush Week? Variant: **what's this – Bush Week?** An Australian c.p., addressed to a man making a (great) noise and a considerable fuss: since the 1920s. Baker records both forms and mentions that no such week exists. Barry Prentice has pointed out that a commoner form is *What do you think this is – Bush Week or Christmas?* and that it is also 'used when someone has produced something very "fishy"'; it occurs in, e.g., Lawson Glassop, *Lucky Palmer*, 1949. This latter sense derives from the country agricultural and pastoral show, when the sharpers fleece the locals.

what do you (or, illiterately yet frequently, **whaddya**) **want – eggs** (or **an egg**) **in your beer?** 'Usually said to someone who is bitching or griping without justifiable cause. I have heard this used only by Marines, but I strongly suspect that it was borrowed from civilian use' (Colonel Albert Moe, 15 June 1975). Therefore, tentatively: C20; civilian become, during WW2, Marine Corps.

what do you want if you don't want money? 'Title of a song, late 1940s–early 1950s. It became a meaningless c.p.' (Paul Beale, 7 March 1975); little used after c. 1965.

what do you want – jam on it? A late C19–20 military c.p., addressed, as a rebuke, to a constant grumbler. As John Brophy wrote in B & P, 1930: 'But this was used just as often ironically, when extra fatigues or working parties took the place of a promised rest, or something fell short of the normal standard.' It had an occasional variant, *d'you want jam on both sides?* The Australian variant is **you want portholes in your coffin?**

what does 'A' do now? What does someone do next? Since c. 1930; by 1975, slightly obsolescent. (Paul Beale, 28 February 1975.)

what does a mouse do when it spins?; and **what was the name of the engine-driver?** These are Cockney c.pp. either derisively or provocatively interrogative. They belong to C20 and are used either to express boredom or to start a discussion or even a bad-tempered argument. The latter phrase derives from the trick of asking many questions about speeds and times; the former, perhaps more often in the version *why is a mouse when it spins?*, has the c.p. 'dovetail' answer, *because the higher the fewer*. (In part, Ramsey Spencer.)

In June 1919, the notable US novelist John Dos Passos (1896–19–), writing from Paris to a Yale freshman, expressed a hope that he was reading something better than the usual authors and ended the paragraph: 'But why in God's name Tennyson and Ruskin? – Why is a mouse when it spins?' I owe this quotation, based on *The Fourteenth Chronicle: Letters and Diaries of John Dos Passos*, ed. by C. T. Ludington and published in 1974 (p. 253), to Professor Harold Shapiro, who, 19 April 1975, tells me that when he 'was in secondary school during the late 1940s', the phrase, in this form, 'was fashionable among some of us boys. There was an answer too: "Because the higher the fewer".' And on 2 May 1975, Professor Shapiro added that, as Dos Passos was at school in England in 1906–7, he may have learnt the phrase at that earlier period.

Cf **how old is Ann(e)?**; **how high is up?** and **do they have ponies down a pit?**

what does that make *me*? – often preceded by **so** – expresses lack of interest or a refusal to participate or to become involved: since the late 1930s. (Laurie Atkinson.)

But it came to Britain from the US, where it had been current since the early 1930s and often (as later in Britain) used in the sense, 'How do I come out of that statement or argument?', or 'That statement or argument isn't very flattering to *me*, is it?' – as in James Eastwood, *The Chinese Visitor*, 1965, '"All bureaucrats are cautious and unenterprising." The very senior Civil Servant ruefully commented, "So what does that make *me*?"'

what else did you get for Christmas? has, since *c.* 1965, been a 'sarcastic remark to someone showing off "a toy", e.g. in exasperation at a roadhog blinding down the outside lane of a motorway in his brand-new Jag, hooting and flashing his lights. General' (Paul Beale, 28 January 1975). The ironic implication is that it isn't a *man*'s car but a *kid*'s plaything.

what gives? and **what gives out?** What's happening? The latter was the property of the RAF in North Italy, 1945. The former, becoming British in or about the same year, had migrated from the US, where current since well before 1939; W & F, who note another sense, 'What did I do to make you say or do that?', suggest origin in Ger. *was ist los?* – but doesn't it rather derive from Ger. *was gibt's?*

what goes up must come down. Several of the friends I've asked about this truism replied, 'Oh, but that's a *proverb*!' Perhaps on its way to becoming a proverb, and certainly obvious and trite enough to have long since done so, it was originally and is still predominantly a c.p., dating, I'd say, from *c.* 1870 (but not improbably much earlier). Ramsey Spencer, 10 May 1969, describes it as 'a C19–20 c.p., commenting with cheerful Newtonian logic on a pregnancy, whether extramarital or not': which suggests that the ultimate origin does, in the fact, reside in the Newtonian dictum of the pull of gravity. Barry Prentice remarks: 'A c.p. that is no longer true.'

what has she got that I haven't (got)? A feminine c.p., originating as an abandoned or jilted wife's or mistress's outcry against a successful rival: since the 1930s. As in the young wife's reproach to her soldier husband, returning from abroad, '*What had she* …?' – and his engaging, if somewhat insensitive, reply, 'Nothing at all, my dear. But it was available.'

what? have you pigs in your belly? (Probably *what* was often omitted.) Current in C18 and occurring in S, 1738, Dialogue I:

NEV[EROUT]: Miss *Notable*; … pray step hither for a Moment.
MISS: I'll wash my Hands and wait on you, Sir; but pray come you hither and try to open this Lock.
NEV: We'll try what we can do.
MISS: We! what, have you Pigs in your Belly?

Miss Notable uses a c.p. to comment adequately upon young Neverout's rather pompous use of the plural 'we'. In general, 'What's wrong with you?'

what ho! she bumps! See **bumps … !**

what is that (or **what's that**) **when it's at home?**; and **who is he** (or **she**) **when he's** (or **she's**) **at home?** C20 tags, implying either derision or incredulity, and signifying 'I've never even heard of her, him, it'. Edwin Pugh uses it in *The Cockney at Home*, 1914, and Dorothy L. Sayers in *Have His Carcase*, 1932, has: 'Haemophilia. What in the name of blazes is that, when it's at home?' Cf the oddly similar quotation from Terence Rattigan, *Harlequinade*, produced in 1948 and published in 1949:

JACK: Social purpose, Mr Burton.
BURTON: Social purpose? Now what the blazes is that when it's at home?

It is, in short, directed esp. at someone employing an unusual or erudite or highly technical or scientific term in a *milieu* unlikely to know its meaning. Cf this, in Julian Symons's *The Players and the Game*, 1972:

'My belief is … that this might be a case of *folie à deux*.'
'And what's that when it's at home?'

[**what is there in it for me?**; and **what's in it for me?** What do I get out of it? How do I profit? Late C19–20. Rather clichés than c.pp.]

what *is* this? International Fuck Your Buddy Week? Paul Beale, 18 July 1974, says:

I haven't heard this phrase for some years now: I think it must have come into the British Army via those units which served alongside the Americans in Korea [1950–3]. It was a useful emollient c.p. in situations where people were getting 'narky' and edgy with each other. 'What is this then? International … ?' [That is, '— you, bud!']

It is therefore probable that the saying had been current in the US Army in 1942–5.

what it is! 'An expression of greeting similar to "what's happening?"' (Folb): the US south-west.

what me! was, in WW1, a frequent greeting between two, or among more than two, soldiers. (B & P, 1931.)

what, *me*? – in *my* state of health? Ted Kavanagh, the script writer for 'ITMA', tells us, in his biography, 1948, of Tommy Handley, that 'There was even a Brighton parson who announced that the subject of his sermon would be: "What *me*, in *my* state of health?"'

From Francis Worsley, the producer, we learn, in his *Itma*, 1948, that this was an 'ITMA' c.p. that caught on, *c.* 1946–50, with the general public.

See also TOMMY HANDLEY CATCH PHRASES.

what next – and next? is contemptuous of an audacious assertion: *c.* 1820–1905. (Ware.)

what o'clock, cock? What's the time, chum?: since *c.* 1955; by 1970, virtually obsolete. From an advertising campaign in which, over several years, this sort of jingle occurred: cf **gently, Bentley** and **see you later, alligator**.

what say?; and **what say you?** The former shortens the latter, which dates from *c.* 1870, but was, by 1975, decidedly obsolescent; the former dates from the 1880s and occurs in those two masters of Cockney speech. W. Pett Ridge (*Minor Dialogues*, 1895) and Edwin Pugh (*Harry the Cockney*, 1912).

It passed into US speech as *what say?*: and Berrey equates it to 'What's the plan?' W & F state that it has been common since *c.* 1920' and that, to distinguish it from a true question, *say* is stressed.

what says the enemy? What's the time?: originally (1789) a quotation, which almost immediately became a c.p., lasting ever since, although little used after WW1 (1914–18). It occurs in Frederick Reynolds, *The Dramatist*, produced in 1789 and published four years later. In Act I, 'Ennui the Timekiller – whose business in life is to murder the hour' soliloquizes thus:

> I've an idea I don't like the Lady Waitfor't – she wishes to trick me out of my match with Miss Courtney, and if I could trick her in return – (*takes out his watch*). How goes the enemy – only one o'clock! I thought it had been that an hour ago.

When he finds that it is, in fact, past two o'clock, Lord Scratch asks, 'And you're delighted because it's an hour', and he replies, 'To be sure I am – my dear friend to be sure I am, the enemy has lost a limb.' In Act III he again asks, 'How goes the enemy? more than half the day over! – tol de roll lol! (*humming a tune*) – I'm as happy as if I was at a fire, or a general riot.'

what shakes? What are the chances? British underworld: *c.* 1830–1900. Hotten, 1859, gives: '"What *shakes*, Bill?" "None."' – that is, there's no chance of our being able to commit a robbery here. From 'to *shake* the dice', to gamble.

what (occasionally **which**) **shall we do – or go fishing?** seems to have arisen in the middle or late 1920s. In one of her two or three best novels, *The Nine Tailors*, 1934, Dorothy L. Sayers offers this example:

> 'What shall we do, or go fishing?'
> 'I'm on; we can but try.'

It went to Australia in the late 1930s; Baker, 1943, calls it 'a rather pointless elaboration of ... "What shall we do?"'. The point is that it's a trick question.

what suit did you give it upon? was an underworld and fringes-of-the-underworld c.p. of *c.* 1790–1850. (Vaux.)

what they say about Chinese girls. See **yes – and what they say ...** .

what time (or **when**) **does the balloon go up?**; with the reply, **the balloon goes up at** (a stated time). When does it happen? Esp., when does the barrage open or the attack begin: 1915, originally military; then, 1919 onwards, also civilian. John Brophy in B & P, 1930, writes: 'What time does the balloon go up? was a favourite way of asking the time fixed for any special parade or "stunt". The balloon going up was equivalent to the chief event of the day.' The reference is to the observation balloons often to be seen behind the lines. By 1935, slightly obsolescent; by 1945, almost obsolete.

what time's Treasury? See **ghost walks** ....

what was the name of the engine-driver? See **what does a mouse do when it spins?**

what *will* they think of next? A c.p. – perhaps exclamatory rather than truly interrogative – either of jocular astonishment or of mildly derisive admiration, when something new has been invented or announced: since the late 1950s. Occasionally modified to **I wonder what they'll think of next!** It arose, I believe, as a humorous aping of a question often asked by the naïve: and therefore it is usually spoken in a slightly ironic tone.

what will you liq? What will you drink? Ware's evidence tends to show that it didn't last very long; say 1905–14, if so long! A pun on *liquor* and *lick*.

what would happen if you were in an accident? is 'a proverbial c.p. used by mothers to children whose underwear is not in perfect condition' (Barry Prentice, 9 June 1975): common, I believe, to Britain and to the entire British Commonwealth of Nations and to former Dominions, e.g. Rhodesia and South Africa; probably going well back into C19. But applied by others than mothers to not only children but also to adult females.

what would shock me would make a pudding crawl. It takes an awful lot to shock me: predominantly feminine: *c.* 1880–1920. 'Men were supposed to be unshockable, anyway' (Laurie Atkinson, 1 September 1971).

what would you do, chums? dates from *c.* 1938. Syd Walker, 'The Philosophic Dustman' who died of appendicitis during WW2, used, with these words, to pose various droll problems in the BBC's radio programme entitled 'Band Wagon'. (EP in *Radio Times*, 6 December 1946.) Little used after *c.* 1950, yet not entirely forgotten even twenty-five years later.

what you can't carry you must drag was, mid C19–early C20, a nautical c.p., applied to clipper ships carrying too much canvas. (Bowen.)

what you don't start you don't miss is an Australian c.p. used about alcohol, sex, drugs, etc.: C20. (Barry Prentice, 1 May 1975.)

what you say goes – all over the town has, since the middle 1940s, been applied to gossips and rumour-mongers. (A. B. Petch, April 1966.) The first part of the phrase = what you say carries great weight, or is unquestioned; there is a considerable pause before the second part is uttered.

what you see is what you get is, when used with humorous irony, an Australian c.p., dating from *c.* 1920. (Barry Prentice, 9 June 1975.)

whatever turns you on (with 'is all right with me' understood) is 'a phrase accepting another's foibles, hobbies or interests, which do not coincide with one's own': since 1972 or early 1973. (Paul Beale, 12 September 1975.)

what's all this in aid of? See **what's this in aid of?**

what's bit (or **bitten**; or usually **biting** or **crawling on** or **eating**) **you?** What's the matter? British soldiers' (1915) become, by 1920, general. John Brophy in B & P, 1930, says:

> Curiosity, though not necessarily sympathy, was conveyed by the query, 'What's biting you?' Varied by *What's bit you?* or *What's crawling on you?* – all obviously metaphorical from the spectacle of the gestures and grimaces of anyone tormented with lice.

Probably it originated in the US, there being a US example dated 1911. Berrey cites two forms, *what's eating you?* and *what's biting you?* The Canadian currency of this phrase (in the form *what's biting you?*) is glossed thus by Douglas Leechman in January 1969: 'What are you complaining about? *or* What irritates you? Not recent.'

what's cooking? What is happening?: Services', esp. air force: since mid 1940; by 1946, a common civilian c.p. From 'What is that smell – what's cooking?' – asked so very often by so many. In 1942–6, often amplified to *what's cooking, good* *looking?* – with the *g*'s often dropped. Adopted from US, where it was employed both as a greeting and to mean 'What's happening?' *or* 'What's going on here? what's being planned?' Esp. in army, among students, among negroes. (W & F; CM.)

what's for tea, Ma? A 'cheerful greeting coined by the character "Ernie Entwistle" of the Knockout Comic in the 1950s' (Mrs Shirley M. Pearce, 23 January 1975): *c.* 1954–65.

what's in it for me? See **what is there in it for me?**

what's in the green bag? 'What is the charge being preferred against me?' (B & L). Since *c.* 1880; if not much earlier; by 1940, obsolete. The brief-bag or -case carried by lawyers used to be coloured green.

what's it in aid of? See **what's this in aid of?**

what's it to you? – What concern is it of yours? – is a US c.p., dating from *c.* 1919, as in Robert Benchley's 'The Questionnaire Craze', originally published by the *Chicago Tribune* in 1930 and reissued in *Chips Off the Old Benchley*, 1949:

> The first question is a simple one. 'How many hours do you sleep each night, on the average?'
> Well, professor, that would be hard to say. I might add 'and what's it to you?' but I suppose there must be some reason for wanting to know.

Berrey, 1942, synonymizes it with 'Mind your own business!'

what's new? What's the news?: British army: 1939 onwards. (PGR.)

what's on your mind? What's the trouble – your difficulty – the question you long to ask?: since the 1920s. From the literal Standard English sense, 'What's worrying or preoccupying you?'

what's shaking? is a US negro form of greeting, roughly equivalent to 'what's happening?': the 1950s. (CM, 1970.)

what's that got to do with the price of fish? In what way is that relevant?: Australian: since *c.* 1930(?). (Barry Prentice, 1 May 1975.)

what's that in aid of? See **what's this in aid of?**

what's that – Scotch mist? See **what do you think that is ...?**

what's that – the population of China? is an Armed Forces' c.p., arising in 1941 and 'deriding a comparatively high service or regimental number' (Laurie Atkinson).

what's that to me? 'A phrase so common that it shows it's a natural one, when people have no interest in a thing. Well, when a feller gets so warm on either side as never to use that phrase at all, watch him, that's all!' (T. C. Haliburton, *The Clockmaker*, 1837). US, esp. New England: C19–20. Hence also British: mid C19–20.

what's that when it's at home? See **what is that when it's at home?**

what's the big idea? What folly – or unpleasant, unwelcome plan – have you in mind? 'Anglicized' *c.* 1930 and originating in US. (*OED* Supp.)

what's the damage? What's the cost or expense?; How much do I owe?: mid C19–20. 'A humorous variation of the earlier *what's the shot?*' (Weekley.)

Apparently it came to Britain from the US: *Am.* 1848, records it, and so does Farmer.

'This c.p. is extremely common in Australia' (Barry Prentice, I May 1975).

what's the diff? – Of what use? *or* What does it matter? – is a US c.p. of *c.* 1930–50, then rapidly decreasing in use. (Berrey.)

what's the difference between a chicken? A 'trick' or bogus puzzle question, to which the 'dovetail' or answer is: *One of its legs is both the same.* Paul Beale, on 21 May 1976, tells me that he first heard it in 1951.

what's the dirt? What's the scandal?: soon weakened to 'What's the news?': Society: since the very early 1930s. It occurs in, e.g., Evelyn Waugh, *A Handful of Dust*, 1934. In the weak sense, not much used since *c.* 1960.

what's the drill? A military version, dating since *c.* 1925, of **what's the form?** What's the procedure, the social custom, the method? Not very general army use until the late 1930s.

what's the dynamite? (or occasionally **lyddite?**) What's the 'row' about?: Society: respectively 1890–9 and 1899–1900. (Ware.) The former derives from the dynamiters' activities in the 1880s; the latter arose during the Boer War.

what's the form? What's it like at, e.g., a house party?: Society: since the early 1920s. Evelyn Waugh, in *A Handful of Dust*, 1934, says of a household:

> 'What's the form?'
> 'Very quiet and enjoyable.'

During the middle 1930s, it became also an army officers' greeting and quickly spread to the other two Services; in the RAF for instance, it signified 'What is the procedure or tactics or strategy?'; and, more generally, 'How're things?' (PGR.) And adopted from army by navy.

what's the good news? In Berrey we find it included in a list of invitations to drink; but the sense broadened to 'What's the news?' Cf:

what's the good word? What's the news? – esp. 'What's the good news?' – US, it dates from *c.* 1910. In Ring Lardner's 'Thompson's Vacation' (Act I), forming part of *First and Last*, 1934 (he had died a year earlier), we find:

> HAINES: Hello there, Thompson.
> THOMPSON: Hello, Mr Haines.
> HAINES: What's the good word?
> THOMPSON: Well—.

It occurs much earlier in John Kendrick Bangs, *A Line o' Cheer for Each Day o' the Year*, 1913; where the entry for 23 April runs:

> THE ANSWER
> 'What's the good word?'
> Now that's a phrase I truly love to hear,
>   And when 'tis heard,
> I always smile and promptly answer 'CHEER!'
>   It holds more warmth and genial glow
>   Than any other word I know.

Damon Runyon and Howard Lindsay use it in *A Slight Case of Murder*, 1935.

what's the mat? What's the matter?: English Public Schools': *c.* 1870–1940. (Ware.) For truncation, cf **what's the diff?**

what's the matter with father? He's all right is a C20 Canadian c.p. (Douglas Leechman, 30 June 1969.) Of vague denotation it has the connotation 'There's nothing really the matter with the person being referred to'.

what's the matter with your hand? was, 1914–18, an army c.p.–addressed, jocularly, to someone lucky enough to be holding an article of food.

what's the news? What's the matter?: esp. 'What's the matter with you, all of a sudden?': late C16–mid C17. As if literal news has been very bad. In *A Woman Is a Weathercock*, produced and published in 1612, Nathaniel Field, at Act IV, Scene ii, writes:

> STRANGE: She said you challenged her, and publicly
> Told you had lain with her; but truth's no wrong.
> POUTS: Truth! 'twas more false than hell, and you shall see me
> (As well as I can repent of any sin)
> Ask her forgiveness for wounding of her name,
> And 'gainst the world recover her lost fame.
> Kind soul! would I could weep to make amends!
> STRANGE: The more base villain thou. [*Strikes him.*]
> POUTS: Ha! what's the news?

what's the score? What sort of weather is it?: RAF pilots': 1939 onwards, but decreasingly after *c.* 1950. From the world of sport. Hence, 'What's the latest "gen" (information)?': RAF: 1941 onwards. Both senses spread to the Commonwealth wartime air forces.

Quite independent is the Suffolk male c.p., probably of late C19–20, and addressed to a man playing or fumbling around his crutch, but within a trousers side-pocket. (A Suffolk correspondent.) From billiards.

what's the strength? What's the news?: Services, whether combatant or protective: 1940 certainly and 1939 probably. It occurs in, e.g., Allan A. Michie and Walter Graebner, *Lights of Freedom*, 1941. Contrast:

what's the strong of it? 'What's the truth?' *and* 'What's the gist of the matter?' Australian: since *c.* 1910. (I didn't hear it used until 1914.) Recorded by Baker.

what's the time? was, *c.* 1880–1960, a juvenile c.p., directed – from the impudence ensured by either cover or distance – at a man whose feet are exceptionally wide apart as he walks. The posture is variously described as *ten to two* (o'clock), (*a*) *quarter to three*, and (*a*) *quarter to one*. F & G, 1925, describe 'a man who turns out his feet more than [is] usual' as *quarter-to-one-feet*.

what's the time by your gold watch and chain? What's the time?: *c.* 1880–1914. (Douglas Leechman, January 1969: 'Heard often in England before 1908.')

what's this blown in? Whom have we here?: C20, but rarely heard after *c.* 1950. Contemptuous. My earliest record is: W. L. George, *The Making of an Englishman*, 1914.

what's this – Bush Week? See **what do you think this is – Bush Week?**

what's this (occasionally **that**) **in aid of?**: **what's all this in aid of?**; and **what's it in aid of?** The second is the predominant post-1945 shape of the first; the first dates from *c.* 1918 and is also the usual US form, mostly used by people conscious of its British origin, as John W. Clark tells me (5 December 1968); the third has been common, esp. in the Services, since the early 1920s.

Meaning 'What's this about?', *or*, sometimes, 'What's the trouble?', the phrase derives from the popular street collections made, during WW1, in this or that good cause.

what's to pay? In *The Baviad and The Maeviad*, 1797, effectively the 2nd edn of both these satires (the latter, 1st edn 1795), William Gifford (1756–1826), editor of the *Quarterly Review* from its inception, 1809, until his retirement, 1824 – reputed 'slasher' of Keats's *Endymion* and of other Romantics – considerable translator, esp. of Juvenal, asked, in a footnote on p. 23, concerning the playwrights Holcroft, Reynolds, Mortin: 'Will posterity believe this facetious triumvirate could think nothing more to be necessary than an external repetition of some contemptible vulgarity, such as That's your sort! Hey, damme! What's to pay? Keep moving, etc.!'

The phrase *what's to pay?* occurred in Frederick Reynold's *Fortune's Fool*, 1796, thus, 'Damme, "what's to pay" is my watch-word while I stay in London' – a sort of charm in every situation or predicament or against every misfortune – and was spoken by the famous actor, William Thomas Lewis (commonly called 'Gentleman' Lewis); it became a c.p. of *c.* 1796–1810. (With thanks to Miss Patricia Sigl, 17 March 1975.)

[**what's up?** – What's the matter? What's the trouble? – cannot itself be regarded as a true c.p.: but it has evoked several 'near'-c.p. rejoinders, **the sky** and **the prices**, the former since *c.* 1920 if not earlier, esp. among juveniles; the latter, since *c.* 1960 and mostly among adults. (A. B. Petch, March 1966.)]

what's up, Doc? is a US c.p. – and included in W & F's list, published in 1960, of seven 'synthetic fad expressions'.

what's with you? – a US c.p. of greeting – means no more than 'How are you?'. W & F think that it is of Yiddish origin.

what's yer fighting weight? and **what's your Gladstone weight?** I'm your man if you want to fight: respectively *c.* 1883–1914, and of Cockney origin; and of 1885–6 only, but of political origin. (Ware.) Cf **what did Gladstone say ... ?**

what's your beef? is the Canadian c.p. form of the slangy US, hence also Canadian, 'What are you beefing [complaining] about?' The US c.p. form is *what's the beef?* – which goes back to the 1920s.

[**what's your poison?** What would you like to drink? Like the virtually synonymous *name your poison!*, it cannot, I think, be classified as a true c.p.]

what's your song, King Kong? is a US negro expression, current during the 1940s and meaning 'How do you feel?'. (CM, 1970.) A jingle.

what's yours is mine – and what's mine is me own is a jocular comment upon have-it-both-ways greed and selfishness: late C19–20.

wheel it on! Bring it on (*or* in); hence 'Let's have it!' It originated, during the late 1930s, in the RAF: and, not surprisingly, it then referred to aircraft; by the middle or, at latest, the late 1940s, it had become a fairly general civilian usage.

when a girl has to go – she has to go! (To *the lavatory* understood.) A feminine c.p., ruefully frank and prettily innocent and usually as 'phoney' as hell. Since during WW2 – let's say *c.* 1943.

[**when Adam was an oakum boy in Chatham Dockyard**; **when coppers** (or **donkeys**) **wore high hats**; and all other such phrases implying a vast antiquity. Not true c.pp.; therefore omitted. Several are genuinely funny; one or two, genuinely witty.]

when are they goin' to burn yer? It 'was called sepulchrally after a rival gang of footballers on a Saturday morning after the callers had lost a match. I heard this in York *c*. 1919. Semantically, I suppose, it is equivalent to "Go to hell!"' (Wilfred Granville, 18 June 1973). North-east England: *c*. 1910–40.

when did you blow in? 'In frequent use. Not recent' (Douglas Leechman, January 1969). Canadian: since (?)*c*. 1920.

when did your last servant die? Don't order me about: mid C19–20. 'Still used, esp. by adults to demanding kids' (Frank Shaw, 25 February 1969).

when do we laugh? See **joke over**.

when do you shine? What time have you been called for?: Canadian railwaymen's: C20. (Douglas Leechman.) That is, to go to work – or to start work – in the morning. Cf **rise and shine!**

when does the balloon go up? See **what time does the balloon go up?**

when father says 'Turn!', we all turn, as a political c.p., was current *c*. 1906–8. It was occasioned by a political picture-postcard, depicting a family sleeping in one large bed, and it referred to a political leader. (Collinson.) But it took on a social connotation: 'A c.p. of father's authority as head of the house, or wife's tribute to, or mockery of, husband's domination' (Laurie Atkinson, 28 March 1975).

when hens make holy water. Never: rural: C16–17. The *OED* cites RH, 1631, 'As our Country Phrase is, When Hens make Holy-water, at new Nevermasse'.

when I come into my Yorkshire estates. When I have the means in a remote and doubtful future: *c*. 1840–1940. (Hotten, 1860.)

when I want a fool I'll send for you. Occurs in S, 1738, Dialogue I:

NEV[EROUT]: So, Miss, you were afraid that Pride should have a Fall.

MISS: Mr *Neverout*, when I want a Fool I'll send for you. This C18 (?until mid C19) c.p. may derive from the C17 proverb, 'He that sends a fool, expects one'.

when I was with Benson; and **when I was with Irving** are sarcastic theatrical c.pp.; rejoinders to boasters and liars among actors; clearly from the literal phrases. Wilfred Granville comments,

In the old days the actor laddies [actors in Victorian melodrama] used to boast that they were in the same cast as Sir Henry Irving at the Lyceum. The stock comment was 'Walking on, I suppose'.

Irving (1838–1905) was, on and off, at the Lyceum for many years.

Sir Frank Benson (1858–1939) was not a great actor: here, the reference is to being a member of his famous Shakespeare company, 1883 onwards. It occurs in, for instance, Allan Monkhouse's *Nothing Like Leather*, 1913.

when in danger, when in doubt – run in circles, scream and shout! This US c.p., current in C20, may well have arisen in the Marine Corps: certainly it was, esp. in WW2, 'used by Marines to criticize some foul up in the navy'. Certainly, too, it passed from either the USMC in particular or the Fighting Forces in general to civilians; and both in the Forces and on the civilian front, 'its application has been to indicate a state of confusion, a general milling about, a lack of leadership, and an absence of definite or positive action'. (Colonel Albert Moe, in letter dated 15 June 1975.) Cf **if in danger ....**

when (or if) in doubt, toss it out! A pharmaceutical, esp. Australian, c.p. of C20.

when it's at home. See **what is that when it's at home?**

when my wife is here, she is my right hand – when my wife is away, my right hand is my wife. A somewhat laboured c.p., applied to male masturbation: C20.

when push comes to shove. If worse comes to worst: US prostitutes': C20. (Murtagh and Harris, *Cast the First Stone*, 1958.)

when roses are red (a significant pause). When girls attain the age of sixteen, they are no longer too young for sexual intercourse: mostly Australian: since the early 1920s. It was prompted by the – esp. in Australia – widely known couplet:

When roses are red, they are ready to pluck;
When girls are sixteen, they are ready to fuck.

Cf the cynical, world-wide c.p.: **if they are big enough, they are old enough.**

when she bumps she bounces occurs since *c*. 1920, either independently or, with preceding **and**, added to **what ho she bumps!** (Frank Shaw, November 1968.)

when shit (generic) (or **the shit** (specific)) **hits the fan**: also **then the shit'll hit the fan**; and **the shit hit the fan**; and **then the shit hits the fan**, apparently the predominant US form. Douglas Leechman says that it is 'a c.p. indicative of grave or exciting consequences': Canadian and US: since *c*. 1930. 'Wait till the major hears that! Then the shit'll hit the fan!' Dr Leechman adds that 'the allusion is to the consequences of throwing this material into an electric fan'. But the original reference, as Norman Franklin in March 1976 reminds me, is to the agricultural muck-spreader.

In *Troubleshooter*, 1971, David Dody writes: '"Otherwise, I'm proud of you, pal. You really emptied your bowels on the table during that last scene. As we used to say in the [US] Navy [during WW2], the shit hit the fan. But good."'

In *Harlequin*, 1974, Morris West writes, '"We'll have it back on the wires in time for the Monday editions here. Same in Europe. Then the shit hits the fan. It might be wise if you went away."'

when (So-and-So) suffers, everybody suffers is 'a c.p. used when a person with a cold, etc., makes everyone else miserable' (Barry Prentice): Australian: since *c*. 1930.

when the (bloody) Duke (or Dook) puts his (bloody) foot down, the (bloody) war will be bloody well over. A WW1 c.p., peculiar to the 62nd Division, the reference being to the divisional sign, a pelican with right foot upraised. (F & G.)

when the eagle shits is an American c.p., used mostly in the Armed Forces, later also in Federal service, and meaning 'on pay day': since *c*. 1942. (*DCCU*.)

when will the ghost walk? See **ghost walks on Friday – the**.

when yer name's on it, it's on was current in London during 'the London Blitz' of 1940–1. 'Genuine Cockney: if the bomb has your name on it, it will get you, no matter what you do, so stop worrying' (Ramsey Spencer, 4 February 1975). Cf **when you gotta go, you gotta go!**

when you dance in France, the last drop always goes down your pants. This low Australian c.p. dates from *c.* 1955 and has three stressed words, pronounced *dahnce – France – pahnts* in derision of those who say *dahnce* and *Frahnce*, régarded by most Australians as affected, even though they say *bahstard* and *cahstrated*. (Barry Prentice.)

On the other hand, 'an American (US) artist gave me this version *c.* 1925: "No matter how much you may wiggle and dance/The last drop inevitably falls in your pants." There was nothing of the long "A" [*ah*] in his version' (Douglas Leechman, April 1967).

when you gotta go, you gotta go! The US usage (since middle 1930s) perhaps comes from the US gangster films of the 1930s; the British usage (since the middle 1940s) perhaps from 'the London Blitz' of 1940–1 (cf **when yer name's on it, it's on**). 'In universal [US] use and, I think, a real c.p.' (John W. Clark, 17 February 1975). But, it is 'now used exclusively – in the States – for going to the lavatory' (Paul Beale, mid March 1975). And see **when you've got to go ...** and **when a girl has to go ....**

when you were (just) a gleam in your father's eye. See **I was** [doing something or other] **when you were a gleam ....**

when you were wearing short (or, intensively, **three-cornered**) **pants**. When you were still a boy or (*three-cornered* = diapers) a baby: Australian: since *c.* 1920. (Barry Prentice.) Prompted by the **before you came up** group of c.pp.

when your mother was cutting bread on you. A variant of **before you came up**.

when you're on (or onto) a good thing, stick to it! Dating from before 1920, it takes the *onto* (or *on to*) form in Britain, the *on* form in Australia.

when (or while) you're talking about me, you're giving somebody else a rest. This mainly Canadian c.p., which implies slander, dates from before 1949.

when you've got to go, you've got to go. Duty calls: Australian: since *c.* 1920. 'Often used in frivolous situations, e.g. *re* a visit to the toilet' (Barry Prentice, 15 December 1975). Cf **when a girl has to go ...** and see **when you gotta go ....**

But in the US, it rather means 'When you have to die, you have to die': since the 1920s. (John W. Clark *et al.*)

when you've seen one, you've seen the lot. They are all the same: C20. (Barry Prentice, 15 December 1975.) As a general statement, it would be a cliché; but it isn't a cliché when it is used by men of females, or by women of males, to mean that when you've seen one sexual organ, you've seen 'em all. (Which is far from being true.)

where did that one go? 'is actually short for *Where did that one go to, Herbert,/Where did that one go?* which comes from a popular wartime song: it was the abbreviation that the soldiers made into a well-used saying and sometimes followed up with: *Theirs or ours?*' (John Brophy, in B & P.) Current in 1915–18 and applied to a shell-burst near by.

where did they dig him up? 'Used in reference to a newcomer who acts queerly' (A. B. Petch, 9 January 1974): since *c.* 1945. Implying that he acts like a zombie.

where did you get that hat? was very popular in Britain *c.* 1885–1914. From a well-known music-hall song, 'Where did you get that hat?/Where did you get that tile?/[Tumpty-tum ...] just the latest style.' The words of another song so titled, words by Joseph J. Sullivan, started in the US, in 1888 and inaugurated a vogue there too. Cf **who's your hatter?**

where did you get that stuff? What a crazy idea!; What crazy ideas!; Where did you hear such crazy nonsense? This US c.p., apparently dating from *c.* 1919, may originally have been students' – as McKnight suggested in 1923. In 1936, in the definitive edn of HLM, Mencken quoted a variant, *where do you ... ?* and included it in a list of c.pp. that possess some appositeness and sense.

where did you get the Rossa? – i.e., the borrowed plumes: current in 1885 only, and borrowed from a notorious New York police trial, Ware tells us.

where do flies go in the winter-time? A C20 c.p., drawn from an immensely popular song. In the *Spectator* of 13 September 1935, a Swanage hotel's advertisement began with these fateful words.

where do we go from here? has two periods, set in two countries and bearing two different nuances. In Britain it dates from *c.* 1945, is serious; it applies to, e.g., the political or social or moral or economic state of the country, as in 'Well, you see what the situation is. So where do we go from here?'; 'In what directions can we improve matters and how shall we go about doing so?' It occurs in, e.g., Alan Gardner's novel, *The Man Who Was Too Much*, 1967, and perhaps more notably in Noël Coward's *Design for Living*, produced in 1932 and published in 1933, at Act I, Scene i:

GILDA: Last year was bad enough. This is going to be far worse.

LEO: Why be scared?

GILDA: Where do we go from here? That's what I want to know.

But the better known sense, at least in the US where it originated, is 'What do we do next?' – as Berrey, 1942, explains it; a meaning loosely synonymous with that of British usage, but employed in very different, often rather trivial, circumstances.

In *DD* Oliver Herford refers to the US usage – to the matured years of that usage – with this entry: 'HEREAFTER. An evasive answer to the GREAT QUESTION: "Where do we go from here?"'

In *The Glory of the Coming*, 1919, Irvin S. Cobb wrote (very near the end of chapter I):

Not a man aboard the *Tuscania*, [carrying, in February 1918, a contingent of US troops for the Fr. front] whether sailor or soldier, showed weakness or fright.... Descending over the side, some of them to be drowned but more of them to be saved, those American lads of ours [glorified] what before then had been a meaningless, trivial jingle.... Perry said: 'We have met the enemy, and they are ours.' Lawrence said: 'Don't give up the ship!' Farragut said: 'Damn the torpedoes, go ahead.' Dewey said: 'You may fire, Gridley, when you are ready.' Our history is full of splendid sea slogans, but I think there can never be a more splendid one that we Americans will cherish than the first line, which is also the title of the song now suddenly freighted with a meaning and a message to American hearts, which our boys sang that black February night in the Irish Sea when two hundred of them ... went over the sides of *Tuscania* to death: 'Where do we go from here, boys, where do we go from here?'

Related to Cobb's passage is this matter from, and about, J. P. Marquand's *H. M. Pulham, Esq.*, serialized, as *Gone Tomorrow*, in *McCall's Magazine*, in 1940, then published as a book in 1941; matter I owe to Professor Harold Shapiro, who, on 15 November 1974, writes from the University of North Carolina at Chapel Hill:

J. P. Marquand, who always made very effective use of catch phrases in his novels, uses this one in Chapter XXI ... headed 'Goodby to All That' ... The chapter opens: 'Now and then, even as late as 1920, it was not difficult to hear someone humming "Where Do We Go from Here"' – and continues with references to the song. But it is quite clear from the next page (p. 225) that the phrase had come into common use by 1920 quite apart from the song. (Marquand is ordinarily very accurate in such matters.) A character gets off the train in Boston and says: 'Well, where do we go from here?' Then the song is picked up again. There are further references later in the same chapter.

Clearly, therefore, the song had achieved an immense popularity by 1918; it was published in 1917, with words by Wenrick and music by Johnson. For some further account of the song, consult – if you happen to be in the US – S. M. Smith and T. Morse's *Good Old Timers*, c. 1922, as Minnie Sears's *Song Index Supplement*, 1934, bids one do.

The song had become popular in Canada by late 1918. Rear-Admiral P. W. Brock tells me that he was familiar with it in late 1918 or very early 1919, while he was a cadet at the Royal Naval College of Canada; that it was sung on 16 October by RNC cadets at Halifax; and that the last two lines of the chorus were

When Pat would see a pretty girl, he'd whisper in her ear
Oh joy! Oh boy! where do we go from here?

where do you get that stuff? See **where did you ....**

where do you think you are – on Daddy's yacht? This c.p. has, since late 1945 or in 1946, been a naval reproof, or snub, to a seaman complaining about the physical conditions or the discipline aboard ship.

where have you been all my life? has expressed exaggerated flattery from a fellow to a girl, or occasionally vice versa, since the early 1920s; it implies 'What I've missed in life until you came along!' Originally US, it doesn't seem to have become well established in Britain and the Commonwealth until c. 1942, but that it was very well established in US by c. 1925 at latest appears from the fact that it could be employed allusively as early as in Clarence B. Kelland's *Dance Magic*, 1927:

'Who is Leach Norcott?'
'Where have you been all our lives? Whoops, my dear! Leach is a bearcat and I don't mean maybe.'

Kelland used the phrase in other novels – e.g., *No Escape*, 1951.

An English example occurs in, e.g., James Eastwood, *The Chinese Visitor*, 1965: 'The girl was obviously attracted, receiving the Grade A treatment, eyes only for you, where've you been all my life, [all] done to a Duty-and-Love routine.'

In Thomas Shadwell's comedy, *Epsom Wells*, 1673, at Act I, Scene ii (lines 540–1 in D. M. Walmsley's edn), occurs an adumbration. Two 'men of wit and pleasure' speak of two girls newly met and respectively admired:

BEV[IL]: By Heaven a Divine Creature!
RAINS: Beyond all comparison. Where have I lived?

The pairing affords an amusing example of the prevalence of thought-patterns in human communication: a mode of thinking determines a similarity in expression. Only an influences fanatic would suggest that someone reading Shadwell was thereby prompted to 'think up' *where have you been all my life?* Cf **does your mother know you're out?**

where it gets dark. This evasive South African underworld c.p., dating since c. 1920, if not a decade or two earlier, is explained in the *Cape Times* of 23 May 1946: 'If he' – a crook – 'has no fixed place of abode, then he lives "where it gets dark".' Origin? Either 'in the native quarter' of a town or city; or semantically related to the New Zealand and Australian cant phrase, *in smoke*, in hiding.

where it was to be had – where the devil had (or got) the friar. See S, 1738, Dialogue I, where Neverout, looking at Miss Notable's handsome ring, asks '... pray, where did you get it?' and she pertly replies, 'Why where it was to be had; where the Devil got the Fryar.' This C17–18 c.p. is explained by a passage in Davenport, 1639: 'Where the devil had the friar, but where was he?' – wherever it happened to be. (Apperson.)

where Maggie wore the beads. She wore them where most women (and now men too) wear them, around the neck; hence 'in the neck', disagreeably, unfortunately, disastrously, fatally – 'where', in short, 'the chicken got the axe', q.v. Current c. 1905–30. (Weekley.)

where men are men and women are glad of it (or **like it**; or **are double-breasted**) are c.p. expressions of the cliché *where men are men*: C20: predominantly US. (Colonel Albert Moe, in a letter dated 15 June 1975.)

where (or **out where**) **the bull feeds** (or **gets his bleeding**, or **bloody, breakfast**). In the outback, the backblocks, a remote country district: Australian: C20. (Baker.)

where the chicken got the axe is the originator of **where Maggie wore the beads**, q.v. Originally American, it began life in 1892, in a song thus titled, the words being by Harry Mayo. It went to England c. 1893 and was slightly obsolescent by 1936, yet not extinct even by 1975, though noticeably moribund. (W. J. Burke, 1975, and Weekley.)

where the deception took place is a C20 c.p., applied to courtship and marriage. It is – as if you needed to be told – a pun on '... where the *reception* took place'. (A. B. Petch, May 1966.)

where the dirty work's done. 'Office, workshop or room where any work or business is carried on. Mostly used jocularly' (A. B. Petch, 18 December 1946): since c. 1919.

where the dogs don't bite, usually preceded by **the place**. Prison; in prison: English, mostly London, underworld: c. 1870–1960. Arthur Morrison *A Child of the Jago*, 1896, has, 'He was marched away, and so departed for the place – in Jago idiom – where the dogs don't bite.'

where the flies won't get it is used when one downs a drink: late C19–20. US before it became British, according to Ware in 1909.

where the nuts came from tends to be heard when either Barcelona or Brazil is mentioned: mostly lower-middle class: C20. (A. B. Petch, 4 January 1974.) Obviously by association with 'Barcelona nuts' and 'Brazil nuts'.

where the pig bit yer! A vaguely minatory, slightly facetious, proletarian version of **bugger you!**: C20. (Frank Shaw, 25 November 1969.)

where was Moses when the light went out? Wilfred Granville, 12 January 1971, says:

A fatuous phrase that was coined, I think, during the First World War Zeppelin raid periods of 1915–16 when the street lights were dimmed and the youths in the 'monkey runs' of the main streets [of London] used to call [it] out when the dimming took place.

It was still heard occasionally as late as the 1930s. But why *Moses*? But the c.p. may have come from the US. Dr Edward Hodnett tells me (19 July 1975) that, in his childhood, if lights went out, children would chant:

Where was Moses when the light went out?
– Down in the cellar eating sauerkraut.

Derivatively, *where were you when the light* (US) – or *lights* (British) – *went out?* is addressed to a couple obviously in love or suspected of venery, or to a male or a female missing a dance and not visible: C20. It occurs in, e.g., John Mortimer's *David and Broccoli*, 1960.

This derivation form probably derives from the music-hall song, 'Where were you when the lights went out?'

where's George? See **George** ....

where's the body? is US, glossed by Berrey as 'why so sorrowful?': *c.* 1920–70.

where's the fire? has, since *c.* 1930, been jocularly addressed to someone in a tearing hurry. Perhaps originally US, as Colonel Albert Moe implies in a letter dated 28 June 1975. On 18 August 1975, Dr Edward Hodnett writes: 'A common salutation by a motorcycle cop on overtaking a speeding motorist and waving him to a halt. By extension when someone is in an unseemly hurry or makes a hasty proposal.' A good example occurs in Hartley Howard, *Room 37*, 1970:

He did it as if he had no time to waste.
I said, 'Where's the fire?'
'Fire, sir?'
'You know darn well what I mean.... Anyway, what's all the rush?'

Cf Alan Gardner, *The Man Who Was Too Much*, 1967:

'I've been trying to find you for hours.'
'We open at nine-thirty and it is not yet midday,' observed Ivan. 'As my American friends might ask – where is the fire?'

But perhaps more revealing is the fact that, in *Still Life*, published in 1936, Noël Coward could write, in Scene III:

MYRTLE: ... I'll trouble you to get out of here double quick....
JOHNNIE: 'Ere, where's the fire – where's the fire?'

where's the war? was, in 1900–1, directed at a street wrangle: London streets'. From scattered fighting in the Boer War. (Ware.)

where's yer white stick? See LIVERPOOL CATCH PHRASES.

where's your violin? – implying 'You need a hair-cut' – was an Australian c.p. of the late 1940s, the 1950s, the earlier 1960s. From a tradition that male musicians wear their hair long. (Barry Prentice.) Once so many males of the Western World began to wear their hair long, such hairiness no longer caused any comment.

whether or no, Tom Collins is a phrase among sailors, signifying, whether you will or not' (W. N. Glascock, *Sailors and*

Saints, 1829, at chapter II, p. 7): very approximately, *c* 1820–50. A variant, perhaps rather the original, is *Tom Collins, whether or no*, occurring in Alfred Burton, *Johnny Newcome*, 1818. (I owe these to Colonel Albert Moe, in a communication of 26 April 1959.)

which is where we came in. See **this is where** ....

which shall we do – or go fishing? See **what shall we do** ...?

which would you rather be – or a wasp? A London schoolchildren's c.p. of *c.* 1905–14. Julian Franklyn compares **or would you rather be a fish?** and adds, 'So far as I remember, there was no standard reply.'

which would you rather – or go fishing? See the preceding entry and **or would you rather be a fish?**

while I'm standing I'm going was a smart c.p. of *c.* 1700–50. It occurs in S, 1738, Dialogue I:

COL[ONEL]: No, Madam, while I'm *standing, I'm going*.

The meaning: 'I'm able and ready to go'. Possible implication: 'I'm still alive'.

while there's life there's soap is a C20 would-be jocular variation, little heard after *c.* 1950, of the old proverb, ... *there's hope*.

while you're talking about me .... See **when you're talking** ....

whiskers down to here, usually preceded by **he has**. A low c.p. (spoken only) of C20; rare after *c.* 1940; obsolete by 1950. Simultaneously with the utterance of *here*, the speaker placed his hand on his trouser flap.

[**white and spiteful**, sometimes preceded by **all**. 'One of my colleagues [recently] returned to work after a bout of 'flu. Asked how she was feeling, she replied, "A bit better than I was, but still white and spiteful".' As applied to women, it originated as a description of a physical and moral condition accompanying menstrual pains. Sometimes *all white and spiteful* refers to a child 'allowed to stay up long past its normal bedtime' (Paul Beale, 30 September 1975): since 1945, at the latest, and probably since *c.* 1900. It teeters between cliché (menstruation) and c.p. (all other applications).]

[**white rabbits!** – often shortened to **rabbits!** A South of England greeting on the first day of every month; equivalent to 'Good luck!' C19–20. Not a true c.p.: it's folklore.]

Whitehall. See **he's been to** ....

whiter than the Whitehouse on the wall. 'Used occasionally for those who support Mrs Whitehouse and Lord Longford' (A. B. Petch, 4 January 1974): 1973–4. In reference to their campaign for purity in films, and in life in general; and with a pun on *whiter than snow* – on the *whiter than white* of detergents advertising – and on the colloquial phrase, *whiter than the whitewash on the wall*. Like most such c.pp., it had a brief life.

who *are* yer (or **you**)? **– who are *you*?** An offensive enquiry and the truculent answer: London streets': 1883 onwards; by 1950, obsolescent. (Ware.)

But, in this remarkable pioneering article, Mackay tells us that *who are you?* succeeded *does your mother know you're out?* as the regnant phrase and then says,

Every alley resounded with it; every highway was musical with it,

'And street to street, and lane to lane flung back
The one unvarying cry.'

The phrase was uttered quickly, and with a sharp sound upon the first and last words, leaving the middle one little more than an aspiration. Like all its compeers which had been extensively popular it was applicable to almost every variety of circumstance.

Apparently *who are you* (or *yer*)? reigned in the middle and later 1830s, and then, as a c.p., disappeared to live, as it were underground, a more modest life; then it reappeared in 1883 and, in a second period of popularity, acquired the dovetail.

who are you calling 'dirty face'? See **who're you ... ?**

'who are you shoving (or pushing)?' said the elephant to the flea. A jocular c.p., uttered by a big – or, at the least, a noticeably bigger man – jostled, or knocked into, by a small man: since *c.* 1920. (A. B. Petch.)

who asked you to put in your two cents' worth? 'Who asked you for an opinion *or* advice?' – esp. when neither advice nor opinion had been sought: US: since *c.* 1945. (W & F.)

who ate (or stole) the cat? Directed at pilferers: mid C19–20; obsolescent by 1920, obsolete by 1950. Probably from an actual incident.

who boiled the bell?; and **who hanged (but usually hung) the monkey?** On the Clyde, both; in the North Country, the latter, supposed to have derived from an incident at Hartlepool. Derisive.

who called the cook a *bastard*? – who called the bastard a *cook*? 'Complementary, but scarcely complimentary, rhetorical remarks passed in disparagement of the cook's efforts' (*SS*): naval and military: since early 1900s. As a private in the Australian Army, WW1, I heard it rather often.

who did yer (or you) say? Levelled at a person of evident, or self-asserting, importance, and uttered by one friend to another, during the 1890s, in the streets of language-inventive London. (Ware.)

who do you think? See **what do you think?**

who do you think you are – Clark Gable? A feminine, esp. teenagers', gibe, addressed to a youth, or a young man, obviously fancying himself as a Lothario: since the 1930s; very common in the 1940s too, although declining in popularity since the famous US film actor's death. Gable had a dashing and debonair, self-assured manner – at least, in the majority of his films. Heard on British TV as late as early January 1972.

who d'you do? is a C20 Liverpool petty crooks' fraternal greeting. Literally, 'whom have you cheated or defrauded recently?' (Frank Shaw, 1 September 1969.)

who got yer (or you) ready? (The *yer* form belongs to Merseyside and several other parts of England.) Literally, 'Who took your ready money?' This is a scornful and deflating phrase: C20. (Frank Shaw, November 1968.) Cf **we had dozens of these.**

who has any land (or lands) in Appleby? See **how lies the land?**

who hit Billy Patterson? See **who struck ... ?**

who ho she bumps. A jocular variant of **what ho ....** (Douglas Leechman, December 1971.)

who hung the monkey? See **who boiled the bell?**

who is at your elbow? A late C17–mid C18 warning to a liar. (BE.) The implication: 'There is One who hears.'

who is he (or she) when he (or she) is at home? See **what is that ... ?**

who is 'she'? A (or the) cat's mother is a variant of **'She' is a cat's mother.**

who kicked your kennel (or pig-sty)? Who asked *you* to interfere?, *or* Mind your own business! A lower-middle-class c.p.: C20. Cf **who pulled your chain?**

who let you out? 'When a person shows himself very cute and clever, another says to him, "Who let you out?" – an ironical expression of fun: as much as to say that he must have been confined in an asylum as a confirmed fool' (P. W. Joyce, *English ... in Ireland*, 1910): Anglo-Irish: late C19–20; by 1940, slightly – by 1960, very – outmoded. Occasionally heard outside of Ireland.

who looks at the mantelpiece when poking the fire? A common rejoinder to an adverse comment about a young woman's face. It has the air of a proverb, cf **a standing prick hath no conscience.** 'I have also heard more than once the callous "You could always stick a sack (or bucket) over her head"' (Paul Beale, 28 January 1975).

who pawned her sister's ship? A Clare Market, London, c.p. of *c.* 1897–9, directed offensively at a woman. Ware shrewdly conjectured *shift* corrupted.

who pulled your chain? Who asked you to interfere?, *or*, less politely Mind your own ruddy business. It dates from *c.* 1910; it was much used by 'the troops' during WW1; and, *c.* 1919, from being somewhat low, it acquired a certain, although modified, social grace – as why should it not? It's genuinely witty. (B & P, 1930.) Clearly from the noise made by the pulling of a w.c. chain.

who put that monkey on horseback without tying his tail? A cheeky, London streets' insult hurled at a bad horseman: (very roughly) *c.* 1760–1830. (Grose, 1788. But in the 3rd edn, 1796, Grose has *legs* for *tail*.)

who robbed the barber? See **that's a rhyme.**

who says so? See **oh, is that so?**

who shot the cat (or the dog)? A stock reproach shouted at the Volunteers: London streets': 1850s and 1860s – and presumably it went underground, to re-emerge in OTCs, where it remained extant until *c.* 1940 at least.

who stole the cat? See **who ate ... ?**

who stole the donkey? – to which a second person would sometimes add **the man in (or with) the white hat**; a man wearing such a hat as a donkey might, in a very hot summer, wear supplies the occasion: *c.* 1835–1900. (The late Professor Arnold Wall, in letter of August 1939.) Said to have arisen from a specific incident.

who stole the goose? '(*People's – provincial.*) Interjection of contempt, which appears to have some erotic meaning, probably of an erotic nature' (Ware, who gives no date: ? C19–early C20.

who stole the mutton? Jeeringly addressed to a policeman: *c.* 1835–60. From the failure of the police to detect the culprit in a theft of mutton. (Brewer.)

who struck (or hit) Billy Patterson? Of this American c.p., M, 1891, cautiously remarks:

... a question no nearer an answer now than when it was

first propounded by a negro minstrel, who offered a pecuniary reward for the man who 'struck his brother Bill'. It ranks ... as a mystery unsolved. Strictly anecdotal; there being several other anecdotes. Edward B. Marks, *They All Sang*, 1934, declares it to have been a minstrel saying derived from an old minstrel sketch. Period? Well, very approximately, *c*. 1885–1910. 'A ludicrous question admitting of no reply.' (R. H. Thornton, *An American Glossary*, 1912.)

who struck Buckley? was, in C19, employed to irritate Irishmen. The origin is obscure, even though Hotten offers a plausible and amusing story.

who suffers? In Act II, Scene ii, of *John Bull, or The Englishman's Fireside*, published 1803, George Colman the Younger causes the Hon. Tom Shuffleton, a young man-about-town, to say to his rural friend, Frank Rochdale, 'Psha! damn it, don't shake your head. Mine's a mere *façon de parler*: just as we talk to one another about our coats: we never say, "Who's your tailor?" We always ask, "Who suffers?"' This, then, would seem to have been, *c*. 1780–1830, a c.p. current among young men of fashion. The tailors *suffered* because they had to wait so long for their bills to be paid.

who told yer (or **you**)? Ironic for 'We *all* know that' or 'Queen Anne's dead': since *c*. 1925. (Frank Shaw, 25 February 1969.)

who told you to say that? A deflating remark 'to a chap trying to be witty. Liverpool: since 1920s' (Frank Shaw, early November 1968) – but not only Liverpool.

who took it out of you? A low London c.p., addressed, *c*. 1890–1914, to a man looking either utterly dejected or washed-out. (Ware.) Sexual implication?

who was the best man here before I came in? 'A jocular expression sometimes heard when a man enters a pub, canteen, etc.' (A. B. Petch, 10 January 1974): since the late 1940s.

who was your lackey last year? In *The Letter Bag of the Great Western*, 1840, T. C. Haliburton, 'Whenever I asked one of them [the crew of a passenger boat] to help me, he said, "It's my turn below": or, "It's my turn on deck"; and, "Who was your lackey last year?" or, "Does your mother know you're out?"' Clearly meaning 'I'm not a servant – do it yourself', this was an English c.p. of *c*. 1820–70.

who were you with last night? This became a c.p. in 1915, originally in the army. Soldiers derived it from the opening line of a very popular music-hall song dating from a few years before WW1. Although the c.p. hasn't been much heard since 1939, it is not yet (1976) obsolete.

Who were you with last night,
Out in the pale moonlight?
It wasn't your sister
And it wasn't your ma –
I saw ya, I saw ya!

The troops sang it either vigorously or with a mock sentimentality. (B & P, 1931.)

who would be a mother?! Feminine: since *c*. 1920, if not very much earlier. (Fernley O. Pascoe, 15 January 1975.)

who would have thought it? occurs in John Day's *Law-Tricks or, Who Would Have Thought It*, 1608; in *P*, 1639, and many times since, for it is characteristic of a fool to ask this question or to say 'I should not have thought it' (*Insipientis dicere, Non putarem*). See Stevenson.

Note that in late C19–20, there was a variant, *whoever would have thought it?*, with *-ever* heavily stressed, and that, in C20, there exists the variant *who'd have thought it?*

who wouldn't sell a farm and go to sea? and **who'd** (or **who'll**) **sell his farm and go to sea?** These are nautically synonymous c.pp. spoken when something very unpleasant or extremely difficult has to be done. Bowen records the former: *Sailors' Slang* says of the latter: 'Old naval expression varied by *sell the pig and buy me out*.' They probably date from *c*. 1870 and were not, even by 1975, extinct.

A variant has been noted earlier in this book of mine.

whoa! carry me out is an occasional variant of **carry me out!**

whoa, Emma! This urban lower-class c.p. was, *c*. 1880–1900, directed at a woman 'of marked appearance or behaviour in the streets' (Ware, who gives it an anecdotal origin). Note, however, that the phrase more probably arose in 1878 or 1879, for, in the former year, Henry Daykins's song, *Whoa, Emma!*, began with the words, 'A saying has come up', as Frank Shaw has informed me (November 1968). Cf **whoa, mare!** Benham cites the longer and perhaps earlier form, *whoa, Emma! mind the paint*. Hence, *c*. 1900–40, a warning to a person of either sex to be careful.

In 1923, McKnight mentions it as a US c.p. 'in vogue not long ago'.

whoa, Jameson! was, in 1896–7, 'an admiring warning against plucky rashness'. From the Jameson Raid, Ware tells us.

whoa, mare! Turn it up! *or* Desist!: *c*. 1920–70. From an old song – and probably of ultimately rural origin. (Frank Shaw, November 1968.) Cf **whoa, Emma!**

whole team. See **he's a whole team.**

who'll sell his farm and go to sea? See **who wouldn't sell a farm ...?**

who're you (or **who yer**) **calling 'dirty face'?** Writing about the latter half of 1916 in his WW1 novel, *Medal without Bar*, 1930, Richard Blaker, from the viewpoint of an Artillery officer, says: '"'Oo yer calling dirty-face" became a standardised pleasantry in the light of a lantern held to a cigarette-stump, from drivers turned muleteer ("the cavalry" as the gunners called them).'

who're you kidding? Who do you think you're fooling? US: C20. Hence British: since *c*. 1919.

who's a pretty boy then? Paul Beale, writing on 25 May 1975, says: 'Conventional form of address to the *psittaci*; may be misapplied' and thus become a c.p. 'I enjoyed a pocket-cartoon showing Count Dracula thus addressing a vampire bat.'

who's afraid of the big bad wolf? is a general, rather vague c.p. of defiance: since 1933. It comes from Ann Ronell's popular song in Walt Disney's *Three Little Pigs*, 1933, according to *BQ*. I think that Benham must be wrong when he cites 'Who's afeared of the Big Bad Wolf?' as a song written *c*. 1936 by Frank Churchill (d. 1942), for W. J. Burke, 23 September 1975, glossed the *Three Little Pigs* song thus, 'This is the song that helped Americans lick the depression of the early 1930s.' The fame of that song – whatever its title – and, still more, the vogue of the phrase may have prompted the titling of Edward Albee's play, *Who's Afraid of Virginia Woolf?* – which, in 1962–3, met with a remarkable, and a remarkably well deserved, success.

who's dead and what's to pay? What's all the fuss about? *or* Why all the fuss and noise? A US c.p. of *c.* 1820–90; by *c.* 1880, adopted in England, where it fell into disuse *c.* 1920. In the 2nd Series (p. 386), 1838, of T. C. Haliburton's *The Clockmaker*, occurs this passage: 'Stop, says I, and tell us what all this everlastin' hubbub is about: who's dead, and what's to pay now?'

R. S. Surtees, *Facey Romford's Hounds*, 1862 (at chapter LXII, 'The Beldon-Ball') has: '"Who's dead, and what's to pay?" demanded Betsey Shannon, pressing forward through the crowd ...'

who's for tennis? See **tennis, anyone?**

who's hoisting my pennants? Who's talking about me?: naval (lower-deck): C20. 'A seaman may ask this when he overhears someone talking about him' (PGR).

who's milking this cow? and **who's robbing this coach?** The former, dating from the late 1940s, is an Australian variant (recorded by Sidney J. Baker in 1959) of the latter; so also perhaps – although it's more probably independent – is it when used in US, as recorded by Berrey in 1942 as a synonym of 'Mind your own business!' Hence, 'Let me get on with the job'.

The Australian version, *who's robbing this coach?*, humorously refers to bushranging and may go back as far as the 1880s. However, as Dr Douglas Leechman says (April 1967, in letter): 'The anecdote from which this phrase derives: The train robbers were robbing the passengers and threatening to rape the women. An altruistic passenger cries, "Spare the women!" An elderly lady turns on him, exclaiming, "Who's robbing this train, anyway?"' It therefore rather looks as if the train, hence coach, version was US in origin and that it soon passed to Canada.

who's smoking cabbage leaves? A mostly Londoners' c.p., addressed to someone smoking a rank cigar: late C19–20. Cf the late C19–early C20 jibe, *flor de cabbagio* (a not entirely unpleasing example of mock-Spanish).

who's that takes my name in vain? – in C19–20, usually **who's that taking ....** Adopted from the Bible, this c.p. has been current since late C17 or very early C18. It occurs in S, 1738, near end of Dialogue I:

NEV[EROUT]: Pray, Madam, smoak [watch closely] Miss yonder biting her Lips, and playing with her Fan.
MISS: Who's that takes my Name in vain?

who's to pay for the broken glass? Who is to pay for the damage (*any* damages)?: late C19–20; by 1930, obsolescent; somewhat revived during the bombing, esp. of London, during WW2; by 1970, however, obsolete.

who's your hatter? was, *c.* 1875–85, a London, esp a Cockney, c.p. Cf **where did you get that hat?**

who's your lady friend? This c.p., current since *c.* 1910, but obsolete by *c.* 1950, derives from a very popular music-hall song of *c.* 1910–11.

whose dog is dead? – variants, **whose dog is a-hanging?** and **whose mare is dead?** Also in the more colloquial form, **whose dog's (whose mare's) dead?** What is the matter *or* fuss? The former dates from C17; obsolete by *c.* 1940. Massinger, 'Whose dog's dead now/That you observe these vigils' is cited by the *OED*. The latter belongs to late C16–mid C18 and was used by Deloney and Shakespeare and Swift. (Apperson.)

whose little girl are you? A playfully jocular address by male to female in an incipient 'pick-up'. Occurs in, e.g., David Craig, *Whose Little Girl Are You?* – a kidnapping 'thriller' – 1974. From the literal query, at, for instance, a children's party.

whose mare's dead? See **whose dog is dead?**

[**why bring *that* up?** Isn't that entirely irrelevant? is the use when the question is indisputably a piece of literal Standard English: but when it is employed to mean 'Isn't it unkind *or* horribly tactless to mention that *or* to remind me (*or* people) of it', it has come to verge upon the status of c.p. – probably from as far back as the 1890s.]

why buy a book when you can join a library? and **you don't have to buy a cow merely because you are fond of** (or **like**, or **need**) **milk**. Cynical male gibes at marriage: the former, Australian, dates from *c.* 1920; the latter, general, since late C19. In the second, Mr Barry Prentice tells me, Australians prefer *just* to *merely*; they also prefer these interrogatives: *if you like milk, why buy a cow?* and *why buy a cow just because you like milk?*

A friend tells me – I needed telling, for I had completely forgotten – that in *The Life and Death of Mr Badman*, 1680, John Bunyan offers some such adumbration as *you don't need to buy a cow merely because you like milk*.

why curls leave home was a short-lived c.p. of *c.* 1950–60; it referred to baldness. (A. B. Petch.) A pun on the literal use of 'Why girls leave home'.

why don't you drop dead? See **drop dead!**

why don't you get wise to yourself (and grow up)? A US fling – very sarcastic and *de haut en bos* – at someone acting childishly: *c.* 1930–45. (Berrey.)

why don't you go back there? Addressed, often illogically, to a praiser of a country other than the speaker's: since the 1920s. (Frank Shaw, 1 April 1969.)

why don't you just rev up and fuck off? Run away and stop bothering me (or us)! Addressed during the latish 1950s to early 1960s by Servicemen to RAF apprentices: 'they wore little brass wheels on their sleeves', Paul Beale says, and on 18 August 1975 adds, 'I'm not sure why we bothered to elaborate so much.

why girls leave home has, since *c.* 1910 or a little earlier, been used to deride a good-looking, esp. if conceited, 'ladies' man'. Contrast **why curls leave home**.

why is a Marine? See **that's the old navy spirit**.

why is a mouse when it spins? See **what does a mouse do when it spins?**

[**why keep a dog and bark yourself (or do your own barking)?** A self-explanatory proverbial saying, rather than c.p., of C18–20.]

why worry? See **I should worry!**

wider the brim, the fewer the acres – the. That station-owner or farmer who wears an exceptionally wide-brimmed hat – known as a lunatic hat – tends to be only a small landowner: Australian: since the 1930s. A lack of intelligence is implied. (Barry Prentice.)

Wigan. See **come from Wigan**.

Wilhelm II much. A bit too much of the Kaiser! – that is, we're getting sick of hearing about the Kaiser. A Society c.p. of 1898. (Ware.) From his numerous activities.

will a duck swim? Certainly! *or* Of course: C19–20; rare after *c.* 1940 and very rare after *c.* 1960. In *Love, Law, and Physic*, *c.* 1830, James Kenney writes:

> DOC[TOR]: Come, then, Mr Log, since you are so resigned, you'll be a guest at the wedding-dinner, at any rate?
> LOG: Will a duck swim?

will she take a stone in her ear? Will she fornicate?: a raffish c.p. of *c.* 1670–1720. In *The Scowrers, A Comedy*, 1691, Thomas Shadwell, at Act II, Scene in the Park, Tope says to Sir William Rant, a young hellion: '... Did you see who went off with your Aunt? is she given to stumble? Will she take a Stone in her Ear?' An ingenious physiological innuendo.

will you have it now or stay (or **wait**) **till you get it?** is addressed to someone either impatient or in a hurry: mid C17–20; the *stay* form belongs to C17–18; the *wait*, to C19–20. The c.p. occurs in S, 1738, early in the Dialogue I:

> NEV[EROUT]: Pray, Miss, fill me another.
> MISS: Will you have it now, or stay till you get it?

Dickens uses it in chapter X of *Pickwick Papers* (1836–7). Probably domestic in origin and certainly, in C20 at least, mainly domestic in usage.

will you shoot? Will you pay for the drinks? Has, since *c.* 1920, been heard in Australian hotel bars. (Baker.) Presumably a pun on slang *shout*, to stand drinks; perhaps, in part, suggested by the next – if, indeed, the next be authentic.

will you short? Will you pay for a tot of spirits? An Australian c.p. of late C19–early C20. (Ware.) Cf the preceding.

will you walk into my parlour, said the spider to the fly arose in the 1880s, from a song thus titled and sung by Kate Castleton. (W. J. Burke, 23 September 1975.) From England, then the rest of Britain, it passed to some of the Dominions that grew into a Commonwealth; I heard it, in New Zealand, *c.* 1902. When exactly it became a c.p., I have been unable to discover; all I can be tolerably sure of is that it was obsolete by the middle 1930s and that it was a c.p. only when applied by the prospective victim to a dubious invitation – or by others commenting on it.

Willie, Willie – wicked, wicked! This was, *c.* 1900–14, a 'satiric street reproach addressed to a middle-aged woman talking to a youth'. Ware derives it from a droll law-suit. Cf **oh, Willie, Willie!**

wim, wigor, and witality (less often **vim, vigor, and vitality**) is a US c.p., current since *c.* 1930 and probably occasioned by a considerable advertising campaign for some health food or some new beverage. (John W. Clark, 17 February 1975.)

wind enough to last a Dutchman a week. More wind than enough: nautical: *c.* 1820–1930. The American sailor, lawyer, author, Richard Henry Dana uses it in his sea classic, *Two Years Before the Mast*, 1840.

wind in your neck! has, in the Services (esp. in the RAF), been, since the 1930s, 'a polite way of asking someone to close a door' (H & P). Contrast:

wind your neck in! Stop talking! Used in the RAF since *c.* 1937. Contrast the preceding entry.

winking at you, usually preceded by **it's**. It – esp. penis or vulva – greets you with a wink: a playful admission of either innocent, because unintentional, or unabashed exposure of the human body: C20.

winter drawers on dates from late C19; I heard it, not in New Zealand but in my second country, Australia, *c.* 1908; very widely used, except among what one used to call 'the nobs', when the onset of winter necessitates a change from cotton to woollen drawers, underpants, knickers, panties, what have you, whether male or female. Obviously it puns the cliché 'winter draws on'.

winter's day. See **he is like a ....**

wipe (or **wipe off**) **your chin!** is an Australian c.p. addressed, since early in C20, to a person suspected of lying. To prevent the 'bullshit' he is talking from getting into the beer he is probably drinking.

But as a US c.p., used 'as a recommendation to be silent – from chin being used to mean speech' (Ware): *c.* 1860–1910. Berrey includes it among 'Disparaging and Sarcastic Flings'.

wire at Mons – on the. See **Mons ....**

wire in and get your name up! Have a go!: proletarian: 1862–*c.* 1914. Ware wrote thus: 'Recommendation to struggle for success, but originally very erotic' and quoted a non-erotic example from *The Referee*, 21 October 1888.

wish I had yer job! is a C20 Cockney c.p., meaning 'I work – or, I have to work – much harder than you do' (Julian Franklyn).

wish in one hand and shit in the other – and see which (hand) gets full first! is another C19–20 Cockney, low c.p.: a retort to someone expressing any wish whatsoever. (Julian Franklyn.)

But this is, I believe, a variant of what seems to have been the C18–early (? mid) C19 form, *wish in one hand and piss in the other – and see...*, if I read correctly this passage from Dialogue I of S, 1738:

> NEV[EROUT]: You'll be long enough before you wish your skin full of Eyelet Holes. [That is, before you wish yourself dead.]
> COL[ONEL]: Wish in one Hand –
> MISS: Out upon you; Lord, what can the man mean?

Miss gives herself away by the haste with which she interrupts the Colonel. Admittedly, however, *piss* may rather have been *prick*.

wit as three folks. See **he has as much wit as three folks**.

with a five-franc note in one hand and his prick in the other was, 1914–18 in France, a soldiers' c.p., applied to those who, immediately on receipt of their week's pay, hastened to a brothel.

with a hook at the end (of it) – accompanied by the speaker crooking a finger. Don't you believe it!: proletarian: C19–early C20. The shorter form is recorded by JB in 1823; the longer occurs in, e.g., Henry Daff Traill (1840–1900), *The New Lucian*, 1884.

with bells on, hence also simply **with bells**. And *how!* – emphatically; in full force; in a joyous mood and dressed in one's best; and so on: US: since *c.* 1909 (W & F), but by 1960 archaic. But also and probably originally British, in nuance 'with lurid or, at the least, picturesque additions': *c.* 1880–1914. See Agatha Christie, *Nemesis*, 1971:

> 'How sad and tragic and terrible it all was. "With bells on," as you might say,' said Miss Marple, using a phrase of her youth [very late C19–early 20]. 'Plenty of exaggeration ...'

Probably from pictures of court jesters: cf **pull the other one – it's got bells on it**.

A jocular masculine US variant, dating from *c.* 1950, is *with balls on* (W & F).

Cf **with knobs on**.

with forty pounds of steam behind him. See **forty pounds** ....

with knobs on is used both adjectivally and adverbially: late C19–20: US, since *c.* 1930. Embellished or with embellishments; generous, generously; vigorous, vigorously; forcible, forcibly; emphatic, emphatically. W & F note: 'Often in "I'll be there with knobs on", in accepting an invitation. From "with bells on". Usually follows an accusation or oath.' Therefore cf **with bells (on)**.

A vulgar, predominantly male, US variation is *with tits on*. (W & F.)

with teeth. John W. Clark, 17 May 1975, says: 'i.e., before I become decrepit with age. Originally, I am pretty sure, said sarcastically by a woman whose fiancé keeps putting off the wedding, and to whom she says, "*I* want to get *married; with teeth*".' It is a US c.p. – dating since the 1930s – only when it is *not* used literally; when, in short, it roughly corresponds to the preceding entry.

with the corner up! Don't believe him: British underworld: *c.* 1930–60. Occurs in, e.g., Robert Fabian, *Fabian of the Yard*. Origin obscure: perhaps cf the underworld *at the corner*, engaged in looking for 'mugs' at street corners in 'shady' districts.

with the help of God and a few Marines. See **by the grace of God** ....

with thumb in bum and mind in neutral, usually preceded by **he goes around with**, is an Australian c.p., dating since *c.* 1950. Paul Beale, 1 October 1974, says:

> I first heard it from an Australian Army officer in the early 1960s – and have enjoyed it ever since as a very useful c.p. to describe an attitude of vacant-minded uninterest. 'What's the new bloke like, then?' – 'Hard to say; he just wanders around all day with his thumb in his bum and his mind in neutral.'

Adopted, *c.* 1965, by the Services in Britain and elsewhere, it has, Paul Beale notes later in that year, been applied rather to 'a "character" who knows how to relax – to let his mind lie fallow – and to refrain from worry and from excessive work'.

within a mile of an oak is a derisive, purposely evasive reply to 'Where do you – or does he (etc.) – live?' Current in late C16–18. (Apperson cites several writers.) Oaks being in late C16 so plentiful in England that most country people did live within a mile of one.

[**without a word of a lie**, emphatic for 'Honestly!', arose late in C19. It teeters on a hair-line between cliché and c.p.: *I* happen to think it a cliché.]

wobbles. See **she wobbles like a drunken tailor**....

Wogs begin at Calais. Thus speaks the insular Englishman. There are some, more parochial still alas, who would narrow the circle even further and say, 'Wogs begin west of Offa's Dyke; West of Pompey; North of Cockfosters; etc.' (Paul Beale, 1 October 1974): since the middle, perhaps the earliest, 1950s.

That is, travelling *from* England, the prejudiced tend to think that foreigners – esp. coloured peoples – begin at Calais. Strictly, a *Wog* is an Indian of India; an Arab; a native of any country from the Levant (but excluding native Jews) to the Indian-Burmese border. The saying arose, I think, among army and RAF 'officer types'.

woman and her husband – a, was, *c.* 1770–1850, applied to 'a married couple, where the woman is bigger than her husband' (Grose, 1788).

women and children first has, since *c.* 1914, been used jocularly on occasions where no emergency exists.

won't run to it! A racing c.p., applied to a horse that has insufficient staying power to gain a place, or even to reach the winning-post: C20; obsolescent by *c.* 1940 and obsolete by *c.* 1950. (Ware.)

won't you come home, Bill Bailey? Used humorously during the first decade of C20. (Collinson.) From the lachrymose, extremely popular song so titled. (I remember my father singing it *c.* 1900–2.)

Wood family – the. See **Mr and Mrs Wood – in front**.

wooden legs are cheap. See **crutches are cheap**.

wool is up and **wool is down** are Australian ruralities, dating from *c.* 1860 but much less frequently heard after *c.* 1945, wool since then being less predominantly the staple product of Australia. (B & L.)

work – I could watch it all day; also **work? I could** .... My immensely well-read friend Oliver Stonor thinks that it may have originated in Jerome K. Jerome's *Three Men in a Boat*, 1889: since *c.* 1890. The Australian version is *I like work – I could watch it all day* (Barry Prentice): since the 1940s.

[**work it up you!** An Australian objurgation not truly a c.p.]

worried as a pregnant fox in a forest fire, with or without **as** preceding. This picturesque Canadian c.p. dates from *c.* 1920. (Douglas Leechman.)

worry – I should. See **I should worry!**

worse in gaol (or **jail**), usually preceded by **there are**. A C20 c.p., admitting that the person concerned might be worse; often self-deprecatory.

worse things happen at sea – in C20 occasionally **can happen** – is a vaguely, often perfunctorily, consolatory c.p., half-serious, quarter-rueful, quarter-jocular; dating since *c.* 1840 if not earlier. It is recorded at 24 August 1852 in a Diary quoted in Joan Fleming, *Screams from a Penny Dreadful*, 1971. (I believe this to be a serious dating.) A good modern example occurs in John Aiken, *Nightly Deadshade*, 1971: '"You mustn't be misled by cloistrophobia," I say to him. "Worse things happen at sea."'

Cf **pity the poor sailor on a night like this!**

worth a guinea a minute. 'With reference to a pair (usually) of persons with a good line in humorous cross-talk. From the fee believed to have been paid by the BBC' (Paul Beale, 12

June 1974). On the analogy of Beecham's Pills, formerly advertised as *worth a guinea a box*.

wotcher, cock, how's yerself! A Cockney c.p. of greeting, very common during the 1940s and 1950s. (Mrs Shirley M. Pearce, 12 January 1975.) I.e., *what cheer, cock....*

[**would!** – he (or she) or you, which is both British and US, meaning 'That's only to be expected of him', cannot, I think, be adjudged a true c.p.]

would lend his arse! See **arse and shite through his ribs**.

would that I had Kemp's shoes to throw after you! I wish I could bring you good luck: C17–early C19. (Grose, 1785.) From a lost topical reference: I suspect to William Kemp (flourished 1600), comic actor and *dancer*.

would you believe. Paul Beale says, 1 October 1974:

> A meaningless prefix (occasionally suffix) to any statement, but usually an answer to a query. 'When am I on guard again?' – 'Would you believe – tonight!' It struck us like a plague in Hong Kong in 1969 or 1970, and I think it originated in some American TV show, possibly the Rowan and Martin 'Laugh-In'.

It occurs, as an Americanism, in David Fletcher, *A Lovable Man*, 1974.

[**would you believe it!** Cliché, not c.p.]

would you for fifty cents? In HLM, 1922, it is listed in a group of c.pp. that, happening 'to strike the popular fancy, are adopted by the mob' and therefore are 'soon worn threadbare and so lose all piquancy and significance'. Later in the same work, Mencken says:

> [it] originated in the ingenious mind of an advertisement writer and was immediately adopted. In the course of time it acquired a naughty significance, and helped to give a start to the amazing button craze of the first years of the century – a saturnalia of proverb and phrase making which finally aroused the guardians of the public morals and was put down by the *polizei*.

[**would you like your daughter to marry one?** Would you like your daughter, who is white, to marry a black man? A post-1945 bigotry that is clearly not a c.p. but a cliché.]

would you mind! is a polite variation of **do you mind!** It occurs in, e.g., Noël Coward's *Pretty Polly Barlow*, 1964.

would you rather be Red or dead? – that is '...communist or dead?' This mostly British c.p. dates from *c*. 1970, but did not become very general until 1973 (Norman Franklin, March 1976.) Cf **better Red than dead**.

would you rather do this than work? has, since *c*. 1920, been humorously addressed to one who is doing some manual work in his own free time – or, even more humorously, to someone busy at his usual job.

wouldn't be in it, with preceding **I** understood. 'I wouldn't take part in it!' An Australian c.p., dating since *c*. 1945. (Barry Prentice.)

wouldn't be seen crossing (or **dead in**) **a forty-acre field with her** (speaker male) or **with him** (speaker female); with preceding **I** either expressed or understood. A c.p. contemptuous or derisive or both; mostly Cockneys'; late C19–20. To a Cockney, forty acres represent a considerable area. Why *forty*? Because it is often employed generically for a largish number.

wouldn't come! A C20 underworld c.p. applied to 'payment refused on the forged cheque' (Val Davis, *Phenomena*, 1941).

wouldn't give you a light, with **he** or **she** understood. He (or she) is extremely mean: Cockney: late C19–20. For one's cigarette or pipe.

wouldn't it! Elliptical for 'Wouldn't it make you angry or disgusted!' Australian: dating since *c*. 1925. (Baker.) Hence, since the 1930s, elliptical for 'Wouldn't it make you laugh?' – as in Jon Cleary, *The Climate of Courage*, 1954, 'Asking your wife if you can write to her. Wouldn't it?'

'"Wouldn't it" was [during WW2] one of the commonest [Australian] expressions of disgust or surprise, being an abbreviation of "Wouldn't it rock you?" and having many variations' (PGR, at the entry 'Digger Slang'). Cf the next two entries.

wouldn't it make you spit blood? (English) (or **... chips?** (Australian)) (or **wouldn't it rot your socks?**) This c.p. indicates, with some emphasis, a superb contempt. The variants date, respectively and only very approximately, from *c*. 1920 to *c*. 1900, to *c*. 1930. (Partly Barry Prentice.) Cf preceding entry and:

wouldn't it rock you? and **wouldn't it rotate you?** Wouldn't it disgust you?; Wouldn't it make you sick?. These phrases arose, *c*. 1941 and *c*. 1942 respectively, among New Zealand and Australian soldiers and then passed to civilians. The earliest record I can supply is J. H. Henderson, *Gunner Inglorious*, 1945 (New Zealand). Clearly the latter c.p. merely elaborates the former; and the former derives from the slangy *rock*, to startle (someone). Cf the two entries preceding this; also cf:

wouldn't that jar you? In HLM Supp 2, it is included in a list of 'the numerous catch-phrases that have little if any precise meaning but simply delight the moron by letting him show that he knows the latest': Mencken does not place it in time: was it the 1930s? For the meaning, cf the preceding entry and:

wouldn't that jar your mother's preserves? A Canadian c.p., expressing surprise and current *c*. 1910. 'Here *jar*, v[erb], means to preserve fruits and vegetables in air-tight jars, with a pun on "shake"' (Douglas Leechman, January 1968). Cf **wouldn't it rock you?**

wouldn't touch it with a red-hot poker, with preceding **I** understood. An Australian c.p., indicative of extreme aversion: C20. (Baker.)

With it goes **wouldn't touch her** (or **him**, or **it**) **with a forty-foot pole**, usually with preceding **I**. Indicating utter contempt or extreme distaste, it isn't – *pace* Baker – solely or even mainly Australian.

[**wouldn't you like to know?** (or **!**), in answer to a direct question: British and US. *Not* a c.p. but an informal cliché.]

wow-wow(-wow)! and **bow-wow!** was a Slade School c.p. of the late 1890s; R. Blaker, *Here Lies a Most Beautiful Lady*, 1936, '"Wow-wow-wow" she gurgled; for "bow-wow" or "wow-wow" was currency in her circle at that time, to denote quiet contempt of an adversary's contempt.'

Contrast **miaow! miaow!**

wrapt up in the tail of his mother's smock, usually preceded by **he was**. A c.p. of *c*. 1760–1830; applied to 'any one remarkable for his success with the ladies' (Grose, 1785). It evolved from *be wrapt* or *wrapped in his mother's smock*, to be born lucky.

write to *John Bull* (or *The Times*) **about it!** If you wish to com-plain, write to the newspapers: respectively *c.* 1910–30 (before *John Bull* turned genteel) and late C19–20. In short, *The Times* version prompted the *John Bull*.

wrong side of the hedge. See **he was on the wrong side ....**

X marks the spot. From being an almost obligatory caption to photographs of 'the scene of the crime', usually murder, it came to be applied to trivialities, e.g. one's room in hotel or boarding-house, and thus, by its frequency, became, *c.* 1925, a c.p.; my own memory of it hardly antecedes the late 1920s. It passed to the US; the earliest US recording I've seen (W & F, 1960) is unrealistically late – the c.p. must have been current there since, I'd guess, the late 1920s or early 1930s.

[**X. Peary Enza does it** is 'a ridiculous malformation of the Latin tag [*Experientia docet*, 'Experience teaches' – 'We learn by experience']. I first heard it about 1912' (Douglas Leechman, January 1969). This and the rather better-known *experience does it* didn't quite 'make the grade'. I've heard neither form since *c.* 1960.]

Yarra – stinking Yarra! See **stinking Yarra!**

ye gods and little fishes! was, *c*. 1884–1912, a lower- and lower-middle-class indication of contempt; from *c*. 1912 until *c*. 1940, a general exclamation, either of derision or of humour. So lofty a phrase found its humble level by way of 'the Transpontine (or Surrey-side) Melodrama' or, as Ware puts it, 'mocking the theatrical appeal to the gods'.

yea big – yea high is a US c.p. – 'a sophisticated fad phrase since *c*. 1955' (W & F). Starting from the literal 'thus big or thus high', indicated by the hands being spread laterally or raised, two contradictory senses derive: 'very large or high, overwhelmingly large or tall'; and, with suitably modified gestures, 'not very big or high' (W & F).

[**yea bo**. Yes. Not a c.p. Strictly one word – the Zulu *yebo*, yes – it was a vogue word of *c*. 1925–30. (W & F.)]

yeah, see you in a while, crocodile. See **see you later, alligator**.

yeah – you could shit a brick. Like hell you could!: Canadian: since *c*. 1930. Suggested by the slangy *shit a brick*, to have an excessively hard stool after a long costive period.

yer blood's worth bottling! An Australian c.p., indicating either very warm approval or hearty congratulations: since *c*. 1950. Russell Braddon, in his Preface to the English edn (1958) of *They're a Weird Mob* (1957) has: 'To Nino Culotta, therefore, in thanks for this book, I say: "Thanks, mate. Yer blood's worth bottling."'

yer mother and father. See **your mother. . . .**

yere they come. See **here they come . . . .**

yes – a cat with two legs. A C18–20, by 1960 obsolescent, domestic c.p. – the housewife's traditional reply to an errant housemaid; beautifully exemplified in S, 1738, early in Dialogue I:

LADY SM[ART]: Go, run Girl, and warm some fresh Cream.
BETTY: Indeed, Madam, there's none left, for the Cat has eaten it all.
LADY SM: I doubt it was a Cat with two Legs.

yes – and what they say about Chinese girls is wrong too (or, occasionally, **is not true** (or **right**) **either**). A C20 c.p., that, in general, supports a statement or an admission, but, in particular, controverts **clever chaps** (or **devils**), **these Chinese**.

'A variant – for what it is worth – met (*c*. 1946) orally only was "and is it true about Western ladies, as Madame . . . asked Mrs . . .". This variant had a short, not very active life' (Ramsey Spencer, 3 September 1973).

The allusion is to the myth (common in the British Army) that, in Chinese females, 'it' is lateral, not vertical.

Originally and still predominantly British, it reached the US by *c*. 1945. Edward Albee employed it allusively in *Who's Afraid of Virginia Woolf?*

See also **clever chaps** (or **devils**), **these Chinese**.

yes – but in the right place is a fast girl's, or a prostitute's, retort to the 'You're cracked' or 'You must be cracked': late C19–20. (I first heard it in 1922 from a man about town.) Cf **cracked in the right place** and

yes – but not the inclination is a jocular – or a saucy – reply, from either sex to the other, to the question, 'Have you the time?'

yes – but only just, short for **yes, that's right – but only just** (with payment understood). In reply to 'Is that the right money?' First heard in 1949 or 1950, but not a c.p. until the late 1950s.

yes, but what have you done for me *lately*? 'Maybe twenty or thirty years old; still widely current,' says John W. Clark, 4 March 1975; on 18 March 1975 he adds:

Very specifically Jewish in *original* allusion, but the kind of Jewish joke that is not anti-Jewish . . . and is first circulated among them, with humorous allusion to qualities particularly attributed to them – in this case, insatiable and single-minded rapacity. The specific story is essentially this. A (relatively) poor and uninfluential Jew visits a rich or influential one, a friend of his, to ask a favor. The friend, weary of his visitor's repeated importunities, names, with exasperation and sarcasm, the many favors he has done him in the past; to which the beggar replies with self-righteous indignation, 'Yes, but what have you done for me *lately?*' Now used here, as a c.p., of any such person, Jewish or Gentile, but always with allusion to this story.

yes, doctor. See **yes, teacher**.

yes, I also know the one about the three bears. 'A sarcastic remark to one who has purveyed a very old, very well known story: since the 1930s' (Julian Franklyn, 20 May 1969). The reference to the Grimms' tale 'The Three Bears' is clear enough.

yes, I don't think! In his *Chosen Words*, the late Ivor Brown mentioned this as a c.p. of the 1930s. Roughly equivalent to 'I'm damn' sure it isn't (*or* wasn't, etc.)'

yes, my arse and your face is the almost obligatory retort, in workshop and offices, to 'Got a match?' ('I want to light a cigarette, or my pipe.'): non-cultured, non-refined, 'pubby': C20. (Laurie Atkinson, late 1974.) I had never heard it, even in the Australian army during WW1, until I came to England in 1921. And certainly not during my Oxford days, 1921–3. 'A Liverpolitan reply to "Have you a match?" obscene' (Frank Shaw. November 1968, an authority on the speech and folklore of Liverpool. C20.)

yes, she gave me a farthing. See **does your mother know you're out?** Cf:

yes, she's with us is another smart stock reply to **does your mother know you're out?** It dates from *c*. 1920.

yes sir, no sir, three bags full, sir has, since *c*. 1910, been a – ?predominantly naval – c.p. applied to or 'describing an over-obsequious person' (Wilfred Granville, 23 January 1969). But has been also used as 'an indignant reaction to someone being bossy but whom one has to obey' (Patricia Newnham, March 1976). It intentionally alters the old nursery rhyme:

Baa, baa, black sheep.
Have you any wool?
Yes sir, yes sir,
Three bags full.

yes, 'stung' is right! That is – or was – an extortionate price or charge: American: *c*. 1910–40. Recorded by S. R. Strait, 'Straight Talk', *Boston Globe* in *c*. 1917. (W. J. Burke, 1976.)

yes, teacher (or, occasionally, **yes, doctor**). A jocularly ironic c.p., addressed to someone who delights in airing his knowledge of general matters or – the latter form – esp. of medical ailments and cures: since *c*. 1910. (A. B. Petch.)

yes, we have no bananas was, during the approximate lustrum or quinquennium, 1923–7, the most widely used of all c.pp. It is based upon that popular song which has, as refrain, those moving and eloquent lines:

Yes, we have no bananas,
We have no bananas today.

It arose in the US, as HLM remarks in the definitive edn, 1936, '[Tad Dorgan] also [besides several immensely popular neologisms] gave the world, "Yes, we have no bananas," though he did not write the song.' Yet it very rapidly caught on in Britain, *teste* Collinson, who writes (in reference to music-hall originations):

Of recent American importations the best (and worst) is perhaps, Yes, we have no bananas. It is interesting to note that this quaint phrase became so widespread as to clamour for expression in circles where least expected, for in 1923 I heard a learned colleague perpetrate the phrase 'Yes, we have no aspirates' in a philological lecture.

But perhaps the most interesting and notable tribute to the song's popularity comes from Will Rogers. In *The Illiterate Digest*, 1924, a collection of humorous speeches and articles, is a piece titled 'The Greatest Document in American Literature'. It begins thus: 'The subject for this brainy Editorial is resolved that, "Is the Song Yes We Have no Bananas the greatest or the worst Song that America ever had?"' And it ends:

I would rather have been the Author of that Banana Masterpiece than the Author of the Constitution of the United States. No one has offered any amendments to it. It's the only thing ever written in America that we haven't changed, most of them for the worst.

The song was written by Frank Silver and Irving Cohn and published in 1923. It is worth recording that the song was revived in Britain during the food shortage prevalent from mid 1940 until late 1946.

yo bad self! See **your bad self!**

yo, Tommy! is glossed thus by Ware: 'Exclamation of condemnation by the small actor [i.e., an actor in minor theatres]. Amongst the lower classes, it is a declaration of admiration addressed to the softer sex by the sterner.'

York Street is concerned (or **there is York Street concerned**). Someone is looking at us very closely: either cant or low slang: *c*. 1780–1830. Prompted by cant *york*, to stare at, to examine.

you ain't 'alf (or **'arf**) **a one!** (or **a caution!**) Addressed to someone very odd, or very much a 'lad' (or female counterpart), or of a quirkish humour that elicits gentle mockery: mostly lower or lower-middle class: at least 1910 to 1930s (Laurie Atkinson, late 1974); in fact *c*. 1890–1939.

you ain't heard (or, the commoner, **seen**) **nothin' yet!** is a US c.p., recorded in 1942 by Berrey, who glosses it thus: 'it is greater, worse, &c., than you think'. Apparently it dates since 1927, for, as Mr W. J. Burke tells me in March 1976, 'Howard E. Smith, in a recent newscast on TV, used [this] old catch phrase ..., and he said it went back to the play *The Barker*, [written] by Kenyon Nicholson and produced on Broadway in 1927.'

According to the *ODQ*, however, the original form was *you ain't heard nothin' yet, folks*, a remark made by Al Jolson in the first talking film, *The Jazz Singer*. Kenyon Nicholson may, of course, have adapted the longer form: one cannot, or should not, be dogmatic about everything so insusceptible to strait-jacketing as a c.p.

It was adopted, in 1944, in Australia, rather in the nuances, 'There are still worse things to come' and, after *c*. 1950, 'There are even better – or more wonderful, more startling – things to come' (Barry Prentice, 31 January 1969); as you might expect, it occurs in Frank Hardy, *Billy Borker Yarns Again*, 1967. But in the Australian Army song, 'Wait Till you Get to New Guinea', composed in 1944 by one of 'the Desert Rats' of Tobruk, occurs the verse

We like ourselves a little bit,
Until to Aussie we get,
'Wait till you get to New Guinea,
You ain't seen nothing yet.'

Recorded in Martin Page's splendid collection, *Songs and Ballads of World War II*, published in 1972 and then as a Panther paperback.

you ain't just whistling 'Dixie'! is a c.p. Americans 'say to someone who has just made a statement with great emphasis and conviction'; the reference is to the song 'Dixie', which 'was the rallying tune of the Confederate soldiers in our Civil War [1861–5]' (W. J. Burke, 9 April 1975). The c.p. could, therefore, have arisen as early as the later 1860s.

you ain't seen nothin' yet. See **you ain't heard nothin' yet.**

you and me both! is a US c.p. of bonhomous agreement – but also of sympathy. 'You hear this expression every day' (W. J. Burke, 13 May 1975). It seems to date from the 1920s. (Berrey, 1942.) Cf **that makes two of us.**

you – and who else? (British and, since *c*. 1930, also US) and the synonymous **you and whose army?** (US and Australian) are phrases of derisive defiance addressed to a quarrelsome opponent: respectively C20 and since *c*. 1944. '"I reckon I can fight you any day."–"Yeah, you and whose army?"' (Barry Prentice.)

you are a calf! You *do* weep a lot, don't you?: *c*. 1910–40. (Manchon.) Probably influenced – perhaps prompted – by Fr. *tu pleures comme un veau*, you weep copiously.

you are a mouth and will die a lip was a low and abusive c.p. of *c*. 1850–80. (Hotten, 1864.) Apparently suggested by the obsolete *mouth*, a noisy, prating, ignorant fellow, and esp. by *mouth almighty*, which, *c*. 1850–1910, signified a noisy and extremely talkative person. Here *lip* = impudence, 'cheek' – cf *lippy*, cheeky, impertinent.

you are a one! – with *are* and *one* emphasized. Either 'You're odd,' *or* 'You're, droll,' or both: originally and still mostly Cockney: since (I'd guess) *c*. 1880 and still extant, although perhaps in the main allusively, as in Charles Drummond's very entertaining detective novel, *A Death at the Bar*, 1972:

> He laughed. ...'Fifty quid or one month under the lock.'
> 'You are a one,' camped Bertie. [Said Bertie in affected mimicry.]

Cf its US counterpart **aren't you the one!** and **you ain't 'arf a one!**

you are a thief and a murderer, you have killed a baboon and stole his face is a c.p. of vulgar and illiterate abuse, recorded by Grose in 1785 and current *c*. 1760–1830.

[**you are all for the hustings**. You're all due for trouble: mid C17–18. Partly a c.p., partly a proverbial saying, it probably derives from *the Hustings*, long the supreme law court of London.]

you are another! (or, more frequently, **you're another!**) A retort, meaning 'You too are a liar', or a rogue, a thief, a coward, a fool, or what you will: C16–20.

R. S. Surtees, *Handley Cross*, 1854, in vol. I, at the chapter 'Serving up a Hunt Dinner', offers this gem:

> Great was the rush! The worthy citizen ... scrambled to his seat at the head of the table, amidst loud cries of 'Sir, this is my Seat. Waiter, take this person out.'
> 'Who are you?'
> 'You're another!'

You're Another served as the title of a comedy by Leicester Buckingham; apparently not listed in the British Library Reference Division catalogue, it was included in Lacy's Acting Edition of Buckingham's *Faces in the Fire*, performed in 1865. In John Bridgeman's *I've Eaten My Friend! A Farce*, performed in 1851, there had been this illuminating passage:

> WIG: ... She only answered it by throwing in my teeth –
> COC: The hair-brush.
> WIG: No, a sort of 'you're another' answer about a certain Sarah Jane ...

It occurs also, as recorded by Farmer and Henley, in Udall, Fielding, Dickens and Sir William Harcourt. In the third, thus: '"Sir," said Mr Pickwick, "you're another."' And in the fourth, thus: 'Little urchins in the street have a conclusive argument. They say, "You're another".' A late C19–early C20 variation is *so's your father*. Note, too, that *you're another* has, in late C19–20, been almost meaningless, yet slightly contemptuous. Cf:

you are Josephus Rex. See **you're joking**.

you are of so many minds you'll never be mad was a semi-proverbial c.p. of mid C16–mid (or perhaps until late) C18. It occurs, as Apperson informs us, both in Ray and in S. Such vacillation precludes the mounting tensions of insanity.

you are sick of the mulligrubs with eating chopped hay seems to have been a c.p. in S's time, to judge by this passage in Dialogue I:

> MISS: Indeed, Madam, I must take my Leave, for I an't well.
> LADY SM[ART]: What, you are sick of the Mulligrubs with eating chopt Hay.

It implies, I think, an imaginary indisposition. Literally, *the mulligrubs* = a stomach-ache.

you are (or **you're** or **he's**) **slower than the second coming of Christ**. A drill-sergeants' 'gag': C20. As John Brophy remarks in B & P, 1931:

> Those drill-sergeants were often violently objurgatory and their choicest clichés cannot be printed, but here are three of the more cultured:
> You shape like a whore at a christening! –
> You are slower than the second coming of Christ. –
> (*At the fixing of bayonets*). Don't look down! You'd soon find the hole if there was ... [hair round it].

I first heard it in Queensland in 1912.

[**you aren't** (or **you're not**) **the only pebble on the beach**, a C20 'deflater' of the addressee's conceit or self-esteem, both British and US (W & F, *you aren't* ...): more of a cliché, or even a proverbial saying, than of a c.p. See also **you're not the only pebble** ...]

you asked for it (, buster)! US: since '*c*. 1950. Probably out of gangster movies and TV, uttered in the act of blasting someone usually addressed as "buster"' (Edward Hodnett, 18 August 1975). You asked – i.e., sought – trouble: now you're getting it! My own impression is that it goes back to the 1920s.

you astonish me! Well, that's pretty obvious, isn't it?: ironic: dating from *c*. 1920 – or perhaps a little earlier.

you beaut! originally – not later than 1925, but not, I think, earlier than *c*. 1910 – indicates a warm approval or even a profound admiration; it came to be occasionally employed in ironic derision. Australian. (Baker, 1943.)

[**you bet!; you bet your (sweet) life!;** also US **you bet you!** or **you betcha!** – meaning 'You may be sure' or 'Assuredly, surely, certainly' and dating probably since the 1860s in US and since the late 1880s in Britain – cannot strictly, I feel, be classified as c.pp.]

you break the King's laws, you stretch without a halter was a Society – and perhaps a donnish – c.p. of C18. See S, 1738, Dialogue I:

> [Colonel stretching himself.]
> LADY SM[ART]: Why, Colonel, you break the King's Laws, you stretch without a Halter.

In the last resort, only the Crown has had – in Britain – the right either to order or to allow a stretching (of the neck), i.e. a hanging.

you can always stoop and pick up nothing. A C20, mostly Cockney, saying, for instance by one friend to another after a quarrel or, esp., by a parent to son or daughter concerning the intended daughter-in-law or son-in-law. It is probably to be included in the small, very revealing, group of domestic c.pp.

you can ax (or **axe**) **me** (occasionally **my**) **arse**. A low verbal snook-cocking, a c.p. of defiance: mid C18–20; by *c*. 1950, slightly obsolescent, and by 1975 obsolete.

you can bet your wife! 'Heard on and off' (A. B. Petch, 4 January 1974): C20. A pun on *you can bet your life* – see **you bet!**

you can call me anything (or **what**) **you like** .... See **call me** ....

you can go off some people, you know is a remark that, dating since *c*. 1960, is 'addressed to, or directed at, someone who has just said or done something to upset [the speaker]. Very common a few years ago, not heard so much now. Perhaps from some radio or TV show' (Paul Beale, 11 December 1974).

[**you can have any colour you like – so long as** (or **provided**) **it's black** is a famous quotation, attributed to Henry Ford concerning the Model T. Ford automobile – not quite a c.p.]

you can have it! (I don't want it is understood. The emphasis lies on *you* and *I*.) I want nothing to do with it; *or* I think so little of it, I'd give it away.

Originally British, with variant *you can keep it!*, it probably arose during the 1890s: it certainly seems to have been current throughout the C20. In B & P, 1930, in the section on 'Chants and Sayings', John Brophy writes:

Much more terse [than the 'Help, help, there's a woman overboard!' concerted chant or collective serial c.p.] was the following dialogue:
A: This is a *bloody* war. What shall we do about it?
B: You can have it! (*or*, You can keep it!)

Americans adopted it, I'd say in 1918–19, from the British Army. Berrey records it as an interjection 'of disapproval'.

you can have my hat! See **carry me out!**

you can hear them change their minds. Dating from the late 1940s, this urban c.p. is applied to those who live in post-war flats and council houses, so thin are the walls.

you can keep it! See **you can have it!**

you can kiss the book on that. It's a dead cert!: a sporting c.p. that dates from late C19. The book is The Book, the Bible, on which solemn oaths are sworn. Cf:

you can put a ring around that one. That's one thing you *can* be sure of: New Zealand: since *c.* 1925. To 'ring' it – preferably in red – so that it stands out on the page.

you can put it where it'll do the most good appears in Berrey's synonymy of 'disparaging and sarcastic flings' (Section 296, paragraph 8, on p. 300, of the 1st edn, 1942). Cf:

you can put (or **shove**) **it where the monkey puts** (or **shoves**) **its nuts.** See **put it where ....**

you can say that again, originally US, soon became also Canadian and then, during the late 1920s, British; it also passed to Australia and New Zealand, probably during the late 1930s and certainly not later than during the latter half of WW2. It indicates a hearty, even a heartfelt, agreement, and amounts to an emphatic 'Yes!' W & F merely refer it to their entry at *you said it* (which they omit to date).

The phrase had by *c.* 1950 become so ingrained in US speechways that, in *Strong Cigars and Lovely Women*, 1951 (a collection of essays and articles reprinted from *Newsweek* of 1949/1950/1951), at the title 'Kefauver Conquers All', John Lardner, that brilliant son of Ring Lardner who died untimely young, could write, 'This year's drought has got real significance, and don't tell me that I can say that again. I know I can. It has got real significance.'

In 1961, Edward Albee, *The American Dream*, uses it thus:

DADDY: I do wish I weren't surrounded by women; I'd like some men around here.
MRS BARKER: You can say that again.

In the *New Yorker* of 28 April 1973, the letterpress to a drawing of indignant husband saying to tactless – or perhaps merely embittered – wife, 'And when I make a self-deprecat-

ing remark, I would appreciate it if you would not join in so fast with "You can say that again!"'

Another good recent US example comes in James Hadley Chase, *Goldfish Have No Hiding Place*, 1974:

I called her house.
When she came on the line, I said, 'Great news about Wally! You must be relieved.'
'Oh, boy! You can say that again.' Shirley sounded very elated.

The survival of **oh, boy!** is worth noting. Moreover, the alert reader will have noticed that, by 1974, both of these c.pp. were clichés as well. Perhaps, however, I may be permitted to interpose a general editorial comment (which the very severe, I think the *ultra*-critical, reviewer may regard as more properly belonging to the Introduction):

There is no such thing as an inviolable and immutable classification of *permanent* inter-distinction between any one and any other of the three groups: c.pp., proverbial sayings, clichés. What's more, the almost infinite number – hence also the variety – of contexts for familiar phrases (a very useful 'umbrella' term) means that a phrase *can* exist simultaneously in any two of these groups. Language, by its very nature, is insusceptible of being straitjacketed.

To take several British examples: *you can say that again* occurs in P. M. Hubbard, *The Holm Oaks*, 1965; Anne Morice, *Death in the Grand Manor*, 1970; Douglas Hurd and Andrew Osmond, *Scotch on the Rocks*, 1971; Reginald Hill, *An Advancement of Learning*, 1971; John Mortimer, *Collaborators*, 1973; John Braine, *The Pious Spy*, 1975.

Late in March 1969, Mr Arthur Gray of New Zealand described this c.p. as 'a strong affirmation of agreement with a speaker, probably introduced from America to NZ during the Second World War. E.g., "He is just a deliberate liar." – "You can say that again."'

Cf **that makes two of us** and:

you can say that in spades has, since *c.* 1945, been a c.p. of heartfelt agreement. John Welcome, *Beware of Midnight*, 1961, has:

He saw me properly then for the first time.... 'You looked bushed. You need a drink.'
'You can say that in spades,' I said. [From the game of bridge.]

Cf the preceding entry.

you can search me! See **search me!**

you can see their breakfasts (their navels) is 'said of girls wearing very low-cut dresses' (Laurie Atkinson, late 1974): perhaps originally Glasgow, but, if so, it spread almost immediately: since the late 1940s (I myself heard it in 1949 or 1950). Noted in the *Observer* Review, 28 January 1973, article 'A Glasgow Gang Observed'.

you can smell my bloody arse! 'A C19–20 Cockney c.p., intended as a crushing conclusion to an argument, but sometimes evoking the still more crushing retort, "I can – from 'ere"' (Ramsey Spencer, 10 May 1969).

Also used as a declaration of defiance. From the olfactory reconnaissance of two dogs becoming acquainted.

you can take it from me! You may accept – *or* take – my word for it: British: since *c.* 1910, if memory serve me faithfully. Often shortened to *take it from me!*

Both forms are also US, with variant *take it straight from me*; they appear in a synonymy of 'Expressions of Affirmation' in Berrey.

I shouldn't care to 'stick my neck out' and assert which usage, the British or the US, preceded the other: but then, it doesn't have to be either – they could be simultaneous flames from a red-hot spontaneous combustion.

you can't beat City Hall is the predominant US original of **you can't fight City Hall**, q.v. W. J. Burke, 13 May 1975, says:

It is used with a shrug of the shoulders and simply means to the person it is addressed to, that a citizen without political pull can't do a thing against petty regulations of Government, injustices, over-taxation, red tape, etc.... But City Hall may mean any bureaucratic organization in a loose sort of way.

you can't beat the system, can you? is a 'c.p. of grievance when authority is believed to oppress' (Laurie Atkinson, late 1974): since *c.* 1955.

you can't do that there 'ere! and **'ere, what's all this?** This pair of C20 c.pp. originated in (often ironical) derision of the rather general illiteracy of the old-style police constable. Contrast **hullo! hullo! hullo!**

you can't fight City Hall. 'An American c.p. that is widely known in Australia. The term "City Hall" is not used [officially] in Australia except in Brisbane' (Barry Prentice, *c.* 15 December 1974). Dr Edward Hodnett thinks that the US c.p. goes back to the corrupt days of Tammany Hall and that it wouldn't now (1 April 1975) be used by the younger generation. But for the wording, see **you can't beat....**

you can't fly on one wing is a US and Canadian invitation – 'frequently heard in bars and at cocktail parties' (W. J. Burke) – to one more drink before departure: since the early-middle 1940s. (Colonel Albert Moe and Dr Douglas Leechman.) From wartime aviation.

[**you can't get away with it**, current since the middle 1950s, occurs, e.g., in John Osborne's *The World of Paul Slickey* (1959), where it forms the chorus of Act II, Scene ix. But it is, I'd say, a cliché rather than a c.p.]

you can't get high enough was, mid C19–early C20, a low jeering comment on a man's failure to achieve something. 'Probably obscene in origin' (F & H).

you can't get the wood, you know. 'A nonsense c.p. from the Goon Show; used nowadays to explain the lack of almost anything' (Paul Beale, 23 March 1975): as a c.p., since the early 1970s.

[**you can't have everything** is usually a cliché, but when used in lighthearted, often also ironic, allusion, it verges on the c.p., as in Noël Coward, *Nude with Violin*, performed and published in 1956, in the opening passage of Act I:

CLINTON: You don't talk like a valet.

SEBASTIEN: You can't have everything.]

you can't have more than the cat and his skin was, *c.* 1870–1920, a somewhat proletarian, somewhat proverbial, Londoners' c.p., on the theme of *having one's cake and eating it*. (Baumann.)

you can't keep a good man down is both US (Berrey) and British. If used literally and seriously, it's an irrefutable cliché; if used humorously, ironically, esp. if self-deprecatingly, it is an irrefutable c.p. (My tentative datings would be:

US, since *c.* 1900; British, since 1918, perhaps via US soldiers.) Edward B. Marks, *They All Sang*, 1934, mentions a song thus titled in 1900, words by M. R. Carey.

you can't lodge here, Ferguson (or **Mr Ferguson**) is a Londoners' c.p., but very short-lived: *c.* 1845–50; expressing either firm refusal or open derision. It arose from the well-publicized difficulties experienced by a drunk – not a drunken – Scot named Ferguson in obtaining lodgings.

you can't play that on me! 'I am not to be thus deceived; I am not a tool or cat's-paw. This c.p. is of Shakespearian descent. "You would play upon me.... 'Sblood, do you think I am easier to be played on than a pipe?"' [Farmer]. Apparently current *c.* 1850–1900. The Shakespearean reference is to *Hamlet*, Act III, Scene ii, lines 380 ff.

you can't take him (less often **her**) **anywhere!**; *without him embarrassing you* understood. 'Exclamation to the company at large *re* one's partner [or companion] who has just done or said something contrary to the accepted custom [or the social code]' (Paul Beale, 28 July 1975). Cf **excuse my pig, he's a friend** and **is he with you?** It dates from *c.* 1945 at the latest.

you can't take it with you is directed at one who, saving money, loses happiness or, at the least, pleasure: C20 in Britain; since *c.* 1920 in US. It occurs in, e.g., S. P. B. Mais, *Cape Sauce*, 1948. Contrast – and cf – **be a devil!**

you can't think! You couldn't possibly imagine it; *or* You'd never believe it; *or* It's incredible: originally and still mostly proletarian Londoners': since *c.* 1770 or a little earlier. Frederick Pilon, *He Would Be a Soldier*, 1776, at Act III, Scene i, Caleb says to Charlotte: 'Suppose you and I go this evening to Bagnigge Wells, and drink tea – the hot rolls are so nice there, you can't think!' In W. Pett Ridge's *Minor Dialogues*, 1895, we read, 'She took up such an 'igh and mighty attitude, you can't think.' This exclamatory c.p. derives from such a sentence as 'You couldn't imagine how I felt'.

you can't win! is a Canadian c.p., dating since *c.* 1950 and 'expressing the impossibility of coming out on top and the futility of kicking against the pricks' (Douglas Leechman). Was it Ring Lardner who, more or less in these words, said, 'The odds are 6–4 against life'? But what spirited person would refuse to accept such odds?

By 1960, at latest, it had become a common British c.p., soon incorporated into everyday speech and writing, as, for instance, in John Hillaby, *Journey through Britain*, 1968:

'From Cornwall?' he said. 'Do you mean to tell me you've walked all the way here?' I nodded. Shaking his head sadly, he said: 'Then all I can say is it's a pity you couldn't be doing something useful.' You can't win.

Cf this from Frederick Nolan's 'thriller', *The Oshawa Project*, 1974: '... The old army rule of Murphy's Law, in itself an extension of the philosophy best described in the words "You can't win" ...'

In a letter of late March 1969, Mr Arthur Gray confirmed that the c.p. was actively current in New Zealand.

Cf:

you can't win them (but usually **'em**) **all!** You can't *always* succeed; You can't win every game or girl or contest or battle; or, as Edward Hodnett (18 August 1975) puts it, 'a philosophical acceptance of defeat, often self-mocking': a US c.p. dating from *c.* 1940 and adopted in Britain *c.* 1955, yet not widely used there before *c.* 1960.

British usage may be exemplified by the following quotations:

James Munro, *The Innocent Bystanders*, 1969, 'He hesitated just a split second too long, and was already starting to turn when Craig's voice spoke behind him. "Be sensible," said Craig. "You can't win them all. Guns on the bed, please."'

Michael Delving, *The Devil Finds Work*, 1970:

Chead was a hamlet.... The pub, Chead House, was neither old nor attractive....

'A quaint little place,' I said.

'Olde Englande,' said Bob, with a grin at me.

'You can't win 'em all,' I said.

In Britain, it carries the dovetail tag: **but one now and again would break the monotony.** (Cyril Whelan, 14 January 1975.)

US examples abound. One will suffice. In *Hail, Hail, the Gang's All Here*, 1971, Ed McBain writes:

'Anything?' Kling asked.

'You can't win 'em all,' O'Brien [a detective] said.

This is perhaps the most satisfactory joint US–British c.p. to have become very widespread since WW2 and looks (in 1976, anyway) likely to endure a long time.

It is well worth while to note John W. Clark's comment, made on 17 May 1975:

'You can't win 'em all' is very common here [the US] as a sort of rueful and more or less humorous self-consolation for an occasional and usually rare defeat or frustration in any kind of contest or contest-like activity.... [Probably] it originated in the language of usually successful (and often crooked) poker players.

Cf **you win a few, you lose a few.**

you come home with your drawers (or **knickers**) **torn**.... See **you'll be telling me, like the girl, that you've fahnd** (or **found**) **a shilling** and **come home with your knickers torn.**

you could have fooled me, with emphasis usually on *me*; often employed with (a mostly gentle) irony, to mean the opposite of what it says: since *c.* 1955. As in Angus Ross, *The London Assignment*, 1972, ' "I'd say you were a very active man. Me, I'm more of the – er – passive type." ... "You could have fooled me," I told him solemnly.'

Of its Australian use, Barry Prentice supplies the gloss, 'I am surprised by your story' (*c.* 15 December 1974).

[**you could have heard a pin drop** may originally have been a c.p., but probably it has always been a proverbial saying: cf *ODEP*.]

[**you could have knocked me down with a feather**. Rather a proverbial saying than a c.p.]

you could piss from one end of the country to the other. A c.p. reference to the (comparatively) small size of England: naturally commoner among natives of the Commonwealth than among Britons: since *c.* 1910; also predictably: used rarely by women.

you could ride bare-arse from London on it is a West Country c.p., alluding to a very blunt knife: late (?mid) C19–20. It has an agreeably rural tang. (With thanks to Mr D. B. Gardner.) Yet it may be urban, for in S, 1738, Dialogue II, occurs this adumbration:

LORD SM[ART]: [*Carving a Partridge.*] Well, one may ride to *Rumford* upon this *Knife*, it is so blunt.

Why Romford? Apparently for the alliteration.

you *could* **say that** is an understatement for 'You could have put it much more strongly and still not be exaggerating': perhaps going back to *c.* 1920, but I didn't hear it – or, rather, notice it as a c.p. – until WW2. (Mr A. B. Petch happily reminded me of it.)

It is as much US as British. Edward Albee, in *Tiny Alice*, performed on 29 January 1964 and published in 1965, has at Act I, Scene ii:

JULIAN: I am a lay brother.

BUTLER: You are *of* the cloth, but have not taken it.

JULIAN [*none too happily*]: You *could* say that.

you could twist my arm. An understated, yet enthusiastic, reply to 'Have a drink!' – current since the 1940s. Also *you have*, or *you've, talked me into it*: since late 1940s. (Frank Shaw, 11 April 1969.)

The latter form occurs at the end of 'The World's Worst Urger' in Frank Hardy's *Billy Borker Yarns Again*, 1967.

you couldn't be more right. This Australian c.p., dating since the late 1930s, indicates the speaker's entire agreement. (Barry Prentice.) A variant, probably deliberate, of **I couldn't agree more.**

you couldn't be served quicker in a cook-shop! 'Housewives' own tribute (richly deserved) to promptness of catering. Edwardian [to my knowledge], but undoubtedly Victorian [in origin]' (Laurie Atkinson, 18 July 1975).

you couldn't blow the froth off a pint; or **you couldn't knock a pint back**; and **you couldn't fight** (or **punch**) **your way out of a paper bag**. C.pp. addressed to a man boasting of his strength or of his abilities at fisticuffs: C20.

The third (*you couldn't fight* ...) is predominantly Australian and has the variant, *you couldn't fight a bag of shit.* Cf:

you couldn't do it in the time. 'A sarcastic comment to a person who threatens to fight' (Baker): Australian: since *c.* 1910. Cf the preceding entry.

you couldn't fight a bag of shit (or **your way out of a paper bag**). See **you couldn't blow ....** and **he couldn't knock ....**

you couldn't hit the side of a barn is addressed to any bad marksman, especially with a rifle shot: late C19–20.

you couldn't see his arse for dust. He departed very hastily indeed, or in a great hurry: late C19–20.

you couldn't throw your hat over the workhouse wall. You have many illegitimate children in there: a Cockney c.p. of C20. The implication is that an attempt to retrieve one's hat thrown over the wall would be to expose oneself to the risk of recognition. Diminishingly popular since mid-1945: it's no longer polite or seemly or befitting human dignity to mention anything so vulgar as a workhouse.

you date! Well, you *are* out of date! – but with the connotation, 'You *are* a queer fish (*or* odd fellow)!': *c.* 1919–30. (Manchon.)

you don't! See **you don't say so!**

you don't get many of those to the pound. Cyril Whelan, February 1975, says that this originated in

a rude joke shared between males as a particularly well

developed pair of female breasts passes by. Like all bawdy jokes it became ubiquitous without any apparent process of communication and is almost impossible to place in time or location with any authority. Possibly, as with 'Kilroy was here', we need to return to the lees of Pompeii to find companion scribblings (sibling scribblings?) – *Marcus hic fuit* – to discover the proper origin.

Not, I think, pre-C20.

you don't have papers on me. You can't serve a writ on me, for, e.g., debt or, esp., for maintenance of an illegitimate child: C20; obsolete by *c.* 1950.

you don't have to be mad to work here – but it helps. As Paul Beale remarked on 21 April 1975: 'It's one of those things like *the impossible we do at once*, instantly memorable and spread through offices and workshops like wildfire. The sort of thing one can buy a printed sign of in a joke shop.' Since *c.* 1960.

you don't have to buy .... See **why buy ....**

you don't know the half of it! was current among US university students during the 1920s (McKnight mentions it) and then more generally.

I don't know when it came to England, but I'd guess the 1940s. On 4 January 1974, Mr A. B. Petch wrote: 'Heard on and off.'

you don't know whether you want a shit or a haircut (or ... **your arsehole's bored or punched**). These two low c.pp. have, in C20, been used, the former to impute befuddlement, the latter to undermine an argument. Hence, with *won't* substituted for *don't*, both have, since *c.* 1910 and in reaction to insult or to horse-play, been spoken either to deter or to intimidate the aggressive party. (Laurie Atkinson.)

you don't know you're born, with emphasis on *born*. 'An old expression still heard' (A. B. Petch, 16 January 1974): since *c.* 1870, if not a generation or two earlier.

you don't look at the mantelpiece while (or **when**) **you're poking the fire**. A male c.p., referring to the male's usual posture and attitude during sexual intercourse: late C19–20. A fairly representative example of the kind of thing one overhears in a reputable 'pub'.

... when you poke the fire occurs in 'Number One' of John Osborne's *The Entertainer*, 1957.

Cf **who looks at the mantelpiece ... ?**

you don't say! – with emphasis usually on *don't* rather than on *say* – is short for **you don't say so!** but it deserves a separate entry, for it has been current since late C19 in Britain and perhaps earlier in US. It expresses astonishment, sometimes amazement, sometimes incredulity; often tinged with irony, as in ' "He's a great man." – "You don't say!" ' As a synonym of 'Fancy that!' it was satirized by *Punch* on 10 October 1973 in the 'feature' titled 'Complete Vocabulary of Spoken English'.

It is recorded by Berrey as being so well established that it labels a brief synonymy indicating surprise or astonishment. A good example occurs in Tom Ardies, *The Man in the White House*, 1971:

'We writer fellows spend a lot of time meditating and contemplating.'

'You don't say?'

'I do say.'

Dr Edward Hodnett, however, on 18 August 1975, explains its US usage as 'a sarcastic equivalent of **sez you!**' And in September 1975, Professor F. E. L. Priestley adjudged it to be obsolete in Canada.

you don't say so (**!** or **?**) Originally US, it became also British in late C19. In *AM*, 1859, we find an entry 'YOU DON'T! for *you don't say so!* i.e. really! indeed! "Mr Grimaldi threw a back somerset out of a three-story window." Now, *you don't!*' Apparently *you don't say so!* dates from early in C19, for it occurs – as a New England c.p. – in John Neal's novel, *The Down-Easters*, 1833, at chapter I, p. 76, thus:

What I tell you is the truth, nevertheless –

Sneks an' spiders! you don't say so!

An early British example comes in Henry Arthur Jones, *The Crusaders*, performed in 1891 and published in 1893, early in Act III:

PALSAM: Sir, a very terrible scandal has occurred, which I shall be compelled to make public.

DICK: You don't say so?

There is even a facetious variation, the jocular *you don't shay sho* (or *so*)*!* : C20. Parodying the drunken pronunciation of the phrase. This has a parallel variation rather than a deliberate variant: *I should shay sho* (or *so*)*.* – as in Ian Hay, *David and Destiny*, 1934: 'I should shay sho! Go right ahead!' These jocularities signify, the former 'Really!' and the latter, 'Certainly!'

Cf the preceding entry.

you don't shit on your own doorstep is a c.p. variation, a realistic alteration, a down-to-earthing of the proverbial 'You don't foul your own nest': late C19–20.

you first, my dear Alfonso (or **Alphonse**). See **after you, Claude**.

you get my goat! was originally American: *c.* 1905; recorded by S. R. Strait in the *Boston Globe*, *c.* 1917, and by W & F, who show it to have been extant in 1960; it still is in 1976, although less common than formerly.

you get nothing for nothing .... See **nothing for nothing ....**

you getting too proud to speak to anyone now? See **are you getting ....**

you give me the balls-ache! (or **you give me a pain in the arse** or **back**, or **balls**, or **neck**, or **penis**, or in one or two other parts or otherwise-named parts of the body not here specified!) I utterly disapprove of your behaviour; I thoroughly disagree with your point of view; or, most frequently, 'You make me tired' – i.e., impatient, disgusted, etc.: C20. The first, third, fourth, sixth being low (yet 'educated' for *prick*): mostly Londoners'.

you got rocks in the head? 'Usually said to one who has made a ridiculous or audacious suggestion or proposal' (W & F, who cite two examples of its use in 1951): US: since the middle 1940s.

you guessed it! is a US expression of affirmation, recorded, 1942, by Berrey, but going back, I'd guess, to early C20.

you had a mother once. See **you once had a mother**.

you have (or **you've got**) **a nice place** (occasionally **set-up**) **here**, 'here' being a house or flat or room or office: US, since the late 1940s, with *place* predominating from *c.* 1965 onwards; adopted in Britain *c.* 1968.

you have another guess coming! You are mistaken, 'You're all wrong!': US: since the 1920s, if not a decade or two earlier.

you have (or **you've**) **been doing naughty things** is a tediously arch C20 bourgeois c.p. addressed to a young couple when, clearly, the wife is pregnant.

you have been to an Irish wedding was, *c.* 1750–1850, addressed to one who has a black eye. Grose, 1788, says, '... Where black eyes are given instead of favours'.

you have been warned is a jocular c.p., current since the 1930s. From the wording of a familiar police admonition. (A. B. Petch, 4 January 1974.)

you have grown a big girl since last Christmas! is a C20 c.p., hardly a cultured address to a girl or even a woman, the reference being to somewhat noticeably large breasts. (Occurs in, e.g., R. Blaker, *Night-Shift*, 1934.)

you have hit it – I believe you are a witch is given by *ODEP* as a proverb, but I'd have said that, originally at least, it was a C18 c.p. Usually ironic, as in S, 1738, Dialogue II:

LADY SM[ART]: Well, but do you hear, that Mrs *Plump* is brought to bed at last?
MISS: And pray, what has God sent her?
LADY SM: Why, guess if you can.
MISS: A Boy, I suppose.
LADY SM: No, you are out, guess again.
MISS: A Girl then.
LADY SM: You have hit it; I believe you are a Witch.

The C20 equivalent is **how did you guess?**

you have (or **you've got**) **it made**. You're on the point of succeeding: US: since *c.* 1920. Adopted in Britain and Australia and New Zealand by *c.* 1944. It has a synonym, current since the middle 1960s (or a little earlier): everything is marvellous for you. (A reminder, March 1976, from Patricia Newnham.) Especially, however, it is addressed to someone who is constantly saying 'It was marvellous' – 'That's marvellous', and in this nuance the *you* is either heavily or, more deadly, lightly yet incisively, emphasized.

you have made a fair speech was, *c.* 1660–1770, a c.p. uttered 'in derision of one that spends many words to little purpose' (BE).

you have your troubles and I have mine is a US c.p., originating in a wartime story (*c.* 1940) of three sailors who succeed in prying a barman loose from a free drink apiece, with the third one facing the barman's indignation by saying, 'Look, buddy, you've got your troubles and I have mine. Now, give me my change and I'll get the hell out of here.' As a c.p., it arose during the late 1940s and is 'used to dismiss someone with a tale of woe'. (Edward Hodnett, 18 August 1975.)

you haven't a dirty pound note or two (that) you don't want, have you? – or ... I suppose? A confirmed borrower's 'touch' or a merely playful request made on the spur of the moment: since the 1920s.

you haven't been in the Service half a dog-watch. A C20 naval c.p. addressed, esp. during WW2, to a newcomer. (*SS*.)

you haven't got the brains you were born with! A derisive C20 c.p., addressed, usually in exasperation, to an exceptionally stupid person.

you haven't seen the half of it yet, or **anything yet**. There's far more to come: C20.

you hear me! Writing in 1889, Farmer says: 'A pleonastic ejaculation of Californian origin. Used to emphasize a statement already made, and to which assent has been given. "Will you go to-night?" "Yes, that's so." "Wa'al, *you hear me!*"' Apparently only *c.* 1880–1910.

you heard! You heard me all right, so don't pretend you didn't! *or* Oh, you understand, so stop pretending!: US, since *c.* 1935; adopted in Britain not later than the middle 1950s. Contrast **I hear you!** In Hugh C. Rae, *The Marksman*, 1971, we read:

'... Ever since I first thought of it.'
'But you didn't think of it, Jack,' Weaver said quietly.
'What!'
'You heard. It's not your idea ...'

But a much earlier example appears in John Mortimer's endearing short play, *Conference*, which forms part of an *avant-garde* symposium of plays: *Sketches from One to Another*, published in 1960 and written by John Mortimer, Norman F. Simpson, Harold Pinter:

JONES (*in the call-box*): This Jones speaking.
TYCOON: Jones, doll, I appreciate your calling. Long time no hear. Have you lost your love for me, Jones?
JONES: Yes.
TYCOON (*appalled*): What did you say? Guess this is a bad connexion.
JONES: You heard.

It also occurs in John Osborne's *A Sense of Detachment*, produced in 1972, published in 1973, early in Act I:

GIRL: You would, you filthy old woman.
OLDER LADY: What did you say?
GIRL: You heard.

you hum it and I'll pick up the tune. See **no! but you hum it** ....

you kid me not! You're telling me! *or* Don't I know it!: US: since *c.* 1940. Adam Hall, *The Berlin Memorandum*, 1965,

'I'm hot,' I said....
'You kid me not,' he grinned quickly.

Cf **I kid you not**.

you kill me! An ironic 'You're so *very* funny!': since middle 1930s. Also, since early 1940s, *you slay me!* Adopted from US, where current since *c.* 1930. Carolyn Weston, *Poor, Poor Ophelia*, 1972, has:

Then he grinned at Krug. 'Just like the bluebird of happiness, Al – it's right here in our own backyard.'
'You kill me, you know that? Bluebird! You really kill me. Okay,' Krug said briskly, 'let's go.'

An English example: Anne Morice, *Death of the Dutiful Daughter*, 1973:

'In the first place you could hop over to Dedley and crack the case yourself, thereby releasing Robin for more important duties.'
'You kill me, Toby.'

In the title story of Noël Coward's *Pretty Polly Barlow*, 1964, an American says to (English) Polly, ' "You slay me!" Rick Barlow laughed, "The way you say things, sort of deadpan." '

You slay me had, by 1975, become sadly outdated; and *you kill me*, slightly obsolescent.

you kill my cat and I'll kill your dog. An exchange of social amenities, in the lower strata: late C19–20; obsolescent by *c.* 1950, well-nigh obsolete by 1976.

[**you know** is a mere conversational stop-gap, not a c.p.]

you know me, Al is a US c.p., meaning 'You can trust me' (Berrey) or 'You can depend on me'. In 1915, there appeared in US a book that almost immediately became famous: Ring Lardner's collection of baseball stories, *You know me, Al* (*A Busher's Letters*) – where *busher* = a 'Bush League' (i.e., inferior grade) baseball player; Al was the recipient of the letters. In 1923, McKnight's excellent book set it on the academic map.

You know me, Al thus extends the synonymous *you know me* (and can therefore trust me), which is itself much rather a cliché than a c.p. The somewhat boastful, entirely self-delusive writer of these letters keeps on saying 'You know me, Al' – as in the letter of 13 May, which ends: 'I will get back in the big league and show them birds something. You know me, Al.'

you know my methods, Watson. The late Professor W. E. Collinson, while at Dulwich College (1901–7) read 'especially the *Sherlock Holmes* stories then appearing in the *Strand Magazine*.... Holmes supplied us with the oft repeated phrase: "You know my methods, Watson, – apply them."' The phrase is extant.

you know the old saying: the Persian Gulf's the arsehole of the world – and Shaiba's half-way up it. This, an army and RAF depreciatory c.p., dates from the 1920s. 'At Shaiba – properly *Sha'aiba* – there was, for many years, a transit camp' (Laurie Atkinson).

But this unwelcome distinction has, since the middle 1920s, been claimed by the RAF for such unpopular, hell-hole, stations as Aden, Basra, Freetown, Sha'aiba (in Iraq) and Suez.

Australians often refer to a place as **the arsehole of the world** if they think it to be inferior in, e.g., climate or amenities to their own city or town.

[**you know what** is, like *you know*, a mere conversational stop-gap: functionally, a phrase-announcer, a statement-usher-in.]

you know what men (or **women**) **are!** See **isn't that just like a man** (or **a woman**)!

you know what they say about Chinese women received the accolade of literature when, in Act II of *Who's Afraid of Virginia Woolf?*, George remarks to Nick, 'All's pretty much the same, anyway ... in spite of what they say about Chinese women.'

The phrase went to the US via US Army officers, who must often have heard it used by British Army officers during WW2. The British Army in general had, since well before WW2, created and then come, or almost come, to believe that Chinese females had vulvas not vertical but lateral.

Cf **clever chaps** (or **devils**) – **these Chinese!** and **yes – and what they say ....**

you know what thought did is a mid C19–20 c.p. If one's interlocutor asks 'What?' one replies **ran away with another man's wife.** This is a euphemistic version of the C18–mid C19 form recorded by Grose, 2nd edn, 1788: '*What did thought do? Lay in bed and besh*t himself, and thought he was up*; reproof to anyone who excuses himself for any breach of positive orders, by pleading that he thought to the contrary.' Cf **what did thought do?**

A C20 variant is recorded by Julian Franklyn (3 January 1968): 'The pert Cockney boy's response is, "No, 'e never! 'E only thought 'e did!"'

you know what you can do with it (or **... what to do with it**) but *with it* is often omitted. 'I don't want it, *you* can stick (*or* shove) it' (in the usual anatomically fundamental nuance): low: since the early 1920s, if not since *c.* 1900 or even earlier; became, in WW2, very popular in the British Armed Forces, whence, on the Exchange system, it passed also to the US Army; hence to US civilians – that is, if they too hadn't already known it. (W & F include, but do not date, it.) Cf the predominantly US euphemism, **you can put it where it will do the most good.**

you know where you can put it. A US synonym (Berrey) of **you can put it where it will do the most good**, q.v. at **you know what you can do with it.**

[**you know who**, for some person unspecified, is a cliché, not a c.p.]

you look good enough to eat has, in late C19–20, been addressed by males to attractive or very pretty females. Cf **he** (or **she**) **looks as if he** (or **she**) **could eat me without salt.**

you lucky people! is that music-hall and BBC comedian Tommy Trinder's 'gag' become a c.p.: since the 1940s (? latish 1930s).

you make a better door than a window. Addressed to a person obstructing the light: US (Berrey, 1942) and New Zealand (*NZS*), both since *c.* 1920 at latest. Cf – **is your father a glazier?**

'you make a muckhill on my trencher,' quoth the bride. You carve a great heap of food for me: *c.* 1650–1750. Ray, 1678; Fuller. (Apperson.)

you make as good music as a wheelbarrow was, in C18, addressed to one who plays a musical instrument very badly, hence also to one who is disagreeably noisy. (Fuller.)

you make me laugh! – late C19–20, sometimes jocularly varied, *c.* 1905–40, to **you make I laugh!** Whereas the former is contemptuously ironic, the latter tended to be mild and good natured. Cf:

you make me tired! You bore me to tears: a US c.p. introduced into Britain in 1898 by the Duchess of Marlborough, 'a then leader of fashion' (Ware). It was glossed thus by M, 1891: '... said to one who tells a stupid story or who bothers a person'; and some fifty years later by Berrey, with the variant *sick.*

you may fire, Gridley, when you are ready. See AMERICAN HISTORICAL BORDERLINERS. Cf the reference in the Irvin S. Cobb quotation made at **where do we go from here?**

you may go back again like a fool as you came was a Society c.p. of C18. See S, 1738, Dialogue I:

NEV[EROUT]: What's the Matter? Whose Mare's dead now?

MISS: Take your Labour for your Pains, you may go back again like a Fool as you came.

Apparently prompted by the C16–19 proverbial *have nothing but labour for one's pains.*

you may have broke (or **you broke**) **your mother's heart but you** (**bloody well**) **won't break mine!** A C20 military c.p. that may have gone back to the Napoleonic Wars, when the drill-sergeants worked miracles upon Wellington's army. As John Brophy remarked in B & P, 1930, it

> was originally a stock phrase of drill-sergeants taking recruits in hand. It was intended both to intimidate and to reassure the new soldiers that the tyrant of the barrack-square was human underneath. A jest widely appreciated and often repeated by privates.

you mean 'similar', sir. 'Eternal barmaid's retort to "same again"' (Frank Shaw, November 1968): a public-house c.p.: C20.

you missed that – as you missed your mother's blessing. You're unlucky: C18. Near the end of Dialogue I of S, 1738, we read:

> [*Miss tries to snatch Mr* Neverout's *Snuff-Box.*]
> NEV: Madam, you miss'd that, as you miss'd your Mother's Blessing.

you must be a good dancer – you are (or **you're**) **so tall.** A US c.p.: C20. Addressed to any tall man. Cf – and see – **how is the weather up there?**

you must be a witch! See **I think you are a witch** and cf **you have hit it** ....

you must be joking or **kidding.** See **you're joking.**

[**you must be mad**, even when used trivially, remains a cliché rather than becomes a c.p.]

[**you must be out of your cotton-picking** (or **tiny**) **mind!** These US expressions date from *c.* 1945 at the latest. The latter is the kind of c.p. you see in the *New Yorker* – the kind that Thurber would have adorned. Originally it belonged either to academic circles or to smart Society; as nearly always happens, it spread both downward and outward, like women's fashions. The former expression is not in the least cultured. But John W. Clark has made it clear that they are clichés and can be used in any person or tense, and are therefore *not* c.pp.]

you must come in with your two eggs a penny and three of them rotten was current throughout C18–19 and into C20. It has the variant ... *five eggs and four of them rotten.* S, 1738, in Dialogue I, has:

> NEV[EROUT]: Come, come, Miss, make much of naught, good Folks are scarce.
> MISS: What, and you must come in with your two Eggs a Penny, and three of them rotten.

Very pertinently cf the US *must you come in with your two cents' worth?* – q.v. at **two cents' worth.** The c.p. implies that the most frequent and copious contributors to a general conversation are precisely those who have the least to contribute and that what they do contribute is, more often than not, tolitesticular.

you must hate yourself! 'Don't be so conceited!' (Berrey, 1942): US: since the 1920s. Variant: *you sure hate yourself!*

you must have been drinking out of a damp glass. See **must have been drinking** ....

you must have been lying in bed barefoot; and **you must have been sleeping near a crack.** A usually male rejoinder to one who has complained of being afflicted with a bad cold: the former, late C19–20, and lower and lower-middle class and the raffish of almost any class; the latter, perhaps from much further back, even as far as C17 – even though I lack examples. The former occurs in, e.g., Ernest Raymond's novel

Mary Leith, 1931. Among the raffish, there is always an innuendo concerning the anatomical cleft.

The latter reason for a severe cold in the head is either jocosely advanced by the sufferer or slyly imputed by a friend. (Frank Shaw, 1 April 1969.)

you must know Mrs Kell(e)y is a c.p. 'with no particular meaning' – addressed to 'a long-winded talker' and deriving from a 'phrase used for two years at all times and places by Dan Leno' (Ware): *c.* 1898–1905.

you must put in your two cents' worth. See **two cents' worth** ....

you must think I'm made of money! and **do you think I'm made of money?** A late C19–20 c.p. rebuke – or an exacerbated remark – either to an importunate borrower or to an extravagant wife. A variation is *you seem to think money grows on trees* or *it doesn't grow on trees* (with , *you know* sometimes added).

you name it! – as in 'He's had a year of mishaps and misfortunes – you name it' (with 'he's experienced it' understood) – has been rather widely used since *c.* 1955, but esp. from 1970 onwards. Very probably elliptical for *you have only to name it.* Contrast:

you name it – we have it. 'Literally, a claim by a firm that they stock everything'; 'hence, we can do anything you need or anything you want done' (Wilfred Granville, 16 May 1969): since the late 1940s. It sounds as if it might have been prompted by the '**You want the best seats – we have them**' slogan of a well-known London firm.

you need your head examined! You must be out of your mind! I suspect that it may go back to the 1890s–early 1900s, when phrenology became fashionable and the science humorously named 'bumps'. In 1971, I had thought it at least obsolescent, yet, on 29 October of that year, I found the c.p. used in Francis Clifford's then recently published novel, *The Blind Side*:

> He took his time. 'You can't seriously –'
> 'Oh, yes.... Why not?'
> Howard snorted. 'You need your head examined.'
> 'Perhaps. But it doesn't alter the facts.'

There is a frequent variation: *you want your head read!* – current since *c.* 1910 and perhaps mostly Australian. Then there's the US variant, recorded by Berrey, 1942: *you'd better have your head examined*: C20.

you never did is a Cockney (hence general lower-strata) c.p. expressive of humorous appreciation or approval or amazement; elliptical for you've never heard or seen the like of it – anything so oddly strange, so very funny, etc: apparently dating since the 1860s or 1870s, it appears in composition (and therefore not, there, strictly a c.p.) in A. Neil Lyon's *Matilda's Mabel*, 1903, 'My dearest Tilda. Such a go you never did! Mr Appleby proposed to me this afternoon!'

you never get a satisfied cock without a wet pussy is a low C20 c.p., of which Mr Laurie Atkinson has shrewdly remarked, 'The crude and the undeniable in juxtaposition are a frequent astringent herb of popular speech' (11 September 1967).

you never know(, you know). You never know what may come of it, you can't *lose* 'em all: mid C19–20, for the shorter form, C20 for the longer. Cf:

you never know your luck! elaborates the preceding c.p.: C20. Strictly, it lies on the boundary between proverb and c.p.; Benham calls it a proverb, Apperson and *ODEP*, 3rd edn, omit it.

The Australian form tends to be a restrictive elaboration: *you never know your luck in a big city.* (Barry Prentice, 1 May 1975.)

you only volunteer once is a sergeant-major's – or a drill-sergeant's – reply to a recuit's remark that he has enlisted voluntarily, the implication being that, once in the Service, he'll obey orders: WW1, and after.

you ought to remember that, once, *you* had a mother; with variants **... that you too ...**, and **... even you ....** This c.p. has, C18 (perhaps late C17)–20, been addressed to a man speaking ill, cynically, callously, of women. In the Dialogue I of S, 1738, we find:

> LADY SM[ART]: But, Colonel, they say that every married Man should believe that there is but one good Wife in the World, and that's his own.
>
> COL[ONEL]: For all that, I doubt, a good wife must be bespoke; for there is none ready made.
>
> MISS: I suppose, the Gentleman's a Woman Hater; but, Sir, I think you ought to remember that once you had a Mother.

you panic me. I think that you – your way of life – your problems and difficulties – are ludicrous: US: since *c.* 1950. W & F, 'The remark is meant to be cruel.'

you pays your money and you takes your choice appeared first – as you might have supposed had you remembered that this weekly has always been prompt to record the customs and curiosities of Cockney speech – in *Punch*; what surprised me is that it came so early as 1846 (X, 16). Used literally (a stallholder's cry to prospective customers), it is obviously not a c.p.; used otherwise, it is. A notable characteristic of this c.p. – an instance, by the way, of what Mr Cyril Whelan has (14 January 1975) called 'costermongery' – is its popularity among literate and illiterate alike.

you play like I fuck. You're a poor sort of card-player: Canadian Army: WW2, and in general low Canadian use for some years earlier, and ever since.

you said a mouthful! Now you really have said something witty or important or strikingly pertinent or otherwise agreeable! In the definitive edn, 1936, of HLM, the author, who said a multitude of worthwhile mouthfuls, includes this c.p. in a brief list of phrases possessing some degree of sense and appositeness and incidentally makes it clear that it had been current since before 1932. Both Berrey, 1942, and W & F, 1960, duly record it.

In Ring Lardner's *First and Last*, 1934 (a year after his death), we read: '"Well Lardy we will have to make it some other time," said Gerry. "You said a mouthful Gerry" was my smiling reply.' This had been anticipated by five years in Irvin S. Cobb's *This Man's World*, 1929. Probably the phrase goes as far back as *c.* 1920, if not a decade, or more, earlier.

Equally mentionable is the fact that as late as 26 May 1973 the *New Yorker* shows, in a saloon, a maudlin, sombre drunk paraphrasing John Donne's 'No man is an island' and the barman admiringly commenting, 'Friend, you sure said a mouthful!'

The phrase was adopted, very late in the 1920s or very early in the 1930s, in Britain, where it tends to become *you've* (said a mouthful), as in H. M. Harwood. *The Man in Possession*, 1930; in Act II, Scene i, where Clara, the maid says to her mistress, 'It *will* be a great change for you, madam' and madam elegantly replies, 'Clara! You've said a mouthful.'

Cf the next, which had probably fathered it, and also **Queen....**

you said it! was adopted in Britain *c.* 1931, via 'the talkies' (as they were then called). It occurs in Dorothy L. Sayers, *Murder Must Advertise*, 1933:

> 'The idea being that ...?'
> 'You said it, chief.'

In 1937, Dodie Smith, *Bonnet over the Windmill*, at Act II, Scene i, has:

> BILLIE [*a woman of 40*]: Funny – anyone can see you're potty about her, but you don't really like her, do you?
> BRIAN: You said it, lady.

In 1942, Evelyn Waugh uses the fairly frequent British variant, *you've said it*, thus in *Work Suspended*:

> 'There's not the money about.'
> 'You've said it.'

Adopted from US, where it arose *c.* 1900.

In Lillian Mortimer's play *No Mother to Guide Her*, performed in 1905 (not published until 1940), in Act II, we read:

> MOTH[ER] J: You have many sweethearts.
> SILAS: You said it.

Already in 1922, HLM, 2nd edn, remarked, 'The favourite affirmations of the army, "I'll say so," "I'll tell the world," "You said it," etc., are ... passing out'; in the definitive edn, 1936, of that famous book, he notes that Tad Dorgan, who died in 1929, appears to have been its begetter; Berrey, 1942, includes it in a synonymy of 'You are right; you speak truly' phrases; W & F, 1960, gloss it 'Emphatically yes; "I agree with you"; "You are right"' – but say nothing of its duration.

you said it – I didn't (with *you* and *I* strongly emphasized). 'If someone speaks insultingly or disparagingly about someone known to the speaker, who probably feels the same way but does not have the guts to say so, this is the rejoinder. That makes one person liable, absolves the other. One hears the expression quite often.' (W. J. Burke, 9 April 1975.) Probably since early C20.

That is the American usage. In Britain, the predominant usage is exemplified when someone addresses the c.p. to one who has spoken derogatorily of *himself*. (The Briticism, as opposed to the Americanism, has been sent by Patricia Newnham, March 1976.)

you said you could do it. See **well, you said ....**

you saved my life. See **you've saved ....**

you say the *nicest* things – a c.p. only when spoken either in graceful irony or with deliberately simpering jocularity, as, since *c.* 1930, it has often been used. See for instance, James Eastwood, *Little Dragon from Peking*, 1967:

> As the music stopped, he [a Japanese] said, 'Very nice, very pleasant. You do not dance like virgin.'
> 'Why, thank you,' Anna said. 'You say the nicest things.'

you say true – will you swallow my knife? Current *c.* 1890–1940. 'I doubt it!' – applied to an impossible story or assertion. The 'swallowing' implies an 'acid test'.

you seem to think money grows on trees. See **you must think** ....

you shall have the King's horse. See **King's horse** ....

you shape like a whore at a christening is a lower classes', whence also an army, esp. a drill-sergeants', c.p., addressed to a (conspicuously) clumsy person: since the 1890s, if not very considerably earlier – to judge by *as demure as a whore* (or *an old whore*) *at a christening*, which was recorded by Grose in 1788 and goes back even earlier.

you shock my mahogany, current only *c.* 1935–50 and, indeed, very little used after 1945, is an example of those sillier c.pp. which the empty-headed affect. It means 'You shock my morals'.

you should pay for them has, since late C19, been addressed to one whose footwear squeaks, supposedly in protest; it is – or was – so well known that a self-conscious wearer may forestall that comment by remarking (*I*) *haven't yet paid for 'em*.

you should see the other fellow! (occasionally **man!**) – often preceded by **but**. Used after a bout of violent fisticuffs and implying that the opponent is in even worse shape: C20 (? also late C19). John Rossiter, *The Victims*, 1971:

'You've been fighting,' she said.

'Yes,' he admitted. 'But you should see the other man.'

[**you should worry!** Ironic: C20. Mostly British. A mere offshoot from *I should worry* and therefore not strictly a c.p.]

you shouldn't have joined! was a WW2 British Armed Forces' c.p., current since *c.* 1930, addressed to a complainer against the Service. (Probably the poor devil had no choice.) Cf **if you can't take a joke** ....

you shouldn't have joined if you can't take a joke. See **if you can't take a joke** ....

you shred it, Wheat. I agree with you – heartily; *or* How very true!: Canadian adolescents': *c.* 1946–7. (In an article published on 24 October 1946 in a Toronto newspaper.) A pun at once on **you said it!** and on *shredded wheat*, the breakfast cereal.

you slay me! See **you kill me!**

you some kind of a nut? 'A rhetorical question put to anyone whose behaviour or appearance seems odd. Derisive, of course. I have heard it for years' (Douglas Leechman, January 1969): US, since *c.* 1915 (a deduction from the entry in W & F); Canadian, since *c.* 1920. Why *nut*? Because, I'd suppose, it's so often *cracked*.

you stick your .... See **I wouldn't stick my walking-stick** ....

you still wouldn't like it on your eye for a wart is a low C20 c.p. 'retort to imputation of undersized penis, but, even more, with boring suggestiveness and knowing wink when anything is thought' – perhaps rather, said to be – 'not big enough' (Laurie Atkinson, 11 September 1967). One of those playfully arch ribaldries which arouse contempt rather than amusement.

you sure slobbered a bibful is a Canadian variation, since *c.* 1938, and New Zealand variation, since *c.* 1943, of the US *you slobbered a bibful* (, *baby*), which, recorded by Berrey, 1942, was itself a modification of **you said a mouthful**. (Mrs Hazel Franklin of Christchurch, New Zealand, supplied the NZ usage in late 1974.)

you take the calls. You're hard to beat; You're formidable: US: *c.* 1900–40. (Edward Hodnett, 18 August 1975.) From the theatre, where, during and after tumultuous applause, the player solely or mainly responsible comes to the front of the stage.

you talk like a halfpenny (or **a penny**) **book** was, *c.* 1880–1914 and esp. among the lower-middle class, addressed to an affected or pedantic or pompous, or a merely very fluent, speaker. But, Frank Shaw once told me, it was (in the *halfpenny* form) current in Liverpool, late C19–mid C20, to mean 'You talk (very) foolishly or stupidly'.

you talked me into it. See **you could twist my arm**.

you tell 'em! You're dead right!: US, whence also Canadian: vogue during the very approximate period, 1924–41; and with an increasingly limited currency right up to the present (mid 1976) – or, in the words of John W. Clark (10 July 1975): 'a c.p., but dead, or nearly so, for, say thirty years, because of overuse'. Probably the original on which the next has been elaborated.

In Philip Hart Dunning and George Abbott, in Act I of *Broadway, A Play*, 1926, used by speakeasy-owner Dolph, to bootlegger Steve, as Colonel A. Moe tells me.

you **tell 'em, kid,** *you* **tell 'em –** *I'm* **bashful** is an American c.p. listed by Berrey, in a synonymy of phrases equivalent to an expression 'of approval and admiration': mid 1930s–40s; The variant '*you* tell 'em, Harry – *I* stutter' seems to have worn better.

you **tell** *me***!** I haven't the faintest idea. Why don't you tell me about it – implying either an answer to a straight question or a denial by one wrongly accused: since the late 1920s. (Prompted by Wilfred Granville, 14 January 1969.)

you tell me and we'll both know – '*I* don't know' – is used when one has been asked a question one is unable to answer: mostly Australian: since *c.* 1950. (Barry Prentice, 1 May 1975.) Cf **that's asking!**

you think you've got the lights of Piccadilly Circus shining out of your arsehole. See **lights of Piccadilly Circus** ....

you too can have a body like mine is a c.p. only when used ironically, as when the speaker is frail or delicate or puny: mid 1930s–*c.* 1970. (I once heard it used with a sort of humorous, self-deprecating boastfulness by an extremely fit, very likable, physical training instructor, in a hut at Technical Training Command, Reading, in 1943.) It comes – as Frank Shaw told me on 1 September 1969 – from a magazine advertisement of Charles Atlas's body-building course.

It had, by 1957, become so widely known that it could be used thus in John Osborne's *Look Back in Anger*:

JIMMY: ... Should I go in for this moral weight lifting ...? I was a liberal skinny weakling. I too was afraid to strip down to my soul, but now everyone looks at my superb physique in envy.

you wanna buy a duck? See **wanna buy a duck?**

you want a little memory-powder. Your memory is bad: Londoners': *c.* 1880–90. (Baumann.)

you want portholes in your coffin! A C20 naval lower-deck c.p., addressed to a man extremely hard to please. (F & G.)

you want the best seats – we have them has been a c.p. since the latish 1920s, as in Stuart Jackman, *Guns Covered with Flowers*, 1973,

> She jumped to her feet and joined the other girls [dancing the can-can] as they lined up across the stage, turned their backs, flipped up their skirts and bent over.
>
> 'There's a sight for sore eyes, squire,' Meyer said happily. 'You want the best seats, we have 'em.'

An allusion to the slogan used by Messrs Keith Prowse, the agents for theatrical – and other – seats. On 18 April 1975, they very kindly sent me a postcard: 'Above phrase first used about 1925. Cannot be more precise. Still in use today.'

you want to know all the ins-and-outs of a nag's arse! 'You're bloody inquisitive!': low Cockney: late C19–20.

you want your head read! See **you need your head examined!**

you were born stupid – you've learnt nothing – and you've forgotten (even) that! A scathing comment: C20. Perhaps predominantly, but far from being only, Australian. (Barry Prentice, who adds that 'it is known in Austria and Germany'.)

you were bred in Brazen Nose College. You are impudent: C18 (? also late C17). (Fuller.) A pun on *brazen-face*, an impudent fellow, and Brasenose College, Oxford.

you were just – British, **you were (still) only** – **a gleam in your father's eye.** That was, or that happened, before you were born: US and British: since the crazy 1920s; but which of the two peoples can claim for it the honour of primogeniture, I haven't been able to discover. The *New Yorker*, 17 July 1971 (p. 31), has 'Of course, at that time you were just a gleam in your father's eye': Mother to barely teen-aged son, in presence of Father, both parents looking as if they were too bored and stodgy ever to have admitted or responded to such concupiscence.

you weren't born – you were pissed up against the wall and hatched in the sun. This c.p., elicited by some such remark as 'Before I was born', is an example of the biting stock wit affected, and beloved, by the unfastidious male half of the proletariat – and others.

you what? – with emphasis on *what*. Literally, this c.p. is elliptical for 'You mean – *what?*' Hence, 'What do you mean?' Hence also 'What did you say *or* do *or* think?' and 'What do you want?' It dates since *c.* 1950 and belongs, socially, to the lower and lower-middle classes and, occupationally, to the fringe of the underworld; it is also affected by those who'd like to be regarded as belonging to the underworld or, at worst, its fringes.

If considered uncritically, it looks like an ordinary ellipsis, yet, as a c.p., it is used derisively and trenchantly.

Laurence Henderson uses it in *Cage until Tame*, 1973:

> 'All right,' his voice was tired, 'how much?'
> 'A hundred grand.' Tolly took pleasure in saying it.
> 'You what?'
> 'Yeah,' Tolly grinned, 'give or take a bit.'

An example can also be found in one of Ted Lewis's novels about roughs and toughs, *Jack Carter's Law*, 1974:

> 'What's the matter? Rather switch than fight?'
> 'You what?'
> 'Forget it.'

you will catch cold at that. A warning to desist: mid C18–mid C19. (Grose, 1788.)

you will die the death of a trooper's horse. This jocular c.p., current probably throughout C18 and into early C19, means 'You will be hanged'. Grose, 1785, explains it thus: 'That is, with your shoes on'.

Cf, therefore, **you will ride a horse foaled by an acorn**, which was an underworld witticism of mid C18–early C19; recorded by Grose, 1788, 'The gallows, called also Wooden and Three-legged mare'.

A grim, a decidedly macabre, sense of humour these Augustan Age criminals had!

you win a few, you lose a few is a wholly US variant, dating since *c.* 1945, of **you can't win 'em all**. (Colonel Albert Moe, 15 June 1975.) It can even be employed allusively as on the last page of Charles Williams's novel, *And the Deep Blue Sea*, 1971: 'She stopped, arrested by something in the attitude of the two figures leaning on the rail, and shrugged. You won a few, you lost a few.'

Professor John W. Clark, 10 July 1975, says:

> Current, and for perhaps 30 years. Having originated as a 'philosophical' or fatalistic remark by a gambler who has just lost a bet (or a games player who has just lost a game ...), it has a raffish aura rather than a sentimental one ... and its persistence is perhaps owing to that fact. Equivalent to 'You can't win 'em all' – which I think is now commoner.

'Have heard. Common gambling observation or experience. A perfectly legitimate item in everyday speech' (Mr W. J. Burke, 18 August 1975).

you won't know yourself! A C20 c.p.: 'You just won't recognize yourself.' Either independently or (as in 'Try on this overcoat – you won't know yourself!) semi-independently.

you won't melt! One of the domestic c.pp., it is addressed to a child objecting to going out, and esp. to running an errand, in the rain: C19–20 and perhaps older.

[**you *won't* – you know!** is a sturdy proletarian retort to, e.g., 'I'll do something or other': probably going far back into C19. But a conventionalism, rather than a c.p., I think. Cf the next.]

[**you would!** is elliptical for 'You would go and do that, curse you!' or 'That's the sort of thing you *would* do!' Probably goes back to C18; a cliché or a conventionalism rather than a c.p. Cf the preceding entry.]

you would not be so soon in my grave. In S, 1738, Dialogue I, occurs this passage:

> [*Neverout rises to take up the Chair and Miss sits in his.*]
> NEV: You would not be so soon in my Grave, Madam.

Apparently a smart c.p. of (say) 1700–60.

[**you wouldn't believe** is a proletarian syntactic conventionalism and it is always used in composition: in short, it isn't autonomous, therefore not a c.p. Probably since mid C19, if not earlier. Dorothy L. Sayers, *Murder Must Advertise*, 1933, 'The edges of the steps get that polished you wouldn't believe.']

you wouldn't chuckle! is an Armed Forces' c.p., dating since *c.* 1938 and originally, as still, meaning 'You wouldn't think so' and then briskly coming, *c.* 1940, to mean also 'You bet I would!'

you wouldn't fool (or **kid**) **me** (or **a fellow**), **would you?** I don't believe it: US: C20. (Berrey.)

you wouldn't fuck (or **rob**) **it**. And that's no lie! An RAF c.p. dating from the mid 1920s. 'Signifies the complete positive to a question or a statement. "It's cold this morning." – "You wouldn't rob it" (or "fuck it")' (Mr R. M. Davidson, in a letter sent to me on 26 September 1942). Semantically, 'You wouldn't do a violence to the truth' – 'You wouldn't rob, i.e. steal from, i.e. defraud the truth, i.e. lie'.

you wouldn't knob it. You wouldn't think so *or* realize it – with the implication that the speaker does know it to be a fact: RAF: since *c.* 1930. Obscurely derivative is the later – since *c.* 1938 – sense, 'You bet I would!' Cf **you wouldn't chuckle!**

you wouldn't read about it. It would amaze you, *or* It beats the band: New Zealand: since *c.* 1935. Also Australian (since late 1930s) – as in Mary Durack, *Keep Him My Country* (Australia), 1955, '"Blimey!" Wilde exclaimed. "You wouldn't read about it."'

John Mortimer, *Marble Arch*, one of the four short plays comprising *Come As You Are*, produced 1970, published 1971, has:

MAX: Good evening, McNee. 'Morning, everyone.

MISS PARKER [a New Zealand journalist]: Gee whiz. You wouldn't read about it. Is his lordship often to be found among your toilet facilities?

LAURA (*still amazed*): No ...

Not the sort of thing you'd expect to read in the newspapers, some truths being, we are solemnly told, stranger than fiction.

you wouldn't rob it. See **you wouldn't fuck it**.

you wouldn't shit me and **don't shit the troops!** These synonymous c.pp., meaning 'I don't believe you', date respectively since the 1920s and, in the Canadian Army, throughout WW2. Here, *shit* = *shit on*, *beshit*.

you'd be far better off in a home was an army c.p. of WW1, but it derived from a late C19–20 civilian saying; by *c.* 1955, slightly obsolescent, but not, even by 1975, extinct. Of its WW1 usage, John Brophy wrote that it 'was sympathetic – in that derisively jocular manner which constituted one of the hall-marks of the soldiers' humour; it fitted almost any occasion on which the man addressed *would* have been far better off in a home' (B & P, 1930).

Rear-Admiral P. W. Brock, on 1 January 1969, says:

This saying was in regular use [in the navy] in 1920–2 because it went so well to the refrain of a march called *El Albanico* (or *Elalbanico*) much in favour with Royal Marine bands. The music almost sang the words itself –

'You'd be far better off in a home,
You'd be far better off in a home,
You'd be far better off in a home,
You'd be far better,
Far better off,
Far better off in a home.'

To that naval comment, add this by Wilfred Granville (16 May 1969): 'Jocular consolatory c.p. to one who is in a bad way, whether in health or in the matter of fortune, especially ill-fortune.'

you'd be (or **get**) **killed in the rush**. Addressed, although not

among the *élite*, to a girl who has just said, 'I wouldn't marry you (even) if you were the last man in the world': C20. It derives from, is the c.p. product of, several scabrously entertaining anecdotes.

you'd better believe it! 'Meaning "Yes, indeed!" Quite recent' (Douglas Leechman, December 1968): Canadian: since *c.* 1960. And on 19 August 1975 F. E. L. Priestley confirmed it.

you'd better have your head examined! See **you need your head examined**.

you'd forget your head if it wasn't screwed on (**properly**) – often preceded by **forget!** – has, since late C19, been addressed to a very forgetful person. I lack an early written reference; I do, however, remember it since *c.* 1901 or 1902 onwards.

you'd get killed in the rush. See **you'd be killed ....**

you'd have been taller if they hadn't turned up so much for feet is a Canadian c.p., current since the 1920s. (Douglas Leechman.)

you'd have died. You would have died of laughing: C20.

you'd only spend it is the traditional c.p. rejoinder to someone remarking 'I'd like, *or* love, to have a lot of money': late C19–20.

you'd soon find it if there was hair (**all**) **round** – or **around** – **it!** See **don't look down ....**

you'll be a long time dead. Enjoy yourself while you can – and while you may: late C19–20. Cf the obsolete proverbial sayings, *she who will not while she may, may not when she would* and *there will be sleeping enough in the grave* and Marvell's 'The grave is a fine and private place,/Yet none, I think, do there embrace.' It has the variant *you're a long time dead*, which occurs in, e.g., 'Number Two' of John Osborne's *The Entertainer*, 1957.

you'll be in dead trouble is common in barrack rooms and workshops 'and such' and it warns someone against the unwisdom of ignoring Standing Orders or the Rules and Regulations or against the stupid tactlessness of annoying the roomful, especially 'its strong men': since *c.* 1925. (Laurie Atkinson, late 1974.)

you'll be lucky – I say, you'll be lucky! was used, sarcastically, in a North Country accent, by comedian Al Read: popular for some years, esp. in the North Country, where it is extant. The versatile Al Read was perhaps better known for his **right, monkey**.

you'll be saying 'arseholes' to the C.O. next. See **eh? – to me!....**

you'll be shot at dawn! 'Used as a jesting expression' to 'anyone in a scrape' (F & G): army: WW1; rarely used in WW2.

you'll be smoking next! What a dissipated fellow – *or* girl – you are!: jocularly commenting upon an act far more audacious or improper: since *c.* 1950 or perhaps as much as twenty years earlier. From the story of that father to whom the neighbours have been complaining that his son has been sexually consorting with their daughters and who feels obliged to say *some*thing to the lad: 'I hear you've been fooling around with the girls. What a young devil you are! Why, dammit, you'll be smoking next!'

you'll be telling me, like the girl, that you've fahnd (or **found**) **a shilling**, which alludes to – indeed, derives from – the rather older **you come home with your drawers** (later **knickers**) **torn and say you found the money**. An 'anecdotal c.p. expression of derisive incredulity' (Laurie Atkinson): Cockneys': C20 – at least until *c.* 1971.

you'll be the death of me! Really, you mustn't be so funny – I'll die laughing: C20. Cf and contrast **you'd have died** and **you'll die**.

you'll bust your kefoofle (or **kerfuffle**) **valve**. An Australian c.p. dating since *c.* 1960 and addressed to someone lifting a heavy weight – i.e., 'You'll bust your appendix.' Probably related to the naval slang term, *foo-foo valve*, an entirely mythical gadget that is always blamed for any mechanical break-down whatsoever. (Barry Prentice, *c.* 6 March 1975.)

you'll die. You'll be vastly amused: *c.* 1670–1740. Elliptical for 'you'll die with laughing', as in Colley Cibber, *The Careless Husband*, 1705, at Act IV, Scene i:

LADY B[ETTY]: Well, my lord, have you seen my Lord Morelove?
LORD F[OPPINGTON]: Seen him! ha, ha, ha, ha! – Oh! I have such things to tell you, Madam – you'll die –.

you'll do yourself out of a job is a jocularity addressed to anyone working very hard: since early C20.

you'll get something you don't want. Addressed to a male, it warns against venereal disease; to a female, pregnancy: C20.

[**you'll get yourself disliked**. '(*Street*, *1878*.) A satirical protest against anyone who is behaving abominably' (Ware, 1909): the grim understatement so weakened that, by *c.* 1930 at latest, it had become a mere cliché.]

you'll have no rest in the airship business until you get the ship into the air. 'An old Royal Naval Air Service c.p., as well as a truism' (Wilfred Granville, late December 1968).

you'll have your work cut out. You'll find it difficult to cope with the work you're causing yourself: a c.p. only when it is addressed – this is its commonest use in Australia – to a mother about to have, or having very recently had, her third or fourth baby. (Barry Prentice, 1 May 1975.) Otherwise it is a cliché.

you'll keep is an Australian variant of **it's only lent**: since *c.* 1950. (Barry Prentice, 31 January 1969.) The *you* is the object lent. But there is a second sense, likewise Australian: 'I'll deal with you later' (Barry Prentice, 1 May 1975).

you'll know me again, won't you? See **do you think you'll know me again?**

you'll speak one word for him and two for yourself. In the Dialogue I of S, 1738, we read:

COL[ONEL]: *Tom*, put on a bold Face for once, and have at the Widow. I'll speak a good Word for you to her.
LADY ANS[WERALL]: Ay, I warrant you'll speak one Word for him, and two for yourself.

This C18 c.p. clearly means that in doing another a good turn, one intends to do oneself an even better.

you'll wake up one of these fine mornings and find yourself dead. An Anglo-Irish c.p., current since late C19, but not much used since *c.* 1945. Implying a fling at Irish humour and esp. at Irish 'bulls'.

your arse is sucking blue mud. You're talking nonsense: Canadian. 'A favourite, *c.* 1920–30. Probably obsolete – I haven't heard it for years. Cf **you're full of shit**'. (F. E. L. Priestley, 19 August 1975.)

your ass! 'means the end or destruction' of the person addressed: US negroes': since *c.* 1950. (CM.) Elliptical for some such phrase as 'You've got your backside caught in the machinery'.

your ass-hole's sucking wind. You don't know what you're talking about: a low C20 Canadian c.p., esp. common in the Canadian Army of WW2. The Canadian *your ass is sucking blue mud* and *your cock's out a foot* are more precise: 'You're in error': since *c.* 1920.

your Aunt Mitty! A US exclamatory c.p. of derision or disbelief, or of a combination of both; W & F tell us that it was popular *c.* 1890 but obsolete by 1960; one can, I believe, narrow it down to late 1880s–early 1900s. But who was Aunt Mitty?

your (or **yo**) **bad self!** 'Addressed to one who has accomplished a remarkable act or piece of work' (CM, 1970): US negroes': since *c.* 1950. Here, *bad* = 'a simple reversal of the white standard, the very best' (CM).

your best friend won't tell you is euphemistic for 'you *stink*' – not in the literal sense ('his best friends won't tell him' about his bad breath) but in either the moral or the social sense: since middle 1960s. From the dentifrice advertisement, 'Her best friends won't tell her'; bad teeth being a frequent cause of bad breath. (Frank Shaw, 25 February 1969.)

your bosom friends are become your backbiters. In the opening dialogue of S, 1738, we read:

[Neverout *scratches his Neck*.]
MISS: Fye, Mr *Neverout*, an't you ashamed? I beg Pardon for the Expression; but I'm afraid your Bosom Friends are become your Backbiters.
NEV: Well, Miss, I saw a Flea once on your Pinner; and a Louse is a Man's Companion, but a Flea is a Dog's Companion. However, I wish you would scratch my Neck with your pretty white Hand.

This C18–early C19 c.p. puns on one's *bosom* – or intimate – *friends* and on *bosom friends* as a euphemism for lice. Cf the contemporary proverbial saying, 'No friend like to a bosom friend, as the man said when he pulled out a louse'; (recorded also by Grose, 1785).

your cock's out a foot. See **your ass-hole's sucking wind**.

your cough's getting better; and **you're coughing better**. Addressed, in C20, to anyone who has just broken wind. Cf **you've a bad cough**.

your custom is out. You can no longer follow your usual practice; the even tenor of your life has been broken: very approximately mid C16–early C17. At ll. 222–3 of A. H. Bullen's edition of George Peele's comedy, *The Old Wives' Tale*, 1595, we read that Erastus, telling Lampriseus how he has buried two wives, says:

And now, neighbour, you of this country say, Your custom is out. But on with your tale, neighbour.

your education has been sadly neglected. See **education**....

your fadder's mustache! On 3 November 1968, my late friend Norris M. Davidson, formerly of Philadelphia, wrote:

It was current some ten or fifteen years ago [i.e., during the middle 1950s]. No one among my limited circle knows its origin, but all agree that it meant much the same thing as '*Sez* you!' or, more agreeably, 'That's what *you* think!' The phrase was always enunciated with a heavy Brooklyn accent and [it] varied between 'Your fadder's muss-tash' – accent on 'muss' and 'me fadder's mustache'. The phrase has lost currency today.

Professor Emeritus F. E. L. Priestley, on 19 August 1975, told me that the Canadian version was *your father's moustache!* and added that it was short-lived: *c.* 1930. Hence, presumably, the American form; perhaps the Canadian version went underground for a decade or more.

your feet won't touch! and the related but not synónymous **your heels won't touch the ground!** The former, meaning 'very quickly indeed', 'in no time at all', is an army, hence later also an air force, c.p., dating since *c.* 1925. 'Any more of that, my lad, and your feet won't touch – you'll soon be up before the CO' (PGR).

The latter is likewise minatory; intended to deter or to intimidate, esp. as a retort upon insult or as a spirited comment on horse-play: since *c.* 1920. (Laurie Atkinson.)

See also **so fast** ....

your guess is as good as mine. Adopted *c.* 1943 from the US, where current since *c.* 1925, is applied to any obscure situation where neither party knows the facts: 'I know as little as you do.' Hartley Howard, *Million Dollar Snapshot*, 1971, uses it:

'If your visitor wanted to discuss business, why didn't he do it during business hours?'
'Your guess is as good as mine.'

Michael Innes, *Appleby at Allington*, 1968, writes:

'But about that treasure, Allington. Do you really suppose there may be anything of the kind buried within or near the castle?'
'Ah!' For a moment Allington hesitated.... 'Your guess is as good as mine.'

And in *The Malcontents*, 1972, C. P. Snow (Lord Snow), writes:

... Saying that he would be back in time for dinner, he was leaving Stephen, when he suddenly thought to ask whether they could get everything in order by Monday. He had planned to return to Cambridge then.
'Your guess is as good as mine,' said Stephen. 'It might be rather a long weekend.'

your heels won't touch the ground. See **your feet** ....

your knees aren't brown is a variant of **get your knees brown**.

your lip's bleeding. What big words you're using! An Australian juvenile c.p., dating since *c.* 1945. (*AS.*) These tongue-twisters are hard to utter clearly.

[**your lips hang in your light**: C16–18. Proverb rather than c.p.]

your mob ... the Emden. See **didn't you sink the Emden?**

your mother and father were never married (or, in Anglo-Irish, **your mother an' father was never married**): a circumlocution for 'You're a bastard', whether literally or figuratively: late C19–20. (Frank Shaw, November 1968.)

your mother wears army boots is a US exclamatory c.p. – at first, i.e. during WW2, very derisive, then jocularly derisive.

An occasional variant: *your sister wears army shoes*, of which Norris M. Davidson has written, 'I dimly remember having heard some nineteen or twenty years ago. It must be a catch phrase, as it makes no sense' (letter dated 16 March 1969).

your nose is bleeding. Your fly is undone: *c.* 1885–1950. By humorous indirection. Contrast **your lip's bleeding**.

your number isn't dry and **your number's still wet.** See **before you come up.**

your pump is good but your (or **the**) **sucker's dry** was, mid C18–early C20, addressed to one who is trying, not very cleverly, to 'pump' another for information. (Grose, 1785.)

your saucepan runs (occasionally **boils**) **over.** You're very saucy: latish C17–18. (BE.)

your sister wears army shoes. See **your mother wears army boots.**

your slip's showing. 'You're giving yourself away by saying or doing that' – applied to a venial fault or not very grave *gaffe*: both British and US: dating since the 1920s.

your store is open. Your fly is open: Canadian: since early 1960s. (Mr D. J. Barr of Almonte, Ontario, in letter of 22 August 1968.) The implication is that all the goods are now either visible or potentially so.

your tiny, tiny mind arose in the US during the 1940s and reached Britain during the late 1950s (but has never been very general there); I associate it particularly with Thurber and the other *New Yorker* wits, who applied it mostly to the supercilious rich male so addressing a luscious, truly dumb, blonde. The insult, originally upper-class only and applied by male to female, lies in the two 'tinies'; it seeped down to the 'middle' middle classes, to be used almost entirely by married or engaged couples quarrelling. (Frank Shaw, 1 September 1969.)

[**your tongue is well hung**; also **your tongue is made of very loose leather**; **your tongue runs on pattens**; and **your tongue runs on wheels**. Respectively C18 (e.g., S); C18 (Fuller); C16–17; and C15–20 (obsolete by *c.* 1940); lying midway between proverbial sayings and c.pp., all meaning 'You're very fluent (*or* glib) of speech'. I think that the last is the only one to have been, or to have become, a true c.p.]

your wheel's going round is a late C19–20 street, esp. juvenile street, c.p. shouted – often with *hoy* and a pause, preceding – at a person travelling by bicycle or car.

you're a better man than I am, Gunga Din. Half-way between famous quotation and c.p. When, however, it is used without reference to, or even consciousness of, its origin in Kipling's poem, *Gunga Din*, in *Barrack-Room Ballads*, 1891, it has, in C20, been, I think, a genuine c.p., as it certainly seems to be in this quotation from Gelett Burgess, *Too Good Looking*, 1936: 'And he was looking at her so queerly. "Well," he said. "You're a better man than I am, Gungha [sic] Din!"'

And as, earlier and even more convincingly, in Maurice Lincoln, '*I, Said the Sparrow*', 1925, '"Well, give the lad my kind regards and tell him that I said 'he's a better man that I am, Gunga Din', will you?"'

you're a big girl now. 'Heard on and off on TV' (A. B. Petch, 21 January 1974): since the early 1960s. But domestically since very much earlier (probably since the 1880s or 1890s) and with the covert intimation 'You're too old, or big, to show so much leg *or* to scratch yourself intimately in public or to ...' Cf **you're getting a big boy now.**

you're a big lad for your age is a jocular c.p., addressed to an apprentice or other youthful worker by his older mates, esp. in factories: late C19–20; decreasingly used since *c.* 1945. Cf:

you're a Fusilier! was, *c.* 1880–1920, a Regular Army c.p. of contempt, addressed by one rifleman to another. Clearly there's a pun on Fusi*lier, liar.*

you're a good man, Charlie Brown. W. J. Burke, 9 April 1975, says it is
> frequently used [in the US] as a compliment, as an acknowledgment of sterling character, based on a Comic Strip character in 'Peanuts' bearing the name Charlie Brown, a modest, good-natured little fellow who is always being picked on by his playmates. There is a popular play based on the character, with the title *You're a Good Man, Charlie Brown*–I believe it is still being revived. The phrase is used frequently to draw a smile from the person so praised, the evocation of the comic strip original being instantly recognized by everyone within hearing distance.... This strip is still going strong in a widely syndicated feature.

you're a good one! is a US c.p., recorded by Berrey, 1942, in a synonym of phrases that are 'disparaging or sarcastic flings'–here, ironic rather than sarcastic. In 1960, W & F wrote thus about certain phrases coined by comedians as 'joke punch lines or as repetitious jokes':
> Thus within the last 15 years such synthetic expressions as *Hey Abbott!, Coming, Mother!, I dood it!* and *you're a good one* have seen some short-lived generalized use.
Elsewhere they included it in a list of 'synthetic fad expressions'.

you're a long time dead. See **you'll be a long time dead.**

you're a poet and don't know it. See **that's a rhyme.**

you're all about – like shit in a field. You're alert and efficient – I *don't* think! Current throughout C20, it is enunciated thus: at first, an apparent compliment, then (the dash) a significant pause – then a weighty jeer.

you're all mouth and trousers has an independent existence, e.g. on radio or TV, but is strictly a euphemism for **you're all prick and breeches**: since *c.* 1955 and *c.* 1920 respectively. It is addressed to a loud-mouthed, blustering fellow. (Laurie Atkinson, 1 July 1964.)

you're all wet! A US c.p., listed by Berrey, 1942, in a synonym of phrasal 'disparaging and sarcastic flings', but going back to at least the 1920s. Here, *wet* is probably elliptical for *wet behind the ears.*

you're another! See **you are another!**

you're as much use as tits on a canary is a 'c.p. hurled at an inefficient player in baseball, or other field sport' (Douglas Leechman): Canadian: since *c.* 1945.

you're awful, but I like you. The vulgarization of a 'gag' used by British comedian Dick Emery, it has become a well-known, although not a madly famous, c.p. (Fernley O. Pascoe, 22 April 1975.) But the original form began 'Oh, you *are* awful'.

you're breaking my heart. See **my heart bleeds for you.**

you're cooking with gas. See **now you're cooking with gas.**

you're coughing better. See **your cough's....**

you're coughing nicely. An affectionately ironic c.p., dating since *c.* 1918.

you're damn' (or darn') tooting. See **too damn' tooting.**

you're fond of a job is, in C20, addressed to one doing a job either another's or unnecessary.

you're full of shit! 'Probably still current in company I no longer frequent. Coarser is **your arse is sucking blue mud**' (F. E. L. Priestley, 19 August 1975): Canadian, perhaps from American (W & F include it, but mention no date): since *c.* 1930 (?).

you're getting a big boy (or **girl**) **now.** (With the latter, cf **you're a big girl now.**) To a boy, a mild, even if slightly contemptuous, reproof for petulance or bad manners; to a girl, for (usually unintentional) immodesty, esp. of dress: late C19–20.

you're getting TV behind has, since the late 1930s, been addressed to a woman very broad in the beam, the implication being that she spends an inordinate time sitting in front of the TV.

you're getting warmer derives from domestic hide-and-seek games and is a c.p. when *otherwise* employed, e.g. in an attempt at logical deduction or in elaboration of a mounting suspicion: C20. (Fernley O. Pascoe, 22 April 1975.)

you're holding up production. You are getting in the way; You are wasting (your own or another's or others') time; You're not being very helpful: RAF: 1940 onwards. The c.p. tried to spread to the army, but never got much of a hold. (EP, *A Glossary of RAF Slang*, early 1945; PGR.)

you're in mourning for the cat. Your finger-nails are filthy: proletarian: C20; by 1970, somewhat outdated.

you're in the wrong pew was current among US university students *c.* 1920 and a few years later. (McKnight.) It is, however, a shortening of *you're in the right church but the wrong pew*, which, *c.* 1909, turned a song title into a c.p. The song was sung in 1900, by Bert Williams; the words were McPherson's; the music Chris Smith's. Cited by Edward B. Marks, *They All Sang*, 1934, as W. J. Burke tells me in a letter dated 23 September 1975.

you're jealous is a jocularly insinuatory retort to 'You're drunk!' I've known it since 1921, and suspect that it goes back to the late C19.

you're joking! and **you must** (or **have to**) **be joking!** and **you've got to be joking!** (Cf **are you kidding?** and the US **no kidding** and **you're** (or **have to, or must, be) kidding!**; also the not-quite-a-c.p., yet potential, indeed imminent c.p., **you're joking, of course?** – which expresses a modified, or even a foolish, optimism – and the Australian **you've got to be kidding.**)

Meaning: 'You *can't* be serious' or 'I can't, I *don't*, believe you're serious': in the British Commonwealth, fully established only since *c* 1950; in the US, the native US forms probably since about the same time and the adopted British forms since *c.* 1960. By the vaguely apprehended yet powerfully operative linguistic processes known as Spontaneous Combustion and Mutual Inter-influencing, it is hardly necessary – come to that, advisable – to separate the British and the US expressions of a universal thought-pattern. Yet it should be noted that, in Britain, *you must be joking* seems to have, in the fact, arisen much earlier than is apparent from the evidence. Grose, 1785, records the c.p., *you are Josephus Rex*, you're joking: by progressive punning, *you are Joseph King* (L. *rex*, a king)–*you are Joe King*–*you are joking*. This at first learned c.p. belongs to the very approximate period, 1760–1900.

Clearly the c.p. usage of *you must be joking* comes straight from the literal use, as in, for instance, Leicester Buckingham's *Faces in the Fire: A Comedy*, performed on 25 February 1865:

> GLAN[VIL]: Doubt her! Oh, no! I often think I should be happier if she loved me less.
>
> MRS H[ARGRAVE] (*laughing*): Well, your grievance has, at any rate, the charm of originality. But you must be joking. (*Glanvil shakes his head.*) No! you are really serious? then you make me uneasy ...

The US *you must be*, or *you're*, *kidding* occurs very neatly in the *New Yorker* of 7 February 1970. It contains a cartoon of the Devil visiting Earth and, to a protesting 'egg-head', exclaiming, *'Persona non grata?* You must be kidding.'

In the same year, the very English W. J. Burley, in his novel, *To Kill a Cat*, writes thus:

> '... What's Fehling playing at?'
>
> 'I don't know you can blame Fehling.'
>
> 'You must be joking.'

A year earlier, a US novelist, Jack D. Hunter wrote in *Spies Inc.*, 1969: 'He gave me one of his long stares. "You must be joking," he said.'

Anne Morice, in *Death of a Gay Dog*, 1971, writes

> 'What a gorgeous room this is,' I said....
>
> 'My dear, you must be joking. When did you ever see anything so pretentious? ... I ask you! Just look at the way he's tarted it up!'

And then, on *c.* 15 December 1974, Barry Prentice attests the Australian form thus: '**you've got to be kidding**. Same meaning as "you must be joking"'. It occurs in, e.g., Alex. Buzo's perturbing play, *Rooted*, performed in 1971.

Here, it's obvious, is a c.p. that, with its variants, merits a little monograph all to itself. 'You must be kidding!'–'On the contrary, I mean it.'

you're kidding. See preceding entry.

you're kneeling on it. Your hair's too long: Guards' regiments': C20.

you're laffin bags. See LIVERPOOL CATCH PHRASES.

you're not here! Exclamation when delivered bowls fall short of the target: South African (the game of bowls): since *c.* 1950 at the very latest. (Professor A. C. Partridge, letter of 18 November 1968.)

you're not just a pretty face. You're not only good-looking, you also have brains: since *c.* 1960. Originally, and still, a compliment to a pretty girl; hence, by the late 1960s, occasionally ironically to a man, even if he isn't handsome, as in James Fraser, *Death in a Pheasant's Eye*, 1972: '"'Greenfingers Brown', they'll be calling you next," Bill Aveyard said. "You're not just a pretty face!"' (A police superintendent to his sergeant.)

you're not kidding! How right you are! Both American, since *c.* 1910 or a little earlier, and Canadian since several years

before WW1. (W & F; F. E. L. Priestley cites its Canadian survival–until at least 19 August 1975.)

you're not on; or, occasionally, **you're on next.** I want nothing to do with you or it; You don't convince me; You've failed: Liverpool: since *c.* 1945. From boxing: 'You've been waiting, and expecting to substitute for an absentee–but you're not needed' (Frank Shaw, *c.* 1965).

you're not paid to think. 'Invariable admonition by NCOs and officers to privates excusing themselves by saying "I thought ..."': (Mr Y. Mindel, MRCVS, on 12 December 1971): army: late C19–20.

you're not Robinson Crusoe. You're not alone, so don't be so damned selfish (*or* unsociable)! Mostly, and probably originally, Australian: since *c.* 1950. On 31 January 1969, Barry Prentice remarked: 'In general use–not confined to surfers or the younger set.'

Also–still predominantly Australian–'You're not alone in *that*': since *c.* 1960. On 15 December 1974, Barry Prentice wrote: 'You are not the only one' and exemplified it thus:

> 'I can't keep up with these amendments.'
>
> 'You're not Robinson Crusoe.'

[**you're not the only pebble on the beach** (C19–20) teeters on the wall that separates clichés from c.pp.; I'd say that it falls on the cliché side. See also **you aren't the only pebble** ... and note that the American song thus titled was sung by Lottie Gibson in 1896, with words by Braisted and music by Carters, as Edward B. Marks mentions in *They All Sang*, 1934. (Thanks to W. J. Burke, 23 September 1975.)]

you're off the grass! You don't stand a chance: cricketers': *c.* 1900–14. (Ware.) Outside the field of play.

you're on my hook. You're getting in my way: an Australian c.p. of *c.* 1946–55. From angling.

you're on next. See **you're not on.**

you're on the pig's back. 'You're living the life of Reilly' (British, originally Anglo-Irish) or 'You have it made' (American). 'The origin of this Anglo-Irish c.p. [dating since latish C19] perhaps lies in the fact that, in early Celtic myth, pigs were sacred' (Frank Shaw, in early November 1968).

you're only making it hard for yourself. 'Jocular double-entendre classic phrase said by one man to the others at horse-play' (Laurie Atkinson, late 1974); but also more widely used, by either sex to its own or the other sex, and in any situation where it makes sense. It must go back at least as far as 1940 and, I suspect, perhaps to *c.* 1910.

you're selling tea! A facetious, mercifully short-lived, perversion of **you're telling me!:** *c.* 1945–55.

you're showing an Egyptian medal. You're showing a fly-button: since mid 1880s; obsolescent by late 1930s and obsolete by mid 1940s. A variant of *c.* 1896–1914 was ... *Abyssinian medal*, from the Abyssinian War of 1893–6. (Ware.) Cf **you're starring in front** and note that all these c.pp. stem from the general **you're showing**–or **wearing**–**a medal**, which probably dates from *c.* 1880 or rather earlier.

you're so full of shit your eyes are brown is a Canadian Army c.p. that, in 1939–45, expressed a truly violent dislike.

you're so sharp you'll be cutting yourself! A late C19–20 c.p. addressed to a smart-tongued person.

you're starring in front is a theatrical variation of the general **you're showing a medal** or **your medals**, q.v. at **you're showing an Egyptian medal**. To any of these, **today** could be appended. The theatrical version has been vouched for by the late Wilfred Granville (6 November 1968) and also by Mr Michael Warwick.

you're telling me! – emphasis on *me*. 'I'm well aware of that'; 'I agree with you heartily': adopted in Britain by 1933 – see an indignant letter in the *Daily Mirror* of that year and cf an advertisement in the 'agony column' of the *Daily Telegraph* on 14 September 1934; in US, it dates since the early 1920s – if not a little earlier – and it duly appears in Berrey, 1942. In 'An Infantry Industry' (*First and Last*, 1934) Ring Lardner cited, as the title of a song, 'You're Telling Me' – apparently being sung in 1932.

In English novels, there are numerous examples; it occurs, for example, several times in Michael Burt's *The Case of the Angel's Trumpets*, 1947. Catherine Aird, *The Complete Steel*, 1969, has:

'It's a bad corner.'
'You're telling me.'

In Tom Lilley, *The 'K' Section*, 1972, a senior British police officer uses it.

you're the doctor – emphasis on *you*. 'Whatever you say – after all, you're the authority on the subject, the expert, the man in charge, and ultimately the responsibility is yours; I'll take your prescription – your word – for it, of course': Canadian and British: since, I'd guess, the 1930s (maybe earlier); certainly I've known it since the middle 1930s. By the middle 1940s, also US. I've noted it in E. V. Cunningham's novel, *Phyllis*, 1962: '"All right, Clancy," he shrugged, "you're the doctor. If that's what she wants, she wants it."' (Clancy is a detective.)

It's just possible that the phrase was originally US.

you're the expert has stemmed from the preceding entry, is both US and British (the entire Commonwealth), and seems to have arisen by the middle 1940s. See, e.g., Philip Gleife, *The Pinchbeck Masterpiece*, 1970:

This time Hank was beaten. 'O.K. – you're the expert.'
'No, but I mingle with the experts – in my job I have to know my stuff.'

you're the top! A c.p. of approval, taken from a comedy, *Anything Goes*, 1935, but not, I think, surviving WW2. Cf the likewise approbatory US *You're* (or *he's*, or *anyone's*) *tops*.

you're too fresh! A US c.p. of *c.* 1870–90. Here, obviously, *fresh* = cheeky, impudent. See the quotation at **pull down your vest!** – recorded in *Am*, 1877.

you're way out in left field! You don't get the point; *or* Your guess couldn't be more wrong: US: C20. 'In baseball, left field is at the furthest distance from the batter, to his left; [literally] it means "You're hopelessly far away from where you should be to catch the batted ball and thus put the batter out"' (John W. Clark, 22 October 1968). Hence, set for a fall, a beating, a defeat; without a chance of winning; in short, 'You're on a loser'.

you're wearing your medal today. See **you're showing an Egyptian medal**.

[**you're welcome** is, when used literally, a cliché, but when it's used trivially and humorously or ironically, it verges on being a c.p., British and US, of C20, as, for instance, in Jean Potts, *An Affair of the Heart*, 1970:

'... How's your head?'
'My what? Oh. Better. Thank you.'
'You're welcome.'

Earlier in Edward Albee, *Tiny Alice*, performed late 1964, published early 1965, at Act II, Scene ii:

LAWYER [*soft sarcasm*]: Thank you.
BUTLER: You're welcome.]

yours if you want it is, among Suffolk males, the standard reply, late C19–20, to **who's shit?**, who has farted? A pun on *who's* (= *who has*) and *whose*. (A Suffolk correspondent, 15 May 1972.)

yours – or clean ones? Addressed by women to a woman exclaiming *knickers!*: mostly Suffolk: C20. Apparently prompted by:

yours or mine? A query addressed to one who has just exclaimed *knackers!*: male, mostly Suffolk: C20. (*Knackers*, slang for testicles. An exclamation, a variant of *balls!*, 'Nonsense!')

This and the two entries preceding it come from the one Suffolk correspondent: and all three exemplify the earthier sort of public-house wit.

yours to a cinder! is a late C19–20, *non*-upper class c.p. ending to a letter, probably either originating in coal-mining areas or prompted by **till hell freezes over**. Clearly, also, the phrases intimate a certain warmth of devotion. By *c.* 1945, obsolete.

you've a bad cough (or **that's a bad cough you have**). Addressed to one who has just broken wind: mostly male: C20.

you've been. Your promised trip – e.g., and esp., in an aircraft – has been cancelled: RAF: since the middle 1930s. (H & P.) Cf **you've had it**.

you've been doing naughty things. See **you have been doing . . . .**

you've been reading my letters is an Australian humorous retort to 'You're a [*figurative*] bastard!' I heard it being used – half a dozen times, at least – while I was serving in the Australian infantry, 1915–19.

The English form is *someone's been looking in my pay-book*, glossed thus (on 18 July 1975): '(In Services) one man has called another, or referred to him as, a bastard': WW2 and since; probably also before.

you've been to an Irish wedding. See **you have been to . . . .**

you've dropped something – too late! the flies have got it has the variant, **you've dropped something – but it would never have lived, its eyes were too far apart**. Whereas the former implies a sweet and sticky substance, the latter – *à la mode macabre ou surréaliste* – implies an unfortunate babe-in-arms. Current since *c.* 1950. (The former supplied by Cyril Whelan; the latter by Paul Beale; both early in 1975.)

you've fixed it up nicely for me. No you don't!; Do you think I'm green? Literally, You've made this arrangement for me *or* You've schemed this – but I'm not falling for it. Proletarian: *c.* 1880–1914. (B & L.) This, I'd say, provides a good example of ironic Cockney humour.

you've forgotten the piano! is a C20 c.p., addressed sarcastically to one who has a great deal of luggage with him, esp. by bus conductors witheringly to passengers.

you've got a nerve! See **of all the nerve!** and cf **you've got your nerve!**

you've got a one-track mind – occasionally elaborated by the addition of **and that's dirt track** – imputes an excessive or, at the least, an absorbed interest in sex; the elaborated form sometimes implies what has been called 'marital buggery'. Since *c.* 1920. Moreover, there is a reference to the dirt track of motorcycle racing.

you've got a smile like a can of worms is a Canadian c.p., expressive of a strong dislike and dating since *c.* 1925. Originally, one suspects, among amateur fishermen. (Douglas Leechman.)

you've got a swinging brick. You have a heart of stone – no emotion, no sentiment, no pity: North of England: since the (?late) 1950s. (David Wharton, 6 June 1966.)

you've got eyes in your head, haven't you? This disparaging c.p. implies in the addressee a slowness of visual understanding and has been current since the 1880s or 1890s.

you've got it all round your neck has, since *c.* 1945, imputed, or even stigmatized, confusion of mind, esp. hesitancy – or outright inability – to complete an explanation. As if it were some impeding garment around the poor fellow's (or girl's) neck.

you've got it made. See **you have it made**.

you've got me, pal! I can't tell you, *or* I can't answer your question; – hence 'I simply don't know': US: since 1920s. (Berrey.) Probably elliptical for 'You've got me guessing'.

you've got one foot in the grave and the other on a banana skin. In the middle 1920s this c.p. was employed by the youthful and the young-mannish supporters of 'soccer' clubs to decide the opinion, the judgment of their elders. (Laurie Atkinson, late 1974.)

you've got something there! You're on to something good; There's much to support what you say; *That's* a darned good idea: since *c.* 1910. Both British and US (Berrey 1942).

you've got to be in it to win it synonymizes the old proverb, 'Nothing venture, nothing win': Australian: since *c.* 1950. (Barry Prentice, *c.* 15 December 1974.) If you've put no money into a lottery or on the pools, you can't win anything. The c.p. exemplifies the ubiquitous attraction of rhyme.

you've got to be joking! See **you're joking!**

you've got to be kidding is a predominantly Australian variant of **you're joking**; it shows US influence and dates from *c.* 1945 or a year or two earlier. (Barry Prentice, *c.* 15 December 1974.)

you've got your nerve! See **of all the nerve!** Also the US **you've got your gall!** – which, even as an Americanism, is less frequent than *you've got your nerve!* Perhaps the commonest of all in Britain and the Commonwealth is *you've got a nerve!*

you've had it! You *won't* get it; You're too late; Your chance – e.g., of a transfer, a promotion, a privilege – has gone (*or* is nil): RAF: since 1937 or 1938; hence in army, since late 1940 or early 1941; by 1944, in fairly general civilian use. (EP in the *New Statesman*, 30 August 1941; H & P; W-J; and EP,

A Glossary of RAF Slang, 1945; PGR). Perhaps elliptical for, or allusive to, 'You've *had* your chance (and didn't, or couldn't, take it)'.

In the third person, *he's had it* can also mean, 'He's been killed' (in a raid) or 'He's been so badly wounded, or is so ill, he stands no chance'. This sense, according to Jock Marshall and Russell Drysdale, *Journey among Men* (p. 17), 1962, 'originated in the Gulf Country of Northern Queensland, where one of us heard it as early as 1929.... It was taken to Europe by Queensland troops or airmen': that is as may be; nevertheless it was already current in the RAF in late 1939.

Also, occasionally, *you've had your time* – 'You're "through"', *or* 'You're too late': RAF only: 1940 onwards, but obsolete by 1950. (Gerald Emanuel, in letter of 29 March 1945.)

This is perhaps the most famous of all c.pp. originated by the RAF, although **it's a piece of cake** must run it fairly close.

you've picked a bad apple – You've made a bad choice – dates from *c.* 1920 but has been little used since *c.* 1960.

you've said it! Yes, indeed!; *or* I agree entirely (with you); *or* You're dead right: adopted, *c.* 1943, by Britain from the US, where it had been current since *c.* 1920 – despite the fact that Berrey, 1942, omits it and W & F, 1960, in the very brief entry they accord to it, don't date it; as early as 1931, the witty Oliver Herford, writer of deft and charming light verse, includes in *The Deb's Dictionary* this entry: 'QUITE (or) "Oh, Quate": British for "You've said it!"'

A British – or rather, a South African – example occurs in James McClure, *The Caterpillar Cop*, 1972:

'But that is a strange thing.'
'You've said it.'

you've saved (occasionally **you saved**) **my life**. That's, or that was, a most timely piece of help: since *c.* 1930. In John Mortimer's *The Judge*, produced and published 1967, in Act I, Scene iii, Serena, having succeeded in begging a cigarette from a strange girl just arrived on the scene, exclaims: ' "Welcome child: you saved my life!" (*Inhales deeply, coughs.*)'

you've shot your granny. John Russell Bartlett, the inaugurator and early editor of the rightly famous book of quotations, also edited, hardly less notably, *DAM* 1848. In the latter – and, please note, it was in the first, *not* the second (or 1859) edn that he did so – he included this c.p., derived it from the literal sense 'By mistake, you've shot your grandmother instead of the person or animal you aimed at', and glossed the c.p. as meaning 'You're deceived in your expectation', *or* 'You haven't at all achieved what you hoped to achieve', *or* esp., 'You're (badly) mistaken': very approximately, *c.* 1830–90.

you've spotted this week's deliberate mistake. Paul Beale, 1 October 1974, says: 'Useful c.p. for any instructor caught out in writing an unwitting error on the blackboard. There are, of course, variations; it originated, I believe, in a radio show some years ago': since the middle or latish 1960s. Isn't this a Cyril Fletcher gag, which has duly risen to the status of c.p.?

you've talked me into it. See **you could twist my arm**.

Z

Zed is a whoreson letter (a late C17 glossarist of cant): ?mid C17–late C18. Because it signifies the end. Probably a reminiscence of Shakespeare's 'Thou whoreson Zed! Thou unnecessary letter!' spoken by Kent to Oswald in *King Lear* at Act II, Scene ii, l. 68 in W. J. Craig's edition.